CHALMERS'

SALE OF GOODS ACT 1979

INCLUDING

THE FACTORS ACTS 1889 & 1890

EIGHTEENTH EDITION

BY

MICHAEL MARK, M.A., B.C.L.

OF THE INNER TEMPLE, BARRISTER

with assistance from

JONATHAN MANCE, B.A.

OF THE MIDDLE TEMPLE, BARRISTER

LONDON
BUTTERWORTHS
1981

England	Butterworth & Co (Publishers) Ltd 88 Kingsway, London WC2B 6AB
Australia	Butterworths Pty Ltd 271–273 Lane Cove Road, North Ryde, NSW 2113 Also at Melbourne, Brisbane, Adelaide and Perth
Canada	Butterworth & Co (Canada) Ltd 2265 Midland Avenue, Scarborough, Ont M1P 4S1
	Butterworth & Co (Western Canada) Ltd 409 Granville Street, Ste 856, Vancouver, BC V6C 1T2
New Zealand	Butterworths of New Zealand Ltd 33–35 Cumberland Place, Wellington
South Africa	Butterworth & Co (South Africa) (Pty) Ltd 152–154 Gale Street, Durban 4001
United States of America	Mason Publishing Company Finch Bldg, 366 Wacouta Street, St. Paul, Minn 55101
	Butterworth (Legal Publishers) Inc 160 Roy Street, Ste 300, Seattle, Wash 98109
	Butterworth (Legal Publishers) Inc 381 Elliot Street, Newton, Upper Falls, Mass 02164

Reprinted 1982

ISBN—Hardcover: 0 406 56448 5
Softcover: 0 406 56449 3

Photo typeset by
Macmillan India Ltd., Bangalore

Printed and bound in Great Britain
by Billing and Sons Limited
Guildford, London, Oxford, Worcester

PREFACE

Since the last edition was published, the main developments in the law have been statutory. In particular, the Sale of Goods Act 1979 has replaced the Sale of Goods Act 1893, drafted by Sir Mackenzie Chalmers, and various amendments mainly enacted between 1967 and 1977.

Statutory protection against unfair contractual terms has also been extended with the passing of the Unfair Contract Terms Act 1977, most of which is reproduced with a commentary in Appendix 1 to this edition.

I have also sought to deal with the further protection for consumers provided by the Consumer Safety Act 1978, by the Consumer Transaction (Restrictions on Statements) Orders 1976 to 1978 and by the Price Markings (Bargain Offers) Order 1979.

The main developments in case law has been in relation to licences and to retention of title clauses.

I have dealt with retention of title clauses in the commentary to s.48 of the Sale of Goods Act 1979, while Mr. Jonathan Mance has greatly expanded the passage on licences in the section on international sale of goods, which he has once again revised. We are indebted to Mr. Jonathan Gaisman for his assistance in this context.

We have sought to state the law on the basis of the reports available as at 1st March 1981, but later cases, including the decision of the House of Lords in *Lexmead* (*Basingstoke*) *Ltd.* v. *Lewis*, have been incorporated where possible.

I should like to thank the staff of Butterworths for their help and co-operation and in particular for their assistance in the tedious and time consuming job of proof reading.

MICHAEL MARK

Lincoln's Inn,
March 1981

INTRODUCTION TO FIRST EDITION (1894)

IT IS difficult to know whether to call this little book a first edition or a second edition. It is a first edition of the Sale of Goods Act, 1893, but it is a reproduction of my book on the Sale of Goods, published in 1890, which was in substance a commentary on the Sale of Goods Bill. The clauses of the Bill, with a few verbal alterations, formed the large type propositions of the book. But though the language of the propositions remains the same, its effect is now very different. Those propositions were only law in so far as they were correct and logical inductions from the decided cases. Now the position is reversed. The propositions have become sections of the Act, and the decided cases are only law in so far as they are correct and logical deductions from the language of the Act. Each case, therefore, must be tested with reference to the Act itself. But it may be none the less useful to the reader to call his attention to the decisions which formed the basis of the various sections, and which were intended to be reproduced in the Act. In so far as the law is unaltered, they are still in point as illustrations.

The history of the Act is as follows: The Bill was originally drafted by me in 1888. I then settled it in consultation with Lord Herschell, who kindly consented to take charge of it. In 1889, Lord Herschell introduced it in the House of Lords, not to press it on, but to get criticisms on it. In 1890 there was no opportunity of proceeding with it, but in 1891 the Bill was again introduced in the Lords, and referred to a Select Committee. It had in the meantime been criticised by Lord Bramwell, Mr. Walter Ker, and other friends, and the Bar Committee had submitted a valuable memorandum on it. In the Lords it was carefully considered by a Select Committee, consisting of Lords Herschell, Halsbury, Bramwell, and Watson. A question arose as to its extension to Scotland, so the Bill stood over till 1892. It was then again introduced in the Lords, and extended to Scotland, on the advice of Lord Watson, who had consulted various Scotch legal authorities. Professor Richard Brown and Mr. Spens of Glasgow took an infinity of pains to suggest the necessary amendments. In 1893 the Bill was again passed through the Lords in the form in which it was settled in 1892. It was then considered by a Select Committee of the House of Commons and further amended. The Committee consisted of Sir Charles Russell, A.-G., Sir R. Webster, Q.C., Mr. Asher, Q.C. (the Scotch Solicitor-General), Mr. Shiress Will, Q.C., Mr. Bousfield, Q.C., Mr. Ambrose, Q.C., and Mr. Mather. Some of the amendments introduced by the Commons were modified on its return to the Lords, and it was finally settled in its present form.

The Bill, in its original form, was drafted on the same lines as the Bills of Exchange Bill. On Lord Herschell's advice it endeavoured to reproduce as exactly as possible the existing law, leaving any amendments that might seem desirable to be introduced in Committee on the authority of the Legislature. So far as England is concerned, the conscious changes effected in the law have been very slight. They are pointed out in the notes to the various sections. As regards Scotland, in some cases the Scottish rule has been saved or enacted for Scotland, in others it has been modified, while in others the English rule has been adopted. These points are noted under the sections as they arise. Scottish law differs from English law mainly by adhering to the Roman law in matters where English law has developed a rule of its own. The Mercantile Law Commission of 1855 reported on this question, and recommended that on certain points the Scotch rule should be adopted in England, while on other points the English rule should be adopted in Scotland. The recommendations of the Commission were partially embodied in the English and Scotch Mercantile Law Amendment Acts of 1856. The result was curious. Either by accident or design certain rules were enacted for England which resembled, but did not reproduce, the Scotch law, while other rules were enacted for Scotland which resembled, but did not reproduce, the English law. The present Act has carried the process of assimilation somewhat further. It is perhaps to be regretted that the process has not been completed; but future legislation may accomplish that. It is always easier to amend an Act than to alter common law. Legislation, too, is cheaper than litigation. Moreover, in mercantile matters, the certainty of the rule is often of more importance than the substance of the rule (*a*). If the parties know beforehand what their legal position is, they can provide for their particular wants by express stipulation. Sale is a consensual contract, and the Act does not seek to prevent the parties from making any bargain they please. Its object is to lay down clear rules for the case where the parties have either formed no intention, or failed to express it.

As regards this edition, I have not attempted to expound or criticise the mass of cases which illustrate or are modified by the Act. Such a work could hardly be undertaken with any prospect of success until the Act has been for some time in operation. I have only sought to indicate the sources of the various provisions in the Act, and to elucidate the general principles of the law of sale by citations from eminent judges. Our common law is rich in the exposition of principles, and these expositions lose none of their value now that the law is codified. A rule can never be appreciated apart from the reasons on which it is founded.

I have compared the main propositions of the English law with the corresponding provisions of the Code Napoleon, which is the model on which most of the Continental Codes have been framed (*b*). On the one

---

(*a*) Cf. *Lockyer* v. *Offley* (1786), 1 T. R. 252, at p. 259.

(*b*) Since the fourth edition of this book was published, Germany has enacted a new civil code for her empire. The German Civil Code of 1900 is a notable addition to legal theory and practice. Its main provisions relating to sale are collected in a sub-heading of the chapter dealing with "Obligatory Relations." But the scheme of the German Code is so widely different from the lines on which the Sale of Goods Act is framed, that any attempt at comparison would be futile, unless explained by a detailed discussion, which would be unsuitable to a small manual such as this.

hand, the scope and effect of a principle are often best brought out by contrast; on the other hand, where any rule of municipal law is found to be generally adopted in other countries, there is a strong presumption that the rule is founded on broad grounds of expediency, and that its application should not be narrowed. The Roman lawyers were justified in attaching a peculiar value to those rules of law which were *juris gentium*. I have also made frequent reference to Pothier's *Traité du Contrat de Vente*. Although published more than a century ago—for Pothier died in 1772—it is still, probably, the best reasoned treatise on the Law of Sale that has seen the light of day. "The authority of Pothier," says BEST, C. J., "is as high as can be had next to the decision of a court of justice in this country" (*c*). This statement must obviously be taken with the qualification that it only holds good when Pothier is discussing some principle of general application; for the law he was particularly dealing with was French law, as modified by the custom of Orleans, before the Code Napoleon.

The references to the Civil Law need little comment. It is the foundation of the Scottish law, and it is an inexhaustible store of legal principles. There is hardly a judgment of importance on the law of sale in which reference is not made to the Civil Law. "The Roman law," says TINDAL, C. J., "forms no rule binding in itself on the subjects of these realms; but in deciding a case upon principle, where no direct authority can be cited from our books, it affords no small evidence of the soundness of the conclusion at which we have arrived, if it prove to be supported by that law—the fruit of the researches of the most learned men, the collective wisdom of ages, and the groundwork of the municipal law of most of the countries of Europe" (*d*). My task of reference in this edition has been much facilitated by Dr. Moyle's excellent monograph on the *Contract of Sale in the Civil Law*, published in 1892.

To facilitate reference to contemporaneous reports, the date of each case cited has been given.

M. D. CHALMERS.

BIRMINGHAM COUNTY COURT,
1894.

(*c*) *Cox* v. *Troy* (1822), 5 B & Ald. 481; *cf. M'Lean* v. *Clydesdale Bank* (1883), 9 App. Cas., at p. 105, *per* LORD BLACKBURN.

(*d*) *Acton* v. *Blundell* (1843), 12 M. & W., at p. 324; *cf. Keighley* v. *Durant*, [1901] A. C., at p. 244.

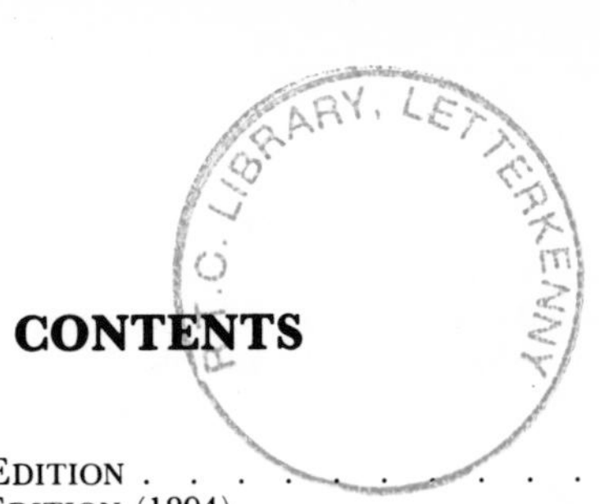

CONTENTS

TABLE OF STATUTES

References in this Table to "*Stats*" are to Halsbury's Statutes of England (Third Edition) showing the volume and page at which the annotated text of the Act will be found. Page references printed in bold type indicate where the Act is set out in part or in full.

PAGE

Consolidated Co. *v.* Curtis & Son, (1892) 1 Q. B. 495; 61 L. J. Q. B. 325 . 159, 258
Continental Contractors, Ltd. *v.* Medway Oil and Storage Co. (1925), 23 Ll. L. Rep. 55, C. A. 35, 184
Continental Grain Export Corporation *v.* S. T. M. Grain, Ltd., [1979] 2 Lloyd's Rep. 460 . . . . . 41, 42
Contract and Trading Co. (Southern), Ltd. *v.* Barbey, [1959] 3 All E. R. 846; [1960] A. C. 244; [1959] 2 W. L. R. 15; 103 Sol. Jo. 1027, H. L.; 17 Digest (Reissue) 509. 329
Conway Brothers and Savage *v.* Mulhern & Co., Ltd. (1901), 17 T. L. R. 730; 39 Digest (Repl.) 502 320
Cooden Engineering *v.* Stanford, [1952] 2 All E. R. 915; [1953] 1 Q. B. 86; [1952] T. L. R. 822; 96 Sol. Jo. 802, C. A.; 17 Digest (Reissue) 184 234
Cooke, *Ex parte, Re* Strachan (1876), 4 Ch. D. 123; 46 L. J. Bcy. 52; 35 L. T. 649; 41 J. P. 180; 25 W. R. 171, C. A.; 5 Digest (Reissue) 772 311
Cooke & Sons *v.* Eshelby (1887), 12 App. Cas. 271; [1886–90] All E. R. Rep. 791; 56 L. J. Q. B. 505; 56 L. T. 673, H. L.; 1 (2) Digest (Reissue) 785 311
Cookson *v.* Knowles, [1978] 2 All E. R. 604; [1979] A. C. 556; [1978] 2 W. L. R. 978; 122 Sol. Jo. 386; [1978] 2 Lloyd's Rep. 315, H. L.; Digest Cont. Vol. E p. 463 322
Cooper, *Ex parte* (1879), 11 Ch. D. 68; 48 L. J. Bcy. 49; 40 L. T. 105; 27 W. R. 518; 4 Asp. M. L. C. 63, C. A.; 39 Digest (Repl.) 763 . . . . . 205, 210
Cooper, *Re, Ex parte* Trustee of Property of Bankrupt *v.* Registrar and High Bailiff of Peterborough and Huntingdon County Courts, [1958] 2 All E. R. 97; [1958] Ch. 922; [1958] 3 W. L. R. 468; 102 Sol. Jo. 635; 5 Digest (Reissue) 886 . 287
Cooper *v.* Bill (1865), 3 H. & C. 722; 12 L. T. 466; 34 L. J. Ex. 161; 39 Digest (Repl.) 746 206
Cooper *v.* Cooper (1888), 13 App. Cas. 88; 59 L. T. 1, H. L.; 22 Digest (Reissue) 677 93
Cooper *v.* Micklefield Coal and Lime Co. (1912), 107 L. T. 457; 12 Digest (Reissue) 724 26
Cooper *v.* Shepherd (1846), 3 C. B. 266; 4 Dow. & L. 218; 15 L. J. C. P. 237; 7 L. T. O. S. 282; 10 Jur. 758; 46 Digest (Repl.) 525 28
Cooper *v.* Shuttleworth (1856), 25 L. J. Ex. 114; 39 Digest (Repl.) 502 . . . 104
Cooper *v.* Stubbs, [1925] 2 K. B. 753; [1925] All E. R. Rep. 643; 94 L. J. K. B. 903; 133 L. T. 582; 41 T. L. R. 614; 69 Sol. Jo. 743; 10 T. C. 29, C. A.; 28 (1) Digest (Reissue) 25 103
Cooper *v.* Willomatt (1845), 1 C. B. 672; [1843–60] All E. R. Rep. 556; 14 L. J. C. P. 219; 5 L. T. O. S. 173; 9 Jur. 598; 3 Digest (Reissue) 488 . . . . . 159, 237
Coote *v.* Jecks (1872), L. R. 13 Eq. 597; 41 L. J. Ch. 599; 7 Digest (Reissue) 32: 319
Cordova Land Co. *v.* Victor Brothers Incorporated, [1966] 1 W. L. R. 793; 110 Sol. Jo. 290 . . . . . 129, 190
Cork Distilleries Co. *v.* G. S. Railway (1874), L. R. 7 H. L. 269; 8 (1) Digest (Reissue) 36 380
Corn Products Co. *v.* Fry, [1917] W. N. 224; 39 Digest (Repl.) 502 320
Cornish *v.* Abington (1859), 4 H. & N. 549; 28 L. J. Ex. 262; 21 Digest (Repl.) 369 163
Cornwal *v.* Wilson (1750), 1 Ves. Sen. 509; 1 (2) Digest (Reissue) 580 . . 196, 197
Cort *v.* Ambergate Ry. Co. (1851), 17 Q. B. 127; 20 L. J. Q. B. 460; 17 L. T. O. S. 179; 15 Jur. 877; 39 Digest (Repl.) 659 . . . . . 20, 226
Cory *v.* Thames Iron Works Co. (1868), L. R. 3 Q. B. 181; [1861–73] All E. R. Rep. 597; 37 L. J. Q. B. 68; 17 L. T. 495; 16 W. R. 456; 39 Digest (Repl.) 815 235
Cottee *v.* Douglas Seaton (Used Cars), Ltd., [1972] 3 All E. R. 750; [1972] 1 W. L. R. 1408; 137 J. P. 1; 116 Sol. Jo. 821; [1972] R. T. R. 509; Digest Supp. 58, 69
Cotton, *Re, Ex parte* Cooke (1913), 108 L. T. 310; 57 Sol. Jo. 343, C. A.; 5 Digest (Reissue) 772. 311

SECTION A

RELATIONSHIP OF SALE AND CONTRACT

Relation of sale to contract generally

The contract of sale is governed in part by principles peculiar to itself, and in part by principles common to contracts generally. The Sale of Goods Act 1979, except incidentally, deals only with the first-mentioned principles. The principles of law which govern contracts generally are outside its scope, but are expressly saved in their application to contracts of sale by s. 62, *post*, unless they are inconsistent with the express provisions of the Act. Further, s. 55, *post*, permits parties to contract out of most of the provisions of the Act, expressly or by necessary implication. Since 1973, there have been stringent restrictions on the capacity of the parties to contract out of the provisions of ss. 12–15 of the Act (*a*). Apart from these restrictions, however, the Act in no way prevents the parties from making what bargain they please (*b*), and by giving legal effect in particular to commercial usage, the development of the law merchant is not impeded. Nor does the Act touch or alter the ordinary law relating to construction and interpretation of written agreements or the admission of parol evidence in relation thereto. Finally, the Act does not touch the tortious liability, in conversion or negligence, of the seller of goods.

If the law of contract were codified, the Sale of Goods Act would form a single chapter in the code.

Intention to create legal relations

An agreement to sell may be made, by express and appropriate terms, binding in honour only, and not in law, but in business dealings a heavy onus of proof lies on the person who alleges that there was no intention to enter into legal relations (*c*). Moreover, specific orders given and accepted under such a general agreement may be enforceable (*d*).

Consideration

Section 1 of the Sale of Goods Act defines a contract of sale as a contract whereby the seller transfers or agrees to transfer the property in goods to the buyer for a money consideration called the price.

(*a*) See Sch. 1, para. 11, of the Sale of Goods Act 1979, *post*, for the restrictions from 1973 to 1978. For restrictions from 1978 see the Unfair Contract Terms Act 1977, *post*, Appendix I.

(*b*) Restrictions are imposed by other legislation: see for example the statutes relating to price control and resale price maintenance, p. 51, *post*, and the consumer protection legislation, p. 53, *post*.

(*c*) *Edwards* v. *Skyways, Ltd.*, [1964] 1 All E. R. 494; [1964] 1 W. L. R. 349.

(*d*) *Rose and Frank* v. *Crompton Brothers*, [1925] A. C. 445.

"Property" and "goods" are defined by s. 61 (1) of the Sale of Goods Act. The goods may be either existing goods owned or possessed by the seller, or goods to be manufactured or acquired by the seller after the making of the contract—see s. 5 of the Sale of Goods Act.

The price is described as "a money consideration", but may by agreement be paid partly with other goods (which are regarded for this purpose as the equivalent of money): see further, p. 82, *post*.

The distinction between contracts for the sale of goods and various similar contracts are examined, in the comment to s. 2 of the Sale of Goods Act, *post*.

The rules for determining the price where none is agreed by the parties, or where they agree to leave it to the valuation of a third party, are considered in ss. 8 and 9 of the Sale of Goods Act.

Statutory price control.—For several years recently, statutory restrictions were imposed on the prices which may be charged on certain goods sold in the course of a business. These restrictions were principally to be found in the Counter-Inflation Act 1973 (*e*). Where goods were unlawfully sold at a price in excess of the maximum permitted under that Act, the contract was not invalid, but the person paying the price may recover the excess unless he was himself liable to punishment in connection with the offence (*f*).

Alteration of customs or excise duties and of value added tax.—By s. 10 of the Finance Act 1901 (*post*, Appendix I), unless otherwise agreed, where after the making of the contract and before the delivery of the goods, a new or increased customs or excise duty is imposed, the amount may be added to the price; and, conversely, where the duty is repealed or lowered, the amount may be deducted from the price. In case of disagreement as to the amount it may be fixed by the Commissioners of Customs and Excise. A similar provision is made by s. 42 of the Finance Act 1972 (*post*, Appendix I) in respect of variations in the rate of value added tax between the date of the contract and the date on which the goods are supplied.

Offer and acceptance

The rules of offer and acceptance apply to contracts of sale in the same way as to contracts generally. The contract of sale must be founded on mutual consent (*g*). The parties must be agreed as to the terms of the contract including the terms upon which the price is to be

---

(*e*) See also Prices Act 1974.

(*f*) S. I. 1973 No. 660, para. 3.

(*g*) Thus the supply of drugs to a patient by the Ministry of Health or by a chemist on payment of a two shilling charge in accordance with a statutory duty is not a sale of goods: *Pfizer Corporation* v. *Ministry of Health*, [1965] 1 All E. R. 450; [1965] A. C. 512; *Appleby* v. *Sleep*, [1968] 2 All E. R. 265; [1968] 1 W. L. R. 948, D. C. See also *Thompson* v. *Ball* (1948), 92 Sol. Jo. 272, D. C. (licensee reluctantly served whisky to food and drugs sampling officer after first refusing to do so because he feared he might otherwise commit the offence of obstructing the officer: no sale).

paid (*h*). The offer and acceptance may be express, or may be implied in whole or in part from the conduct of the parties.

Frequently, goods are bought and sold without any agreement being made as to the price of the goods. In such a case, s. 8 (2) of the Sale of Goods Act provides that the buyer must pay a reasonable price. The circumstances in which s. 8 (2) applies, or in which apart from s. 8 (2) the court will imply a term that the goods should be sold at a reasonable price are discussed in the comment to s. 8 (2), *post*.

Mistake

Section 62 (2) of the Sale of Goods Act preserves the rules of the common law relating to the effect of mistake on a contract for the sale of goods, save insofar as they are inconsistent with the express provisions of the Act (*i*).

The law of mistake is of little practical importance in relation to the sale of goods, but questions occasionally arise where a fraudulent buyer has disguised his identity, in relation to s. 23 of the Sale of Goods Act, for if by reason of the fraud the contract is void for mistake, the fraudulent buyer acquires no title to the goods, and therefore can give no title even to one who buys from him in good faith. See further the comment to s. 23, *post*.

Questions may also arise whether a contract for the sale of specific goods is void or may be avoided because at the time it was made the goods did not exist and had never existed, or perhaps were so defective that the seller could not perform his obligations under the contract by delivering them. See further the comment to s. 6, *post*.

Capacity

Section 3 of the Sale of Goods Act specifically provides that capacity to buy and sell is regulated by the general law concerning capacity to contract, and to transfer and acquire property, subject to a proviso relating to the sale of necessaries. The general law concerning capacity to contract and to transfer and acquire property is discussed in the comment to s. 3 of the Sale of Goods Act, *post*.

Formalities

There are no special formalities required for most contracts for the sale of goods, except where the sale is made on credit terms to an individual and the credit is less than £5,000. In such cases, except insofar as the agreement is exempted by regulations made under s. 16 of the Consumer Credit Act 1974, the seller must comply with the

---

(*h*) For conflicting conditions of order see *Butler Machine Tool Co., Ltd.* v. *Ex-Cell-O Corporation (England), Ltd.*, [1979] 1 All E. R. 965; [1979] 1 W. L. R. 401, C. A. Contrast *Unity Finance* v. *Hammond* (1965), 109 Sol. Jo. 70 (a hire purchase agreement where the parties were not *ad idem* as to the size of the weekly payments) and see further the comment to s. 8 of the Sale of Goods Act, *post*.

(*i*) The saving may relate to s. 6 of the Sale of Goods Act, but see the comment to that section, *post*.

requirements of that Act (*k*). See further s. 4 of the Sale of Goods Act, *post.*

If, however, the parties have put a contract of sale into writing, the ordinary rules of evidence apply. The general rule is that parol evidence is inadmissible to contradict, add to, or vary the terms of the written instrument; but such evidence is admissible to explain it, and, in explaining it, to annex incidents thereto (*l*).

The general rule is subject to certain exceptions. Thus (1) Parol evidence is always admissible to avoid a contract, as for instance by showing that it was induced by fraud (*m*), or founded on such mistake as to prevent what appears to be a contract from ever having been a contract at all (*n*); (2) Parol evidence is admissible to show that a written agreement which purports to be unconditional was in fact executed with the intention that it should only take effect as a contract on the performance of a condition precedent (*o*); (3) A written agreement may in general (*p*) be modified by a subsequent oral agreement; (4) A written agreement can always be rescinded or abrogated by a subsequent oral agreement (*q*); (5) Parol evidence may be admitted to show that a written agreement is subject to a collateral oral warranty, provided that this is not inconsistent with the writing (*r*).

Moreover, the general rule only applies where the writing is intended to constitute the contract itself, and not merely a note or memorandum of it (*s*).

(*k*) Under Consumer Credit Act 1974, Sch. 3, the relevant provisions will come into force on dates to be appointed. As yet none of the provisions have been brought into force. The Act also repeals the Hire-Purchase Act 1965 from a date to be appointed under s. 192 (4) of that Act. As yet no date has been appointed, and credit sale and conditional sale agreements coming within the Hire-Purchase Act 1965 must comply with the formalities required by ss. 5–10 of that Act.

(*l*) *Phipson on Evidence* (12th ed.), Chs. 33–35; *Cross on Evidence* (5th ed.), pp. 608 *et seq.*; *Bristol Tramways Co.* v. *Fiat Motors, Ltd.*, [1910] 2 K. B. 831, at p. 838, *per* FARWELL, L. J. As to incidents annexed by usage, see *Syers* v. *Jonas* (1848), 2 Exch. 111 (usage to sell by sample); *Brown* v. *Byrne* (1854), 3 E. & B. 703 (usage to deduct discount); *Field* v. *Lelean* (1861), 6 H. & N. 617, Ex. Ch. (usage not to deliver till time of payment arrives); *Produce Brokers Co.* v. *Olympia Oil and Cake Co.* [1917], 1 K. B. 320, C. A. (appropriation by original seller passed on the sub-buyer after loss); but see as to the limitations of usage, p. 15, *post.* See further, notes to *Wigglesworth* v. *Dallison*, 1 Smith L. C. (13th ed.) 597.

(*m*) *Chanter* v. *Hopkins* (1838), 4 M. & W. 399, at p. 406; *Kennedy* v. *Panama Mail Co.* (1867), L. R. 2 Q. B. 580; *Dobel* v. *Stevens* (1825), 3. L. J. (O. S.) K. B. 89.

(*n*) P. 3, *ante.*

(*o*) *Moore* v. *Campbell* (1854), 10 Exch. 323; *Murray* v. *Earl of Stair* (1823), 2 B. & C. 82; *Latch* v. *Wedlake* (1840), 11 Ad. & El. 959; *Clever* v. *Kirkman* (1875), 33 L. T. 672; *Lindley* v. *Lacey* (1864), 17 C. B., N. S. 578; *Guardhouse* v. *Blackburn* (1866), L. R. 1 P. & D. 109; *Pym* v. *Campbell* (1856), 25 L. J. Q. B. 277.

(*p*) But not if the agreement is one required by law to be in writing: *Goss* v. *Lord Nugent* (1833), 2. L. J. K. B. 127.

(*q*) Even if it is one required by law to be in writing: *Morris* v. *Baron & Co.*, [1918] A. C. 1, H. L.

(*r*) *Morgan* v. *Griffith* (1851), L. R. 6 Ex. 70; *De Lassalle* v. *Guildford*, [1901] 2 K. B. 215.

(*s*) *Allen* v. *Pink* (1838), 4 M. & W. 140.

An oral express term will override a written exemption clause (*t*), if made by the seller or by an agent with actual or ostensible authority to agree it (*u*).

A contract of sale, like other contracts, may be made retrospective in effect, so as to activate earlier dealings between the parties (*a*).

Representations

In the course of the formation of a contract of sale, representations may be made by either party which may have the following consequences:—

(1) The representation may be a mere expression of opinion, or a mere commendation by the seller of his wares—what is often called a "puff". Such a representation will give rise to no civil liability (*b*). An expression of opinion or a puff may however amount to or be treated as a trade description for the purposes of the Trade Descriptions Act 1968 so that, if the opinion is wrong or the puff is unjustified, the representants may be guilty of the offence of applying a false trade description under s. 1 of that Act (*c*).

(2) The representation may or may not become incorporated into the contract. Whether or not it does will depend upon the intention of the parties (*d*). If made in the course of negotiations for a contract for the purpose of inducing the other party to act on it, and it actually induces him to act on it, it is *prima facie* a term of the contract (*e*).

(*t*) *Couchman* v. *Hill*, [1947] 1 All E. R. 103, C. A.; [1947] K. B. 554, applied and approved in *Harling* v. *Eddy*, [1951] 2 All E. R. 212, C. A.; [1951], 2 K. B. 739; *J. Evans & Son, Ltd.* v. *Andrea Merzario*, [1976] 2 All E. R. 930; [1976] 1 W. L. R. 1078, C. A.

(*u*) An agent will not have such ostensible authority if the buyer is put on notice by a written document that he has no such authority before the contract is made or the terms agreed: *Jacobs* v. *Morris*, [1902] 1 Ch. 816, C. A.; *Overbrooke Estates, Ltd.* v. *Glencombe Properties, Ltd.*, [1974] 3 All E. R. 511; [1974] 1 W. L. R. 1335, explaining *Mendelssohn* v. *Normand, Ltd.*, [1969] 2 All E. R. 1215; [1970] 1 Q. B. 177, C. A.

(*a*) *Trollope and Colls, Ltd.* v. *Atomic Power Constructions*, [1962] 3 All E. R. 1035, 1040; [1963] 1 W. L. R. 333, 339–340.

(*b*) *Scott* v. *Hanson* (1829), 1 Russ. & M. 128; *Dimmock* v. *Hallett* (1866), 36 L. J. Ch. 146; *Magennis* v. *Fallon* (1828), 2 Mol. 561 at p. 588; Spencer Bower & Turner: *Actionable Misrepresentation* (3rd ed.), paras. 29–35, 49–51.

(*c*) See further p. 56, *post*.

(*d*) *Hopkins* v. *Tanqueray* (1854), 15 C. B. 130; *Bannerman* v. *White* (1861), 10 C. B. N. S. 844; *Routledge* v. *McKay*, [1954] 1 All E. R. 855; [1954] 1 W. L. R. 615, C. A.; *De Lassalle* v. *Guildford*, [1901] 2 K. B. 215, C. A.; criticised as incomplete in *Heilbutt* v. *Buckleton*, [1913] A. C. 30; *Couchman* v. *Hill*, [1947] 1 All E. R. 103; [1947] K. B. 554, C. A.; *Birch* v. *Paramount Estates, Ltd.*, cited in *Oscar Chess* v. *Williams*, [1957] 1 All E. R. 325; [1957] 1 W. L. R. 370, C. A.; *Dick Bentley Productions, Ltd.* v. *Harold Smith* (*Motors*), *Ltd.*, [1965] 2 All E. R. 65; [1965] 1 W. L. R. 623, C. A.; *J. Evans & Son, Ltd.* v. *Andrea Merzario, supra*. A representation which is not incorporated in the contract is sometimes (and confusingly) called a "mere" representation.

(*e*) It is for the maker of the representation to rebut this inference by showing that it really was innocent, in that he was in fact innocent of fault in making it, and that it would not be reasonable in the circumstances for him to be bound by it: *Dick Bentley Productions* v. *Harold Smith, supra, per* Lord DENNING, M. R. As to the classification of terms, see p. 8, *post*. As to representations in sales brochures, compare *Murray* v. *Sperry Rand Corporation*,

(a) If it is a condition, the other party will be entitled (*f*) to rescind if it is broken;

(b) If it is only a warranty, the other party will in the event of a breach be entitled only to damages for the breach of warranty.

(c) If it is neither a condition nor a warranty, but an "intermediate" term, the rights of the other party upon its breach will depend upon all the circumstances (*g*).

(d) The right, if any, of the other party to rescind for misrepresentation is not lost just because the misrepresentation has become a term of the contract (*h*).

(3) Whether or not incorporated into the contract, the representation may be made before or at the time of contracting about some existing fact or past event, and be one of the causes inducing the making of the contract (*i*). In that event,

(a) if the representation prove to be false in a material respect (regardless of whether or not made fraudulently), equity will *prima facie* (*k*) allow the party who has been misled to rescind the contract (*l*); but where the misrepresentation was not fraudulent, the court or an arbitrator has a discretion to award damages in lieu of rescission if of the opinion that it would be

---

[1979] 23 O. R. (2d) 456 (where representations in the manufacturers' and distributors' sales brochures were held to amount to collateral warranties by them upon which a purchaser from a retailer could sue) with *Lambert* v. *Lewis*, [1980] 1 All E. R. 978; [1980] 2 W. L. R. 299, C. A. (where a retailer was held not to be entitled to sue a manufacturer upon similar representations when he had not bought direct from the manufacturer – an appeal to the House of Lords was dismissed on other grounds—see *Lexmead* (*Basingstoke*) *Ltd.* v. *Lewis* (1981) Times, 9th April).

(*f*) Subject of course to s. 11 (2) and s. 11 (4) of the Sale of Goods Act, *post*: see generally *Wallis* v. *Pratt & Haynes*, [1911] A. C. 394.

(*g*) See p. 8, *post*.

(*h*) Misrepresentation Act 1967, s. 1, *post*, Appendix I.

(*i*) As to inducement and materiality see Spencer Bower and Turner: *Actionable Misrepresentation*, Ch. VI.

(*k*) But subject to the limitations imposed on the equitable remedy: thus there will be no rescission if the plaintiff has delayed too long (*Leaf* v. *International Galleries*, [1950] 1 All E. R. 693; [1950] 2 K. B. 86, C. A.); or has otherwise affirmed the contract (*Long* v. *Lloyd*, [1958] 2 All E. R. 402; [1958] 1 W. L. R. 753; and see the cases on affirmation for the purposes of s. 18, rule 4 and s. 35 of the Sale of Goods Act, *post*); or where *restitutio in integrum* is no longer possible (*Glasgow South Western Rail. Co.* v. *Boyd and Forrest*, [1915] A. C. 526; *cf. Freeman* v. *Consolidated Motors, Ltd.* (1968), 69 D. L. R. (2d) 581 (trade-in car sold by motor dealer before buyer sought to rescind contract of which trade-in formed part)); or where third party rights would be prejudiced (*Oakes* v. *Turquand* (1867), L. R. 2 H. L. 325); as to the onus of proof, see *Steedman* v. *Frigidaire Corpn.*, [1933] 1 D. L. R. 161, P. C.; *Zien* v. *Field* (1964), 41 D. L. R. (2d) 394. Prior to 1967 it was doubtful whether a party could rescind for innocent (as opposed to fraudulent) misrepresentation once the contract had been executed. It is now settled by s. 1 of the Misrepresentation Act 1967, *post*, Appendix I, that the right to rescind will not be lost just because the contract has been performed. See generally Spencer Bower & Turner, *op. cit.*,.Chs. XIII–XIV.

(*l*) In theory, therefore, a party faced with a breach of condition has two distinct and independent rights to rescind: one for breach of condition and the other for material misrepresentation. In practice, however, it is difficult to imagine a case where the latter remedy would avail him if the former did not: as DENNING, L. J., pointed out in *Leaf* v. *International Galleries*, [1950] 1 All E. R. 693, at p. 695; [1950] 2 K. B. 86, at pp. 90–91, "it is

equitable to do so, having regard to the nature of the misrepresentation and the loss that would be caused by it if the contract were upheld, as well as to the loss that rescission would cause to the other party (*m*);

(b) if the representation was made fraudulently, the party deceived will be entitled to damages for the tort of deceit (*n*), and also to rescind the contract (*o*);

(c) if the representation was not made fraudulently, but was made in such circumstances that had it been fraudulent, the person making it would have been liable to damages, then that person will be so liable unless he proves that he had reasonable grounds to believe and did believe up to the time the contract was made that the facts represented were true (*p*);

(d) the representation may create an estoppel against its maker (*q*);

(e) whether or not the representation was made fraudulently the representor may be guilty of an offence under the Trade Descriptions Act 1968 if the misrepresentation was made in the course of a business (*r*).

Although the decision to rescind should normally be communicated to the other contracting party (*s*), this may not be essential at any rate where that other party is a rogue who has deliberately absconded. In such a case it is sufficient if the rescinding party takes all possible steps to recover the goods (*t*). It may be that this is also the position in other

---

to be remembered that an innocent misrepresentation is much less potent than a breach of condition . . . if a claim to reject for breach of condition is barred, it seems to me *a fortiori* that a claim to rescission on the ground of innocent misrepresentation is also barred." It is possible that the effect of s. 3 of the Misrepresentation Act 1967, *post*, Appendix I, is that the right to rescind for breach of condition may be excluded, while the right to rescind for misrepresentation is not. See further the comment to that section, *post*.

(*m*) Misrepresentation Act 1967, s. 2 (2), *post*, Appendix I.

(*n*) *Levy* v. *Langridge* (1838), 4 M. & W. 337, Ex. Ch.; *Derry* v. *Peek* (1889), 14 App. Cas. 337, and see the notes to s. 62 (2) of the Sale of Goods Act, *post*. Damages for deceit should compensate the plaintiff for all the actual damage directly flowing from the fraudulent inducement and are not limited to such as may reasonably be supposed to have been in the contemplation of the parties: *Doyle* v. *Olby*, [1969] 2 All E. R. 119; [1969] 2 Q. B. 158, C. A.

(*o*) But the goods must be rejected within a reasonable time after the fraud is discovered: *Kwei Tek Chao* v. *British Traders*, [1954] 1 All E. R. 779; [1954] 2 Q. B. 459.

(*p*) Misrepresentation Act 1967, s. 2 (1), *post*, Appendix I. There may also be a claim for damages for negligent misrepresentation: *Esso Petroleum, Ltd.* v. *Mardon*, [1976] 2 All E. R. 5; [1976] Q. B. 801, C. A.; *Howard Marine and Dredging Co., Ltd.* v. *A. Ogden & Sons*, [1978] 2 All E. R. 1134; [1978] Q. B. 574, C. A.

(*q*) *Maddison* v. *Alderson* (1883), 8 App. Cas. 467, at p. 473; *cf.* the comment to s. 21 of the Sale of Goods Act, *post*.

(*r*) See p. 56, *post*.

(*s*) *Scarf* v. *Jardine* (1882), 7 App. Cas. 345, at p. 361; *Kerr on Fraud and Mistake* (7th ed.), p. 530; Spencer Bower & Turner, *op. cit.*, para. 239.

(*t*) *Car and Universal Finance Co., Ltd.* v. *Caldwell*, [1964] 1 All E. R. 290; [1965] 1 Q. B. 525, C. A.; *Newtons of Wembley, Ltd.* v. *Williams*, [1964] 3 All E. R. 532; [1965] 1 Q. B. 560, C. A. But *cf. MacLeod* v. *Kerr*, 1965 S. L. T. 358, where the Court of Session took a different view; see also 29 M. L. R. 442.

cases where the communication of the intention to rescind cannot readily be effected (*u*).

Terms of the contract

Conditions and warranties contrasted.—The Sale of Goods Act draws throughout a distinction between the terms "condition" and "warranty," and defines the circumstances under which a condition may be treated as a warranty.

This distinction had often been insisted on, but seldom observed by judges and text-writers before the Act. As used in the Act, "condition" is the equivalent of the old term "dependent covenant", while "warranty" is equivalent to the old term "independent covenant".

A warranty is defined by s. 61 (1) of the Sale of Goods Act (as regards England and Ireland, but not Scotland) as an agreement with reference to goods which are the subject of a contract of sale, but collateral to the main purpose of such contract, the breach of which gives rise to a claim for damages, but not to a right to reject the goods and treat the contract as repudiated.

No express definition of "condition" is given by the Act, but it is defined by inference as a term in the contract the breach of which gives rise to a right to repudiate the contract. Whether a given stipulation is a condition or a warranty is a question of construction and intention, and not of terminology: see s. 11 of the Sale of Goods Act, *post*.

Relation to general law of contract.—Sections 10 to 15 of the Sale of Goods Act deal with conditions and warranties peculiar to the law of sale. But the Act must be regarded as a single chapter in the general law of contract, and it therefore does not attempt to deal with the law of representations, conditions, and warranties to the extent that they are governed by considerations common to the whole field of contract. In so far as sale is regulated by the general law of contract, the rules which apply are saved by s. 62 (2), *post*, except insofar as they are inconsistent with the express provisions of the Act.

In other classes of contract, many terms may be neither conditions nor warranties as defined above, but "intermediate terms", and the question whether a breach by one party of such an "intermediate" term entitles the other party to treat the contract as repudiated turns upon the seriousness of the breach in all the circumstances (*a*). In such other contracts, the nature of the term is determined from the contract and the surrounding circumstances.

In contracts for the sale of goods, where terms are implied by ss. 12–15 of the Act, they must be either conditions or warranties although similar terms in other contracts may be of the intermediate kind

---

(*u*) *Car and Universal Finance Co., Ltd.* v. *Caldwell, supra.*

(*a*) See the judgment of DIPLOCK, L.J., in *Hong Kong Fir Co., Ltd.* v. *Kawasaki*, [1962] 1 All E. R. 474, at pp. 485–9; [1962] 2 Q. B. 26, at pp. 65–73; *Schuler A. G.* v. *Wickman Machine Tool Sales, Ltd.*, [1973] 2 All E. R. 39; [1974] A. C. 235, H. L.; *Daulatram Rameshwarlall* v. *European Grain & Shipping, Ltd.*, [1971] 1 Lloyd's Rep. 368; *Bremer Handelgesellschaft m.b.h.* v. *Vanden Avenne-Izegem*, [1978] 2 Lloyd's Rep. 109, H. L.

(*b*). Indeed, the whole Act, and particularly s. 11 (3), appears to have been drafted on the assumption that a term has either to be a condition or a warranty, but there is nothing in the Act so inconsistent with the existence of such intermediate terms as to prevent the ordinary rules of common law from applying in respect of them except in the case of terms implied by ss. 12–15 of the Act (*c*).

Express agreement.—Sale is a consensual contract, and the parties may alter at will the obligations which the law implies from the general nature of the contract. BLACKBURN, J., discussing the correlative obligations of payment and delivery, says,

> "There is no rule of law to prevent the parties from making any bargain they please" (*d*);

and BRETT, L. J., says,

> "Merchants are not bound to make their contracts according to any rule of law" (*e*).

Interpretation and construction.—There is no canon of construction peculiar to contracts of sale.

> "The rule of construction applicable in general to all written contracts is, that they are to be construed according to the real intention of the parties, to be collected from the language they have used; that effect is to be given, if possible, to every word used, and that every word is to be interpreted according to its natural and ordinary meaning, unless such construction would be contrary to the manifest intention of the parties, or would necessarily lead to some contradiction or absurdity. But this rule, though applicable to contracts in general, must be received with some qualification, when the contract or a portion of the contract in question consists of an incomplete sentence, ambiguous in its terms, and upon which a literal construction of every word would either be impracticable or would leave the contract indeterminable and uncertain. And such is the case with the contract in question, which I think is to be construed according to what we can collect to have been the substantial intention of the parties, applying our common sense, and such knowledge as we may possess, to the language in which they have expressed themselves" (*f*).

In construing a contract, the court must place itself in thought in the

---

(*b*) Cf. *Harbutt's Plasticine, Ltd.* v. *Wayne Tank and Pump Co., Ltd.*, [1970] 1 All E. R. 225; [1970] 1 Q. B. 447, C. A.

(*c*) *Cehave N. V.* v. *Bremer Handelsgesellschaft m.b.h.*, [1975] 3 All E. R. 739; [1976] Q. B. 44, C. A.; *Daulatram Rameshwarlall* v. *European & Shipping, Ltd.*, *supra*. See further the comment to s. 11(3) of the Sale of Goods Act, *post*.

(*d*) *Calcutta Co.* v. *De Mattos* (1863), 32 L. J. Q. B. 322, at p. 328; see the passage cited at length, *post*, Appendix II, Note B.

(*e*) *Honck* v. *Muller* (1881), 7 Q. B. D. 92, at p. 103, C. A. For an extreme application of this principle, see *Lancaster* v. *Turner & Co.*, [1924] 2 K. B. 222 (effect of "invoicing back clause" in case of seller's default).

(*f*) *Per* KELLY, C. B. in *Coddington* v. *Paleologo* (1867), L. R. 2 Exch. 193, at p. 200; *cf. Honck* v. *Muller* (1881), 7 Q. B. D. 92, at p. 103, *per* Lord ESHER; *Champanhac & Co., Ltd.* v. *Waller & Co., Ltd.*, [1948] 2 All E. R. 724.

same factual situation as that in which the parties were when the contract was made (*g*).

Section 55 (2) of the Sale of Goods Act, *post* (*h*), expressly provides that an express condition or warranty does not negative a condition or warranty implied by the Sale of Goods Act unless inconsistent with it. But this probably does no more than restate the position at common law (*i*).

Exemption clauses.—At common law a party to a contract may by a suitably worded exemption clause (*k*) exclude or limit his liability for breach of any term of the contract. Formerly, this was also the case in a contract for the sale of goods, and before 1973 s. 55 of the Act, *post*, provided that any implied condition or warranty may be negatived or varied by express agreement, course of dealing or usage. That right has now been severely restricted by the Unfair Contract Terms Act 1977 (*l*), repealing and replacing the amendments effected to s. 55 by s. 4 of the Supply of Goods (Implied Terms) Act 1973 in relation to attempts by a seller to limit or exclude his liability in respect of the conditions and warranties implied by ss. 12–15 of the Act (*m*). The restrictions apply to all contracts for the sale of goods except international supply contracts (*n*).

Fundamental breach and exemption clauses.—A fundamental breach of contract is a breach or a number of breaches rendering the purported performance of a contract quite different from that which the contract contemplated (*o*).

In recent years the view has been put forward that no exemption clause could relieve a party to a contract from liability for a fundamental breach (*p*). But it has now been settled by the House of Lords in *Suisse Atlantique Société D'Armement Maritime S. A.* v. *N. V. Rotterdamsche Kolen Centrale* (*q*) and re-affirmed in *Photo Production, Ltd.* v. *Securicor Transport, Ltd.* (*r*) that this view was wrong. To cover a case of

(*g*) *Reardon Smith Line, Ltd.* v. *Hansen–Tangen*, [1976] 3 All E. R. 570; [1976] 1 W. L. R. 989, H. L.; *Bunge, S. A.* v. *Kruse*, [1977] 1 Lloyd's Rep. 492.

(*h*) Formerly s. 14 (4). The present s. 55 (2) was introduced into the Sale of Goods Act 1893 by s. 4 of the Supply of Goods (Implied Terms) Act 1973.

(*i*) *Mody* v. *Gregson* (1868), L. R. 4 Exch. 49, at p. 53, Ex. Ch.; approved, *Drummond* v. *Van Ingen* (1887), 12 App. Cas. 284, at p. 294, *per* Lord HERSCHELL. *Cf. Bigge* v. *Parkinson* (1862), 7 H. & N. 955.

(*k*) In several cases the need for clear language in provisions designed to limit or exclude the ordinary rights of the buyer has been emphasised: see, *e.g. Wallis* v. *Pratt*, [1911] A. C. 394; *Pollock* v. *McRae*, 1922 S. C. 192, H. L.; *Baldry* v. *Marshall*, [1925] 1 K. B. 260; *Alison & Co.* v. *Wallsend Slipway and Engineering Co.* (1927), 43 T. L. R. 323, C. A.; *Modiano Bros. & Son* v. *Pearson & Co., Ltd.* (1929), 34 Ll. L. Rep. 52; *Webster* v. *Higgin*, [1948] 2 All E. R. 127.

(*l*) *Post*, Appendix I.

(*m*) See further the comment to s. 55, *post*.

(*n*) As defined in s. 26 of the Unfair Contract Terms Act 1977, *post*, Appendix I.

(*o*) *Suisse Atlantique Société D'Armement Maritime S. A.* v. *N. V. Rotterdamsche Kolen Centrale*, [1966] 2 All E. R. 61; [1967] 1 A. C. 361, H. L.

(*p*) *E.g., Karsales (Harrow), Ltd.* v. *Wallis*, [1956] 2 All E. R. 866; [1956] 1 W. L. R. 936.

(*q*) [1966] 2 All E. R. 61; [1967] 1 A. C. 361; and see 29 M. L. R. 546.

(*r*) [1980] 1 All E. R. 556; [1980] A. C. 827, H. L.

fundamental breach, an exemption clause could, it seems, take one of three forms: it might limit liability in the event of such a breach, for example, by limiting the quantum of damages payable or by limiting the time within which a particular remedy would be available to an injured party (*s*); or it might exclude liability; or it might make permissible what would otherwise be a fundamental breach (*t*).

But the courts will only interpret exemption clauses as extending to cases of fundamental breach if they are worded in clear and unambiguous terms (*u*). Indeed, even when they are so worded, they must still be construed in conjunction with the contract as a whole (*a*) and until recently their terms have been read down where they could be applied literally without creating an absurdity or defeating the main object of the contract (*b*).

> "There is a strong, though rebuttable, presumption that in inserting a clause of exclusion or limitation in their contract the parties are not contemplating breaches of fundamental terms and such clauses do not apply to relieve a party from the consequences of such a breach even where the contract continues in force. This result has been achieved by a robust use of a well-known canon of construction, that wide words which taken in isolation would bear one meaning must be so construed as to give business efficacy to the contract and the presumed intention of the parties, upon the footing that both parties are intending to carry out the contract fundamentally" (*c*).

But now that Parliament has intervened to limit the effect of exemption clauses (*d*) it seems that the courts will be less willing than before to place a strained construction upon words in an exemption clause, particularly in the case of a commercial dispute between businessmen capable of looking after their own interests and deciding how risks ought to be borne (*e*).

(*s*) *Suisse Atlantique Société Maritime S. A.* v. *N. V. Rotterdamsche Kolen Centrale.* [1966] 2 All E. R. at p. 92; [1967] 1 A. C. at p. 431; *H. & E. Van der Sterren* v. *Cibernetics (Holdings)* Pty., Ltd. (1970), 44 A. L. J. R. 157 (H. C. of Aus.).

(*t*) *Cf.* the division adopted by DIPLOCK, L. J., in *Hardwick Game Farm* v. *Suffolk Agricultural and Poultry Producers Association, Ltd.*, [1966] 1 All E. R. 309, 346; [1966] 1 W. L. R. 287, 341. The third case is not strictly speaking an exemption clause, but permits the performance of the contract in a way which would otherwise be held not to have been contemplated by the parties. For an unsuccessful attempt to construe a clause in this way, see *Glynn* v. *Margetson & Co.*, [1893] A. C. 351.

(*u*) *Suisse Atlantique Société D'Armament Maritime S. A.* v. *N. V. Rotterdamsche Kolen Centrale, supra.* For examples of such clauses see *R. W. Green, Ltd.* v. *Cade Bros. Farms*, [1978] 1 Lloyds Rep. 602; *Photo Production, Ltd.* v. *Securicor Transport, Ltd.*, [1980] 1 All E. R. 556; [1980] A. C. 827, H. L.; *Woollatt Fuel and Lumber* v. *Matthews Group* (1978), 83 D. L. R. (3d) 137.

(*a*) *Ibid.*, [1966] 2 All E. R. at pp. 67, 81; [1967] 1 A. C. at pp. 392, 413–414; applied in *Western Tractors* v. *Dyck* (1969), 7 D. L. R. (3d) 535; *Barker* v. *Inland Truck Sales* (1970), 11 D. L. R. (3d) 469.

(*b*) *Ibid.*, [1966] 2 All E. R. at p. 71; [1967] 1 A. C. at p. 398, per Lord REID; *H. & E. Van der Sterren* v. *Cibernetics (Holdings) Pty., Ltd.* (1970), 44 A. L. J. R. 157 (H. C. of Aus.)

(*c*) *Ibid.*, [1966] 2 All E. R. 89; [1967] 1 A. C. 427, *per* Lord UPJOHN.

(*d*) See the Unfair Contract Terms Act 1977, partially reproduced *post*, Appendix I.

(*e*) *Photo Production, Ltd.* v. *Securicor Transport, Ltd.*, [1980] All E. R. 556; [1980] A. C.

The principles involved in determining whether an exemption clause ought to be read down would appear to be those involved in determining whether any term ought to be implied into a contract (*f*). Thus the language which the parties have used in an exemption clause is not so to be modified unless it is necessary to give effect to what the parties must be understood to have intended (*g*).

In construing a contract with a view to ascertaining what the parties intended, the court may be more inclined to read down a clause in standard printed conditions imposed upon an ignorant buyer, than a clause in clear language agreed between two parties negotiating on an equal footing (*h*).

These principles of construction do not apply to an agreed damage clause inserted for the benefit of both parties (*i*).

In applying these principles, it would seem that while a suitably drafted clause may (*k*) expressly provide for the delivery of beans instead of peas, or may (*l*) limit the damage in the event of peas not being delivered, it is still not possible to go so far as to provide that the seller is not obliged to deliver the contract goods at all, or that he shall not be liable for failure to do so.

> "One may safely say that the parties cannot, in a contract, have contemplated that the clause should have so wide an ambit as in effect to deprive one party's stipulations of all force; to do so would be to reduce the contract to a mere declaration of intent" (*m*).

Implied terms.—A distinction must be drawn between the implication of terms

> "based on an intention imputed to the parties from their actual circumstances",

as discussed below, and that of a term

> "which does not depend on the actual intention of the parties but on a rule of law, such as the terms, warranties or conditions which, if not expressly

---

827, H. L.; *R. W. Green, Ltd.* v. *Cade Bros. Farms*, [1978] 1 Lloyds Rep. 602.

(*f*) *Post*, p. 13; and see *R. G. Maclean, Ltd.* v. *Canada Vickers, Ltd.* (1971), 15 D. L. R. (3d) 15.

(*g*) *H. & E. Van der Sterren* v. *Cibernetics (Holdings) Pty., Ltd.* (1970), 44 A. L. J. R. 157 (Sale of goods; Clause limiting time within which buyer could make claim in relation to the goods sold).

(*h*) *Ibid., Photo Production, Ltd.* v. *Securicor Transport, Ltd., supra*; and see *Thornton* v. *Shoe Lane Parking, Ltd.*, [1971] 1 All E. R. 686; [1971] 2 Q. B. 163, C. A.; but *cf. Kenyon Son & Craven, Ltd.* v. *Baxter Hoare & Co., Ltd.*, [1971] 2 All E. R. 708, at p. 720; [1971] 1 W. L. R. 519, at p. 533.

(*i*) *Suisse Atlantique Société D'Armement Maritime S. A.* v. *N. V. Rotterdamsche Kolen Centrale*, [1966] 2 All E. R. 61; [1967] 1 A. C. 361; and *cf. G. H. Renton & Co., Ltd.* v. *Palmyra Trading Corporation of Panama*, [1956] 3 All E. R. 957; [1957] A. C. 149.

(*k*) Subject to s. 3 (2) (b) of the Unfair Contract Terms Act 1977, *post*, Appendix I.

(*l*) Subject to ss. 3 (2) (a) and 6 (2) of the Unfair Contract Terms Act 1977, *post*, Appendix I.

(*m*) *Suisse Atlantique Société D'Armement Maritime S. A.* v. *N. V. Rotterdamsche Kolen Centrale*, [1966] 2 All E. R. 92; [1967] 1 A. C. 432, *per* LORD WILBERFORCE.

excluded, the law imports, as for instance under the Sale of Goods Act and the Marine Insurance Act" (*n*).

There are many cases in which the courts must pronounce upon rights and obligations of parties to a contract which have not been expressly provided for by the parties themselves and are not implied by operation of law. In such cases, the court is often asked to imply a term into the contract, and it will generally do so, though always with great caution, if it is clear from the nature of the transaction that the parties must have intended such a term to be a part of the contract, and if in all the circumstances it is a reasonable term (though this last consideration alone is not enough); but the court will always be careful not to make for the parties a contract they have not made themselves.

"The court does not make a contract for the parties. The court will not even improve the contract which the parties have made for themselves, however desirable the improvement might be. The court's function is to interpret and apply the contract which the parties have made for themselves . . . An unexpressed term can be implied if and only if the court finds that the parties must have intended that term to form part of their contract: it is not enough for the court to find that such a term would have been adopted by the parties as reasonable men if it had been suggested to them: it must have been a term that went without saying, a term necessary to give business efficacy to the contract, a term which, although tacit, formed part of the contract which the parties made for themselves" (*o*).

But the court is not concerned to decide what the parties actually intended. A term will not be implied merely because both parties independently intended such a term to be incorporated in the contract, if in fact it was not referred to by either party and could not be described as "going without saying".

"The judicial task is not to discover the actual intention of each party; it is to decide what each was reasonably entitled to conclude from the attitude of the other" (*p*).

Course of dealing.—The phrase "course of dealing" means:

"that past business between the parties raises an implication as to the terms to be implied into a fresh contract, where no express provision is made on the point at issue" (*q*).

(*n*) *Luxor* v. *Cooper*, [1941] 1 All E. R. 33, at p. 52; [1941] A. C. 108, at p. 137, *per* Lord WRIGHT.

(*o*) *Trollope and Colls, Ltd.* v. *North West Metropolitan Regional Hospital Board*, [1973] 2 All E. R. 260, at p. 267; [1973] 1 W. L. R. 601, at p. 609, per Lord PEARSON. And see *B. P. Refinery Pty., Ltd.* v. *Shire of Hastings* (1978), 52 A. L. J. R. 20, P. C.

(*p*) *McCutcheon* v. *David MacBrayne*, [1964] 1 All E. R. 430, at p. 433; [1964] 1 W. L. R. 125, at p. 128, *per* Lord REID; *British Crane Hire Corporation* v. *Ipswich Plant Hire, Ltd.*, [1974] 1 All E. R. 1059; [1975] Q. B. 303, C. A. For the "officious bystander" text see *Shirlaw* v. *Southern Foundries*, [1939] 2 All E. R. 113, at p. 124; [1939] 2 K. B. 206, at p. 227; affirmed *sub nom. Southern Foundries* v. *Shirlaw*, [1940] 2 All E. R. 445; [1940] A. C. 701; *Luxor* v. *Cooper*, [1941] 1 All E. R. 33, at p. 52; [1941] A. C. 108, at p. 137, *per* Lord WRIGHT.

(*q*) *Pocahontas Fuel Co.* v. *Ambatielos* (1922), 27 Com. Cas. 148, at p. 152, *per* MCCARDIE, J.

Thus where a tradesman regularly charged a customer interest on debts due for over three years and the customer never objected, the customer was taken to have agreed to pay interest on all such debts with that tradesman (*r*).

The problem whether a term or terms should be implied into a contract as a result of a course of dealing, where no term could have been implied if the contract had been an isolated transaction, has most frequently arisen in recent years where one of the parties has written "Conditions of Contract" but the parties conclude a contract without any express reference to them, for example because they are contained in a document which is given to the other party only after the contract is concluded.

In such cases, the terms will be incorporated only if the parties by their conduct must be taken to have agreed that they should form part of the contract (*s*). It is irrelevant that the other party has not read the terms on the documents previously supplied to him, provided that he knew that that the documents contained terms which the party supplying the documents intended should be part of the contract between them, or at least that the party supplying the documents had taken reasonable steps to draw them to his attention (*t*).

But the terms will not normally be incorporated if the contract in question is materially different from the earlier contracts (*u*), nor if the earlier contracts were few and infrequent (*a*), nor if the document containing the terms is not one which the other party would expect to contain terms, and in fact he did not realise that it contained them (*b*), particularly if the party seeking to impose the terms ought to have realised that they would not or might not have come to the attention of the representative of the other party responsible for entering into the contracts (*c*).

(*r*) *Re Marquis of Anglesey, Willmot* v. *Gardner*, [1901] 2 Ch. 548, C. A.

(*s*) *Hardwick Game Farm* v. *Suffolk Agricultural Association, Ltd.*, [1966] 1 All E. R. 309, at pp. 322, 344–355; [1966] 1 W. L. R. 287, at pp. 308, 338–340; *sub nom. Henry Kendall & Sons* v. *William Lillico & Sons, Ltd.*, [1968] 2 All E. R. 444, at pp. 474–475, 481, 496; [1969] 2 A. C. 31, at pp. 104–105, 112–113, 130, H. L. See also as to the effect of terms contained in an invoice or confirmation note, 33 M. L. R. 518; Spencer Bower & Turner, *Estoppel by Representation* (3rd ed.), para 107; and see the judgment of Lord WRIGHT in *Hillas & Co.* v. *Arcos, Ltd.* (1932), 38 Com. Cas. 23.

(*t*) *Henry Kendall & Sons* v. *William Lillico & Sons, Ltd., supra; Mendelssohn* v. *Normand*, [1969] 2 All E. R. 1215; [1970] 1 Q. B. 177, C. A.

(*u*) *McCutcheon* v. *David MacBrayne*, [1964] 1 All E. R. 430; [1964] 1 W. L. R. 125, H. L. But it may be possible to infer a common understanding that the purchase was to be on the current conditions of one of the parties provided these were reasonable: *Farmway, Ltd.* v. *Bird*, unreported, 3rd October 1974, C. A.

(*a*) *Hollier* v. *Rambler Motors*, [1972] 1 All E. R. 399; [1972] 2 Q. B. 71, C. A. (3 or 4 occasions over 5 years).

(*b*) *Cf. Chapelton* v. *Barry Urban District Council*, [1940] 1 All E. R. 356; [1940] 1 K. B. 532, C. A.

(*c*) See *D. J. Hill & Co. Pty., Ltd.* v. *Walter H. Wright Pty., Ltd.*, [1971] V. R. 749; and compare *British Crane Hire Corporation, Ltd.* v. *Ipswich Plant Hire, Ltd.*, [1974] 1 All E. R. 1059; [1975] Q. B. 303, C. A. (two previous transactions, neither of which were known to the Manager placing the order: *semble* no sufficient course of dealing); *Grayston Plant, Ltd.*

Even where no course of dealing can be established, however, the standard terms of one party may be incorporated into a contract if from the conduct of the parties a common understanding can be shown to have existed between them that the contract should be on the usual conditions of one of them. Such an understanding may exist between parties of equal bargaining power in the same trade where the other party knows, and it is common knowledge in the trade, that such conditions are always imposed even though they are sometimes sent to the other party only after the agreement is made (*d*).

Usage.—Usage, says Lord BLACKBURN, when it is properly proved—

> "is to be considered as part of the agreement; and if the agreement be in writing, though the custom is not written it is to be treated exactly as if that unwritten customary clause had been written out at length" (*e*).

A usage may affect transactions either in a particular trade or a particular place and binds all those who participate in such transactions whatever the nature of their callings and in whatever capacity they do business (*f*).

To have effect, the usage must—

(1) be legal (*e*);

(2) be reasonable (*e*);

(3) be sufficiently certain that it would not be void for uncertainty if an express term of the contract (*f*);

(4) be generally accepted by those who habitually do business in the trade or market concerned and be so generally known that an outsider, who makes reasonable enquiries could not fail to be aware of it (*g*);

(5) not have been expressly or impliedly excluded by the agreement of the parties, as, for instance, where it is inconsistent with a written term of the contract (*h*);

(6) not be—

> "so inconsistent with the nature of the contract to which it is sought to be applied as that it would change its nature altogether, or as to change its intrinsic character" (*i*).

---

v. *Plean Precast, Ltd.*, 1976 S. C. 206, where the Court of Session held that the test was whether the party seeking to rely on the conditions had done what was reasonably sufficient to bring their existence to the other party's attention and that on the facts that test was not satisfied although there had been a course of twelve dealings in three months.

(*d*) *British Crane Hire Corporation, Ltd.* v. *Ipswich Plant Hire, Ltd., supra.* The equality of bargaining power is presumably relevant to the question whether the other party can be taken to have assented to the terms being incorporated into the contract, but it would not seem to be essential.

(*e*) *Tucker* v. *Linger* (1883), 8 App. Cas. 508, at p. 511.

(*f*) *Kum* v. *Wah Tat Bank*, [1971] 1 Lloyd's Rep. 439, P. C.

(*g*) *Kum* v. *Wah Tat Bank, supra*; and see *Robinson* v. *Mollet* (1875), L. R. 7 H. L. 802.

(*h*) *Produce Brokers Co.* v. *Olympia Oil & Cake Co.*, [1916] 1 A. C. 314; *Re Sutro & Co.*, [1917] 2 K. B. 348, C. A.; *Thomas Borthwick (Glasgow), Ltd.* v. *Faure Fairclough, Ltd.*, [1968] 1 Lloyd's Rep. 16; *Kum* v. *Wah Tat Bank, supra.*

(*i*) *Per* BRETT, J., in *Robinson* v. *Mollet* (*supra*), at p. 819. See also *per* WILLES, J. in the same case at (1870), L. R. 5 C. P. 646, *sub nom. Mollet* v. *Robinson.*

Illegality

The common law rules relating to the effect of illegality upon a contract are saved by s. 62 (2) of the Sale of Goods Act, *post*.

When illegality is apparent on the face of the transaction the court must take cognisance of it, though the defence of illegality is not set up (*k*); and similarly the court must take cognisance when the illegality becomes apparent from the evidence (*l*). But when the illegality is not apparent, it must be pleaded (*m*). Speaking generally, a contract is illegal when it is prohibited by statute or is contrary to public policy, as where it is for an illegal or immoral purpose which is known to both parties (*n*), or is intended by both parties to be performed in an illegal manner (*o*). If only one party has in mind the illegal or immoral purpose, or the intention to perform the contract in an illegal manner, and the other party does not know of his illicit designs, the contract is not illegal (*p*), and may be enforced by the innocent party, but not by the guilty party (*q*). Where, on the other hand, the contract itself (as opposed to its purpose or mode of performance) is prohibited by statute, and the prohibition is made in the public interest, neither party can enforce the contract, even though one party was unaware of the facts constituting the illegality (*r*).

(*k*) *Re North West Salt Co.*, [1913] 3 K. B. 422, C. A.; reversed, [1914] A. C. 461.

(*l*) *Snell* v. *Unity Finance, Ltd.*, [1963] 3 All E. R. 50; [1964] 2 Q. B. 203, C. A.; *Lipton* v. *Powell*, [1921] 2 K. B. 51, at p. 58; as to the duty of an arbitrator, see *David Taylor & Son, Ltd.* v. *Barnett*, [1953] 1 All E. R. 843; [1953] 1 W. L. R. 562, C. A.

(*m*) *Lipton* v. *Powell*, [1921] 2 K. B. 51.

(*n*) It is sufficient if the facts which give rise to the illegality are known to both parties even if one or both of them fails to realise that those facts constitute an offence: *Belvoir Finance Co.* v. *Stapleton*, [1970] 3 All E. R. 664; [1971] 1 Q. B. 210, C. A.; *cf. Southern Industrial Trust, Ltd.* v. *Brooke House Motors, Ltd.* (1968), 112 Sol. Jo. 798, C. A. (H.P. transaction: illegality of H.P. agreement through fraud of seller and customer; finance company entitled to enforce sale agreement with seller, being unaware of the fraud or illegality); *Mason* v. *Clarke*, [1955] 1 All E. R. 914; [1955] A. C. 778, H. L. (receipt required for unlawful purpose of which party giving receipt was unaware; innocent party not debarred from enforcing contract). As to good morals the rule is *ex turpi causâ non oritur actio; cf. Pearce* v. *Brooks* (1866), L. R. 1 Exch. 213 (supply of goods, not necessaries, to known prostitute). See the judgment of ATKIN, L. J., in *Rawlings* v. *General Trading Co.*, [1921] 1 K. B. 635, C. A., as to restraint of trade.

(*o*) See *Archbolds (Freightage), Ltd.* v. *Spanglett, Ltd.*, [1961] 1 All E. R. 417; [1961] 1 Q. B. 374, C. A.; *Mason* v. *Clarke, supra.* It is sufficient to debar the innocent party from enforcing the contract if, after the contract has been entered into, he becomes aware that the other party intends to perform the contract in a manner which the innocent party knows to be unlawful, and participates in the unlawful performance, for example by standing by and sanctioning it when by objecting he might prevent it: *Ashmore Benson Pease & Co., Ltd.* v. *A. V. Dawson, Ltd.*, [1973] 2 All E. R. 856; [1973] 1 W. L. R. 828, C. A.

(*p*) *Marles* v. *Philip Trant & Sons, Ltd.*, [1953] 1 All E. R. 651; [1954] 1 Q. B. 29, C. A.

(*q*) *Alexander* v. *Rayson*, [1936] 1 K. B. 169; *St. John Shipping Corporation* v. *Joseph Rank, Ltd.*, [1956] 3 All E. R. 683, at p. 687; [1957] 1 Q. B. 267, at p. 283. But if the guilty party did not have the unlawful intention to perform the contract illegally when the contract was made, he can enforce the contract, provided that in so doing he does not have to disclose that he committed an illegal act: *St. John Shipping Corpn.* v. *Joseph Rank, Ltd., supra.*

(*r*) *Re Mahmoud and Ispahani*, [1921] 2 K. B. 716, C. A.; *Archbolds (Freightage), Ltd.* v. *S. Spanglett, Ltd.*, [1961] 1 All E. R. 417; [1961] 1 Q. B. 374, C. A.; *Yin* v. *Sam*, [1962] A. C. 304, P. C. See also *St. John Shipping Corpn.* v. *Joseph Rank, Ltd., supra; Fenton* v. *Scotty's Car Sales*, [1968] N. Z. L. R. 929.

Normally it is for the person alleging illegality to prove it (*s*). Where a contract is capable of two constructions and the effect of one is to render it illegal, the other construction will be given to it *ut res magis valeat quam pereat* (*t*). So too, where a contract can be performed either legally or illegally the presumption is that it will be performed legally (*u*). Where the property in goods is transferred in pursuance of an illegal transaction, then, at least if the contract has been fully executed, it remains in the transferee notwithstanding the illegality (*a*), even if the transferee has never taken possession of the goods (*b*). As to illegality by subsequent legislation or outbreak of war, see p. 18, *post*.

Many statutory offences in connection with the sale of goods have been created in recent years. In general, however, the statutes creating the offences have provided that a contract is not to be void or unenforceable by reason only of such offences (*c*).

Impossibility

There are cases common to the whole field of contract where performance is excused on the ground of impossibility. As a general rule, if a man makes a contract he must fulfil its conditions or pay damages. It is no excuse that he cannot get the goods he has contracted to deliver (*d*), or that he can only obtain them at a prohibitive price (*e*), or that they can only be shipped by a much longer sea route than the parties contemplated at the time of contracting (*f*), or that they cannot be shipped because the agreed shipping line failed to provide a vessel to load in the agreed month of shipment (*g*). If he wishes to be safe he must protect himself by express stipulation (*h*). But there are cases of *vis major*,

---

(*s*) *Hire Purchase Furnishing Co.* v. *Richens* (1887), 20 Q. B. D. 387.

(*t*) *Cf. Wong* v. *Beaumont Property Trust, Ltd.*, [1964] 2 All E. R. 119; [1965] 1 Q. B. 173, C. A. (construction of lease).

(*u*) *Lewis* v. *Davidson* (1839), 4 M. & W. 654, at p. 657; *Waugh* v. *Morris* (1873), L. R. 8 Q. B. 202, at p. 208; applied in *Maschinenfabrik Seydelmann K. G.* v. *Presswood Brothers, Ltd.*, [1966] 1 O. R. 316.

(*a*) *Singh* v. *Ali*, [1960] 1 All E. R. 269; [1960] A. C. 167, P. C.; *Chettiar* v. *Chettiar*, [1962] 1 All E. R. 494; [1962] A. C. 294, P. C.

(*b*) *Belvoir Finance Co.* v. *Stapleton*, [1970] 3 All E. R. 664; [1971] 1 Q. B. 210, C. A.

(*c*) See further p. 54, *post*.

(*d*) *Hale* v. *Rawson* (1858), 4 C. B., N. S., 85; *Re Weis & Co.*, [1916] 1 K. B. 346; *Blackburn Bobbin Co.* v. *Allen & Sons, Ltd.*, [1918] 2 K. B. 467, C. A.; *Produce Brokers Co.* v. *Weis & Co.* (1918), 87 L. J. K. B. 472; *Sargant & Sons* v. *Paterson & Co.* (1923), 129 L. T. 471 (intended port of shipment closed by enemy); *Intertradex S. A.* v. *Lesieur-Tourteaux S.a.r.l.*, [1977] 2 Lloyd's Rep. 146 (supplier of seller unable to fulfil contract with seller because raw materials not available).

(*e*) *Exportelisa S.A.* v. *Rocco Giuseppe*, [1978] 1 Lloyd's Rep. 433.

(*f*) *Tsakiroglou & Co., Ltd.* v. *Noblee & Thorl G.m.b.H.*, [1961] 2 All E. R. 179; [1962] A. C. 93, H. L.

(*g*) *Thomas Borthwick (Glasgow), Ltd.* v. *Faure Fairclough, Ltd.*, [1968] 1 Lloyd's Rep. 16.

(*h*) *New Zealand Shipping Co.* v. *Société des Ateliers de France*, [1919] A. C. 1; *per* Lord LOREBURN in *Tennants (Lancashire), Ltd.* v. *Wilson & Co.*, [1917] A. C. 495, at p. 510. The following cases illustrate how particular stipulations of this kind have been construed by the courts: *Matsoukis* v. *Priestman & Co.*, [1915] 1 K. B. 681 (provision for payment of £10 in respect of any day in which performance was late, "force majeure" excepted); *Peter Dixon & Sons* v. *Henderson & Co.*, [1919] 2 K. B. 778, C. A. (suspension of delivery if

independent of any particular contract, which excuse performance. For example, if the goods which a man has contracted to sell are requisitioned by the Government before delivery, he is absolved from his obligation to deliver them (*i*).

Supervening illegality.—Again, if a contract, legal in its inception, is prohibited by or under an Act of Parliament before its fulfilment, the obligation is dissolved (*k*). A declaration of war by this country operates as an Act of Parliament prohibiting all intercourse with the enemy (*l*). If a contract made before war involves intercourse with the enemy for its due performance, the contract is dissolved, and a clause purporting to suspend its operation during war is null and void (*m*). As to who is an enemy, see p. 91, *post.*

The provisions of s. 1 of the Law Reform (Frustrated Contracts) Act 1943 apply to these cases, because the impossibility does not arise from the fact that the goods have perished.

Continental lawyers recognise *force majeure* as excusing the performance of a contract on the principle of act of state. English judges formerly rested the defence of *vis major* on the fiction of an implied condition forming the basis of the contract between the parties (*n*). This fiction has now largely been abandoned. The current test is whether a situation has arisen which renders performance of the contract a thing radically different from that which the parties undertook (*o*). Though

---

"hindered" by war, etc.); *Clark* v. *Cox McEuen & Co.* (*1919*), [1921] 1 K. B. 139, C. A. (contract to be cancelled if vessel lost before declaration of shipment); *Re Comptoir Commercial Anversois*, [1920] 1 K. B. 868, C. A. (contract to be at an end in the event of "hostilities preventing shipment"); *Wills & Sons* v. *Cunningham & Co.*, [1924] 2 K. B. 220 (scope of clause "unforeseen circumstances excepted"); *Brauer* v. *Clark*, [1952] 2 All E. R. 497, C. A. (sale subject to export licence); *Smyth* v. *Lindsay*, [1953] 2 All E. R. 1064 (contract to be cancelled if fulfilment rendered impossible by "prohibition of export"); and see note "Licences", p. 39, *post.*

(*i*) *Re Shipton, Anderson & Co.*, [1915] 3 K. B. 676, and see *Bank Line* v. *Capel & Co.*, [1919] A. C. 435 (charter party frustrated by requisitioning of ship); but *cf. Port Line, Ltd.* v. *Ben Line Steamers, Ltd.*, [1958] 1 All E. R. 787; [1958] 2 Q. B. 146 (a time charter for thirty months of which a little over seventeen months have expired is not frustrated by a requisitioning which would be expected to, and does in fact, last three to four months); and see also *Hong Kong Fir Shipping Co., Ltd.*, v. *Kawasaki Kisen Kaisha, Ltd.*, [1962] 1 All E. R. 474; [1962] 2 Q. B. 26, C. A. As to a temporary embargo on export, see *Millar & Co.* v. *Taylor & Co.*, [1916] 1 K. B. 402, C. A. See further, *post*, p. 40.

(*k*) *Metropolitan Water Board* v. *Dick Kerr & Co.*, [1918] A. C. 119 (building contract); *MacMaster* v. *Cox & Co.*, 1920 S. C. 566; reversed, 1921 S. C. 24 (H. L.) (sale); *Kursell* v. *Timber Operators, Ltd.*, [1927] 1 K. B. 298.

(*l*) *Esposito* v. *Bowden* (1857), 7 E. & B. 763, at p. 781, Ex Ch.

(*m*) *Ertel Bieber & Co.* v. *Rio Tinto Co.*, [1918] A. C. 260; *Ottoman Bank* v. *Jebara*, [1928] A. C. 269 (completion did not involve intercourse with enemy). As to c.i.f. contracts, see *Karberg* v. *Blythe Green & Co.*, [1916] 1 K. B. 495, C. A.; *Krupp* v. *Orconera Iron Ore Co.* (1919), 88 L. J. Ch. 304.

(*n*) *Taylor* v. *Caldwell* (1863), 3 B. & S. 826, and see the authorities collected in *Blackburn Bobbin Co.* v. *Allen & Sons*, [1918] 1 K. B. 540; affirmed [1918] 2 K. B. 467, C. A. As to *vis major* and "act of God," see *Nugent* v. *Smith* (1876), 1 C. P. D. 423, at p. 429, C. A.

(*o*) *Davis Contractors* v. *Fareham Urban District Council*, [1956] 2 All E. R. 145; [1956] A. C. 696; *Tsakiroglou & Co., Ltd.* v. *Noblee & Thorl G.m.b.H.*, [1961] 2 All E. R. 179; [1962] A. C. 93; *Ocean Tramp Tankers Corporation* v. *V/O Sovfracht*, [1964] 1 All E. R. 161;

vis major may excuse performance of a contract, it cannot be relied on to justify the variation of a contract (*p*).

Law Reform (Frustrated Contracts) Act 1943.—The Act does not deal in any way with the general law of frustration as a cause of the discharge of contracts. What it does is to make certain provisions about what shall happen once a contract governed by English law has become impossible of performance or been otherwise frustrated, and the parties thereto have for that reason been discharged from the further performance of the contract. The Act applies only to contracts governed by English law, and it applies to contracts to which the Crown is a party in like manner as to contracts between subjects, s. 2 (2), *post*, Appendix I. There are certain contracts to which the Act does not apply at all, and special provision is made for contracts capable of being severed, and for contracts containing express provisions about frustration; see s. 2, *post*, Appendix I.

The Act applies to contracts of sale of goods in the same way as it applies to other contracts governed by English law (*q*), but subject to the exceptions contained in s. 2 (5) (c), *post*, Appendix I, which provides that the Act shall not apply to contracts to which s. 7 of the Sale of Goods Act applies or to any other contract for the sale, or sale and delivery, of specific goods, where the contract is frustrated through the goods perishing.

No doubt the reason for thus excluding the application of the Act in the two cases there specified is that the case of impossibility by the perishing of the goods is peculiar to the law of sale, and the special rules applicable to the perishing of specific goods have been long established and are well understood by the commercial community, so that there is no point in disturbing them. It is now clear that s. 7 of the Sale of Goods Act does not apply to specifically described goods.

Rescission or variation

A contract of sale may be rescinded by a subsequent agreement, which may be oral (*r*) or in writing, and which may rescind the former contract either expressly or by necessary implication. The latter will be the case if the second contract is inconsistent with the first to an extent which goes to its very root (*s*). Rescission may also be implied from the parties' course of conduct (*t*) or from the fact that neither party has insisted upon performance for a long time after the contract was made (*u*). Variation of the original contract must be carefully distinguished from rescission:

[1964] 2 Q. B. 226, C. A.; *Amalgamated Investment Property Co.* v. *John Walker*, [1976] 3 All E. R. 509; [1977] 1 W. L. R. 164, C. A.

(*p*) *Brooke Tool Manufacturing Co.* v. *Hydraulic Gears Co.* (1920), 89 L. J. K. B. 263 (delivery delayed by war conditions; buyers refused to accept delayed delivery. Sellers have no action for the price).

(*q*) As to the general application of the Act, see *B. P. Exploration Co.* v. *Hunt* (*No. 2*), [1979] 1 W. L. R. 783; affirmed on appeal (1981), 125 Sol. Jo. 165, C. A.

(*r*) *Goss* v. *Lord Nugent* (1833), 5 B. & Ad. 58; *Morris* v. *Baron & Co.*, [1918] A. C. 1; *British and Beningtons, Ltd.* v. *North West Cachar Tea Co.*, [1923] A. C. 48.

(*s*) *Morris* v. *Baron & Co.*, [1918] A. C. 1, at p. 27; *British and Beningtons, Ltd.* v. *N. W. Cachar Tea Co.*, [1923] A. C. 48.

(*t*) *Bruner* v. *Moore*, [1904] 1 Ch. 305, at p. 312; *Hartley* v. *Hymans*, [1920] 3 K. B. 475.

(*u*) *Pearl Mill Co.* v. *Ivy Tannery Co.*, [1919] 1 K. B. 78; *Fisher* v. *Eastwoods*, [1936] 1 All E. R. 421.

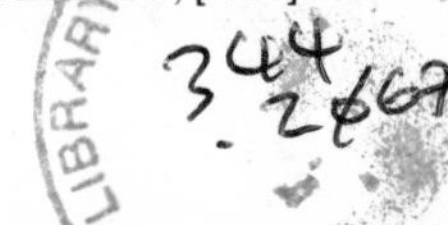

"In the first case there are no such executory clauses in the second arrangement as would enable you to sue upon that alone if the first did not exist; in the second you could sue on the second arrangement alone, and the first contract is got rid of either by express words to that effect, or because, the second dealing with the same subject-matter as the first but in a different way, it is impossible that the two should be both performed" (*a*).

Waiver.—A distinction must also be drawn between variation of a contract and the mere waiver by one party of the performance of a stipulation in the contract. If a stipulation operates for the benefit of both parties it can only be altered by mutual consent (*b*). But a party may always waive unilaterally a stipulation which is for his own benefit alone (*c*). Thus if a seller at the request of the buyer postpones delivery, or a buyer at the request of the seller does not insist upon delivery at the stipulated time, there is no variation of the contract though it may affect the measure of damages (*d*). Where the fulfilment of a condition by one party is prevented by the other, the condition is waived (*e*); and the wrongful repudiation of a contract by one party may operate as a waiver of conditions precedent to be performed by the other (*f*).

It seems that where a party does waive a stipulation, he cannot afterwards treat the non-performance of that stipulation as giving him the right to rescind the contract (*g*), and where there is what may be called a continuing waiver he must give the other party reasonable notice of his intention to insist in the future on the performance of the stipulation, in order that the other party may have an opportunity of complying with it (*h*).

(*a*) *Morris* v. *Baron & Co.*, [1918] A. C. 1, at p. 26; *Goss* v. *Lord Nugent* (1833), 5 B. & Ad. 58, at pp. 65, 66. It will be found that all the cases in which evidence of the new oral arrangement was rejected were cases of attempted variation.

(*b*) *Maine Spinning Co.* v. *Sutcliffe & Co.* (1917), 87 L. J. K. B. 382 ("delivery d.o.b. Liverpool"); *Fibrosa S. A.* v. *Fairbairn Lawson Combe Barbour, Ltd.*, [1941] 2 All E. R. 300; [1942] 1 K. B. 12, C. A. ("delivery c.i.f. Gdynia").

(*c*) See, e.g., *Hartley* v. *Hymans*, [1920] 3 K. B. 475. As to waiver of a condition before examination of the goods, see *per* ATKIN, L. J., in *Moore & Co.* v. *Landauer & Co.* (1921), 26 Com. Cas. 267, at p. 276, C. A.

(*d*) *Hickman* v. *Haynes* (1875), L. R. 10 C. P. 598 (forbearance of seller); *Potts & Co.* v. *Brown McFarlane & Co.* (1925), 30 Com. Cas. 64, H. L. (demand of inspection extending time of delivery); *Levey* v. *Goldberg*, [1922] 1 K. B. 688 (postponement of time of delivery at buyer's request); *Besseler Waechter Glover & Co.* v. *South Derwent Coal Co., Ltd.*, [1938] 1 K. B. 408 (postponement of delivery dates); *cf. Ogle* v. *Vane* (1868), L. R. 3 Q. B. 272, Ex. Ch. (forbearance of buyer to buy in against the seller on the latter failing to deliver at the contract time). See also p. 233, *post.*

(*e*) *Mackay* v. *Dick* (1881), 6 App. Cas. 251; followed, *Kleinert* v. *Abosso Mining Co.* (1913), 58 Sol. Jo. 45, P. C. *Cf. New Zealand Shipping Co.* v. *Société des Ateliers*, [1919] A. C. 1, at p. 6, *per* Lord FINLAY.

(*f*) *Cort* v. *Ambergate Rail. Co.* (1851), 17 Q. B. 127; *Braithwaite* v. *Foreign Hardwood Co.*, [1905] 2 K. B. 543, C. A. See s. 31, *post*, and notes.

(*g*) *Harlow and Jones* v. *Panex* (*International*), *Ltd.*, [1967] 2 Lloyd's Rep. 509. See also *Bentsen* v. *Taylor*, [1893] 2 Q. B. 274, 283.

(*h*) *Tyers* v. *Rosedale Co.* (1875), L. R. 10 Exch. 195, Ex. Ch.: *Panoutsos* v. *Raymond Hadley Corporation of New York*, [1917] 2 K. B. 473, applied in *Plasticmoda S.P.A.* v. *Davidsons, Ltd.*, [1952] 1 Lloyd's Rep. 527. See also *Rickards* v. *Oppenheim*, [1950] 1 All E. R. 420, C. A.; [1950] 1 K. B. 616. As to quasi-estoppel, see now *Ajayi* v. *R. T. Briscoe* (*Nigeria*),

A party will be treated as having waived a stipulation if his conduct is reasonably interpreted by the other party and relied on by him as amounting to a waiver, provided that it clearly and unambiguously bears that interpretation, even if the first party did not intend to waive the stipulation (*i*).

Where a party is already in breach of a stipulation in a contract, the other party cannot, strictly speaking, waive performance of that stipulation. He may, however, waive one or more of his remedies arising out of the breach. Thus, if a buyer is entitled to reject goods on a certain ground, but so conducts himself as to lead the other to believe that he is not relying on that ground, he cannot afterwards reject the goods on that ground, at any rate if it would be unfair or unjust to allow him to do so (*k*).

An accord and satisfaction after breach is often referred to as waiver. Thus a new contract may be made after breach, and such new contract in itself may be an accord and satisfaction, though often it is merely an accord, and there is no satisfaction until it is performed. In this last case it cannot be sued on, and does not operate to discharge the original contract. Where, however, the new contract is itself the accord and satisfaction it can be sued on, and also provides a complete answer to an action on the original contract. An assent to accept a substituted mode of performance has also been held not to constitute a variation of the contract (*l*).

Performance of the contract

The law relating to the performance of a contract for the sale of goods is codified in Part IV of the Sale of Goods Act 1979. The rules there laid down apply in the absence of contrary agreement between the parties.

Duties of the seller.—The basic duty of the seller is to deliver the goods to the buyer in accordance with the terms of the contract (*m*). Delivery is defined by s. 61 (1) of the Sale of Goods Act as the voluntary transfer of

---

Ltd., [1964] 3 All E. R. 556; [1964] 1 W. L. R. 1326, P. C., where the earlier decisions are reviewed; *W. J. Alan & Co., Ltd.* v. *El Nasr Export and Import Co.*, [1972] 2 All E. R. 127; [1972] 2 Q. B. 189, C. A.

(*i*) *Woodhouse A. C. Israel Cocoa, Ltd. S. A.* v. *Nigerian Produce Marketing Co.*, [1972] 2 All E. R. 271; [1972] A. C. 741, H. L.; *Finagrain S. A.* v. *Kruse*, [1976] 2 Lloyd's Rep. 508; *cf. Spiro* v. *Lintern*, [1973] 3 All E. R. 319; [1973] 1 W. L. R. 1002, C. A.

(*k*) *Panchaud Frères S. A.* v. *Establissements General Grain Co.*, [1970] 1 Lloyd's Rep. 53, C. A., where Lord DENNING, M. R., at p. 57, treated this rule as an example of estoppel by conduct. WINN, L. J., on the other hand considered, at p. 59, that it was not an example of estoppel or quasi-estoppel, but may rather be "an inchoate doctrine stemming from the manifest convenience of consistency in pragmatic affairs negativing any liberty to blow hot and cold in commercial conduct." See also *Bentsen* v. *Taylor*, [1893] 2 Q. B. 274, 283; *Toepfer* v. *Cremer*, [1975] 2 Lloyd's Rep. 118, C. A.; *The Vladimir Ilich*, [1975] 1 Lloyd's Rep. 322.

(*l*) *Leather Cloth Co.* v. *Hieronimus* (1875), L. R. 10 Q. B. 140 (change of route); doubted in *Hartley* v. *Hymans*, [1920] 3 K. B. 475, at p. 493; *Sanday & Co., Ltd.* v. *Shipton Anderson & Co., Ltd.* (1926), 25 Ll. L. Rep. 508; see also the judgment of SCRUTTON, L. J., in *British Russian Gazette* v. *Associated Newspapers*, [1933] 2 K. B. 616, 643, C. A.

(*m*) Sale of Goods Act 1979, s. 27, *post*.

possession from one person to another (*n*). The rules as to delivery are set out in ss. 28–32 of the Sale of Goods Act, *post.*

It is also of the essence of a contract of sale that the seller should transfer the property in the goods to the buyer. The time at which the property is transferred depends upon the intention of the parties, provided that where the contract is for the sale of unascertained goods, no property in the goods can be transferred to the buyer until the goods are ascertained (*o*). Rules for ascertaining the intention of the parties are set out in ss. 17 and 18 of the Sale of Goods Act, *post.*

Where the seller is not the absolute owner of the goods at the date of the contract of sale, he may still be able to perform his obligations under the contract if—

(1) He is authorised by the owner of the goods to sell them on his behalf;

(2) he possesses some special common law or statutory power of sale or is selling under the order of a court of competent jurisdiction (*p*);

(3) he acquires the right to sell the goods before the time when the property is to pass (*q*).

In each of the above cases the seller is acting perfectly lawfully in selling the goods, even though in the first two cases they do not belong to him.

(4) He is selling goods which he has no right to sell, but the buyer obtains a good title by reason either of the law of estoppel or of one of the statutory provisions enabling an apparent owner to dispose of goods as if he were the true owner (*r*).

In such a case, the true owner will have no recourse against the buyer (who will generally therefore have no cause for complaint on that ground against the seller (*s*)), but the true owner will normally be able to recover damages from the seller who will have converted his property (*t*).

Duties of the buyer.—It is the duty of the buyer to accept the goods and to pay for them in accordance with the terms of the contract (*u*). In the absence of agreement to the contrary, payment and delivery are concurrent conditions (*a*).

(*n*) See further as to the different forms which delivery may take, *post*, p. 263.

(*o*) Sale of Goods Act 1979, s. 16, *post.* For the extent to which a buyer can acquire an equitable interest in goods before the property in them passes to him, see the comment to s. 16.

(*p*) For examples of such powers of sale, see note (*u*) at p. 160, *post.* The validity of such sales is not affected by anything in the Sale of Goods Act 1979: see s. 21 (2) (b) of that Act.

(*q*) Sale of Goods Act 1979, s. 12 (1).

(*r*) Such statutory provisions are unaffected by the Sale of Goods Act 1979: see s. 21 (2) (a) of that Act.

(*s*) But he may be able to recover any costs incurred in resisting the true owner's claim—see the comment to s. 12 of the Sale of Goods Act, *post.*

(*t*) For the true owner's right to waive the tort and claim the price from the seller in an action for money had and received, see *post*, p. 28.

(*u*) Sale of Goods Act 1979, s. 27, *post.*

(*a*) *Ibid.*, s. 28, *post.*

As to payment generally, see the comment to s. 49 of the Sale of Goods Act, *post*. As to payment by banker's irrevocable letter of credit, see *post*, p. 42.

Rules as to acceptance are set out in ss. 34–37 of the Sale of Goods Act, *post*.

Remedies for breach of contract

Rights of unpaid seller against the goods.—The unpaid seller retains rights over the goods so long as he retains possession of them, even if the property in them has passed to the buyer. Where the property in the goods has passed to the buyer, the unpaid seller in possession has a lien over the goods for the price, and where the property has not passed to the buyer, he has a right of withholding delivery similar to and co-extensive with his right of lien. These rights will be lost if they are once waived (*b*).

The unpaid seller has also the right, if the seller becomes insolvent, to stop the goods in transit after he has parted with possession of them (*c*), but circumstances in which this right is of value are rare.

Where the unpaid seller exercises his right of lien or stoppage in transit, he acquires a limited right to re-sell the goods in the circumstances set out in s. 48 (3) of the Sale of Goods Act, *post*. He may, of course, under the terms of the contract of sale, reserve for himself a more extensive right to re-sell the goods if the buyer makes default, and s. 48 (4) of the Sale of Goods Act, *post*, provides for such a case (*d*). He may also provide under the terms of the contract of sale that although the buyer obtains possession of the goods, property in them shall not pass to him until the price is paid or some other condition is satisfied. In this case, if the buyer repudiates his obligations under the contract the seller may be able to claim back the goods (*e*).

Other rights of the seller.—In the circumstances set out in s. 49 of the Sale of Goods Act, *post*, and the comment thereto the seller may sue the buyer for the price of the goods. Except in those cases, he is entitled only to damages for non-acceptance of the goods sold, which are calculated in accordance with the principles set out in s. 50 of the Sale of Goods Act, *post*. If the buyer wrongfully fails to take delivery of the goods or delays in so doing, the seller may also be entitled under s. 37 of the Sale of Goods Act, *post*, to a reasonable charge for the care and custody of the goods.

The seller's right to special damages and to interest on the price or on damages awarded are preserved by s. 54 of the Sale of Goods Act, *post*. The principles on which such damages or interest are awarded are those

---

(*b*) Sale of Goods Act 1979, ss. 39–43, *post*.

(*c*) *Ibid*., ss. 44–46, *post*.

(*d*) As to re-sale by buyer and seller generally, where a right of lien or stoppage in transit has been exercised, see *ibid*., ss. 47–48, *post*.

(*e*) P. 218, *post*. But his rights in this respect may be restricted if the agreement is within the Consumer Credit Act 1974, p. 66, *post*, or, pending its repeal under the provisions of the Consumer Credit Act, is within the Hire-Purchase Act 1965.

which apply in contract generally. As to special damages, see further the comment to s. 54 of the Sale of Goods Act, *post*. As to interest, see further s. 3 of the Law Reform (Miscellaneous Provisions) Act 1934 and the comment thereon, *post*, Appendix I.

As to mitigation of damages, see p. 249, *post*.

As to the rate of exchange where the price or charges have to be calculated in a foreign currency, see p. 252, *post*.

Deposit.—Sometimes part of the price is prepaid by way of security when the contract is entered into. The money so prepaid is called a deposit. The return of the deposit in case the sale goes off is usually a matter of agreement, but in the absence of a different agreement the deposit is forfeited if the sale goes off through the buyer's fault (*f*). "The deposit," says Lord MACNAGHTEN,

> "serves two purposes: if the purchase is carried out it goes against the purchase-money; but its primary purpose is this: it is a guarantee that the purchaser means business" (*g*).

In deciding whether a payment in advance is a deposit or a part payment which can be recovered if the sale goes off, regard must be had to all the surrounding circumstances (*h*).

Remedies of the buyer.—If the seller fails to deliver any goods, or delivers goods which the buyer rejects as not being in conformity with the contract, the buyer may have available one or more of the following remedies:

(1) He may sue for damages for non-delivery—see s. 51 of the Sale of Goods Act, *post*.

(2) If the price has been paid by him, he may recover it in an action for money had and received for a consideration which has wholly failed, and in special circumstances a seller might be held to be a trustee of the purchase price for the buyer until he delivers the goods. See further p. 252, *post*.

(3) Where the buyer cannot be adequately compensated in damages, he may sometimes sue for specific performance of the contract. This right is set out in s. 52 of the Sale of Goods Act, *post*, in the case of specific or ascertained goods. The Sale of Goods Act does not deal with specific performance of a contract for the sale of unascertained

---

(*f*) *Howe* v. *Smith* (1884), 27 Ch. D. 89, C. A. See the history of the law of earnest and deposit traced by FRY, L. J., at p. 94. *Cf. Roberts and Cooper, Ltd.* v. *Salvesen & Co.*, 1918 S. C. 794; *Alexander* v. *Webber*, [1922] 1 K. B. 642 (secret agreement for commission between seller and buyer's servant; buyer entitled to recover his deposit because contract avoided by seller's fraud); *Dies* v. *British and Finance Corporation, Ltd.*, [1939] 1 K. B. 724; *cf. R. V. Ward, Ltd.* v. *Bignall*, [1967] 2 All E. R. 449; [1967] 1 Q. B. 534, C. A., overruling *Gallagher* v. *Shilcock*, [1949] 1 All E. R. 921; [1949] 2 K. B. 765. But note that a deposit may be recoverable where it would be unconscionable in equity for it to be forfeited: *Stockloser* v. *Johnson*, [1954] 1 All E. R. 630; [1954] 1 Q. B. 476, C. A.; *Steedman* v. *Drinkle*, [1916] 1 A. C. 275, P. C.; *Re Dagenham (Thames) Dock Co., ex p. Hulse* (1873), 8 Ch. App. 1022.

(*g*) *Soper* v. *Arnold* (1889), 14 App. Cas. 429, at p. 435.

(*h*) *Elson* v. *Prices Tailors, Ltd.*, [1963] 1 All E. R. 231; [1963] 1 W. L. R. 287.

goods, but in special cases the remedy is available on general equitable principles (*i*).

(4) If the goods are specific or ascertained, and under the terms of the contract the buyer is entitled to immediate possession of them, he may claim them in an action for wrongful interference—see p. 236, *post.*

(5) In a clear case, if the seller is prosecuted and convicted of an offence committed by him in connection with the contract, the buyer may be able to obtain compensation under s. 35 of the Powers of Criminal Courts Act 1973 (*k*) for any loss or damage resulting from that offence. He may also be able to recover compensation if the seller is convicted of another offence and asks for an offence committed in connection with the contract to be taken into account by the court in determining sentence.

Where the seller is in breach of some other condition of the contract, the buyer may treat the contract as repudiated by such breach, at least in the great majority of cases (*l*), and may then recover damages for breach of contract. He may also recover the price, if he has paid it, in an action for money had and received for a consideration which has wholly failed—see p. 252, *post.*

If the buyer accepts the goods delivered although they are not in conformity with the contract, or otherwise elects, or is bound (*m*), to treat a breach of condition as a breach of warranty, then he may sue for damages for breach of warranty (*n*), or he may set off the damages in diminution or extinction of the price, and claim in respect of any further damage he may have suffered by reason of the breach (*o*).

As to the measure of damages for breach of warranty, see s. 53 of the Sale of Goods Act, *post.* As to special damages and mitigation of damages, see s. 54 of the Sale of Goods Act, *post.* As to interest, see s. 3 of the Law Reform (Miscellaneous Provisions) Act 1934, Appendix I, *post.*

Assignment of contract of sale

There is no provision in the Sale of Goods Act which deals with the assignment of contracts of sale. Such contracts can therefore be assigned subject to the conditions applicable in the case of other contracts. If the assignment is to be a legal assignment the provisions of s. 136 of the Law of Property Act 1925 must be complied with. But this section, which replaces s. 25 (6) of the Judicature Act 1873,

> "does not enlarge the class of choses in action, the assignability of which was previously recognised either at law or in equity" (*p*).

The simplest cases arise where the goods have been delivered and the

---

(*i*) See further the comment to s. 52, *post.*
(*k*) Appendix I, *post.*
(*l*) See p. 8, *ante.*
(*m*) See s. 11 of the Sale of Goods Act, *post.*
(*n*) *Ibid.*, s. 53 (1) (b).
(*o*) *Ibid.*, s. 53 (1) (a).
(*p*) *Tolhurst* v. *Associated Portland Cement Manufacturers, Ltd.*, [1902] 2 K. B. 660, at p. 676.

right to receive the price is assigned, or where, the price having been paid, the right to receive the goods is assigned. In both these cases the assignor has performed his part of the contract, and the obligation of the other party to the contract is varied to this extent only, that he must pay the price or deliver the goods to the assignee instead of to the person with whom he contracted. The rule is the same where the price is not due at the date of the assignment; the right to receive it when due can be assigned (*q*). Apparently an assignment of part of a debt or other legal chose in action is not effectual to transfer the legal right to that part which is assigned, but operates in equity only, with the result that the assignee could not sue in his own name (*r*). The whole debt may be assigned at law, however, so that the assignee may sue in his own name, in consideration of a covenant by the assignee to pay a percentage of any sum recovered (*s*).

But the contract may provide for a series of deliveries, or the quantity, quality, or the time of the delivery may depend on the wishes or needs of the parties. In these cases, where neither party has performed his part of the contract, there can be no assignment where the duties which were owed to the assignor would be made more onerous by being transferred to the assignee, or where the rights to be assigned are essentially personal. Thus where A agreed to supply B with all the eggs he should require for manufacturing purposes for a year, and B purported to assign his right to a limited company, it was held that the contract was personal, for A's liability was measured by the personal requirements of B (*t*).

Similarly where deliveries of coal were to be made by a company over a long period, and credit was to be given, the company were held to be entitled to refuse to supply an assignee on the ground that the giving of credit was a personal matter in that particular case (*u*). The obligation to pay, like obligations to do work or deliver goods, cannot always be performed vicariously (*a*).

But where A contracted to supply for fifty years all the chalk that a company required at a certain works, and that company assigned the benefit of the contract to a larger company, it was held that the latter could enforce the contract because the amount of the deliveries was to be ascertained by reference to the needs of certain stated works, and was thus not personal to the original contracting company (*b*). The first

(*q*) *Brice* v. *Bannister* (1878), 3 Q. B. D. 569.

(*r*) *Re Steel Wing Co., Ltd.*, [1921] 1 Ch. 349; *Williams* v. *Atlantic Assurance Co., Ltd.*, [1933] 1 K. B. 81.

(*s*) *Ramsey* v. *Hartley*, [1977] 2 All E. R. 673; [1977] 1 W. L. R. 686, C. A.

(*t*) *Kemp* v. *Baerselman*, [1906] 2 K. B. 604; see also *International Fibre Syndicate* v. *Dawson* (1901), 3 F. (Ct. of Sess.) 32.

(*u*) *Cooper* v. *Micklefield Coal & Lime Co.* (1912), 107 L. T. 457.

(*a*) *Ibid.*, at p. 458. See also *Johnson* v. *Raylton* (1881), 7 Q. B. D. 438, C. A., where there was held to be an implied term that a manufacturer contracting to supply specific goods must supply goods of his own manufacture.

(*b*) *Tolhurst* v. *Associated Portland Cement Manufacturers*, [1903] A. C. 414; see also the judgment of COLLINS, M. R., in the same case in the Court of Appeal, [1902] 2 K. B. 660, at pp. 668, 669.

company did not get rid of its liability to pay should the second company fail to do so, nor is the original contractor bound to look to the assignee in any way for the discharge of duties owed to him (*c*).

In any case it is only the benefit of a contract which can be assigned. The assignor cannot get rid of his obligations. The most he can do is to perform them through his assignee, he himself remaining liable (*d*).

Assignment must be carefully distinguished from novation which is the substitution, with the consent of all parties, of a new contract for a previously existing one. The parties to the new contract may be different from those to the old one.

Quasi-Contracts of Sale

The Sale of Goods Act deals only with contracts of sale, properly so called. But there are certain quasi-contracts of sale which require to be noted. By a quasi-contract of sale is meant a transaction to which, independently of the will of the parties, the law annexes consequences similar to those which result from a sale (*e*). For example:—

(1) *Satisfied judgment for wrongful interference with goods.*—The torts of conversion, or trover, and trespass to goods are now included in a general statutory description of torts resulting in damage to goods or to an interest in goods, namely "wrongful interference with goods" (*f*). The tort of detinue has been abolished (*g*). The relief available in proceedings for wrongful interference against a person who is in possession or in control of goods is—

(a) an order for delivery of the goods and payment of any consequential damage, or

(b) an order for delivery of the goods, but giving the defendent the alternative of paying damages by reference to the value of the goods, together in either alternative with payment of any consequential damages, or

(*c*) damages (*h*).

Where damages are, or would fall to be, assessed on the footing that the claimant is being compensated for the whole of his interest in the goods (subject to any reduction for contributory negligence) payment of the assessed damages or settlement of the claim for damages, extinguishes the claimant's title to that interest (*i*).

In effect, this is a statutory re-statement of the common law rule that when the substance of the action is conversion, judgment recovered by

---

(*c*) See the useful summary by ATKIN, J., in *Sorrentino Fratelli* v. *Buerger*, [1915] 1 K. B 307, at pp. 312, 313.

(*d*) *British Waggon Co.* v. *Lea* (1880), 5 Q. B. D. 149, C. A.; especially at p. 154.

(*e*) As to implied contracts where there is consent in fact, though not expressed, see ss. 3 and 8 of the Sale of Goods Act, *post*.

(*f*) Torts (Interference with Goods) Act 1977, s. 1.

(*g*) *Ibid.*, s. 2.

(*h*) *Ibid.*, s. 3.

(*i*) *Ibid.*, s. 5.

the plaintiff for damages estimated on the footing of the full value of the goods and satisfied, either voluntarily by the defendant or by execution, operates as a sale of the goods by the plaintiff to the defendant as from the time when the judgment is satisfied (*k*).

In detinue also the defendant had at common law the power to defeat the plaintiff's claim to the return of the goods and to satisfy the judgment by paying their value (*l*), so that, in the words of JESSEL, M. R.,

> "the theory of the judgment in an action of detinue is that it is a kind of involuntary sale of the plaintiff's goods to the defendant. The plaintiff wants to get his goods back and the Court gives him the next best thing, that is the value of the goods" (*m*).

This defect was remedied by s. 78 of the Common Law Procedure Act 1854, now replaced by R. S. C., O. 45, rr. 4, 13 (3); but the Court still had a discretion and could refuse to compel the defendant to return the goods (*n*).

An unsatisfied judgment does not transfer the property in any of these cases (*o*).

(2) *Waiver of tort.*—It has been held that where a plaintiff has been induced, by the fraud of a third person, to sell goods to an insolvent buyer, and such third person has afterwards obtained the goods himself, the plaintiff may waive the tort, and treat the transaction as a sale to such third person (*p*).

Again, there are other cases where, when one person has wrongfully obtained possession of the goods of another, as when they have been sold to him by a third person who had no right to sell them, the owner of the goods may waive the tort, and treat the transaction as a sale by himself to the person who has got the goods (*q*). So, too, as against the person who has thus wrongfully sold the goods and received the price, "the

---

(*k*) *U.S.A.* v. *Dollfus Mieg*, [1952] 1 All E. R. 572; [1952] A. C. 582 at p. 622 *per* Lord TUCKER, (trover); *Cooper* v. *Shepherd* (1846), 3 C. B. 226 (trover); *Brinsmead* v. *Harrison* (1871), L. R. 6 C. P. 584 (trover); and *cf.* the note to *Holmes* v. *Wilson* (1839), 10 Ad. & El. 503, at p. 511. It may of course be that there is someone who claims through the defendant and thus has a better title than he. If, for example, A takes goods from B and sells them to C, it is clear that satisfaction made by A to B will operate as a sale to C.

(*l*) See *Eberle's Hotels Co.* v. *Jonas* (1887), 18 Q. B. D. 459, at p. 468.

(*m*) *Ex p. Drake* (1877), 5 Ch. D. 866, at p. 871, C. A.

(*n*) *Peruvian Guano Co.* v. *Dreyfus Bros. & Co.*, [1892] A. C. 166, at p. 176; *Whiteley* v. *Hilt*, [1918] 2 K. B. 808, at pp. 819, 824, C. A.; *Cohen* v. *Roche*, [1927] 1 K. B. 169, at pp. 179–181.

(*o*) *Ex p. Drake, supra* (detinue); *Ellis* v. *Stenning*, [1932] 2 Ch. 81 (trover). In *Bradley* v. *Ramsay & Co.* (1912), 106 L. T. 771, C. A., where goods were sent on approval to the defendant and the plaintiff claimed their return in an action for detinue, judgment was entered by consent for the plaintiff; but on the facts (distinguishing *Brinsmead* v. *Harrison* (*supra*)) it was held to be in substance a judgment for the price of the goods, and consequently, though it was not satisfied, the property in the goods was transferred.

(*p*) *Hill* v. *Perrott* (1810), 3 Taunt, 274.

(*q*) *A.-G.* v. *Nissan*, [1969] 1 All E. R. 629, at pp. 651–652; [1970] A. C. 179, at p. 228, *per* Lord PEARCE: *cf. Dickenson* v. *Naul* (1833), 4 B. & Ad. 638; *Allen* v. *Hopkins* (1844), 13 M. & W. 94.

owner may waive the tort and recover the proceeds in an action for money had and received" (*r*). "If the servant of a company," says Lord SUMNER,

> "acting ultra vires of the company converts a stranger's chattel, and, having sold it, pays the proceeds into the company's account as its servant, I suppose an action for conversion would lie against the servant, and for money had and received against the company" (*s*).

(3) *Sale by estoppel.*—So, too, there may be a sale by estoppel. Suppose a defendant sells specific goods to one person, and the documents of title to the goods to another person, he would be liable to both, though a doubt might arise as to which person would be entitled to the goods themselves. Likewise, a person holding himself out as the buyer may be liable as such, and a person who stands by and lets his goods be sold is bound by the sale (*t*).

For further instances of quasi-contract, see the notes to s. 3 of the Sale of Goods Act, *post*.

(*r*) *Arnold* v. *Cheque Bank* (1876), 1 C. P. D. 578, at p. 585. This will be the position where "the plaintiff in truth treats the wrongdoer as having acted as his agent, overlooks the wrong, and by consent of both parties is content to receive the proceeds," *per* Lord ATKIN in *United Australia, Ltd.* v. *Barclays Bank*, [1940] 4 All E. R. 20, at p. 36; [1941] A. C. 1 at p. 28; overruling the dictum of BOVILL, C. J., in *Smith* v. *Baker*, [1873] L. R. 8 C. P. 350 at p. 355; and the dicta of A. L. SMITH, L. J., in *Rice* v. *Reed*, [1900] 1 Q. B. 54 at pp. 65–66, C. A.; and distinguishing *Verschures Creameries, Ltd.* v. *Hull and Netherlands Steamship Co., Ltd.*, [1921] 2 K. B. 608. Where, however, there is no true election between two inconsistent rights, the institution of proceedings against one tortfeasor for money had and received will not bar a subsequent action against another for a separate tort, at any rate so long as there is no satisfied judgment in the first action: *United Australia, Ltd.* v. *Barclays Bank* (*supra*).

(*s*) *Att.-General* v. *De Keyser's Hotel*, [1920] A. C. 508, at p. 556.

(*t*) As to estoppel and the passing of property, see the comment to s. 21, of the Sale of Goods Act, *post*.

SECTION B

INTERNATIONAL CONTRACTS OF SALE

A. Customary international contracts

The most common forms of international contract for the sale of goods are f.o.b. (free on board), c.i.f. (at a price to cover cost, insurance and freight) and ex-ship. Others are f.a.s. (free alongside), f.o.b. stowed (free on board and stowed), c. and f. (where the seller is not obliged to arrange insurance), delivered (where the seller undertakes that the goods will be delivered at, for example, the buyer's place of business) and ex-works. The ordinary incidents of f.o.b., c.i.f. and ex-ship contracts are described below. These incidents *prima facie* follow if a contract is described as f.o.b., c.i.f. or ex-ship (*a*). But upon a true construction of the remainder of the contract they may be, and commonly are, varied, sometimes to the point where the abbreviation f.o.b., c.i.f. or ex-ship merely indicates the mode of calculating the price. Thus hybrid f.o.b./c.i.f. contracts (*b*) or c.i.f./ex-ship contracts (*c*) are common.

A contract may, on its true construction be capable of performance at one or the other party's option either as f.o.b. contract or as a c.i.f. contract (*d*).

Save for delivered and ex-works contracts, the forms of contract mentioned above contemplate the shipment of goods by sea. Nonetheless f.o.b., c.i.f. and the other abbreviations are sometimes used in relation to contracts for sale where, for example, the goods are to be sent by road or air or combined transport from the seller to the buyer. The abbreviations will in such a case retain importance as indications as to the division of costs, as to responsibility for insurance (*e*), as to risk, and, usually, as to the time when property is to pass. But many of the incidents of a contract for carriage by sea cannot be relevant in such a context. For example, it is unlikely that there will be a document of title equivalent to a bill of lading. Thus, the seller will not have the protection of a document which he can hold until the price is paid, so

---

(*a*) *N. V. Handel My. J. Smiths Import-Export* v. *English Exporters* (*London*), *Ltd.*, [1957] 1 Lloyd's Rep. 517 (f.o.b.); *Frebold* v. *Circle Products, Ltd.*, [1970] 1 Lloyd's Rep. 499, C. A. (f.o.b.); *Comptoir d'Achat et de Vente du Boerenbond Belge S/A* v. *Luis de Ridder*, [1949] 1 All E. R. 269, at p. 274; [1949] A. C. 293, at p. 311 (c.i.f.). In *Law and Bonar* v. *British American Tobacco*, [1916] 2 K. B. 605, a printed clause inconsistent with what were otherwise c.i.f. terms was disregarded.

(*b*) See *The Parchim*, [1918] A. C. 157, P. C.; *President of India* v. *Metcalfe Shipping Co., Ltd.*, [1969] 1 All E. R. 861; [1969] 2 Q. B. 123; on appeal, [1969] 3 All E. R. 1549; [1970] 1 Q. B. 289, C. A.

(*c*) See *The Gabbiano*, [1940] P. 166.

(*d*) See *Comptoir d'Achat* v. *Luis de Ridder*, *supra*.

(*e*) *Lindon Tricotagefabrik* v. *White & Meacham*, [1975] 1 Lloyd's Rep. 384 (Sale c.i.f. Customer's warehouse; goods stolen before delivery: sellers not entitled to price because they failed to tender insurance documents).

preventing the buyer from obtaining the goods in the meantime. A seller will not therefore be fully protected in such a case unless he agrees with both the buyer and the carrier that actual delivery by the carrier to the buyer is to be withheld pending payment of the price (*f*) or unless he obtains collateral protection (*g*).

(1) F.o.b. contracts.—In the absence of suitable (*h*) provision to the contrary (*i*), the buyer must nominate a ship and the port of shipment (*k*), and notify the seller when it will be likely to arrive (*l*). Where shipment is to be within a certain period, the buyer must notify the seller of the likely arrival date of the nominated ship in such time as will enable the seller to bring forward or make available and ship the goods within that period (*m*). This is a condition precedent to the seller's duty to bring goods to or make them available for loading at the port (*n*). The arrival and readiness to load of the ship by the date agreed

---

(*f*) In *Frebold* v. *Circle Products*, [1970] 1 Lloyd's Rep. 499, C. A., such a provision was treated as reserving the seller's right of possession only, and not the property in the goods, after shipment.

(*g*) *E.g.* the right to draw on a letter of credit under which the Bank agrees to accept an air or road consignment note, or the intervention on a confirming house or of a guarantor. If the seller reserves title but not possession under the contract, this will not assist him if the buyer resells or otherwise disposes of the goods to somebody who takes them in good faith and without notice of the seller's interest, at least where English law is the proper law of the second disposition—see s. 9 of the Factors Act 1889, *post.*

(*h*) *Bunge* v. *Tradax England, Ltd.*, [1975] 2 Lloyd's Rep. 235.

(*i*) Provision to the contrary is very common: see *Ian Stach* v. *Baker Bosley*, [1958] 1 All E. R. 542, at p. 544; [1958] 2 Q. B. 130, at p. 132. The classic f.o.b. contract has developed into a "flexible instrument": *Pyrene* v. *Scindia Navigation Co., Ltd.*, [1954] 2 All E. R. 158; [1954] 2 Q. B. 402.

(*k*) An f.o.b. contract which stipulated a range of ports by the words "f.o.b. . . . good Danish port" was thus not void for uncertainty: *David T. Boyd & Co., Ltd.* v. *Louca*, [1973] 1 Lloyd's Rep. 209.

(*l*) *J. J. Cunningham, Ltd.* v. *Munro & Co., Ltd.* (1922), 28 Com. Cas. 42, at p. 45; *Harlow and Jones, Ltd.* v. *Panex (International), Ltd.*, [1967] 2 Lloyd's Rep. 509, esp. at pp. 526–528. The buyer may change his mind and later nominate a different vessel: *Agricultores Federados Argentinos Sociedad Cooperative* v. *Ampro S.A. Commerciale Industrielle et Financière*, [1965] 2 Lloyd's Rep. 157. *Quaere* as to the postion if the seller has in the meantime acted on the former nomination: see *J. J. Cunningham, Ltd.* v. *Munro & Co., Ltd.*, *supra*, at p. 46.

(*m*) *J. J. Cunningham, Ltd.* v. *Munro & Co., Ltd.*, *supra; F. E. Napier* v. *Dexters, Ltd.* (1926), 26 Ll. L. Rep. 184, C. A.; *Bunge* v. *Tradax England, Ltd.*, [1975] 2 Lloyd's Rep. 235; *Bremer* v. *Rayner*, [1978] 2 Lloyd's Rep. 73. Where the sale contract stipulates a loading rate, the seller is entitled after expiry of the notice to sufficient time within the shipment period to load at that rate: *Bunge Corporation* v. *Tradax Export S. A.*, [1980] 1 Lloyd's Rep. 294. *A fortiori* such time must also remain after the ship's actual arrival and readiness to load. But damages for the buyer's failure to nominate such a ship, and so accept delivery, will be assessed as at the end of the shipment period: *Kyprianou* v. *Pim*, [1977] 2 Lloyd's Rep. 570.

(*n*) *Sutherland* v. *Allhusen* (1866), 14 L. T. 666; *Anglo-African Shipping Co., Ltd.* v. *J. Mortimer, Ltd.*, [1962] 1 Lloyd's Rep. 81 at p. 92; and see on appeal, [1962] 1 Lloyd's Rep. 610, at pp. 615, 622–623, C. A.; *Bunge Corporation* v. *Tradax Export S. A.*, [1980] 1 Lloyd's Rep. 294, C. A. Bringing goods to the port contemplates that the seller will be holding them elsewhere. But the place of shipment may itself be the place where the parties contemplate that the goods will be held, as in the case of a sale of oil f.o.b. a refinery. See also *The "Al Hofuf"*, [1981] 1 Lloyd's Rep. 81.

(if any) is *prima facie* of the essence of an f.o.b. contract (*o*). On the ship's arrival, the seller must deliver the goods on board at his own expense (*p*). Thereafter the goods are at the buyer's risk, and he is responsible for the freight and any subsequent charges (*q*). "The seller," says HAMILTON, L. J.,

> "puts the goods safely on board, pays the charge for doing so, and for the buyer's protection, but not under a mandate to send, gives up possession of them to the ship 'only upon the terms of a reasonable and ordinary bill of lading or other contract of carriage (*r*). There his contractual liability as seller ceases, and delivery to the buyer is complete so far as he is concerned' " (*s*).

The buyer under an f.o.b. contract cannot claim delivery of the goods before shipment (*t*). There is no rule that the goods must be examined before shipment. The proper place for examination depends on the circumstances of the particular contract (*u*). Upon shipment the goods must be in such a condition that they can endure the normal journey and can be merchantable, and fit for any relevant purpose made known to the seller, on arrival and for a reasonable time thereafter to enable them to be disposed of or used (*a*). It has been stated that, if the seller ships goods in circumstances in which he retains all rights over and title to goods, he does not fulfil his obligations under an f.o.b. contract (*b*). There are, however, many cases where a seller under an f.o.b. contract has been held to retain rights over and title to the goods after shipment to secure the contract price, for example by taking the bill of lading to his own order (*c*). It is a question of fact in each case whether the seller,

---

(*o*) *The Osterbek*, [1972] 2 Lloyd's Rep. 341, at p. 351.

(*p*) Strictly across the ship's rail: *Pyrenne* v. *Scindia Navigation Co., Ltd.*, [1954] 2 All E. R. 158, at p. 161; [1954] 2 Q. B. 402, at p. 414.

(*q*) *Stock* v. *Inglis* (1884), 12 Q. B. D. 564, at p. 573; affirmed sub nom. *Inglis* v. *Stock* (1885), 10 App. Cas. 263, at p. 271; see also 19 Mod. L. R. 417, and, for a discussion on the various types of f.o.b. contract, 3 Business L. R. 256.

(*r*) See s. 32 (2) of the Sale of Goods Act, *post*.

(*s*) *Wimble* v. *Rosenberg & Sons*, [1913] 3 K. B. 743, at p. 757. *Cf. Re L. Sutro, Heilbut Symons & Co.*, [1917] 2 K. B. 348, C. A. (printed contract alleged usage as to alternative route); *Cunningham, Ltd.* v. *Robert Munro & Co., Ltd.* (1922), 28 Com. Cas. 42, at p. 45 (general statement of principles of law applicable to f.o.b. contract); see also *Ian Stach* v. *Baker Bosley, Ltd.*, [1958] 1 All E. R. 542; [1958] 2 Q. B. 130.

(*t*) *Maine Spinning Co.* v. *Sutcliffe & Co.* (1917), 87 L. J. K. B. 382.

(*u*) *Boks & Co.* v. *Rayner & Co.* (1921), 37 T. L. R. 519, affirmed by C. A., *ibid.*, 800; *cf. Scaliaris* v. *Ofverberg & Co.* (1921), 37 T. L. R. 307, C. A.; *Bragg* v. *Villanova* (1923), 40 T. L. R. 154 (goods shipped f.o.b. Tarragona, but not inspected there); *Mantovani* v. *Carapelli*, [1978] 2 Lloyd's Rep. 63, affirmed [1980] 1 Lloyd's Rep. 375, C. A.

(*a*) *Mash and Murrell* v. *Joseph I. Emmanuel, Ltd.*, [1961] 1 All E. R. 485; [1961] 1 W. L. R. 862; reversed on facts, [1962] 1 All E. R. 77, *n*; [1962] 1 W. L. R. 16, C. A. This implied term applies also to c.i.f. and other contracts where the goods are to be subject to transit before use; see, *e.g.*, *Commercial Fibres* v. *Zabaida*, [1975] 1 Lloyd's Rep. 27. See further, s. 33 of the Sale of Goods Act, *post*.

(*b*) *Wait* v. *Baker* (1848), 2 Exch. 1, at p. 8; *Browne* v. *Hare* (1853), 3 H. & N. 484; (1859), 4 H. & N. 822. See also *Gabarron* v. *Kreeft* (1875), L. R. 10 Ex. 274.

(*c*) *The Parchim*, [1918] A. C. 157, P. C.; *Frebold* v. *Circle Products, Ltd.*, [1970] 1 Lloyd's Rep. 499, C. A.

by so acting, retains not only the possession of the goods (*d*), but also the title to them (*e*), but as the price is sufficiently secured by retaining possession of the goods, special circumstances would seem to be required to rebut the *prima facie* inference that the parties intend the title to the goods to pass on shipment (*f*).

Where payment is by irrevocable letter of credit, property passes at the latest when payment is made against presentation of the documents by the seller to the bank.

(2) C.i.f. contracts.—Under an ordinary c.i.f. contract the seller has

> "firstly to ship at the port of shipment goods of the description contained in the contract (*g*); secondly, to procure a contract of affreightment under which the goods will be delivered at the destination contemplated by the contract (*h*); thirdly, to arrange for an insurance upon the terms current in the trade which will be available to the buyer; fourthly, to make out an invoice as described by BLACKBURN, J., in *Ireland* v. *Livingston* (*i*), or in some similar form; and finally to tender these documents to the buyer (*k*), so that he may know what freight he has to pay, and obtain delivery of the goods if they arrive, or recover for their loss if they are lost on the voyage" (*l*).

(*d*) As in *The Sorfareren* (1915), 114 L. T. 46, and in the cases cited in the preceding note.

(*e*) As in *Wait* v. *Baker, supra; Turner* v. *Liverpool Docks Trustees* (1851), 6 Exch. 543; *Ogg* v. *Shuter* (1875), 1 C. P. D. 47.

(*f*) *Frebold* v. *Circle Products, Ltd.*, [1970] 1 Lloyd's Rep. 499, C. A. This inference necessarily weakens the contrary inference to be drawn in a bill of lading case under s. 19 (2) of the Sale of Goods Act, *post*, if the bill is made out to the seller's order, but in principle s. 19 (2) would seem to cover f.o.b. contracts; see *The Parchim, supra*, at pp. 170–171. It has been said that the retention of possession alone would be inadequate to enable the seller to raise finance—*See per* Lord WRIGHT in *Smyth* v. *Bailey*, [1940] 3 All E. R. 60, at p. 68. But the right to the physical possession of the goods can be transferred for this purpose, as in *Mirabita* v. *Imperial Ottoman Bank* (1878), 3 Ex. D. 164, and *The Parchim, supra*. For conflicting views as to the extent to which a seller may retain rights over goods after placing them on board ship, see Carver, *British Shipping Laws* (12th ed.), Vol. 3, para. 1066; Sassoon, *British Shipping Laws*, Vol. 5, para. 391. As to the reservation of a right of disposal of goods generally after they have been appropriated to a contract, see s. 19 of the Sale of Goods Act 1893, *post*.

(*g*) Alternatively, unless the contract otherwise provides, the seller may acquire the goods afloat after their shipment from the port of shipment: *Ross T. Smyth & Co.* v. *Bailey Son & Co.*, [1940] 3 All E. R. 60, at pp. 67–68; see also *Vantol* v. *Fairclough Dodd and Jones*, [1955] 1 Lloyd's Rep. 546, 552; [1956] 2 Lloyd's Rep. 437, 447, H. L.; *Lewis Emanuel* v. *Sammut*, [1959] 2 Lloyd's Rep. 629.

(*h*) But the seller does not promise that the goods will be delivered at their destination. The risk of loss or damage is on the buyer as from the shipment. The seller does however give the implied undertaking as to their condition on shipment discussed at note (*a*) on p. 32.

(*i*) (1872), L. R. 5 H. L. 395, at p. 406.

(*k*) Tender must be as soon as possible after shipment: *Sharpe & Co.* v. *Nosawa & Co.*, [1917] 2 K. B. 814 (reviewing earlier cases). *Quaere* what the position is when the seller acquires goods afloat. There is no absolute duty to tender the documents prior to the vessel's arrival, or before charges are incurred on the goods at the port of destination: *Sanders* v. *Maclean* (1883), 11 Q. B. D. 327.

(*l*) *Biddell Brothers* v. *E. Clemens Horst Co.*, [1911] 1 K. B. 214, at p. 220, *per* HAMILTON, J., and see *ibid.*, [1911] 1 K. B. 934, at p. 952, *per* KENNEDY, L. J., whose dissenting

It is sometimes said that a c.i.f. contract is a contract for the sale of documents rather than a sale of goods (*m*); but the cases show that it is a contract for the sale of insured goods, lost or not lost, to be implemented by the transfer of proper documents (*n*).

In the normal c.i.f. contract the property in the goods only passes upon transfer of the documents (*o*), except in special cases, for example where no right of disposal is reserved and property passes on shipment (*p*). Further, in a c.i.f. sale of goods "in bulk" (*q*) property cannot pass until the goods sold have become ascertained usually on or after discharge (*r*).

The risk in the goods passes on or as from shipment in the case of specific goods (*s*). With a sale of unascertained or future goods, there must be a measure of appropriation of goods to the contract before the risk can pass (*t*). Once such appropriation occurs, the risk passes retrospectively as from shipment, but it would seem that if the goods have already been lost before appropriation, the appropriation will not be effective (*u*).

Shipment must be effected within the time stated in the contract, if any, or within a reasonable time (*a*). In commercial contracts for the sale of goods a stipulated time for shipment is *prima facie* of the essence

---

judgment was approved, [1912] A. C. 18; *Johnson* v. *Taylor Bros.*, [1920] A. C. 144, at p. 156 (suggesting six requisites). See also *Landauer* v. *Craven*, [1912] 2 K. B. 94; *Groom* v. *Barber*, [1915] 1 K. B. 316; *Karberg* v. *Blythe Green & Co.*, [1916] 1 K. B. 495, at p. 513, C. A.

(*m*) *Arnhold Karberg & Co.* v. *Blythe, Green, Jourdain & Co.*, [1915] 2 K. B. 379, at p. 388; but see on appeal at [1916] 1 K. B. 495, at p. 510.

(*n*) *Smyth* v. *Bailey*, [1940] 3 All E. R. 60, H. L.; *The Gabbiano*, [1940] P. 166, at p. 174, approving the passage in the text.

(*o*) "In this course of business, the general property in the goods remains in the seller until he transfers the bills of lading": *Smyth* v. *Bailey*, [1940] 3 All E. R. 60, H. L., *per* Lord WRIGHT, at p. 68. Where payment is cash against documents, property will not pass until payment is made, despite endorsement and delivery of the bill of lading: *Ginzberg* v. *Barrow Haematite Steel Co., Ltd.*, [1966] 1 Lloyd's Rep. 343, at p. 348, and s. 19(3) of the Sale of Goods Act.

(*p*) See *The Albazero*, [1974] 2 All E. R. 906 (where the seller reserved the right of disposal until the posting of the documents to the buyer); affirmed on this point: [1975] 3 All E. R. 21; [1977] A. C. 774, C. A.; reversed [1976] 3 All E. R. 129; [1977] A. C. 774, H. L.

(*q*) *I.e.*, the sale of an unascertained part of a larger cargo on board a vessel.

(*r*) See the comment to s. 16 of the Sale of Goods Act, *post.*

(*s*) Or retrospectively as from shipment in the case of specific goods acquired afloat: see *Comptoir D'Achat et de Vente du Boerenland Belge S/A* v. *Luis de Ridder*, [1949] 1 All E. R. 269 at p. 274; [1949] A. C. 293, at p. 309, *per* Lord PORTER; *The "Galatia"*, [1979] 2 Lloyd's Rep. 450, at p. 455; affirmed [1980] 1 Lloyd's Rep. 453, C. A.

(*t*) "Appropriation" is here used in the sense of the seller binding himself to deliver particular goods or documents relating to them or to make delivery of part of a particular bulk shipment or documents relating to it; see *Benjamin's Sale of Goods*, paras. 1503, 1549.

(*u*) See *Couturier* v. *Hastie* (1856), 5 H. L. Cas. 673, H. L., where the contract would seem to have been a c.i.f. contract. See also Benjamin, *op. cit.*, paras. 1549–1550, 1565.

(*a*) *Landauer* v. *Craven*, [1912] 2 K. B. 94, at p. 105; *Thomas Borthwick (Glasgow), Ltd.* v. *Bunge & Co., Ltd.*, [1969] 1 Lloyd's Rep. 17, at p. 28; and s. 29(3) of the Sale of Goods Act, *post.*

(*b*). Even if no such time is expressly stipulated, the implied duty to ship within a reasonable time is probably also, *prima facie*, a condition (*c*).

The documents must likewise be tendered to the buyer within the time stated in the contract, if any, or, otherwise, with reasonable despatch after the seller has destined the goods to the buyer (*d*).

The transfer of proper documents has four elements: first, all the documents called for in the contract must be tendered (*e*); second, the documents must be of the type discussed below and be valid on tender (*f*); third, they must in the case of the bill of lading show, and in the case of the policy and invoice relate to, goods of the contractual description (*g*); fourth, the statements in the documents must be accurate. As to the third and fourth heads, it is not enough to tender documents which purport to relate to the shipment of the contractual goods. If they do so only because they are inaccurate, their tender is a breach of contract by the seller. The seller is also in breach for not shipping the contractual goods. The two breaches are separate (*g*). The fact that the goods shipped do not comply with the contract does not necessarily make the documents inaccurate. Many contracts call for documents giving only the barest description, and this description may be perfectly accurate. But it would seem that a buyer can reject even accurate documents, if he can show that the goods to which they relate do not comply with the contract, since the seller owes a duty to ship or acquire afloat goods of the contract description, and is not entitled to tender documents relating to any but such goods (*h*).

A buyer who initially rejects documents alleging wrongly that they are inaccurate or inadequate may subsequently justify his rejection by showing non-compliance of the goods with the contract at the time of the initial rejection (*i*).

(*b*) *Bowes* v. *Shand* (1877), 2 App. Cas. 455; *Bunge* v. *Tradax*, [1980] 1 Lloyd's Rep. 294; and see the comment to s. 10 of the Sale of Goods Act, *post*.

(*c*) *Thomas Borthwick* v. *Bunge, supra; McDougall* v. *Aeromarine of Emsworth*, [1958] 3 All E. R. 431, at pp. 438, 439.

(*d*) *Sanders* v. *Maclean* (1883), 11 Q. B. D. 327; *Landauer* v. *Craven*, [1912] 2 K. B. 94; *Johnson* v. *Taylor Bros.*, [1920] A. C. 144; *Toepfer* v. *Lenersan-Poortman*, [1978] 2 Lloyd's Rep. 555, at p. 558; [1980] 1 Lloyd's Rep. 143, C. A.; *S. I. A. T. Di Del Ferro* v. *Tradax Overseas S. A.*, [1978] 2 Lloyd's Rep. 470, at p. 493.

(*e*) *Libau Wood Co.* v. *H. Smith & Sons* (1930), 37 Ll. L. Rep. 296.

(*f*) *Arnhold Karberg & Co.* v. *Blythe Green & Co.*, [1916] 1 K. B. 495, C. A.

(*g*) *Finlay & Co., Ltd.* v. *Kwik Hoo Tong Handel Matschappij*, [1929] 1 K. B. 400; *Chao* v. *British Traders and Shippers*, [1954] 1 All E. R. 779; [1954] 2 Q. B. 459; but see *Panchaud Frères S. A.* v. *Établissement General Grain Co.*, [1970] 1 Lloyd's Rep. 53, C. A. As to the measure of damages recoverable when a buyer pays against inaccurate documents believing them to be accurate, see *Chao* v. *British Traders and Shippers, supra*.

(*h*) *Cf. Taylor* v. *Oakes, Roncoroni & Co.* (1922), 38 T. L. R. 349, at p. 351; affirmed on appeal, 38 T. L. R. 517; *Dean* v. *O'Day* (1927), 39 C. L. R. 330. The buyer cannot claim to wait until the goods arrive in order to inspect them before deciding whether or not to accept the documents: *E. Clemens Horst* v. *Biddell Brothers*, [1912] A. C. 18, H. L. For a contrary view to that in the text, see *Gulamali Abdul Hussain* v. *Mohammed Yousuf*, [1953] 1 Mad. L. J. R. 504, at p. 507.

(*i*) *Taylor* v. *Oakes, Roncoroni & Co., supra*; *British and Beningtons, Ltd.* v. *North West Cachar Tea Co.*, [1923] A. C. 48, H. L.; *Continental Contractors* v. *Medway* (1925), 23 Ll. L. Rep. 55, 124.

Provided he can do so within a reasonable time of shipment, a seller whose tender of documents is justifiably rejected may obtain and tender fresh documents (*k*). If necessary, and provided there has been no appropriation of particular goods to the contract (*l*), these may relate to fresh goods (*m*).

If the goods shipped do not correspond with the contract description, there is a breach of the contract when the goods are shipped (*n*). A distinction has, however, to be made between the contract description and words in the contract which serve merely to identify the goods (*o*). In case of non-delivery, the seller is in breach for failing to ship, or acquire afloat, the contractual goods (*p*), but for the purpose of assessment of damages, and unless the contract otherwise provides, the relevant breach is that which occurs at the time when (*q*) and the place where (*r*) the documents ought to have been tendered.

Damages for non-delivery fall *prima facie* to be calculated by the market value of similar goods at the latter time and place (*s*).

Apart from contrary provision, or to a contrary practice in the particular trade (*t*), the contract of affreightment (almost invariably evidenced by a bill of lading) must cover the whole transit and be transferable, so that the buyer may be in a position to claim delivery and to sue for any breach (*u*). The bill of lading must be issued "on shipment", meaning at the time of shipment or without undue delay in the ordinary course of business thereafter; and the shipping documents

---

(*k*) *Libau Wood Co.* v. *H. Smith & Sons, Ltd.* (1930), 37 Ll. L. Rep. 296. See also *The Vladimir Ilich*, [1975] 1 Lloyd's Rep. 322 (impossible appropriation by seller).

(*l*) See *Kleinjan Holst N. V. Rotterdam* v. *Bremer Handelsgesellschaft m.b.h. Hambourg*, [1972] 2 Lloyd's Rep. 11.

(*m*) *Borrowman* v. *Free* (1878), 4 Q. B. D. 500; *Getreide Import* v. *Itoh*, [1979] 1 Lloyd's Rep. 592.

(*n*) *Parker* v. *Schuller* (1901), 17 T. L. R. 299, C. A.; *Crozier & Co.* v. *Auerbach*, [1908] 2 K. B. 161, C. A.; *Libau Wood Co.* v. *H. Smith & Sons, Ltd.* (1930), 37 Ll. L. Rep. 296.

(*o*) *Reardon Smith Line, Ltd.* v. *Hansen-Tangen*, [1976] 3 All E. R. 570; [1976] 1 W. L. R. 989, H. L.; *Sanko Steamship Co., Ltd.* v. *Kano Trading, Ltd.*, [1978] 1 Lloyd's Rep. 156.

(*p*) *Johnson* v. *Taylor Bros.*, [1920] A. C. 144.

(*q*) *Sharpe & Co.* v. *Nosawa & Co.*, [1917] 2 K. B. 814; distinguished on the special facts, *Produce Brokers Co.* v. *Weis & Co.* (1918), 87 L. J. K. B. 472.

(*r*) *Biddell Bros.* v. *E. Clemens Horst Co.*, [1911] 1 K. B. 934, 961, C. A. And the non-delivery of the documents may be treated as the breach for the purpose of R. S. C., O. 11, r. 1 (g), which was altered to its present form to meet the decision in *Johnson* v. *Taylor Bros.*, [1920] A. C. 144.

(*s*) *Sharpe & Co.* v. *Nosawa & Co.*, [1917] 2 K. B. 814; and see the comment to s. 51 of the Sale of Goods Act, *post*. As to damages in a foreign currency, see the comment to s. 54 of that Act, *post*.

(*t*) *Bunstall* v. *Grimsdale* (1906), 11 Com. Cas. 280, at p. 290; *N. V. Meyer* v. *Aune*, [1939] 3 All E. R. 168..

(*u*) *Hansson* v. *Hamel & Horley* (1921), 26 Com. Cas. 236, C. A.; affirmed [1922] 2 A. C. 36; *N. V. Arnold Meyer* v. *Aune* (1939), 64 Ll. L. Rep. 121. As to the presence of transhipment terms, see *Holland Colombo Trading Society, Ltd.* v. *Segu Mohamed Alawdeen*, [1954] 2 Lloyd's Rep. 45, at p. 53; *Soproma S.p.A.* v. *Marine and Animal By-Products Corpn.*, [1966] 1 Lloyd's Rep. 367, at p. 388–389. The bill of lading must also evidence a contract for the whole transit; the buyer is not obliged to speculate or investigate, or accept assurances outside the bill of lading: *S. I. A. T.* v. *Tradax Overseas S. A.*, [1980] 1 Lloyd's Rep. 53, C. A.

must be "reasonably and readily fit to pass current in commerce" (*a*). The bill must evidence shipment "on board" (*b*), except in trades where a received for shipment bill of lading is shown to be usual (*c*).

The buyer may refuse to accept an enemy bill of lading though the contract was entered into before the outbreak of war (*d*).

The goods must be covered by an effective policy of insurance (*e*), and even if the goods arrive safely this condition is not dispensed with (*f*). On the other hand, there is a valid tender under the contract if the proper documents be tendered after knowledge that the goods have been lost, but the goods must be covered by a policy which can be assigned to the buyer. An open cover taken out by the seller protecting all goods shipped by him is not enough (*g*). A contract by the seller to insure cattle sent abroad against "all risks" is not satisfied by taking out a Lloyds' "all risks" policy if the policy contains the "free of capture and seizure" clause (*h*). If the seller has effected a proper insurance under a c.i.f. policy, he may retain for his own benefit "increased value" policies which he has subsequently taken out (*i*). If an English buyer purchases goods from a foreigner abroad on c.i.f. terms, he cannot demand an

---

(*a*) *Hansson* v. *Hamel & Horley*, *supra; S. I. A. T.* v. *Tradax Overseas S. A.*, [1978] 2 Lloyd's Rep. 470, 492–493 and [1980] 1 Lloyd's Rep. 53, at p. 62, deciding, *inter alia*, that an altered bill is bad tender, if altered other than by way of correction before issue of a minor clerical error. But, if the bill is clear, the fact that it is in unusual form, or contains unusual words will not necessarily make it "unfit to pass current in commerce": see *The "Galatia"*, [1979] 2 Lloyd's Rep. 450, at p. 456; [1980] 1 Lloyd's Rep. 453, C. A.

(*b*) *Diamond Alkali Corporation* v. *Bourgeois*, [1921] 3 K. B. 443.

(*c*) *Weis* v. *Produce Brokers* (1921), 7 Ll. L. Rep. 211, C. A.; *United Baltic Corpn.* v. *Burgett & Newsam* (1921), 8 Ll. L. Rep. 190, 191, C. A.

(*d*) *Karberg* v. *Blythe Green & Co.*, [1916] 1 K. B. 495, C. A.; *cf. Duncan Fox & Co.* v. *Schrempft*, [1915] 3 K. B. 355, C. A.

(*e*) *Cantiere Meccanico Brindisino* v. *Constant* (1912), 17 Com. Cas. 182, 192; *Loders & Nucoline, Ltd.* v. *Bank of New Zealand* (1929), 33 Ll. L. Rep. 70 (term in contract providing for "insurance at contract price" is not satisfied by separate insurances on freight and goods); *Diamond Alkali Corporation* v. *Bourgeois*, [1921] 3 K. B. 443 (certificate of insurance insufficient); *Scott (Donald) & Co.* v. *Barclays Bank*, [1923] 2 K. B. 1, C. A. (certificate of insurance not an "approved insurance policy"). Even if a certificate of insurance is accepted, the seller impliedly warrants that the assertions in it are true, and that he will produce, or procure the production of, the policy referred to in the certificate: *Harper & Co.* v. *Mackechnie & Co.*, [1925] 2 K. B. 423. Where the contract provides for a certificate of insurance, a cover note will not suffice; *Promos S. A.* v. *European Grain and Shipping*, [1979] 1 Lloyd's Rep. 375.

(*f*) *Orient Co., Ltd.* v. *Brekke*, [1913] 1 K. B. 531. *Cf. Re Denbigh Cowan & Co. & Atcherley & Co.* (1921), 90 L. J. K. B. 836, C. A.

(*g*) *Manbre Saccharine Co.* v. *Corn Products Co.*, [1919] 1 K. B. 198. *Cf. Wilson Holgate & Co.* v. *Belgian Grain Co.*, [1920] 2 K. B. 1, as to an alleged usage.

(*h*) *Yuill* v. *Robson*, [1908] 1 K. B. 270, C. A. (cattle sent from Buenos Aires and seized by Natal Government on account of disease). But distinguish *Vincentelli* v. *Rowlett* (1911), 105 L. T. 411 ("all risks" policy not covering improper stowage for which ship is liable). As to scope and limits of ordinary "all risks" policy, see *British and Foreign Marine Ins. Co.* v. *Gaunt*, [1921] 2 A. C. 41, at p. 57. As to war risks, see *Groom* v. *Barber*, [1915] 1 K. B. 316, when the contract ran "war risk for buyer's account"; *Law and Bonar* v. *American Tobacco Co.*, [1916] 2 K. B. 605 (c.i.f. contract made before war).

(*i*) *Strass* v. *Spillers & Bakers*, [1911] 2 K. B. 759; but distinguish *Landauer* v. *Asser*, [1905] 2 K. B. 184.

English policy, but he may reject the goods if the policy tendered does not specify the risks (*k*).

After the documents have been taken up by the buyer, the seller may still incur liability (*e.g.* under a charterparty) in respect of matters such as discharge which are the buyer's responsibility if the contracts of sale and affreightment are on "free out" terms. Sale contracts therefore often include provisions to protect the seller, *e.g.* an indemnity against any demurrage which the seller may have to pay to shipowners arising from discharge below the charter rate (*l*) or even an independent demurrage code in the sale contract (which may or may not be back-to-back with that in the charter (*m*). A simple indemnity against demurrage will not, however, suffice if the seller utilizes a ship which he has on time-charter, since slow discharge will then involve him in extra hire, not demurrage (*n*).

(3) "Ex-ship" contracts.—"In the case of a sale 'ex-ship'," says Lord SUMNER,

> "the seller has to cause delivery to be made to the buyer from a ship which has arrived at the port of delivery, and has reached a place therein which is usual for delivery of goods of the kind in question. The seller has therefore to pay the freight or otherwise to release the shipowner's lien, and to furnish the buyer with an effectual direction to the ship to deliver. Till this is done the buyer is not bound to pay for the goods. Till this is done he may have an insurable interest in profits, but none that can correctly be described as an interest 'upon goods,' nor any interest which the seller, as seller, is bound to insure for him" (*o*).

The inclusion of terms based on the assumption that the goods will arrive does not necessarily make what is otherwise a c.i.f. contract into an ex-ship contract (*p*). The contract will, however, be an ex-ship contract if it is quite clear that arrival is a condition of payment (*q*). This will generally, if not always, be the case where under a contract nominally c.i.f. a buyer is, in accordance with a usual practice, merely given a delivery order addressed by the seller to his agents at the port of arrival (*r*).

(4) "Ex-store" contracts.—A contract to deliver "ex-store" does not cover a delivery "ex-lighter" or "ex-quay"; but the exact scope of the contract is somewhat indefinite (*s*).

(*k*) *Malmberg* v. *Evans & Co.* (1924), 29 Com. Cas. 235; affirmed 30 Com. Cas. 107, C. A., on the particular facts without deciding the general point.

(*l*) *Suzuki & Co.* v. *Companhia Mercantile Internacional* (1921), 8 Ll. L. Rep. 174; 9 Ll. L. Rep. 171, where a cesser clause in the charter meant the seller had no such liability.

(*m*) *Houlder Bros.* v. *Commissioner of Public Works*, [1908] A. C. 276; *French Govt.* v. *Sanday* (1923), 16 Ll. L. Rep. 238.

(*n*) *Mallozzi* v. *Carapelli*, [1976] 1 Lloyd's Rep. 407.

(*o*) *Yangtsze Ins. Association* v. *Lukmanjee*, [1918] A. C. 585, at p. 589, P. C.

(*p*) *Re Denbigh Cowan & Co. & Atcherley & Co.* (1921), 90 L. J. K. B. 836; *Plaimar, Ltd.* v. *Waters Trading Co., Ltd.* (1945), 72 C. L. R. 304 (High Ct. of Aus.); *Fragano* v. *Long* (1825), 4 B. & C. 219, considered in *The Pantanassa*, [1970] 1 All E. R. 848; [1970] P. 187.

(*q*) *Dupont* v. *British S. A. Co.* (1901), 18 T. L. R. 24; *Polenghi* v. *Dried Milk Co.* (1904), 10 Com. Cas. 42; *The Pantanassa*, [1970] 1 All E. R. 848.

(*r*) *See Comptoir d'Achat* v. *Luis de Ridder*, [1949] 1 All E. R. 269; [1949] A. C. 293, H. L.

(*s*) *Fisher Reeves & Co.* v. *Armour & Co.*, [1920] 3 K. B. 614, C. A.

B. Licences

The import or export of goods under international contracts of sale frequently requires the permission of a governmental authority in the form of an import or export licence. Where this is the case, the parties will usually provide in the contract which of them is to apply for the necessary licence and what is to happen if the application is refused.

If the contract is altogether silent about licences, or is expressed to be "subject to licences" without providing who is to obtain them, a term is usually implied (*t*) making this the duty of one party or the other (*u*). The tendency is to cast the duty upon the party best qualified, by knowledge of the necessary facts or otherwise, to obtain the licence (*a*). Thus, in a sale of turpentine f.a.s. Lisbon, where the seller knew that the buyer wished to export to East Germany, and where the only person who could apply for the necessary export licence was the seller's supplier, whose identity the seller deliberately withheld from the buyer, it was held to be the seller's duty to procure the licence (*b*). The buyer was not bound to change the contemplated destination to one for which an export licence could be obtained, at least where he was only requested to do so towards the end of the contractual shipment period. On the other hand, where jute was sold f.o.b. Dundee, and the seller had no knowledge of its destination, which might have been to another U.K. port or to a foreign port, the duty to apply for an export licence was held to be on the buyer (*c*).

Once it is determined, from the words of the contract or by implication, who is to apply for the licences, there is a separate question, again depending on the circumstances of the particular case, whether the duty is an absolute one (*d*) or, more usually, whether it is only to use all reasonable diligence to obtain the necessary licences (*e*). Performance of the contract in the latter case is only excused if the duty has been performed but no licence has been obtained (*f*) or if no steps which

(*t*) See the note on implied terms, p. 12, *ante*.

(*u*) *Cassidy* v. *Osuustukkukauppa*, [1957] 1 All E. R. 484.

(*a*) *Brandt* v. *Morris*, [1917] 2 K. B. 784, as explained in *Pound* v. *Hardy*, [1956] 1 All E. R. 639; [1956] A. C. 588.

(*b*) *Pound* v. *Hardy*, *supra*.

(*c*) *McMaster & Co.* v. *Cox, McEuen & Co.* 1921 S. C. (H. L.) 24 (where the export licence was required by legislation enacted after the contract was made). See also *Mitchell Cotts & Co.* v. *Hairco, Ltd.*, [1943] 2 All E. R. 552 (property having passed to buyer upon tender of shipping documents, buyer was importer of goods, and responsible for obtaining import licence).

(*d*) As in *Partabmull* v. *Sethia*, [1951] 2 All E. R. 352 *n.*, H. L.; *Cassidy* v. *Osuustukkukauppa*, [1957] 1 All E. R. 484; and *Toprak Mahsulleri Ofisi* v. *Finograin Compagnie*, [1979] 2 Lloyd's Rep. 98, at pp. 107, 108. See also the special clause considered in *Czarnikow, Ltd.* v. *Rolimpex*, [1979] A. C. 351, H. L.

(*e*) *Re Anglo-Russian Merchant Traders and Batt*, [1917] 2 K. B. 679, at p. 686, C. A.; *Brauer* v. *Clark*, [1952] 2 All E. R. 497, C. A.; *Pound* v. *Hardy* (*supra*). Where the contract is silent, the duty imposed is almost invariably only to use all reasonable diligence: *Coloneale Import–Export* v. *Loumidis*, [1978] 2 Lloyd's Rep. 560, and *semble* that where the contract is "subject to licence," the duty cannot be absolute—see the dictum of DEVLIN, J., in *Cassidy* v. *Osuustukkukauppa* (*supra*), at p. 488.

(*f*) *Taylor* v. *Landauer*, [1940] 4 All E. R. 335; *Société D'Avances Commerciales* v. *Besse*, [1952] 1 Lloyd's Rep. 242; *Brauer* v. *Clark* (*supra*).

could have been taken would have led to a licence being obtained (*g*). The other party may have a duty to co-operate with the party applying for a licence, for example by supplying necessary information, at least if requested to do so (*h*).

If an absolute prohibition of export supervenes upon a contract which provides for cancellation in such an event, and the seller receives notice during the contractual period for shipment that such a prohibition will be imposed, he is not discharged from performance unless he does everything possible to ship before the prohibition comes into force (*i*).

Numerous cases have come before the courts on contracts containing clauses providing for cancellation or extension in the case of supervening events such as prohibition of export, or hindrance or delay affecting shipment in circumstances constituting "*force majeure*". Such clauses are intended to apply in circumstances not amounting to frustration. The cases turn to a considerable extent upon the wording of the particular clauses. The following conclusions may, however, be drawn:

(1) Clauses covering "hindrance" of performance by specified events apply if such an event occurs giving rise to "obstacles which it would be really difficult to overcome" (*k*). Clauses covering "prevention" or "prohibition" by specified events have been said to require proof of legal or physical impossibility of performance (*l*).

(2) Such a clause may apply generally as where the export of goods of the contract description is prohibited, or may deal particularly with the effects of *force majeure* on the seller's actual intended performance.

(3) Where such a clause applies generally,

(a) the seller need not show that, but for the prohibition, he would have been able to perform (*m*);

(b) he must show that the prohibition was such as to prevent

(*g*) In either case, the onus of proof is upon the party upon whom the duty lay to show that he ought to be excused; this is a particularly difficult task in the latter case: *Windschluegl* v. *A. Pickering & Co.* (1950), 84 Ll. L. R. 89, at p. 95; *Société d' Avances Commerciales* v. *Besse, supra*; but see *Provimi* v. *Warinco*, [1978] 1 Lloyd's Rep. 67 and 373, C. A., where the onus was satisfied. In *Agroexport State Enterprise for Foreign Trade* v. *Compagnie Européene de Céréals*, [1974] 1 Lloyd's Rep. 499, a government decision just before the shipment date to refuse further export licences was no excuse for a seller who had already had several months in which to obtain a licence. In *Malik Co.* v. *Central European Trading Agency, Ltd.*, [1974] 2 Lloyd's Rep. 279, the seller had failed to apply for several months, and although he did everything possible thereafter, he failed to discharge the onus upon him.

(*h*) *Pound* v. *Hardy*, [1956] 1 All E. R. 639; [1956] A. C. 588, at pp. 608, 611.

(*i*) *Smyth* v. *Lindsay*, [1953] 2 All E. R. 1064, distinguishing *Re Anglo-Russian Merchant Traders* v. *Batt* (*supra*), where the prohibition came into effect without prior notice.

(*k*) *Tennants* (*Lancaster*), *Ltd.* v. *Wilson & Co.*, [1917] A. C. 495; *Dixon & Son* v. *Henderson Craig & Co.*, [1919] 2 K. B. 778; *Reardon Smith* v. *Ministry of Agriculture*, [1961] 2 All E. R. 577; [1962] 1 Q. B. 42, C. A.; but see on appeal [1963] 1 All E. R. 545; [1963] A. C. 691, H. L.

(*l*) *Tennants* v. *Wilson, supra*, at p. 509. But commercial impracticability may, it seems, also constitute prevention or prohibition: see *e.g.* *Bremer* v. *Mackprang*, [1979] 1 Lloyd's Rep. 221, at p. 224; and head (3) below.

(*m*) *Bremer* v. *Vanden*, [1978] 2 Lloyd's Rep. 109, at pp. 114, 121 and 131, H. L. It may be open to the buyer to prove the contrary: *per* Viscount DILHORNE at p. 121.

performance of the contract in any manner permitted by its terms which it would be practicable and commercially sensible to expect him to adopt (*n*);

(c) he must also establish that he did not in fact have available to him for performance goods already afloat or within any exceptions to the embargo (*o*);

(d) where he intended before the embargo to fulfil the contract using goods bought in, he must also, it seems, show that the originally intended shipper (and, possibly, any intermediate sellers) had no such goods available (*p*);

(e) where he receives prior notice that an embargo is likely to be imposed with effect part-way through the contractual shipment period, he must do everything reasonably possible to ship before the prohibition comes into force (*q*). But it is a matter of degree whether the likelihood of an embargo affecting performance is sufficiently strong to oblige him to accelerate shipment in this way (*r*);

(f) where he has sufficient goods available to him to fulfil part but not all of his relevant commitments, he can still probably rely upon a prohibition clause to protect him, provided that he appropriates the goods which are available "in a way which the trade would consider to be proper and reasonable" – whether the basis is pro-rata, chronological order of contracts or some other (*s*). There may be more than one reasonable course of action open to a seller.

(4) Under a clause dealing with the particular effects of *force majeure* on the seller's intended performance:

(a) The seller must prove that the *force majeure* event relied upon in fact prevented (or hindered or delayed as the case is) the shipment of goods which he could and would otherwise have delivered.

(*n*) *Warinco* v. *Fritz Mauthner*, [1978] 1 Lloyd's Rep. 151, C. A.; *Exportelisa* v. *Giuseppe*, [1978] 1 Lloyd's Rep. 433, C. A., giving the examples of shipment from a different port or by utilizing a different supplier. In commodity trading where an embargo supervenes purchase of goods already afloat is, generally, not expected: *Tradax* v. *Andre*, [1976] 1 Lloyd's Rep. 416, C. A.; *Bremer* v. *Vanden, supra*. The same applies to goods already on lighters or in course of loading and excepted from the embargo: *Bunge* v. *Kruse*, [1979] 1 Lloyd's Rep. 279.

(*o*) *Tradax* v. *Andre, supra; Bremer* v. *Mackprang*, [1979] 1 Lloyd's Rep. 221, C. A.; *Andre* v. *Blanc*, [1979] 2 Lloyd's Rep. 427, C. A.; *Continental Grain Export Corporation* v. *S.T.M. Grain, Ltd.*, [1979] 2 Lloyd's Rep. 460; *Toepfer* v. *Schwarze*, [1980] 1 Lloyd's Rep. 385, C. A.

(*p*) *Bremer* v. *Mackprang, supra; Bunge* v. *Deutsche Conti*, [1979] 2 Lloyd's Rep. 435, C. A., (where the seller, at the date of embargo, had made no arrangements to buy in). See too *Tradax* v. *Cook* (1979), 30th July as yet unreported, GOFF, J. considering *Bunge* v. *Deutsche Conti, supra*.

(*q*) See note (*i*), *supra*.

(*r*) *Tradax* v. *Andre*, [1976] 1 Lloyd's Rep. 416, at pp. 424 and 426, C. A.; *Continental* v. *S.T.M.*, [1979] 1 Lloyd's Rep. 460, at pp. 474–475.

(*s*) *Tradax* v. *Andre*, [1976] 1 Lloyd's Rep. 416, at p. 423, C. A.; *Intertradex* v. *Lesieur-*

(b) If the seller can show prohibition, hindrace or delay affecting the shipment of particular goods (or goods from a particular source) he may not need to show that there were no, or no practicable, alternative means of performance. He must still satisfy the conditions in paragraph (3) (c), (d) and, where appropriate, (e) above, in relation to the particular goods which he intended for delivery (*t*).

(c) In other circumstances a seller may still be able to rely upon the clause if he can satisfy, in their full width similar general conditions to those mentioned in paragraph (3) (b) to (f) above (*u*).

C. Exchange control

Section 33 of the Exchange Control Act 1947, *post*, Appendix I, provides that where Treasury consent is required for the performance of any term of a contract, then, except insofar as it may be shown to be inconsistent with the intention of the parties, it is an implied condition in the contract that the term should not be performed except insofar as that consent is given or not required (*a*). See further the comment to that section, *post*.

D. Payment by Banker's Irrevocable Letters of Credit

Where seller and buyer carry on business in different countries, the contract of sale frequently provides for the seller to be paid through a bank. The most common provision is for payment by means of an irrevocable letter of credit, which has the considerable advantage to the seller that, provided he complies with its terms, he is assured of payment. If the letter of credit is in terms at variance in material respects with those of the contract of sale, and is accepted by the seller, the effect will be to amend the contract of sale (*b*).

An irrevocable letter of credit is an undertaking issued by the buyer's bank by which the bank promises the seller to pay the price of goods upon presentation of specified documents, either in cash or by negotiating or accepting drafts presented by the seller with documents. The specified documents will almost invariably include the bill or bills

---

Torteaux, [1977] 2 Lloyd's Rep. 146; [1978] 2 Lloyd's Rep. 509, C. A.; *Bremer* v. *Mackprang*, [1979] 1 Lloyd's Rep. 221, C. A.

(*t*) *European Grain* v. *Rayner*, [1970] 2 Lloyd's Rep. 239; *Avimex S. A.* v. *Dewulf*, [1979] 2 Lloyd's Rep. 57; *Continental Grain* v. *S. T. M.*, [1979] 2 Lloyd's Rep. 460, at p. 473.

(*u*) See note (*p*), *supra*. But if he leaves it uncertain whether or not he intended to ship any particular goods, or goods from any particular source, affected by the *force majeure* event, he cannot excuse himself from liability: *Bremer* v. *Mackprang* (*No. 2*) (1979), GOFF, J. judgment given 30th July, as yet unreported.

(*a*) Since October 1979, consent has been dispensed with in relation to almost all dealings: see now the Exchange Control (General Exemption) Order 1979 (S. I. 1979 No. 1660).

(*b*) *W. J. Alan & Co., Ltd.* v. *El Naso Export–Import Co.*, [1972] 2 All E. R. 127; [1972] 2 Q. B. 189, C. A.; *Ets. Soules* v. *International Trade Development Co.*, [1979] 2 Lloyd's Rep. 122, at p. 132; on appeal [1980] 1 Lloyd's Rep. 179, C. A.; *Ficom S. A.* v. *Soc. Cadex Limitador*, [1980] 2 Lloyd's Rep. 118.

of lading relating to the goods sold, and in the case of a c.i.f. contract the requisite policy of insurance, and may include such other documents as certificates of quality and origin.

The buyer's bank may instruct another bank in the seller's country to advise the seller of the opening of the letter of credit (*c*). This second bank may "confirm" the credit to the seller, thus adding its own personal liability to that of the issuing bank. Confirmation by a bank in the seller's own country is frequently a term of the contract (*d*).

Where the contract of sale stipulates for payment by an irrevocable letter of credit, it is the duty of the buyer to open such a credit prior to the earliest date for shipment, whether the contract is c.i.f. (*e*) or f.o.b. (*f*). It has been said that the credit must be opened a reasonable time before the first date for shipment (*g*), but this has been questioned (*h*). Failure to open the credit in time is a repudiation of the contract of sale (*i*).

The bank must comply strictly with the instructions given to it by the buyer as to the terms of the credit to be opened, and must take proper care to ensure that the documents when presented comply strictly with those terms (*k*). Otherwise the bank may sacrifice its right to indemnity from the buyer. But if the documents on reasonable examination appear on their face to comply, the bank is entitled to its indemnity even if the documents are in fact forgeries (*l*).

Bills of lading tendered by the seller to the bank must be clean, i.e. they must be free of express clauses indicating defects in the goods' condition upon shipment (*m*). "Received for shipment" bills of lading

---

(*c*) There may indeed be a chain of banks.

(*d*) See, *e. g.*, *Enrico Furst & Co.* v. *W. E. Fischer, Ltd.*, [1960] 2 Lloyd's Rep. 340. For the position of a "confirming house", see *Rusholme and Bolton and Hadfield* v. *Read, S. G.*, [1955] 1 All E. R. 180; *Sobell Industries* v. *Cony Bros.*, [1955] 2 Lloyd's Rep. 82.

(*e*) *Pavia & Co. S. P. A.* v. *Thurmann-Neilson*, [1952] 1 All E. R. 492; [1952] 2 Q. B. 84, C. A. See *Sinason-Teicher* v. *Oilcakes and Oilseeds Trading Co.*, [1954] 3 All E. R. 468, C. A. for an analogous case of a bank guarantee of payment upon presentation of documents.

(*f*) *Ian Stach* v. *Baker Bosley*, [1958] 1 All E. R. 542; [1958] 2 Q. B. 130. In the case of f.o.b. contracts there is no difference in this respect between "classic" f.o.b. contracts, where the seller need take no step towards shipment until he has had instructions from the buyer, and contracts where it is for the seller to arrange shipping space.

(*g*) *Sinason-Teicher Inter American Grain Corporation* v. *Oilcakes and Oilseeds Trading Co.*, [1954] 3 All E. R. 468, at p. 472, *per* DENNING, L. J.

(*h*) *Ian Stach* v. *Baker Bosley, Ltd.*,[1958] 1 All E. R. 542; [1958] 2 Q. B. 130, at pp. 141, 144. See also *Alexandria Cotton and Trading Co. (Sudan), Ltd.* v. *Cotton Co. of Ethiopa, Ltd.*, [1963] 1 Lloyd's Rep. 576, where ROSKILL, J., said that he did not regard the rule as finally settled by the authorities.

(*i*) *Ian Stach* v. *Baker Bosley, supra.*

(*k*) The "*de minimis*" rule does not apply: see *Rayner & Co., Ltd.* v. *Hambros Bank, Ltd.*, [1943] 1 K. B. 37; *Moralice (London), Ltd.* v. *E. D. & F. Man*, [1954] 2 Lloyd's Rep. 526; *Cehave N. V.* v. *Bremer Handelsgesellschaft m.b.H.*, [1975] 3 All E. R. 739; [1976] Q. B. 44, C. A.

(*l*) *Gian Singh & Co., Ltd.* v. *Banque de l'Indochine*, [1974] 2 All E. R. 754; [1974] 1 W. L. R. 1234, P. C.

(*m*) As to "clean" bills, see *British Imex Industries, Ltd.* v. *Midland Bank, Ltd.*, [1958] 1 All E. R. 264; [1958] 1 Q. B. 542; *Cehave N. V.* v. *Bremer Handelsgesellschaft m.b.H., supra; The "Galatia"*, [1979] 2 Lloyd's Rep. 450; [1980] 1 Lloyd's Rep. 453, C. A.

and bills incorporating the terms of a charterparty are not acceptable for tender under letters of credit (*n*).

The extent to which the seller may look to the buyer direct for the price will depend upon the construction of the sale contract (*o*). The *prima facie* position appears to be as follows:

(1) Payment by letter of credit is, where agreed, the primary mode of payment to which the seller must if possible look (*o*).

(2) If the seller is unable to obtain payment under the letter of credit, he may look to the buyer direct for payment unless either there is a clear stipulation to the contrary, or the seller was himself responsible for failing to obtain payment under the letter of credit (*p*).

(3) The buyer has a duty to the seller under the contract to provide a letter of credit in accordance with its terms and to take every reasonable step, at least, to ensure that the Bank will pay on presentation under the letter of credit. If the buyer fails to perform this duty, and as a result the Bank fails to pay, then the seller would seem to be entitled to claim damages from the buyer equivalent to the price, even if the contract provides that he should not be entitled to look to the buyer direct for the price.

The opening of an irrevocable letter of credit gives rise to a contract between the issuing bank (and, if there is one, the confirming bank) on the one hand, and the seller on the other (*q*). This contract is governed by the terms of the letter of credit and is entirely separate from the contract of sale and from the buyer's contract with the issuing bank. Under this contract with the seller the bank must pay against documents (or honour or accept drafts as appropriate) provided the documents are on their face good. The bank cannot withhold payment because of the nature or condition of the goods. If the buyer has any complaint on this score, he must bring an action for damages against the

(*n*) *Enrico Furst & Co.* v. *W. E. Fischer, Ltd.*, [1960] 2 Lloyd's Rep. 340, at pp. 345–346. The credit itself will usually expressly insist upon "on board" bills. See also Arts. 17 and 18 of the Uniform Customs and Practice for Documentary Credits (1962 Revision).

(*o*) *W. J. Alan & Co.* v. *El Nasr Export & Import Co.*, [1972] 2 All E. R. 127; [1972] 2 Q. B. 189, C. A., *Saffaron* v. *Société Minière Cafrika* (1958), 100 C. L. R. 231 (H. C. of Aus.), *Soproma S. p. A.* v. *Marine Animal By-Products Assocn.*, [1966] 1 Lloyd's Rep. 367; *E. D. & F. Man* v. *Nigerian Sweets*, [1977] 2 Lloyd's Rep. 50.

(*p*) *Maran Road Saw Mill* v. *Austin Taylor Co., Ltd.*, [1975] 1 Lloyd's Rep. 156, at p. 159; *Newman Industries* v. *Indo-British Industries*, [1956] 2 Lloyd's Rep. 219; revd. on other grounds: [1957] 1 Lloyd's Rep. 211, C. A., where the bank's refusal to pay was arguably justified under the letter of credit, but SELLERS, J. held that even if it was justified, the seller could sue the buyer direct, because the buyer should have rectified the position with the bank so as to accord with the sale contract; *E. D. & F. Man* v. *Nigerian Sweets, supra*. In *Saffaron* v. *Société Minière Cafrika* (1958), 100 C. L. R. 231, the High Court of Australia suggested that the only circumstance in which a seller might forfeit the price would be if it was his fault that payment under the letter of credit had not been forthcoming. But even in such a case as that, there seems no good reason why the buyer should not pay the price unless he has been prejudiced by the seller's default.

(*q*) *Urquhart, Lindsay & Co., Ltd.* v. *Eastern Bank, Ltd.*, [1922] 1 K. B. 318; *Hamzeh Malas & Sons* v. *British Imex Industries, Ltd.*, [1958] 1 All E. R. 262; [1958] 2 Q. B. 127, C. A. Consideration can clearly be found in the seller's acting on the credit by bringing the

seller (*r*). In general, he cannot prevent the seller from presenting the necessary documents to the bank for payment, nor can he prevent the bank from paying the seller (*r*). Thus, an injunction will not be granted to restrain such presentation on payment except perhaps in circumstances where it could be clearly established that the documents presented were forged or that the person presenting them was acting fraudulently in circumstances where there was no right to payment; mere suspicion or the possibility of fraud will not justify an interlocutory injunction in this context (*s*).

The bank is, however, entitled to refuse payment if the documents presented are forged or the request for their payment is made fraudulently in circumstances where there is no right to payment (*t*). The bank itself may thus, it appears, raise such a defence even though the buyer may be unable to oblige it to do so (*u*). A bank which has paid on forged or fraudulently presented documents can after discovering this also recover the money as paid under a mistake of fact, and may be able to set off its claim to such recovery against other sums otherwise payable under the credit (*a*).

In principle, the bank would also seem to be justified in refusing payment if the contract of sale is illegal (*b*).

If the bank wrongfully fails to pay under the letter of credit, the seller may recover from the bank the amount which should have been paid, usually with interest (*c*), upon retendering the documents (*d*). If instead

---

goods forward for shipment. As to the proper law of this contract see *Offshore International S. A.* v. *Banco Central S. A.*, [1976] 3 All E. R. 749; [1977] 1 W. L. R. 399.

(*r*) *Hamzeh Malas & Sons* v. *British Imex Industries, Ltd., supra.*

(*s*) *Discount Records* v. *Barclays Bank*, [1975] 1 All E. R. 1071; [1975] 1 W. L. R. 315; *Harbottle Coal Co., Ltd.* v. *National Westminster Bank*, [1977] 2 All E. R. 862; [1978] 1 Q. B. 146; *Edward Owen Engineering Ltd.* v. *Barclays Bank International Ltd.*, [1978] 1 All E. R. 976; [1978] 1 Q. B. 159, C. A.; *The "American Accord"*, [1979] 1 Lloyd's Rep. 267.

(*t*) *Edward Owen* v. *Barclays Bank, supra; The "American Accord", supra; Etablissement Esefka* v. *Central Bank of Nigeria*, [1979] 1 Lloyd's Rep. 445. These cases follow the rule laid down in the United States: see *Sztejn* v. *J. Henry Schroder Banking Corpn.* (1941), 31 N. Y. S. (2d) 631 (reviewing earlier decisions). See also *Société Metallurgique d'Anbrives and Villerupt* v. *British Bank for Foreign Trade* (1922), 11 Ll. L. Rep. 168, at p. 170; *Hamzeh Malas & Sons* v. *British Imex Industries, Ltd.*, [1958] 1 All E. R. 262, at p. 263; [1958] 2 Q. B. 127, at p. 130, C. A. *Old Colony Trust Co.* v. *Lawyers' Title and Trust Co.* (1924), 297 F. 152 also suggests that in the United States the bank would be able to reject forged documents, even when presented by *bona fide* holders for value. The Uniform Commercial Code – Letters of Credit (1962 version), s. 5–114, assimilates forged documents with valid but fraudulent documents in those states which apply it.

(*u*) *The "American Accord", supra*, at p. 277; *Etablissement Esefka* v. *Central Bank of Nigeria, supra.*

(*a*) *Etablissement Esefka* v. *Central Bank of Nigeria, supra.*

(*b*) See p. 16, *ante.*

(*c*) Now under the Law Reform (Miscellaneous Provisions) Act 1934, s. 3, *post*, Appendix I. See also the cases cited at n. (*d*), *post*. There is also a right at law to interest on an overdue banker's draft, as with other negotiable instruments.

(*d*) As in *Belgian Grain and Produce Co.* v. *Cox & Co. (France), Ltd.* (1919), 1 Ll. L. Rep. 256, C. A.; *Stein* v. *Hambro's Bank of Northern Commerce* (1921), 9 Ll. L. Rep. 507. It was suggested in *Société Metallurgique d'Anbrives and Villerupt* v. *British Bank of Foreign Trade* (1922), 11 Ll. L. Rep. 168, that if the buyer would be able to reject the goods on arrival for

the seller re-sells the goods and claims damages from the bank, then the seller would seem to be under a duty to the bank to take reasonable steps to mitigate his loss when re-selling (*e*). If the credit covers several instalments, failure to pay in respect of one shipment may amount to repudiation of the whole credit, in which case the seller may accept the repudiation and claim damages (*f*).

It is a term of the contract between the buyer and the bank (to be implied if not expressed) that the bank will not only open the credit, but will pay the seller in accordance with its terms, so that if the bank evinces an intention not to pay the seller, the buyer is relieved from his obligation to the bank to put it in funds to meet the credit (*g*).

E. Performance Guarantees

Buyers sometimes require sellers to provide a performance guarantee or bond in respect of some or all of the sellers' obligations (*h*).

A guarantee in the strict sense of the word would involve an undertaking by a third party to answer to the buyer in the case of default by the seller – and the buyer would have to establish the default against the seller and/or guarantor. But the documents considered by the courts in recent cases have been issued at the seller's request by or through the seller's bank in terms promising to pay or repay sums to the buyer at the buyer's demand – *i.e.* on the buyer's assertion that such sums were due.

The courts have treated such documents as analogous to letters of credit. Save in the event of a clearly established fraud by the buyer the seller cannot claim to restrain the bank paying on the buyer's demand; and the bank itself cannot unless it can establish fraud have any defence to the buyer's claim to payment. If the buyer makes a claim for which there is no justification under the sale contract, which the bank pays and in respect of which the seller then has to indemnify the bank, the seller's only remedy is to reclaim from the buyer under the sale contract the monies thus disbursed (*h*)

F. Confirming Houses

Another means by which a buyer may provide his seller with security of payment is by use of a confirming house, usually carrying on its business in the seller's country. The buyer, who may or may not have been in direct contact with the seller, instructs the confirming house, in

---

non-compliance with the contract, damages against the bank for failure to pay against documents might be nominal, on the ground of circuity of action. *Sed quaere.*

(*e*) The seller's right to resell and claim damages would seem to be governed by principles analogous to those set out in s. 48(3) of the Sale of Goods Act, *post.*

(*f*) *Urquhart, Lindsay & Co.* v. *Eastern Bank, Ltd.*, [1922] 1 K. B. 318, where it was said that the buyer owed no duty to mitigate his damages by letting the documents go against part payment.

(*g*) *Sale Continuation, Ltd.* v. *Austin Taylor & Co., Ltd.*, [1967] 2 All E. R. 1092; [1968] 2 Q. B. 849.

(*h*) *Harbottle* v. *National Westminster Bank*, [1977] 2 All E. R. 862; [1978] 1 Q. B. 146; *Edward Owen* v. *Barclays Bank*, [1978] 1 All E. R. 976; [1978] 1 Q. B. 159, C. A.; *Howe Richardson Scale Co., Ltd.* v. *Polimex-Cekop*, [1978] 1 Lloyd's Rep. 161, C. A.

return for a commission, either simply to place the order with the seller in its own name or to add its confirmation to the buyer's order form and send the same to the seller.

In both cases the confirming house is, as regards the seller, a principal to the purchase (*i*) but, as regards the buyer, it acts as an agent with a corresponding right to indemnity (*k*). Its position is thus distinct from that of a *del credere* agent (whose liability to the seller only arises in the event of the buyer's insolvency). It is, however, submitted that since in both cases the confirming house acts on the buyer's instructions for a commission, the buyer is also a party (whether disclosed or undisclosed) to the contract of purchase, and could (for example) be sued by the seller in the event of the confirming house's default (*l*).

A different situation exists where a confirming house intervenes in such a way as to give rise to a back-to-back sales first by the supplier to the confirming house, and then by the confirming house to the ultimate buyer. This is only distinguished from an ordinary sale and resale in that the confirming houses reward consists of a commission on the suppliers' sale price.

G. Conflict of laws

A distinction must be drawn here between (1) questions arising out of the law of contract, and (2) questions arising out of the law of property. The former concern such matters as capacity, formalities, essential validity, construction, discharge, and illegality; the latter cover such things as the passing of property and risk, lien, and stoppage *in transitu*.

(1) Questions arising out of the law of contract are generally determined by the "proper law" of the contract. The contract may or may not provide what the proper law shall be. Where it does not so provide, either expressly or by influence in all the circumstances, the proper law is "the system of law by reference to which the contract was made or that with which the transaction has the closest and most real connection" (*m*). In determining which system of law this is, it is necessary to consider the terms of the contract, the situation of the

(*i*) *Rusholme Bolton and Roberts Hadfield, Ltd.* v. *S. G. Read & Co.*, [1955] 1 All E. R. 180; [1955] 1 W. L. R. 146; *Sobell Industries, Ltd.* v. *Cory Brothers, Co., Ltd.*, [1955] 2 Lloyd's Rep. 82; *cf. Maran Road Saw Mill* v. *Austin Taylor & Co., Ltd.*, [1975] 1 Lloyd's Rep. 156.

(*k*) *Anglo-African Shipping, Co., Ltd.* v. *J. Mortimer, Ltd.*, [1962] 1 Lloyd's Rep. 610, C. A., pointing out that confirming houses often act in additional capacities on behalf of the buyer, *e.g.* as forwarding agents.

(*l*) *Rusholme* v. *S. G. Read, supra*, is sometimes regarded as an authority where the confirming house although instructed to purchase by the buyer was not authorised to create a contract between supplier and buyer—see *Benjamin's Sale of Goods*, para. 2123. This is not easy to follow in principle, and, it is submitted, PEARCE, J. certainly did not intend to decide that no contract existed at all between the supplier and Australian buyers, merely that there was no such contract made by the indent which such buyers had sent direct to the supplier prior to the confirming house's confirmation. PEARCE, J. expressly described the confirming house as the buyer's agent at pp. 183 and 150 and both agent and principal (whether disclosed or undisclosed) may be liable on a purchase—see *Bowstead on Agency* (14th ed.), Article 112.

(*m*) *Bonython* v. *Commonwealth of Australia*, [1951] A. C. 201, 219, P. C.; *re United Railways of Havana and Regla Warehouses*, [1960] 2 All E. R. 332; [1961] A. C. 1007;

parties, and generally all the surrounding facts (*n*). These will include where the contract was made, where it is to be performed (*o*), the nature and situation of the subject matter, the language in which it is written, the system of law to which any legal terms used belong (*p*), the currency in which any payments are to be made, and the selection of arbitrators from some particular country (*q*).

The expressed intention of the parties as to the proper law of their contract will be given effect, save where their choice is illegal or contrary to public policy (*r*).

It is common for parties to choose English arbitration or jurisdiction in relation to contracts which have little or no other connection with England. Such choice is a strong indication that the parties also intend English law as the proper law (*s*), but it is not conclusive and may therefore be over ridden if other indications point clearly to some different system of law.

For questions as to *capacity*, see the note "conflict of laws" to s. 3, *post*.

A contract is valid as to *form* so long as it complies with the requisite formalities either of its proper law or of the *lex loci contractus* (*t*).

Questions of essential validity, construction and discharge are always governed by the proper law of the contract (*u*).

A contract which is *illegal* under its proper law is always void; and if it is valid under its proper law it will still not be enforced in England if it is contrary to English public policy (*a*) or, at least where English law is the proper law (*b*), in so far as performance would be illegal by the law of the place of performance (*c*).

Cheshire and North's *Private International Law* (10th ed.), pp. 195 *et seq*.; Dicey and Morris *Conflict of Laws* (10th ed.), p. 769.

(*n*) *The Assunzione*, [1954] 1 All E. R. 278, 289; [1954] P. 150, 175; *Coast Lines* v. *Hwdig and Veder*, [1972] 1 All E. R. 451; [1972] 2 Q. B. 34, C. A.

(*o*) *Chatenay* v. *Brazilian Submarine Telegraph Co.*, [1891] 1 Q. B. 79.

(*p*) *James Miller & Partners, Ltd.* v. *Whitworth Street Estates, Ltd.*, [1970] 1 All E. R. 796; [1970] A. C. 583, H. L.

(*q*) *Hamlyn* v. *Talisker Distillery*, [1894] A. C. 202; *Compagnie d'Armement Maritime S.A.* v. *Compagnie Tunisienne de Navigations S.A.*, [1970] 3 All E. R. 71; [1971] A. C. 572, H. L.

(*r*) See, *e.g.*, Dicey and Morris, *loc cit.*, rule 145, sub-rule 1; Cheshire and North, *loc cit.*, pp. 199 *et seq*.; *N. V. Kwik Hoo Tong* v. *James Finlay & Co., Ltd.*, [1927] A. C. 604; *Vita Food Products, Incorporated* v. *Unus Shipping Co., Ltd.*, [1939] 1 All E. R. 513; [1939] A. C. 277, P. C. (refusing to follow the earlier decision of the Court of Appeal in *The Torni*, [1932] P. 78); *re Helbert Wagg & Co.*, [1956] 1 All E. R. 129, 136; [1956] Ch. 323, 341; *Mackender* v. *Feldia A.G.*, [1966] 3 All E. R. 847, C. A.; 56 L. Q. R. 320.

(*s*) *Compagnie d'Armement Maritime S.A.* v. *Compagnie Tunisienne de Navigation S.A.*, [1970] 3 All E. R. 71; [1971] A. C. 572, H. L., explaining and disapproving statements in *Tzortzis* v. *Monark Line A/B*, [1968] 1 All E. R. 949; [1968] 1 W. L. R. 406, C. A.

(*t*) Dicey and Morris, *loc cit.*, rule 150; *Albeko Schumaschinen A.-G.* v. *Kamborian Shoe Machine Co.* (1961), 111 L. Jo. 519; 10 I. C. L. Q. 908.

(*u*) *P. & O.* v. *Shand* (1865), 3 Moo. P. C. C. N. S. 272 (essential validity); *Jacobs* v. *Crédit Lyonnais* (1884), 12 Q. B. D. 589, C. A. (discharge).

(*a*) *Kaufman* v. *Gerson*, [1904] 1 K. B. 591, C. A.

(*b*) Cheshire and North, *loc. cit.*, pp. 224–230.

(*c*) *Ralli Bros.* v. *Compania Naviera &c.*, [1920] 1 K. B. 614; [1920] 2 K. B. 287, C. A.; *cf. Foster* v. *Driscoll*, [1929] 1 K. B. 470, C. A. (partnership agreement to smuggle intoxicating liquor into United States); *Regazzoni* v. *Sethia*, [1957] 3 All E. R. 286; [1958] A. C. 301; (c.i.f. contract illegal by law of country of export).

All rules of *procedure* and *evidence* are governed by the *lex fori*, the law of the court in which the action is brought. This includes the admissibility of evidence, the means of proving particular facts, the time within which an action must be brought, rights of set-off and counterclaim, remedies for breach, joinder of parties, the effect of recovering judgment, and execution. Hence in an action in England all English rules of procedure and evidence apply (*d*) and all such foreign rules are ignored. The test seems to be that if the foreign rule bars the remedy only, the English court ignores it as procedural; but if it makes the contract itself void, it will be recognised as a rule of substance (*e*).

(2) Passing to questions arising out of the law of property, subject to certain qualifications, the English rule has generally been taken to be that if personal property be disposed of in a manner binding according to the law of the country where it is (the *lex situs*), that disposition is binding in England (*f*). Thus where the master of a ship wrongfully sold the cargo by auction in Norway, but in such circumstances as to give a good title in Norway, the sale was held valid, although the cargo subsequently came to England (*g*); the title to a stolen horse bought in market overt in Ireland would be recognised in Scotland (*h*); and the validity of a pledge is determined by the law of the country where the goods were pledged (*i*). *Locus regit actum* is a rule of wide application.

H. Foreign law

In the absence of evidence to the contrary, foreign law is presumed to be the same as English law. If the foreign law differs, and the difference is relied on, it must be proved as a question of fact (*k*). But the effect of the evidence as to the foreign law is a matter for the judge, and not for the jury, if any (*l*). In referring to foreign laws, it should be noted that some continental codes distinguish traders from non-traders, and

---

(*d*) See, *e.g.*, *Leroux* v. *Brown* (1852), 12 C. B. 801 (decided on a repealed part of s. 4 of the Statute of Frauds 1677); *D'Almeida Araujo Lda.* v. *Becker & Co., Ltd.*, [1953] 2 All E. R. 288; [1953] 2 Q. B. 329; *In the Estate of Fuld* (*No. 3*), *Hartley* v. *Fuld*, [1965] 3 All E. R. 776; [1966] 2 W. L. R. 717; and see *James Miller & Partners, Ltd.* v. *Whitworth Street Estates, Ltd.*, [1970] 1 All E. R. 796; [1970] A. C. 583, H. L. (English contract—arbitration in Scotland by Scottish arbieter governed as to procedure by Scottish law); *Miliangos* v. *George Frank* (*No. 2*), [1977] Q. B. 489.

(*e*) *Alves* v. *Hodgson* (1797), 7 Term Rep. 241.

(*f*) *Embiricos* v *Anglo-Austrian Bank*, [1905] 1 K. B. 677, at p. 683, C. A.; *Re Korvine's Trust*, [1921] 1 Ch. 343, 348 (*donatio mortis causâ*); Dicey and Morris, *Conflict of Laws* (10th ed.) Rule 79; Cheshire and North, *loc. cit.*, pp. 520 *et seq.*; 22 I. C. L. Q. 213. British ships constitute a statutory exception to this rule.

(*g*) *Cammell* v. *Sewell* (1860), 5 H. & N. 728, Ex. Ch.; applied in *Winkworth* v. *Christie Manson and Woods*, [1980] 1 All E. R. 1121; [1980] 2 W. L. R. 937; and *cf. Alcock* v. *Smith*, [1892] 1 Ch. 238, C. A. (bill of exchange taken in execution abroad).

(*h*) *Todd* v. *Armsur*, 1882 9 R. (Ct. of Sess.) 901.

(*i*) *City Bank* v. *Barrow* (1880), 5 App. Cas. 664, at p. 667.

(*k*) *The Parchim*, [1918] A. C. 157, at pp. 160, 161, *per* Lord PARKER. As to expert evidence to prove the foreign law, see *Phipson on Evidence* (12th ed.), pp. 1232–1237; *Cross on Evidence* (5th ed.), pp. 633–636. *Cf. Perlak Petroleum Co.* v. *Deen*, [1924] 1 K. B. 111, 115 (evidence of foreign law by non-expert inadmissible).

(*l*) Supreme Court of Judicature (Consolidation) Act 1925, s. 102; (25 Halsbury's

modify or supplement the general law of the country as regards commercial transactions.

I. Uniform Law on International Sales Act 1967

This Act is designed to incorporate into the law of the United Kingdom the Uniform law on the International Sale of Goods, which governs the obligations of the seller and buyer arising from a contract of sale to which it applies, and the Uniform Law for the Formation of Contracts for the International Sale of Goods, which is concerned with the formation of such contracts. The laws were the subject of Conventions drawn up at The Hague in 1964.

The two Uniform Laws relate to international sales as defined in Article 1 of the First Law. Save that the definition in Article 1 is limited to contracts between parties whose places of business are in different Contracting States, it is identical to that which was contained in s. 62 (1) of the Sale of Goods Act 1893, and it is similar to the definition of international supply contracts in s. 26 of the Unfair Contract Terms Act 1977, *post*, Appendix I. By Article 4 of the First Law parties can also choose this law as the proper law of their contract whether or not the parties' places of business or habitual residences are in different states and whether or not such states are parties to the Conventions, but, in relation to a contract made between 18th May 1973 and 1st February 1978, only to the extent that it does not affect the application of ss. 12 to 15, 55 and 56 of the Sale of Goods Act 1979 and, in relation to a contract made on or after 1st February 1978, only to the extent that it does not affect the application of ss. 12 to 15 of the Sale of Goods Act 1979 (*m*).

An Order in Council has been made (*n*) applying the Laws from 18th August 1972, but this would not seem to have had any great effect to date in that:

(1) The Order further declares pursuant to s. 1 (3) of the Act that the Laws will apply to a contract affected by this Act only if chosen by the parties to that contract; and

(2) Only six States have been declared to be contracting parties under the Order: Belgium, Israel, Italy, the Netherlands, San Marino, and the United Kingdom.

Statutes (3rd Edn.) 744) as to the High Court; County Courts Act 1959, s. 97 (5 Halsbury's Statutes (3rd Edn.) 362), as to County Courts; the Administration of Justice Act 1920, s. 15 (6 Halsbury's Statutes (3rd Edn.) 358), as to other courts.

(*m*) Uniform Laws on International Sales Act 1967, s. 1 (4), as substituted by the Sale of Goods Act 1979, Sch. 2, para. 15.

(*n*) S. I. 1972 No. 973.

SECTION C

STATUTORY CONTROLS OVER THE SALE OF GOODS

I PRICE MAINTENANCE

At common law, unless he has otherwise bound himself by contract, a man may sell at any price he pleases, and to undersell trade rivals he may offer goods at a loss (*a*); moreover, so long as it is not in unreasonable restraint of trade (*b*) he can attach a condition to such a sale that the goods shall not be resold by the buyer below some specified price (*c*).

This position has been radically altered by statute, currently the Resale Prices Act 1976 and by Article 85 of the Treaty of Rome as enacted by s. 2 of the European Communities Act 1972.

Under the 1976 Act, where a term or condition establishing or providing for the establishment of minimum resale prices is attached or agreed in relation to a sale by a supplier to a dealer (*d*), it is void and unlawful (*e*) except in the case of:

(i) goods to be resold outside the United Kingdom (*e*);

(ii) goods exempted by the Restrictive Practices Court from the provisions of the Resale Prices Act 1976 in exercise of its powers under s. 14 of that Act (*f*).

The 1976 Act does not preclude a supplier, or an association or person on his behalf, notifying to dealers or otherwise publishing "recommended" resale prices for his goods (*g*).

Even in cases within the two exceptions, (i) and (ii), set out above to the 1976 Act, re-sale price maintenance agreements will frequently be unenforceable by virtue of Article 85. Article 85 (1) applies to all agreements, decisions and concerted practices between undertakings

---

(*a*) *Ajello* v. *Worsley*, [1898] 1 Ch. 274, 280.

(*b*) *Petrofina* (*Great Britain*), *Ltd.* v. *Martin*, [1966] 1 All E. R. 126; [1966] Ch. 146, C. A.; *Esso Petroleum Co., Ltd.* v. *Harper's Garage* (*Stourport*), *Ltd.*, [1967] 1 All E. R. 699; [1968] A. C. 269, H. L.

(*c*) *Elliman* v. *Carrington*, [1901] 2 Ch. 275. As to enforcement of these conditions at common law, see *Sorrell* v. *Smith*, [1925] A. C. 700; *Hardie & Lane, Ltd.* v. *Chilton*, [1928] 2 K. B. 306, disapproving *R.* v. *Denyer*, [1926] 2 K. B. 258, C. C. A.

(*d*) See the definitions of "supplier" and "dealer" in s. 11 (1) of the Resale Prices Act 1964; 37 Halsbury's Statutes (3rd Edn.) 167.

(*e*) Resale Prices Act 1976, s. 14. The unlawfulness is not criminal, but entitles the Crown to seek injunctive or other appropriate relief and may give third parties a cause of action for breach of statutory duty: s. 25. Collective agreements between suppliers or dealers, or their associations which aim indirectly to enforce resale price maintenance are also made unlawful in circumstances defined in ss. 1 to 8 of the 1976 Act.

(*f*) *I.e.*, books and medicaments.

(*g*) S. 9 (2).

which affect undertakings between member states and have as their object or effect the prevention, restriction or distortion of competition within the Common Market, including *inter alia* those fixing purchase or selling prices or any other trading conditions. Such agreements, decisions and practices must be notified to the Commission (*h*).

Agreements within category (i) mentioned above will thus commonly be caught by Article 85; so, too, agreements within category (ii) will commonly be caught insofar as they fix the price or conditions of sale in the United Kingdom from elsewhere in the Common Market. By concession (*i*) agreements to which only two undertakings are parties and which only restrict resale prices or conditions are not subject to notification, but they are still unenforceable if they materially affect trade between member states. The Commission has, however, stated that it considers minor agreements outside Article 85. For this purpose, minor agreements are agreements where (a) the products involved represent less than 5 per cent of the volume of such products in the area of the Market affected and (b) the aggregate turnover of the parties (if commercial undertakings) does not exceed 20,000,000 units of account (one unit being equal to a little over 1 U.S. dollar) (*k*). Infringements of Article 85 are punishable by fine. The commission may by decision (which would no doubt be enforced by injunction) require termination of an infringement (*l*).

Where resale price maintenance is still lawful any conditions as to the price at which goods sold by a supplier may be resold can be enforced against any person not party to the original sale who subsequently acquires the goods with notice of the condition as if he had been a party to the sale (*m*). "Notice" here seems to mean no more than sufficient, rather than actual, notice, so that it is enough for the supplier to prove that he took all reasonable steps to bring the condition to the notice of the defendant (*n*).

The remedy is by injunction or "any other relief which may be granted" (*o*). The court acts in accordance with acknowledged general principles in determining whether to grant an injunction (*p*). The remedy is not available against persons who acquire the goods otherwise than for the purpose of re-sale in the course of business, or their sub-

(*h*) Common Market Regulations, Regulation 17 (1962), art. 4 (1).

(*i*) *Ibid.*, art. 4 (2).

(*k*) Notice of 27th May 1970, J. O. 1970 C 84/1.

(*l*) Regulation 17 (1962), arts. 3, 15 and 16.

(*m*) Resale Prices Act 1976, s. 26. At common law such a condition was not binding on subsequent buyers, even with notice (*Dunlop Pneumatic Tyre Co.* v. *Selfridge & Co.*, [1915] A. C. 847) except it seems in the case of patented articles known to be sold under a restrictive licence: (*National Phonograph Co. of Australia* v. *Menck*, [1911] A. C. 336, 347, P. C.; *Columbia Phonograph Co.* v. *Regent Fittings Co.* (1913), 30 R. P. C. 484).

(*n*) *Goodyear Tyre and Rubber Co.* (*Great Britain*) v. *Lancashire Batteries*, [1958] 3 All E. R. 7; [1958] 1 W. L. R. 857, C. A.; distinguishing *County Laboratories* v. *Mindel*, [1957] 1 All E. R. 806; [1957] Ch. 295.

(*o*) Resale Prices Act 1976, s. 26 (5).

(*p*) *Gallaher, Ltd.* v. *Supersafe Supermarkets* (1964), L. R. 5 R. P. 89; *cf.* 1956 Public Law 320, *n.* 15.

purchasers (*q*), nor is it available against persons selling goods pursuant to an order of any court, or their sub-purchasers (*r*).

II CONSUMER PROTECTION

There is now a wide range of statutes for the protection of the consumer, governing a wide range of matters. Many deal with sales of specific types of goods (*s*). Others are of general application.

Those of general application or which are potentially of general application include the Consumer Protection Acts 1961 and 1971 and the Consumer Safety Act 1978; the Weights and Measures Act 1963; the Trade Descriptions Acts 1968 and 1972; the Unsolicited Goods and Services Act 1971; the Fair Trading Act 1973 and the Consumer Credit Act 1974.

As most of these statutes have broadly similar provisions as to who may be liable and what defences may be available to a person charged with an offence, and as to their general enforcement, these aspects are discussed separately in relation to all the statutes.

The rights of the buyer where the seller has committed a statutory offence

The position of a buyer where the seller has committed a statutory offence in the course of selling goods to him would seem to be as follows:

(1) The buyer will be entitled to the same remedies for misrepresentation and for breach of contract, if any, as he would have had if the statutory offence had not existed.

(2) In some cases a warranty on the part of the seller is implied into the contract that he has complied with the provisions of the statute in question (*t*). In such cases, the buyer may be entitled to claim damages from the seller for breach of that warranty.

(3) Where the seller owes a statutory duty to the buyer to comply with a statutory requirement, and is in breach of that duty, the buyer (*u*) may claim damages from the seller in respect of its breach. But it would seem that in relation to consumer protection statutes, the seller will only owe such a duty to the buyer if the statute expressly so provides (*a*).

(*q*) Resale Prices Act 1976, s. 26 (3).

(*r*) *John Mackintosh & Sons* v. *Baker's Bargain Stores* (*Seaford*), *Ltd.*, [1965] 3 All E. R. 412; [1965] 1 W. L. R. 1182 (sale by liquidator of company being wound up by the court).

(*s*) See, *e.g.*, Food and Drugs Act 1955; Plant Variety and Seeds Act 1964; Farm and Garden Chemicals Act 1967; Agriculture Act 1970.

(*t*) See, *e.g.*, Plant Varieties and Seeds Act 1964, s. 17; Agriculture Act 1970, s. 72.

(*u*) The statutory duty may be owed to others as well as the buyer, as under the Consumer Protection Acts 1961 and 1971, and the Consumer Safety Act 1978, discussed p. 54; *post*, in which case those others may also claim damages for its breach.

(*a*) *Square* v. *Model Farm Dairies* (*Bournemouth*), *Ltd.*, [1939] 1 All E. R. 259; [1939] 2 K. B. 365, C. A. (Food and Drugs (Adulteration) Act 1928); *London Armoury Co., Ltd.* v. *Ever Ready Co.* (*Great Britain*), *Ltd.*, [1941] 1 All E. R. 364; [1941] 1 K. B. 742 (Merchandise Marks Act 1926); *Badham* v. *Lambs, Ltd.*, [1945] 2 All E. R. 295; [1946] K. B. 45 (road traffic legislation regarding sale of car in unroadworthy condition); *J. Bollinger* v. *Costa*

(4) The buyer may in some cases be able to claim that the contract is void or unenforceable by the seller because it was illegal or because he intended to perform it in an illegal manner (*b*). But several of the statutes expressly provide that a contract shall not be unenforceable or void just because a seller commits an offence under that statute (*c*).

(5) If the seller is prosecuted for the offence, or if he is convicted of some other offence, and the offence from which the buyer has suffered loss is taken into account in determining sentence, then the buyer may be awarded compensation by the court which sentences the seller (*d*).

Consumer Protection Acts 1961 and 1971

These Acts empower the Secretary of State to make such regulations in respect of prescribed classes of goods and component parts of goods "as are in his opinion expedient to prevent or reduce risk of death or personal injury" (*e*). As the scope of potential consumer protection extends only to risk of physical injury, their effect is more limited than the title of the Acts would suggest. The Secretary of State has no power under them to protect consumers' economic interests.

The Acts have been repealed from a date to be fixed (*f*), but the regulations made under them presently remain in force. These relate to gas and electric fires, oil heaters, oil lamps, nightdresses, stands for carry cots, domestic electric appliances having a mains lead with three wires, electric blankets, electrical equipment, cooking utensils, pencils and graphic instruments, toys, glazed ceramic ware, children's hood cords, babies' dummies, perambulators and push chairs and cosmetic products.

Section 2 (1) of the 1961 Act prohibits the sale or possession for the purpose of selling of any goods which do not comply with the requirements of regulations made under s. 1 of the Act. Section 2 (2) deals in similar terms with component parts. The duty to comply with s. 2 is owed to every person who may be affected by a failure to comply with the requirements in question (*g*), and a person who commits an offence under s. 2 is not only liable to prosecution, but may be sued for breach of statutory duty by anybody affected by the contravention.

Brava Wine Co., Ltd., [1959] 3 All E. R. 800, at p. 813; [1960] Ch. 262, at p. 287 (Merchandise Marks Acts); *H. P. Bulmer, Ltd.* v. *J. Bollinger* (1975), *Times*, 20th May (Trade Descriptions Act 1968). Section 26 (a) of the Fair Trading Act 1973 expressly provides that contravention of an order made by the Secretary of State under s. 22 of that Act, concerning a consumer trade practice, should not entitle any person affected to bring any civil claim. See further, p. 62, *post*.

(*b*) See generally, p. 16, *ante*.

(*c*) See, *e.g.*, Plant Variety and Seeds Act 1964, s. 17 (5); Trade Descriptions Act 1968, s. 35; Agriculture Act 1970, ss. 68 (8), 71 (4); Fair Trading Act 1973, s. 26; Consumer Credit Act 1974, s. 170; Consumer Safety Act 1978, s. 6 (4).

(*d*) Powers of Criminal Courts Act 1973, s. 35, Appendix I, *post*.

(*e*) Consumer Protection Act 1961, s. 1 (a).

(*f*) Consumer Safety Act 1978, s. 10 (1), Sch. 3.

(*g*) Consumer Protection Act 1961, s. 3.

Any term of an agreement which purports to exclude or restrict or has the effect of excluding or restricting, any obligation imposed by or by virtue of s. 2, or any liability for breach of such an obligation is void (*h*)

Consumer Safety Act 1978

This Act came into force on 1st November 1978 (*i*). It empowers the Secretary of State to make safety regulations containing a wide range of provisions for the purpose of securing that goods are safe (*k*) or that appropriate information is provided and inappropriate information is not provided in respect of goods.

To date, such regulations have been made in respect of children's nightwear, balloon making compounds and tear gas capsules.

Section 3 (1) of the Act empowers the Secretary of State to make prohibition orders prohibiting persons from supplying or offering to supply, agreeing to supply, exposing for supply or possessing for supply goods which the Secretary of State considers are not safe and which are described in the orders, and certain goods designed to be used as component parts of such unsafe goods. The section further empowers the Secretary of State to serve on any person a prohibition notice prohibiting him from so dealing with unsafe goods which are specified in the notice, and to serve on any person a notice to warn requiring the person to publish a warning about unsafe goods specified in the notice.

It is an offence to contravene any of the regulations, or a prohibition order, prohibition notice or notice to warn.

By s. 6 (2) of the Act, any obligation imposed on a person by safety regulations or a prohibition order or a prohibition notice is a duty owed by him to any other person who may be affected by a failure to perform the obligation, and a breach of that duty is actionable. By s. 6 (2), an agreement is void so far as it would have the effect of excluding or restricting such an obligation or liability for breach of such an obligation.

The Weights and Measures Acts 1963 to 1979

Part I of the 1963 Act as amended establishes units and standards of measurement. Part II provides that only these units may be "used for trade" (*l*). Part III deals with public weighing and measuring equipment. Part IV contains important provisions for consumer protection.

Section 21 empowers the Department of Trade and Industry to make orders and regulations for certain transactions in goods: for example, to sell by weight or measure, net or gross, only in prescribed quantities, to require marking of quantities and, sometimes, to require certain written

---

(*h*) Consumer Protection Act 1961, s. 3 (1A), inserted by s. 30 (1) of the Unfair Contract Terms Act 1977, *post*, Appendix I.

(*i*) Consumer Safety Act 1978 (Commencement No. 1) Order 1978, S. I. 1978 No. 1445.

(*k*) As defined in s. 9 (4) of the Act.

(*l*) "Used for trade" is defined very widely by s. 9, Weights and Measures Act 1963.

documents. Where under the Act goods may only be sold by quantity as expressed in a particular manner, and they are sold, exposed or offered for sale in some other manner, an offence is committed (*m*). It is also an offence to cause other people so to act (*n*). Section 23 provides that in certain circumstances, the quantity of goods sold must be stated in writing.

Section 24 prohibits short weight or measure. Section 24 (1) makes it an offence to deliver or cause to be delivered a lesser quantity than that purported to be sold or than corresponds with the price charged. Section 24 (2) makes it an offence for any person, in connection with the sale or purchase of goods, to make any misrepresentation (*o*) either by word of mouth or otherwise as to the quantity of the goods or to do any other act calculated to mislead (*p*) a person buying or selling the goods as to the quantity thereof.

Trade Descriptions Acts 1968 and 1972

By s. 1 of the Trade Descriptions Act 1968 any person who, in the course of a trade or business (*q*), either applies a false trade description to any goods or supplies or offers to supply any goods to which a false trade description is applied is, subject to the provisions of that Act, guilty of an offence.

Trade description.—A trade description is an indication, direct or indirect, and by whatever means given of any of the matters set out in s. 2 of the 1968 Act (*r*). These are quantity (*s*), size or gauge; method of manufacture, production, processing or re-conditioning; composition; fitness for purpose, strength, performance, behaviour or accuracy; any other physical characteristics; testing by any person and results of such testing; approval by any person or conformity with a type approved by any person; place or date of manufacture, production, processing, or reconditioning; person by whom manufactured, produced, processed or reconditioned; or other history, including previous ownership or use.

"Indication" is much wider than "representation", and covers conduct and signs of many different kinds (*t*).

(*m*) Weights and Measures Act 1963, s. 22.

(*n*) *Ibid.*, s. 22 (1) (b).

(*o*) Such misrepresentation need not be made pursuant to a contract or by a party to a contract: *Collett* v. *Co-op Wholesale Society, Ltd.*, [1970] 1 All E. R. 274; [1970] 1 W. L. R. 250, D. C.

(*p*) An act is calculated to mislead if it is "likely to deceive or mislead": *Collett* v. *Co-op Wholesale Society, Ltd.*, *supra*.

(*q*) See the note to the definition of "business" in s. 61 (1) of the Sale of Goods Act 1979, *post*.

(*r*) Descriptions or marks applied in pursuance of certain Acts concerned with agriculture and horticulture and certain descriptions dealt with under the Food and Drugs Act 1955 are expressly excluded by s. 2 (4)–(5) of the 1968 Act as amended.

(*s*) Defined by s. 2 (3) to include length, width, height, area, volume, capacity, weight and number.

(*t*) *Doble* v. *David Greig, Ltd.*, [1972] 2 All E. R. 195; [1972] 1 W. L. R. 703, D. C. But it must be an indication of one of the matters specified in s. 2: *Cadbury, Ltd.* v. *Halliday*, [1975] 2 All E. R. 226; [1975] 1 W. L. R. 649, D. C. ("extra value" not of itself a trade description).

False trade description.—A false trade description is a trade description which is false to a material degree or which, though not false, is misleading, that is to say, likely to be taken for such an indication of any of the matters specified in s. 2 of the 1968 Act as would be false to a material degree (*u*). The expression also includes anything which, though not a trade description, is likely to be taken for an indication of any of those matters, and, as such an indication, would be false to a material degree (*a*).

A trade description may be false even though there is no intent to mislead a customer (*b*) and even though the goods are of equal (*c*) or superior (*d*) quality to that indicated by the description. The test is whether the description is false, not whether the bargain is fair (*e*).

In deciding whether a trade description is false, the courts will take a broad view of all the circumstances (*f*) and consider whether in those circumstances it is likely to mislead. An offence may be committed if a trade description is capable of being misunderstood, even though many more customers are not misled by it (*g*). In general, it seems that no evidence need be adduced that anybody was misled, but where it is not clear on the face of it that the description is false or misleading, then the prosecution must prove that members of the public were in fact misled (*g*).

Applying a trade description goods.—A person applies a trade description to goods if he affixes or annexes it to or in any manner marks it on or incorporates it with the goods themselves or anything in or with which the goods are supplied; or if he places the goods in, on or with anything which the trade description has been affixed or annexed to, marked on or incorporated with, or if he places any such thing with the goods; or if he uses the trade description in any manner likely to be taken as referring to the goods (*h*). Also, where goods are supplied in pursuance of a request in which a trade description is used and the circumstances are such as to make it reasonable to infer that the goods are supplied as goods corresponding to that trade description, the person supplying the

---

(*u*) Trade Descriptions Act 1968, s. 3 (2). A *bona fide* but incorrect opinion may be a false trade description; *Holloway* v. *Cross* (1980), Times, 20th November, D. C.

(*a*) *Ibid.*, s. 3 (3).

(*b*) *Mear* v. *Baker* (1954), 118 J. P. 483, D. C.; *R.* v. *Reiss*, [1957] Crim. L. R. 404.

(*c*) *Kirshenboim* v. *Salmon and Gluckstein*, [1898] 2 Q. B. 19, D. C.

(*d*) *Thornley* v. *Tuckwell (Butchers), Ltd.*, [1964] Crim. L. R. 127, D. C.

(*e*) *Furniss* v. *Scholes*, [1974] R. T. R. 133, D. C.

(*f*) See *e.g. Evans* v. *British Doughnut Co., Ltd.*, [1944] 1 All E. R. 158; [1944] K. B. 102, D. C.; *White Hudson & Co.* v. *Asian Organisation, Ltd.*, [1965] 1 All E. R. 1040; [1964] 1 W. L. R. 1466, P. C. (get up of sweets more important than printed words); *Donnelly* v. *Rowlands*, [1971] 1 All E. R. 9; [1971] 1 W. L. R. 1600, D. C. (dairyman used milk bottles embossed with name of owners of bottles and foil cap with his own name and address. Held: in context, and in absence of evidence that anybody had been misled, name of owner on bottles was not false trade description).

(*g*) *Doble* v. *David Greig, Ltd.*, [1972] 2 All E. R. 195; [1972] 1 W. L. R. 703, D. C.

(*h*) Trade Descriptions Act 1968, s. 4 (1). An oral statement may amount to the use of a trade description: s. 4 (2). Unauthorised user by an employee in connection with the employer's business would seem to amount to user by the employee: *Richardson* v. *Baker*, [1976] R. T. R. 56, D. C.

goods is deemed to have applied that trade description to the goods (*i*).

A person may apply a false trade description without realising that it is false (*k*). Indeed, it has been held that if one partner applies a false trade description, another partner who has no knowledge of the transaction in which it is applied may also be guilty of applying it (*l*).

A buyer as well as a seller may apply a trade description to goods, and if he does so in the course of a business, and it is false, then he commits the offence of applying a false trade description to goods (*m*).

But the courts have implied some limitations to the offence of applying a false trade description which are not to be found in the very wide wording of s. 1 (1) (a) of the 1968 Act. On a literal interpretation of that section, the context in which the trade description is applied would seem to be irrelevant. In *Wickens Motors* (*Gloucester*) v. *Hall* (*n*), however, it was held that no offence under s. 1 (1) (a) was committed if the false trade description was not applied in connection with the sale or supply of goods (*o*).

At least where the trade description is already on the goods or packaging when they come into the hands of the seller, he will not be held to have applied that description if he has disclaimed any responsibility as to its accuracy before the goods are supplied (*p*) in a form as bold, precise and compelling as the trade description itself (*q*). It would seem that the trade description is not applied if both parties know that it cannot be relied on and act on that basis (*r*).

Supplies or offers to supply any goods.—Goods are supplied when the seller notifies the buyer that they are available for delivery, or in the absence of such notification when they are actually delivered (*s*).

(*i*) Trade Descriptions Act 1968, s. 4 (3).

(*k*) *Taylor* v. *Smith*, [1974] Crim. L. R. 200, D. C.; *Tarleton Engineering* v. *Nattrass*, [1973] 3 All E. R. 699; [1973] 1 W. L. R. 1261, D. C.

(*l*) *Clode* v. *Barnes*, [1974] 1 All E. R. 1166; [1974] 1 W. L. R. 544, D. C. This would seem to be because the knowledge of one partner is imputed to all the partners. But *cf. Cottee* v. *Douglas Seaton* (*Used Cars*), *Ltd.*, [1972] 3 All E. R. 750; [1972] 1 W. L. R. 1408, D. C. where a car had been damaged and the damage concealed by a previous owner. The seller was not aware of the damage when he sold the car, and it was held by the Divisional Court that he had not applied the false trade description. See also the defence under s. 24 (3) of the 1968 Act.

(*m*) *Fletcher* v. *Budgen*, [1974] 2 All E. R. 1243; [1974] 1 W. L. R. 1056, D. C.

(*n*) [1972] 3 All E. R. 759; [1972] 1 W. L. R. 1418, D. C.

(*o*) Or, presumably, the provision of services. But it is sufficient to constitute an offence if the person applying the false trade description has an interest in the fate of the goods: *Fletcher* v. *Sledmore* (1973), L. G. R. 179, where A sold a car to B, and then recommended the car to C who was considering buying it from B.

(*p*) Or, presumably, contracted to be supplied.

(*q*) *Norman* v. *Bennett*, [1974] 3 All E. R. 351; [1974] 1 W. L. R. 1229, D. C.; Cf. *Doble* v. *David Greig*, [1972] 2 All E. R. 195; [1972] 1 W. L. R. 703, D. C. (notice displayed at cash desk at supermarket held ineffective); *Waltham Forest London Borough Council* v. *Wheatley* (*No. 2*), [1978] R. T. R. 333 (notice behind proprietor's desk insufficient). See also *Zawadski* v. *Sleigh*, [1975] R. T. R. 113, D. C. (disclaimer by auctioneer whether on own behalf or on behalf of seller, may be sufficient if bold enough to contradict false trade description).

(*r*) *Norman* v. *Bennett*, *supra*.

(*s*) *Rees* v. *Munday*, [1974] 3 All E. R. 506; [1974] 1 W. L. R. 1284, D. C.

A person exposing goods for supply or having goods in his possession for supply is deemed to offer to supply them (*t*). Accordingly, an offence is committed if the false trade description is applied to the goods displayed in a shop even if it is corrected before the goods leave the shop (*u*).

Trade descriptions used in advertisements.—Where in an advertisement (*a*) a trade description is used in relation to any class of goods, it is to be taken as referring to all goods of the class whether or not in existence when the advertisement is published:

(a) in determining whether the offence has been committed of applying a false trade description to any goods; and

(b) where goods of the class are supplied or offered to be supplied by a person publishing or displaying the advertisement, also in determining whether the offence has been committed of supplying or offering to supply any goods to which a false trade description is applied (*b*).

In determining for this purpose what goods come within any particular class, regard is to be had not only to the form and content of the advertisement, but also to the time, place, manner, and frequency of its publication, and all other matters making it likely or unlikely that a person to whom the goods are supplied would think of the goods as belonging to the class in relation to which the trade description is used in the advertisement (*c*).

Additional powers of Department of Trade and Industry.—The Department of Trade and Industry has power in certain circumstances by order:

(a) to assign definite meanings to expressions used in relation to goods (*d*);

(b) to impose requirements for securing that goods are marked with or accompanied by specified information or instructions and to regulate or prohibit the supply of goods with respect to which the requirements are not complied with (*e*);

(c) to require advertisements of goods to contain or refer to specified information concerning the goods (*f*).

False or misleading indications as to price of goods.—It is an offence for any

(*t*) Trade Descriptions Act 1968, s. 6.

(*u*) *Haringey London Borough Council* v. *Piro Shoes, Ltd.*, [1976] Crim. L. R. 462, D. C. And see *Stainthorpe* v. *Bailey*, [1979] Crim. L. R. 677. *R.* v. *Hammertons Cars, Ltd.*, [1976] 3 All E. R. 758 is somewhat misleading in this respect as it deals only with the supply of goods and not with an offer to supply them.

(*a*) Defined by s. 39 (1) of the Trade Descriptions Act 1968 to include a catalogue, a price list and a circular.

(*b*) Trade Descriptions Act 1968, s. 5 (1)–(2).

(*c*) *Ibid.*, s. 5 (3).

(*d*) *Ibid.*, s. 7.

(*e*) *Ibid.*, s. 8.

(*f*) *Ibid.*, s. 9.

person offering to supply goods (*g*) to give, by whatever means, any false indication (*h*) to the effect that the price at which goods are offered is equal to or less than either a recommended price or the price at which the goods or goods of the same description were previously offered by him, or that the price is less than such a price by a specified amount (*i*). It is also an offence for such a person to give any indication likely to be taken as an indication that the goods are being offered at a price less than that at which they are in fact being offered (*k*). These offences will only be committed, however, if the offer to supply goods is made in the course of a trade or business (*l*).

Where a price list gives one price, but a higher price is charged, this is *prima facie* evidence of an offence in the absence of any satisfactory explanation (*m*). If the lower price is for cash sales only this should be indicated on the price list or an offence may be committed (*n*).

The Trade Descriptions Act 1972.—This Act requires that the origin of certain imported goods should be conspicuously indicated in certain cases where those goods have applied to them a United Kingdom name or mark, or a name or mark which is likely to be taken for a United Kingdom name or mark (whether or not such a United Kingdom name or mark actually exists) (*o*).

Offences under the Trade Descriptions Acts and civil liability for misrepresentation.—The offences created by the Trade Descriptions Acts are thus very wide. A seller may commit such an offence even though he has done nothing which would render him liable to the buyer for misrepresentation. In particular:

(*g*) "Offer to supply" is defined by s. 6 of the 1968 Act: see *ante*, p. 59. In this context the expression also includes advertising goods as available for supply.

(*h*) See p. 57, *ante*. Anything likely to be taken as such an indication is sufficient for this purpose: see s. 11 (3) (c) of the 1968 Act. Advertising a price without any reference to value added tax may, if that tax is not included in the advertised price, be an offence: *Richards* v. *Westminster Motors, Ltd.*, (1975), 119 Sol. Jo. 626, D. C.

(*i*) Trade Descriptions Act 1968, s. 11 (1). Unless the contrary is made clear, an indication that goods were previously offered at a particular price or at a higher price is to be treated as an indication that they were so offered by the person giving the indication and that that offer was made for at least 28 consecutive days within the preceding 6 months: s. 11 (3) (a). Also, unless the contrary is made clear, an indication as to a recommended price is to be treated as an indication that the price is recommended by the manufacturer or producer and that it is recommended generally for supply by retail in the area in which the goods are offered: s. 11 (3) (b).

(*k*) Trade Descriptions Act 1968, s. 11 (2). See further, p. 57, *ante*.

(*l*) *John* v. *Mathews*, [1970] 2 All E. R. 643; [1970] 2 Q. B. 443, D. C.

(*m*) *Whitehead* v. *Collett*, [1975] Crim. L. R. 53, D. C.

(*n*) Compare *Read Bros. Cycles (Leyton), Ltd.* v. *Waltham Forest London Borough Council*, [1978] R. T. R. 397, D. C.; *Barnes* v. *Watts Tyre & Rubber Co., Ltd.*, [1978] R. T. R. 405, D. C.

(*o*) Section 1. The requirement does not apply if the name or mark is neither visible in the state in which the goods are supplied or offered nor likely to become visible on such inspection as may reasonably be expected to be made of the goods by a person to whom they are to be supplied (s. 1 (2)). The Secretary of State has power under s. 1 (5) to relax the requirements of s. 1 if satisfied that the interests of persons in the United Kingdom to whom such goods may be supplied would not be materially impaired by his so doing and that it is desirable for him to do so.

(1) A mere puff may be a false trade description (*p*).
(2) No representation need be made. Any indication is sufficient (*q*).
(3) There need be no intention that the trade description should be relied on by the buyer (*r*).
(4) The seller may be guilty of an offence even if the buyer suffers no loss (*s*).
(5) A potential seller may be guilty of an offence even if the goods are not sold (*t*), and nobody is influenced by it (*u*).

The Unsolicited Goods and Services Acts 1971 and 1975

These Acts seek to protect people to whom goods are sent or delivered without being asked for. Section 1 of the 1971 Act provides that in certain circumstances the receiver of unsolicited goods may use, deal with or dispose of them as if they were an unconditional gift to him. Any rights of the sender are thereby extinguished. The particular circumstances are defined by s. 1 (2).

It is a criminal offence for a person to make a demand for payment (*a*) for what he knows are unsolicited goods, if he has no reasonable cause to believe there is a right to payment (*b*). It is also a criminal offence in such a case to threaten to bring any legal proceedings with a view to obtaining payment for unsolicited goods, or to threaten to invoke or invoke or cause to be invoked any other collection procedure to obtain payment (*c*).

The Fair Trading Act 1973

One of the objects of this Act is to protect the interests of consumers generally without having to introduce fresh legislation every time a new abuse appears.

Section 1 of the Act provides for the appointment of a Director-General of Fair Trading. His functions are set out in s. 2 of the Act, and include the keeping under general review of commercial activities which relate to the supply of goods and services and which may adversely affect the economic interests of consumers. He is also under a

---

(*p*) See, *e.g.*, *Robertson* v. *Dicicco*, [1972] R. T. R. 431 ("beautiful car"); *Hawkins* v. *Smith*, [1978] Crim. L. R. 578 (car in "showroom condition"); *Furniss* v. *Scholes*, [1974] R. T. R. 133, D. C. (car in "really exceptional condition throughout"). But *cf.* Treitel (1968), 31 M. L. R. 662. A statement of opinion will also be a false trade description if it is likely to be taken for an indication of any of the matters specified in s. 2 of the 1968 Act: see s. 3 of that Act.

(*q*) *Doble* v. *David Greig, Ltd.*, [1972] 2 All E. R. 195; [1972] 1 W. L. R. 703, D. C.

(*r*) *Mear* v. *Baker* (1954), 118 J. P. 483, D. C.; *R.* v. *Reiss*, [1957] Crim. L. R. 404.

(*s*) *Thornley* v. *Tuckwell* (*Butchers*), *Ltd.*, [1964] Crim. L. R. 127, D. C.

(*t*) As where they are only offered for sale: see ss. 1 and 6 of the 1968 Act.

(*u*) *Taylor* v. *Smith*, [1974] R. T. R. 190, D. C.

(*a*) Orders made under the 1971 Act, as amended by the 1975 Act, set out regulations to be complied with, if an invoice or similar document is not to be treated as a demand for payment: 1975 S. I. Nos. 731, 732.

(*b*) Section 2 (1) of the 1971 Act.

(*c*) Section 2 (2) of the 1971 Act.

duty to receive and collate evidence relating to such activities which may adversely affect other interests of consumers.

The Act also creates the Consumer Protection Advisory Committee (*d*). The Secretary of State or any other Minister, or the Director-General of Fair Trading may refer to the Advisory Committee the question whether a "consumer trade practice" (*e*) affects the economic interests of consumers (*f*). If the Director-General refers such a question to the Advisory Committee, he may in certain circumstances include proposals for recommending to the Secretary of State that he should exercise his powers with respect to that consumer trade practice (*g*).

In such a case, the Secretary of State may, after receiving the report of the Advisory Committee, by an order made by statutory instrument give effect to the proposals as set out in the original reference or as modified by the Advisory Committee (*h*). Contravention of such an order is a criminal offence (*i*).

Additional functions of the Director-General for the protection of consumers are contained in Part III of the Act. Where a person carries on a business and in the course of that business persists in a course of conduct which is detrimental to consumers' interests (*k*) and which is unfair to consumers, the Director-General must use his best endeavours to obtain from such person a written assurance that he will discontinue that course of conduct (*l*). Two types of conduct are regarded as unfair for this purpose. First, if the course of conduct consists of contraventions of a duty enforceable by criminal proceedings, whether or not such duty relates to consumers, and whether or not a conviction in respect thereof has been secured (*m*). Second, an unfair course of conduct also consists of any breach of contract or other duty enforceable by civil proceedings, whether or not civil proceedings have in fact been brought (*n*).

If such an assurance is not forthcoming, or is given and is then not observed, the Director-General has power to bring proceedings against that person before the Restrictive Practices Court (*o*). If that person does not give a proper undertaking to the Court, and if it appears that he is likely to persist in his course of conduct, the Court may make an order under s. 37 of the Act directing him to refrain from continuing that course of conduct.

(*d*) Fair Trading Act 1973, s. 3.
(*e*) As defined in *ibid.*, s. 13.
(*f*) *Ibid.*, s. 14.
(*g*) *Ibid.*, s. 17.
(*h*) *Ibid.*, s. 22.
(*i*) *Ibid.*, s. 23.
(*k*) Whether those interests are economic interests or interests in respect of health, safety or other matters; s. 34 (1) (a).
(*l*) *Ibid.*, s. 34 (1).
(*m*) *Ibid.*, s. 34 (2).
(*n*) *Ibid.*, s. 34 (3).
(*o*) *Ibid.*, s. 35. In certain circumstances the proceedings may be brought in another court: see s. 41.

The rest of the Act is primarily concerned with monopoly situations and other uncompetitive practices, apart from Part XI which empowers the Secretary of State to make regulations concerning pyramid selling, and provides for the enforcement of those regulations.

The Consumer Transactions (Restrictions on Statements) Order 1976.—This order (*p*) was made by the Secretary of State under s. 22 of the Fair Trading Act. As subsequently amended (*q*) it makes unlawful certain practices by persons acting in the course of a business which might mislead consumers (*r*) as to their rights.

Notices and advertisements.—Article 3 (a) and (b) of the Order prohibit such persons from

(1) displaying a notice at any place where consumer transactions (*s*) are effected (whether wholly or partly) or

(2) publishing or causing to be published any advertisement (*t*) which is intended to induce persons to enter into consumer transactions where the notice or advertisement contains a statement purporting to apply in relation to such consumer transactions a term which would be void by virtue of s. 6 or s. 20 of the Unfair Contract Terms Act 1977 (*u*) if applied to some or all such consumer transactions.

Other statements.—Article 3 (c) and (d) and article 4 further prohibit such persons from supplying to a consumer pursuant to or in connection with the carrying out of such a consumer transaction goods bearing, or goods in a container (*a*) bearing, any of the following:

(1) a statement which either (a) is a term of that consumer transaction and which is void by virtue of, or inconsistent with the provisions of s. 6 or s. 20 of the Unfair Contract Terms Act or (b) which would be so void or inconsistent if it were a term of that transaction;

(2) a statement about the rights that the consumer has against that person or about the obligations to the consumer accepted by that

---

(*p*) S. I. 1976 No. 1813.

(*q*) By the Consumer Transactions (Restrictions on Statements) (Amendment) Order 1978, S. I. 1978 No. 127.

(*r*) "Consumer" means a person acquiring goods otherwise than in the course of a business but does not include a person who holds himself out as acquiring them in the course of a business: see art. 2 (1) of the 1976 Order.

(*s*) Defined by art. 2 (1) of the 1976 Order as substituted by art. 4 of the 1978 Order to include a sale of goods (other than an auction sale, a sale by competitive tender, and a sale arising by virtue of a contract for the international sale of goods as originally defined in s. 62 (1) of the Sale of Goods Act 1893 as amended by the Supply of Goods (Implied Terms) Act 1973) where the goods are of a type ordinarily bought for private use or consumption and are sold to a person who does not buy or hold himself out as buying them in the course of a business.

(*t*) Including a catalogue and a circular: see art. 2 (1) of the 1976 Order.

(*u*) *Post*, Appendix I. The wording is curious as no term is in fact rendered void by s. 6 of the 1977 Act.

(*a*) "Container" includes any form of packaging of goods whether by way of wholly or partly enclosing the goods or by way of attaching the goods to, or winding the goods round, some other article, and in particular includes a wrapper or confining band.

person in relation to the goods (*b*) being rights or obligations that arise if the goods are defective or are not fit for a purpose or do not correspond with a description unless there is close to that statement a clear and conspicuous statement to the effect that the first statement does not or will not affect the statutory rights of a consumer (*c*).

Such persons are also prohibited from furnishing to a consumer in connection with the carrying out of a consumer transaction or to a person likely, as a consumer, to enter into such a transaction a document which includes a statement of the kind described in paragraphs (1) and (2) above. In the case of a statement of the kind described in paragraph (1) the prohibition is absolute, and in the case of a statement of the kind described in paragraph (2) it is subject to the proviso there set out.

Statements by manufacturers, wholesalers etc.—Article 5 relates to goods which are not supplied directly to consumers but which are intended by the supplier to be, or might reasonably be expected by him to be, the subject of a subsequent consumer transaction. It provides that the supplier shall not

(1) supply such goods if they bear, or are in a container bearing, a statement which sets out or describes or limits obligations (*d*) accepted or to be accepted by him in relation to the goods (*e*); or

(2) furnish a document in relation to the goods which contains such a statement (*f*)

unless there is close to any such statement another clear and conspicuous statement to the effect that the first statement does not or will not affect the statutory rights of a consumer.

The Prices Act 1974

Section 4 of this Act empowers the Secretary of State, after consultation in accordance with s. 2 (6) of the Act, to make provision by an Order made by statutory instrument for securing that prices are indicated on or in relation to goods offered or exposed for sale by retail.

Such an order may make provision for any of the following matters:

(a) the manner in which any price is to be indicated;

(b) the unit or units of measurement by reference to which the price is to be expressed; and

(c) where value added tax is payable, the manner in which that tax is to be indicated.

(*b*) Whether legally enforceable or not.

(*c*) "Statutory rights" in relation to the sale of goods means the rights arising by virtue of ss. 13 to 15 of the Sale of Goods Act 1979, *post*—see art. 2 of the 1976 Order and s. 17 (2) of the Interpretation Act 1978.

(*d*) Whether legally enforceable or not.

(*e*) This provision is only contravened if the goods become the subject of a consumer transaction, as defined in *n*. (*s*), *ante*.

(*f*) This provision is only contravened if the document has been furnished to a consumer in relation to goods which were the subject of a consumer transaction, or to a person likely to become a consumer pursuant to such a transaction.

The order may make different provisions in relation to different circumstances and may contain supplementary provisions.

The order currently in force is the Price Marking (Bargain Offers) Order 1979 (*g*). Articles 2 and 3 of that Order apply in relation to the sale of goods where a person indicates that any goods are or may be for sale by retail (*h*). That person may not, on or in relation to those goods, indicate a price for their sale in such a manner that the indication includes any statement (however framed and whether express or implied) that the price indicated is lower than—

(a) a value ascribed to the goods; or

(b) the amount of another price for the sale of goods of the same description (*i*) unless that other price falls within one of the following exceptions:

(i) A particular price which the person giving the indication proposes to charge or has charged in the ordinary course of business on the same or on other identified premises (*k*) or which that person has reasonable cause for believing has been charged in the ordinary course of business by another identified person (*k*) in identified circumstances (*l*) and has no reason for believing has ceased to be a price at which that person is prepared to do business in those circumstances. The price quoted in such a case may be one for goods of the same description (*i*) in a specified different condition or quantity (*m*).

(ii) A particular price applicable to the sale of goods of the same description (*i*) by the person giving the indication upon specified different terms as to the time or manner of payment or in specified different circumstances or in a specified different condition or quantity (*m*) or to any person who is not within a class or description of persons for sales to whom the indicated price is expressed to apply.

(iii) In a case where the indicated price applies to goods when

---

(*g*) S. I. 1979 No. 364, as amended by the Price Marking (Bargain Offers) (Amendment) Order 1979, S. I. 1979 No. 633, and the Price Marking (Bargain Offers) (Amendment No. 2) Order 1979, S. I. 1979 No. 1124. There are also special orders applying to various types of food and drink, and to petrol.

(*h*) Article 2 (1) (a). The prohibition does not apply to persons who give an indication of a price only as (a) independent compilers of reports or surveys relating to prices including that price or (b) a publisher or distributor of a publication or an exhibitor or broadcaster of a film or radio or T. V. broadcast. Nor does it apply to a statement relating to a maximum permitted price or charge which is indicated pursuant to any enactment or community obligation (art. 2 (2)).

(*i*) Goods are taken to be of the same description as other goods if those other goods are, by reason of their construction or composition or of a purpose for which they may be used, of a description with which the goods may reasonably be compared: art. 7 (1) (a). Note that by virtue of art. 5 (2), this prohibition does not apply to the amount of the price for the sale of goods which are exempt goods for the purposes of the Retail Prices Act 1976.

(*k*) The person or the premises, as the case may be, must be identified in the indication: art. 7 (3) (a).

(*l*) The circumstances must be specified in the indication: art. 7 (3) (b).

(*m*) The condition or quantity must be specified in the indication: art. 7 (3) (b).

supplied with other specified goods or with specified services, a particular price for the sale of the goods without those other goods or services or with specified goods or services.

(iv) Except in the case of goods specified in the Schedule to Order 1 as amended (*n*), comparison may be made with a retail price recommended or suggested by any person in the course of business (*o*).

The Consumer Credit Act 1974

This Act, which is presumably being brought into force in stages (*p*), establishes for the protection of consumers a new system of credit control administered by the Director-General of Fair Trading. It replaces the previous legislation relating to moneylenders, pawnbrokers and hire purchase traders and their transactions.

With certain limited exceptions (*q*), the Act is concerned only with consumer credit agreements. A consumer credit agreement is an agreement between an individual (*r*), the debtor, and any other person, the creditor, by which the creditor provides the debtor with credit not exceeding £5,000 (*s*). Some provisions of the Act apply to all consumer credit agreements; others apply only to regulated agreements, that is consumer credit agreements which are not exempted under s. 16 of the Act. Regulated agreements are further subdivided by ss. 11–13 of the Act to take account of the purpose for which credit was given. The most important category for the purposes of the sale of goods is the debtor-creditor-supplier agreement which is a regulated consumer credit agreement to finance a transaction between the debtor and the creditor, or which is made under pre-existing arrangements between the creditor and a supplier (*t*) to finance a transaction between the debtor and the supplier.

Credit includes a cash loan and any other form of financial accommodation (*u*).

(*n*) The Schedule, as amended by S. I. 1979 No. 1124, lists goods under the following categories: beds, electrically powered and similar domestic appliances and apparatus, consumer electronic goods, carpets and furniture.

(*o*) Article 5 (1).

(*p*) By statutory instruments made under s. 192 of the Act.

(*q*) See in particular the provisions as to extortionate credit bargains in ss. 137–140 of the Act.

(*r*) By s. 189 (1) of the Act, "individual" includes a partnership or other unincorporated body of persons not consisting entirely of bodies corporate. Companies and other bodies corporate cannot therefore be debtors under the Act except as members of such partnerships or other unincorporated bodies.

(*s*) Or such other sum as may be fixed by order under s. 181 of the Act. An item forming part of the total charge for the credit, as determined by regulations under s. 20 of the Act is not to be treated as credit even though time is allowed for its payment: s. 9 (4) of the Act.

(*t*) Or in some cases in contemplation of future arrangements: s. 12 of the Act. "Supplier" means any other person than the debtor and includes a person to whom the rights and duties of a supplier have passed by assignment or operation of law or (in relation to a prospective agreement) the prospective supplier: s. 189 (1) of the Act. "Arrangements between a creditor and a supplier" are defined by s. 187 of the Act.

(*u*) Section 9 (1).

In relation to regulated agreements, the Act regulates the activities both of those who provide credit in the course of a business (*a*), and of those engaged in an ancillary credit business. An ancillary credit business is any business so far as it comprises or relates to credit brokerage, debt-adjusting, debt-counselling, debt-collecting or the operation of a credit reference agency. The various terms are defined in s. 145 of the Act, but the principal activity in relation to the sale of goods is credit brokerage, which is the effecting of introductions of individuals desiring to obtain credit to persons who in the course of their business enter into agreements providing individuals with credit not exceeding £5,000 (*b*). Thus sellers who assist buyers to acquire their goods by introducing them to a finance house are credit brokers, and their dealings as credit brokers are regulated by the Act.

The detailed provisions of the Act are beyond the scope of this book. It provides for the licensing of most consumer credit businesses (*c*) and ancillary credit businesses (*d*) and regulates or empowers the Secretary of State to regulate virtually everything done in the course of such businesses. It also confers upon debtors rights which they would not otherwise have to be given information (*e*), to withdraw from agreements (*f*), to complete payments ahead of time and to terminate agreements (*g*). It also gives to a debtor who has obtained credit under a debtor-creditor-supplier agreement the right to hold the creditor liable for any misrepresentation or breach of contract by the supplier where the creditor is acting in the course of a business and the claim relates to items with a cash price of £30 to £10,000 each.

Extortionate credit agreements.—By s. 137 of the Act (*h*), the court has power to re-open any agreement by which any person provides an individual with credit of any amount, and which is extortionate, so as to do justice between the parties.

A credit bargain is extortionate if it requires the debtor or a relative of his to make payments (whether unconditionally or on certain contingencies) which are grossly exorbitant or if it otherwise grossly contravenes ordinary principles of fair dealing. All relevant consider-

---

(*a*) By s. 189 (1), "business" includes profession or trade, and by s. 189 (2), a person is not to be treated as carrying on a particular type of business merely because occasionally he enters into transactions belonging to a business of that type. *Cf.* the definition of business in s. 61 (1) of the Sale of Goods Act 1979, *post.*

(*b*) Or such other sum as may be fixed by order under s. 181 of the Act. There is an exception where the agreement under which the credit is provided is exempted by an order of the Secretary of State under s. 16 (5) (a) of the Act on the ground that the number of payments to be made by the debtor does not exceed the number specified for that purpose in the order.

(*c*) A consumer credit business is defined by s. 189 (1) of the Act as "any business so far as it comprises or relates to the provision of credit under regulated consumer credit agreements".

(*d*) Sections 21–42, 147–150.

(*e*) Sections 55, 76–79, 103, 107–110, 157–159.

(*f*) Sections 67–73.

(*g*) Sections 94–104.

(*h*) Brought into force on 16th May 1977 by the Consumer Credit (Commencement No. 2) Order 1977.

ations are to be taken into account, and some are specified in s. 138 of the Act.

By s. 171 (7) of the Act, if it is alleged by a debtor or surety that a credit bargain is extortionate, it is for the creditor to prove the contrary.

If a credit bargain is re-opened, the court has wide powers to do whatever is necessary, including altering the terms of the credit agreement and setting aside the whole or any part of any obligation imposed on the debtor or any surety, for the purpose of relieving the debtor or surety from payment of any sum in excess of that fairly due and reasonable: s. 139 (2) of the Act.

Persons liable to prosecution

Offences by corporations.—Under most consumer protection statutes where an offence has been committed by a body corporate with the consent or connivance of, or is attributable to any neglect on the part of, any director, manager, secretary or other similar officer (*i*) of the body corporate, that person as well as the body corporate commits an offence (*k*). A similar provision is contained in s. 20 of the Trade Descriptions Act 1968, but under that section the offence must have been committed with the consent *and* connivance of the officer charged.

Accomplices.—Section 21 of the Trade Descriptions Act 1968 makes it an offence in some circumstances for a person in the United Kingdom to assist in or induce the Commission in any other country of certain acts in respect of goods which would constitute an offence under s. 1 or s. 12 of that Act if the acts were committed in the United Kingdom.

In addition, the usual common law rules as to accomplices will apply to offences under consumer protection statutes.

Act or default of another person.—Where the commission by any person of an offence under Part IV of the Weights and Measures Act 1963, or under the Trade Descriptions Acts 1968 and 1972, or under s. 23 of the Fair Trading Act 1973, or under s. 3 of the Consumer Protection Act 1961 (*l*) or under s. 2 of the Consumer Safety Act 1978 is due to the act or default of some other person, that other person is also guilty of the

---

(*i*) In a case under the Restrictive Trade Practices Act 1956, "manager" and "officer" were held not to include the branch manager of a local retail outlet: *Registrar of Restrictive Trades Practices* v. *W. H. Smith & Son, Ltd.*, [1969] 3 All E. R. 1065; [1969] 1 W. L. R. 1460, C. A. *Cf. Tesco Supermarkets, Ltd.* v. *Nattrass*, [1971] 2 All E. R. 127; [1972] A. C. 153, H. L.

(*k*) See s. 107, Food and Drugs Act 1955; s. 3 (3), Consumer Protection Acts 1961 and 1971; s. 50, Weights and Measures Act 1963; s. 5, Unsolicited Goods and Services Act 1971; s. 132, Fair Trading Act 1973; s. 169, Consumer Credit Act 1974; and s. 7 (4), Consumer Safety Act 1978.

The Food and Drugs Act 1955, Consumer Protection Acts 1961 to 1971, Weights and Measures Act 1963 and Trade Descriptions Act 1968 all provide that "director" in relation to any statutory body corporate under national ownership or in relation to a body corporate whose affairs are managed by its members means a member of that body corporate. The Unsolicited Goods and Services Act 1971, the Fair Trading Act 1973, the Consumer Credit Act 1974 and the Consumer Safety Act 1978 have similar provisions, but only where the affairs of a body corporate are managed by its members.

(*l*) As amended by s. 1 of the Consumer Protection Act 1971.

offence, whether or not proceedings are taken against the principal offender (*m*). For this purpose, the meaning of "other person" does not appear to be restricted in any way, and means any individual or corporate body. Thus, where the offence is committed by a corporate body, proceedings may be brought against any person, including an employee of the body, whatever his position in it.

There must be a sufficient connection between the act or default and the offence committed. What is a sufficient connection will no doubt have to be determined on the facts of each case, but in one case where A sold a car to B on which the mileage recorded was incorrect, and B resold it to C with the same mileage recorded, it was held that the false trade description applied by B was not due to the act or default of A (*n*).

The other person cannot be convicted under any of the foregoing provisions if the person alleged to have committed the principal offence is shown to have committed no offence (*o*). But it has been held that, in the case of an offence under the Trade Descriptions Act 1968, there is still an offence capable of being due to the act or default of another person if the principal offender's only defence is under s. 24 of that Act (*p*). The position would seem to be the same under the Fair Trading Act 1973 where the only defence is under s. 25 of that Act, which is identical to s. 24 of the Trade Descriptions Act. Under s. 3 (2B) of the Consumer Protection Act 1961 (as amended) the defence is wider and less technical, and it is not clear whether the position would be the same (*q*).

Section 27 (4) of the Weights and Measures Act 1963 and s. 113 (3) of the Food and Drugs Act 1955 are similar in effect though different in phraseology and approach.

Defences

The offences created by the consumer protection legislation are in general offences of strict liability. A person may be guilty of an offence even though he has no intention to commit it. Where defences are created by the legislation, it is for the person charged to prove the facts which will constitute a defence.

Broadly similar defences are provided by s. 113 (1) of the Food and Drugs Act 1955, s. 3 (2B) of the Consumer Protection Act 1961 as amended by the Consumer Protection Act 1971, ss. 26 (1) and 27 (1) of the Weights and Measures Act 1963, s. 24 of the Trade Descriptions Act

---

(*m*) Section 27 (2), Weights and Measures Act 1963 as substituted by Weights and Measures Act 1979, s. 20, Sch. 5; s. 23, Trade Descriptions Act 1968; s. 24, Fair Trading Act 1973; s. 3 (2A), Consumer Protection Act 1961; s. 2, Consumer Safety Act 1978.

(*n*) *Tarleton Engineering* v. *Nattrass*, [1973] 3 All E. R. 699; [1973] 1 W. L. R. 1261, D. C. See also *Cadbury, Ltd.* v. *Halliday*, [1975] 2 All E. R. 226; [1975] 1 W. L. R. 649, D. C. (manufacturer and retailer); *K. Lill Holdings* v. *White*, [1979] R. T. R. 120, D. C.; *Meah* v. *Roberts*, [1978] 1 All E. R. 97; [1977] 1 W. L. R. 1187, D. C.

(*o*) *Cottee* v. *Douglas Seaton* (*Used Cars*), *Ltd.*, [1972] 3 All E. R. 750; [1972] 1 W. L. R. 1408, D. C.

(*p*) *Coupe* v. *Guyett*, [1973] 2 All E. R. 1058; [1973] 1 W. L. R. 669, D. C.

(*q*) See these defences considered, *post*.

1968, s. 25 of the Fair Trading Act 1973, and s. 168 of the Consumer Credit Act 1974 and s. 2 (6) of the Consumer Safety Act 1978.

The due diligence defence.—Under s. 3 (2B) of the Consumer Protection Act 1961, s. 26 (1) of the Weights and Measures Act 1963 (as substituted by para. 7 of Schedule 5 to the Weights and Measures Act 1979) and s. 2 (6) of the Consumer Safety Act 1978, it is a defence for a person charged with an offence under that Act to prove that he took all reasonable precautions and exercised all due diligence to avoid the commission of the offence. These two requirements frequently appear in the defences available under the other Acts, but are there subject to further qualifications. While they must be taken together, the first, "reasonable precautions" refers to the setting up of a proper system of work, and the second, "due diligence" refers to the proper supervision of that system (*r*).

To establish that he took reasonable precautions and exercised due diligence, the person charged must show, and apparently need only show, that he acted without negligence (*s*). But the standard of care required would seem to be a high one (*t*).

A person running a business must devise a system which could rationally be said to be so designed that the commission of the offence could be avoided (*u*). A paper scheme, perfunctorily enforced would be inadequate (*a*). If, however, a proper scheme is devised and it is properly supervised, a failure in the scheme due to the default of an employee will not prevent the owner of the business from establishing the defence (*b*).

It is a question of fact in all cases whether a person has taken reasonable precautions or exercised due diligence. It is not necessary to show how the offence came to be committed, although it may be desirable to do so to help to show that all reasonable precautions were taken.

Act or default of another person.—Under other statutory provisions the

---

(*r*) *Tesco Supermarkets, Ltd.* v. *Nattrass*, [1971] 2 All E. R. 127; [1972] A. C. 153, H. L.

(*s*) *Ibid.*, at pp. 155 and 199, *per* Lord DIPLOCK.

(*t*) Thus it will not normally be sufficient to obtain a written undertaking from a foreign manufacturer that goods comply with safety regulations if it is possible to have a sample of the goods analysed: *Taylor* v. *Lawrence Fraser* (*Bristol*), [1978] Crim. L. R. 43, D. C. Nor is it normally a sufficient answer to a charge under s. 1 of the Trade Descriptions Act 1968, where an odometer reading in a car is false, simply to have examined the car to see whether the mileage shown is consistent with the condition of the car, without making further enquiries: *Lewis* v. *Mahoney*, [1977] Crim. L. R. 436, D. C. Nor are enquiries sufficient if they are unproductive: *Simmons* v. *Potter*, [1975] R. T. R. 347, D. C. See also *Wandsworth London Borough Council* v. *Bentley*, [1980] R. T. R. 429, D. C. (odometer reading: no disclaimer and no inquiry of previous owner, a very reputable company: no defence). As to the defence under s. 24 (3) of the 1968 Act that reasonable diligence would not have revealed the error, see *Crook* v. *Howells*, [1980] R. T. R. 434, D. C.: *Barker* v. *Hargreaves* (1981), 125 Sol. Jo. 165, D. C.

(*u*) *Tesco Supermarkets, Ltd.* v. *Nattrass*, *supra.*, at pp. 140 and 180, *per* Lord MORRIS.

(*a*) *Ibid.*, at pp. 135 and 174, *per* Lord REID.

(*b*) *Ibid.*, where the appellants were able to rely on the defence provided by s. 24 of the Trade Descriptions Act 1968 as the offence was committed due to the default of one of

defence is only available if other requirements are satisfied. Under s. 24 of the Trade Descriptions Act 1968, s. 25 of the Fair Trading Act 1973 and s. 168 of the Consumer Credit Act 1974 it must also be proved that the act or omission of the person charged was due to a mistake, or reliance on information supplied to him, or to the act or default (*c*) (or omission) of another person, or to an accident or some other cause beyond his control.

Section 113 (1) of the Food and Drugs Act 1955 and s. 27 (1) of the Weights and Measures Act 1963 require not only that the person charged must prove that he has used all due diligence, but also that he must prove that the commission of the offence was due to the act or default (*c*) of another person. It is not sufficient to show that the offence *may* have been due to the other person's act or default (*d*).

Where a retailer seeks to rely for his defence on one of these sections to show that the contravention was due to the act or default of a middleman, the middleman may in his turn rely for his defence on the same section to show that it was due to the act or default of the manufacturer. The section, once used, is not exhausted (*e*).

The other person may be a servant or agent or other person who is under the control of the person charged (*f*). Thus in the case of a company, an employee who is not within the "brain area" of the company is another person for this purpose, unless perhaps he is responsible for devising or supervising the system devised to avoid the commission of the offence (*g*).

Under these various sections, the person charged must give the

---

their shop managers. See also *Beckett* v. *Kingston Brothers (Butchers), Ltd.*, [1970] 1 All E. R. 715; [1970] 1 Q. B. 606, D. C., where the managing director of the company wrote a special letter to his area managers, requiring all turkeys which had been mistakenly labelled "Norfolk King Turkey" to be remarked "Danish", and this was held sufficient to exonerate the company when one of the turkeys was subsequently sold under the wrong label. But in *Sherratt* v. *Geralds the American Jewellers* (1970), 114 Sol. Jo. 147, jewellers obtained watches, marked "waterproof" from their suppliers. When charged under s. 1 (1) (b) of the Trade Descriptions Act 1968 with supplying goods to which a false trade description was applied, they sought to rely upon s. 24 of that Act. It was held that they were not entitled to do so, because it was not enough for them to rely, however reasonably, on the reputation or experience of their wholesale suppliers. Where the person charged is only a dealer but not an expert, he is not excused from taking steps which to experts might be reasonable: *Sutton London Borough* v. *Perry Sanger & Co., Ltd.* (1971), 135 J. P. Jo. 239. Where a car is sold and the mileage indicated on the odometer amounts to a false trade description under the Trade Descriptions Act 1968, the person charged can no longer say that he has taken all reasonable precautions to avoid the commission of an offence unless he has issued a disclaimer in a sufficiently clear form: *Simmons* v. *Potter*, [1975] R. T. R. 347, D. C., distinguishing *Naish* v. *Gore*, [1971] 3 All E. R. 737. For disclaimers, see *supra*, p. 59.

(*c*) In *Tesco Supermarkets, Ltd.* v. *Nattrass*, *supra*, Lord DIPLOCK, at pp. 153 and 196–197 defined a default in this context as a failure to act which constitutes a breach of a legal duty to act.

(*d*) *Moore* v. *Ray*, [1950] 2 All E. R. 561; [1951] K. B. 58.

(*e*) *British Fermentation Products, Ltd.* v. *British Italian Trading Co., Ltd.*, [1942] 2 All E. R. 256; [1942] 2 K. B. 145.

(*f*) *Hall* v. *Farmer*, [1970] 1 All E. R. 729, *per* Lord PARKER, C. J.

(*g*) *Tesco Supermarkets, Ltd.* v. *Nattrass*, [1971] 2 All E. R. 127; [1972] A. C. 153, H. L.

prosecution the statutory notice of his intention to allege that the commission of the offence was due to the act or default of another person or to reliance on information supplied by another person. If it is then shown that the contravention was due to the act or default of that other person (*h*), he may be convicted (*i*) of the offence.

Penalties

Penalties for offences under the different statutes vary, Under s. 106 of the Food and Drugs Act 1955, except where otherwise provided (*k*), the maximum penalty is a fine of £100 and three months' imprisonment, plus £5 for each day in the case of a continuing offence. Under s. 52 of the Weights and Measures Act 1963 (*l*) penalties range from a maximum of £200 to £1,000 and two years' imprisonment.

Section 18 of the Trade Descriptions Act 1968 and s. 23 of the Fair Trading Act 1973 provide a maximum fine of £400 on summary conviction and an unlimited fine (*m*) plus imprisonment for up to two years on conviction on indictment. Section 167 of and Schedule 1 to the Consumer Credit Act 1974 provides for fines of £50—£400 on summary conviction, and for an unlimited fine and imprisonment of from one to two years on conviction on indictment.

An offender may also be ordered as part of his sentence to compensate any person who has suffered loss as a result of the offence (*n*).

It has been said (*o*) that a sentence of imprisonment, whether suspended or not, is not normally justified for a contravention of a provision of the Trade Descriptions Act 1968 unless the offender is guilty of dishonesty, and this will presumably also apply under other consumer protection legislation.

Notification of conviction or judgment to Director-General of Fair Trading

Where a person is convicted of an offence in any criminal proceedings or has a judgment given against him in civil proceedings, and it appears to the court that having regard to the functions of the Director-General

---

But a person who sells only as an agent or broker for a disclosed principal cannot by selling be guilty of an act or default to which the commission of an offence by the principal is due: *Lester* v. *Balfour Williamson Merchant Shippers*, [1953] 1 All E. R. 1146; [1953] 2 Q. B. 168, D. C.

(*h*) It has been held under s. 24 of the Trade Descriptions Act 1968 that it is not necessary in order to prove that the offence was due to the act or default of another person to identify the precise persons responsible provided the person charged can show that he has done all that was reasonably to be expected by way of enquiry and investigation to identify the other person: *McGuire* v. *Sittingbourne Co-operative Society*, [1976] Crim. L. R. 268, D. C.

(*i*) Unless he has a defence: *e.g.*, that the information preferred against him was outside the time limit as in *R.* v. *Bicester Justices, ex parte Unigate, Ltd.*, [1975] 1 All E. R. 449; [1975] 1 W. L. R. 207, D. C.

(*k*) *E.g.* s. 8 (4) of that Act.

(*l*) As amended by s. 18, Weights and Measures Act 1979.

(*m*) See *R.* v. *Churchill* (*No. 2*), [1966] 2 All E. R. 215; [1967] 1 Q. B. 190.

(*n*) See s. 35, Powers of Criminal Courts Act 1973, *post*, Appendix I.

(*o*) *R.* v. *Haesler*, [1973] R. T. R. 486, C. A.

under Part III of the Fair Trading Act 1973 or under the Consumer Credit Act 1974 that the conviction or judgment should be brought to his attention, and that it may not be brought to his attention unless arrangements are made by the court, then the court may make such arrangements although the proceedings have been finally disposed of (*p*).

Enforcement of consumer protection legislation

The Food and Drugs Act 1955.—Section 87 of the Food and Drugs Act 1955 imposes a duty to prosecute in respect of contraventions of the provisions of that Act in some cases on the Minister of Agriculture, and in other cases on local councils, but enforcement of most provisions is in the hands of the food and drug authorities (*q*). The Act does not prohibit private prosecutions, but contemplates that prosecutions will ordinarily be instituted by food and drug authorities (*r*). There is no duty for these authorities to prosecute automatically in every case. They are required to use their discretion and consider whether the public interest will be served by a prosecution. Indeed, it has been said that where a prosecution does not serve the general interests of consumers, justices may think fit to grant an absolute discharge even though the Act has been contravened (*s*).

The Weights and Measures Acts 1963 to 1979.—Private prosecutions may not be brought under these Acts. The acts are administered by local weights and measures authorities through their appointed inspectors (*t*), and it is provided by s. 51 of the 1963 Act that proceedings for any offence under the Acts shall not be instituted except by or on behalf of a local weights and measures authority or the chief office of police for a police area.

The Trade Descriptions Acts 1968 to 1972.—Private prosecutions may be brought under these Acts, but as with the Food and Drugs Act 1955, it is clearly contemplated that private prosecutions will not normally be brought. The duty of enforcement is imposed on the local weights and measures authorities (*u*). If any such authority fails to discharge its

(*p*) Fair Trading Act 1973, s. 131; Consumer Credit Act 1974, s. 166. A Home Office Circular (No. 10/1975) has been sent to Clerks to Magistrates' Courts setting out the information required. It is reproduced in N. L. J. Vol. 125, p. 131. Arrangements have also been made between the office of Fair Trading and local authorities for the outcome of prosecutions brought by local weights and measures authorities to be notified to the Director-General.

(*q*) As defined in s. 88 of the 1955 Act.

(*r*) *Smedleys, Ltd.* v. *Breed*, [1974] 2 All E. R. 21, 33; [1974] A. C. 839 *per* Viscount DILHORNE.

(*s*) *Ibid.*, at pp. 34 and 856, *per* Viscount DILHORNE. *Cf.* s. 109 (1) of the 1955 Act which provides that certain government departments may initiate proceedings "where the general interests of consumers are affected", and s. 127 of that Act which gives the Minister of Agriculture power to authorise a prosecution if he is of the opinion that the failure of a food and drugs authority to prosecute affects the general interests of consumers.

(*t*) Weights and Measures Act 1963, s. 41.

(*u*) Trade Descriptions Act 1968, s. 26. But s. 26 (5) provides that in Scotland the procurator fiscal shall be responsible for the initiation of proceedings. Similar provision as to enforcement is contained in s. 27 of the Fair Trading Act 1973 in respect of an order made under s. 22 of that Act, and in s. 161 (1) of the Consumer Credit Act 1974 in respect of that

functions properly, complaint may be made to the Department of Trade and Industry which may cause a local enquiry to be held (*a*).

Where a local weights and measures authority intends to institute proceedings under these Acts, or under s. 23 of the Fair Trading Act 1973, or under the Consumer Credit Act 1974, it must give the Director-General of Fair Trading notice of such intended proceedings together with a summary of the facts on which the charge is to be founded (*b*).

Where a charge is being considered under the Trade Descriptions Acts in respect of facts which also constitute an offence under Part IV of the Weights and Measures Act 1963, then except in the case of proceedings under s. 23 of the 1968 Act special provisions contained in the Weights and Measures Act must be complied with, and the time limit for prosecutions is three months instead of the normal twelve months (*c*) under s. 19 of the 1968 Act. There are also special restrictions on the admissibility of evidence where the act or omission alleged constitutes an offence under the food and drugs laws (*d*).

Powers of the relevant authorities

Under each Act, the relevant authorities have wide powers to make test purchases (*e*), and to enter premises and inspect, and in some cases seize, goods and documents (*f*). Where goods were seized, and during their detention they are lost or damaged or they deteriorate, the owner is entitled to be compensated for the loss suffered unless he is convicted of an offence (*g*).

It is an offence to obstruct the work of authorised officers (*h*).

Act and regulations made under it. In addition to the local weights and measures authorities, the Director-General of Fair Trading also has a duty to enforce the provisions of the 1973 and 1974 Acts and orders and regulations made under them.

(*a*) Trade Descriptions Act 1968, s. 26 (3). The Secretary of State has a similar power under s. 161 (4) of the Consumer Credit Act 1974.

(*b*) Fair Trading Act 1973, s. 130; Consumer Credit Act 1974, s. 161 (2).

(*c*) The normal time limit in summary proceedings: see s. 19 (2) of the 1968 Act. The time limit in summary proceedings is only six months in some cases: see s. 19 (4) of the 1968 Act and s. 104 of the Magistrates Court Act 1952. Where proceedings are brought by way of indictment, the time limit for commencing them is three years from the date of the offence or one year from its discovery by the prosecutor: s. 19 (1) of the 1968 Act.

(*d*) Trade Descriptions Act 1968, s. 22 (2).

(*e*) Weights and Measures Act 1963, s. 32; Weights and Measures Act 1979, s. 4 (2), Sch. 2, para. 5 (c); Trade Descriptions Act 1968, s. 27; Fair Trading Act 1973, s. 28; Consumer Credit Act 1974, s. 164; Consumer Safety Act 1978, s. 5 (3); Sch. 2, para. 2; and *cf.* Food and Drugs Act 1955, s. 91 (powers of sampling).

(*f*) Food and Drugs Act 1955, ss. 9, 100; Weights and Measures Act 1963, s. 48, as amended by Weights and Measures Act 1979, Sch. 5, para. 13; Weights and Measures Act 1979, s. 4 (2), Sch. 2, paras. 1–4; Trade Descriptions Act 1968, s. 28; Fair Trading Act 1973, s. 29; Consumer Credit Act 1974, s. 162; Consumer Safety Act 1978, Sch. 2, para. 3.

(*g*) See Food and Drugs Act 1955, ss. 9 (4), 211; Trade Descriptions Act 1968, s. 33; Fair Trading Act 1973, s. 32; Consumer Credit Act 1974, s. 163; Consumer Safety Act 1978, Sch. 2, para. 15.

(*h*) Food and Drugs Act 1955, s. 105; Weights and Measures Act 1963, s. 49; Weights and Measures Act 1979, s. 4 (2), Sch. 2, para. 6; Trade Descriptions Act 1968, s. 29; Fair Trading Act 1973, s. 30; Consumer Credit Act s. 165; Consumer Safety Act 1978, Sch. 2, para. 10.

SECTION D

THE SALE OF GOODS ACT 1979

(1979, c. 54)

An Act to consolidate the law relating to the sale of goods (*a*).

[6th December 1979]

The law relating to the sale of goods was first codified by the Sale of Goods Act 1893. Section 4 of the 1893 Act, relating to the need for certain contracts to be evidenced in writing, was repealed in 1954. Section 24, relating to the revesting of property in stolen goods on the conviction of the offender was repealed by the Theft Act 1968. Other amendments were made to the 1893 Act by the Misrepresentation Act 1967, the Supply of Goods (Implied Terms) Act 1973, the Consumer Credit Act 1974, and the Unfair Contract Terms Act 1977.

The Sale of Goods Act 1979 consolidates these amendments, re-enacting the 1893 Act as amended with the exception of s. 26 of that Act. The language of the consolidating Act is substantially that of the 1893 Act, but some changes have been made in an attempt to "modernise" some expressions.

Canon of construction.—The canon for construing a codifying Act was discussed by the House of Lords in a case on the Bills of Exchange Act 1882 (*b*). "I think," says Lord HERSCHELL,

> "the proper course is in the first instance to examine the language of the statute, and to ask what is its natural meaning, uninfluenced by any considerations derived from the previous state of the law; and not to start with inquiring how the law previously stood, and then, assuming that it was probably intended to leave it unaltered, to see if the words of the enactment will bear an interpretation in conformity with this view."

But, of course, as he proceeds to point out, if any provision be of doubtful import, resort to the previous state of the law would be perfectly legitimate (*c*).

On the 1893 Act, Lord ALVERSTONE, C. J., said:

> "I think it is very important to bear in mind that the rights of people in regard to these matters depend now upon statute. To a large extent the old

---

(*a*) Short title "The Sale of Goods Act 1979," see s. 64, *post*.

(*b*) 3 Halsbury's Statutes (3rd Edn.) 188.

(*c*) *Bank of England* v. *Vagliano*, [1891] A. C. 107, at p. 145. *Cf. Bristol Tramways Co.* v. *Fiat Motors Co., Ltd.*, [1910] 2 K. B. 831, at p. 836, C. A.; *Wimble* v. *Rosenberg & Sons*, [1913] 3 K. B., at p. 757, C. A.; *In re Wait*, [1927] 1 Ch. 606, at pp. 630–631; *Laurie & Morewood* v. *Dudin & Sons*, [1926] 1 K. B. 223, at p. 234. But note the criticism of PALLES, C. B., in *Wallis* v. *Russell*, [1902] 2 I. R. 585, at p. 590, and see the savings of common law in s. 61 of the 1893 Act, re-enacted in s. 62, *post*.

law, I will not say has been swept away, but it has become unnecessary to refer to it (*d*)."

In practice, however, the courts sometimes applied the pre-1893 law even where the 1893 Act appears to be inconsistent with such a course (*e*).

Similar canons of construction apply to a consolidating Act. The House of Lords has recently re-affirmed the rule that a self-contained statute, whether consolidating previous law, or so doing with amendments, should be interpreted if reasonably possible without regard to its antecedents. Recourse should only be had to the earlier legislation where there is a real and substantial difficulty or ambiguity which classical methods of construction cannot resolve. It is only where there is such a difficulty or ambiguity that recourse may be had to the rule that a consolidating Act (insofar as it merely re-enacts) does not change the law (*f*).

The provisions of the 1979 Act must be read with and subject to the provisions of the Interpretation Act 1978 (*g*), which apply to all Acts of Parliament passed after 1889 (*h*). By s. 6 of the 1978 Act, unless the contrary intention appears, singular words include the plural, and *vice versa*; by Schedule 1 "person" includes a body of persons, corporate or unincorporate; and "writing" includes typing, printing, lithography, photography, and other modes of representing or reproducing words in a visible form and expressions referring to writing are construed accordingly.

The Sale of Goods Act is divided into Parts, and those Parts are again subdivided by various headings. Regard must be had to these divisions in construing the Act (*i*).

PART I

CONTRACTS TO WHICH ACT APPLIES

1. Contracts to which Act applies.—(1) This Act applies to contracts of sale of goods made on or after (but not to those made before) 1 January 1894.

(2) In relation to contracts made on certain dates, this Act applies subject to the modification of certain of its sections as mentioned in Schedule 1 below.

(*d*) *Wallis* v. *Pratt & Haynes*, [1911] A. C. 394, at p. 398.

(*e*) See *Reid* v. *Metropolitan Police Commissioner*, [1973] 2 All E. R. 97; [1973] 2 Q. B. 551, C. A. applying the rules as to market overt set out in *Co. Inst.*, Vol. II, p. 713, which appear wholly inconsistent with s. 22 of the Act, *post*.

(*f*) *Farrell* v. *Alexander*, [1976] 2 All E. R. 721; [1977] A. C. 59, H. L.

(*g*) Repealing and replacing the Interpretation Act 1889.

(*h*) Interpretation Act 1978, Sch. 2, Pt. I.

(*i*) *Inglis* v. *Robertson*, [1898] A. C. 616, at p. 630; and see *Qualter Hall & Co., Ltd.* v. *Board of Trade*, [1961] 3 All E. R. 389; [1962] Ch. 273, C. A.; *Elliott* v. *Grey*, [1959] 3 All E. R. 733; [1960] 1 Q. B. 367, D. C.

(3) Any such modification is indicated in the section concerned by a reference to Schedule 1 below.

(4) Accordingly, where a section does not contain such a reference, this Act applies in relation to the contract concerned without such modification of the section.

Derivation.—This section is new.

Definitions.—For "contract of sale" and "goods", see s. 61 (1), *post*.

Cross references.—For provisions in respect of things done before 1st January 1894, see Sch. 4, paras. 5, 6, *post*.

COMMENT

This Act seeks to consolidate the Sale of Goods Act 1893, except s. 26, and amendments to that Act effected by the Misrepresentation Act 1967, the Misrepresentation Act (Northern Ireland) 1967, the Supply of Goods (Implied Terms) Act 1973, the Consumer Credit Act 1974 and the Unfair Contract Terms Act 1977.

Unlike most consolidating Acts, which apply only from a date following their enactment, this Act seeks to regulate retrospectively every contract for the Sale of Goods since the 1893 Act came into force on 1st January 1894.

Subsection (1) of this section excludes contracts of sale of goods made before that date (*k*).

In relation to contracts of sale made between 1894 and the various dates on which amendments to the 1893 Act took effect, this Act seeks to preserve the law as it was when those contracts were made by re-enacting in the First Schedule the relevant provisions of the 1893 Act in their unamended form (apart from minor drafting amendments) and by applying those provisions to such contracts.

Further, certain provisions of the present Act, re-enacting amendments effected to the 1893 Act by the Consumer Credit Act 1974, will only come into force on a date to be appointed and the provisions applicable until that date are also set out in the First Schedule.

PART II

FORMATION OF THE CONTRACT

Contract of Sale

2. Contract of sale.—(1) A contract of sale of goods is a contract by which the seller transfers or agrees to transfer

(*k*) Section 63 of the 1893 Act, the commencement provision, was repealed as spent by the Statute Law Revision Act 1908.

the property in goods to the buyer for a money consideration, called the price (*l*).

(2) There may be a contract of sale between one part owner and another (*m*).

(3) A contract of sale may be absolute or conditional.

(4) Where under a contract of sale the property in the goods is transferred from the seller to the buyer the contract is called a sale.

(5) Where under a contract of sale the transfer of the property in the goods is to take place at a future time or subject to some condition thereafter to be fulfilled the contract is called an agreement to sell (*n*).

(6) An agreement to sell becomes a sale when the time elapses or the conditions are fulfilled subject to which the property in the goods is to be transferred (*o*).

Derivation.—Section 1 of the 1893 Act.

Definitions.—For "buyer," "contract of sale," "goods," "property," "seller" and "sale," see s. 61 (1), *post*.

Cross-references.—*Cf.* ss. 8 and 9, *post* (price), and s. 49, *post* (action for the price).

COMMENT

This section appears to be purely declaratory.

Subsections (1) and (2).—*Seller and buyer must be different persons.*—The essence of sale is the transfer of the property in a thing from one person to another for a price. Hence it has been said that if a man purchase his own goods there is no sale, whether or not he knows that they are his (*p*). But one co-owner may sell to another, a partner may

---

(*l*) See note "Hire purchase, credit-sale and conditional sale agreements", p. 84, *post*.

(*m*) As to sale by a co-owner to a third party, and the remedies of co-owners *inter se*, see *post*, notes to s. 21. As to sale of undivided moiety of specific chattel, creating co-ownership, see *Marson* v. *Short* (1835), 2 Bing. N. C. 118.

(*n*) *Cf. Heilbutt* v. *Hickson* (1872), L. R. 7 C. P. 438, at p. 449; *Lee* v. *Butler*, [1893] 2 Q. B. 318, C. A.; *Marten* v. *Whale*, [1917] 2 K. B. 480, at p. 484, C. A.; 34 Halsbury's Laws (3rd Edn.) 19.

(*o*) *Bishop* v. *Shillito* (1819), 2 Barn. & Ald. 329 *n*. (special condition); *Rohde* v. *Thwaites* (1827), 6 B. & C. 388, at p. 393 (appropriation of goods to contract); *Bianchi* v. *Nash* (1836), 1 M. & W. 545 (special condition). *Cf. Mischeff* v. *Springett*, [1942] 2 All E. R. 349; [1942] 2 K. B. 331.

(*p*) 2 *Black. Com.* (1st ed.), p. 450; *Bell* v. *Lever Bros., Ltd.*, [1932] A. C. 161, *per* Lord ATKIN at p. 218; *Moore* v. *Singer Manufacturing Co.*, [1904] 1 K. B. 820, C. A. (distrainor buying at auction goods distrained); *Plasycoed Collieries Co.* v. *Partridge, Jones & Co.*, [1912] 2 K. B. 345 (distrainor taking goods at appraised value and using them); *Tunstall* v. *Steigmann*, [1962] 2 All E. R. 417; [1962] 2 Q. B. 593, C. A. (where A sells his business to a limited company wholly owned and controlled by him, the business is no longer "carried on by" A for the purposes of the Landlord and Tenant Act 1954).

sell to his firm, and the firm may sell to a partner (*q*), and there are clearly certain quasi-exceptions to the rule; for instance, when a man's goods are sold under an execution or distress he may himself become the purchaser. So, too, a bankrupt may buy back his own goods from the trustee,

> "though the trustee, the auctioneer, or any one bearing a fiduciary character . . . is precluded from becoming a purchaser by the general policy of the law which prohibits an agent from selling to himself" (*r*).

The true position seems to be this: buyer and seller must be different persons, but where one person has by law the right to sell another person's goods, that other person may purchase his own goods. As to bids at auction on behalf of seller, see s. 58, *post*.

Cognate or ambiguous contracts.—Whether a given contract be a contract of sale or some other kind of contract is a question of substance and not of form. It is the duty of the court to look behind the form of a transaction and to ascertain its real substance (*s*), and where the true transaction is impeachable by or unenforceable against one of the parties to the litigation the court will treat as a nullity a document designed by the parties to it to mask the true nature of the transaction (*t*). Thus it depends on the real meaning and nature of the transaction whether it is to be construed as a contract of sale or an invitation to enter into a contract of sale (*u*); as a contract of sale or a mere guarantee for the price (*a*); as a contract of sale or a bailment on trust (*b*); as a contract of "sale or return", or a contract of *del credere* agency (*c*); as a contract of sale or a contract for sale on commission (*d*); as a contract of sale or a contract of loan on security or mortgage (*e*); as a contract of sale or a

---

(*q*) For power to assign personal property to self and others, see Law of Property Act 1925, s. 72; 27 Halsbury's Statutes (3rd Edn.) 451.

(*r*) *Kitson* v. *Hardwick* (1872), L. R. 7 C. P. 473, at p. 478; *cf. Armstrong* v. *Jackson*, [1917] 2 K. B. 822 (broker); *Hocker* v. *Waller* (1924), 29 Com. Cas. 296, 298 (agent for sale on commission).

(*s*) *Stoneleigh Finance, Ltd.* v. *Phillips*, [1965] 1 All E. R. 513; [1965] 2 Q. B. 537, C. A.; *St. Margaret's Trusts* v. *Castle*, [1964] C. L. Y. 1685, C. A.

(*t*) But the design must be that of *both* parties: *Yorkshire Railway Wagon Co.* v. *Maclure* (1882), 21 Ch. D. 309, 314, *per* JESSEL, M. R.; *Stoneleigh Finance* v. *Phillips, supra; Kingsley* v. *Sterling Industrial Securities, Ltd.*, [1966] 2 All E. R. 414; [1966] 2 W. L. R. 1265, C. A.; *Bennett* v. *Griffin Finance*, [1967] 1 All E. R. 515; [1967] 2 Q. B. 46, C. A.; *Snook* v. *London and West Riding Investments, Ltd.*, [1967] 1 All E. R. 518; [1967] 2 Q. B. 786, C. A.; *cf. Re Watson, Ex p. Official Receiver in Bankruptcy* (1890), 25 Q. B. D. 27, C. A.; and see the rule in the case of a bill of sale in 4 Halsbury's Laws of England (4th Edn.), paras. 616, 662.

(*u*) *Harvey* v. *Facey*, [1893] A. C. 552; *Pharmaceutical Society of Great Britain* v. *Boots Cash Chemists (Southern), Ltd.*, [1953] 1 All E. R. 482, C. A.; [1953] 1 Q. B. 401.

(*a*) *Hutton* v. *Lippert* (1883), 8 App. Cas. 309, P. C.

(*b*) *South Australian Ins. Co.* v. *Randell* (1869), L. R. 3 P. C. 101.

(*c*) *Re Nevill, Ex. p. White* (1871), 6 Ch. App. 397; affirmed *sub nom. Towle & Co.* v. *White* (1873), 21 W. R. 465, H. L.; *Weiner* v. *Harris*, [1910] 1 K. B. 285, C. A. See the English and Scottish cases reviewed in *Michelin Tyre Co.* v. *Macfarlane*, 1917 55 Sc. L. R. 35, H. L.

(*d*) *The Prinz Adalbert*, [1917] A. C. 586, P. C. For a hybrid contract of sale and agency, see *The Kronprincessin Cecilie* (1917), 33 T. L. R. 292, P. C.

(*e*) *Ex p. Harvey & Co.* (1890), 7 Morrell, 138; *Re Watson* (1890), 25 Q. B. D. 27, C. A.;

mere wager (*f*); as a contract of sale or a contract for work and materials; as a contract of sale or a contract of hiring, including the so-called hire-purchase agreement which is a contract of hiring coupled with an option to purchase (*g*); as a contract of sale or a contract to do work as an agent (*h*); as a contract of sale or a licence to get mineral products from land (*i*); as a contract of sale or a pledge to bankers (*k*); as a contract of sale or a contract of agistment (*l*); as a contract of sale or a contract to procure and carry goods (*m*); or as a contract of sale or an option in one party to force a sale (*n*). By s. 62(4), *post*, it is expressly provided that

> "the provisions of this Act relating to contracts of sale do not apply to any transaction in the form of a contract of sale which is intended to operate by way of mortgage, pledge, charge, or other security."

The question whether a given contract be a contract of sale or some other allied form of contract, though often difficult to determine, is of practical and not merely of theoretical importance.

Work and materials.—The principal practical differences between such a contract and one of sale are that, terms are implied into the former only in accordance with the general law of contract and not under this Act (*o*), and that the right to treat the contract as at an end as a result of a breach by the other party may in some cases depend upon the nature of the contract (*p*).

Opinions have differed much about the test for distinguishing between these two contracts (*q*), but the general rule deducible from the

---

Madell v. *Thomas*, [1891] 1 Q. B. 230, C. A.; *Wheatley's Trustee* v. *Wheatley, Ltd.* (1901), 85 L. T. 491; *Maas* v. *Pepper*, [1905] A. C. 102 (bill of sale cases); *Polsky* v. *S. & A. Services*, [1951] 1 All E. R. 185; affirmed [1951] 1 All E. R. 1062, C. A. ("hire purchase" documents executed where true transaction was loan on security of motor car), and cases there cited.

(*f*) *Rourke* v. *Short* (1856), 5 E. & B. 904 (alternative price as a wager).

(*g*) See p. 84, *post*.

(*h*) *Dixon* v. *London Small Arms Co.* (1876), 1 App. Cas. 632, at pp. 645, 648, 654; *Lamb (W. T.) & Sons* v. *Goring Brick Co., Ltd.*, [1932] 1 K. B. 710.

(*i*) *Morgan* v. *Russell & Sons*, [1909] 1 K. B. 357.

(*k*) *The Orteric*, [1920] A. C. 724, P. C. (bill of exchange, with bill of lading attached, "sold" to bank).

(*l*) *Re Woodward, Ex p. Huggins* (1886), 54 L. T. 683.

(*m*) *Cobbold* v. *Caston* (1824), 1 Bing. 399.

(*n*) *Manders* v. *Williams* (1849), 4 Exch. 339; *Bianchi* v. *Nash* (1836), M. & W. 545; *Marten* v. *Whale*, [1917] 2 K. B. 480.

(*o*) For the nature of the conditions and warranties implied into a contract for work and materials and the circumstances in which such conditions and warranties will be implied, see *Young & Marten, Ltd.* v. *McManus Childs, Ltd.*, [1968] 2 All E. R. 1169; [1969] 1 A. C. 454, H. L.; *Gloucestershire County Council* v. *Richardson*, [1968] 2 All E. R. 1181; [1969] 1 A. C. 480, H. L.; *Samuels* v. *Davis*, [1943] 2 All E. R. 3; [1943] K. B. 526, C. A.; *Ingham* v. *Emes*, [1955] 2 All E. R. 740; [1955] 2 Q. B. 366, C. A. For a case in which the warranty of fitness was excluded by the circumstances see *Helicopter Sales (Australia) Pty., Ltd.* v. *Rotor Works Pty., Ltd.*, [1974] 4 A. L. R. 77 (High Ct. of Aus.). For restrictions on the exclusion of terms contained in or implied into a contract for work and materials see ss. 3 and 7 of the Unfair Contract Terms Act 1977.

(*p*) See p. 8, *ante*.

(*q*) See, *e.g.* *Robinson* v. *Graves*, [1935] 1 K. B. 579, C. A.; *Lyle* v. *Ajax Distributing Agency Pty., Ltd.* (1975), 11 S. A. S. R. 9.

cases seems to be that if the main object of the contract is the transfer from A to B, for a price, of the property in a thing in which B had no previous property, then the contract is a contract of sale; but if the real substance of the contract is the performance of work by A for B, it is a contract for work and materials notwithstanding that the performance of the work necessitates the use of certain materials and that the property in those materials passes from A to B under the contract (*r*). Thus a contract to make two sets of false teeth to fit the person ordering them (*s*), a contract for a mink jacket to be made from skins selected by the customer (*t*) and a contract to provide and lay fitted carpets (*u*) have been held to be contracts of sale; but a contract to print 500 copies of a treatise, the printer supplying the paper (*a*) and a contract for the manufacture and supply of oil storage tanks (*b*) have both been held to be contracts for work and materials. A contract to paint a picture may be one of sale or of work and materials, depending upon the facts of each case (*c*).

This general rule would seem to be subject to an exception where the goods supplied are to be affixed to land before the property in them passes. Such a contract is not one by which the seller transfers or agrees to transfer the property in goods, for the goods lose their character of "goods" as defined by s. 62, *post*, upon being attached to the land. The contract cannot, therefore, be for the sale of goods (*d*).

Gift.—Where goods are transferred by one person to another without any price or other consideration being given in return, the transaction is called a gift (*e*). Where a gift of goods is not effected by deed (*f*), it is incomplete and ineffectual until delivery to the donee of the thing intended to be given. The intention to transfer the property is of no avail

(*r*) The difficulty is an old one and was much debated by the Roman lawyers. See *Inst. III*, 24, 4, and De Zulueta, *The Roman Law of Sale*, pp. 15, 16. See also 1 L. Q. R. 8.

(*s*) *Lee* v. *Griffin* (1861), 30 L. J. Q. B. 252.

(*t*) *Marcel (Furriers), Ltd.* v. *Tapper*, [1953] 1 All E. R. 15; [1953] 1 W. L. R. 49.

(*u*) *Philip Head & Sons, Ltd.* v. *Showfronts, Ltd.*, [1970] 1 Lloyd's Rep. 140.

(*a*) *Clay* v. *Yates* (1856), 1 H. & N. 73.

(*b*) *R. and J. Dempster, Ltd.* v. *Motherwell Bridge and Engineering Co.*, 1964 S. L. T. 353; see also *Grafton* v. *Armitage* (1845), 2 C. B. 336 (contract for A to devise method of curving metal tubing; use by A of his own materials); *Anglo-Egyptian Navigation Co.* v. *Rennie* (1875), L. R. 10 C. P. 271 (contract to make and supply machinery for ship and to alter the engines of the ship according to specification); contrast *Cammell Laird & Co., Ltd.* v. *Manganese Bronze and Brass Co., Ltd.*, [1934] A. C. 402 (contract to make ships' propellers: sale of goods).

(*c*) *Isaacs* v. *Hardy* (1884), Cab. & El. 287; *Robinson* v. *Graves*, [1935] 1 K. B. 579, C. A.; and see *Newman* v. *Lipman*, [1950] 2 All E. R. 832; [1951] 1 K. B. 333, D. C., where the position of a photographer was argued but not decided. In Australia a contract to have photographs taken has been held to be a contract for work and materials, not sale of goods: *Lyle* v. *Ajax Distributing Agency Pty., Ltd.* (1975), 11 S. A. S. R. 9.

(*d*) *Collins Trading Co. Pty.* v. *Maher*, [1969] V. R. 20, where, however, the property in an oil heater to be installed in a house was held to have passed before it was installed; *cf. Clark* v. *Bulmer* (1843), 11 M. & W. 243 (steam engine to be completed and affixed to land). See also *Benjamin's Sale of Goods*, para. 36.

(*e*) As to "free gifts" given with goods sold, see *Esso* v. *Customs and Excise Commissioners*, [1976] 1 All E. R. 117; [1976] 1 W. L. R. 1, H. L.

(*f*) *Re Seymour* [1913], 1 Ch. 475, C. A.

(*g*). So again, a gift must be distinguished from a declaration of trust. In the case of a gift there must be a transfer of possession, in the case of a declaration of trust the trustee must retain, and intend to retain, the control. An inchoate gift falls between the two (*h*).

Exchange of goods or barter.—Where the consideration for the transfer of the property in goods from one person to another consists of the delivery of other goods, the contract is not a contract of sale, but is a contract of exchange or barter (*i*). But if the consideration for such a transfer consists partly of the delivery of goods (the goods being regarded as the equivalent of a certain sum of money) and partly of the payment of money, it is a contract of sale (*k*). Thus if the buyer in such a case fails to deliver the goods, the seller's proper remedy is not an action for detinue but an action for that part of the price which the goods represent (*l*). The contract may also be a contract of sale even where the goods delivered in part exchange are not regarded as the equivalent of money (*m*). Similarly if the contract may be performed either by the delivery of goods or the payment of money, it seems that the contract is a contract of sale (*n*). But where the goods were supplied on the terms that they were to be paid for by the bill of a third party, without recourse to the buyer if the bill was dishonoured, the contract was treated as one of exchange, rather than of sale (*o*). A contract for the supply of goods in exchange for vouchers redeemable by a third party has, however, been held to be a contract for the sale of goods (*p*).

When a statute refers in terms to contracts of sale (as, for instance, the Sale of Goods Act or the Stamp Act), it seems clear that it would have no application to contracts of exchange. Section 5 of the Factors Act 1889, *post*, for its special purpose, draws a distinction between sales and exchanges. Apart from statute, however, it seems that the rules of law

---

(*g*) *Cochrane* v. *Moore* (1890), 25 Q. B. D. 57, C. A. (attempted gift of undivided fourth part of a racehorse); see also 6 L. Q. R. 446; *Kilpin* v. *Ratley*, [1892] 1 Q. B. 582; *Cain* v. *Moon*, [1896] 2 Q. B. 283, 289; *Stoneham* v. *Stoneham*, [1919] 1 Ch. 149 (all cases on constructive delivery). As to the suggested rights of a donee, in the case of an incomplete gift, against persons other than the donor, see Pollock's *Essays in the Law*, chap. v. (gifts without delivery).

(*h*) *Cf. Richards* v. *Delbridge* (1874), L. R. 18 Eq. 11.

(*i*) *Harrison* v. *Luke* (1845), 14 M. & W. 139.

(*k*) *Forsyth* v. *Jervis* (1816), 1 Stark. 437; *Sheldon* v. *Cox* (1824), 3 B. & C. 420; *Aldridge* v. *Johnson* (1857), 7 E. & B. 885; *Chappell & Co., Ltd.* v. *Nestlé Co., Ltd.*, [1959] 2 All E. R. 701, at p. 709; [1960] A. C. 87, at p. 109, *per* Lord REID; and see *Flynn* v. *Mackin*, [1974] I. R. 101, where the Irish Supreme Court ruled that an agreement to supply a new car for an old car plus cash was barter not sale, there being no evidence of any agreement to buy the new car for an agreed price.

(*l*) *Forsyth* v. *Jervis* (*supra*); *Dawson* (*Clapham*), *Ltd.* v. *Dutfield*, [1936] 2 All E. R. 232.

(*m*) *Routledge* v. *Mackay*, [1954] 1 All E. R. 855; [1954] 1 W. L. R. 615, C. A.; *Buckley* v. *Lever Brothers, Ltd.*, [1953] 4 D. L. R. 16 (special offer of clothes pegs for cash plus wrappers); *Clarke* v. *Reilly* (1962), 96 I. L. T. R. 96 (exchange of new car for old car plus cash).

(*n*) *South Australian Insurance Co.* v. *Randell* (1869), L. R. 3 P. C. 101.

(*o*) *Read* v. *Hutchinson* (1813), 3 Camp. 352.

(*p*) *Davies* v. *Customs and Excise Commissioners*, [1975] 1 All E. R. 309; [1975] 1 W. L. R. 204, D. C., where *Read* v. *Hutchinson*, *supra*, was not cited to the court. The decision would seem to be justifiable only on the ground that if the vouchers were not met, the seller could

relating to sales apply in general to contracts of barter or exchange; but the question has been by no means fully worked out (*q*).

Trading stamps.—Section 3 of the Trading Stamps Act 1964 (*r*) provides for the redemption of trading stamps for cash. If they are nevertheless redeemed for goods, s. 4 of the 1964 Act (*s*) implies warranties on the part of the promoter of the trading stamps scheme similar to the provisions of the new ss. 12 and 14 (2) of the Sale of Goods Act 1893. These warranties are implied notwithstanding any terms to the contrary on which the redemption is made.

Liquor sold in clubs.—Where intoxicating liquor, which is *bona fide* the property of a club, is supplied to a member of the club, who pays for it, the transaction, though resembling a sale, is not a sale within the meaning of the Licensing Acts. In substance the member is consuming his own property, and the mode of payment is a matter of internal arrangement regulated by the rules of the club (*t*).

Subsection (3).—As the contract of sale is consensual, it follows that it may be either absolute or conditional, as the parties may please. The conditions inserted by the parties may be either conditions precedent or conditions subsequent. In the apt phraseology of the Continental and Civil lawyers, a contract of sale may be either a sale pure and simple, transferring the property absolutely to the buyer, or it may be subject to a "suspensive" or "resolutive" condition (*u*). The division of conditions into those which are suspensive and those which are resolutive is convenient, because those terms mark clearly the distinction between an agreement for sale which is to become an actual sale on the fulfilment of a particular condition, and an actual sale passing the property to the buyer, but subject to defeasance on the happening of some specified event. When goods are sold by weight or measure, the weighing and measuring are suspensive conditions, and if goods be sent on approval, the approval of the buyer constitutes a suspensive condition (see s. 18, rules (3) and (4), *post*). But if goods be

---

claim the price from the person acquiring the goods—a possibility which it is unlikely that the parties contemplated.

(*q*) See *Fairmaner* v. *Budd* (1831), 7 Bing. 574; *Emanuel* v. *Dane* (1812), 3 Camp. 299; *La Neuville* v. *Nourse* (1813), 3 Camp. 350. The Bill originally contained a clause applying its provisions *mutatis mutandis* to exchanges, but it was cut out by the Commons Select Committee. In Scotland the rule as to passing of risk in a contract of exchange has been held to be the same as it was under Scottish common law in a contract of sale: *Widenmeyer* v. *Burn Stewart & Co., Ltd.*, 1967 S. L. T. 129 (Ct. of Sess.) where the rules as to passing of property are also discussed.

(*r*) As amended by the Decimal Currency Act 1969, Sch. 2; 40 Halsbury's Statutes (3rd Edn.) 316; and the Consumer Credit Act 1974, Sch. 4, paras. 24–26 (not yet in force).

(*s*) As substituted by s. 16 (1) of the Supply of Goods (Implied Terms) Act 1973.

(*t*) *Graff* v. *Evans* (1882), 8 Q. B. D. 373, 378; *cf. Newman* v. *Jones* (1886), 17 Q. B. D. 132 (unauthorised sale by steward to person not a member of club); as to status of member of proprietary club, see *Baird* v. *Wells* (1890), 44 Ch. D. 661; and see further Paterson's *Licensing Acts* (88th ed.), pp. 625, *et seq.*

(*u*) French Civil Code, art. 1584, and see further arts. 1181–1184, defining these conditions; *cf.* De Zulueta, *The Roman Law of Sale*, pp. 28–30; *Murdoch* v. *Greig*, 1889 16 R. (Ct. of Sess.) 396.

sold by auction with a condition that they may be re-sold if not paid for within twenty-four hours, the condition is resolutive (*a*). So too a term which allows the buyer to return goods if they do not correspond with a warranty is resolutive (*b*). As a contract of sale may be conditional, the parties may attach such consequences as they see fit to the non-fulfilment of the condition. They may stipulate that in the event of non-fulfilment both parties shall be discharged from their obligations, or that the seller shall not be bound to deliver, or that the buyer shall not be bound to pay the price (*c*). Conditions may also be implied by other statutes; see, for example, s. 33(1) of the Exchange Control Act 1947 (*d*).

In *Christopher Hill, Ltd.* v. *Ashington Piggeries, Ltd.* (*e*), the plaintiffs had agreed in May 1960 to supply food for the defendants' mink made up in accordance with the defendants' formula, orders to be placed by the defendants from time to time as they required the food. Subsequently the defendants placed a number of orders for the food. The Court of Appeal held that having regard to ss. 1 and 5 of the Sale of Goods Act 1893, the agreement of May 1960 was a conditional contract of sale, the condition being the placing of orders by the defendants as and when they required the food. The subsequent orders were not themselves separate contracts of sale.

Hire-purchase, credit-sale and conditional sale agreements.—A hire-purchase agreement, whereby goods are let on hire with a proviso that they shall become the property of the hirer when a certain amount has been paid, may be an agreement for sale (*f*). If so, it will of course be a conditional agreement to buy for the purposes of the Sale of Goods Act 1979. A conditional agreement to buy must be distinguished from an option to buy (*g*). By s. 61 of the Sale of Goods Act 1979, "buyer" means a person who buys or agrees to buy goods. There must therefore be a consent to buy as well as a consent to sell. It follows that a hirer with an option to buy is not a "person having agreed to buy goods" within s. 9 of the Factors Act 1889 (*h*). The hire-purchase transaction is essentially different, both in practice and in its legal incidents, from the ordinary

---

(*a*) See *Lamond* v. *Davall* (1847), 9 Q. B. 1030; and *cf.* s. 48 (4), *post.*

(*b*) *E. G.*, *Head* v. *Tattersall* (1871), L. R. 7 Exch. 7; for a peculiar restrictive condition containing a term for novation, see *Grissell* v. *Bristowe* (1868), L. R. 3 C. P. 112. *Cf. The Ripon City*, [1897] P. 226 (conditional sale of ship); *Wyllie* v. *Povah* (1907), 12 Com. Cas. 317, 321 (goods sold while at sea, in case of non-arrival the contract to be void).

(*c*) *Calcutta Co.* v. *De Mattos* (1863), 32 L. J. Q. B. 322, at p. 328. *Cf. New Zealand Shipping Co.* v. *Société des Ateliers de France*, [1919] A. C. 1 (stipulation in a contract that it should be void in a certain event); *The Vesta*, [1921] 1 A. C. 774, at p. 784 (sale with a condition enabling buyer to call upon seller to re-purchase).

(*d*) *Post*, Appendix I.

(*e*) [1969] 3 All E. R. 1496, C. A.; reversed on other grounds: [1971] 1 All E. R. 847; [1972] A. C. 441, H. L.

(*f*) *Lee* v. *Butler*, [1893] 2 Q. B. 318, C. A.; *Muirhead* v. *Dickson*, 1905 7 F. (Ct. of Sess.) 686; *A.-G.* v. *Pritchard* (1928), 97 L. J. K. B. 561; *Taylor* v. *Thompson*, [1930] W. N. 16.

(*g*) See *Marten* v. *Whale*, [1917] 2 K. B. 480, C. A.

(*h*) *Helby* v. *Matthews*, [1895] A. C. 471; nor within s. 25 of the Sale of Goods Act 1979: *Belsize Motor Supply Co.* v. *Cox*, [1914] 1 K. B. 244; *cf. Felston Tile Co., Ltd.* v. *Winget*,

sale of goods and it is therefore considered as being outside the scope of this book. Credit-sale agreements, however, although usually entered into in practice in circumstances similar to those of hire-purchase agreements, and although governed in some respects by the Hire-Purchase Act 1965 (*i*) and by the Consumer Credit Act 1974 are for the most part governed by the general law relating to the sale of goods.

Conditional sale agreements are hybrid in character. They are contracts of sale and are thus generally subject to the Sale of Goods Act, but by virtue of the provisions of the Hire-Purchase Act 1965 (*i*) certain sections of the Sale of Goods Act do not apply or are limited in their application. These agreements are also akin to hire-purchase agreements and several provisions relating to hire-purchase agreements are extended to them in the Hire-Purchase Act 1965 (*i*).

To the extent that they are governed by the law relating to sale of goods, credit-sale and conditional sale agreements are dealt with in this book.

Mortgage of goods.—A mortgage is sometimes called a conditional sale, but, as CAVE, J., has pointed out, a sale with a condition for re-sale to the original seller need have nothing to do with a mortgage (*k*). In a mortgage there is no sale of the goods and there is a debt always due from the mortgagor to the mortgagee, until it has been satisfied by payment or foreclosure (*k*). A mortgage of goods may be defined as a transfer of the general property in goods from mortgagor to mortgagee in order to secure a debt (*l*). This Act has no application to any mortgage, even though clad with the form of a contract of sale; see s. 62 (4), *post.* If a mortgage of goods be in writing, it usually comes within the Bills of Sale Acts 1878 and 1882 (*m*). But it seems that goods might be mortgaged by parol (*n*). If that be so, such a mortgage apparently comes under neither this Act nor the Bills of Sale Acts; for the latter Acts strike only at documents, and not at the transactions themselves (*o*).

Ltd., [1936] 3 All E. R. 473, C. A.; *St. Margaret's Trust* v. *Castle*, [1964] C. L. Y. 1685, C. A.

(*i*) The Hire-Purchase Act 1965 has been repealed by Sch. 5 of the Consumer Credit Act 1974 as from a date to be appointed pursuant to s. 192 (4) of that Act. As yet no date has been appointed and the 1965 Act remains in force. For the effect of the Consumer Credit Act 1974 on contracts for the sale of goods where credit is given by the seller, see p. 66, *ante*.

(*k*) *Beckett* v. *Tower Assets Co.*, [1891] 1 Q. B. 1, at p. 25; *cf. Manchester, Sheffield and Lincolnshire Rail Co.* v. *North Central Wagon Co.* (1888), 13 App. Cas. 554; and *Joblin* v. *Watkins and Roseveare, Ltd.*, [1949] 1 All E. R. 47.

(*l*) *Keith* v. *Burrows* (1876), 1 C. P. D. 722, at p. 731, *per* LINDLEY, J.; *Ex p. Hubbard* (1886), 17 Q. B. D. 690 at p. 698, *per* BOWEN, J. A Memorandum of a pledge of goods containing a power of sale is not a mortgage for stamp duty purposes: *Re Attenborough* (1855), 11 Exch. 461.

(*m*) 3 Halsbury's Statutes (3rd Edn.) 261.

(*n*) *Flory* v. *Denny* (1852), 7 Exch. 581 (no deed is necessary), and *cf. Reeves* v. *Capper* (1838), 5 Bing. N. C. 136; *Redhead* v. *Westwood* (1888), 59 L. T. 293; *Ramsay* v. *Margrett*, [1894] 2 Q. B. 18; *London and Yorkshire Bank* v. *White* (1895), 11 T. L. R. 570. There appears to be no statute requiring a mortgage of goods to be in writing.

(*o*) *North Central Wagon Co.* v. *Manchester, Sheffield and Lincolnshire Rail Co.* (1887), 35 Ch. D. 191, at p. 206, C. A.

Letters of hypothecation.—A letter of hypothecation of imported goods need not be registered as a bill of sale (*p*). The term "hypothecation" is somewhat loosely used. It usually denotes an equitable charge, without possession but not amounting to a mortgage (*q*).

Pledge.—A pledge may be defined as a delivery or bailment of goods by one person to another in order to secure payment of a debt (*r*). If the pledgor makes default in paying the debt the pledgee may sell the goods after notice to the pledgor (*s*). A pledge differs from a mortgage—(1) because the mortgagor may retain possession, while a pledge must be delivered to the pledgee; (2) because the mortgagee obtains the general property in the goods, while the pledgee only obtains a special property necessary to secure his rights (*t*). Note a wider definition of pledge given by s. 1 (5) of the Factors Act 1889, *post*, for the purposes of that Act.

Subsections (4) and (5).—The definition of "sale" has been criticised as failing to distinguish a contract, by which a right *in personam* is created, from a conveyance, by which a right *in rem* is transferred. But the language of English law is inveterate, an agreement to sell being known as an executory contract of sale, while a sale is known as an executed contract of sale.

The term "contract of sale" thus includes both actual sales and agreements for sale. It is important to distinguish clearly between the two classes of contract. An agreement to sell, or, as it is often called, an executory contract of sale, is a contract pure and simple; whereas a sale, or, as it is called for distinction, an executed contract of sale, is a contract plus a conveyance. By an agreement to sell a right *in personam* is created, by a sale a right *in rem* also is transferred. Where goods have been sold (even though not delivered), and the buyer makes default, the seller may sue for the contract price on the count of "goods bargained and sold", but where an agreement to buy is broken, the seller's normal

---

(*p*) Bills of Sale Act 1890; 3 Halsbury's Statutes (3rd Edn.) 270; as amended by Bills of Sale Act 1891 (3 Halsbury's Statutes (3rd Edn.) 271). As to registration of charges created by limited companies, see ss. 95–106 of the Companies Act 1948; 5 Halsbury's Statutes (3rd Edn.) 189 *et seq.*, as amended by the Companies Act 1980, Sch. 3, para. 15, and *Ladenburg & Co.* v. *Goodwin*, [1912] 3 K. B. 275 (hypothecation of proceeds of exported goods = charge on book debts); *Reed on Bills of Sale Acts* (14th ed.), pp. 78, 206.

(*q*) *Hart's Law of Banking* (4th ed.), p. 909; *Fisher and Lightwood's Law of Mortgages* (7th ed.), p. 112; *cf. Ex p. North Western Bank* (1872), L. R. 15 Eq. 69, at p. 73.

(*r*) *Story on Bailments* (9th ed.), pp. 7, 286; *cf. Blundell Leigh* v. *Attenborough*, [1921] 1 K. B. 382, 389 (nature of pledge and constructive delivery), reversed on inference of fact, but approved as to law, [1921] 3 K. B. 235, 239, C. A.

(*s*) *Story on Bailments* (9th ed.), p. 308, and see generally the notes to *Coggs* v. *Bernard*, 1 Smith L. C. (13th ed.), pp. 175, 201. The power of a pledgee to sell without the intervention of any court is peculiar to English law; see *The Odessa*, [1916] 1 A. C. 145, at p. 158, P. C. As to Scotland, see Green's *Encyclopædia of Scots Law*, tit. "pledge."

(*t*) *Halliday* v. *Holgate* (1868), L. R. 3 Exch. 299, see *per* WILLES, J.; *Ex p. Hubbard* (1886), 17 Q. B. D. 690, at p. 698; *Re Morritt* (1866), 18 Q. B. D. 222, at p. 232; see a mere lien distinguished from a pledge, *Donald* v. *Suckling* (1866), L. R. 1 Q. B. at p. 612; *cf. Howes* v. *Ball* (1827), 7 B. & C. 481 (hypothecation); and see pledge and sale contrasted, *Burdick* v. *Sewell* (1884), 13 Q. B. D. 159, at p. 175, C. A., and 10 App. Cas. 74, at p. 93.

remedy is an action for unliquidated damages (*u*). If an agreement to sell be broken by the seller, the buyer has only a personal remedy against the seller. The goods are still the property of the seller, and he can dispose of them as he likes; they may be taken in execution for his debts, and, if he becomes bankrupt, they pass to his trustee. But if there has been a sale, and the seller breaks his engagement to deliver the goods, the buyer has not only a personal remedy against the seller, but also remedies in respect of the goods themselves, such as the actions for wrongful interference with goods under the Tort (Interference with Goods) Act 1977. In many cases, too he can follow the goods into the hands of third parties. Again, if there be an agreement for sale, and the goods are destroyed, the loss as a rule falls on the seller, while if there has been a sale, the loss as a rule falls upon the buyer, though the goods have never come into his possession. See s. 20, *post*.

Subsection (6).—By s. 61, *post*, the term "sale" includes a bargain and sale, as well as a sale and delivery (*a*). According to the Civil Law which, with some statutory modifications, prevailed in Scotland before the 1893 Act, the property in the goods sold did not pass to the buyer until delivery (*b*), and then only if the price was paid or security found or credit given. But English law has rejected the objective test of delivery, and has adopted the rule that the property in the goods may be transferred by the contract itself if the parties so intend (*c*). The parties may make whatever bargain they please, and the law will give effect to it. When the parties express their intention clearly no difficulty arises. The contract may pass the property at once, or at a future time, or contingently on the performance of some condition (*d*). But in many cases the parties either form no intention on the point, or fail to express it. To meet such cases the Courts worked out a series of more or less artificial rules for determining when the property is to be deemed to pass, according to the imputed intention of the parties. These rules are now reproduced in s. 18 of the Act, *post*.

3. Capacity to buy and sell.—(1) Capacity to buy and sell is regulated by the general law concerning capacity to contract, and to transfer and acquire property (*e*).

(*u*) For exceptions see the comment to s. 49, *post*.

(*a*) As to the old distinction between the action for goods bargained and sold and the action for goods sold and delivered, see Bullen and Leake, *Prec. of Plead.* (3rd ed.), pp. 38–39; see also *Colley* v *Overseas Exporters*, [1921] 3 K. B. 302, 309–310, *per* McCardie, J.

(*b*) See *McBain* v. *Wallace* (1881), 6 App. Cas. 588, at pp. 605, 608, and Moyle's *Sale in the Civil Law*, p. 110.

(*c*) See *Blackburn on Sale* (1st ed.), pp. 187–197, who finds traces of the rule as far back as the time of Edward IV. The history of the question is treated exhaustively in the judgment in *Cochrane* v. *Moore* (1890), 25 Q. B. D. 57, C. A. (gift of a horse).

(*d*) *Johnson* v. *Macdonald* (1842), 9 M. & W. 600 (sale subject to arrival of ships with goods on board); *McEntire* v. *Crossley* (1895), A. C. 457, at p. 463 (hire-purchase). See s. 17, *post*, and *cf. The Parchim*, [1918] A. C. 157, *per* Lord Parker at pp. 160, 161.

(*e*) English law, unlike some continental codes, draws no general distinction between traders and non-traders.

(2) Where necessaries are sold and delivered to a minor or to a person who by reason of mental incapacity or drunkenness is incompetent to contract, he must pay a reasonable price for them (*f*).

(3) In subsection (2) above "necessaries" means goods suitable to the condition in life of the minor or other concerned person (*g*) and to his actual requirements at the time of the sale and delivery (*h*).

ILLUSTRATION

Clothes to the value of £145, including eleven fancy waistcoats, are supplied by a tailor to an infant undergraduate at Cambridge. The tailor must show that the goods were suitable to the condition in life of the infant and also that they were suitable to his actual requirements at the time of the sale and delivery (*i*).

Derivation.—Section 2 of the 1893 Act.

Definitions.—For "delivery," "property," and "sale," see s. 61 (1), *post*.

Cross-reference.—*Cf.* s. 8, *post* (reasonable price).

COMMENT

Capacity to contract must be distinguished from authority to contract. Capacity means power to bind oneself; authority means power to bind another. Capacity is part of the law of status; authority is part of the law of principal and agent. Capacity is usually a question of law; authority is usually a question of fact. This section deals only with the question of capacity to buy and sell. As regards authority to buy or sell on behalf of another there appears to be nothing peculiar to the contract of sale, except the provisions of the Factors Acts, *post*. On this subject, therefore, the reader is referred to general works on the law of Agency and Partnership, though certain special cases of authority are, for convenience, considered below. Section 62 (2), *post*, contains an express saving for the law of principal and agent.

Capacity.—The section is probably declaratory. As COTTON, L. J., has pointed out, when necessaries are supplied to a person who is incompetent to contract, the obligation to pay for them is quasi-

---

(*f*) *Ryder* v. *Wombwell* (1868), L. R. 4 Exch. 32, at p. 38, Ex. Ch. Lord BLANESBURGH in *Keane* v. *Mount Vernon Colliery Co.*, [1933] A. C. 309 at p. 328 said that the whole jurisprudence on this subject will be found in the judgment of WILLES, J., in this case (jewellery).

(*g*) *Ibid.; Peters* v. *Fleming* (1840), 6 M. & W. 42, at p. 46, *per* PARKE, B., and p. 48, *per* ALDERSON, B.

(*h*) *Barnes* v. *Toye* (1884), 13 Q. B. D. 410; *Johnstone* v. *Marks* (1887), 19 Q. B. D. 509, C. A.

(*i*) *Nash* v. *Inman*, [1908] 2 K. B. 1, at p. 5, C. A.

contractual and does not result from the agreement between the parties (*k*). He cannot bind himself to pay for them, but it is for his benefit that he should have them, and the law therefore will see that a fair price is paid therefor.

Mental patient.—As a rule, a contract made with a person who, at the time of contracting, is mentally disordered (*l*) to an extent such that his free and full consent is vitiated, cannot be enforced against him if the other contracting party knew the state of his mind; but such a person will still be under a quasi-contractual liability to pay for necessaries supplied to him (*m*).

Drunken man.—A contract made by a man is voidable at his option if, when he made it, he was so drunk as not to know what he was doing, and this fact was known to the other contracting party (*n*). But as POLLOCK, C. B., says, a drunkard is liable "when sober, for necessaries supplied to him when drunk" (*o*).

Infant or minor.—The term "minor" is the Scottish equivalent of the English term "infant." Since 1969, infants in England may also be described as minors (*p*). By s. 1 of the Infants Relief Act 1874 (*q*)

> "all contracts . . . for goods supplied, or to be supplied, other than contracts for necessaries, and all accounts stated with infants shall be absolutely void."

These words are apparently to be interpreted as meaning that all contracts imposing upon the infant the obligation to pay for goods other than necessaries shall be unenforceable against him whether the goods have been supplied to him in pursuance of the contract or not. "Absolutely void," does not mean that the transaction was wholly without effect, for it has been held in England that property in the goods can pass to the infant under the transaction (*r*). But the precise effect of those words is unclear. If they mean more than that the contract is voidable at the option of the infant, so that the adult party to the contract is not bound, then they have altered the common law rule to the prejudice of the infant. But the infant cannot claim specific

---

(*k*) *Re Rhodes* (1890), 44 Ch. D. 94, at pp. 105–107, C. A. See also *per* FLETCHER MOULTON, L. J., in *Nash* v. *Inman*, [1908] 2 K. B. 1, at p. 8, C. A.

(*l*) The expression comes from the Mental Health Act 1959; 25 Halsbury's Statutes (3rd Edn.) 42 and now presumably takes the place of the expressions "lunatic" and "person of unsound mind" in former use.

(*m*) *Re Rhodes* (1890), 44 Ch. D. 94, C. A. (necessaries); *Imperial Loan Co.* v. *Stone*, [1892] 1 Q. B. 599, C. A. (promissory note signed by defendant as surety); *York Glass Co., Ltd.* v. *Jubb* (1926), 134 L. T. 36, C. A. (contract for purchase of land). As to contracts by mentally disordered persons generally, see 17 L. Q. R. 147.

(*n*) *Gore* v. *Gibson* (1845), 13 M. & W. 623; *Matthews* v. *Baxter* (1873), L. R. 8 Exch. 132.

(*o*) *Gore* v. *Gibson* (1845), 13 M. & W. 623, at p. 625; see also *West Ham Union* v. *Pearson* (1890), 62 L. T. 638 (supply of necessaries to man suffering from delirium tremens).

(*p*) Section 12, Family Law Reform Act 1969.

(*q*) 17 Halsbury's Statutes (3rd Edn.) 412.

(*r*) *Stocks* v. *Wilson*, [1913] 2 K. B. 235; *Watts* v. *Seymour*, [1967] 1 All E. R. 1044; [1967] 2 Q. B. 647, D. C. In Canada it has been held that "absolutely void" prevents the passing of the property: *Prokopetz* v. *Richardson's Marina, Ltd.* (1978), 93 D. L. R. (3d) 442.

performance (*s*). Moreover, if an infant buys and pays for goods which are not necessaries he cannot recover the money he has paid (*t*), unless there has been a total failure of consideration (*u*). And if the infant has not paid for the goods which have been delivered to him he cannot be sued for their conversion, which would be possible if the property had not passed to him (*a*). It might, however, be held that in such cases the infant acquired the property not by virtue of the contract, but because there had been a delivery with the intention of passing the property (*b*) which would be operative even if the contract were void. Only a definite judical decision can settle the question. The language of that Act is consistent with the view that an infant might be liable on an executory contract to supply him with necessaries, and in a case where an infant contracted to go on a billiard tour which involved the supply of necessaries to him, HAMILTON, L. J., said he could not see

> "why a contract which is in itself binding, because it is a contract for necessaries not qualified by unreasonable terms, can cease to be binding merely because it is still executory" (*c*).

But an infant has never yet been held liable for breach of contract to accept necessaries, nor for necessaries bargained and sold but not delivered, and it will be observed that by the language of s. 2 it is necessary that the goods should be sold and delivered. The definition of necessaries also assumes that the goods have been delivered. As the law makes the contract for the infant, and for his benefit, he is only liable to pay a reasonable price, and not any price he may have been led to agree to.

An infant may marry, so he may make himself liable for necessaries supplied to his family (*d*). Theoretically, at any rate, English law, unlike Scottish law, "knows of no distinction between infants of tender and of mature years" (*e*).

Even where an infant has obtained goods in pursuance of a contract induced by his fraud, the seller cannot recover the price of the goods in

---

(*s*) *Lumley* v. *Ravenscroft*, [1895] 1 Q. B. 683, C. A.; 73 L. Q. R. 200; 74 L. Q. R. 99.

(*t*) *Hamilton* v. *Vaughan*, [1894] 3 Ch. 589, at p. 594. *Cf. Pearce* v. *Brain*, [1929] 2 K. B. 310 (a case of barter).

(*u*) *Valentini* v. *Canali* (1889), 24 Q. B. D. 166; *cf. Steinberg* v. *Scala* (*Leeds*), Ltd., [1923] 2 Ch. 452 (contract for sale of shares voidable at the infant's option). And see *Chaplin* v. *Leslie Frewin* (*Publishers*), [1965] 3 All E. R. 764, 770; [1966] Ch. 71, 90, *per* Lord DENNING, M. R.

(*a*) *Stocks* v. *Wilson*, [1913] 2 K. B. 235.

(*b*) *Simpson* v. *Nicholls* (1838), 3 M. & W. 240, at p. 244; and see the view expressed by LUSH, J., in *Stocks* v. *Wilson*, [1913] 2 K. B. 235.

(*c*) *Roberts* v. *Gray*, [1913] 1 K. B. 520, at p. 530, C. A.

(*d*) *Chapple* v. *Cooper* (1844), 13 M. & W. 252, at p. 259, *per* ALDERSON, B. (infant widow liable for husband's funeral expenses).

(*e*) *Morgan* v. *Thorne* (1841), 7 M. & W. 400, at p. 408, *per* PARKE, B. But obviously necessaries for a child of seven, and for a youth of seventeen, must stand on a different footing. As to Scotland, see Green's *Encyclopædia of Scots Law*, tits. "Minor" and "Sale".

any form of action, though perhaps on equitable principles the infant may be compelled to return the goods, or, if he has sold them, to account for the proceeds of the sale (*f*). Conversely, where an infant has contracted to sell goods and has received the price but not delivered the goods, or has delivered goods of an inferior quality, he cannot be sued either for damages or for the return of the price as money had and received (*g*), and, it is submitted, the effect of this rule cannot be avoided by framing the action in tort (*h*).

Meaning of necessaries.—A somewhat artificial definition of necessaries has been gradually evolved by the cases, and is now embodied in the concluding paragraph of the section. It is for the judge to explain to the jury the legal meaning of necessaries, and for the jury to say whether in any particular case the goods supplied are necessaries. But it is a question of law for the judge to determine in the first instance whether there is any evidence to go to the jury (*i*), and most of the reported cases are cases deciding whether there was any evidence, having regard to all the circumstances, which was fit to be considered, and are not to be taken as deciding that a particular article is or is not a necessary (*k*). The burden of proving that the goods supplied were necessaries lies on the party seeking to enforce the contract (*l*).

Articles of mere luxury are always excluded, though luxurious articles of utility are sometimes allowed (*m*).

Married women.—The Married Women (Restraint upon Anticipation) Act 1949 (*n*), abolished the last remaining incapacities of married women.

Enemy.—At common law an alien enemy is a person who carries on business or voluntarily resides in hostile territory, which includes territory permanently occupied by the enemy (*o*). Locality, and not nationality, furnishes the test (*p*). But by statute enemy status may be

(*f*) *Stocks* v. *Wilson*, [1913] 2 K. B. 235; *Leslie* v. *Sheill*, [1914] 3 K. B. 607, C. A. For the general rule that an infant's contract, unenforceable at law, cannot be enforced by the device of suing him in tort, see *Jennings* v. *Rundall* (1799), 8 Term Rep. 335; *Fawcett* v. *Smethurst* (1914), 84 L. J. K. B. 473; but *cf. Burnand* v. *Haggis* (1863), 14 C. B., N. S., 45; *Ballett* v. *Mingay*, [1943] 1 All E. R. 143; [1943] K. B. 281.

(*g*) *Cowern* v. *Nield*, [1912] 2 K. B. 419.

(*h*) *Leslie* v. *Sheill*, [1914] 3 K. B. 607, C. A. The contrary was suggested in *Cowern* v. *Nield* (*supra*), but this seems inconsistent with the views expressed in *Leslie* v. *Sheill*. See especially *per* KENNEDY, L. J., at p. 621.

(*i*) *Nash* v. *Inman*, [1908] 2 K. B. 1, C. A.; *cf. Stocks* v. *Wilson*, [1913] 2 K. B. 235, at p. 241.

(*k*) See, *e.g.*, *Elkington & Co., Ltd.* v. *Amery*, [1936] 2 All E. R. 86.

(*l*) *Nash* v. *Inman*, *supra*.

(*m*) *Chapple* v. *Cooper* (1844), 13 M. & W. 252, at p. 258; cited with approval in *Keane* v. *Mount Vernon Colliery Co.*, [1933] A. C. 309, at pp. 326, 327. And see *Clyde Cycle Co.* v. *Hargreaves* (1898), 78 L. T. 296 (racing bicycle a necessary); *Hewlings* v. *Graham* (1901), 70 L. J. Ch. 568 (cartridges and jewellery for girl friend not necessaries).

(*n*) 17 Halsbury's Statutes (3rd Edn.) 131.

(*o*) *Sovfracht* v. *Van Udens Scheepvaart*, [1943] 1 All E. R. 76; [1943] A. C. 203.

(*p*) *Janson* v. *Driefontein Consolidated Mines*, [1902] A. C. 484, at p. 505; *Porter* v. *Freudenberg*, [1915] 1 K. B. 857, C. A. As to a British registered company under enemy control, which gives it enemy status, see *The Daimler Co.* v. *Continental Tyre Co.*, [1916] 2 A.

imposed on enemy nationals and other persons having hostile associations outside enemy territory; see, *e.g.*, The Trading with the Enemy Act 1939 (*q*).

An enemy may be sued, and, as he may be sued, he may defend and appeal if judgment is given against him when defendant, but as a general rule (except by licence from the Crown) an enemy cannot sue in a British court or be the *actor* in any legal proceeding (*r*).

If an enemy has a right of action which accrued before war, the right is suspended during war, but revives when peace is declared (*s*). For example, if goods are sold and delivered by a German firm to an English firm before war, no action for the price can be maintained during war (*t*). As soon as war is declared all commercial intercourse with the enemy is prohibited, and if and in so far as any contract is executory, and its due fulfilment would involve intercourse with the enemy, the contract is dissolved. See p. 18, *ante*, and the Law Reform (Frustrated Contracts) Act 1943, in Appendix I, *post*.

C. 387, and see the Trading with the Enemy Act 1939, as to enemy-controlled corporations.

(*q*) It is outside the scope of this book to deal with the general subject of trading with the enemy, as to which see generally Howard, *Trading with the Enemy* (1943).

(*r*) *Porter* v. *Freudenberg*, [1915] 1 K. B. 857, C. A.; *Ex p. Marum* (1915), 84 L. J. K. B. 1893. But an alien enemy may be joined *pro forma* as a plaintiff in a partnership action: *Rodriguez* v. *Speyer Brothers*, [1919] A. C. 59; and an interned enemy may sue: *Schaffenius* v. *Goldberg*, [1916] 1 K. B. 284, C. A. For cases arising out of the last war, see *Sovfracht* v. *Van Udens Scheepvaart*, [1943] 1 All E. R. 76; [1943] A. C. 203 (affirming the general rules as to an enemy plaintiff's incapacity to sue as laid down in *Porter* v. *Freudenberg, supra*); *Eichengruen* v. *Mond*, [1940] 3 All E. R. 148, C. A.; [1940] Ch. 785 (power to strike out enemy plaintiff's statement of claim delivered before outbreak of war if frivolous and vexatious); *re Churchill & Co., Ltd. and Lonberg*, [1941] 3 All E. R. 137 (as to service on enemy defendant); *Schering, Ltd.* v. *Stockholms Enskilda Bank A.B.*, [1946] 1 All E. R. 36; [1946] A. C. 219 (war does not abrogate or discharge a debt incurred before the declaration of war and so obligation to pay and right to recover are only suspended). See also *Arab Bank, Ltd.* v. *Barclays Bank (D.C. & O.)*, [1954] 2 All E. R. 226; [1954] A. C. 495; *Vamvakas* v. *Custodian of Enemy Property*, [1952] 1 All E. R. 629; [1952] 2 Q. B. 183 (difference between meaning of "enemy" under the Statute and at common law discussed). *Maerkle* v. *British & Continental Fur Co., Ltd.*, [1954] 3 All E. R. 50 (statement of claim struck out as disclosing no reasonable cause of action since the plaintiffs were "enemies" at time of transaction and by Trading with the Enemy (Custodian) Order 1951, the property concerned vested in the custodian of enemy property); *Kuenigl* v. *Donnersmarck*, [1955] 1 All E. R. 46; [1955] 1 Q. B. 515 (an English company may be prejudiced if under enemy control in that it may have enemy character conferred upon it, but it remains English and still subject to English law). *Bevan* v. *Bevan*, [1955] 2 All E. R. 206; [1955] 2 Q. B. 227 ("enemy" plaintiff succeeded in action for maintenance due under separation agreement of 1932, since the agreement continued to subsist at common law—public policy not requiring its termination on the outbreak of war—and so defendant was subject to s. 7 of the 1939 Act and should have paid the sum due to the Custodian).

(*s*) *Janson* v. *Driefontein Consolidated Mines*, [1902] A. C. 484, at p. 499; *Porter* v. *Freudenberg*, [1915] 1 K. B. 857, at p. 873, C. A. Under the old form of pleading, the plea of "alien enemy" was usually raised by a dilatory plea and perhaps could not be raised by a plea in bar.

(*t*) *Wolf & Sons* v. *Carr Parker & Co.* (1915), 31 T. L. R. 407, C. A. Note a Scottish case, which goes further than English law by allowing a former alien enemy to recover a prepaid instalment of the price where the contract was dissolved by war; *Cantiere San Rocco* v. *Clyde Shipbuilding Co.*, [1924] A. C. 226.

Registration of business names.—Speaking generally, a person or firm may trade in any name that person or firm likes to adopt. But under the Registration of Business Names Act 1916, an individual who carries on business in any name other than his own, and a firm whose firm name does not disclose the names of all the partners, must register the name in which the business is carried on and give the particulars required by the Act. By s. 8 of the Act, if default is made in complying with the provisions of the Act, the defaulter cannot maintain any action to enforce any contract made or entered into in relation to the business unless the court, for cause shown, grants him relief (*u*).

Conflict of laws.—There is only one English case dealing with this aspect of capacity: *Male* v. *Roberts* (*a*), decided over 180 years ago, in which Lord ELDON is reported to have referred the question to "the laws of that country where the contract arises." In that case, the *lex loci contractus* was the same as the proper law, and both the decision and the report are unsatisfactory in many respects. There are dicta in other English cases some of which favour the *lex loci contractus* as determining capacity (*b*), and some the *lex domicilii* (*c*).

Of the various views put forward in these cases, in decisions in other common law jurisdictions (*d*), and by modern text-book writers, the best seems to be that questions of capacity to enter into mercantile or commercial contracts should fall to be decided by the proper law of the contract (*e*).

Agency.—*Power of wife to bind husband.*—

Where husband and wife are living together, there is a presumption of fact that the wife has the husband's authority to pledge his credit for necessaries (*f*). This presumption may be rebutted by the husband in the following ways at least:

(a) by proof that the tradesman concerned had been expressly warned not to supply the wife with goods on credit;

(b) by proof that the wife was already adequately supplied with necessaries (*g*);

(c) by proof that the wife had an adequate allowance for the purchase of necessaries (*h*);

(d) by proof that the wife had been expressly forbidden by the

---

(*u*) As to the scope of this enactment, see *Daniel* v. *Rogers*, [1918] 2. K. B. 228, C. A.; *Watson* v. *Park Royal*, [1961] 2 All E. R. 346; [1961] 1 W. L. R. 727.

(*a*) (1800), 3 Esp. 163.

(*b*) *E.g.*, *Sottomayor* v. *de Barros* (1877), 3 P. D. 1, 5; *Cooper* v. *Cooper* (1888), 13 App. Cas. 88, 99, 100.

(*c*) *E. g.*, *Simonin* v. *Mallac* (1860), 2 Sw. & Tr. 67; *Sottomayor* v. *de Barros* (1879), 5 P. D. 94; *Baindail (otherwise Lawson)* v. *Baindail*, [1946] 1 All E. R. 342; [1946] P. 122, C. A.

(*d*) See these reviewed in Dicey and Morris, *Conflict of Laws* (10th ed.), Rule 147.

(*e*) *Charron* v. *Montreal Trust* (1958), 15 D. L. R. (2d.) 240.

(*f*) *Debenham* v. *Mellon* (1880), 6 App. Cas. 24, especially at pp. 32, 36 and 37; *Miss Gray, Ltd.* v. *Earl of Cathcart* (1922), 38 T. L. R. 562 (all the exceptions reviewed).

(*g*) *Seaton* v. *Benedict* (1828), 5 Bing. 28.

(*h*) *Morel* v. *Earl of Westmorland*, [1904] A. C. 11.

husband to pledge his credit (*i*), but if the husband has on previous occasions held his wife out as having authority to bind him, he will be estopped from relying on an express prohibition unless he has given express notice of it to the tradesman concerned (*k*).

But if the wife has separate estate and credit is given solely to her, the husband is not liable (*l*).

Formerly, a wife could also pledge her husband's credit for necessaries in certain circumstances as an agent of necessity (*m*). This power has now been abolished by s. 41 (1) of the Matrimonial Proceedings and Property Act 1970 (*n*).

Divorced woman.—A woman who is divorced, or who is judicially separated from her husband, is on the same footing as a single woman.

Mistress.—When a woman is living with a man as his wife, she has, while so living with him, the like authority to pledge his credit for necessaries as if she were married to him (*o*).

Parent and child.—A father is not liable for necessaries supplied to his infant child without his authority, nor is the mother, though she have separate estate (*p*). But authority or ratification is inferred on slight evidence (*q*).

Master of ship.—The master of a ship has implied authority to bind the owner for the price of necessaries supplied for the ship (*r*).

Clubs and messes.—A member of a club is not liable for goods supplied to the club unless he has expressly or impliedly authorised the supply, and in determining that question the rules of the club are relevant (*s*). A commanding officer, as such, is not liable for goods ordered by the Mess Committee (*t*).

(*i*) *Jolly* v. *Rees* (1863), 15 C. B., N. S., 628.

(*k*) *Jetley* v. *Hill* (1884), Cab. & El. 239; see also *Hunt* v. *Blaquiere* (1829), 5 Bing. 550, at p. 560; *Swan & Edgar* v. *Mathieson* (1910), 103 L. T. 832.

(*l*) *Callot* v. *Nash* (1923), 39 T. L. R., 291. The mere fact that the wife has separate estate does not negative the husband's liability.

(*m*) See p. 27 of the 15th edition of the present work.

(*n*) 40 Halsbury's Statutes (3rd Edn.) 836.

(*o*) *Ryan* v. *Sams* (1848), 12 Q. B. D. 460.

(*p*) *Mortimore* v. *Wright* (1846), 6 M. & W. 482, 486 (father); *Hodgens* v. *Hodgens* (1837), 4 Cl. & F. 323, 375, H. L. (mother with separate estate).

(*q*) *Baker* v. *Keen* (1819), 2 Stark. 501; *Bazeley* v. *Forder* (1868), L. R. 3 Q. B. 559.

(*r*) *Mackintosh* v. *Mitcheson* (1849), 4 Exch. 175. As to the nature of the master's contract when he draws a bill for the price, see *The Ripon City*, [1897] P. 226, at p. 231; *Pocahontas Fuel Co.* v. *Ambatielos* (1922), 27 Com. Cas. 148 (master's authority to draw, course of dealing). The price of necessaries supplied to a ship may be also recovered by action *in rem* against the ship: *The Mogileff*, [1921] P. 236.

(*s*) *Leake on Contracts* (8th ed.), p. 395; *Wertheimer on Clubs* (6th ed.), p. 63 *et seq.*; 6 Halsbury's Laws (4th Edn.) paras. 268 *et seq.*

(*t*) *Lascelles* v. *Rathbun* (1919), 35 T. L. R. 347, C. A.; *cf. Cross* v. *Williams* (1862), 31 L. J. Ex. 145 (goods supplied to Volunteer Corps where there was authority).

Formalities of the Contract

4. How contract of sale is made.—(1) Subject to this and any other Act (*u*), a contract of sale may be made in writing (either with or without seal), or by word of mouth, or partly in writing and partly by word of mouth (*a*), or may be implied from the conduct of the parties (*b*).

(2) Nothing in this section shall affect the law relating to corporations.

Derivation.—Section 3 of the 1893 Act.

Definitions.—For "contract of sale," see s. 2(1), *ante*, and s. 61(1), *post*. For "writing," see Sch. 1 and Sch. 2, para. 4(2) of the Interpretation Act 1978.

COMMENT

A written offer to sell goods may be orally accepted, and *vice versa*. Where a man goes into a restaurant, orders a dinner and eats it, obviously there is a sale though no mention be made of buying, or selling, or price. If, however, the parties have put a contract of sale into writing, the ordinary rules of evidence apply. See as to these rules, p. 4, *ante*.

Corporations.—Limited companies and, in England and Wales, all other corporations now contract exactly like private persons (*c*). But a contract which is required to be made in a special form, and which a private individual might vary or discharge without formalities, can only be varied or discharged by a limited company or other corporation in the manner it can be made (*d*).

Subject Matter of Contract

5. Existing or future goods.—(1) The goods which form the subject of a contract of sale may be either existing goods, owned or possessed by the seller, or goods to be manufactured or acquired by the seller after the making of the contract of sale, in this Act called future goods (*e*).

(2) There may be a contract for the sale of goods, the

(*u*) See the Merchant Shipping Act 1894, ss. 24, 26, 65; as amended by the Merchant Shipping Act 1965, Sch. 2; transfer of British ships and shares therein by bill of sale only. *Cf. Manchester Ship Canal Co.* v. *Horlock*, [1914] 2 Ch. 199, C. A. (ship sunk in fairway, sold by harbour authority).

(*a*) *Lockett* v. *Nicklin* (1848), 2 Exch. 93.

(*b*) *Brogden* v. *Metropolitan Rail. Co.* (1877), 2 App. Cas. 666.

(*c*) Companies Act 1948, s. 32; Corporate Bodies' Contracts Act 1960.

(*d*) Companies Act 1948, s. 33 (3); Corporate Bodies' Contracts Act 1960, s. 1 (3).

(*e*) *Ajello* v. *Worsley*, [1898] 1 Ch. 274. (I have no piano by Ajello in stock and the maker has refused to supply me with one, yet I may contract to sell you such an article since I might be able to obtain one from another dealer.)

acquisition of which by the seller depends upon a contingency which may or may not happen (*f*).

(3) Where by a contract of sale the seller purports to effect a present sale of future goods, the contract operates as as an agreement to sell the goods (*g*).

Derivation.—Section 5 of the 1893 Act.

Definitions.—For "contract of sale," "goods," and "seller," see s. 61 (1), *post*. The definition of "future goods" is also repeated in that subsection.

History.—*Subsection* (1).—The Roman lawyers doubted whether an agreement to sell "future goods" constituted a contract of sale, but it is long since any such question has been raised in English law (*h*). The term "future goods" is not a very happy one, but the alternative "after-to-be-acquired goods" was impossible.

Subsection (2).—There is very little English authority on the point. "No doubt," says MARTIN, B., "a man may buy the chance of obtaining goods," but he then goes on to say that in the case he was dealing with the plaintiff bought the goods themselves (*i*). Perhaps the doubtful case of *Bagueley* v. *Hawley* (*k*) may be explained on the ground that the plaintiff there bought another man's bargain at an auction for what it was worth, and not the goods themselves (*l*).

In *Howell* v. *Coupland* (*m*), there was a contract to supply 200 tons of potatoes to be grown on a particular farm and the crop failed. It was held that neither party was liable under the contract, as performance was impossible.

It was the opinion of Sir MCKENZIE CHALMERS that this rule was preserved by s. 7, *post*, but it has now been held (*n*) that it is either embodied in this subsection or else is preserved as one of the common law principles retained by s. 62 (2), *post* (*o*).

Subsection (3).—There was one case in which it was supposed at common law that future goods could be assigned. It was said that a man might sell future goods which had a "potential existence," and that then

---

(*f*) *Watts* v. *Friend* (1830), 10 B. & C. 446 (sale of crop not yet sown); *Hale* v. *Rawson* (1858), 4 C. B. N. S., 85 (sale of goods contingent on safe arrival of ship carrying them); see p. 17, *ante*, and see also comment to s. 2(3), *ante*, and s. 7, *post*.

(*g*) *Lunn* v. *Thornton* (1845), 1 C. B. 379 (trover for furniture); *cf. Heseltine* v. *Siggers* (1848), 1 Exch. 856 ("bought and sold" in relation to stock may mean *agreed* to be bought or sold).

(*h*) *Hibblewhite* v. *M'Morine* (1839), 5 M. & W. 462, at p. 466. Section 7 of the Statute of Frauds (Amendment) Act 1828 (Lord Tenterden's Act; 9 Geo. 4, c. 14, *repealed*), at any rate, concluded the question in England.

(*i*) *Buddle* v. *Green* (1857), 27 L. J. Ex. 33, at p. 34 (goods in hands of wharfinger).

(*k*) (1867), L. R. 2 C. P. 625.

(*l*) *Cf. Chapman* v. *Speller* (1850), 14 Q. B. 621 (sale by sheriff and sub-sale).

(*m*) (1876), 1 Q. B. D. 258.

(*n*) *Sainsbury, Ltd.* v. *Street*, [1972] 3 All E. R. 1127; [1972] 1 W. L. R. 834.

(*o*) For those principles, see *Taylor* v. *Caldwell* (1863), 3 B. & S. 826; *Appleby* v. *Myers* (1867), L. R. 2 C. P. 651.

the legal property in them would pass to the buyer as soon as they came into actual existence. Goods were supposed to have a potential existence if they would naturally grow out of anything already owned by the seller. For instance, it was said a man might sell the wool to be grown on sheep which he then had, but not the wool on sheep which he was going to buy (*p*). There seems to be no rational distinction between one class of future goods and another (*q*).

COMMENT

Assignment of "future goods".—The conditions under which an ordinary agreement to sell becomes a sale are dealt with in s. 2, *ante*, and ss. 16–20, *post*. But sometimes a contract purports presently to assign goods to be acquired in the future (*r*). In such case the legal property in the goods does not pass to the buyer unless and until the seller does some act irrevocably appropriating them to the contract (*s*), or the buyer takes possession of them under a licence to seize, which is equivalent to a delivery by the seller (*t*). But if the goods assigned be sufficiently described to become specific or ascertained goods on acquisition by the seller, the equitable interest in them passes to the buyer as soon as they are so acquired (*u*):

> "A man cannot in equity, any more than at law, assign what has no existence. A man can contract to assign property which is to come into existence in the future, and when it has come into existence equity, treating as done that which ought to be done, fastens upon that property, and the contract to assign thus becomes a complete assignment" (*a*).

It is only the equitable interest which passes to the buyer by the contract; hence his rights are liable to be defeated if, before he gets the legal property in the goods, the seller disposes of them to a second purchaser without notice, who thus first obtains the legal estate (*b*).

If there is a contract for the sale of future goods and only part of those goods come into existence, it is a question of construction of the contract in all the circumstances whether the seller is bound to deliver and the buyer to accept those goods or whether the contract is discharged (*c*).

(*p*) *Grantham* v. *Hawley* (1615), Hobart Rep. 132, 2 Roll. 48, pl. 20.

(*q*) It might possibly be contended that goods having a potential existence do not come within the definition of "future goods," inasmuch as they accrue to the seller, and are not "acquired by" him.

(*r*) See such a contract distinguished from an agreement to sell *plus* a licence to seize: *Reeve* v. *Whitmore* (1863), 4 De G. J. & S. 1.

(*s*) *Langton* v. *Higgins* (1859), 4 H. & N. 402 (sale of future crop).

(*t*) *Congreve* v. *Evetts* (1854), 10 Exch. 298; *Hope* v. *Hayley* (1856), 5 E. B. 830.

(*u*) *Re Wait*, [1927] 1 Ch. 606, C. A., explaining *Holroyd* v. *Marshall* (1862), 10 H. L. Cas. 191; *cf. Tailby* v. *Official Receiver* (1888), 13 App. Cas. 523. But see further the discussion of *re Wait* in the comment to s. 16, *post*.

(*a*) *Collyer* v. *Isaacs* (1881), 19 Ch. D. 342, at pp. 351, 354, C. A.

(*b*) *Joseph* v. *Lyons* (1884), 15 Q. B. D. 280, C. A.; *Hallas* v. *Robinson* (1885), 15 Q. B. D. 288, C. A. (bill of sale cases).

(*c*) *Sainsbury* v. *Street*, [1972] 3 All E. R. 1127; [1972] 1 W. L. R. 834 (seller not excused

6. Goods which have perished.—Where there is a contract for the sale of specific goods, and the goods without the knowledge of the seller have perished at the time when the contract is made, the contract is void (*d*).

Derivation.—Section 6 of the 1893 Act.

Definitions.—For "contract of sale," see s. 2 (1), *ante*, and s. 61 (1), *post*. For "goods," "seller" and "specific goods," see s. 61 (1), *post*.

Cross-reference.—*Cf.* the narrower s. 7, *post*, which applies only to agreements to sell.

COMMENT

The rule in this section has at different times been said to be based either on the ground of common mistake (*e*), or on the ground of impossibility of performance, or on an implied condition precedent that the goods exist (*f*). The rule is confined to the case of specific goods. Generic goods, that is to say, goods defined by description only, come within the maxim *genus numquam perit* (*g*).

The rules of the common law are expressly preserved by s. 62 (2), *post*, except insofar as they are inconsistent with the express provisions of the Act. The common law rule embodied in this section appears to be that if the parties contract that one of them shall do something which without any fault on his part and without the knowledge of either of them at the time is impossible, then the contract is void (*h*), but it will not be void if one of the parties warrants that performance is possible (*i*). Generally, a

---

from delivering lesser quantity if buyer willing to take it).

(*d*) *Couturier* v. *Hastie* (1856), 5 H. L. Cas. 673 (cargo of corn).

(*e*) *Bell* v. *Lever Brothers*, [1932] A. C. 161, 217; and see *Barrow Lane and Ballard, Ltd.* v. *Phillip Phillips and Co., Ltd.*, [1929] 1 K. B. 574, at p. 582 (total failure of consideration and mistake).

(*f*) *Bell* v. *Lever Brothers, supra*, at p. 224; *Solle* v. *Butcher*, [1949] 2 All E. R. 1107, at p. 1119; [1950] 1 K. B. 671, at p. 681.

(*g*) *Re Thornett and Fehr and Yuills*, [1921] 1 K. B. 219; *Hayward Brothers* v. *Daniel* (1904), 91 L. T. 319.

(*h*) See *e.g. Cox* v. *Prentice* (1815), 3 M. & S. 344; *Couturier* v. *Hastie, supra; Clifford* v. *Watts* (1870), L. R. 5 C. P. 577; *Griffith* v. *Brymer* (1903), 19 T. L. R. 434 (contract to hire room to watch coronation of Edward VII; coronation cancelled before contract made; contract void). The mistake must be fundamental (*Bell* v. *Lever Bros., Ltd.*, [1932] A. C. 161, H. L.). There is, however, no clear authority as to what mistakes in relation to the sale of goods will be fundamental, other than a mistake as to their existence. See further *Benjamin's Sale of Goods*, paras. 218–224. "Void" in this context has commonly been assumed to mean of no effect whatsoever. But it is not always used in this sense, and both at common law and when used in statutes has been construed as meaning "voidable" at the option of one or both parties; see, *e.g., Cox v. Prentice, supra, per* BAYLEY, J.; and see generally *Stroud's Judicial Dictionary* (4th ed.)., p. 2951.

(*i*) *Clifford* v. *Watts* (1870), L. R. 5 C. P. 577, at pp. 585, 588. This case was one of those cited by Sir McKenzie Chalmers, who does not appear to have regarded this section as altering the common law: see the 1st edition of this work at p. 10, and the 2nd edition at p. 16. See also *Produce Brokers Co.* v. *Olympia Oil and Cake Co.*, [1917] 1 K. B. 320, 330, C. A. (custom that buyer must accept seller's appropriation although goods at time of appropriation were lost); *Produce Brokers Co.* v. *Olympia Oil and Cake Co.* (1914), 84 L. J. K. B. 1153, C. A., and [1916] 1 A. C. 314 (arbitrator may find custom). *Cf.* Treitel, *Law of Contract* (5th ed.), pp. 207, 208, where it is suggested that s. 6 cannot be excluded.

seller will not be treated as warranting the existence of goods (*k*), but such a warranty has been implied by the High Court of Australia in a case where the goods never existed (*l*).

There is no authority as to the meaning of "perish" in relation to this section, but it has been held at first instance in relation to s. 7 that rotten potatoes which cannot be used are still potatoes so long as they are in a form which permits of their being called potatoes (*m*). The case has, however, been criticised (*n*). Probably, the precise meaning of "perish" is academic, for if goods have so deteriorated that at common law the contract is void, or in the case of s. 7 avoided, then it will be irrelevant whether they have perished within the meaning of this section or s. 7.

If the basis of the rule is as stated above, there seems no reason why the situation should differ, in the absence of some special agreement, where for some other reason than the fact that goods have perished, by reason of facts for which neither party is responsible and of which neither was aware, the seller cannot perform and does not purport to perform his obligations under the contract (*o*). Indeed, even if the contract is not void, it may be set aside in equity "if the parties were under a common misapprehension either as to facts or as to their relative and respective rights, provided that the misapprehension was fundamental and that the party seeking to set it aside was not himself at fault" (*p*).

But if the goods are defective, and the seller nevertheless supplies them (*q*), he warrants that they are of the contract quality, and will no longer be able to treat the contract as void.

(*k*) *Barrow Lane and Ballard, Ltd.* v. *Phillip Phillips and Co., Ltd.*, [1929] 1 K. B. 574, at p. 582.

(*l*) *McRae* v. *Commonwealth Disposals Commission* (1950), 84 C. L. R. 377.

(*m*) *Horn* v. *Minister of Food*, [1948] 2 All E. R. 1036.

(*n*) Atiyah, *Sale of Goods* (5th ed.), p. 46. *Cf. Rendell* v. *Turnbull* (1908), 27 N. Z. L. R. 1067, where there was a contract for the sale of 75 tons of table-potatoes, which, unknown to the seller, were at the time of the contract unfit for human consumption. The contract was held to be void because the potatoes had ceased to be "table-potatoes".

(*o*) It has been said that mistakes as to quality are not fundamental (see *Benjamin's Sale of Goods*, para. 220, and cases there cited). But if the defect is such that it would be a breach of contract to tender the goods in that condition, and the defect is irremediable, it is difficult to see why the rights of the parties should turn on the philosophical question whether the goods still permit of being called by their original description. In *Couturier* v. *Hastie*, *supra*, it was assumed on the basis of *Barr* v. *Gibson* (1838), 3 M. & W. 390, that the contract would not be void if the goods still existed in a defective condition, but *Barr* v. *Gibson* was decided on the basis that there was no implied warranty of the good quality or condition of the chattel sold—see at p. 399. While there are authorities that a mistake as to quality will not in general affect the validity of a contract (see *Benjamin's Sale of Goods*, para. 220) in none of those authorities would the defect in quality have meant that the seller could not perform his obligations under the contract. Moreover, if the seller does not warrant that the goods exist when the contract is made (see n. (*k*), *supra*) it is a little difficult to see why he sould be responsible for their quality at that stage.

(*p*) *Solle* v. *Butcher*, [1949] 2 All E. R. 1107, at p. 1120; [1950] 1 K. B. 671, at p. 693, *per* DENNING, L.J. This statement of principle was held by GOFF, J., in *Grist* v. *Bailey*, [1966] 2 All E. R. 875; [1967] Ch. 532, to have been the basis of the decision in *Solle* v. *Butcher* and to be binding on him. But this remedy is discretionary and subject to the usual limitations on the equitable remedy of rescission.

(*q*) It has been held in relation to the Trade Descriptions Act 1968 that goods are

There may be some cases where upon the true construction of the contract the buyer may have the option of taking incomplete or damaged goods (*r*).

7. Goods perishing before sale but after agreement to sell.—Where there is an agreement to sell specific goods and subsequently the goods, without any fault on the part of the seller or buyer, perish (*s*) before the risk passes to the buyer, the agreement is avoided (*t*).

Derivation.—Section 7 of the 1893 Act.

Definitions.—For "contract of sale," see s. 2 (1), *ante*, and s. 61 (1), *post*. For "buyer," "fault," "goods," "seller" and "specified goods," see s. 62 (1), *post*.

Cross-references.—*Cf*. s. 20, *post* (risk generally), and s. 33, *post* (risk where distant delivery).

COMMENT

"Specific goods".—It was the opinion of Sir McKenzie Chalmers that this section applies to specifically described goods, whether in existence at the time the contract was made or not. He cited the opinion of MELLISH, L. J., in *Howel* v. *Coupland* (*u*), where there was a contract to supply 200 tons of potatoes to be grown on a particular farm and the crop failed, that

> "This is not like the case of a contract to deliver so many goods of a particular kind, where no specific goods are to be sold. Here there was an agreement to sell and buy 200 tons out of a crop to be grown on specific land, so that it is an agreement to sell what will be, and may be called specific things; therefore neither party is liable if the performance becomes impossible."

This involved giving to the word "specific" in the section a meaning which differs from that given in the definition clause, and it has now been held in *Sainsbury, Ltd.* v. *Street* (*a*), that this section does not apply to such a contract but that the decision in *Howell* v. *Coupland* would be

---

supplied when they are delivered or in some cases when the buyer is notified that they are available for delivery; *Ress* v. *Munday*, [1974] 3 All E. R. 506; [1974] 1 W. L. R. 1284, D. C. In the context of s. 14, *post*, "supplied" would seem to involve at least the seller parting with possession of the goods.

(*r*) *Cf. Sainsbury* v. *Street*, [1972] 3 All E. R. 1127; [1972] 1 W. L. R. 834. But see *Barrow Lane and Ballard* v. *Phillip Phillips & Co.*, [1929] 1 K. B. 574, at p. 583 (sale of 700 bags of nuts, 109 of which perished before the contract; buyer could not be compelled to take 591 bags).

(*s*) See comment to s. 6, *ante*.

(*t*) *Elphick* v. *Barnes* (1860), 5 C. P. D. 321 (death of a horse delivered on sale or return).

(*u*) (1876), 1 Q. B. D. 258, at p. 262.

(*a*) [1972] 3 All E. R. 1127; [1972] 1 W. L. R. 834, adopting the opinion of ATKIN, L. J. in *re Wait*, [1927] 1 Ch. 606, at p. 630, C. A.

covered by s. 5 (2), *ante*, or by the common law principles retained by s. 62 (2), *post*, of the Act (*b*).

See as to frustration of contracts generally, p. 17, *ante*.

The present section deals with a case of impossibility peculiar to the law of sale, and it is to be noted that the provisions of s. 1 of the Law Reform (Frustrated Contracts) Act 1943 (*post*, Appendix I) do not apply to any contract to which s. 7 of the Sale of Goods Act applies (*c*).

The Price

8. Ascertainment of price.—(1) The price in a contract of sale may be fixed by the contract, or may be left to be fixed in a manner agreed by the contract, or may be determined by the course of dealing between the parties (*d*).

(2) Where the price is not determined as mentioned in subsection (1) above the buyer must pay a reasonable price (*e*).

(3) What is a reasonable price is a question of fact dependent on the circumstances of each particular case.

Derivation.—Section 8 of the 1893 Act.

Definitions.—For "contract of sale," see s. 2 (1), *ante*, and s. 61 (1), *post*.

Cross-references.—*Cf.* s. 9, *post* (sale at valuation), and s. 49, *post* (action for price).

History.—The doctrine of implied or reasonable price seems to be an original development of English law. The rule of Roman law was that the price, or the mode of fixing it, must be expressed in the contract itself (*f*). If the price was not fixed, the contract was classed as innominate.

According to Roman law, the price must be a serious price (*g*), but English courts have always declined to enquire into the adequacy of any *bona fide* consideration.

Comment

The "price" of a thing is its agreed or estimated value expressed in terms of the currency of the country.

(*b*) For these principles, see *Taylor* v. *Caldwell* (1863), 3 B. & S. 826; *Appleby* v. *Myers* (1867), L. R. 2 C. P. 651.

(*c*) Or to any contract for the sale of specific goods which is frustrated by the fact that the goods have perished: s. 2 (5) (c).

(*d*) *Arcos, Ltd.* v. *Aronson* (1930), 36 Ll. L. Rep. 108 (price to be decided by arbitration); *Gibraltar Packers, Ltd.* v. *Basic Economy and Development Corporation*, [1966] 1 Lloyd's Rep. 615. As to usage to deduct discount, see *Brown* v. *Byrne* (1854), 3 E. & B. 703.

(*e*) *Valpy* v. *Gibson* (1847), 4 C. B. 837, 864; *cf. Jewry* v. *Busk* (1814), 5 Taunt. 302; *Mack and Edwards (Sales), Ltd.* v. *McPhail Brothers* (1968), 112 Sol. Jo. 211, C. A.

(*f*) *Inst. III.*, 23.

(*g*) De Zulueta, *The Roman Law of Sale*, pp. 19–20.

"The technical term which has been invariably adopted for the numerical expression of the values of commodities, in terms of the standard, is 'price'" (*h*).

Where the alleged contract provided for "prices to be agreed upon from time to time," the House of Lords held that there was no contract at all, but a mere agreement to agree, and s. 8 (2) could only be brought into play where the contract was totally silent about the price (*i*). The principle seems to be that there is no contract unless the price is determined by the contract or is determinable otherwise than by a fresh agreement between the parties (*k*).

The further the parties have gone on with their contract, the more ready are the courts to imply any reasonable term to give effect to their intentions (*l*). In one recent case, the parties had disagreed as to the price, but the seller had nonetheless delivered, and the buyer accepted and used the goods. The Court of Appeal held that had the "contract" been executory, there would have been no contract, but since the goods had been delivered, there was a necessary implication from the conduct of the parties that the buyer would pay a reasonable price (*m*).

In another case, the contract was for the sale of certain land at a price fixed by the contract, and also of all the petrol required from time to time at a petrol filling station "at a price to be agreed by the parties in writing from time to time". The contract contained an arbitration clause providing for the submission to arbitration of any dispute or difference on "the subject matter or construction" of the agreement; it was held that a term must be implied in the agreement, under the

---

(*h*) Scott's *Money and Banking*, p. 34. As to legal tender, see p. 223, *post*. As to varying meanings of the term "Currency," see *Banque Belge* v. *Hambrouck*, [1921] 1 K. B. 321, at p. 326. As to foreign currencies, see *post*, notes to s. 54.

(*i*) *May and Butcher* v. *R.*, [1934] 2 K. B. 17 *n.*, H. L. (decided in 1929). *Cf. Hillas* v. *Arcos* (1932), 38 Com. Cas. 23, H. L.; *Scammell* v. *Ouston*, [1941] 1 All E. R. 14; [1941] A. C. 251; *British Bank for Foreign Trades* v. *Novimex*, [1949] 1 All E. R. 155, C. A.; [1949] 1 K. B. 623; *Loftus* v. *Roberts* (1902), 18 T. L. R. 532 (explaining the older cases), and the judgment of DENNING, L. J., in *Nicolene* v. *Simmonds*, [1953] 1 All E. R. 822; [1953] 1 Q. B. 543.

(*k*) In Scotland the Court of Session has held that, in very special circumstances and where the contract was not one of sale, the price might not be a material element at all, and the contract might still be enforceable even though it provided for "the prices to be mutually settled at a later and appropriate date": *R. and J. Dempster, Ltd.* v. *Motherwell Bridge and Engineering Co., Ltd.*, 1964 S. L. T. 353. The clause of the Sale of Goods Bill 1893 originally provided that the price might "be left to be fixed by subsequent arrangement"; but these words were struck out in Committee.

(*l*) *F. & G. Sykes (Wessex), Ltd.* v. *Fine Fare, Ltd.*, [1967] 1 Lloyd's Rep. 53, C. A.

(*m*) *Mack and Edwards (Sales), Ltd.* v. *McPhail Brothers* (1968), 112 Sol. Jo. 211, C. A. This case is perhaps an example of a quasi-contractual obligation to pay a reasonable price for goods supplied in the absence of a binding contract—*cf.* the obligation of a person lacking capacity to contract to whom necessaries are supplied, s. 3 (2), *ante*. In *McCarthy Milling Co., Ltd.* v. *Elder Packing Co., Ltd.* (1973), 33 D. L. R. (3d.) 52, a price less than the full market price was agreed on the common assumption, for which the buyer was responsible, that the seller would receive the difference by way of Government subsidy. The subsidy was paid, but it later turned out that the goods were ineligible and the seller had to repay the subsidy. The buyer was held liable as a matter of quasi-contract to pay the amount of the subsidy to the seller. See also *Cox* v. *Prentice* (1815), 3 M. & S. 344.

doctrine of *The Moorcock* (*n*), that the petrol should be sold at a reasonable price and that if any dispute arose as to what was a reasonable price it must be determined by arbitration (*o*).

A reasonable price is not necessarily the market price. It is a price which must be fair and just to both parties (*p*).

Presumably if the price was subsequently fixed by the parties, the court would hold that it was a reasonable price. Marine insurance policies are often effected "at a premium to be arranged" (*q*). A similar question arises there.

Yet another case is put by BLACKBURN, J., who says:

> "Where the price is not ascertained, and it could not be ascertained with precision in consequence of the thing perishing, nevertheless the seller may recover the price, if the risk is clearly thrown on the purchaser, by ascertaining the amount as nearly as you can" (*r*).

Such a case, however, would today fall within the section, since it arises only where the contract lays down the manner in which the price is to be fixed.

An alternative price, if in the nature of a wager, avoids the contract for being a gaming one (*s*).

For the effect on the price of an alteration of customs or excise duty, or of the rate of value added tax, see p. 2, *ante*.

For the law relating to deposits, see p. 24, *ante*.

For the law relating to price control and price maintenance, see p. 51, *ante*.

For the offence under the Trade Descriptions Act 1968 of giving a misleading indication as to the price of goods, see p. 59, *ante*.

Credit sale and conditional sale agreements.—See the special provisions about these in ss. 5 and 6 of the Hire-Purchase Act 1965 and in the Consumer Credit Act 1974 (*t*).

(*n*) (1889), 14 P. D. 64, C. A.; but see the note "Implied Terms", p. 12, *ante*.

(*o*) *Foley* v. *Classique Coaches, Ltd.*, [1934] 2 K. B. 1, C. A.; and see *F. & G. Sykes* (*Wessex*), *Ltd.* v. *Fine Fare, Ltd.*, [1967] 1 Lloyd's Rep. 53, C. A.; contrast the arbitration clause in *May and Butcher* v. *R.*, [1934] 2 K. B. 17 *n.*, H. L.

(*p*) *Acabel* v. *Levy* (1834), 10 Bing. 376, at p. 383, *per* TINDAL, C. J.; *Glynwed Distribution, Ltd.* v. *Koronka*, 1977 S. L. T. 65 (Ct. of Sess.): A sold and delivered steel to B. A was selling foreign steel but did not say so. B thought he was buying U.K. steel but did not stipulate for it. The price of U.K. steel was controlled and was less than foreign steel. A reasonable price was held to be between the price of U.K. steel and the price of foreign steel.

(*q*) See Marine Insurance Act 1906, s. 31; 17 Halsbury's Statutes (3rd Edn.) 852.

(*r*) *Martineau* v. *Kitching* (1872), L. R. 7 Q. B. 436, at pp. 455, 456 (sugar sold at so much per cwt. and destroyed after it had come at buyer's risk but before it could be weighed). *Cf. Castle* v. *Playford* (1872), L. R. 7 Exch. 98, at pp. 99, 100.

(*s*) *Rourke* v. *Short* (1856), 5 El. & Bl. 904; *cf. Brogden* v. *Marriott* (1836), 3 Bing. N. C. 88; *Ironmonger & Co.* v. *Dyne* (1928), 44 T. L. R. 497, at p. 499. As to speculative contracts in "futures," see *Forget* v. *Ostigny*, [1895] A. C. 318, at p. 323, P. C.; and *Re Gieve*, [1899] 1 Q. B. 794, C. A. (wagering contract *plus* contract for sale of stock); *Universal Stock Exchange* v. *Strachan*, [1896] A. C. 166; *Cooper* v. *Stubbs*, [1925] 2 K. B. 753, C. A. (both sides must bet); *Woodward & Co.* v. *Wolfe*, [1936] 3 All E. R. 529 ("futures" brokers do not bet).

(*t*) The Hire-Purchase Act 1965 has been repealed by Schedule 5 to the Consumer

9. Agreement to sell at valuation.—(1) Where there is an agreement to sell goods on the terms that the price is to be fixed by the valuation of a third party, and he cannot or does not make the valuation, the agreement is avoided (*u*); but if the goods or any part of them have been delivered to and appropriated by the buyer he must pay a reasonable price for them (*v*).

(2) Where the third party is prevented from making the valuation by the fault of the seller or buyer, the party not at fault may maintain an action for damages against the party at fault.

ILLUSTRATION

In 1966 A agreed to purchase from B for 5 years all the flour required by A for his bakery business at the maximum price fixed for the time being pursuant to the Australian Profiteering Prevention Acts 1948 to 1959. In 1967 flour ceased to be subject to these maximum prices. Held: the agreement is suspended and is not enforceable at the suit of either party. No agreement can be implied to pay a reasonable price or a price fixed by any other body (*a*).

Derivation.—Section 9 of the 1893 Act.

Definitions.—For "contract of sale," see s. 2 (1), *ante*, and s. 61 (1), *post*. For "action," "buyer," "delivery," "fault," "goods" and "seller," see s. 61 (1), *post*.

Cross-reference.—*Cf.* s. 8, *ante* (reasonable price).

COMMENT

The rule stated in subsection (2) appears to be a particular instance of the general common law rule stated by Lord ATKIN in *Southern Foundries* v. *Shirlaw* (*b*):

> "if a party enters into an arrangement which can only take effect by the continuance of an existing set of circumstances . . . I look on the law to be that . . . there is an implied engagement on his part that he shall do nothing of his own motion to put an end to that state of circumstances, under which alone the agreement can be operative."

Credit Act 1974 from a date to be appointed under s. 192 (4) of that Act. So far no date has been appointed, and the Hire-Purchase Act 1965 continues in force. There are also special provisions in the Consumer Credit Act 1974 dealing with the price of goods sold on credit under agreements which are regulated agreements within the meaning of that Act (as to which see p. 66, *ante*).

(*u*) *Thurnell* v. *Balbirnie* (1837), 2 M. & W. 786 (damages); *Vickers* v. *Vickers* (1867), L. R. 4 Eq. 529 (specific performance); *Fry on Specific Performance* (6th ed.), §§ 357 *et seq*. If the valuer fails to act, there is no right of action, since there is no implied warranty that he shall act: *Cooper* v. *Shuttleworth* (1856), 25 L. J. Ex. 114.

(*v*) *Clarke* v. *Westrope* (1856), 18 C. B. 765.

(*a*) *Re Nudgee Bakery Pty., Ltd.'s Agreement*, [1971] Qd. R. 24.

(*b*) [1940] 2 All E. R. 445, at p. 454; [1940] A. C. 701 at p. 717, quoting and approving

In a case before the Act where one of the parties prevented his valuer from acting, PAGE WOOD, V.C., refused him specific performance, on the ground that there was no contract to enforce, and saying that the court had adopted this principle from the civil law (*c*).

In some cases the party in fault may be restrained from preventing the valuer from acting (*d*).

There is also an implied term that neither contracting party will do anything unfair to secure an advantageous decision. A decision unfairly obtained cannot be relied on by the party who was behaved unfairly (*e*).

Valuation as used in this section must be distinguished from arbitration. Arbitration presupposes a dispute or difference, and while a reference to valuers may be an arbitration this will be so only where a dispute exists which it is intended to determine by a process of judicial enquiry. Essentially a valuation is intended to prevent a dispute (*f*).

Conditions and Warranties

10. Stipulations about time.—(1) Unless a different intention appears from the terms of the contract stipulations as to time of payment are not of the essence of a contract of sale (*g*).

(2) Whether any other stipulation as to time is of the essence of the contract or not depends on the terms of the contract (*h*).

(3) In a contract of sale "month" prima facie means calendar month (*i*).

---

the words of COCKBURN, C. J., in *Stirling* v. *Maitland* (1864), 5 B. & S. 841, at p. 852. *Cf. Universal Cargo Carriers* v. *Citati*, [1957] 2 All E. R. 70; [1957] 2 Q. B. 401.

(*c*) *Vickers* v. *Vickers* (1867), L. R. 4 Eq. 529, at p. 535. See *Inst. III.*, 23, where it is said "*Sin autem ille qui nominatus est vel non potuerit vel noluerit pretium definire, tunc pro nihilo esse venditionem quasi nullo pretio statuto.*"

(*d*) See *Fry on Specific Performance* (6th ed.), §§ 1157, 1158, and *Smith* v. *Peters* (1875), L. R. 20 Eq. 511 (mandatory order).

(*e*) *Essoldo* v. *Ladbroke Group* (1976), Times, 21 Dec.

(*f*) *Russell on Arbitration* (18th ed.), pp. 45–46, 48–50; Hogg's *Arbitration*, pp. 9–11, where the cases are collected.

(*g*) *Martindale* v. *Smith* (1841), 1 Q. B. 389; and see *United Dominions Trust (Commercial), Ltd.* v. *Eagle Aircraft Services, Ltd.*, [1968] 1 All E. R. 104; [1968] 1 W. L. R. 74, C. A. For the rule in connection with sales of land, see *Smith* v. *Hamilton*, [1950] 2 All E. R. 928; [1951] Ch. 174; *Re Barr's Contract, Moorwell Holdings* v. *Barr*, [1956] 2 All E. R. 853; [1956] Ch. 551. For the rule in connection with an option to purchase shares, see *Hare* v. *Nicoll*, [1966] 1 All E. R. 285; [1966] 2 Q. B. 130, C. A.

(*h*) See the cases cited in notes (*r*) and (*s*), p. 107, *post*.

(*i*) *Cf.* Bills of Exchange Act 1882, s. 14 (4); 3 Halsbury's Statutes (3rd Edn.) 197. In ordinary legal documents "month" at common law primarily meant lunar month: *Bruner* v. *Moore*, [1904] 1 Ch. 305, but in a particular trade it might by usage have a special trade meaning: *Bissell* v. *Beard* (1873), 28 L. T. 740 (iron trade). Now, by s. 61 of the Law of Property Act 1925 (27 Halsbury's Statutes (3rd Edn.) 437), it means calendar month in all deeds, contracts, wills, orders and other instruments made after 1st January 1926, "unless the context otherwise requires."

ILLUSTRATIONS

(1) Sale of beans; goods to be shipped and bill of lading to be dated in December and/or January, and bill of lading to be *prima facie* evidence of date of shipment. The buyer may refuse to accept the goods if the bill of lading is dated 2nd February, even though the goods were shipped on 30th January (*k*).

(2) Contract for sale of grain to be shipped from River Plate on ship "expected to be ready to load late September." The ship was not ready to load till the middle of November, and the sellers had no reasonable ground for stating that she would be ready in September. The buyer may refuse to accept the goods (*l*).

Derivation.—Section 10 of the 1893 Act.

Definitions.—For "contract of sale," see s. 2 (1), *ante*, and s. 61 (1), *post*.

Cross-references.—Section 28 (payment and delivery concurrent conditions); s. 31 (payment in contracts involving delivery by instalments); s. 48 (3) (seller may make time of payment of the essence). For a general note on conditions and warranties, see p. 8, ante. For their history, see Note A, *post*, Appendix II.

COMMENT

Stipulations as to time of payment.—When the contract provides for the opening of a confirmed credit, *prima facie* it must be opened at the latest by the beginning of the agreed shipment period, and where a shipment date is given it must be opened a reasonable time before that date (*m*).

If a discount is agreed upon for payment within a stated period, the full price becomes payable at the end of that period if the reduced price has not then been paid (*n*).

In determining whether time is of the essence, the court will take into account the nature of the property involved and the intention of the parties (*o*).

Notwithstanding this section, where an unpaid seller has a lien over

---

(*k*) *Re General Trading Co.* (1911), 16 Com. Cas. 95. *Cf. Kwei Tek Chao* v. *British Traders and Shippers*, [1954] 1 All E. R. 779; [1954] 2 Q. B. 459; see also *Heskell* v. *Continental Express*, [1950] 1 All E. R. 1033, and *Macpherson Train* v. *Ross*, [1955] 2 All E. R. 445; [1955] 1 W. L. R. 640.

(*l*) *Sanday & Co.* v. *Keighley, Maxted & Co.* (1922), 91 L. J. K. B. 624.

(*m*) *Plasticmoda* v. *Davidsons*, [1952] 1 Lloyd's Rep. 527; *Pavia* v. *Thurmann-Nielson*, [1952] 1 All E. R. 492; [1952] 2 Q. B. 84, C. A. (c.i.f. contract); *Sinason-Teicher* v. *Oilcakes and Oilseeds Trading Co.*, [1954] 3 All E. R. 468, C. A.; *Ian Stach* v. *Baker Bosley*, [1958] 1 All E. R. 542; [1958] 2 Q. B. 130 (f.o.b. contract). But see *Alexandria Cotton and Trading Co.* (*Sudan*), *Ltd.* v. *Cotton Co. of Ethiopia, Ltd.*, [1963] 1 Lloyd's Rep. 576, where ROSKILL, J., said that he did not regard the rule as finally settled by the authorities. See further, p. 43, *ante*.

(*n*) *Amos and Wood* v. *Kaprow* (1948), 64 T. L. R. 110.

(*o*) *Cf. Hare* v. *Nicoll*, [1966] 1 All E. R. 285; [1966] 2 Q. B. 130, C. A. In commodity contracts the buyer's obligation will normally be to take up and pay for the documents of title on the day agreed, time being of the essence: *Toepfer* v. *Lenersan-Poortmann N. V.*, [1980] 1 Lloyd's Rep. 143, C. A.

perishable goods or has stopped them in transit, time of payment is of the essence, and if no time of payment is specified, the buyer must tender the price within a reasonable time—see s. 48 (3), *post*. Likewise, where the goods are not perishable, such an unpaid seller may make time of the essence by giving notice to the buyer of his intention to re-sell, in which case the buyer must also tender the price within a reasonable time (*p*).

See the special provisions as to credit-sale and conditional sale agreements in the Hire-Purchase Act 1965 (*q*).

Other stipulations as to time.—As regards stipulations other than those relating to the time of payment, time is of the essence of the contract, in most mercantile transactions (*r*) and in some non-mercantile transactions (*s*). Thus, where there was a contract for the sale of twenty-five tons of pepper, "name of vessel or vessels, marks and particulars to be declared within sixty days of date of bill of lading," COTTON, L. J., says,

> "It was argued that the rules of Courts of Equity are now to be regarded in all Courts, and that equity enforced contracts though the time fixed therein for completion had passed. This was in the cases of contracts, such as purchases and sales of land, where, unless a contrary intention could be collected from the contract, the Court presumed that time was not an essential condition. To apply this to mercantile contracts would be dangerous and unreasonable. We must therefore hold that the time within which the pepper was to be declared was an essential condition of the contract" (*t*).

Where a stipulation as to time is of the essence, the party in whose favour it operates may waive it unilaterally. He can then make it of the essence again only by giving reasonable notice, in clear terms, of his intention to do so (*u*).

When time of delivery is an essential condition it is often referred to in

---

(*p*) *R. V. Ward* v. *Bignall*, [1967] 2 All E. R. 449; [1967] 1 Q. B. 534, C. A.; and see p. 218, *post*.

(*q*) 30 Halsbury's Statutes (3rd Edn.) 61. The 1965 Act has been repealed from a date to be appointed by Sch. 5 to the Consumer Credit Act 1974, but so far no date has been appointed.

(*r*) *Bowes* v. *Shand* (1877), 2 App. Cas. 455, at p. 463, *per* Lord CAIRNS; *Elmdove, Ltd.* v. *Keech* (1969), 113 Sol. Jo. 871, C. A. (time presumed to be of the essence unless circumstances show otherwise); *Bunge* v. *Tradax*, [1980] 1 Lloyd's Rep. 294, at pp. 305, 306 (where time is of the essence a stipulation as to time has effect as a condition); *Toepfer* v. *Lenersan-Poortmann N. V.*, [1980] 1 Lloyd's Rep. 143 (commodity contracts); *cf. Paton* v. *Payne*, 1897 35 Sc. L. R. 112, H. L. (time not essential); *Hartley* v. *Hymans*, [1920] 3 K. B. 475, at p. 484 (time essential); *Brooke Tool Manufacturing Co.* v. *Hydraulic Gears Co.* (1920), 89 L. J. K. B. 263 (effect of delay caused by Government action where delivery by a certain date expressly stipulated); *Aron & Co.* v. *Comptoir Wegimont*, [1921] 3 K. B. 435 (effect of delay caused by strike where there is express obligation to ship during October). And see *United Dominions Trust (Commercial), Ltd.* v. *Eagle Aircraft Services, Ltd.*, [1968] 1 All E. R. 104; [1968] 1 W. L. R. 74, C. A. See also *ante*, p. 34.

(*s*) *McDougall* v. *Aeromarine of Emsworth*, [1958] 3 All E. R. 431; [1958] 1 W. L. R. 1126.

(*t*) *Reuter* v. *Sala* (1879), 4 C. P. D. 239, at pp. 246, 249, C. A. See also *Berg & Sons* v. *Landauer & Co.* (1925), 42 T. L. R. 142.

(*u*) *Rickards* v. *Oppenheim*, [1950] 1 All E. R. 420; [1950] 1 K. B. 616, C. A.; see also *Panoutsos* v. *Raymond Hadley*, [1917] 2 K. B. 473, C. A.; *Plasticmoda* v. *Davidsons*, [1952] 1

the cases as part of the description of the goods. But the Act treats the two conditions as distinct (*a*); *cf.* s. 13, *post*.

11. When condition to be treated as warranty.—(1) Subsections (2) to (4) and (7) below do not apply to Scotland and subsection (5) below applies only to Scotland.

(2) Where a contract of sale is subject to a condition to be fulfilled by the seller, the buyer may waive the condition, or may elect to treat the breach of the condition as a breach of warranty and not as a ground for treating the contract as repudiated (*b*).

(3) Whether a stipulation in a contract of sale is a condition, the breach of which may give rise to a right to treat the contract as repudiated, or a warranty, the breach of which may give rise to a claim for damages but not to a right to reject the goods and treat the contract as repudiated, depends in each case on the construction of the contract (*c*); and a stipulation may be a condition, though called a warranty in the contract (*d*).

(4) Where a contract of sale is not severable (*e*), and the buyer has accepted the goods or part of them (*f*), the breach of a condition to be fulfilled by the seller can only be

---

Lloyd's Rep. 527; *Furst (Enrico) & Co.* v. *W. E. Fischer, Ltd.*, [1960] 2 Lloyd's Rep. 340; *Soproma S. p. A.* v. *Marine and Animal By-Products Corporation*, [1966] 1 Lloyd's Rep. 367; *Sunstrum Ranching Co., Ltd.* v. *International Building Systems*, [1975] 4 W. W. R. 86; *Toprak* v. *Finagrain*, [1979] 2 Lloyd's Rep. 98, C. A. As to waiver generally, see p. 20, *ante*.

(*a*) See *Aron & Co.* v. *Comptoir Wegimont* (*supra*), at p. 440, *per* McCardie, J.; *Wilson* v. *Wright*, [1937] 4 All E. R. 371, at p. 373, *per* Mackinnon, L. J.; and *Macpherson* v. *Ross*, [1955] 2 All E. R. 445.

(*b*) *Ellen* v. *Topp* (1851), 6 Exch. 424, at p. 431; *Behn* v. *Burness* (1863), 3 B. & S. 751, Ex. Ch.; *Wallis* v. *Pratt* [1911], A. C. 394; (applied, *Harling* v. *Eddy*, [1951] 2 All E. R. 212, C. A.; [1951] 2 K. B. 739) and judgment of Fletcher Moulton, L. J., in the court below: [1910] 2 K. B. 1003, 1012, C. A.; *Sullivan* v. *Constable* (1932), 48 T. L. R. 369, C. A. (election by buyer to treat breach of condition as warranty); and see s. 53, *post*. As to waiver generally, see p. 20, *ante*.

(*c*) *Graves* v. *Legg* (1854), 9 Exch. 709; *Behn* v. *Burness* (1863), 3 B. & S. 751, at p. 754, Ex. Ch. For suggested tests for distinguishing a condition from a warranty, see *Heilbutt, Symons & Co.* v. *Buckleton*, [1913] A. C. 30; *Bentsen* v. *Taylor*, [1893] 2 Q. B. 274, at p. 281, *per* Bowen, L. J.; *Harrison* v. *Knowles and Foster*, [1917] 2 K. B. 606, at p. 610; *Wilson* v. *Wright*, [1937] 4 All E. R. 371, at p. 373, *per* Mackinnon, L. J.; *Oscar Chess* v. *Williams*, [1957] 1 All E. R. 325; [1957] 1 W. L. R. 370, C. A.; and see other cases cited in Appendix II, Note A. See also p. 8, *ante*.

(*d*) *Wallis* v. *Pratt*, [1911] A. C. 394, at p. 397.

(*e*) As to severable contracts, see *Jackson* v. *Rotax Motor and Cycle Co.*, [1910] 2 K. B. 937, 947, C. A.; *J. Rosenthal & Sons, Ltd.* v. *Esmail*, [1965] 2 All E. R. 860; [1965] 1 W. L. R. 1117, H. L.; and s. 31, *post*.

(*f*) *Graves* v. *Legg* (1854), 9 Exch. 709, at p. 717; *Behn* v. *Burness* (1863), 3 B. & S. 751, Ex. Ch.; *Heilbutt* v. *Hickson* (1872), L. R. 7 C. P. 438, at p. 450. For the meaning of "acceptance", see ss. 34 (1) and 35, and the illustrations and comment to them, *post*.

treated as a breach of warranty, and not as a ground for rejecting the goods and treating the contract as repudiated (*g*), unless there is an express or implied term of the contract to that effect (*h*).

(5) In Scotland, failure by the seller to perform any material part of a contract of sale is a breach of contract, which entitles the buyer either within a reasonable time after delivery to reject the goods and treat the contract as repudiated, or to retain the goods and treat the failure to perform such material part as a breach which may give rise to a claim for compensation or damages (*i*).

(6) Nothing in this section affects a condition or warranty, whose fulfilment is excused by law by reason of impossibility or otherwise (*k*).

(7) Paragraph 2 of Schedule 1 below applies in relation to a contract made before 22 April 1967 or (in the application of this Act to Northern Ireland) 28 July 1967.

Derivation.—Section 11 of the 1893 Act as amended by s. 4 of the Misrepresentation Act 1967 and, in the case of Northern Ireland, s. 4 of the Misrepresentation Act (Northern Ireland) 1967. Paragraph 2 of Schedule 1, *post*, re-enacts s. 11 (1) (c) of the 1893 Act as it was until 1967, in relation to contracts made before the amendments came into force.

The subsections in the 1893 Act have been renumbered as follows:

1893 Act	1979 Act
s. 11 (1) (a)	11 (2)
s. 11 (1) (b)	11 (3)
s. 11 (1) (c)	11 (4)
s. 11 (2)	11 (5)
s. 11 (3)	11 (6)

Definitions.—For "contract of sale," see s. 2 (1), *ante*, and s. 61 (1), *post*. For "buyer," "delivery," "goods," "property," "seller," "specific goods," and "warranty," see s. 61 (1), *post*.

(*g*) In *Wallis* v. *Pratt*, [1910] 2 K. B. 1003, C. A., FLETCHER MOULTON, L. J. (whose dissenting judgment was upheld in the House of Lords: [1911] A. C. 394) said at p. 1013 that there was no reason to suppose that the Act intended that these should be the only modes in which a buyer could effectively bar himself from taking advantage of the choice of remedies given in the case of a breach of a condition.

(*h*) *Bannerman* v. *White*, [1861] 10 C. B. N. S. 844; and see 19 Mod. L. R. 315.

(*i*) *Couston* v. *Chapman* (1872), L. R. 2 Sc. & Div. 250; *Aird* v. *Pullan*, 1904 7 F. (Ct. of Sess.) 258; *Nelson* v. *William Chalmers & Co.*, 1913 S. C. 441; *Pollock* v. *Macrae*, 1922 S. C. 192 (H. L.); *Mechans, Ltd.* v. *Highland Marine Charters, Ltd.*, 1964 S. C. 48 (Ct. of Sess.).

(*k*) See ss. 6 and 7, *ante*; *Baily* v. *De Crespigny* (1869), L. R. 4 Q. B. 180, at p. 185. As to dissolution of contracts by war, see cases cited, p. 18, *ante*; as to impossibility, see p. 17, *ante*. See also the Law Reform (Frustrated Contracts) Act 1943, and s. 33 (1) of the Exchange Control Act 1947, *post*, Appendix I.

Cross-references.—For a general note on conditions and warranties, see *ante*, p. 8. For the history of conditions and warranties, see Note A, *post*, Appendix II. *Cf.* ss. 16 to 18, *post* (passing of property), ss. 34 and 35, *post* (acceptance), and s. 53, *post* (remedy for breach of warranty).

COMMENT

Subsection (2).—For the buyer to waive a condition altogether, he must make a representation to the seller that he has no objection to the goods as they are, and the seller must act as a result of that representation in a manner different from that in which he would otherwise have acted (*l*). See further as to waiver, p. 20, *ante*.

Subsection (3).—The Act reflects, in the context of the law of sale of goods, the division of contractual terms into conditions and warranties which was contended for by judges and text-book writers at the time of its enactment. The modern common law has moved away from such a rigid division in relation to contracts generally, and has re-assented that the majority of contractual stipulations are neither conditions nor warranties, but are intermediate stipulations, the effect of which depends upon the nature of the breach (*m*). These rules of common law are preserved by s. 62 (2), *post*, except insofar as they are inconsistent with the express provisions of the Act, apply to provisions in contracts for the sale of goods other than the terms implied by ss. 12–15, *post* (*n*).

Where one party is in breach of a term of a contract for the sale of goods the position is therefore as follows:

(1) The contract may expressly provide that in the event of the breach of the term the other party is entitled to terminate the contract or, in the case of the buyer, reject the goods.

(2) Even if there is no express provision to that effect, the other party may still be so entitled upon the proper construction of the contract.

(3) Whether he is so entitled because the term is described as a "condition" depends upon whether that word is used as a code for "shall be entitled to repudiate the contract or reject the goods" or in some other sense.

(4) In all those sections of this Act which create implied conditions the word condition is by definition a code word for "breach of this term will entitle the buyer to reject the goods" subject to any other relevant provision of the Act.

(5) In other cases the court has decided that breach of some specific

(*l*) *Toepfer* v. *Warinco*, [1978] 2 Lloyd's Rep. 569, at p. 576.

(*m*) In *Cehave N. V.* v. *Bremer Handelgesellschaft m.b.h.*, [1975] 3 All E. R. 739, 766; [1976] Q. B. 44, 84, ORMROD, L. J., in a judgment with which ROSKILL, L. J., agreed, doubted whether there was in fact a third category of stipulations rather than that a buyer was entitled to reject goods where by virtue of a breach or breaches of warranty *de facto* the consideration for his promise had been wholly destroyed. *Cf.* the comment to s. 31 (2), *post*.

(*n*) *Cehave N. V.* v. *Bremer Handelgesellschaft m.b.h., supra*; *Tradax Internacional S. A.* v. *Goldschmidt, S. A.*, [1977] 2 Lloyd's Rep. 604. See further p. 8, *ante*. For a note on the history of conditions and warranties, see Appendix II, Note A, *post*.

terms gives rise of itself to a right in the other party to repudiate the contract.

(6) In cases under heads (4) and (5) the consequences of the breach are assumed to go to the root of the contract and to justify repudiation.

(7) In other cases of breach, the other party may treat the contract as repudiated or reject the goods if the events produced by the breach are such that the breach goes to the root of the contract (*o*).

Subsection (4).—Where, under this subsection, the buyer has lost his right to reject and sues for damages, he is still suing for a breach of condition, not for breach of warranty, and will not be barred by a clause in the contract which provides against actions for breach of warranty (*p*). For this subsection to apply, the contract must not be severable at the time when the buyer has to decide how to treat the breach of condition. If the contract is not severable then, it is irrelevant that it could have been severed at an earlier time (*q*).

For the meaning of "acceptance," see ss. 34 (1) and 35, *post*. For the rules as to the passing of property in a sale of specific goods, see s. 18, *post*.

Conditional sale agreements.—Section 11(4) does not apply to conditional sale agreements which are agreements for consumer sales (*r*).

Subsection (5).—In Scotland, no distinction was drawn between conditions and warranties, and the right of rejection was much larger than in England. This right is preserved by the Act (*s*). On the other hand, the *actio quanti minoris* was much restricted in Scotland, and when the buyer could return the goods he was not allowed to keep them and

---

(*o*) *Cehave N. V.* v. *Bremer Handelgesellschaft m.b.h., supra*, at pp. 766, 767 and 84, *per* ORMROD, L. J.

(*p*) *Wallis* v. *Pratt*, [1911] A. C. 394; *Baldry* v. *Marshall*, [1925] 1 K. B. 260; *Barker (Junior) & Co.* v. *Agius, Ltd.* (1927), 33 Com. Cas. 120; *Sullivan* v. *Constable* (1932), 48 T. L. R. 369, C. A.; *Couchman* v. *Hill*, [1947] 1 All E. R. 103, C. A.; [1947] K. B. 554; *Harling* v. *Eddy*, [1951] 2 All E. R. 212, C. A.; [1951] 2 K. B. 739; *Nicholson and Venn* v. *Smith Marriott* (1947), 177 L. T. 189; but *cf. Wilkinson* v. *Barclay*, [1946] 2 All E. R. 337, *n.*, C. A.

(*q*) *J. Rosenthal & Sons, Ltd.* v. *Esmail*, [1965] 2 All E. R. 860; [1965] 1 W. L. R. 1117, H. L.

(*r*) Supply of Goods (Implied Terms) Act 1973, s. 14 (1). "Consumer sale" has the same meaning here as under s. 55 of the Sale of Goods Act as set out in para. 11 of Sch. 1, *post*: see s. 15 (1) of the 1973 Act, as amended by para. 17 of Sch. 2, *post*. In the case of conditional sale agreements, a breach of condition to be fulfilled by the seller is, in England, Wales and Northern Ireland, to be treated as a breach of warranty if (but only if) it would be so treated if it formed part of a corresponding hire-purchase agreement; see s. 14 (2) of the 1973 Act. The relevant provisions of the 1973 Act at present define conditional sale agreement and hire-purchase agreement by reference to the Hire-Purchase Act 1965, but by virtue of s. 192 (4) of and Sch. 4 to the Consumer Credit Act 1974, from a date to be appointed, ss. 14 and 15 of the 1973 Act have been amended to bring them into line with the Consumer Credit Act 1974.

(*s*) In *Millars of Falkirk, Ltd.* v. *Turpie*, 1976 S. L. T. (Notes) 66, the Court of Session left open the question whether a buyer could rely on a minor defect which the seller was willing to remedy but which involved a breach of a condition implied by s. 14 (2) or s. 14 (3), *post*, as allowing him to reject the goods under this subsection.

sue for damages. Now he has this right, subject to the conditions specified by s. 59, *post*.

12. Implied undertakings as to title, etc.—(1) In a contract of a sale, other than one to which subsection (3) below applies, there is an implied condition on the part of the seller that in the case of a sale he has a right to sell the goods, and in the case of an aggrement to sell he will have such a right at the time when the property is to pass.

(2) In a contract of sale, other than one to which subsection (3) below applies, there is also an implied warranty that—

(a) the goods are free, and will remain free until the time when the property is to pass, from any charge or encumbrance not disclosed or known to the buyer before the contract is made, and

(b) the buyer will enjoy quiet possession of the goods except so far as it may be disturbed by the owner or other person entitled to the benefit of any charge or encumbrance so disclosed or known.

(3) This subsection applies to a contract of sale in the case of which there appears from the contract or is to be inferred from its circumstances an intention that the seller should transfer only such title as he or a third person may have.

(4) In a contract to which subsection (3) above applies there is an implied warranty that all charges or encumbrances known to the seller and not known to the buyer have been disclosed to the buyer before the contract is made.

(5) In a contract to which subsection (3) above applies there is also an implied warranty that none of the following will disturb the buyer's quiet possession of the goods, namely—

(a) the seller;

(b) in a case where the parties to the contract intend that the seller should transfer only such title as a third person may have, that person;

(c) anyone claiming through or under the seller or that third person otherwise than under a charge or encumbrance disclosed or known to the buyer before the contract is made.

(6) Paragraph 3 of Schedule 1 below applies in relation to a contract made before 18 May 1973.

ILLUSTRATIONS

(1) An auctioneer sells by auction a piano seized under a distress warrant. The buyer knows that the piano is sold under a distress. Prior to 1973, it was held that if the warrant turned out to be invalid, the auctioneer was not liable because the circumstances were such as to show an intention to exclude the operation of s. 12 of the 1893 Act(*t*). It would seem, however, that this defence is no longer available to the auctioneer, for he intends to transfer such title as the party distrained upon might have. There is therefore an implied warranty, which by virtue of s. 6 (1) of the Unfair Contract Terms Act 1977, *post*, Appendix I (*u*), cannot be excluded, that the party distrained on will not disturb the buyer's quiet possession of the goods: see s. 12 (5)(b).

(2) A offers a motor car to B, who cannot buy it himself. C asks B to buy the car and then immediately re-sell it to him. It turns out that the car was stolen. The circumstances were such as to exclude the operation of the original s. 12 of the 1893 Act as between B and C (*a*), and this would still seem to be the case as the claim by the true owner would not involve any breach by B of warranties implied by the new s. 12 (4) and (5).

(3) Sale of 3,000 tins of preserved milk, some of which are labelled "Nissly brand." This is admitted to be an infringement of the N. Company's trademark. The buyer can either reject the consignment, or take off the labels and claim damages for the reduced sale value: "if a vendor can be stopped by process of law from selling, he has not the right to sell" (*b*).

(4) In 1967, P files a specification for a patent for apparatus for marking roads. The specification is published in November 1970 and the patent is granted and sealed in 1972. In January 1970, M sells to V similar apparatus, which infringes P's patent. P takes steps to prevent V from using the apparatus. M is liable to V for damages for breach of the warranty of quiet possession (*c*).

(5) Purchase of motor-car which is used for some months. It then turns out that the car had been stolen, and the buyer restores it to its owner. Although he has had some months' use of it he can recover the full price from the seller as money paid on a consideration which has wholly failed (*d*).

Derivation.—Section 12 of the 1893 Act as substituted by s. 1 of the Supply of Goods (Implied Terms) Act 1893. The original s. 12 and the substituted section are both reproduced in Sch. 1, para. 3, *post*. The

---

(*t*) *Payne* v. *Elsden* (1900), 17 T. L. R. 161.

(*u*) Replacing s. 55 (3) of the 1893 Act as amended by s. 4 of the Supply of Goods (Implied Terms) Act 1973.

(*a*) *Warming's Used Cars, Ltd.* v. *Tucker*, [1956] S. A. S. R. 249.

(*b*) *Niblett* v. *Confectioners' Materials Co.*, [1921] 3 K. B. 387, C. A.; overruling *Monforts* v. *Marsden* (1895), 12 R. P. C. 266 (machine made under invalid patent). Note that "right to sell" is therefore wider than "right to pass the property in."

(*c*) *Microbeads AG* v. *Vinhurst Road Markings, Ltd.*, [1975] 1 All E. R. 529; [1975] 1 W. L. R. 218, C. A.

(*d*) *Rowland* v. *Divall*, [1923] 2 K. B. 500, 505, C. A.

subsections in the substituted s. 12 of the 1893 Act have been renumbered as follows:

1893 Act	1979 Act
s. 12 (1) (a)	12 (1)
s. 12 (1) (b)	12 (2)
s. 12 (2)	12 (3)
s. 12 (2) (a)	12 (4)
s. 12 (2) (b)	12 (5).

Definitions.—For "contract of sale," see s. 2 (1), *ante*, and s. 61 (1), *post*. For "buyer," "goods," "property," "seller" and "warranty," see s. 61 (1), *post*.

Cross-references.—For a general note on conditions and warranties, see p. 8, *ante*. For their history, see Note A, *post*, Appendix II. For their effect, see s. 11, *ante*. *Cf.* ss. 16, 17 and 18, *post* (passing of property); ss. 21 to 26 and the Factors Acts, *post* (transfer of title); and the Unfair Contract Terms Act 1977, *post*, Appendix I.

COMMENT

Formerly the rule was stated to be that on a sale of specific goods there was no implied warranty of title, and that, in the absence of fraud, the seller was

> "not liable for a bad title unless there was an express warranty, or an equivalent to it by declaration or conduct" (*e*).

But as Lord Campbell said in 1851, "the exceptions have well-nigh eaten up the rule" (*f*) and the original s. 12 (1) of the 1893 Act (*g*) may be regarded as declaratory.

The new sub-ss. (1) and (2) are similar to the original sub-ss. (1)–(3) in the 1893 Act, but while the former provisions would be excluded if the circumstances were such as to show a different intention, the condition and warranty implied by the new sub-ss. (1) and (2) cannot be excluded, except in the case of an international supply contract, unless the contract is one to which sub-s. (3) applies (*h*). In practice, the cases in which, before 1973, implied undertakings as to title were negatived mainly arose out of sales by sheriffs or forced sales by public auction, where the circumstances were such as to indicate that the seller was only selling such right as he might have in the goods. A sheriff selling an execution debtor's goods, or an auctioneer who, to the knowledge of the buyer, was selling goods seized under a distress warrant gave no

(*e*) *Per* PARKE, B., in *Morley* v. *Attenborough* (1849), 3 Exch. 500, at p. 512 (auction sale of forfeited pledges).

(*f*) *Sims* v. *Marryat* (1851), 17 Q. B. 281, at p. 291 (sale of copyright).

(*g*) Reproduced in Sch. 1, para. 3, *post*.

(*h*) See s. 6 (1) of the Unfair Contract Terms Act 1977, *post*, Appendix I. International supply contracts are defined in s. 26 of that Act, *post*, Appendix I.

implied undertaking as to title (*i*). He was only responsible if he *knew* that he had no title to sell (*k*).

The implied condition as to title.—The right to sell is wider than the right to pass property. If a seller can be stopped by process of law from selling, he has not the right to sell (*l*).

A contract of sale is a contract to transfer the property in goods (*m*). If the seller fails to transfer the property in the goods, there is a total failure of consideration and the buyer is entitled on discovering the true facts to treat the contract as at an end and recover the full purchase even though he has enjoyed the use of the goods (*n*). In such a case the buyer owes nothing to the seller for the use of the goods (*o*).

This is so even if, after the buyer has rescinded the contract, the property in the goods is acquired by the seller (*p*). But it may be different if, before the buyer rescinds, the seller acquires the property in the goods. In such a case, there is probably no total failure of consideration, for the buyer retains, and is entitled to retain the goods against all the world, but as the seller was in breach of the implied condition that he had the right to sell, the buyer may claim damages, and, subject to s. 11 (4), may treat the contract as repudiated (*q*).

(*i*) *Ex p. Villars* (1874), 9 Ch. App. 432, at p. 437 (sheriff); *Payne* v. *Elsden* (1900), 17 T. L. R. 161 (*ante*, illustration 1); and see *Warming's Used Cars, Ltd.* v. *Tucker*, [1956] S. A. S. R. 249 (*ante*, illustration 2); *Niblett* v. *Confectioners' Materials Co.*, [1921] 3 K. B. 387, 401; *cf.* s. 5, *ante*.

(*k*) *Peto* v. *Blades* (1814), 5 Taunt. 657; *cf. Dorab Ally* v. *Abdool Azeze* (1878), L. R. 5 Ind. App. 116. See also the provisions of s. 15 of the Bankruptcy and Deeds of Arrangement Act 1913 (3 Halsbury's Statutes (3rd Edn.) 18), as explained by the Court of Appeal in *Curtis* v. *Maloney*, [1950] 2 All E. R. 982; [1951] 1 K. B. 736.

(*l*) *Niblett* v. *Confectioners' Materials Co.*, [1921] 3 K. B. 387, C. A.; overruling *Monforts* v. *Marsden* (1895), 12 R. P. C. 266 (machine made under invalid patent); *J. Barry Winsor and Associates* v. *Belgo-Canadian Manufacturing Co.* (1976), 76 D. L. R. (3d) 685 (sale of lamps to retailer which, because of safety defects, the seller could have been injuncted from selling by or at the instance of an inspector under the Canadian Electrical Energy Inspection Act).

(*m*) Section 2, *ante*.

(*n*) *Rowland* v. *Divall*, [1923] 2 K. B. 500, C. A.

(*o*) *Warman* v. *Southern Counties Car Finance Corporation, Ltd.*, [1949] 1 All E. R. 711; [1949] 2 K. B. 576.

(*p*) *Butterworth* v. *Kingsway Motors*, [1954] 2 All E. R. 694; [1954] 1 W. L. R. 1286.

(*q*) When the seller acquires the property in the goods, the contract with the buyer is "fed" so that the buyer then acquires a good title to the goods: *Whitehorn Brothers* v. *Davison*, [1911] 1 K. B. 463 at pp. 475, 481, 486, C. A.; *Blundell-Leigh* v. *Attenborough*, [1921] 3 K. B. 235 at pp. 240, 242, C. A.; *Butterworth* v. *Kingsway Motors*, [1954] 1 W. L. R. 1286, at p. 1295; *Patten* v. *Thomas Motors Pty., Ltd.* (1965), 66 S. R. (N. S. W.) 458. In *Bennett* v. *Griffin Finance*, [1967] 2 Q. B. 46, at p. 50, WINN, L. J., expressly reserved the point, but it was not argued before him and no authorities appear to have been cited. For a different view to that in the text see *West (H. W.), Ltd.* v. *McBlain*, [1950] N. I. 144. The statement in *Rowland* v. *Divall*, [1923] 2 K. B. 500, at pp. 506–507, that s. 11 (1) (c) of the 1893 Act (now s. 11 (4) of the 1979 Act) was inapplicable to sales without title was made with reference to a situation in which there was a total failure of consideration, and there seems no reason why s. 11 (4) of the 1979 Act should not apply to a situation where there is no such failure. In *Denis Geary Motors* v. *Hunter Stores Finance*, [1979] Qd. R. 207, a person who had no right to sell certain goods sold them to two different purchasers and then acquired the legal title to them. It was held that the equitable interest of the first purchaser prevailed.

It would also seem clear (*r*) that a seller who has not got any right to sell, but who is able to give a good title to the buyer by reason of, for example, s. 8 or s. 9 of the Factors Act 1889, *post*, is in breach of the condition implied by s. 12 (1). The buyer may suffer no damage from the breach, as he gets a good title to the goods. But if he is put to expense establishing his title, this may be recoverable as damages from the seller, and in any event he is under no duty to the seller to mitigate his damages in a doubtful case by engaging in complicated litigation to determine whether he has indeed acquired a good title (*s*).

The warranty of freedom from encumbrances and of quiet possession.—This warranty is similar to those formerly implied by s. 12 (2) and (3) of the 1893 Act before 1973. It protects a buyer where the seller has a right to sell but the goods are subject to the rights of a third party (*t*).

The warranty as to quiet possession appears to give the buyer a contractual remedy if the seller himself wrongfully seizes the goods (*u*). It would also seem to allow the buyer a longer period of limitation than the other provisions of this section since time does not begin to run until the buyer's possession is disturbed.

It had been suggested (*a*) that this warranty ought to be limited in the same way as the covenent by a vendor for quiet enjoyment of real property, but this suggestion has now been disapproved by the Court of Appeal (*b*).

Contracts to transfer only such title as the seller or a third party may have.—Although sellers are not able to exclude the provisions of this section, they may make it clear to the buyer that they are only selling such title as they or some third person may have. If they make this clear, the condition and warranty implied by s. 12 (1) and (2) do not apply and instead the more limited warranties set out in s. 12 (3)–(5) will be implied. As these relate only to freedom from

---

(*r*) But *cf.* ATKIN, L.J., in *Niblett* v. *Confectioners' Materials, Ltd.*, [1921] 3 K. B. 387, at p. 401; *Benjamin's Sale of Goods*, para. 264.

(*s*) *Pilkington* v. *Wood*, [1953] 2 All E. R. 810; [1953] Ch. 770. The buyer may in theory be able to rescind even if his title is not open to question, for the seller will still have had no right to sell the goods, and will therefore be in breach of the condition implied by section 12 (1). In practice, there are not likely to be many occasions when the buyer will wish to avail himself of this right.

(*t*) *Lloyds and Scottish Finance, Ltd.* v. *Modern Cars and Caravans* (*Kingston*), *Ltd.*, [1964] 2 All E. R. 732; [1966] 1 Q. B. 764; *Microbeads A. G.* v. *Vinhurst Road Markings, Ltd.*, [1975] 1 All E. R. 529; [1975] 1 W. L. R. 218, C. A. (patent published after date of sale), *ante*, illustration (4).

(*u*) *Monforts* v. *Marsden* (1895), 12 R. P. C. 266, at p. 269; *Niblett* v. *Confectioners' Materials Co., Ltd.*, [1921] 3 K. B. 387, at p. 403, *per* ATKIN, L. J.; *Healing* (*Sales*) *Pty., Ltd.* v. *Inglis Electric Pty., Ltd.* (1968), 121 C. L. R. 584 (H. C. of Aus.); but *cf. Anderson* v. *Ryan*, [1967] I. R. 34, where it was held that a buyer seeking to establish a breach of the former sub-s. (2) had to show that he did not get a right to quiet possession by virtue of the sale.

(*a*) *Niblett* v. *Confectioners' Materials Co., Ltd.*, [1921] 3 K. B. 387, at p. 403, *per* ATKIN, L. J.

(*b*) *Microbeads A. G.* v. *Vinhurst Road Markings, Ltd.*, [1975] 1 All E. R. 529; [1975] 1 W. L. R. 218, C. A.

encumbrances and quiet possession, it follows that the condition implied by s. 12 (1) that the seller has a right to sell can in practice be wholly excluded notwithstanding s. 6 of the Unfair Contract Terms Act 1977 (*c*), if the seller makes it clear that he is only selling such title as he may have.

The intention may be expressed or it may be inferred from the circumstances. Circumstances from which such an intention may be inferred will presumably be similar to those (discussed above) in which, prior to 1973, the implied undertaking as to title was negatived (*d*). But the consequences will not necessarily be the same as before 1973, as appears from illustrations (1) and (2) to this section, *ante*.

Damages.—Damages for breach of the conditions and warranties implied by this section include consequential losses directly and naturally resulting from the breach. These have been held to include the cost of overhauling a typewriter subsequently returned to its true owner (*e*), costs of litigation reasonably undertaken (*f*) and the costs of paying customs duty on a car which was impounded by the Customs and Excise because it had been illegally imported (*g*). See further as to general principles on assessing damages, ss. 53 and 54, *post*.

13. Sale by description.—(1) Where there is a contract for the sale of goods by description, there is an implied condition that the goods will correspond with the description (*h*).

(*c*) *Post*, Appendix I.

(*d*) Under s. 12 (2) (a), the warranty implied is that the goods *are free* and will remain free until the time when the property is to pass from encumbrances not disclosed or known to the buyer. This is wider than the original s. 12 (3) of the 1893 Act, under which the warranty was merely that the goods shall be free from encumbrances which are not declared or known to the buyer. The practical effect is probably the same. The seller will now be in breach of warranty if he does not disclose all charges and encumbrances affecting the goods, but it is difficult to conceive of a situation in which the buyer will suffer any loss recoverable under s. 12 (2) which would not have been recoverable under the original s. 12 (2) or (3) of the 1893 Act.

(*e*) *Mason* v. *Burningham*, [1949] 2 All E. R. 134; [1949] 2 K. B. 545, C. A. But, following the decision in *Greenwood* v. *Bennett*, [1972] 3 All E. R. 586; [1973] 1 Q. B. 195, C. A., the plaintiff might well have been entitled to insist on being reimbursed the cost of the repairs before handing over the typewriter to the true owner, and if in any future case a purchaser has unreasonably failed to avail himself of such a right against the true owner, he may be precluded from recovering from the seller what he should have recovered from the owner. See also s. 6 of the Torts (Interference with Goods) Act 1977, which provides for an allowance to be made in respect of improvements in the assessment of damages for wrongful interference.

(*f*) *Bowmaker (Commercial)* v. *Day*, [1965] 2 All E. R. 856*n*.; [1965] 1 W. L. R. 1396.

(*g*) *Stock* v. *Urey*, [1954] N. I. 71; but it is difficult to see why the purchaser in that case was held to be entitled to pay more than the value of the car to the customs. In general, unless a purchaser can show that he acted reasonably in paying more than the value of the goods to recover them, he ought not to recover the excess from the seller: *cf. Darbishire* v. *Warran*, [1963] 3 All E. R. 310; [1963] 1 W. L. R. 1067, C. A.

(*h*) *Shepherd* v. *Kain* (1821), 5 B. & Ald. 240; *Josling* v. *Kingsford* (1863), 13 C. B., N. S., 447; *Borrowman* v. *Drayton* (1876), 2 Ex. D. 15, C. A.

(2) If the sale is by sample as well as by description, it is not sufficient that the bulk of the goods corresponds with the sample if the goods do not also correspond with the description (*i*).

(3) A sale of goods is not prevented from being a sale by description by reason only that, being exposed for sale or hire, they are selected by the buyer.

(4) Paragraph 4 of Schedule 1 below applies in relation to a contract made before 18 May 1973.

ILLUSTRATIONS

(1) A agrees to buy a second-hand reaping machine, which he has never seen, but which the seller assures him to have been new the previous year, and to have been used only to cut about fifty acres. This is a sale by description, and if the machine does not correspond with the description, A may reject it (*k*).

(2) Contract for sale of large overboots, described as "waders". A sample is sent to the buyer before he places his order. The "waders" were not articles known to ordinary commercial trading and formed part of the anti-gas equipment which had been made for the Government during the Second World War. The slightest examination of them would have cast great doubt upon any inference that they were waterproof. The buyer did not rely on the description. The sale is not a sale by description (*l*).

(3) Contract for the sale of East African copra cake. The goods are accepted and resold but are subsequently found to be so adulterated with castor oil as to be poisonous to cattle. The goods do not correspond with their description in that they are a mixture of copra cake and castor oil and are useless for any purpose for which copra cake could be expected to be used. The sellers are not protected by a clause in the contract to the effect that the "goods are not warranted free from defect rendering same unmerchantable which would not be apparent on reasonable examination, any statute or rule of law notwithstanding" (*m*).

(4) A sells to B a food compounded in accordance with an agreed formula. This is a sale by description. The formula includes herring meal. A uses herring meal which (unknown to either party) is contaminated by dimethylnitrosamine (D.M.N.A.) produced by a chemical reaction following the use of sodium nitrite as a preservative. D.M.N.A. (unknown to either party) is

---

(*i*) *Nichol* v. *Godts* (1854), 10 Exch. 191 (foreign refined rape oil); *Azémar* v. *Casella* (1867), L. R. 2 C. P. 677, Ex. Ch. (long staple Salem cotton); *Steels and Busks* v. *Bleecker Bik & Co.*, [1956] 1 Lloyd's Rep. 228 (pale crepe rubber, quality as previously delivered). See further s. 15, *post*, as to sale by sample.

(*k*) *Varley* v. *Whipp*, [1900] 1 Q. B. 513.

(*l*) *Travers* v. *Longel* (1947), 64 T. L. R. 150.

(*m*) *Pinnock Brothers* v. *Lewis & Peat*, [1923] 1 K. B. 690; as explained in *Ashington Piggeries, Ltd.* v. *Christopher Hill, Ltd.*, [1971] 1 All E. R. 847; [1972] A. C. 441, H. L.; see also *Robert A. Munro & Co.* v. *Meyer*, [1930] 2 K. B. 312, at pp. 326–328 ("goods to be taken with all faults and defects at valuation" does not exclude the section and applies only to goods answering the trade description), applied *Champanhac & Co., Ltd.* v. *Waller & Co., Ltd.*, [1948] 2 All E. R. 724; *E. & S. Ruben, Ltd.* v. *Faire Bros. & Co., Ltd.*, [1949] 1 All E. R. 215; [1949] 1 K. B. 254. See also the passage on fundamental breach and exemption clauses, p. 10, *ante*.

toxic to mink, for which, as A knows, B requires the food. The food corresponds with its description. D.M.N.A. is not an extraneous substance added to herring meal. It is just herring meal gone wrong (*n*).

(5) A sells seed to B as "English sainfoin" on the terms that "seller gives no warranty express or implied as to growth, description, or any other matters." B re-sells to C. The seed is sown and turns out to be giant sainfoin. The seed does not correspond with the description, and B may recover damages from A as in a case of breach of warranty (*o*).

(6) Contract for purchase of 3,000 tins of canned fruit from Australia, to be packed in cases each containing 30 tins. When the goods are tendered in London, a substantial part is tendered in cases containing 24 tins. It has been held that the buyer may reject the whole (*p*), but this decision has been stigmatised as technical and due for re-examination by the House of Lords (*q*).

(7) Contract for purchase of a number of "new Singer cars" providing that "all conditions and warranties implied by statute, common law, or otherwise" be excluded. One of the cars delivered is a used car: the sellers are in breach because the description "new Singer car" is an express, not an implied, term (*r*).

(8) Contract for sale of Australian canned peaches "afloat per s.s. Morton Bay due London approx. June 8th." Ship at that time already known not to be due until June 19th; in fact she arrives June 21st. Clause is part of description and buyers are entitled to reject (*s*).

Derivation.—Section 13 of the 1893 Act. Subsection (3) was introduced as s. 13 (2) (*t*) into the 1893 Act by s. 2 of the Supply of Goods (Implied Terms) Act 1973. Subsections (1) and (2) together formed s. 13 (1).

Definitions.—For "contract of sale," see s. 2 (1), *ante*, and s. 61 (1), *post*.

Cross-references.—For the classification of terms in a contract for the sale of goods, the doctrine of fundamental breach, and the construction of exemption clause, see p. 8 *et seq.*, *ante*. For their effect see s. 11, *ante*. *Cf.* s. 18, rule 5, *post* (passing of property in unascertained goods sold by description). For restrictions on contracting out of the provisions of this section, see ss. 6, 26, Unfair Contract Terms Act 1977, *post*, Appendix I.

(*n*) *Ashington Piggeries, Ltd.* v. *Christopher Hill, Ltd.*, [1971] 1 All E. R. 847; [1972] A. C. 441, H. L.

(*o*) *Wallis* v. *Pratt*, [1911] A. C. 394, approving the dissenting judgment of FLETCHER MOULTON, L. J. at [1910] 2 K. B. 1011.

(*p*) *Re Moore & Co.* v. *Landauer & Co.*, [1921] 2 K. B. 519, C. A.; *cf. Manbre Saccharine Co.* v. *Corn Products Co.*, [1919] 1 K. B. 198, at p. 207.

(*q*) *Reardon Smith* v. *Hansen-Tangen*, [1976] 3 All E. R. 570, at p. 576; [1976] 1 W. L. R. 989, at p. 998.

(*r*) *Andrews Bros., Ltd.* v. *Singer & Co., Ltd.*, [1934] 1 K. B. 17. It would seem that the case might equally well have been decided on the basis of breach of a fundamental term: see *per* PARKER, L. J. in *Karsales (Harrow)* v. *Wallis*, [1956] 2 All E. R. 866, at p. 871 (a hire purchase case); and 77 L. Q. R. 98.

(*s*) *Macpherson Train* v. *Ross*, [1955] 2 All E. R. 445.

(*t*) The new sub-s. (2) probably did not change the law: see, *e.g.*, *Grant* v. *Australian Knitting Mills*, [1936] A. C. 85, at p. 100, P. C., and the cases cited at p. 120, note (*a*).

COMMENT

Sale by description.—Where goods are described by the contract, and the buyer contracts in reliance on that description, there is a sale by description even if the goods be specific. CHANNELL, J., has said:

> "The term 'sale of goods by description' must apply to all cases where the purchaser has not seen the goods, but is relying on the description alone" (*u*).

And it may apply even where he has seen and selected the goods, if the deviation of the goods from the description is not apparent (*a*). The only sales not by description are sales of specific goods *as such*. Specific goods may be sold as such when they are sold without any description, express or implied; or where any statement made about them is not essential to their identity; or where, though the goods are described, the description is not relied upon, as where the buyer buys the goods such as they are (*b*). The fact that a sale is a sale by sample does not prevent it from being a sale by description also (*c*). Where a sale is not a sale by sample but the seller sends a sample of the goods to the buyer, the sample will be taken into account as evidence of the description given by the seller (*d*).

Section 6 of the Unfair Contract Terms Act 1977 (*e*) provides that, except in the case of international supply contracts (*f*), liability for breach of the condition implied by this section cannot be excluded or restricted (*g*) by reference to any contract term as against a person dealing as a consumer (*h*), and in other cases can be excluded or restricted by reference to a contract term only in so far as the term satisfies the requirement of reasonableness (*i*).

But, quite apart from the provisions of the Unfair Contract Terms Act, an exemption clause will not normally be construed as relieving a seller from liability for failing to supply goods corresponding with the contract description. Thus, where there is a sale by description and the

---

(*u*) *Varley* v. *Whipp*, [1900] 1 Q. B. 513, at p. 516; *Daniels and Daniels* v. *White and Sons and Tarbard*, [1938] 4 All E. R. 258; *Armaghdown Motors, Ltd.* v. *Grays Motors, Ltd.*, [1963] N. Z. L. R. 5.

(*a*) *Beale* v. *Taylor*, [1967] 3 All E. R. 253; [1967] 1 W. L. R. 1193, C. A. *Cf. Medway Oil and Storage Co.* v. *Silica Oil Corporation* (1928), 33 Com. Cas. 195, H. L.; *Godley* v. *Perry*, [1960] 1 All E. R. 36; [1960] 1 W. L. R. 9; *Elder Smith Goldsbrough Mort, Ltd.* v. *MacBride*, [1976] 2 N. S. W. L. R. 631, where the text was cited with approval ("breeding bull" sterile).

(*b*) *Benjamin on Sale* (7th Edn.), p. 641, cited with approval by SELLERS, J. in *Travers* v. *Longel* (1947), 64 T. L. R. 150. *See* also *Christopher Hill, Ltd.* v. *Ashington Piggeries, Ltd.*, [1969] 3 All E. R. 1496, at p. 1511, C. A.; reversed on other grounds: [1971] 1 All E. R. 847; [1972] A. C. 441, H. L.

(*c*) *Nichol* v. *Godts* (1854), 10 Exch. 191; *Harrison and Jones* v. *Bunten and Lancaster*, [1953] 1 All E. R. 903; [1955] 1 Q. B. 646.

(*d*) *Boshali* v. *Allied Commercial Exporters, Ltd.*, [1961] Nigeria L. R. 917, P. C.

(*e*) *Post*, Appendix I.

(*f*) As defined in s. 26 of that Act, *post*, Appendix I.

(*g*) Exclusion of the condition itself and certain other provisions are also negated by s. 13 of the 1977 Act, *post*, Appendix I.

(*h*) Dealing as a consumer is defined by s. 12 of the 1977 Act, *post*, Appendix I.

(*i*) The requirement of reasonableness is set out in s. 11 of the 1977 Act, *post*, Appendix I.

goods tendered or delivered do not answer the description, the seller cannot take advantage of any term in the contract merely to protect him from liability for defects in the things sold (*k*). It is for this reason that it is misleading to say, as the Act does, that it is a condition of the contract that the goods should correspond with the description. If this obligation were merely a condition of the contract, it would be possible to exclude it by such an exemption clause (*l*). But the true position is that if a seller delivers goods which do not correspond with the contract description he had not merely broken a condition of the contract but has entirely failed to perform it. As Lord ABINGER said, as long ago as 1838,

> "If a man offers to buy peas of another, and he sends him beans, he does not perform his contract; but that is not a warranty; there is no warranty that he should sell him peas; the contract is to sell peas, and if he sends him anything else in their stead, it is a non-performance of it" (*m*).

It follows that the crucial question to decide in a particular case is often whether words used in the contract with reference to the goods sold form part of the description under which the goods are sold, or amount only to a condition or warranty against the breach of which the seller can protect himself, or are no more than a means of identifying the goods (*n*). Thus if a seller contracts to sell, "round mahogany logs" with an exemption clause which protects him against breaches of condition, and then tenders logs which are mahogany but square, the first question will be whether the shape of the logs formed part of their contractual description, and this will be a question of construction of the particular contract. Once it is decided that contractual words do form part of the description, it remains necessary to decide whether the defect complained of is sufficient to prevent the goods from answering that description, and this will be a question of fact in each case. Where there is a recognised trade description, the proper test is whether the goods comply with the description by the standard generally applied and accepted in the trade (*o*).

Once there is a misdescription however small then subject to the *de minimis* rule the buyer is entitled to reject the goods if he acts in time (*p*).

Failure on the part of the seller to deliver goods which correspond with the contract description may also have the effect of preventing the property from passing (*q*).

(*k*) Similarly where there is a sale by sample no such exemption clause can absolve the seller from his obligation to deliver goods which correspond with the sample: *Champanhac & Co., Ltd.* v. *Waller & Co., Ltd.*, [1948] 2 All E. R. 724.

(*l*) *L'Estrange* v. *Graucob, Ltd.*, [1934] 2 K. B. 394, shows clearly that a seller can effectively protect himself from liability for breach of a condition if he uses appropriate words.

(*m*) *Chanter* v. *Hopkins* (1838), 4 M. & W. 399, at p. 404; Lord BLACKBURN used the same illustration in *Bowes* v. *Shand* (1877), 2 App. Cas. 455, at p. 480.

(*n*) *Rearden Smith* v. *Hansen Tangen*, [1976] 3 All E. R. 570; [1976] 1 W. L. R. 989, H. L.

(*o*) *Steels and Busks* v. *Bleecker Bik & Co.*, [1956] 1 Lloyd's Rep. 228.

(*p*) *Rapalli* v. *Take*, [1958] 2 Ll. R. 469, C. A.

(*q*) *Varley* v. *Whipp*, [1900] 1 Q. B. 513 (though the possible effect of s. 11 (4) does not

Relation to s. 14.—Where the article tendered answers the description, the buyer must, apart from some warranty, express or implied, take the risk as to its quality and condition (*r*). Thus a person purchasing "safety glass" flying goggles gets what he contracts to get if the glass is of the kind generally understood to be meant by that term, and it is not a condition of the contract that the glass should be absolutely safe (*s*).

The implied conditions of merchantableness and fitness for a particular purpose were formerly treated as part of the description, but the 1893 Act treated them as distinct and the fact that goods are merchantable is not a proper test to apply in determining whether goods satisfy a contract description (*t*).

14. Implied undertakings as to quality or fitness.—(1) Except as provided by this section and section 15 below and subject to any other enactment (*u*), there is no implied condition or warranty as to the quality or fitness for any particular purpose of goods supplied under a contract of sale (*a*).

(2) Where the seller sells goods in the course of a business, there is an implied condition that the goods supplied under the contract are of merchantable quality, except that there is no such condition—

(a) as regards defects specifically drawn to the buyer's attention before the contract is made; or

(b) if the buyer examines the goods before the contract is made, as regards defects which that examination ought to reveal.

---

appear to have been argued in this case). *Cf.* the dictum of GAVAN DUFFY, J., in *O'Connor* v. *Donnelly*, [1944] Ir. Jur. Rep. 1, at p. 8.

(*r*) *Barr* v. *Gibson* (1838), 3 M. & W. 390; *cf. Ward* v. *Hobbs* (1878), 4 App. Cas. 13.

(*s*) *Grenfell* v. *E. B. Meyrowitz, Ltd.*, [1936] 2 All E. R. 1313, C. A. But if a misleading description is used in the course of a business, an offence may be committed under the Trade Descriptions Act 1968; see p. 56, *ante*.

(*t*) *Arcos* v. *E. A. Ronaasen & Son*, [1933] A. C. 470.

(*u*) See, for example, note (*t*) at p. 53, *ante*.

(*a*) As to the words "supplied under a contract of sale," see the comment to sub-s. (2), *post*. For conditions imported into contracts for work and labour, see *Myers* v. *Brent Cross Service Co.*, [1934] 1 K. B. 46, D. C.; *Samuels* v. *Davis*, [1943] 2 All E. R. 3, C. A.; [1943] 1 K. B. 526; *Ingham* v. *Emes*, [1955] 2 All E. R. 740; [1955] 2 Q. B. 366, C. A.; *Young and Marten, Ltd.* v. *McManus Childs, Ltd.*, [1968] 2 All E. R. 1169; [1969] 1 A. C. 454, H. L.; *Gloucestershire County Council* v. *Richardson*, [1968] 3 All E. R. 1181; [1969] 1 A. C. 480, H. L.; as to contracts of hire and hire purchase, see *Drury* v. *Buckland*, [1941] 1 All E. R. 269, C. A., the remarks of McNAIR, J., in *Andrews* v. *Hopkinson*, [1956] 3 All E. R. 422, at p. 426; [1957] 1 Q. B. 229, at p. 237; *Yeoman Credit, Ltd.* v. *Apps*, [1961] 2 All E. R. 281; [1962] 2 Q. B. 508, C. A.; *Astley Industrial Trust* v. *Grimley*, [1963] 2 All E. R. 33; [1963] 1 W. L. R. 584, C. A.; *Charterhouse Credit Co.* v. *Tolly*, [1963] 2 All E. R. 432, 440; [1963] 2 Q. B. 683, 707, C. A.

(3) Where the seller sells goods in the course of a business and the buyer, expressly or by implication, makes known—

(a) to the seller, or
(b) where the purchase price or part of it is payable by instalments and the goods were previously sold by a credit-broker to the seller, to that credit broker,

any particular purpose for which the goods are being bought, there is an implied condition that the goods supplied under the contract are reasonably fit for that purpose, whether or not that is a purpose for which such goods are commonly supplied, except where the circumstances show that the buyer does not rely (*b*), or that it is unreasonable for him to rely, on the skill or judgment of the seller or credit-broker.

(4) An implied condition or warranty about quality or fitness for a particular purpose may be annexed to a contract of sale by usage.

(5) The preceding provisions of this section apply to a sale by a person who in the course of a business is acting as agent for another as they apply to a sale by a principal in the course of a business, except where that other is not selling in the course of a business and either the buyer knows that fact or reasonable steps are taken to bring it to the notice of the buyer before the contract is made.

(6) Goods of any kind are of merchantable quality within the meaning of subsection (2) above if they are as fit for the purpose or purposes for which goods of that kind are commonly bought as it is reasonable to expect having regard to any description applied to them, the price (if relevant) and all the other relevant circumstances.

(7) Paragraph 5 of Schedule 1 below applies in relation to a contract made on or after 18 May 1973 and before the appointed day, and paragraph 6 in relation to one made before 18 May 1973.

(8) In subsection (7) above and paragraph 5 of Schedule 1 below references to the appointed day are to the day appointed for the purposes of those provisions by an order of the Secretary of State made by statutory instrument.

(*b*) *Ashford S. C.* v. *Dependable Motors*, [1961] 1 All E. R. 96; [1961] A. C. 336, P. C. (reliance by corporation: one agent makes known the purpose; another decides to buy).

ILLUSTRATIONS

Subsection (2).—(1) Plaintiff goes into a beer-house which he knows is tied to Holden & Co., and asks for beer. Beer contaminated with arsenic is supplied to him, and he is injured in consequence. This is a breach of condition and the seller is liable in damages (*c*).

(2) B by a written contract buys from Fiat Motors, Ltd. a Fiat motor omnibus, which he has inspected, and orders the chassis of six more. He explains orally that they are required for heavy traffic on hilly roads. When the cars are delivered they break down and are unfit for the traffic required. The seller is liable in damages because (1) the cars are not fit for the particular purpose required, and (2) the cars must be "merchantable," which they are not (*d*).

(3) Contract for the sale of 600 motor horns as required. The buyer accepts the first lot delivered. He rejects the rest as they are nearly all dented and scratched owing to bad packing. The motor horns could be repaired at a small expense. The contract is severable, and the buyer may reject the subsequent deliveries as the horns are unmerchantable (*e*).

(4) Plaintiff buys groundnut meal from the defendant for use as an ingredient in poultry foods. The meal is poisonous and many of the birds to which the poultry foods are fed die. The meal could safely be used in smaller inclusions for feeding to certain classes of poultry, and to certain other livestock. Before 1973, the meal was held to be of merchantable quality (*f*). But this may no longer be the case as it would not seem to be "as fit for the purpose or purposes for which goods of that kind are commonly bought as it is reasonable to expect", see s. 14 (6).

(5) A buys a new car from B. The car has minor defects which are not dangerous and are easily remediable under the manufacturer's guarantee. The seller is willing to remedy them. The car is merchantable and is not rendered unmerchantable just because the first attempt to remedy the defects is unsuccessful (*g*).

(6) A buys a second hand car from B for £295. The normal top price for a car of that make and age is £275. The car is in very poor condition and is either not roadworthy or hardly roadworthy. A judge is entitled to conclude that the car is not of merchantable quality as defined in s. 14 (6) (*h*).

Subsection (3).

(7) Plaintiff asks defendant for a hot-water bottle, and inquires whether it will stand boiling water. Defendant sells him an American rubber bottle, saying it will stand hot but not boiling water. The bottle, which was got for plaintiff's wife, bursts and injures her. The jury find that the bottle was not fit for use as a hot-water bottle. There is a breach of condition, and the seller is liable in damages (*i*).

(*c*) *Wren* v. *Holt*, [1903] 1 K. B. 610, C. A. As to measure of damages, see *Bostock* v. *Nicholson*, [1904] 1 K. B. 725, C. A., and s. 53, *post*.

(*d*) *Bristol Tramways Co.* v. *Fiat Motors, Ltd.*, [1910] 2 K. B. 831, C. A.

(*e*) *Jackson* v. *Rotax Motor and Cycle Co.*, [1910] 2 K. B. 937, C. A.

(*f*) *Henry Kendall & Sons* v. *William Lillico & Sons, Ltd.*, [1968] 2 All E. R. 444; [1969] 2 A. C. 31, H. L.; see also *Labrecque* v. *Saskatchewan Wheat Pool*, [1980] 3 W. W. R. 558 (weedkiller of merchantable quality although it damaged certain crops as well as killing weeds, but seller liable in negligence for failing to warn of danger to crops).

(*g*) *Millars of Falkirk* v. *Turpie*, 1976 S. L. T. (Notes) 66 (Ct. of Sess.).

(*h*) *Towerbrook, Ltd.* v. *Williams* (1976), unreported, Transcript 426, C. A.

(*i*) *Priest* v. *Last*, [1903] 2 K. B. 148, C. A. *Cf. Geddling* v. *Marsh*, [1920] 1 K. B. 668 (mineral water bottle).

(8) Plaintiff buys milk from a milk dealer for family use. The milk account book supplied to plaintiff contains a statement of the precautions taken to keep the milk pure. The milk contains the germs of typhoid fever, and plaintiff's wife becomes infected and dies. This is a breach of condition, and the milk dealer is liable in damages (*k*).

(9) A tells B that he can supply him with bunkering coal to suit his steamers. B says he will give an order, but that the order must come through L, the coal merchant with whom he deals. This conversation is repeated to L, who gives the order. If coal unfit for bunkering is supplied and rejected, A cannot sue L for the price (*l*).

(10) Sale of 500 tons of coal for bunkering steamship *Manchester*. It is known that the only available supply is from coal now at sea as there is a railway strike on. The coal is delivered, and found to be quite unsuitable for bunkering the *Manchester*. There is an implied condition of suitability, and the seller is liable in damages (*m*).

Derivation.—Subsections (1), (2), (4) and (5) are taken from s. 14 of the 1893 Act as substituted by s. 3 of the Supply of Goods (Implied Terms) Act 1973. Subsection (3) is taken from s. 14 (3) of the 1893 Act as substituted by Sch. 4, para. 3 of the Consumer Credit Act 1974 with effect from a date to be fixed. Subsection (6) is taken from s. 62 (1A) of the 1893 Act, which was inserted by s. 7 (2) of the Supply of Goods (Implied Terms) Act 1973.

Section 14 is to come into force on a day to be appointed under s. 14 (8) and until that time the version of s. 14 set out in para. 5 of Sch. 1, *post*, represents the law. Most of the provisions in that version are identical to those set out in sub-ss. (1) to (6) above, the only differences being in sub-s. (3) where the references to credit-brokers are omitted. Instead, similar provisions are incorporated in sub-s. (7) of that version by reference to persons conducting negotiations antecedent to an agreement for sale under which the price or part of it is payable by instalments.

Definitions.—For "contract of sale," see s. 2 (1), *ante*, and s. 61 (1), *post*. For "business," "buyer," "credit-broker," "goods," "quality," "seller" and "warranty," see s. 61 (1), *post*.

Cross-references.—For a general discussion as to terms of contracts, fundamental breach, and exemption clauses, see p. 8, *ante*. For the history of conditions and warranties, see Note A, *post*, Appendix II. For restrictions on exemption clauses, see the Unfair Contract Terms Act 1977, *post*, Appendix I. *Cf.* s. 34, *post* (buyer's right to examine).

History.—In a case of 1838 where a ship was bought while on a voyage, and had stranded, though she was not a total wreck, PARKE, B. said:

"In the bargain and sale of an existing chattel, by which the property passes,

---

(*k*) *Frost* v. *Aylesbury Dairy Co.*, [1905] 1 K. B. 608, C. A.; *Jackson* v. *Watson & Sons*, [1909] 2 K. B. 193, C. A. (tinned salmon: death of plaintiff's wife).

(*l*) *Crichton* v. *Love*, 1908 S. C. 818.

(*m*) *Manchester Liners, Ltd.* v. *Rea, Ltd.*, [1922] 2 A. C. 74.

the law does not, in the absence of fraud, imply any warranty of the good quality or condition of the chattel so sold" (*n*).

The old rule of *caveat emptor*—let the buyer take care—probably owed its origin to the fact that in early times nearly all sales of goods took place in market overt (*o*). Its policy was at one time defended on the ground that it tended to diminish litigation (*p*), but its scope was limited in the course of the 19th century, as the courts became more willing to imply terms that the goods should be of merchantable quality when the buyer had no opportunity of examining them (*q*) and that they should be fit for the purpose for which they were intended if the buyer made known that purpose to the seller so as to show that he relied on his skill and judgment (*r*). Its scope was further limited by the wording of the original s. 14 of the 1893 Act (*s*), particularly as subsequently interpreted by the courts (*t*).

Ultimately in 1969, the Law Commission recommended extensive changes to this section in its Report on Amendments to the Sale of Goods Act 1893 (*u*), and these recommendations were largely adopted and enacted in s. 3 of the Supply of Goods (Implied Terms) Act 1973, which substituted a new section for the original one.

The new section was amended by the Consumer Credit Act 1974, from a date to be appointed, as a consequence of the repeal by that Act of the Hire Purchase Acts and the introduction of a new system of consumer credit control, but no date was appointed prior to the repeal of the 1893 Act.

Scope for the rule of *caveat emptor* still remains where the circumstances envisaged by the present section are not satisfied.

Scotland.—In Scotland formerly, it was held that the seller guaranteed the buyer against all latent defects. But by s. 6 of the Mercantile Law Amendment (Scotland) Act 1856, it was provided that if the seller did not know the goods to be defective or of bad quality, the goods, with all faults, should be at the risk of the purchaser unless there was an express warranty or unless the goods were expressly sold for a particular specified purpose. This enactment was intended to assimilate Scottish to English law, but it laid down a narrower rule for the former country. Now a uniform rule is laid down for both countries.

(*n*) *Barr* v. *Gibson* (1838), 3 M. & W. 390, at p. 399, a decision perhaps even then already against the trend of judicial opinion: see *Benjamin on Sale* (8th ed.), p. 612.

(*o*) *Morley* v. *Attenborough* (1849), 3 Exch. 500, at p. 511.

(*p*) Mercantile Law Commission 1855, 2nd Report, p. 10.

(*q*) *Jones* v. *Just* (1868), L. R. 3 Q. B. 197, reviewing the earlier authorities.

(*r*) *Randall* v. *Newson* (1877), 2 Q. B. D. 102, C. A., reviewing the earlier authorities.

(*s*) See the 2nd edition of this work at p. 30.

(*t*) See the comment to this section in the 16th edition of this work.

(*u*) Law Com. No. 24.

COMMENT

Exemption Clauses.—Section 6 of the Unfair Contract Terms Act 1977 (*a*) provides that except in the case of international supply contracts (*b*), the conditions implied by this section cannot be excluded or restricted (*c*) by reference to any contract term as against a person dealing as a consumer (*d*) and in other cases can be excluded or restricted by reference to a contract term only insofar as the term satisfies the requirement of reasonableness (*e*).

Subsection (2).—The original subsection in the 1893 Act (*f*) read "Where goods are bought by description from a seller who deals in goods of that description (whether he be the manufacturer or not), there is an implied condition that the goods shall be of merchantable quality; provided that if the buyer has examined the goods, there shall be no implied condition as regards defects which such examination ought to have revealed".

The condition implied by the present subsection differs from the condition of merchantable quality formerly implied in the following respects:

(1) The original provision only applied when the goods were bought by description. It is no longer necessary that the goods should be bought by description.

(2) The original provision applied only where the seller dealt in goods of that description. Now it is sufficient that the seller sells the goods in the course of a business (*g*). This would include a sale of goods which are totally different from any the seller has dealt in previously. Indeed, it is unnecessary that the seller should ever have sold any goods previously.

It is not clear whether a sale of all or part of the capital equipment of a business will necessarily be a sale in the course of a business. But it is not necessary that the seller should be in business as a vendor or dealer. It is sufficient if the sale was an integral part of the business in question (*h*).

(3) Before 1973, the requirement that the goods should be of merchantable quality was frequently the subject of litigation. A number of definitions were put forward, but following two

(*a*) *Post*, Appendix I.

(*b*) Excluded from s. 6 by s. 26 of the 1977 Act, *post*, Appendix I.

(*c*) Exclusion of the conditions themselves and certain other provisions are also negated by s. 13 of the 1977 Act, *post*, Appendix I.

(*d*) Dealing as a consumer is defined by s. 12 of the 1977 Act, *post*, Appendix I.

(*e*) The requirement of reasonableness is set out in s. 11 of the 1977 Act, *post*, Appendix I.

(*f*) Reproduced in para. 6 of Sch. 1, *post*.

(*g*) "Business" is defined by s. 61 (1), *post*, to include a profession and the activities of any government department or local or public authority. For the meaning of "in the course of a business" see *Borough of Havering* v. *Stevenson*, [1970] 3 All E. R. 609; [1970] 1 W. L. R. 1375, D. C.

(*h*) *Borough of Havering* v. *Stevenson, supra*.

decisions of the House of Lords, it appeared that as a general rule (*i*), goods would be of merchantable quality if in the form in which they were tendered they would be used by a reasonable man for some purpose for which goods of the same quality and same general character and designation would normally be used, so as to be saleable under the description by which they were sold at a price not substantially less than the contract price (*k*).

"Merchantable quality" is now defined by sub-s. (6), which reproduces the definition first introduced into the 1893 Act (as s. 62 (1A) of that Act) by s. 7 (2) of the Supply of Goods (Implied Terms) Act 1973. Under this definition goods are of merchantable quality if they are as fit for the purpose or purposes for which goods of that kind are commonly bought as it is reasonable to expect having regard to any description applied to them, the price (if relevant) and all the other relevant circumstances.

" 'Merchantable . . .' is a composite quality comprising elements of description, purpose, condition and price. The relevant significance of each of those elements will vary from case to case according to the nature of the goods in question and the characteristics of the market which exists for them" (*l*).

The pre-1973 decisions on the meaning of "merchantable quality" no longer represent the law (*m*), but a number of dicta in the course of those decisions are still relevant in considering how to apply the new statutory definition. Thus, if goods are offered for sale at a very cheap price, this is an indication that they might well not be as fit for the purposes for which such goods are commonly bought as most goods of that description (*n*) though that inference may not be made if the seller

---

(*i*) It would be dangerous to treat this definition as universally accurate: see *Henry Kendall & Sons* v. *William Lillico & Sons, Ltd.*, [1968] 2 All E. R. at p. 451; [1969] 2 A. C. at p. 77, *per* Lord REID; *B. S. Brown & Son, Ltd.* v. *Craiks, Ltd.*, [1970] 1 All E. R. at p. 825; [1970] 1 W. L. R. at p. 754, *per* Lord REID.

(*k*) *B. S. Brown, Ltd.* v. *Craiks, Ltd.*, [1970] 1 All E. R. 823; [1970] 1 W. L. R. 752, H. L. Their Lordships adopted the definition given by Lord WRIGHT in *Cammell Laird & Co.* v. *Manganese Bronze and Brass Co., Ltd.*, [1934] A. C. 402, at p. 430, as amended by Lord REID in *Henry Kendall & Sons* v. *William Lillico & Sons, Ltd.*, [1968] 2 All E. R. at p. 451; [1969] 2 A. C. at pp. 76–77, but modified it in two respects: by allowing that the price element may be material (thus meeting criticisms of Lords GUEST, PEARCE and WILBERFORCE in *Kendall* v. *Lillico*); and by holding that it was not necessary that the goods should be usable for some purpose for which they—the contract goods—were normally used, provided they were usable for some purpose for which goods of the same general character and designation would normally be used. See also *Cehave N. V.* v. *Bremer Handelgesellschaft m.b.h.*, [1975] 3 All E. R. 739; [1976] Q. B. 44; 85 L. Q. R. 74, C. A.

(*l*) *Cehave N. V.* v. *Bremer Handelgesellshaft, supra, per* ORMROD, L. J., at pp. 763 and 80.

(*m*) *Lee* v. *York Coach & Marine*, [1977] R. T. R. 35, C. A.; *McDonald* v. *Engine Garage* (1975), unreported, Court of Appeal transcript 422A, *per* JAMES and BRIDGE, L. JJ. But see the different view of Lord DENNING, M. R. in the same case and in *Cehave N. V.* v. *Bremer Handelgesellschaft m.b.h., supra.*

(*n*) *Cf. B. S. Brown, Ltd.* v. *Craiks, Ltd.*, [1970] 1 All E. R. 823, at pp. 825, 828, 830–831; [1970] 1 W. L. R. 752, at pp. 754–755, 757–758, 760.

offers some other explanation for their cheapness, or if it is reasonable to draw some other inference from the circumstances (*o*).

Further, if goods are fit for the purpose or purposes for which they are bought but because of defects their value is less than their price this will not by itself and without considering any other circumstances mean that they are not of merchantable quality, particularly if there is a provision in the contract giving the buyer an allowance in respect of the defects in question (*p*).

On the other hand it may no longer be sufficient that the goods can be used for one purpose for which goods of that kind can normally be used, if it is reasonable in all the circumstances to expect them to be fit for some other purpose as well (*q*). Moreover, the degree of fitness which it is reasonable to expect would normally seem to be such a degree as would enable them to be safely used in the light of existing knowledge (*r*).

When goods have only one use in the ordinary course of things, and are not fit for that use, they are not merchantable (*s*).

Where a buyer orders an article under a trade name, he will normally be taken to have ordered it as manufactured at the date of the order (*t*), and its merchantable quality must therefore be determined on that basis.

If there is a condition of merchantable quality and the seller knows that the goods will undergo transit of a substantial duration, the condition requires that the goods be in such a state at the start of the transit that they will remain merchantable throughout normal transit to their destination, and for a reasonable time thereafter to allow for their disposal (*u*). So, too, if the seller knows the goods will need to be stored for a time before use or resale, they must remain of merchantable

---

(*o*) As, for example, if they are part of a clearance sale, or are described as shop soiled and no indication is given that they are sub-standard.

(*p*) *Cehave N. V.* v. *Bremer Handelgesellschaft*, [1975] 3 All E. R. 739; [1976] Q. B. 44; 85 L. Q. R. 74, C. A.

(*q*) Accordingly, cases such as *Kendall* v. *Lillico, ante*, illustration (4), and *Canada Atlantic Grain Export Co.* v. *Eilers* (1929), 35 Com. Cas. 90 would probably be decided differently today. But see *Cehave N. V.* v. *Bremer Handelgesellschaft, supra, per* Lord DENNING, M. R.

(*r*) As to the relevance before 1973 of after acquired knowledge as to the way the goods could safely be used, see *Kendall* v. *Lillico* at [1968] 2 All E. R. 478; [1969] 2 A. C. 108–109, *per* Lord GUEST, but *cf.* the dissenting judgment of Lord PEARCE at [1968] 2 All E. R. 486–487; [1969] 2 A. C. 118–119. Lord REID and Lord MORRIS, although agreeing in the result with Lord GUEST, do not appear to support his reasoning: see at [1968] 2 All E. R. 453, 469; [1969] 2 A. C. 79, 98. See further 86 L. Q. R. 167.

(*s*) *Grant* v. *Australian Knitting Mills, Ltd.*, [1936] A. C. 85.

(*t*) *Harris & Sons* v. *Plymouth Varnish and Colour Co., Ltd.*, (1933), 49 T. L. R. 521.

(*u*) *Beer* v. *Walker* (1877), 46 L.J. Q. B. 677; *Mash & Murrell* v. *Emanuel*, [1961] 1 All E. R. 485; [1961] 1 W. L. R. 862, reversed on the ground that the transit was not a normal one in fact: [1962] 1 All E. R. 77; [1962] 1 W. L. R. 16, C. A. ; *Hardwick Game Farm* v. *Suffolk Agricultural and Poultry Producers Association, Ltd.*, [1964] 2 Lloyd's Rep. 227, 270, *per* HAVERS, J., *Cordova Land Co.* v. *Victor Brothers Incorporated*, [1966] 1 W. L. R. 793. But see *Oleificio Zucchi S.p.A.* v. *Northern Sales, Ltd.*, [1965] 2 Lloyd's Rep. 496, 517, 518; 28 M. L. R. 189; and *cf.* s. 33, *post.*

quality, when properly stored, for long enough to give the buyer a reasonable opportunity of dealing with them (*a*).

The condition of merchantable quality extends to all goods supplied under the contract. This includes not only the goods contracted to be sold, but also all goods supplied in purported compliance with the contract (*b*) including containers (*c*).

If a trader who buys goods may be injuncted from selling them because the labels infringe another's trade marks, then they are not of merchantable quality (*d*). But it was held before 1973 that goods were not unmerchantable merely because their condition rendered them unsaleable in a foreign country to which the seller knew that the buyer intended to export them (*e*). Those decisions turned on the meaning of merchantable quality under the original section 14 (2) in the 1893 Act. The new definition is different, but unless there are special circumstances, as, for example, that the seller not only knew that the goods were intended for export, but also knew the legal requirements of the country to which they were being exported, it would not be reasonable to expect the goods to comply with special requirements of the local foreign law. The goods would therefore be of merchantable quality, as they would be as fit for the purpose or purposes for which such goods are commonly bought as it is reasonable to expect. Similarly, under the new subsection there is no condition of merchantable quality as regards defects specifically drawn to the buyer's attention before the contract is made. There was no equivalent provision before 1973, but it seems clear that this was also the position under the earlier subsection.

Examination.—Under the original subsection there was no implied condition if the buyer had examined the goods as regards any defect which ought to have been revealed by such examination. The new proviso (b) makes it clear that this exception now only applies if the examination preceeded the contract.

Generally, the implied condition will only be excluded in respect of defects which ought to have been revealed by the examination actually made (*f*). It may be, however, that the buyer's conduct will show that

---

(*a*) *Georgetown Seafoods, Ltd.* v. *Usen Fisheries* (1977), 78 D. L. R. (3d) 542.

(*b*) *Wilson* v. *Rickett Cockerell & Co., Ltd.*, [1954] 1 All E. R. 868; [1954] 1 Q. B. 598, C. A.

(*c*) *Geddling* v. *Marsh*, [1920] 1 K. B. 668; *MacLean* v. *People's Gas Supply Co., Ltd.*, [1940] 4 D. L. R. 433 (Sup. Ct. of Can.); *Niblett* v. *Confectioners Materials Co.*, [1921] 3 K. B. 387, C. A. As to free gifts, see *Esso* v. *Customs and Excise Commissioners*, [1976] 1 All E. R. 117; [1976] 1 W. L. R. 1, H. L.

(*d*) *Niblett* v. *Confectioners Materials Co.*, [1921] 3 K. B. 387, C. A. On the same principle, goods which cannot be resold in their existing packaging without infringing the Trade Descriptions Act 1968 are probably not of merchantable quality if supplied to a trader for resale.

(*e*) *Sumner Permain & Co.* v. *Webb & Co., Ltd.*, [1922] 1 K. B. 55, C. A.; *Phoenix Distributors* v. *Clarke*, [1966] 2 Lloyds' Rep. 285; affirmed [1967] 1 Lloyd's Rep. 518, C. A.

(*f*) *Bristol Tramways Co.* v. *Fiat Motors, Ltd.*, [1910] 2 K. B. 831, C. A.; and see *Canadian Yacht Sales* v. *MacDonald*, [1977] 2 Lloyd's Rep. 298 (where it would have taken a chemical analysis to reveal a defect in a yacht) and *cf.* the rule that a misrepresentation made in negotiating a contract is no less actionable because an opportunity to examine has been

he was willing to take the risk of any defects not revealed by a partial inspection which would have been apparent upon a full one, and in such a case the seller may not be liable for such defects (*g*).

Subsection (3).—The original subsection (1) in the 1893 Act (*h*) read "Where the buyer, expressly or by implication, makes known to the seller the particular purpose for which the goods are required, so as to show that the buyer relies on the seller's skill or judgment, and the goods are of a description which it is in the course of the seller's business to supply (whether he be the manufacturer or not), there is an implied condition that the goods shall be reasonably fit for such purpose, provided that in the case of a contract for the sale of a specific article under its patent or other trade name there is no implied condition as to its fitness for any particular purpose".

The present condition differs from the former condition in the following respects:

(1) The new provision applies whenever a seller sells goods in the course of a business (*i*). Before 1973 the goods had to be of a description which it was in the course of the seller's business to supply, but this requirement was broadly interpreted. Accordingly, even under the old law, generally, where a seller deliberately dealt in goods for the purpose of his business, he made it part of his business to supply such goods for the purposes of the original s. 14 (1) of the 1893 Act (*k*).

It was sufficient if the goods were of a kind which the seller supplied in the course of his business even though he had never sold goods of that exact description (*l*). It was not clear whether a person who sold goods in the course of his business of a kind which he had not previously supplied came within the original s. 14 (1), but the position probably was that if by entering the contract he was making it part of his business to supply such goods, and *a fortiori* if he had already acquired the goods with a view to selling them, then the subsection applied (*m*), though in such a case it may have been harder for the buyer to show that he

---

afforded to the other party and has been refused—see *e.g.*, *Redgrave* v. *Hurd* (1881), 20 Ch. D. 1, C. A.

(*g*) *Cf. Thornett and Fehr* v. *Beer & Son*, [1919] 1 K. B. 486, where a full examination was agreed to and an opportunity for such an examination was afforded to the buyer, but without the seller's knowledge the buyer failed to avail himself of it. In view of the clear wording of the new subsection, it is doubtful whether the condition will now be excluded in such a case except where the buyer is estopped from asserting that he did not examine the goods.

(*h*) Now reproduced in para. 6 of Sch. 1, *post*.

(*i*) See comment to s. 14 (2), *ante*, and s. 61 (1), *post*.

(*k*) *Buckley* v. *Lever Brothers, Ltd.*, [1953] 4 D. L. R. 16 ("special offer" of clothes pegs by detergent manufacturer); but contrast *Rahtjen* v. *Stern G. M. C. Trucks* (1976), 66 D. L. R. (3d) 566 (Manit. C. A.).

(*l*) *Ashington Piggeries, Ltd.* v. *Christopher Hill, Ltd.*, [1971] 1 All E. R. 847, H. L.; *Spencer Trading Co., Ltd.* v. *Devon*, [1947] 1 All E. R. 284.

(*m*) *Ashington Piggeries, Ltd.* v. *Christopher Hill, Ltd.*, *supra* at p. 876, *per* Lord WILBERFORCE, and *cf.* at p. 885, *per* Lord DIPLOCK.

relied on the seller's skill and judgment, and the court may more readily have held the implied condition to have been excluded by the course of dealing between the parties.

Where the buyer relied on the seller's skill and judgment only in relation to certain components of the goods, it would seem to have been sufficient if it was in the course of the seller's business to supply those components (*n*).

(2) The condition was previously implied where the buyer made known to the seller the particular purpose for which the goods were required so as to show that he relied on the seller's skill and judgment (*o*). The new provision puts the burden on the seller to show that the buyer did not rely on his skill or judgment or that in all the circumstances it was unreasonable for the buyer to rely on his skill or judgment. Previously it was sufficient to prove that he did rely on the seller's skill and judgment, whether or not such reliance was reasonable.

(3) The original sub-s. (1) was subject to a proviso which excluded any implied condition as to fitness for a particular purpose where a specified article was sold under its patent or trade name. This proviso has now been repealed, but in determining whether the circumstances show that a buyer did not rely, or that it was unreasonable for him to rely, on the seller's skill or judgment, the fact that he asked for a specific make of goods may still be relevant (*p*). Even before 1973, moreover, the proviso would not apply unless the buyer ordered the goods under a patent or trade name in such a way as to show that he was not relying on the seller's skill or judgment (*q*).

Any particular purpose.—There is no magic in the word "particular". A communicated purpose, if stated with reasonably sufficient precision, will be a particular purpose (*r*). A purpose may be in wide terms or it may be circumscribed or narrow. The less circumscribed the purpose, the less circumscribed as a rule, will be the range of goods which are reasonably fit for such purpose (*s*).

Reasonable fitness.—The implied undertakings as to fitness for a particular purpose and merchantable quality must be construed reasonably. Very minor complaints will be disregarded (*t*).

(*n*) *Ashington Piggeries, Ltd.* v. *Christopher Hill, Ltd.*, [1971] 1 All E. R. at pp. 855, 868.

(*o*) The new subsection reads "*any* particular purpose".

(*p*) *Cf. Daniels and Daniels* v. *White & Sons, and Tarbard*, [1938] 4 All E. R. 258, at p. 263 ("I want a bottle of R. White's lemonade").

(*q*) *Baldry* v. *Marshall*, [1925] 1 K. B. 260, C. A.; *Bristol Tramways Co.* v. *Fiat Motors, Ltd.*, [1910] 2 K. B. 831, C. A.

(*r*) *Henry Kendall & Sons* v. *William Lillico & Sons, Ltd.*, [1968] 2 All E. R. at pp. 465, 475, 482–483, 490; [1969] 2 A. C. at pp. 93, 105, 114, 123.

(*s*) *Henry Kendall & Sons* v. *William Lillico & Sons, Ltd., per* Lord PEARCE at [1969] 2 A. C. 114; [1968] 2 All E. R. 483.

(*t*) *Bristol Tramways Co.* v. *Fiat Motor Co., Ltd.*, [1910] 2 K. B. 831, at p. 841, C. A.; *Rapalli* v. *K. L. Take, Ltd.*, [1958] 2 Lloyd's Rep. 469, C. A.; *cf. Millars of Falkirk* v. *Turpie*, 1976 S. L. T. (Notes) 67 (*ante*, illustration (5)).

Reasonable fitness is a question of fact. In deciding the question of fact the rarity of the unsuitability should be weighed against the gravity of the consequence (*u*).

All relevant factors must be taken into account. Thus, if a car is sold for immediate use upon the roads which cannot safely be driven, it is not reasonably fit for the purpose intended, possibly even if it could have been made fit at small expense (*a*). But if it is sold on the footing that it is not or may not be safe to drive so that the buyer receives adequate warning of known or possible defects, there would be no implied condition that it was fit to be driven in its existing condition (*b*). In the case of second-hand goods a buyer should realise that defects will appear sooner or later. Thus, where a second-hand Jaguar was sold for £950 on the basis that it might need a repair to its clutch costing £25, but in fact a more serious repair was necessary costing £45, the car was held still to be reasonably fit for the purpose for which it was bought (*c*). But when another Jaguar was sold as being of exceptional quality and hardly run-in, although the representations were not taken literally, they were taken into account by the Court of Appeal in holding that the car was not fit for the purpose intended because the engine was in fact "clapped out" at the time of the sale and broke up completely after being driven a further 2300 miles (*d*).

Where the goods sold are fit for the purpose for which they are bought only if certain precautions are taken, and the buyer cannot be assumed to know this, they will not be reasonably fit if sold without any warning to the buyer to take those precautions (*e*).

Reliance.—"The buyer's reliance is a question of fact to be answered by examining all that was said and done with regard to the proposed transaction on either side from its first inception to the conclusion of the agreement to purchase" (*f*).

Before 1973, in order to succeed, the buyer had to show that in all the circumstances a reasonable man in the shoes of the seller would have realised that he was being relied on (*g*). In many cases it was sufficient if

(*u*) *Henry Kendall & Son* v. *William Lillico & Sons*, [1968] 2 All E. R. at p. 483; [1969] 2 A. C. at p. 115, *per* Lord PEARCE.

(*a*) *Lee* v. *York Coach and Marine*, [1977] R. T. R. 35, esp. at pp. 42, 43, C. A.

(*b*) As in *Carr* v. *G. and B. Auto Mart, Ltd.*, [1978] 5 W. W. R. 361 (sale of used car which both parties knew had not been driven for years "as is—no warranty"); and see *Hurley* v. *Dyke*, [1979] R. T. R. 265, H. L. (dangerous car sold at auction "as seen with all its faults and without warranty" and a seller who knew the car might be dangerous, but did not know that it was, was held to have discharged his duty of care to third parties by fair warning).

(*c*) *Bartlett* v. *Sidney Marcus, Ltd.*, [1965] 2 All E. R. 753; [1965] 1 W. L. R. 1013, C. A.

(*d*) *Crowther* v. *Solent Motor Co.*, [1975] 1 All E. R. 139; [1975] 1 W. L. R. 30, C. A.

(*e*) *Willis* v. *F. M. C. Machinery and Chemicals, Ltd.* (1976), 68 D. L. R. (3d) 127; and see *Lem* v. *Barotto Sports, Ltd.* (1976), 69 D. L. R. (3d) 276; *Vacwell Engineering* v. *B. D. H. Chemicals*, [1969] 3 All E. R. 1681; [1971] 1 Q. B. 88; compromised on appeal: [1970] 3 All E. R. 553; [1971] 1 Q. B. 111, C. A.

(*f*) *Medway Oil and Storage Co., Ltd.* v. *Silica Gel Corpn.* (1928), 33 Com. Cas. 195, at p. 196, *per* Lord SUMNER.

(*g*) *Henry Kendall & Sons* v. *William Lillico & Sons, Ltd.*, [1968] 2 All E. R. at p. 455; [1969] 2 A. C. at p. 81, *per* Lord REID.

the buyer made known to the seller the particular purpose for which he required the goods (*h*). The onus is now on the seller to show that the buyer did not rely on him or that it was unreasonable for the buyer to rely on him.

"It is clear that the reliance must be brought home to the mind of the seller, expressly or by implication. The reliance will seldom be express: it will usually arise by implication from the circumstances: thus to take a case of a purchase from a retailer, the reliance will in general be inferred from the fact that a buyer goes to the shop in the confidence that the tradesman has selected his stock with skill and judgment: the retailer need know nothing about the process of manufacture: it is immaterial whether he be manufacturer or not: the main inducement to deal with a good retail shop is the expectation that the tradesman will have bought the right goods of a good make . . ." (*i*).

But it would seem that no such inference can be drawn where two equally knowledgeable merchants are dealing with each other, just because one makes known to the other the purpose for which he requires the goods (*k*). In such a case, something more must be shown to prove reliance, as in *Henry Kendall & Sons* v. *William Lillico & Sons, Ltd.* (*l*), where the sellers had acquired goods from a new source and recommended them to the buyers.

Reliance is not excluded because the seller may not himself have seen the goods he is selling (*m*). It has been said, however, that reliance will more readily be inferred where the article is to be used in an unchanged state, or where the seller specialises in the manufacture of such articles for a clear purpose, than where the material is a raw material or a material manufactured in bulk and capable of being used, and in fact used, for a large variety of purposes in the manufacture of other articles (*n*).

Partial reliance.—The reliance on the seller's skill and judgment need not be exclusive of all reliance on anything else (*o*), and s. 14 has been held to cover a case in which the materials from which certain

---

(*h*) *Ashington Piggeries, Ltd.* v. *Christopher Hill, Ltd.*, [1971] 1 All E. R. at pp. 861, 877; *Teheran-Europe Co., Ltd.* v. *S. T. Belton (Tractors), Ltd.*, [1968] 2 All E. R. 886; [1968] 2 Q. B. 545, C. A. As to the position where the buyer asks for the goods of a specified manufacturer, *cf. Young and Marten* v. *McManus Childs, Ltd.*, [1968] 3 All E. R. 1169; [1969] 1 A. C. 454, H. L.

(*i*) *Grant* v. *Australian Knitting Mills, Ltd.*, [1936] A. C. 85, at p. 99. See also *Teheran-Europe Co., Ltd.* v. *S. T. Belton, Ltd.*, [1968] 2 All E. R. at p. 894; [1968] 2 Q. B. at p. 560, *per* DIPLOCK, L. J.

(*k*) *Henry Kendall & Sons* v. *William Lillico & Sons, Ltd.*, [1968] 2 All E. R. at pp. 457, 491–492; [1969] 2 A. C. at pp. 84, 124–125.

(*l*) [1968] 2 All E. R. 444; [1969] 2 A. C. 31, H. L., where it was said to be sufficient that a reasonable seller would have realised that he was inviting the buyer to rely on his skill and judgment.

(*m*) *Henry Kendall & Sons* v. *William Lillico & Sons, Ltd.*, *supra*, especially *per* Lord PEARCE at [1969] 2 A. C. 116; [1968] 2 All E. R. 484.

(*n*) *Steels and Busks* v. *Bleecker Bik & Co.*, [1956] 1 Lloyd's Rep. 228, at p. 235.

(*o*) *Medway Oil and Storage Co., Ltd.* v. *Silica Gel Corp.* (1928), 33 Com. Cas. 195, H. L.; *Manchester Liners* v. *Rea, Ltd.*, [1922] 2 A. C. 74.

propellors were to be made, and certain dimensions, were specified by the buyer, other details being left to the seller's judgment. It was said that it was not necessary that the buyer should rely exclusively on the skill and judgment of the seller for every detail in the production of the goods, and that it is enough if reliance is placed on his skill and judgment to some substantial extent and that the unfitness of which complaint is made arises from matters in regard to which reliance was placed on the seller (*p*).

The condition implied is that the goods are reasonably fit for the purpose made known to the seller to the extent to which the buyer relied upon the seller's skill and judgment. A seller will not be held liable when the unsuitability arises from some special state of affairs relating to the buyer, of which the seller had no reason to be aware or in respect of which no reliance was placed on the seller (*q*). Thus, a buyer who asks for lawn seed for his garden cannot rely on this subsection merely because his own lawn has some peculiar characteristic known only to him, unless he has made known that characteristic to the seller in circumstances which would bring the subsection into force (*r*). But it would appear to be sufficient if the seed was not suitable for at least one type of lawn upon which the seed could fairly and reasonably have been expected to have been used (even, perhaps, if the lawn upon which it was used was not of that type) or if the seller should reasonably have contemplated that it was not unlikely that the seed would be used upon a lawn having a characteristic such as that possessed by the buyer's lawn (*s*).

Unreasonable to rely.—It is not possible to consider all the circumstances in which it may be unreasonable for the buyer to rely on the seller's skill or judgment, but in general it will probably be unreasonable for one party to rely on another if in all the circumstances he ought to appreciate that a reasonable man in the shoes of the seller would not realise that he was being relied on (*t*).

It may also be unreasonable to rely on a seller's skill or judgment in respect of matters which are or ought to be known to the buyer to be outside the normal scope of such a seller's experience. This may be the case either because the particular purpose is not one of which the seller

(*p*) *Cammell Laird & Co., Ltd.* v. *Manganese Bronze & Brass Co., Ltd.*, [1934] A. C. 402; *Ashington Piggeries, Ltd.* v. *Christopher Hill, Ltd.*, [1971] 1 All E. R. 847; [1972] A. C. 441, H. L.: compare *Dixon Kerly, Ltd.* v. *Robinson*, [1965] 2 Lloyd's Rep. 404.

(*q*) *Ashington Piggeries, Ltd.* v. *Christopher Hill, Ltd.*, [1971] 1 All E. R. 847; [1972] A. C. 441, H. L.; *Griffiths* v. *Peter Conway, Ltd.*, [1939] 1 All E. R. 685 (purchase of Harris tweed coat by woman with abnormally sensitive skin who did not disclose this fact to the seller); *Venus Electric, Ltd.* v. *Brevel Products, Ltd.* (1978), 85 D. L. R. (3d) 282 (Ont. C. A.).

(*r*) *Teheran-Europe Co., Ltd.* v. *S. T. Belton, Ltd.*, [1968] 2 All E. R. at pp. 895–896; [1968] 2 Q. B. at p. 563, *per* SACHS, L. J.; and see *Ashington Piggeries, Ltd.* v. *Christopher Hill, Ltd.*, [1971] 1 All E. R. 847, at p. 873, *per* Lord WILBERFORCE.

(*s*) *Cf. Christopher Hill, Ltd.* v. *Ashington Piggeries, Ltd.*, [1969] 3 All E. R. at p. 1523, C. A.; reversed on the facts, [1971] 1 All E. R. 847; [1972] A. C. 441, H. L., where the onus of proof is discussed.

(*t*) *Cf. Henry Kendall & Sons* v. *William Lillico & Sons*, [1968] 2 All E. R. 444, at p. 455; [1969] 2 A. C. 31, at p. 81.

can be expected to have sufficient knowledge to enable him to consider whether the goods are fit for that purpose (*u*) or because the buyer knows that the seller does not normally sell goods of the type in question and has no special skill or judgment in relation to such goods and did not originally acquire them for the purpose of resale (*a*). Also, if the purpose is not made known to the seller with sufficient particularity to enable him to identify the characteristics which the goods would need to possess in order to be fit for that purpose, it will be unreasonable to rely on his skill or judgment, unless it is within the seller's ostensible sphere of expertise to recognise that such further details are required to avoid the risk of defects (*b*).

Credit-Brokers.—The provision concerning credit-brokers was introduced into the 1893 Act by the Consumer Credit Act 1974 (*c*), from a date to be appointed under s. 192 (4) of that Act. It will now take effect from a date to be appointed under sub-s. (8), *supra*. It is designed to cover situations where a prospective buyer wishes to obtain goods on credit, and the prospective seller wishes to obtain the purchase price at once. The prospective seller therefore sells the goods to a finance company or other person willing to provide credit, and the finance company or other person then re-sells the goods to the prospective buyer on credit terms.

When the provision is brought into force, if the prospective seller carries on a business of credit-brokerage (*d*), and if the prospective buyer makes known to him the purpose for which the prospective buyer requires the goods, then the condition of fitness for purpose will be implied into the contract of sale between the prospective buyer and the finance company, except where the circumstances show that the prospective buyer did not rely, or that it was unreasonable for him to rely on the skill or judgment of the credit-broker.

It will be a question of fact in each case whether the prospective seller is or is not carrying on a business of credit-brokerage, and the onus would seem to be on the prospective buyer to prove that he does carry on such a business (*e*). If the prospective seller does not carry on such a business, then the condition will not be implied into the contract between the finance company and the prospective buyer just because the prospective buyer makes known to the prospective seller the purpose for which the goods are being bought. This will be so even though the prospective seller is acting in the course of a business is selling the goods to the finance company.

(*u*) *Cf.* the cases cited at n. (*q*), *supra*.

(*a*) As where they form part of the capital assets of a business.

(*b*) *Cf. Venus Electric, Ltd.* v. *Brevel Products, Ltd.* (1978), 85 D. L. R. (3d) 282.

(*c*) S. 192 (3); Sch. 4.

(*d*) Such a business must be licensed under Part III of the Consumer Credit Act 1974 insofar as it falls within the definition of credit brokerage in s. 145 (2) of that Act, unless it is within the limited exceptions contained in the Consumer Credit Act (Commencement No. 4) Order 1977 (S. I. 1977 No. 2163).

(*e*) For the definition of "business," see s. 61 (1), *post*.

Sale by Sample

15. Sale by Sample.—(1) A contract of sale is a contract for sale by sample where there is an express or implied term to that effect in the contract.

(2) In the case of a contract for sale by sample there is an implied condition—

(a) that the bulk will correspond with the sample in quality (*f*);

(b) that the buyer will have a reasonable opportunity of comparing the bulk with the sample (*g*);

(c) that the goods will be free from any defect, rendering them unmerchantable, which would not be apparent on reasonable examination of the sample (*h*).

(3) In subsection 2 (c) above "unmerchantable" is to be construed in accordance with section 14 (6) above.

(4) Paragraph 7 of Schedule 1 below applies in relation to a contract made before 18 May 1973.

ILLUSTRATIONS

(1) Sale by sample, goods to be paid for in cash on arrival in exchange for shipping document. An opportunity to inspect is not a condition precedent to payment, and payment does not prejudice the right of rejection if the bulk does not correspond with the sample (*i*).

(2) Sale by sample of a quantity of maroon twill. A part of the twill supplied is inferior to sample. The buyer may reject the whole, or may retain the whole, claiming damages for the portion inferior to sample, but he cannot keep the part equal to the sample and reject the other part (*k*).

(3) Sale of Government surplus balloons, goods to be "as sample taken away" and to be sold "with all faults and imperfections." The sellers are still bound to deliver a bulk which corresponds with the sample, but *semble* the exemption clause may protect them (subject now to the provisions of the Unfair Contract Terms Act 1977 (*l*)) against imperfections in the sample which would not be apparent on reasonable examination (*m*).

(*f*) *Parker* v. *Palmer*, [1821] 4 B. & Ald. 387, at p. 391. Even if only a simple process is required to make the bulk correspond with the sample, it does not correspond with the sample: *Ruben* v. *Faire*, [1949] 1 All E. R. 215; [1949] 1 K. B. 254.

(*g*) *Lorymer* v. *Smith* (1822), 1 B. & C. 1.

(*h*) *Heilbutt* v. *Hickson* (1872), L. R. 7 C. P. 438, at p. 456; *Mody* v. *Gregson* (1868), L. R. 4 Exch. 49; *Drummond* v. *Van Ingen* (1887), 12 App. Cas. 284 and *cf.* proviso to s. 14 (2), *ante*.

(*i*) *Polenghi* v. *Dried Milk Co.* (1904), 92 L. T. 64; *cf. Heilbutt* v. *Hickson* (1872), L. R. 7 C. P. 438; *Biddell Brothers* v. *E. Clemens Horst Co.*, [1911] 1 K. B. 934, *per* KENNEDY, L. J.; reversed, [1912] A. C. 18 (c.i.f. contract).

(*k*) *Aitken* v. *Boullen*, 1908 S. C. 490; *aliter* if the contract be severable: *Jackson* v. *Rotax Motor and Cycle Co.*, [1910] 2 K. B. 937, C. A.; and see s. 30 (3), *post*, and the cases about delivery of wrong quantity or mixed goods.

(*l*) *Post*, Appendix I.

(*m*) *Champanhac & Co., Ltd.* v. *Waller & Co., Ltd.*, [1948] 2 All E. R. 724.

Derivation.—Section 15 of the 1893 Act. The definition of unmerchantable in sub-s. (3) derives from the definition introduced into the 1893 Act as s. 62 (1A) by s. 7 (2) of the Supply of Goods (Implied Terms) Act 1973.

Definitions.—For "contract of sale," see s. 2 (1), *ante*, and s. 61 (1), *post*. For "buyer," "goods" and "quality," see s. 61 (1), *post*. For "merchantable quality", see s. 14 (6), *ante*.

Cross-references.—For a general note on conditions and warranties, see p. 8, *ante*. For their history, see Note A, *post*, Appendix II. For their effect, see s. 11, *ante*. *Cf.* s. 13 *ante* (sale by description and sample); s. 34, *post* (buyer's right to examine); and the Unfair Contract Terms Act 1977, *post*, Appendix I (exclusion of implied terms and conditions).

COMMENT

Exemption Clauses.—Section 6 of the Unfair Contract Terms Act 1977 (*n*) provides that, except in the case of international supply contracts (*o*), the conditions implied by this section cannot be excluded or restricted (*p*) by reference to any contract term as against a person dealing as a consumer (*q*) and in other cases can be excluded or restricted by reference to a contract term only insofar as the term satisfies the requirement of reasonableness (*r*).

Subsection (1).—Evidence of usage is admissible to show that a sale was by sample, though the written contract may be silent on the point (*s*). On the other hand, the exhibition of a sample during the making of the contract does not necessarily make it a contract for sale by sample; it must be shown to be a term of the contract that the sale is a sale by sample, and if the contract is reduced to writing this term must be included in the writing (*t*).

"The office of a sample," says Lord MACNAGHTEN,

> "is to present to the eye the real meaning and intention of the parties with regard to the subject-matter of the contract which, owing to the imperfection of language, it may be difficult or impossible to express in words. The sample speaks for itself. But it cannot be treated as saying more than such a sample would tell a merchant of the class to which the buyer belongs, using due care and diligence, and appealing to it in the ordinary way, and with the knowledge possessed by merchants of that class at the time" (*u*).

(*n*) *Post*, Appendix I.

(*o*) Excluded from s. 6 by s. 26 of the 1977 Act, *post*, Appendix I.

(*p*) Exclusion of the conditions themselves and certain other provisions are also negated by s. 13 of the 1977 Act, *post*, Appendix I.

(*q*) Dealing as a consumer is defined by s. 12 of the 1977 Act, *post*, Appendix I.

(*r*) The requirement of reasonableness is set out in s. 11 of the 1977 Act, *post*, Appendix I.

(*s*) *Syers* v. *Jonas* (1848), 2 Exch. 111.

(*t*) *Meyer* v. *Everth* (1814), 4 Camp. 22 (sugar described in bought note); *Gardiner* v. *Gray* (1815), 4 Camp. 144 (waste silk sold under written contract).

(*u*) *Drummond* v. *Van Ingen* (1887), 12 App. Cas. 284, at p. 297; *cf. Mody* v. *Gregson*

Subsection (2) (a).—Text writers and the older cases speak of the term that the bulk shall agree with the sample as a warranty, collateral to the contract (*v*). The Act, following Benjamin (*a*), prefers to treat it as a condition and not a warranty. The parties may, however, agree that the term shall be treated as a warranty and not as a condition (*b*). Subject to the effect of such a special agreement, however, if the seller fails to deliver goods which correspond with the sample, he is not merely in breach of a term of the contract, but is entirely failing to perform it, in the same way as if the goods do not correspond with their description. Accordingly, even where a seller may rely on an exemption clause, he cannot take advantage of a term in the contract designed merely to protect him from liability for defects in the thing sold (*c*).

"Quality" here is confined to such qualities as are apparent on an ordinary examination of the sample as usually carried out in the trade (*d*).

Subsection (2) (b).—*Prima facie* the place of delivery is the place for comparing the bulk with the sample (*e*). But this presumption may be rebutted and BRETT, J., has expressed the opinion that

> "such a contract always contains an implied term that the goods may under certain circumstances be returned; that such term necessarily contains certain varying or alternative applications, and, amongst others, the following, that, if the time of inspection, as agreed upon, be subsequent to the time agreed for the delivery of the goods, or if the place of inspection, as agreed upon, be different from the place of delivery, the purchaser may, upon inspection at such time and place, if the goods be not equal to sample, return them *then and there* on the hands of the seller" (*f*).

Subsection (2) (c).—A reasonable examination is such an examination as, in the case of a sale to a trader, is ordinarily carried out in that trade (*g*). Reasonable does not mean practicable (*h*).

Before the 1893 Act, there was a conflict of judicial opinion whether a merchant who was not a manufacturer was to be responsible for a latent

---

(1868), L. R. 4 Exch. 49, at p. 53, *per* WILLES, J.

(*v*) *E.g., Parker* v. *Palmer* (1821), 4 B. & Ald. 387, at p. 391, *per* ABBOTT, C. J.

(*a*) *Benjamin on Sale* (4th ed.), p. 936.

(*b*) *Heyworth* v. *Hutchinson* (1867), L. R. 2 Q. B. 447; *Re Walkers and Shaw*, [1904] 2 K. B. 152.

(*c*) *Champanhac & Co., Ltd.* v. *Waller & Co., Ltd.*, [1948] 2 All E. R. 724 (*ante*, illustration (3)). See further as to fundamental breach and exemption clauses, p. 10, *ante*.

(*d*) *Hookway* v. *Alfred Isaacs & Sons*, [1954] 1 Lloyd's Rep. 491; *Steels and Busks* v. *Bleecker Bik & Co.*, [1956] 1 Lloyd's Rep. 228; and see *Ashington Piggeries, Ltd.* v. *Christopher Hill, Ltd.*, [1971] 1 All E. R. 847, at pp. 856, 892; [1972] A. C. 441, 470–471, 514, H. L.

(*e*) *Perkins* v. *Bell*, [1893] 1 Q. B. 193, C. A. (barley delivered at T. station).

(*f*) *Heilbutt* v. *Hickson* (1872), L. R. 7 C. P. 438, at p. 456; *cf. Grimoldby v. Wells* (1875), L. R. 10 C. P. 391, at p. 395, *per* BRETT, J. This was also the law in Scotland: *Couston* v. *Chapman* (1872), L. R. 2 Sc. & Div. 250, at p. 254, *per* Lord CHELMSFORD (wine sold by auction).

(*g*) *Hookway* v. *Alfred Isaacs & Sons*, [1954] 1 Lloyd's Rep. 491; *Steels and Busks* v. *Bleecker Bik & Co.*, [1956] 1 Lloyd's Rep. 228; and see *Ashington Piggeries Ltd.*, [1971] 1 All E. R. 847 at pp. 856, 892; [1972] A. C. 441, at pp. 470–471, 514, H. L.

(*h*) *Godley* v. *Perry*, [1960] 1 All E. R. 36; [1960] 1 W. L. R. 9.

defect which examination of the sample failed to disclose (*i*). There is now no distinction between a manufacturer and anybody else, and in *Godley* v. *Perry* (*k*) a wholesaler and an importer were held to have been in breach of this subsection.

PART III

EFFECTS OF THE CONTRACT

Transfer of property as between seller and buyer

16. Goods must be ascertained.—Where there is a contract for the sale of unascertained goods no property in the goods is transferred to the buyer unless and until the goods are ascertained.

ILLUSTRATION

A, having 200 sacks of flour in a warehouse, sells 50 to B, receives the price and gives B a delivery order. B presents the delivery order at the warehouse and gets a storage warrant in exchange. Nothing is done to appropriate any particular 50 sacks to the contract. No property in any of the sacks passes to B, and if A becomes bankrupt his trustee can claim the whole of the flour (*l*).

Derivation.—Section 16 of the 1893 Act.

Definitions.—For "contract of sale," see s. 2 (1) *ante*, and s. 61 (1), *post*. For "buyer," "goods" and "property," see s. 61 (1), *post*; and compare also "future goods" and "specific goods" defined in that section.

COMMENT

This section is declaratory. "In the case of executory contracts," said BOVILL, C. J.,

> "where the goods are not ascertained or may not exist at the time of the contract, from the nature of the transaction, no property in the goods can pass to the purchaser by virtue of the contract itself; but where certain goods have been selected and appropriated by the seller, and have been approved and assented to by the buyer, then the case stands as to the vesting of the property very much in the same position as upon a contract for the sale of goods which are ascertained at the time of the bargain" (*m*).

(*i*) *Cf. Parkinson* v. *Lee* (1802), 2 East, 314 (no liability) with *Randall* v. *Newson* (1877), 2 Q. B. D. 102, at p. 106 (liability).

(*k*) [1960] 1 All E. R. 36; [1960] 1 W. L. R. 9.

(*l*) *Hayman* v. *M'Lintock*, 1907 S. C. 936; *Laurie & Morewood* v. *Dudin & Sons*, [1926] 1 K. B. 223; finally disposing of *Whitehouse* v. *Frost* (1810), 12 East, 614.

(*m*) *Heilbutt* v. *Hickson* (1872), L. R. 7 C. P. 438, at p. 449, BYLES, J. concurring. For a case about the passing of property, where a person paid a yearly sum for the property in scrap which he agreed to clear from artillery ranges, see *Gale* v. *New*, [1937] 4 All E. R. 645, C. A.

"A contract to sell unascertained goods," says Lord LOREBURN "is not a complete sale, but a promise to sell" (*n*).

Unascertained goods.—Unascertained goods, that is to say, goods defined by description only, must be distinguished from specific goods, that is to say, goods identified and agreed upon at the time when the contract is made (*o*). Suppose A agrees to sell to B "fifty Southdown sheep," no property in any sheep can pass to B till the sheep are appropriated to the contract. A fulfils his contract by delivering at the appointed time any fifty Southdown sheep. But if he agreed to sell "*the* fifty Southdown sheep now in my field" he could not keep his contract by delivering any others, and the property might pass at once if the parties so intended.

Part of specific whole.—Although the buyer may have an undivided interest in the whole for insurance purposes (*p*), he can acquire no property in the goods before the goods are ascertained. The sale of an unascertained portion of a larger ascertained quantity of goods passes no property to the buyer till that portion is identified and appropriated to the contract. "If," says BAYLEY, B.,

> "I agree to deliver a certain quantity of oil as 10 out of 18 tons no one can say which part of the whole quantity I have agreed to deliver until a selection is made. There is no individuality until it has been divided" (*q*).

This is so even if the seller has contracted to sell the remainder of the goods to other buyers (*r*). Nor will he acquire any equitable interest in the whole (*s*). But a seller can confer such an interest on the buyer by creating a trust of the whole. No special form is required to create such a trust (*t*), but the person creating the trust must clearly evince his intention to create it, and must identify both the subject and object of the trust (*u*). In *Re Wait* (*a*), ATKIN, L. J., left open the possibility that a direction by the seller to the person holding the goods to deliver part of

---

(*n*) *Badische Anilin Fabrik* v. *Hickson*, [1906] A. C. 419, at p. 421.

(*o*) See the definition of specific goods in s. 61 (1), *post*. Note also that specific goods may be sold by description; see comment to s. 13, *ante*.

(*p*) *Inglis* v. *Stock* (1885), 10 App. Cas. 263, H. L.

(*q*) *Gillett* v. *Hill* (1834), 2 Cr. & M. 530, at p. 535; *Boswell* v. *Kilborn* (1862), 15 Moo. P. C. C. 309 (hops not separated from larger bulk); *Hayman* v. *M'Lintock*, 1907 S. C. 936 (sale of a number of sacks of flour from a larger number housed in a third party's store); *Kursell* v. *Timber Operators, Ltd.*, [1927] 1 K. B. 298 (all trees in a forest conforming to certain measurements); *in Re Wait*, [1927] 1 Ch. 606 (500 tons of wheat out of parcel of 1000 tons); *Wardar's (Import and Export) Co., Ltd.* v. *Norwood & Sons, Ltd.*, [1968] 2 All E. R. 602; [1968] 2 Q. B. 663, C. A. (600 cartons of kidneys out of a consignment of 1500 cartons).

(*r*) *Healy* v. *Howlett & Sons*, [1917] 1 K. B. 337, D. C.

(*s*) *Ibid.* The same conclusion must result from the decision in *Re Wait*, [1927] 1 Ch. 606, C. A.

(*t*) *Cf. Re Kayford, Ltd.*, [1975] 1 All E. R. 604; [1975] 1 W. L. R. 279, where the purchase price of goods which had not been delivered was held on the special facts of that case to be held on trust by the seller for the buyer.

(*u*) See *Snell's Principles of Equity* (27th ed.), p. 111.

(*a*) [1927] 1 Ch. 606, C. A.

them to the buyer might in some circumstances amount to an equitable assignment of them which the buyer could enforce against the bulk (*b*).

Specific or ascertained goods.—Where the goods are specific or have been ascertained, the property in the goods normally passes, by virtue of s. 17, *post*, at such time as the parties to the contract intend it to pass (*c*), and in this context, the rules for ascertaining their intention set out in s. 18, *post*, may be relevant.

It would seem to be at least arguable, however, that even where the property has not passed, the buyer in these circumstances can acquire an equitable interest in the property, so that, for example, if the seller becomes insolvent after the buyer has paid all or part of the price, the buyer may assert his interest in the goods rather than simply prove for his debt in the liquidation (*d*).

The buyer might also in some cases acquire a right to the immediate possession of the goods sufficient to enable him to bring an action against the seller for conversion if the seller fails to deliver them (*e*).

Goods which are part of a specific whole may become ascertained if they are set aside or marked in some way so as to be allocated to a particular contract (*f*). They may also become ascertained if the remainder of the bulk is disposed of leaving only sufficient goods to fulfil the contract with the buyer (*g*).

Goods mixed.—If the goods sold have been ascertained, and the property has passed to the buyer, his rights cannot be affected by the fact that the seller has afterwards mixed the goods sold with other goods (*h*).

17. Property passes when intended to pass.—(1) Where there is a contract for the sale of specific or

---

(*b*) [1927] 1 Ch. 606, at pp. 633–634.

(*c*) In *Re Yorkshire Joinery Co., Ltd.* (1967), 111 Sol. Jo. 701, materials supplied were incorporated in a building with the result that property passed notwithstanding a term of the contract to the contrary.

(*d*) In *Re Wait*, [1927] 1 Ch. 606, the Court of Appeal held 2–1 that a buyer did not acquire such an interest merely by contracting to buy part of a parcel of goods. But Lord HANWORTH, M. R., one of the majority clearly contemplated that the buyer might claim an equitable interest in the goods once they were ascertained. In this he agreed with SARGANT, L. J., who dissented on the point at issue in the action. ATKIN, L. J., at p. 639, thought differently, on the ground that the common law position was altered by the Sale of Goods Act, but it does not appear to have been the intention of Sir MacKenzie Chalmers to alter the common law position in this respect when drafting the Act: see the 2nd edition of this work at p. 16, substantially reproduced in the comment to s. 5, *ante*, under the heading "Assignment of 'future goods'".

(*e*) P. 236, *post*.

(*f*) See the cases on appropriation reviewed in *Federspiel* v. *Twigg* [1975] 1 Lloyd's Rep. 240. See also *Re Wait, supra, per* ATKIN, L. J., at p. 630.

(*g*) *Wait & James* v. *Midland Bank* (1926), 31 Com. Cas. 172.

(*h*) *Aldridge* v. *Johnson* (1857), 7 E. & B. 885; *Hayman* v. *M'Lintock*, 1907 S. C. 936; but *cf. Spence* v. *Union Mar. Ins. Co.* (1868), L. R. 3 C. P. 427, as to goods of different owners mixed during carriage, where a tenancy in common was held to arise. As to the limits of this doctrine, see *Sandeman & Sons* v. *Tyzack and Branfoot Steamship Co., Ltd.*, [1913] A. C. 680.

ascertained goods (*i*) the property in them is transferred to the buyer at such time as the parties to the contract intend it to be transferred (*k*).

(2) For the purpose of ascertaining the intention of the parties regard shall be had to the terms of the contract (*l*), the conduct of the parties and the circumstances of the case (*m*).

ILLUSTRATIONS

(1) Contract to build a ship to be classed A1 at Lloyd's, to be paid for after completion. The vessel as she is constructed, and the materials from time to time intended for her, whether in the building yard or elsewhere, to be the property of the purchasers. This is a contract for a complete ship. The buyer obtains no property in iron plates at the railway station marked for the ship, and creditors of the buyer cannot attach them (*n*).

(2) Contract to build a ship, instalments of price to be paid as work proceeds, and buyer to have the right to inspect and superintend construction, delivery to be considered complete after satisfactory official trial. This is a contract for a complete ship, and no property passes to the buyer before the official trial (*o*).

(3) A in England agrees with B in England to sell him a quantity of patented dye stuffs, delivery to be made at Basle in Switzerland. A procures the goods abroad, and has them forwarded to Basle, where his agent holds them at B's disposal. If B assents to this, the property in the goods thereupon passes to B (*p*).

(4) B offers to buy a parcel of diamonds from a foreign firm. The diamonds are sent by post with a bill drawn on the buyer and an invoice marked "settled by acceptance." If the bill of exchange is not accepted, the ownership of the diamonds remains in the seller (*q*).

(5) Sale of car by auction. Buyer offers to pay by cheque, and is allowed to remove the car upon signing a form which provides that the property will not

---

(*i*) Similar principles apply to a contract for the sale of unascertained goods: *Ginzberg* v. *Barrow Haematite Steel Co., Ltd. and McKellor*, [1966] 1 Lloyd's Rep. 343. "'Ascertained' probably means identified in accordance with the agreement after the time a contract of sale is made": *per* ATKIN, L. J., in *Re Wait*, [1927] 1 Ch. 606, at p. 630.

(*k*) *Reid* v. *Macbeth & Gray*, [1904] A. C. 223. *Cf. Dennant* v. *Skinner*, [1948] 2 All E. R. 29; [1948] 2 K. B. 164; see also *City Motors* (1933) *Proprietary, Ltd.* v. *Southern Aerial Proprietary, Ltd.* (1961), 106 C. L. R. 477.

(*l*) For cases depending on the inference to be drawn from the terms of the contract, see *Re Anchor Line* (*Henderson Brothers*), *Ltd.*, [1936] 2 All E. R. 941; [1937] 1 Ch. 1, C. A.; *Cheetham & Co.* v. *Thornham Spinning Co.*, [1964] 2 Lloyd's Rep. 17 (retention of shipping documents pending payment); *President of India* v. *Metcalfe Shipping Co., Ltd.*, [1969] 1 All E. R. 861; [1969] 2 Q. B. 123; on appeal, [1969] 3 All E. R. 1549; [1970] 1 Q. B. 289, C. A. (term as to passing of risk).

(*m*) *The Parchim*, [1918] A. C. 157, at pp. 161, 162, P. C.

(*n*) *Reid* v. *Macbeth & Gray*, [1904] A. C. 223; see at p. 230 for the principle. No question was raised in this case about the property in the uncompleted ship. *Cf. Re Blyth Shipbuilding Co.*, [1926] Ch. 494, at p. 505.

(*o*) *Sir J. Laing* v. *Barclay & Co.*, [1908] A. C. 35.

(*p*) *Badische Anilin Fabrik* v. *Hickson*, [1906] A. C. 419 (there is no "vending" in England within the meaning of the Patent Acts).

(*q*) *Saks* v. *Tilley* (1915), 32 T. L. R. 148, C. A.; *cf.* s. 19 (3), *post*.

pass until the cheque has been met. The property has already passed at the fall of the hammer, and the form is of no effect (*r*).

(6) A selects goods in a supermarket and takes them to the cash desk. The price is £185, but the cash register records only £85, being incapable of recording over £100. A pays £85, knowing it is not the true price, and removes the goods. The manager of the supermarket is supervising at the cash desk. Although normally it is the intention of the parties in this type of case that the property shall not pass until the price is paid, the property here passes to A upon payment of £85, because the manager intended the property so to pass (*s*).

Derivation.—Section 17 of the 1893 Act.

Definitions.—For "contract of sale," see s. 2 (1), *ante*, and s. 61 (1), *post*. For "buyer," "goods," "property" and "specific goods," see s. 61 (1), *post*; compare also the definition of "future goods" in that section.

History.—By the Civil Law, the property in goods did not pass by virtue of a contract of sale until delivery (*t*). But, as soon as the parties were agreed on the subject-matter and the price, and there were no suspensive conditions, there was an *emptio perfecta*, the result of which was that the risk passed to the buyer, and he acquired a *jus ad rem*, though not a *jus in re*. The Scottish common law followed this rule, but by the Mercantile Law Amendment (Scotland) Act 1856, s. 1 (now repealed), when goods had been sold but not delivered, the seller's creditors could not attach them, and a sub-vendee was entitled to demand the goods subject to satisfying the seller's lien for the price. The effect was, that when in England the property in goods would pass to the buyer, the same results followed in Scotland, though those results were arrived at in a different manner (*u*). Under the 1893 Act, and under this Act, the same rule applies to both countries.

Comment

By English law the property may pass by the contract itself, if such be the intention of the parties. In other words, the contract may include a conveyance. "Where, by the contract itself," says Parke, B.,

> "the vendor appropriates to the vendee a specific chattel, and the latter thereby agrees to take that specific chattel and to pay the stipulated price, the parties are then in the same situation as they would be after a delivery of goods in pursuance of a general contract. The very appropriation of the chattel is equivalent to delivery by the vendor, and the assent of the vendee to take the specific chattel and to pay the price is equivalent to his accepting

---

(*r*) *Dennant* v. *Skinner & Collom*, [1948] 2 All E. R. 29; [1948] 2 K. B. 164.

(*s*) *Lacis* v. *Cashmarts*, [1969] 2 Q. B. 400, D. C.; *cf*. *Pilgram* v. *Rice-Smith*, [1977] 1 W. L. R. 671, D. C. (fraudulent sale at undervalue by shop assistant to friend a nullity); *Kaur* v. *Chief Constable for Hampshire* (1981), Times, 30th January (sale at undervalue because price ticket incorrect—mistake known to purchaser who concealed true price ticket. Held: contract voidable, not void, and property passed).

(*t*) Moyle's *Justinian* (5th ed.) p. 210, citing *Cod*. 2, 3, 20.

(*u*) *McBain* v. *Wallace* (1881), 6 App. Cas. 588, at p. 618; *Seath* v. *Moore* (1886), 11 App. Cas. 350, at pp. 370, 380. See, too, *Blackburn on Sale* (1st ed.), pp. 187–197.

possession. The effect of the contract, therefore, is to vest the property in the bargainee" (*a*).

Whether this be a satisfactory explanation or not, the rule is undoubted, and is as old as the year books (*b*). The section is thus declaratory. CHANNELL, J.'s comment on it was:

"It is impossible to imagine a clause more vague than this, but I think it correctly represents the state of the authorities when the Act was passed" (*c*).

18. Rules for ascertaining intention.—Unless a different intention appears (*d*), the following are rules for ascertaining the intention of the parties as to the time at which the property in the goods is to pass to the buyer.

Rule 1.—Where there is an unconditional contract for the sale of specific goods in a deliverable state (*e*), the property in the goods passes to the buyer when the contract is made, and it is immaterial whether the time of payment or the time of delivery, or both, be postponed (*f*).

Rule 2.—Where there is a contract for the sale of specific goods and the seller is bound to do something to the goods for the purpose of putting them into a deliverable state, the property does not pass until the thing is done (*g*) and the buyer has notice that it has been done.

Rule 3.—Where there is a contract for the sale of specific goods in a deliverable state but the seller is bound to

---

(*a*) *Dixon* v. *Yates* (1833), 5 B. & Ad. 313, at p. 340.

(*b*) For a discussion of its policy, see 2nd Report of Mercantile Law Commission 1855, pp. 9, 42; *Blackburn on Sale* (1st ed.), pp. 187–197; and for its history, see *Cochrane* v. *Moore* (1890), 25 Q. B. D. 57, C. A. (attempted gift of a fourth share of a horse).

(*c*) *Varley* v. *Whipp*, [1900] 1 Q. B. 513, at p. 517.

(*d*) *Turley* v. *Bates* (1863), 2 H. & C. 200 (intention of parties that property should pass immediately although the goods had still to be weighed); *Young* v. *Matthews* (1866), L. R. 2 C. P. 127 (intention of parties that property should pass immediately although some of the goods were still unfinished); *Re Anchor Line (Henderson Brothers), Ltd.*, [1936] 2 All E. R. 941; [1937] 1 Ch. 1 (terms of contract showing a different intention); *Lambert* v. *G. & C. Finance Corporation* (1963), 107 Sol. Jo. 666 (retention of car log book showed absence of intention to pass property in car); *Cheetham & Co.* v. *Thornham Spinning Co.*, [1964] 2 Lloyd's Rep. 17 (retention of shipping documents pending payment); *Lacis* v. *Cashmarts*, [1969] 2 Q. B. 400, D. C. illustration (6) to s. 17, *ante*); *President of India* v. *Metcalfe Shipping Co., Ltd.*, [1969] 1 All E. R. 861; [1969] 2 Q. B. 123; on appeal, [1969] 3 All E. R. 1549; [1970] 1 Q. B. 289, C. A. (term as to passing of risk); and see generally pp. 4, 9 and 12, *ante*.

(*e*) *Philip Head* v. *Showfronts, Ltd.*, [1970] 1 Lloyd's Rep. 140, *post*, illustration 10.

(*f*) *Tarling* v. *Baxter* (1827), 6 B. & C. 360. See the rule stated and contrasted with the Civil Law and Scottish common law in *Seath* v. *Moore* (1886), 11 App. Cas. 350, at p. 370.

(*g*) *Rugg* v. *Minett* (1809), 11 East, 210; *Acraman* v. *Morrice* (1849), 8 C. B. 449; *Boswell* v. *Kilborn* (1862), 15 Moo. P. C. C. 309; *Young* v. *Matthews* (1866), L. R. 2 C. P. 127, at p. 129.

weigh, measure, test, or do some other act or thing with reference to the goods for the purpose of ascertaining the price, the property does not pass until the act or thing is done (*h*) and the buyer has notice that it has been done.

Rule 4.—When goods are delivered to the buyer on approval or on sale or return or other similar terms (*i*) the property in the goods passes to the buyer—

(a) When he signifies his approval or acceptance to the seller or does any other act adopting the transaction (*k*);

(b) if he does not signify his approval or acceptance to the seller but retains the goods without giving notice of rejection, then, if a time has been fixed for the return of the goods, on the expiration of that time, and, if no time has been fixed, on the expiration of a reasonable time (*l*).

Rule 5.—(1) Where there is a contract for the sale of unascertained or future goods by description, and goods of that description (*m*) and in a deliverable state (*n*) are unconditionally (*o*) appropriated to the

---

(*h*) *Hanson* v. *Meyer* (1805), 6 East, 614; *Zagury* v. *Furnell* (1809), 2 Camp. 239. Goods of this kind were known in Scottish law as "fungibles." *Cf.* Bell's *Principles of the Law of Scotland* (9th ed.), § 137.

(*i*) *Polar Refrigeration Service, Ltd.* v. *Moldenhauer* (1967), 61 D. L. R. (2d) 463 (air-conditioning equipment: fitness for stated purpose a condition precedent); *Tiffin* v. *Pitcher*, [1969] C. L. Y. 3234 (sale of van conditional on replacement of engine and subsequent fitness for intended purpose); *R.* v. *Justelius*, [1973] 1 N. S. W. L. R. 471 (advance subscription order for books, recipient to return them within 7 days or pay for them; company's practice to treat recipient as debtor if goods not returned. Held: "on similar terms" to sale or return, so that property in the books passed to recipient after 7 days).

(*k*) *Swain* v. *Shepherd* (1832), 1 M. & Rob. 233; Bell's *Inquiries into the Contract of Sale of Goods and Merchandise*, p. 111; *cf.* s. 35, *post.*

(*l*) *Moss* v. *Sweet* (1851), 16 Q. B. 493; *cf. Beverley* v. *Lincoln Gas Co.* (1837), 6 A. & E. 829; *Elphick* v. *Barnes* (1880), 5 C. P. D. 321 (death of horse delivered on sale or return); *Re Ferrier, ex p. the Trustee* v. *Donald*, [1944] Ch. 295 (goods taken in execution after delivery on sale or return); *Poole* v. *Smith's Car Sales (Balham), Ltd.*, [1962] 2 All E. R. 482; [1962] 1 W. L. R. 744, C. A. What is a reasonable time is a question of fact—see s. 59, *post.*

(*m*) *Cf. Thornley* v. *Tuckwell (Butchers), Ltd.*, [1964] Crim. L. R. 127 (English lamb appropriated to contract for the sale of New Zealand lamb: no property passes).

(*n*) *Philip Head* v. *Showfronts, Ltd.*, [1970] 1 Lloyd's Rep. 140, *post*, illustration (10).

(*o*) So that where, as in the case of the usual c.i.f. contract, the seller retains the documents against payment of the price, his notice of appropriation does *not* pass the property: *Smyth* v. *Bailey*, [1940] 3 All E. R. 60, H. L. Goods are unconditionally appropriated even if the buyer expressly reserves the right to reject the goods after delivery if they are defective, provided the right reserved is no wider than that which he would possess in any event under s. 35, *post: Pullman Trailmobile* v. *Hamilton Transport* (1979), 23 O.R. 553.

contract, either by the seller with the assent of the buyer or by the buyer with the assent of the seller, the property in the goods then passes to the buyer (*p*); and the assent may be express or implied, and may be given either before or after the appropriation is made (*q*).

(2) Where, in pursuance of the contract, the seller delivers the goods to the buyer or to a carrier or other bailee or custodier (whether named by the buyer or not) for the purpose of transmission to the buyer, and does not reserve the right of disposal (*r*), he is to be taken to have unconditionally appropriated the goods to the contract (*s*).

ILLUSTRATIONS

Rule 1.—(1) Contract for the sale of a stack of hay made on January 6; price to be paid on February 4, but hay not to be removed until May 1. On January 20 the stack is destroyed by fire. The property and risk passed when the contract was made, and the loss falls on the buyer (*t*).

Rule 2.—(2) Sale of condensing engine. It is to be severed from the realty and delivered free on rail at a specified price. It is damaged in transit before it reaches the railway. The property does not pass, as when it reaches the railway it is not in a deliverable state (*u*).

Rule 3.—(3) A sells 160 bags of cocoa to B at 59*s*. per load of 60 lbs., knowing that B will resell to X, and that the weights will be tested at X's place of business. This checkweighing is not suspensive of the contract of sale, nor a condition precedent to the property passing to B (*a*).

Rule 4.—(4) A delivers goods to B on sale or return. B pledges the goods. This adopts the sale, and the property passes to the buyer. A therefore cannot recover the goods from the pawnbroker (*b*).

(5) A delivers goods to B on sale for cash or return, the goods to remain the property of A till settled for or charged. C tells B he can find a customer for them, but, instead of doing so, he pawns them with D. A can recover the goods from D, the pawnbroker (*c*).

(*p*) See, in illustration, *Rohde* v. *Thwaites* (1827), 6 B. & C. 388; *Aldridge* v. *Johnson* (1857), 7 El & Bl. 885; *Langton* v. *Higgins* (1859), 4 H. & N. 402; *Doak* v. *Bedford*, [1964] 1 All E. R. 311; [1964] 2 Q. B. 587; *Edwards* v. *Ddin*, [1976] 3 All E.R. 705; [1976] 1 W.L.R. 942, D. C.; *Morton-Norwich Products, Inc.* v. *Intercen, Ltd.*, [1978] R. P. C. 501; and see principle fully discussed, and authorities reviewed, in *Federspiel* v. *Twigg*, [1957] 1 Lloyd's Rep. 240, and in *Widenmeyer* v. *Burn Stewart & Co., Ltd.*, 1967 S. L. T. 129 (Ct. of Sess.)

(*q*) *Campbell* v. *Mersey Docks* (1863), 14 C. B., N.S., 412; *cf. Godts* v. *Rose* (1855), 17 C. B. 229, at p. 237; *Aldridge* v. *Johnson* (*supra*); *Jenner* v. *Smith* (1869), L. R. 4 C. P. 270.

(*r*) See *Smyth* v. *Bailey*, [1940] 3 All E. R. 60, H. L.

(*s*) For statement of principle, see *Mirabita* v. *Imperial Ottoman Bank* (1878), 3 Ex. D. 164, C. A.; *Napier* v. *Dexters* (1926), 26 Ll. L. Rep. 62; and see Note B, Appendix II, *post*.

(*t*) *Tarling* v. *Baxter* (1827), 6 B. & C. 360.

(*u*) *Underwood* v. *Burgh Castle Cement Syndicate*, [1922] 1 K. B. 343, C. A.

(*a*) *Nanka Bruce* v. *Commonwealth Trust*, [1926] A. C. 77, P. C.

(*b*) *Kirkham* v. *Attenborough*, [1897] 1 Q. B. 201, C. A.; *London Jewellers, Ltd.* v. *Attenborough*, [1934] 2 K. B. 206, C. A.

(*c*) *Weiner* v. *Gill*, [1905] 2 K. B. 172, affirmed [1906] 2 K. B. 574, C. A.; *R.* v. *Eaton*

(6) A delivers diamonds to B on sale or return, and B delivers them to C on the like terms. C delivers them to D, and while they are in D's custody they are lost. As B cannot return the diamonds to A, he has by his dealing with them adopted the transaction and is liable for the price (*d*).

(7) Two days after goods are delivered by A to B on sale for cash or return within a week, execution is levied on B's goods on behalf of two creditors and the goods in question are seized. Once the goods have been seized, B no longer "retains" them within the meaning of s. 18, r. 4 (b); thus they have not become B's property, so that A is entitled to recover them (*e*).

Rule 5.—(8) A in England writes to B at Basle in Switzerland for a packet of patent dye, to be sent by parcel post. B posts the packet to A. The property passes to A as soon as the packet is posted in Basle (*f*).

(9) B orders 140 bags of rice from A, pays for them and asks for delivery. A sends him a delivery order for 125, and asks him to send for the remaining 15 at A's place of business. B waits a month before sending for them, and in the meantime they are stolen. The property in the 15 bags has passed to B, and he must bear the loss (*g*).

(10) A orders carpets from B to be laid by B on A's premises. B delivers carpets to A's premises, but before B can lay them they are stolen. The carpets are not in a deliverable state and the property in them has not passed to A (*h*).

Derivation.—Section 18 of the 1893 Act.

Definitions.—For "contract of sale," see s. 2 (1), *ante*, and s. 61 (1), *post*. For "bailee," "buyer," "delivery," "future goods," "goods," "property," "seller" and "specific goods," see s. 61 (1), *post*. For "deliverable state," see s. 61 (5), *post*.

Cross-references.—*Cf.* p. 30, *ante* (shipping contracts); ss. 2 (1), 8 and 9, *ante* (price); s. 1 (2), *ante* (conditional and unconditional contract); s. 2 (4)–(6), *ante* (passing of property); s. 10, *ante* (time of payment); s. 13, *ante* (sale by description); s. 19, *post* (right of disposal); s. 28, *post* (payment and delivery); s. 35, *post* (acceptance and rejection); s. 55, *post* ("different intention"); s. 59, *post* (reasonable time a question of fact); and Note B, Appendix II, *post* (delivery to carrier).

Comment

As the English courts have rejected the objective test of delivery for marking the time when the property is to pass, they have been forced to lay down more or less arbitrary rules for fixing the moment when the property is to be held to pass in cases where the parties have either formed no intention on the point, or have failed to express it.

(1966), 50 Cr. App. Rep. 189; *cf. Edwards* v. *Vaughan* (1910), 26 T. L. R. 545, C. A. The terms of the special contract took the case out of rule 4. Cozens-Hardy, M.R., at p. 546, said that "a transaction on sale or return was not a case where a person was in possession under an agreement to buy within s. 25 of the Sale of Goods Act 1893." See also *Kempler* v. *Bravingtons, Ltd.* (1925), 133 L. T. 680, C. A. (reviewing previous cases).

(*d*) *Genn* v. *Winkel* (1912), 107 L. T. 434.

(*e*) *Re Ferrier, ex p. the Trustee* v. *Donald*, [1944] Ch. 295.

(*f*) *Badische Anilin Fabrik* v. *Basle Chemical Works*, [1898] A. C. 200, at pp. 203, 204.

(*g*) *Pignataro* v. *Gilroy*, [1919] 1 K. B. 459. For converse case, see *Healy* v. *Howlett & Sons*, [1917] 1 K. B. 337.

(*h*) *Philip Head* v. *Showfronts, Ltd.*, [1970] 1 Lloyd's Rep. 140.

The rules laid down by this section apply unless a contrary intention appears (*i*). It has, however, been said that very little is now needed to give rise to the inference that the property in specific goods is to pass only on delivery or payment (*k*).

Rule 1.—*Specific goods.*—See note to s. 17, *ante*. The first four rules deal only with specific goods.

Rule 2.—The final words, "and the buyer has notice thereof," were added to the 1893 Bill in Committee on a suggestion from Scotland that it was unfair that the risk should be transferred to the buyer without notice. It is to be noted that this rule is negative. The case of an article which the seller is to manufacture for the buyer is sometimes treated as coming under this rule, but it generally comes under Rule 5. If a man orders a watch to be specially made for him, it is clear that the watchmaker may, if he likes, make two such watches, and that he keeps his contract by delivering either of them (*l*). PARKE, B., has pointed out that there may be an intermediate state of things. An article may be in course of manufacture, and the parties may have so far agreed upon it that the seller would break his contract if he delivered any other article, but there may be no intention that the property in it should pass before its completion (*m*). Unless a different intention be clearly shown, the rule is that the property in an article, which the seller is to make or complete for the buyer, does not pass until the article is delivered in a finished state, or until it is ready for delivery and is approved by the buyer in that state (*n*).

At one time the courts seemed inclined to reverse the presumption in the case of shipbuilding contracts, where the ship was to be paid for by stated instalments as the work progressed (*o*); but in a subsequent case in the House of Lords it was held that there was no sound distinction between the case of a ship and any other manufactured article (*p*). These decisions depend upon the particular terms of the contracts with which they deal, and are not to be regarded as inconsistent (*q*).

If the specific goods sold are attached to, or form part of, realty at the time of the contract, and are to be severed by the buyer, the property will only pass when they are severed (*r*).

(*i*) See cases cited at p. 145, *n.* (*d*).

(*k*) *Ward* v. *Bignall*, [1967] 2 All E. R. 449, at p. 453; [1967] 1 Q. B. 534, at p. 545, *per* DIPLOCK, L.J.

(*l*) *Cf. Atkinson* v. *Bell* (1828), 8 B. & C. 277, and *Xenos* v. *Wickham* (1866), L. R. 2 H. L. 296, at p. 316, *per* WILLES, J.

(*m*) *Laidler* v. *Burlinson* (1837), 2 M. & W. 602, at pp. 610, 611 (ship in course of building); *Wait* v. *Baker* (1848), 2 Exch. 1, at pp. 8, 9.

(*n*) *Clarke* v. *Spence* (1836), 4 A. & E. 448, at p. 466 (ship in course of building), reviewing the previous cases. As to an article begun by one person and finished by another, see *Oldfield* v. *Lowe* (1829), 9 B. & C. 73, at p. 78 (machinery).

(*o*) *Woods* v. *Russell* (1822), 5 B. & Ald. 942.

(*p*) *Seath* v. *Moore* (1886), 11 App. Cas. 350, at pp. 370, 380 (ship and its fittings); *Story on Sale*, § 316a, and notes to s. 17, *ante*.

(*q*) *Re Blyth Shipbuilding Co.*, [1926] Ch. 494, C. A. (reviewing all the earlier cases).

(*r*) *Jones* v. *Earl of Tankerville*, [1909] 2 Ch. 440, 442; *Kursell* v. *Timber Operators*, [1927] 1 K. B. 298, C. A.

Rule 3.—As to the concluding words, "and the buyer has notice thereof," see note to last rule. Lord BLACKBURN, in his work on *Sale* (*s*), states this rule without confining its operation to acts to be done by the seller, and regards it as a rule arbitrarily adopted from the Roman law, where it was a logical deduction from the principle that there could be no sale until the price was fixed. But the Court of Exchequer in 1863 reviewed the cases, and came to the conclusion that the rule should be qualified, as in the text, by confining it to acts to be done by the seller (*t*). The 1893 Act adopted this view, and the rule is now so confined. If the buyer were bound by the contract to do the weighing, it would be a matter of construction, having regard to s. 17 and s. 18, rule 1, when the property passed. A mere right of the buyer to weigh is immaterial (*u*). And if the parties have agreed on a provisional estimate of the total amount payable, to be more exactly calculated when the goods can be weighed, a common intention may be inferred that the transfer of the property shall not depend upon such weighing (*a*).

Rule 4.—*Sale or return, etc.*—When goods are sent on trial, or on approval, or on sale or return, the clear general rule is that the property remains in the seller till the buyer adopts the transaction, but it is quite competent to the parties to agree that the property shall pass to the buyer on delivery, and that, if he does not approve the goods, the property shall then revest in the seller (*b*). To use the language of continental lawyers, the condition on which the goods are delivered may be either suspensive or resolutive.

In some trades the usage is that when goods are delivered on fourteen days' approval, the property does not pass to the buyer on the expiration of that time, but the seller at any time after the fourteen days can call on the buyer either to take or to return the goods at once.

A transaction on sale or return is not a transaction where a person is in possession of the goods under an agreement to buy within s. 25 of the Act (*c*), nor does it become a sale because the goods perish or are damaged while in the possession of the bailee otherwise than by his act or default (*d*).

A delivery on sale or return within the meaning of the Rule may contemplate a sale to the transferee, or to a third party (*e*).

As to factors to be taken into account in determining what is a

---

(*s*) 1st ed., p. 152.

(*t*) *Turley* v. *Bates* (1863), 2 H. & C., 200.

(*u*) *Nanka Bruce* v. *Commonwealth Trust*, [1926] A. C. 77, P. C., and *cf. Tansley* v. *Turner* (1835), 2 Bing. N.C. 151.

(*a*) *Martineau* v. *Kitching* (1872), L. R. 7 Q. B 436; *cf. Anderson* v. *Morice* (1874), L. R. 10 C. P. 58; and see also *Castle* v. *Playford*, (1872) L. R. 7 Ex. 98.

(*b*) *Cf. Head* v. *Tattersall* (1871), L. R. 7 Exch. 7.

(*c*) *Edwards* v. *Vaughan* (1910), 26 T. L. R. 545, at p. 546, C. A.

(*d*) *Elphick* v. *Barnes* (1880), 5 C. P. D. 321 (death of horse on sale or return); see also the remarks of WILLMER, L.J., in *Poole* v. *Smith's Car Sales* (*Balham*), *Ltd.*, [1962] 2 All E. R. 482 at p. 489; [1962] 1 W. L. R. 744 at p. 753, C. A.

(*e*) See *Poole* v. *Smith's Car Sales* (*Balham*), (*supra*).

reasonable time within which to reject goods, see the comment to s. 35, *post*.

Rule 5.—*Generic goods.*—When there is a contract for the sale of unascertained goods, and the goods are afterwards selected by the buyer, or if selected by the seller are approved by the buyer, no difficulty arises. The difficulty comes when the seller makes the selection pursuant to an authority derived from the buyer; and it is often a nice question of law whether the acts done by the seller merely express a revocable intention to appropriate certain goods to the contract, or whether they show an irrevocable exercise of a right of election.

> "The general rule seems to be that when, from the nature of an agreement, an election is to be made, the party who is by the agreement to do the first act, which from its nature cannot be done till the election is determined, has authority to make the choice in order that he may perform his part of the agreement: when once he has performed the act the choice has been made and the election irrevocably determined; till then he may change his mind as to what the choice shall be, for the agreement gives him till that time to make his choice" (*f*).

The expression that the property in the goods passes by their "appropriation to the contract," though consistently used in the modern cases, is not a fortunate one. In the first place, as PARKE, B., has pointed out, the term is used in two senses. It may mean that the goods are so far appropriated that the seller would break his contract by delivering any other goods, though they still remain his property, or it may, and usually does, mean that the goods are finally appropriated to the contract so as to pass the property in them to the buyer (*g*). In the second place, if the decisions be carefully examined, it will be found that in every case where the property has been held to pass, there has been an actual or constructive delivery of the goods to the buyer (*h*). If the term "delivery" had been substituted for "appropriation," probably less difficulty would have arisen; and it seems a pity that this was not done.

The difficulty in the shipbuilding cases usually arises in regard to appropriation.

(*f*) *Blackburn on Sale* (1st ed.), p. 128, citing *Heyward's Case* (1595), 2 Coke, 35a, where it is said, "the certainty and thereby the property begins by election."

(*g*) *Wait* v. *Baker* (1848), 2 Exch. 1, at p. 8.

(*h*) This passage was approved by PEARSON, J., in *Federspiel* v. *Twigg & Co.*, [1957] 1 Lloyd's Rep. 240 at pp. 255–256, subject to the possible qualification that there may be after such constructive delivery an actual delivery still to be made by the seller under the contract. In *Wardar's* (*Import and Export*) *Co., Ltd.* v. *W. Norwood & Sons, Ltd.*, [1968] 3 All E. R. 602; [1968] 2 Q. B. 663, C. A., the Court of Appeal left open the question whether there was an unconditional appropriation of frozen kidneys when these were removed from a cold store and placed on the pavement to await collection. It seems improbable that there was such an appropriation, since this would have meant that the seller would have committed a breach of contract and a wrongful interference with the buyer's goods if for any reason he subsequently sold those kidneys elsewhere and supplied other kidneys to the buyer. *Cf. Flynn* v. *Mackin*, [1974] I.R. 101, where the Irish Supreme Court held that there had been no unconditional appropriation of a car by a seller who was driving it to the buyer to deliver it, as he could legally have sold it *en route* and supplied another one to the buyer.

"For appropriation I think there must be some definite act, such as the affixing of the property to the vessel itself, or some definite agreement between the parties which amounts to an assent to the property in the materials passing from the builders to the purchasers" (*i*).

Under s. 20, *post*, risk normally passes with property. It is relevant, therefore, to consider whether in all the circumstances risk has passed (*k*).

Delivery to carrier.—The commonest method of appropriating goods to a contract is by delivering them to a carrier, and then, if there be authority so to deliver them, and the seller does not reserve the right of disposal (*l*),

"the moment the goods which have been selected in pursuance of the contract are delivered to the carrier, the carrier becomes the agent of the vendee, and such a delivery amounts to a delivery to the vendee; and if there is a binding contract between the vendor and the vendee . . . then there is no doubt that the property passes by such delivery to the carrier. It is necessary, of course, that the goods should agree with the contract" (*m*).

19. Reservation of right of disposal.—(1) Where there is a contract for the sale of specific goods or where goods are subsequently appropriated to the contract, the seller may, by the terms of the contract or appropriation (*n*), reserve the right of disposal of the goods until certain conditions are fulfilled; and in such a case, notwithstanding the delivery of the goods to the buyer, or to a carrier or other bailee or custodier for the purpose of transmission to the buyer, the property in the goods does not pass to the buyer until the conditions imposed by the seller are fulfilled (*o*).

(2) Where goods are shipped, and by the bill of lading the goods are deliverable to the order of the seller or his agent, the seller is prima facie to be taken to reserve the right of disposal (*p*).

(*i*) *Re Blyth Shipbuilding Co.*, [1926] Ch. 494; *per* SARGANT, L.J., at p. 518.

(*k*) *Federspiel* v. *Twigg & Co., supra.*

(*l*) As he does in the ordinary c.i.f. contract, by holding the documents against the price: *Smyth* v. *Bailey*, [1940] 3 All E. R. 60, H. L.

(*m*) *Wait* v. *Baker* (1848), 2 Exch. 1, at p. 8 (unindorsed bill of lading); *Napier* v. *Dexters, Ltd.* (1926), 26 Ll. L. Rep. 62; *Wardar's (Import and Export) Co., Ltd.* v. *W. Norwood & Sons, Ltd.*, [1968] 2 All E. R. 602; [1968] 2 Q. B. 663, C. A.; and see Note C, Appendix II, *post*.

(*n*) See, *e.g.*, *Wait* v. *Baker* (1848), 2 Exch. 1; *Ogg* v. *Shuter* (1875), 1 C. P. D. 47 (property reserved by terms of contract); *Turner* v. *Liverpool Docks* (1851), 6 Exch. 543 (property reserved by terms of appropriation).

(*o*) *Mirabita* v. *Imperial Ottoman Bank* (1878), 3 Ex. D. 164, *per* COTTON, L.J. See also *The Annie Johnson*, [1918] p. 154, at p. 163.

(*p*) *Ogg* v. *Shuter* (1875), 1 C. P. D. 47, C. A.; *Mirabita* v. *Imperial Ottoman Bank* (1878), 3 Ex. D. 164, at p. 172, C. A. But see *The Parchim*, [1918] A. C. 157. In *Joyce* v. *Swann* (1864), 17 C. B., N. S., 84, and in *Browne* v. *Hare* (1853), 3 H. & N. 484; (1859), 4 H. & N. 822, the inference was negatived.

(3) Where the seller of goods draws on the buyer for the price, and transmits the bill of exchange and bill of lading to the buyer together to secure acceptance or payment of the bill of exchange, the buyer is bound to return the bill of lading if he does not honour the bill of exchange, and if he wrongfully retains the bill of lading the property in the goods does not pass to him (*q*).

ILLUSTRATIONS

(1) A consigns goods to B by ship, and draws on him for the price. He discounts the bill with a bank, indorses the bill of lading in blank, and authorises the bank to hand the bill of lading to B when he accepts the bill of exchange. Apart from any special terms in the contract, the property in the goods is transferred to B when he accepts the bill of exchange (*r*).

(2) A contracts to sell goods to B, and ships them under bills of lading made out to order of A upon a ship chartered by A for B. A then draws a bill of exchange on B. He discounts it with a bank, lodging the bill of lading with the bank. B is notified by the bank to which he tenders the price. The bank refuses the tender and sells elsewhere. Held: A's appropriation was subject only to payment on tender. Property therefore passed to B when he tendered the price, and the bank is liable in conversion (*s*).

(3) A contracts to sell goods to B, and arranges the shipment of the goods to B under a bill of lading naming A as consignee. A and B are associated companies and payment is to be made on credit terms. A has no intention of securing the price, but intends to reserve the right, if necessary, to divert the goods to another customer. Property only passes when the possibility of diverting the goods ceases when A posts the bill of lading to B (*t*).

Derivation.—Section 19 of the 1893 Act.

Definitions.—For "contract of sale," see s. 2 (1), *ante*, and s. 61 (1), *post*. For "buyer," "delivery," "goods," "property," "seller" and "specific goods," see s. 61 (1), *post*.

(*q*) *Shepherd* v. *Harrison* (1871), L. R. 5 H. L. 116, see at p. 133, *per* Lord CAIRNS; *Cahn* v. *Pockett's Bristol Channel Co.*, [1899] 1 Q. B. 643, at p. 656, C. A. The same principle underlies *Saks* v. *Tilley* (1915), 32 T. L. R. 148, C. A., where diamonds were posted to a buyer, together with a bill of exchange for acceptance and an invoice marked "settled by acceptance". For the position where the seller's agent credits the seller and then sends the bill of lading and a bill of exchange for acceptance to the buyer, see *Jordesen & Co. and Kahn* v. *London Hardwood Co., Ltd.* (1913), 19 Com. Cas. 164; *Barton Thompson* v. *Vigers Brothers* (1906), 19 Com. Cas. 175; *Churchill and Sim* v. *Goddard*, [1936] 1 All E. R. 675; [1937] 1 K. B. 92.

(*r*) *The Prinz Adelbert*, [1917] A. C. 586, P. C.; *cf. The Derfflinger No. 2* (1918), 87 L. J. P. C. 195; *The Miramichi*, [1915] P. 71; *The Orteric*, [1920] A. C. 724, 733, P. C. See also *The Vesta*, [1921] A. C. 774, 783 where the property was held to have passed although the seller was obliged to take goods back if "found unsuited."

(*s*) *Mirabita* v. *Imperial Ottoman Bank* (1878), 3 Ex. D. 164. Had the seller's intention throughout been to deprive the buyer of the goods, rather than to pass them to him against payment, the result would have been different; see *per* COTTON, L.J., especially at pp. 172–173 and the cases cited at n. (*b*) on p. 32, *supra*.

(*t*) *The Albazero*, [1974] 2 All E. R. 906; affirmed on this point [1975] 3 All E.R. 21, C.A.; reversed [1976] 3 All E.R. 129; [1977] A. C. 774, H. L., where the presumption was applied in the light of evidence of the seller's actual intention.

Cross-references.—*Cf.* ss. 8 and 9, *ante* (price); s. 25, *post* (buyer in possession); s. 43 (1), *post* (seller's lien); s. 32, *post*, and Note B, *post*, Appendix II (delivery to carrier); and the commentary on f.o.b. and c.i.f. contracts, *ante*, pp. 30 *et seq.*

COMMENT

This section, like the preceding sections, deals only with the transfer of the property in goods as between seller and buyer, and does not affect the protection afforded to innocent third parties by s. 25 and the Factors Acts, *post* (*u*), all of which prevail over the present section. COTTON, L.J.'s summary of the law upon which the equivalent section in the 1893 Act was largely based was as follows:

> "In the case of such a contract [*i.e.*, a contract for the sale of unascertained goods], the delivery by the vendor to a common carrier, or, (unless the effect of the shipment is restricted by the terms of the bill of lading), shipment on board a ship of, or chartered for, the purchaser is an appropriation sufficient to pass the property. If, however, the vendor, when shipping the articles which he intends to deliver under the contract, takes the bill of lading to his own order, and does so not as agent, or on behalf of the purchaser, but on his own behalf, it is held that he thereby reserves to himself a power of disposing of the property, and that consequently there is no final appropriation, and the property does not on shipment pass to the purchasers. . . . If the vendor deals with, or claims to retain the bill of lading, in order to secure the contract price, as when he sends forward the bill of lading with a bill of exchange attached, with directions that the bill of lading is not to be delivered to the purchaser till acceptance or payment of the bill of exchange, the appropriation is not absolute, but until acceptance of the draft, or payment or tender of the price, is conditional only, and until such acceptance or payment or tender, the property in the goods does not pass to the purchaser" (*a*).

This passage is however open to one observation: it does not cover the intermediate situation where the seller intends to reserve not his title, but simply a right to possession as security for the price, by taking the bill of lading in his own name (*b*).

The question whether any and if so what right of disposal is reserved is a question of fact (*c*). Relevant factors would include the seller's wishes (i) to secure payment or (ii) to raise money by pledge of shipping documents or (iii) to reserve the right to deliver or direct the cargo to another customer (*d*).

After loss of both title and the right to possession (*e.g.* after transfer of the shipping documents to the buyer), the unpaid seller may still be able to exercise the right of stoppage in transitu if the buyer becomes

---

(*u*) *Cahn* v. *Pockett's Bristol Channel Co.*, [1899] 1 Q. B. 643, C. A.

(*a*) *Mirabita* v. *Imperial Ottoman Bank* (1878), 3 Ex. D. 164, at p. 172; see also at p. 170, *per* BRAMWELL, L.J. *Cf. Ex p. Banner* (1876), 2 Ch. D. 278.

(*b*) *The Parchim*, [1918] A. C. 157, H. L., and other cases considered, p. 32, *ante*.

(*c*) See p. 32, *ante*.

(*d*) See *The Albazero*, illustration (3), *ante*.

insolvent (*e*) but subject to the rights of any bona fide sub-buyer or pledgee from the buyer (*f*).

20. Risk *prima facie* passes with property.—(1) Unless otherwise agreed (*g*), the goods remain at the seller's risk until the property in them is transferred to the buyer, but when the property in them is transferred to the buyer the goods are at the buyer's risk whether delivery has been made or not (*h*).

(2) But where delivery has been delayed through the fault of either buyer or seller the goods (*i*) are at the risk of the party at fault as regards any loss which might not have occurred but for such fault (*k*).

(3) Nothing in this section affects the duties or liabilities of either seller or buyer as a bailee or custodier of the goods of the other party (*l*).

ILLUSTRATIONS

(1) Furs delivered "on approval" with invoice. They are stolen by burglars. By the custom of the fur trade the goods are at the risk of the person ordering them on approval. The seller can recover the invoice price from the person to whom he delivered them (*m*).

(2) Sale of potatoes in clamp, delivery instructions to be given by buyer in 6 months, property to pass and payment to be completed on delivery. Seller undertakes to take reasonable care of the potatoes until delivery. The potatoes rot, although the seller takes reasonable care. Held: risk on buyer,

---

(*e*) *Schotsman* v. *Lancs and Yorkshire Rail Co.* (1867), L. R. 2 Ch. App. 332, at p. 337; *Lyons* v. *Hoffnung* (1890), 15 App. Cas. 391, H. L. See further, s. 45, *post*.

(*f*) See s. 47 (2), *post*.

(*g*) *Martineau* v. *Kitching* (1872), L. R. 7 Q. B. 436; *Castle* v. *Playford* (1872), L. R. 7 Exch. 98; *Inglis* v. *Stock* (1885), 10 App. Cas. 263 (f.o.b. contract).

(*h*) For examples of seller's risk, see *Head* v. *Tattersall* (1871), L. R. 7 Exch. 7, see at p. 14; *Elphick* v. *Barnes* (1880), 5 C. P. D. 321, at p. 326 (death of horse delivered on sale or return). For examples of buyer's risk, see *Rugg* v. *Minett* (1809), 11 East, 210 (sale of goods in warehouse, sellers agreeing to pay rent for 30 days; goods destroyed by fire within this period); *Tarling* v. *Baxter* (1827), 6 B. &. C. 360 (sale of standing hay, not to be cut by buyer before 1st May. Had seller undertaken to cut hay, property and risk would not have passed); *Sweeting* v. *Turner* (1871), L. R. 7 Q. B. 310 (risk of landlord distraining on goods sold); *cf. Widenmayer* v. *Burn Stewart & Co., Ltd.*, 1967 S. L. T. 129 (Ct. of Sess.) (a case of barter).

(*i*) "the goods" = contractual goods assembled by the seller for the purpose of fulfilling the contract and making delivery: *Demby Hamilton & Co.* v. *Barden*, [1949] 1 All E. R. 435.

(*k*) *Martineau* v. *Kitching* (1872), L. R. 7 Q. B. 436, at p. 456; *per* BLACKBURN, J., *Demby Hamilton & Co.* v. *Barden* (*supra*).

(*l*) *Cf. Head* v. *Tattersall* and *Elphick* v. *Barnes* (*supra*); *Poole* v. *Smith's Car Sales, Ltd.*, [1962] 2 All E. R. 482, at p. 489; [1962] 1 W. L. R. 744, at p. 753, *per* WILLMER, L.J.; *Wiehe* v. *Dennis Brothers* (1913), 29 T. L. R. 250 (pony left in possession of seller for a few days; seller liable as gratuitous bailee even if property and risk had passed).

(*m*) *Bevington* v. *Dale* (1902), 7 Com. Cas. 112.

who must pay for the potatoes as the risk and property are separated by the agreement (*n*).

(3) Sale of 120,000 gallons of white spirit out of 200,000 in a tank on wharf. No appropriation to the contract is made, but a delivery warrant is issued to the buyer, and the wharfingers attorn to the buyer. The warrant is not acted on for some months, and in the meantime the spirit deteriorates. The loss falls on the buyer (*o*).

(4) Agreement for sale of 30 tons of apple juice to be delivered weekly on buyer's instructions. Buyer fails to give instructions for last 10 tons, which seller has put in casks ready for delivery. The juice goes putrid as a result. Although property remains in the seller, the loss was the fault of the buyer and is at his risk (*p*).

Derivation.—Section 20 of the 1893 Act, which took the form of a single provision with two provisos. The first proviso is now sub-s. (2) and the second proviso is now sub-s. (3).

Definitions.—For "buyer," "delivery," "fault," "goods," "property" and "seller," see s. 61 (1), *post.*

Cross-references.—*Cf.* ss. 6 and 7, *ante* (goods perishing before sale); ss. 32 (2), (3) and 33, *post* (goods sent by carriers); s. 37, *post* (neglect or refusal to take delivery); and s. 55 (1), *post* ("unless otherwise agreed").

History.—

The expression "*might* not have occurred" was substituted for "*would* not have occurred" in the first proviso in the 1893 Bill (now sub-s. (2)) at the instance of Lord WATSON. Although it is probably not true to say that it shifts the onus of proof on to the party at fault, it lessens the onus of proof on the innocent party (*q*).

COMMENT

"As a general rule," says BLACKBURN, J.,

> "*res perit domino*, the old Civil law maxim, is a maxim of our law, and, when you can show that the property passed, the risk of the loss *primâ facie* is in the person in whom the property is. If, on the other hand, you go beyond that and show that the risk attached to one person or the other, it is a very strong

(*n*) *Horn* v. *Minister of Food*, [1948] 2 All E. R. 1036.

(*o*) *Sterns* v. *Vickers*, [1923] 1 K. B. 78, C. A. The Court of Appeal left open the question whether property had passed, but it would seem that no legal property is acquired by a purchaser in such circumstances, although it is just possible that he might acquire an interest in equity in special circumstances; see further the comment to s. 16, *ante*. The finding that risk passed was based on the consideration that the seller had done all that he agreed to do, the wharfinger had attorned, and the buyers were free to take delivery when they wished. *Cf. J. J. Cunningham, Ltd.* v. *Robert Munro, Ltd.* (1922), 28 Com. Cas. 42 (bran deteriorates while waiting in lighters for buyer's ship; seller's risk, as buyer's contractual obligation to take delivery has not arrived); *Comptoir etc. du Boerenbond Belge* v. *Luis de Ridder*, [1949] 1 All E. R. 269; [1949] A. C. 293.

(*p*) *Demby Hamilton & Co.* v. *Barden*, [1949] 1 All E. R. 435.

(*q*) *Denby Hamilton & Co.* v. *Barden, supra.*

argument for showing that the property was meant to be in him. But the two are not inseparable. . . ." (*r*).

The parties may expressly agree that the risk shall pass to the buyer before the property in the goods passes or that the property shall pass before the risk.

Such an agreement may also be implied from the terms of the contract and the surrounding circumstances. Thus, risk may pass to the buyer before the property passes and even before the goods are delivered where the contract provides that the seller should take reasonable care of the goods until delivery (*s*), where the goods are an unascertained part of a larger bulk and the buyer has every opportunity to take delivery but elects not to (*t*), in f.o.b. contracts where property is reserved after shipment (*u*), and in c.i.f. contracts (*a*).

Risk will also frequently pass to the buyer once the goods are delivered to him even though the property in the goods is to remain in the seller until the price is paid (*b*). But the risk does not normally pass to a potential buyer where goods are delivered on sale or return (*c*).

In the absence of an express agreement to that effect, risk will rarely remain with the seller once the property in the goods has passed to the buyer except to a limited extent under sub-s. (2) of this section, where the seller is in default in delivering the goods, and under the special provisions of s. 32 (3), *post*, where transit by sea is involved (*d*).

Where the buyer is entitled to reject goods because of a breach of contract by the seller, and does reject them, so that the property in them revests in the seller, it would seem that the seller must bear any loss arising from damage to or deterioration of the goods even while the goods were temporarily the property of the buyer (*e*), provided at least that the loss was not the fault of the buyer.

Duties of bailee.—When the seller remains in possession of the goods after the property in them has passed to the buyer, or when the buyer gets possession of the goods before the property and risk pass, as in

---

(*r*) *Martineau* v. *Kitching* (1872), L. R. 7 Q. B. 436, at pp. 454, 456; discussed and approved, *The Parchim*, [1918] A. C. 157, at p. 168, P. C. BLACKBURN, J.'s citation of the maxim *res perit domino* is misleading as to Roman Law, under which, as a general rule, risk passed as soon as the parties were agreed on a specific article and the price, but property passed only on delivery, and sometimes not even then: see *Moyle's Justinian* (5th ed.) p. 434.

(*s*) *Horn* v. *Minister of Food*, illustration (2), *ante*.

(*t*) *Stern* v. *Vickers*, illustration (3), *ante*.

(*u*) P. 32, *ante*, and see the comment to s. 19, *ante*.

(*a*) P. 34, *ante*.

(*b*) *Cf. Comptoir d'Achat et de Vente du Boerenbond Belge S. A.* v. *Luis de Ridder*, [1949] 1 All E. R. 269; [1949] A. C. 293, H. L.; and see *Benjamin's Sale of Goods*, para. 405. Even where risk does not pass, the buyer will owe a duty of care as bailee of the goods—see *post*. As to reservation of title clauses, see the comment to s. 48, *post*.

(*c*) *Cf. Bevington* v. *Dale*, illustration (1), *ante*, where a trade custom to the contrary was proved.

(*d*) There is no reported authority, but it may be that a similar principle to that in s. 32 (3) will also apply where transit by land or air is involved.

(*e*) *Head* v. *Tattersall* (1871), L. R. 7 Exch. 7.

the case of goods on trial, the party in possession is in each case a bailee (*f*).

The duty of a bailee is to take reasonable care of the goods, and to have them available undamaged for delivery up when agreed or required unless he is prevented from doing so without any fault on his or his servants' part (*g*). The onus is upon the bailee to prove that any loss or damage to goods occurred without any failure on his part to take reasonable care (*h*). Further, in the case of a bailment under contract (as where a seller is in possession of the goods before property and risk pass) the bailee's promise probably is that reasonable care will be taken by himself, his servants or agents (*i*).

The absence of any reward is only one of the issues taken into account in assessing the degree of care required (*k*). Reward in this sense exists where by an agreement of sale one or other of the parties is to have possession without property even though no specific sum is to be paid for such custody.

A buyer who rightfully rejects goods is an involuntary bailee if the seller refuses to retake, and is therefore perhaps only under a duty to avoid wilful or reckless damage (*l*).

A seller in possession under s. 37 following a buyer's failure to collect within a reasonable time, however, probably owes a duty of reasonable care since he has a right to charge for his care and custody.

Although s. 20 (3) does not expressly refer to these situations, a seller remaining in possession after the risk, but before property passes, or a buyer in possession after property but before risk passes, must also be responsible for loss or damage arising in consequence of his failure to take reasonable care of the goods. Where neither property nor risk has passed under an agreement to sell specific goods, a seller in possession is also responsible for loss or, no doubt, damage due to his fault: see s. 7, *ante*.

Passing of risk but not property.—A purchaser to whom the property in the goods has not yet passed and who is not entitled to possession of them has been held to have no right of action in negligence against a third party who carelessly damages or destroys them even though the risk has passed to him (*m*).

(*f*) See *Wiehe* v. *Dennis Bros.* (1913), 29 T. L. R. 250.

(*g*) *Houghland* v. *R. R. Low* (*Luxury Coaches*), *Ltd.*, [1962] 2 All E. R. 159; [1962] 1 Q. B. 694, C. A.; *Morris* v. *C. W. Martin & Sons, Ltd.*, [1965] 2 All E. R. 725; [1966] 1 Q. B. 716, C. A.

(*h*) *Ibid.*; *Coldman* v. *Hill*, [1919] 1 K. B. 443; *The Sansei Maru*, [1979] 1 Lloyd's Rep. 11, P. C.

(*i*) *B. R. S.* v. *Arthur Crutchley & Co., Ltd.*, [1968] 1 All E. R. 811, C. A.; *Morris* v. *C. W. Martin & Sons, Ltd., supra*, at pp. 731 and 728 respectively.

(*k*) See *Houghland* v. *R. R. Low* (*Luxury Coaches*), *Ltd., supra*. If there is any distinction in principle between the duties of a bailee for reward and a gratuitous bailee, it is a very fine one: *The Sansei Maru, supra*.

(*l*) *Howard* v. *Harris* (1884), 1 Cab. & El. 253; but see *Newman* v. *Bourne and Hollingsworth* (1915), 31 T. L. R. 209.

(*m*) *Margarine Union G.m.b.H.* v. *Cambay Prince S.S. Co., Ltd.*, [1967] 3 All E. R. 775; [1969] 1 Q. B. 219. Such a purchaser will commonly have contractual rights—see s. 1 of

As property and risk are separable, it follows that property and insurable interest may be separable. If goods are at a person's risk, he has an insurable interest, whether he has any property in the goods or not (*n*). And if he has the property in the goods, he has an insurable interest whether they are at his risk or not (*o*).

A provision in a contract that the risk shall not pass until a time necessarily later than the time when property would normally pass, provides a powerful indication that the property in the goods was not intended by the parties to pass until the later date (*p*).

Accessories or accretion.—The converse of the rule *res perit domino* also holds good, and any fruits or increase of the thing sold belong *prima facie* to the party who has the property in it.

> "Any calamity befalling the goods after the sale is completed must be borne by the purchaser, and, by parity of reasoning, any benefit to them is his benefit, and not that of the vendor" (*q*).

Transfer of Title

21. Sale by person not the owner.—(1) Subject to this Act (*r*), where goods are sold by a person who is not their owner, and who does not sell them under the authority or with the consent of the owner, the buyer acquires no better title to the goods than the seller had (*s*), unless the owner of the goods is by his conduct precluded from denying the seller's authority to sell.

(2) Nothing in this Act affects—

---

the Bills of Lading Act 1855, *post*, Appendix I, and "*The Dona Mari*", [1973] 2 Lloyd's Rep. 366.

(*n*) As to the insurable interest of seller and buyer respectively, see *Anderson* v. *Morice* (1876), 1 App. Cas. 713; *Colonial Ins. Co.* v. *Adelaide Marine Insurance Co.* (1886), 12 App. Cas. 128, at p. 135; Chalmers' *Marine Insurance Act 1906* (5th ed.), pp. 11 *et seq.*

(*o*) *Inglis* v. *Stock* (1885), 10 App. Cas. 263, at p. 270.

(*p*) *President of India* v. *Metcalfe Shipping Co., Ltd.*, [1969] 1 All E. R. 861; [1969] 2 Q. B. 123; on appeal, [1969] 3 All E. R. 1549; [1970] 1 Q. B. 289, C. A.

(*q*) *Sweeting* v. *Turner* (1871), L. R. 7 Q. B. 310, at p. 313, *per* BLACKBURN, J.

(*r*) See ss. 22 to 25, *post*.

(*s*) For principle, see *Colonial Bank* v. *Whinney* (1886), 11 App. Cas. 426, at pp. 435, 436, *per* Lord BLACKBURN. For illustrations, see *Cooper* v. *Willomatt* (1845), 1 C. B. 672 (fraudulent sale by bailee); *Lee* v. *Bayes* (1856), 18 C. B. 599 (stolen goods sold by auction); *Consolidated Co.* v. *Curtis & Son* (1892), 1 Q. B. 495, 498 (goods included in bill of sale sold by auction); *The Telegrafo* (1871), L. R. 3 P. C. 673, at p. 685 (goods taken by piracy); *Cundy* v. *Lindsay* (1878), 3 App. Cas. 459 (goods obtained by fraud and resold); *Helby* v. *Matthews*, [1895] A. C. 471 (wrongful disposition by hirer under hire-purchase agreement). But if a person acquires goods in good faith and spends money in improving them, the true owner will not be able to recover them without giving credit for the improvements; *Greenwood* v. *Bennett*, [1972] 3 All E. R. 586; [1973] 1 Q. B. 195, C. A. For a criticism of this case, see 1973 J. B. L. 64. See also s. 6 of the Torts (Interference with Goods) Act 1977, which provides for an allowance to be made in respect of improvements in the assessment of damages for wrongful interference.

(a) the provisions of the Factors Acts or any enactment enabling the apparent owner of goods to dispose of them as if he were their true owner (*t*);

(b) the validity of any contract of sale under any special common law or statutory power of sale or under the order of a court of competent jurisdiction (*u*).

ILLUSTRATIONS

Subsection (1).—(1) A, a timber merchant, instructs the dock company with whom his timber is warehoused to accept delivery orders signed by his clerk. The clerk has a limited authority to sell to known customers. The clerk in an assumed name sells some of the timber to B, who knows nothing of A, or of the clerk under his real name. The clerk carries out the fraud by giving the dock company orders for the transfer of timber into his assumed name, and then in that name giving delivery orders to B. A can recover the value of the timber from B since the clerk, having no title to the timber, could give none to B. A has not held the clerk out to B as having his authority to sell, so that no question of estoppel can arise (*a*).

(*t*) See the Factors Act 1889, the Factors (Scotland) Act 1890, and the Bills of Lading Act 1855, *post*; the Bankruptcy Act 1914, ss. 38 and 38A (reputed ownership); 3 Halsbury's Statutes (3rd Edn.) 87; as limited by the Hire-Purchase Act 1965, s. 53; 30 Halsbury's Statutes (3rd Edn.) 61; see also the Hire-Purchase Act 1964, ss. 27–29, both in their present form and as substituted, from a date to be appointed by Sch. 4, para. 22 of the Consumer Credit Act 1974, which enable a *bona fide* private purchaser of a car which is the subject of a hire-purchase agreement to obtain a good title; and for certain purposes the Bills of Sale Act 1878, *post*, Appendix I; *Lamb* v. *Wright & Co.*, [1924] 1 K. B. 857 (reputed ownership in case of hire-purchase agreement).

(*u*) As to pawnee, see *Martin* v. *Reid* (1862), 11 C. B., N. S., 730, at p. 736, *per* WILLES, J.; *Pigot* v. *Cubley* (1864), 15 C. B., N. S., 701. As to the power of a carrier to sell as agent of necessity, see *Sims & Co.* v. *Midland Railway*, [1913] 1 K. B. 103 (perishable goods). As to distrainor, see Woodfall's *Landlord and Tenant* (26th ed.), 436 *et seq*. As to sheriff, see s. 15, Bankruptcy and Deeds of Arrangement Act 1913, as explained in *Curtis* v. *Maloney*, [1950] 2 All E. R. 982; [1951] 1 K. B. 736, C. A., and *Dyal Singh* v. *Kenyan Insurance, Ltd.*, [1954] A. C. 287, P. C. (sales under execution); *Doe* v. *Donston* (1818), 1 B. & Ald. 230 (sale after expiration of office); *cf. Batchelor* v. *Vyse* (1834), 4 M. & Sc. 552 (excessive sale): *Manders* v. *Williams* (1849), 4 Exch. 339 (sale by sheriff of goods on sale or return); *Jones Brothers* v. *Woodhouse*, [1923] 2 K. B. 117 (sale by sheriff of goods on hire-purchase). As to master of ship, see *The Gratitudine* (1801), 3 Ch. Rob. 240, at p. 259, and *Kaltenbach* v. *Mackenzie* (1878), 3 C. P. D. 467, at p. 473. As to order of Court, see R. S. C., O. 29, r. 4. As to goods left with innkeeper, see the Innkeepers Act 1878; 17 Halsbury's Statutes (3rd Edn.) 815; the Hotel Proprietors Act 1956; 17 Halsbury's Statutes (3rd Edn.) 816; and *Chesham* v. *Beresford Hotel* (1913), 29 T. L. R. 584; *Marsh* v. *Commissioner of Police*, [1944] 2 All E. R. 393; [1945] K. B. 43. As to executor or administrator, see Williams and Mortimer: *Executors Administrators and Probate*, pp. 615–629. As to trustee in bankruptcy, see ss. 55, 56 of the Bankruptcy Act 1914; 3 Halsbury's Statutes (3rd Edn.) 106, 108. As to sale by warehouseman for non-payment of his charges, see *Willets* v. *Chaplin & Co.* (1923), 39 T. L. R. 222.

(*a*) *Farquharson Brothers* v. *King & Co.*, [1902] A. C. 325. Contrast *Canadian Laboratory Supplies* v. *Engelherd Industries* (1979), 97 D. L. R. (3d) 1, where the defendant buyer dealt with the agent for several years because he was P's employee acting, as the buyer believed, with authority from P on behalf of a "customer" of P who turned out to be fictitious. The Supreme Court of Canada held that although there had been no holding out by P in respect of earlier dealings, there had been such a holding out in respect of later dealings.

(2) A cotton broker innocently buys certain bales of cotton from a person who has fraudulently obtained them and who has himself no title to them, thinking they may suit an old customer. He afterwards sells and delivers the cotton to that customer. He is liable to the true owner for the conversion of the cotton (*b*).

(3) X wishes to obtain an advance on the security of his car. He goes to a car dealer and signs a form by which he makes an application to a finance company to hire the car on H. P. terms. The form contains a statement that the car is the sole unencumbered property of the car dealer. The car dealer then sells the car to the finance company. X is estopped from denying the car dealer's title to sell the car as its owner (*c*).

(4) M, a car dealer, displays a number of cars for sale. To the knowledge of P, another car dealer, some of these cars are the property of a finance company which has authorised M to sell them. Unknown to P this authority is withdrawn. M sells cars to P othewise than in the ordinary course of business, representing them to be his own unencumbered property. They are in fact the property of the finance company. The finance company is not estopped from denying M's title to the cars (*d*).

Subsection (2).—(3) The high bailiff of a County Court seizes certain goods under a warrant of execution. X, who is the true owner, claims them, but does not make the required deposit. The high bailiff sells them, and the price is duly paid into court. The purchaser acquires a good title under s. 135 of the County Courts Act 1959 (*e*).

(4) Consignment of perishable goods (tomatoes) from Jersey to London. Delivery is interrupted at Weymouth by a railway strike. The Railway Company sells the goods at Weymouth without communicating with the London buyers. The company is liable in damages, as in these circumstances it is not an agent of necessity (*f*).

Derivation.—Section 21 of the 1893 Act.

Definitions.—For "contract of sale," see s. 2 (1), *ante*, and s. 61 (1), *post*. For "buyer," "Factors Acts," "goods," and "seller," see s. 61 (1), *post*.

Cross-references.—*Cf.* s. 12, *ante* (seller's warranty of title, etc.); and ss. 22 to 25, *post* (transfer of title).

COMMENT

Subsection (1).—"The general rule of law," says WILLES, J.,

(*b*) *Hollins* v. *Fowler* (1875), L. R. 7 H. L. 757; see s. 23, *post*, as to voidable titles.

(*c*) *Stoneleigh Finance* v. *Phillips*, [1965] 1 All E. R. 513; [1965] 2 Q. B. 537, C. A.; *cf. Mercantile Credit* v. *Hamblin*, [1964] 3 All E. R. 592; [1965] 2 Q. B. 242, C. A.

(*d*) *Motor Credits* (*Hire Finance*), *Ltd.* v. *Pacific Motors Pty., Ltd.* (1963), 109 C. L. R. 87; reversed on another ground; *sub nom. Pacific Motor Auctions Proprietary, Ltd.* v. *Motor Credits* (*Hire Finance*), *Ltd.*, [1965] 2 All E. R. 105; [1965] A. C. 867.

(*e*) *Goodlock* v. *Cousins*, [1897] 1 Q. B. 558, C. A. (a decision under s. 156 of the County Courts Act 1888, now replaced by the Act above referred to: 7 Halsbury's Statutes (3rd Edn.) 389).

(*f*) *Springer* v. *Great Western Rail Co.*, [1921] 1 K. B. 257, C. A. See note on agent of necessity, *post*.

"is undoubted, that no one can transfer a better title than he himself possesses. *Nemo dat quod non habet*" (*g*).

In a case under the Factors Act 1842, BLACKBURN, J., says:

"At common law a person in possession of goods could not confer on another, either by sale or by pledge, any better title to the goods than he himself had. To this general rule there was an exception of sales in market overt [*see now* s. 22, *post*], and an apparent exception where the person in possession had a title defeasible on account of fraud [*see now* s. 23, *post*]. But the general rule was that, to make either a sale or a pledge valid against the owner of the goods sold or pledged, it must be shown that the seller or pledger had authority from the owner to sell or pledge, as the case might be. If the owner of the goods had so acted as to clothe the seller or pledger with apparent authority to sell or pledge, he was at common law precluded, as against those who were induced *bonâ fide* to act on the faith of that apparent authority, from denying that he had given such an authority, and the result as to them was the same as if he had really given it. But there was no such preclusion as against those who had notice that the real authority was limited" (*h*).

No title by finding.—The finder of lost goods acquires no title as against the true owner, and can give none except by sale in market overt.

"If a person leaves a watch or a ring on a seat in the park or on a table at a café, and it ultimately gets into the hands of a *bona fide* purchaser, it is no answer to the true owner to say that it was his carelessness, and nothing else, that enabled the finder to pass it off as his own" (*i*).

The saying that "findings are keepings" is not a maxim of the law. A person who finds goods and converts them to his own use, having reason to believe, at the time of finding, that the owner can be discovered by taking reasonable steps, may be guilty of theft (*k*). Presumably if goods are voluntarily abandoned, anyone taking possession becomes the owner in the full sense of the term, as was the case in the Civil Law (*l*).

Estoppel.—It sometimes happens that a man is precluded by his conduct from denying the truth of a particular state of affairs.

"Where one man by his words or conduct wilfully causes another to believe in the existence of a certain state of things, and induces him to act on that belief, so as to alter his own previous position, the former is concluded from

---

(*g*) *Whistler* v. *Forster* (1863), 14 C. B., N. S., 248, at p. 257; *Banque Belge* v. *Hambrouck*, [1921] 1 K. B. 321, at p. 329, C. A.

(*h*) *Cole* v. *North Western Bank* (1875), L. R. 10 C. P. 354, at p. 362; approved *Colonial Bank* v. *Whinney* (1886), 11 App. Cas. 426, at pp. 435, 436 (reputed ownership); *cf. City Bank* v. *Barrow* (1880), 5 App. Cas. 664, at p. 677, as to Roman and old French law, and Canadian law.

(*i*) *Farquharson Brothers* v. *King & Co.*, [1902] A. C. 325, at p. 336. But a finder has a good title against everyone except the true owner: *Armory* v. *Delamirie* (1721), 1 Str. 505. See the law fully discussed in *Hannah* v. *Peel*, [1945] 2 All E. R. 288; [1945] K. B. 509.

(*k*) Under the Theft Act 1968; 8 Halsbury's Statutes (3rd Edn.) 782; as to what amounts to conversion by finder, see *Hollins* v. *Fowler* (1875), L. R. 7 H. L. 757, at p. 766.

(*l*) *Inst. II*, 1, 47; but see *Hibbert* v. *McKiernan*, [1948] 1 All E. R. 860, D. C.; [1948] 2 K. B. 142.

averring against the latter a different state of things as existing at the same time" (*m*).

Moreover, as PARKE, B., said in 1848,

"By the term wilfully . . . we must understand . . . at least that he means his representation to be acted upon, and that it is acted upon accordingly; and if, whatever a man's real meaning may be, he so conducts himself that a reasonable man would take the representation to be true, the party making the representation would be equally precluded from contesting its truth; and conduct by negligence or omission when there is a duty cast upon a person by usage of trade or otherwise to disclose the truth may often have the same effect" (*n*).

Applying this rule to the circumstances envisaged by the present subsection, the question to be asked is:

"whether the true owner of the goods has so invested the person dealing with them with the indicia of property as that when an innocent person enters into a negotiation with the person to whom these things have been entrusted with the indicia of property the true owner of the goods cannot afterwards complain that there was no authority to make such a bargain" (*o*).

It is a question of fact whether the true owner has so invested the seller with the indicia of property. It is not enough that the true owner has carelessly allowed them to come into the hands of the seller (*p*). There must normally be a representation by the owner either that he has no interest in the goods, or that the seller has authority to sell the goods on his behalf in the manner in which he purports to (*q*), or that the seller is

---

(*m*) *Pickard* v. *Sears* (1837), 6 Ad. & El. 469, at p. 474.

(*n*) *Freeman* v. *Cooke* (1848), 18 L. J. Ex. 114, 119; and see *Gregg* v. *Wells* (1839), 10 Ad. & El. 90; *Cornish* v. *Abington* (1859), 4 H. & N. 549; *Wester Moffat Colliery Co.* v. *Jeffrey & Co.*, 1911 S. C. 346 (Ct. of Sess.); *Seton* v. *Lafone* (1887), 19 Q. B. D. 68, at p. 72, C. A.

(*o*) *Henderson & Co.* v. *Williams*, [1895] 1 Q. B. 521, at p. 525, *per* Lord HALSBURY; *Knights* v. *Wiffen* (1870), L. R. 5 Q. B. 660; but *cf. Farquharson Brothers* v. *King & Co.*, [1902] A. C. 325; *Mercantile Bank of India, Ltd.* v. *Central Bank of India, Ltd.*, [1938] 1 All E. R. 52; [1938] A. C. 287, P. C., not following *Commonwealth Trust* v. *Akotey*, [1926] A. C. 72, P. C.; *Jerome* v. *Bentley*, [1952] 2 All E. R. 114. And see *Wah Tat Bank, and Overseas Chinese Banking Corporation, Ltd.* v. *Chan Chen Kum and Hua Siang Steamship Co.*, [1967] 2 Lloyd's Rep. 437; on appeal, [1971] 1 Lloyd's Rep. 439, P. C. See also *Gillett* v. *Hill* (1834), 2 Cr. & M. 530 (wharfinger accepting delivery order estopped from denying he had the goods); *Laurie and Morewood* v. *Dudlin & Sons*, [1926] 1 K. B. 223 (warehouseman not estopped by mere receipt of delivery order); *Coventry* v. *Gt. Eastern Rail Co.* (1883), 11 Q. B. D. 776 (two delivery orders for same goods); *Cohen* v. *Mitchell* (1890), 25 Q. B. D. 262, C. A. (sale by bankrupt, trustee not intervening); *Waller* v. *Drakeford* (1853), 1 E. & B. 749; *Patterson Motors* v. *Riley* (1966), 56 D. L. R. (2d.) 278; 18 L. Q. R. 159; Atiyah, *Sale of Goods* (5th ed.), p. 184; Spencer Bower & Turner, *Estoppel by Representation* (3rd ed.), paras. 73–80.

(*p*) *Farquharson Brothers* v. *King & Co.*, [1902] A. C. 325, P. C.; *Jerome* v. *Bentley*, [1952] 2 All E. R. 114.

(*q*) *Motor Credit (Hire Finance), Ltd.* v. *Pacific Motors Pty., Ltd.* (1963), 109 C. L. R. 87 (*ante*, illustration (4)); reversed on another ground, *sub nom. Pacific Motor Auctions Proprietary, Ltd.* v. *Motor Credits (Hire Finance), Ltd.*, [1965] 2 All E. R. 105; [1965] A. C. 867, P. C.; *Spencer* v. *North Country Finance Co.*, [1963] C. L. Y. 212.

the owner of the goods (*r*) or is otherwise entitled to dispose of them (*s*), and that representation must be acted upon by the buyer to his detriment.

The nature of the estoppel may be important. If the true owner has represented that the seller is owner of the goods, then the buyer will be able to rely on this representation whatever the circumstances of the sale, provided, of course, that he acts in good faith (*t*). If, on the other hand, the true owner has only represented that the seller had authority to sell the goods as his agent then he will be able to recover them if they are sold in a manner not covered by the seller's ostensible authority as agent (*u*).

A mere omission to act on the part of the true owner will not preclude him from denying the seller's authority to sell unless on the facts the owner owes a duty of care to the purchaser and is in breach of that duty (*a*).

But if the true owner becomes aware, even after a contract has been entered into, that some other person has contracted to sell his property, he owes a duty of care to the purchaser to disclose to him the fact that that other person was not entitled so to act. If he does not disclose the true position to the purchaser, then he may be held to have represented to the purchaser by his conduct that the other person was entitled to act as he did, and if as a result the purchaser acts in a manner which would be to his disadvantage if the true owner were thereafter to assert his rights, then the true owner will be estopped from so asserting his rights (*b*).

Where a person signs a document and parts with it so that it may come into other hands, he has a responsibility, that of the normal man of prudence, to take care what he signs, which if neglected precludes him

---

(*r*) *Eastern Distributors, Ltd.* v. *Goldring*, [1957] 2 All E. R. 525; [1957] 2 Q. B. 600, C. A.; *Stoneleigh Finance, Ltd.* v. *Phillips*, [1965] 1 All E. R. 513; [1965] 2 Q. B. 537, C. A. (*ante*, illustration (3)); *Lloyds and Scottish Finance, Ltd.* v. *Williamson*, [1965] 1 All E. R. 641; [1965] 1 W. L. R. 404, C. A.; *cf. Mercantile Credit Co., Ltd.* v. *Hamblin*, [1964] 3 All E. R. 592; [1965] 2 Q. B. 242, C. A. If A gives B his car together with his registration book he does not thereby hold out B as having authority to sell the car: *Central Newbury Car Auctions* v. *Unity Finance*, [1956] 3 All E. R. 905; [1957] 1 Q. B. 371, C. A.; *J. Sargent (Garages), Ltd.* v. *Motor Auctions (West Bromwich), Ltd.*, [1977] R. T. R. 121, C. A.

(*s*) As in *Canadian Laboratory Supplies* v. *Engelhard Industries* (1979), 97 D. L. R. (3d) 1 (Sup. Ct. of Can.), noted, p. 160, *n.* (*a*), *ante*.

(*t*) *Lloyds and Scottish Finance, Ltd.* v. *Williamson*, [1965] 1 All E. R. 641; [1965] 1 W. L. R. 404, C. A.

(*u*) *Motor Credit (Hire Finance), Ltd.* v. *Pacific Motors Pty., Ltd.* (1963), 109 C. L. R. 87 (*ante*, illustration (4)); reversed on another ground, *sub nom. Pacific Motor Auctions Proprietary, Ltd.* v. *Motor Credits (Hire Finance), Ltd.*, [1965] 2 All E. R. 105; [1965] A. C. 867, P. C.; *Davey* v. *Paine Brothers (Motors), Ltd.*, [1954] N. Z. L. R. 1122. *Raffoul* v. *Essanda, Ltd.* (1970), s. 72 S. R. (N. S. W.) 633.

(*a*) *Moorgate Mercantile Co., Ltd.* v. *Twitchings*, [1976] 2 All E. R. 641; [1977] A. C. 890, H. L.

(*b*) *Spiro* v. *Lintern*, [1973] 3 All E. R. 319; [1973] 1 W. L. R. 1002, C. A.; and see *Commercial Bank of Wales* v. *Illingworth* (1978), unreported (Court of Appeal transcript No. 72 of 1978).

from denying his liability under the document according to its tenor (*c*). Where the owner of goods, by signing a document and giving it to the seller, enables the seller to hold himself out as having authority to sell, he will be precluded from denying the seller's authority to sell unless he can prove that he acted carefully (*d*).

By virtue of this subsection, where the owner is precluded by his conduct from denying the seller's authority to sell, the buyer acquires a good title to the goods and not merely a right to plead an estoppel (*e*).

In *Snook* v. *London and West Riding Investments, Ltd.* (*f*), the defendants were allowed to rely on an estoppel although it was not expressly pleaded, all necessary facts being proved.

Subsection (2).—*Special power.*—One person is sometimes invested by law with a special power to dispose of another person's property. For instance, a pawnbroker may sell unredeemed pledges; and a landlord who has duly distrained for rent may sell the goods so distrained. See the authorities collected in the footnote to sub-s. (2) (b), *ante*.

Agent of necessity.—It has always been held that the master of a ship may, in case of necessity, dispose of the ship and cargo and it has now been held that

> "the law as to the power of sale and the duty to take care of the goods which is laid down in the case of a carrier by sea applies to a carrier by land where the necessary conditions giving rise to such a power and duty exist,"

and

> "the conditions necessary . . . are—(1) that a real necessity must exist for the sale, and (2) that it must be practically impossible to get the owner's instructions in time as to what shall be done" (*g*).

The exact limits of the doctrine are uncertain, but the only cases in which agency of necessity has been held to arise are cases in which there has been a previously existing contractual relationship between the parties giving rise to some duty on the one to take care of the other's goods.

Dicta favouring an extension of the doctrine to cases in which no such duty could be implied have been disapproved (*h*).

(*c*) *Saunders* v. *Anglia Building Society*, [1970] 3 All E. R. 961, at pp. 972, 973; [1971] A. C. 1004, at p. 1027, *per* Lord WILBERFORCE.

(*d*) *United Dominions Trust, Ltd.* v. *Western*, [1975] 3 All E. R. 1017; [1976] Q. B. 513, C. A.; *Mercantile Credit* v. *Hamblin*, [1964] 3 All E. R. 592; [1965] 2 Q. B. 242, C. A.; *Commercial Bank of Wales* v. *Illingworth*, *supra*. See also *General & Finance Facilities* v. *Hughes* (1966), 110 Sol. Jo. 847, which must, however, be read in the light of *Saunders* v. *Anglia Building Society*, *supra*.

(*e*) *Eastern Distributors, Ltd.* v. *Goldring*, [1957] 2 All E. R. 525; [1957] 2 Q. B. 600, C. A.; *Mercantile Credit Co., Ltd.* v. *Hamblin*, [1964] 3 All E. R. 592; [1965] 2 Q. B. 242, C. A.

(*f*) [1967] 1 All E. R. 518; [1967] 2 Q. B. 786, C. A.

(*g*) *Sims & Co.* v. *Midland Railway*, [1913] 1 K. B. 103, at p. 112; approved in *Springer* v. *Great Western Rail. Co.*, [1921] 1 K. B. 257. See also *Sachs* v. *Miklos*, [1948] 1 All E. R. 67, C. A.; [1948] 2 K. B. 23; *Munro* v. *Willmott*, [1948] 2 All E. R. 983; [1949] 1 K. B. 295.

(*h*) *Jebara* v. *Ottoman Bank*, [1927] 2 K. B. 254, at pp. 270, 271, commenting on *Prager* v. *Blatspiel*, [1924] 1 K. B. 566, where McCARDIE, J., reviewed the cases and favoured an extension of the doctrine.

Co-owners.—The law relating to co-owners, who are not partners, is rather obscure. Probably a co-owner, in the absence of estoppel or authority from the other co-owners, could only transfer his own share (*i*). If one co-owner sells and retains the whole price, the remedy of the others at law against him is doubtful, unless the sale confers a good title to the whole. If co-owners cannot agree as to the possession or use of the goods owned in common the only remedy in equity was to apply for an injunction or for a receiver and sale (*k*), but now by s. 188 of the Law of Property Act 1925 (*l*) the court has power to order a division on the application of persons interested in a moiety or upwards of such chattels. In a case in 1892, A sold a half-share in a gold snuff-box to B, on the terms that A was to retain possession till resale on joint account, and afterwards handed the box to B to sell it at Christie's. B, instead of selling, deposited the box with H, to whom he owed money. It was held that A could recover the box from H (*m*).

It seems that if two or more persons agree to purchase goods on joint account, notice to the one who effects the purchase of any defect in title of the seller affects the others also (*n*). Further,

> "Any partner, co-adventurer, agent, or any other person in any position of trust must make no profit out of his position without the knowledge of his principals, and in particular cannot sell his own goods to his principals without fully disclosing his own personal interest in the matter" (*o*).

As to co-adventurers in Scotland, see Green's *Encyclopædia of Scots Law*, tit. "Co-adventurers."

22. Market overt.—(1) Where goods are sold in market overt, according to the usage of the market, the buyer acquires a good title to the goods, provided he buys them in good faith and without notice of any defect or want of title on the part of the seller (*p*).

(2) This section does not apply to Scotland (*q*).

(*i*) See *re Tamplin, Ex p. Barnett* (1890), 7 Morr. 70. As to partners, who *prima facie* are agents for each other, see the Partnership Act 1890, ss. 5 and 6; 24 Halsbury's Statutes (3rd Edn.) 505, 506. See also *Mann* v. *D'Arcy*, [1968] 2 All E. R. 172; [1968] 1 W. L. R. 893; *R.* v. *Bonner*, [1970] 2 All E. R. 97; [1970] 1 W. L. R. 838, C. A.

(*k*) *Lindley on Partnership* (9th ed.), pp. 38–41. There are very special conditions as to ships; see *ibid.*, p. 37; *cf. Nicol* v. *Cooper* (1896), 1 Com. Cas. 410 (sale of ship by managing owner, rights of dissenting shareholder).

(*l*) 27 Halsbury's Statutes (3rd Edn.) 605.

(*m*) *Nyberg* v. *Handelaar*, [1892] 2 Q. B. 202, C. A.

(*n*) *Oppenheimer* v. *Frazer*, [1907] 2 K. B. 50, 76, C. A.

(*o*) *Kuhlirz* v. *Lambert Bros., Ltd.* (1913), 108 L. T. 565, at p. 567 (co-adventure in sale of coal to Austrian Government).

(*p*) *The Case of Market Overt* (1596), 5 Co. Rep. 83 b; Tudor's *Merc. Cases* (3rd ed.), p. 274, and notes; distinguished, *Bishopsgate Motor Finance Co.* v. *Transport Brakes, Ltd.*, [1949] 1 All E. R. 37, C. A.; [1949] 1 K. B. 322; and see *Crane* v. *London Dock Co.* (1864) 5 B. & S. 313; *per* BLACKBURN, J., at p. 320, as to the usage of the market; *cf. Vilmont* v. *Bentley* (1886), 18 Q. B. D. 322, at p. 331. See also 31 L. Q. R. 270 as to the City of London.

(*q*) See *Todd* v. *Armsur*, 1882 9 R. (Ct. of Sess.) 901, as to conflict of laws, when it was held that a title acquired as the result of a sale in market overt in England will be

(3) Paragraph 8 of Schedule 1 below applies in relation to a contract under which goods were sold before 1 January 1968 or (in the application of this Act to Northern Ireland) 29 August 1967.

ILLUSTRATIONS

(1) Stolen sheep are brought to an auctioneer to sell, and are sold by him in market overt. The buyer is protected, but the auctioneer is liable for conversion (*r*).

(2) A motor-car is put up for auction in a statutory market by its bailee under a hire-purchase agreement. It remains unsold, but the bailee later sells it by private treaty in the same market, as is customary there. The buyer gets a good title, as the rules of market overt can apply in a market established by statutory powers and the sale need not be by a trader (*s*).

(3) Two stolen antique chandeliers are offered for sale in market overt on 21st October. One is sold at 4.30 p.m. on the same afternoon to a *bona fide* purchaser, having been exposed on the stall for only a few minutes. The other is exposed daily until 21st December when it is sold to another *bona fide* purchaser. The first sale was before sunset. The second sale was after sunset. The first buyer gets a good title; the second buyer does not (*t*).

Derivation.—Section 22 (1) and (3) of the 1893 Act. Section 22 (2) of that Act, which excluded the sale of horses from s. 22, was repealed by Sch. 3 of the Criminal Law Act 1967, together with the Sale of Horses Acts 1555 and 1588 (*u*).

Definitions.—For "buyer," "goods," and "seller", see s. 61 (1), *post*; for "good faith," see s. 61 (3), *post*.

Cross-references.—*Cf.* s. 12, *ante* (seller's warranty of title, etc.); and s. 21, *ante*, and ss. 23 to 25, *post* (transfer of title).

---

recognised in Scotland. For Scottish cases as to horses, see Green's *Encyclopædia of Scots Law*, tit. "Horses."

(*r*) *Delaney* v. *Wallis* (1884), 15 Cox C. C. 525.

(*s*) *Bishopsgate Motor Finance Co.* v. *Transport Brakes, Ltd.*, [1949] 1 All E. R. 37, C. A.; [1949] 1 K. B. 322.

(*t*) See *Reid* v. *Metropolitan Police Commissioner*, [1973] 2 All E. R. 97; [1973] Q. B. 551, C. A. The Court of Appeal appears to have arrived at this decision because it felt that despite the finding of the County Court Judge, the buyer had not been *bona fide*. The Court applied an ambiguous statement in *Co. Inst.*, Vol. II, pp. 713–714. In so doing it appears to have disregarded the wording of this section, and the principles of construing a codifying statute, set out at page 75, *ante*. The decision also runs contrary to the recommendations of the Law Reform Committee in its Report on the Transfer of Title to Chattels (Cmnd. 2958), that the law of market overt should be extended to all shops. It would also seem to lead to further anomalies in applying the law of market overt to many important markets which operates wholly or partly during the night. Such markets are, of course, generally well lit by electric lighting.

The other exceptions set out in *Co. Inst.* need not be referred to here, as they are embodied either in the text of this section or in the decisions based upon it, or are clearly no longer law.

(*u*) The repeals implemented one of the recommendations of the Law Reform Committee in its Report on the Transfer of Title to Chattels (Cmd. 2958). See also [1956] Current Legal Problems 113.

COMMENT

Subsection (1).—The rules of market overt do not apply in Scotland or Wales (*a*), or the United States, and in England they only apply to a limited class of retail transactions.

All shops in the city of London are market overt, for the purposes of their own trade, provided that the goods are sold in the ordinary hours of business on business days between sunrise and sunset (*b*), and the whole transaction takes place in the open part of the shop. Thus a wharf in the city is not market overt (*c*), and a sale by sample is not within the custom, because the whole transaction must take place in the open market, and not merely the formation of the contract (*d*). So, too, a sale of jewellery to a tradesman in his showroom is not within the custom (*e*). Nor is the sale of a stolen watch in a first floor auction room where unredeemed pledges are sold periodically (*f*).

Outside the city of London, markets with the custom of market overt may exist by grant or prescription, and it seemed at one time that the custom did not apply to a market established by a local Act (*g*). However, the Court of Appeal have now held that a sale between private persons in a statutory market can be a sale in market overt if made in accordance with the usage of the market (*h*).

23. Sale under voidable title.—When the seller of goods has a voidable title to them, but his title has not been avoided (*i*) at the time of the sale, the buyer acquires a good title to the goods, provided he buys them in good faith and without notice of the seller's defect of title (*k*).

(*a*) See The Laws in Wales Act 1542, s. 47; 6 Halsbury's Statutes (3rd Edn.) 460.

(*b*) *Reid* v. *Metropolitan Police Commissioner*, [1973] 2 All E. R. 97; [1973] Q. B. 551, C. A.; see illustration (3), *ante*.

(*c*) *Wilkinson* v. *King* (1809), 2 Camp. 335.

(*d*) *Crane* v. *London Dock Co.* (1864), B. & S. 313.

(*e*) *Hargreave* v. *Spink*, [1892] 1 Q. B. 25; *cf. Ardath Tobacco Co.* v. *Ocker* (1931), 47 T. L. R. 177.

(*f*) *Clayton* v. *Le Roy*, [1911] 2 K. B. 1031; reversed on another ground [1911] 2 K. B. 1046, C. A.

(*g*) *Moyce* v. *Newington* (1878), 4 Q. B. D. 32, at p. 34, *per* COCKBURN, C. J.; and see *Lee* v. *Bayes* (1856), 18 C. B. 599 (sale by auction at horse repository).

(*h*) *Bishopsgate Motor Finance Co.* v. *Transport Brakes, Ltd.* (*supra*), *where Moyce* v. *Newington (supra)* was not followed.

(*i*) For avoidance, see *Clough* v. *London and Northwestern Rail. Co.* (1871), L. R. 7 Ex. 26; see also illustration (6) to this section and the footnote thereto.

(*k*) *Cundy* v. *Lindsay* (1878), 3 App. Cas. 459, at p. 464, *per* Lord CAIRNS; *cf. Robin and Rambler Coaches* v. *Turner*, [1947] 2 All E. R. 284; *Car and Universal Finance Co., Ltd.* v. *Caldwell*, [1964] 1 All E. R. 290; [1965] 1 Q. B. 525, C. A. (sale by dealer to finance, company in course of hire-purchase transaction); see also *Stoneleigh Finance, Ltd.* v. *Phillips*, [1965] 1 All E. R. 513; [1965] 2 Q. B. 537, C. A.; *Pollock on Possession*, pp. 203, 204; O. W. Holmes' *The Common Law*, lecture 9 (void and voidable contracts). The onus of proving notice or want of good faith is on the former owner: *Whitehorn Brothers* v. *Davison*, [1911] 1 K. B. 463, C. A.; *secus* as to the proviso to s. 2 (1) of the Factors Act 1889, *post*. The Law Reform Committee in its report on the Transfer of Title to Chattels (Cmd. 2958) recommended that it should be for the purchaser to prove that he bought in good faith.

ILLUSTRATIONS

(1) B has a room at 37 Wood Street. There is a reputable firm in the same street trading as "W. Blenkiron & Co." B orders goods in the name of "Blenkiron & Co." and A, thinking he is dealing with "W. Blenkiron & Co.," supplies them. There is no contract between A and B, and B cannot give any title to a sub-purchaser (*l*).

(2) B induces A to send him jewellery on approval by falsely representing that he has a good customer for it. He then pledges the goods with C. B then induces A to sell him the goods on credit, saying that he cannot ask his customer for cash before delivery. A cannot avoid the sale to B and recover the goods from C unless he can affect C with notice of the fraud (*m*).

(3) X goes to a jeweller and agrees to buy a ring. Pretending to be Sir G. B., he draws a cheque in that name and gives it in payment for the ring, which he is allowed to take away. X then pledges the ring with a pawnbroker, who takes it in good faith. The pawnbroker gets a good title, for there was a *de facto* contract between the jeweller and X (*n*).

(4) A motor-car obtained by fraud is sold to B, who buys it in good faith and without notice. B sells it to C, who had notice of the fraud, but was not a party to it. C gets a good title to the car (*o*).

(5) P advertises a car for sale. X comes to see it and says he likes it. He introduces himself as G, a well-known actor. P and X agree a price of £450. X writes a cheque and says he wants the car at once. P asks for proof of identity. X shows him a pass to Pinewood Studios with a photo of X, the name G, and an address. P then lets X have the car and log book. The cheque is not met but the car is resold to D. There is a voidable contract between P and X. The mistake as to identity was here merely a mistake as to an attribute of the buyer. X was therefore able to give a good title to D (*p*).

(6) A rogue obtains a motor car by fraud, and deliberately absconds. On discovering the fraud the seller immediately does everything possible to discover the rogue, and informs the police and the Automobile Association. Subsequently the rogue sells the car to another rogue who sells it to a *bona fide* purchaser. The first sale has been avoided and the *bona fide* purchaser acquires no title to the car under this section (*q*).

(*l*) *Cundy* v. *Lindsay* (1878), 3 App. Cas. 459.

(*m*) *Whitehorn Brothers* v. *Davison*, [1911] 1 K. B. 463, C. A.; discussed and approved, *Folkes* v. *King*, [1923] 1 K. B. 282, C. A.; distinguished, *Heap* v. *Motorists Advisory Agency, Ltd.*, [1923] 1 K. B. 577 (larceny by trick). As to seller's right to avoid a fraudulent purchase as against the buyer's trustee in bankruptcy, see *Ex p. Ward*, [1905] 1 K. B. 465; *Tilley* v. *Bowman, Ltd.*, [1910] 1 K. B. 745.

(*n*) *Phillips* v. *Brooks*, [1919] 2 K. B. 243; as explained in *Lake* v. *Simmons*, [1927] A. C. 487, at p. 501; and see *Barclays Bank* v. *Okenarhe*, [1966] 2 Lloyd's Rep. 87.

(*o*) *Peirce* v. *London Horse and Carriage Repository*, [1922] W. N. 170, C. A.

(*p*) *Lewis* v. *Averay*, [1971] 3 All E. R. 907; [1972] 1 Q. B. 198, C. A.; distinguishing *Ingram* v. *Little*, [1960] 3 All E. R. 332; [1961] 1 Q. B. 31, C. A., where on very similar facts it was held that there was no contract between the seller and the rogue, and that the seller could recover the car from the person to whom the rogue sold it. See further 1972 J. B. L. 151.

(*q*) *Car and Universal Finance Co., Ltd.* v. *Caldwell*, [1964] 1 All E. R. 290; [1965] 1 Q. B. 525, C. A.; but *cf. Newtons of Wembley* v. *Williams*, [1964] 3 All E. R. 532; [1965] 1 Q. B. 560, C. A., where the rogue conveyed a good title by virtue of the operation of ss. 2 and 9 of the Factors Act 1889, *post*. For a conflicting decision of the Court of Session, see *Macleod* v. *Kerr*, 1965 S. L. T. 358; 29 M. L. R. 442. The Law Reform Committee in its report on the transfer of Title to Chattels (Cmd. 2958) recommended that a seller should not be able to avoid a sale until he has informed the buyer of his decision.

Derivation.—Section 23 of the 1893 Act.

Definitions.—For "buyer," "goods," "sale" and "seller," see s. 61 (1), *post*. For "good faith," see s. 61 (3), *post*.

Cross-references.—*Cf.* s. 12, *ante* (seller's warranty of title, etc.); and ss. 21 and 22, *ante*, and ss. 24 and 25, *post* (transfer of title).

COMMENT

Many cases to which this section applies will also fall within s. 25, *post*, and s. 9 of the Factors Act 1889. But the present section will also operate where the seller is not in possession, where his voidable title is not derived from a sale, or where he is a buyer in possession and the sale is not one made in the ordinary course of the business of a mercantile agent.

The section in terms deals with a seller, but a precisely similar rule applies to a pledgor (*r*), and to the creator of an equitable right by an incomplete pledge (*s*).

> "If the chattel has come into the hands of a person who professed to sell it, by a *de facto* contract, that is to say, a contract which has purported to pass the property to him from the owner of the property, there the purchaser will obtain a good title, even although afterwards it should appear that there were circumstances connected with that contract which would enable the original owner of the goods to reduce it and to set it aside" (*t*).

Such circumstances may include fraud, duress or undue influence; but where in fact no property has passed to the seller under the first transaction, the section has no application (*u*). Thus if the original seller believed that his purchaser was (*a*), or was acting on behalf of (*b*), some other person, then if the identity of the other contracting party was in all the circumstances so important that the proper inference was that there was no intention to contract with anybody else (*c*), then the purchaser will get no title. But if, as will normally be the case where the parties meet, the mistake as to identity was in all the circumstances merely a mistake as to an attribute of the purchaser, then the purchaser will get at least a voidable title to the goods (*d*), for where a fraudulent misrepresentation, even as to an attribute of the purchaser (*e*), has

(*r*) *Whitehorn Brothers* v. *Davison*, [1911] 1 K. B. 463, C. A.

(*s*) *Attenborough* v. *St. Katherine's Dock Co.* (1878), 3 C. P. D. 450, C. A.

(*t*) *Cundy* v. *Lindsay* (1878), 3 App. Cas. 459, at p. 464.

(*u*) *Cundy* v. *Lindsay* (1878), 3 App. Cas. 459.

(*a*) *Ingram* v. *Little*, [1960] 3 All E. R. 332; [1961] 1 Q. B. 31, C. A.; *Boulton* v. *Jones* (1857), 2 H. & N. 564 (purchaser mistaken as to identity of seller); *Cundy* v. *Lindsay* (*supra*); *cf. Macleod* v. *Kerr*, 1965 S. L. T. 358 (Ct. of Sess.); 29 M. L. R. 442; *Porter* v. *Latec Finance Proprietary, Ltd.* (1964), 38 A. L. J. R. 184.

(*b*) *Hardman* v. *Booth* (1862), 32 L. J. Ex. 105.

(*c*) *Cf. Lewis* v. *Averay*, [1971] 3 All E. R. 907; [1972] 1 Q. B. 198, C. A.

(*d*) *Lewis* v. *Averay*, *supra*.

(*e*) *King's Norton Metal Co.* v. *Edridge Merrett & Co.* (1897), 14 T. L. R. 98, C. A. But compare *Newborne* v. *Sensolid (Great Britain), Ltd.*, [1953] 1 All E. R. 708; [1954] 1 Q. B. 45, C. A.; followed: *Black* v. *Smallwood* (1966), 117 C. L. R. 52 (H. C. of Austr.). See also *Wickberg* v. *Shatsky* (1969), 4 D. L. R. (3d) 540.

induced a contract of sale, or the creation of a power to pass the property (*f*), a third party taking before avoidance of the transaction will get a good title.

If the original seller only intended to pass possession without intending to create any power to pass a title (*g*), or intended to deal with some other property (*h*), no title will pass.

It follows that, broadly speaking, where goods are obtained by conduct which would before the Theft Act 1968 came into force have amounted to larceny by a trick (*i*) no property passes, but where the obtaining is by false pretences a voidable title is created (*k*). This distinction was formerly of importance in connection with the Factors Acts and s. 25, *post*. If a mercantile agent gets possession of goods, intending at the time to misappropriate them, he has clearly committed larceny by a trick, for the common law judges held that in such circumstances the owner's apparent consent to the agent's possession was negatived (*l*). It was then much doubted (*m*) whether, that being so, the owner could be held to have consented to possession by the agent for the purposes of the Factors Acts. However, the better view is that Parliament did not have "any intention of applying the artificial distinctions of the criminal law to a commercial transaction," and that the consent necessary for the operation of the Factors Acts is only consent in fact (*n*).

If the transaction which passes the voidable title is subsequent in time to the disposition to the innocent third party, this section will still apply, for there is then a feeding of the third party's title (*o*).

24. Seller in possession after sale.—Where a person having sold goods continues or is in possession of the goods, or of the documents of title to the goods, the delivery or transfer by that person, or by a mercantile agent acting

---

(*f*) *Whitehorn Brothers* v. *Davison* (*supra*).

(*g*) *Whitehorn Brothers* v. *Davison* (*supra*); *Folkes* v. *King*, [1923] 1 K. B. 282, C. A.

(*h*) *Morrisson* v. *Robertson*, 1908 S. C. 332.

(*i*) See Pollock and Wright, *Possession in the Common Law*, pp. 218–219; *Russell on Crime* (12th ed.) pp. 941 *et seq.*; *Ingram* v. *Little*, (*supra*) at pp. 349 and 69 respectively.

(*k*) In *Whitehorn Brothers* v. *Davison* (*supra*) and *Folkes* v. *King* (*supra*), the Court decided in each case that there was no larceny by a trick and accordingly a voidable contract.

(*l*) *Oppenheimer* v. *Frazer & Wyatt*, [1907] 2 K. B. 50, at pp. 71–72, C. A.

(*m*) *Cahn* v. *Pockett's Bristol Steam Packet Co.*, [1899] 1 Q. B. 643 at p. 659, C. A.; *Oppenheimer* v. *Frazer*, [1907] 2 K. B. 50, C. A.; *per* ATKIN L. J., in *Lake* v. *Simmons*, [1926] 2 K. B. 51 at pp. 70–71, C. A.

(*n*) *Folkes* v. *King* (*supra*); *Pearson* v. *Rose and Young*, [1950] 2 All E. R. 1027; [1951] 1 K. B. 275, C. A.; *Du Jardin* v. *Beadman*, [1952] 2 All E. R. 160; [1952] 2 Q. B. 712; and *per* DEVLIN, L. J., in *Ingram* v. *Little* (*supra*) at pp. 349 and 70 respectively. This view has been followed in New Zealand: *Davey* v. *Paine Brothers* (*Motors*), *Ltd.*, [1954] N. Z. L. R. 1122. See also [1957] Crim. L. R. pp. 28 and 96; the question was left open by Lord SUMNER in *Lake* v. *Simmons*, [1927] A. C. 487 at pp. 510, 511.

(*o*) *Whitehorn Brothers* v. *Davison*, (*supra*); on the question of feeding title, see also *Butterworth* v. *Kingsway Motors*, [1954] 2 All E. R. 694.

for him, of the goods or documents of title under any sale, pledge, or other disposition thereof, to any person receiving the same in good faith and without notice of the previous sale, has the same effect as if the person making the delivery or transfer were expressly authorised by the owner of the goods to make the same.

25. Buyer in possession after sale.—(1) Where a person having bought or agreed to buy goods obtains, with the consent of the seller, possession of the goods or the documents of title to the goods, the delivery or transfer by that person, or by a mercantile agent acting for him, of the goods or documents of title (*p*), under any sale, pledge, or other disposition thereof, to any person receiving the same in good faith and without notice of any lien or other right of the original seller in respect of the goods, has the same effect as if the person making the delivery or transfer were a mercantile agent in possession of the goods or documents of title with the consent of the owner.

(2) For the purposes of subsection (1) above—

(a) the buyer under a conditional sale agreement is to be taken not to be a person who has bought or agreed to buy goods, and

(b) "conditional sale agreement" means an agreement for the sale of goods which is a consumer credit agreement within the meaning of the Consumer Credit Act 1974 under which the purchase price or part of it is payable by instalments, and the property in the goods is to remain in the seller (notwithstanding that the buyer is to be in possession of the goods) until such conditions as to the payment of instalments or otherwise as may be specified in the agreement are fulfilled.

(3) Paragraph 9 of Schedule 1 below applies in relation to a contract under which a person buys or agrees to buy goods and which is made before the appointed day.

(*p*) It seems that these need not be the same documents of title as those of which the buyer has obtained possession with the consent of the seller: see *per* SALMON, J. in *Mount* v. *Jay & Jay*, [1959] 3 All E. R. 307, at p. 311; [1960] 1 Q. B. 159 at pp. 168–169.

(4) In subsection (3) above and paragraph 9 of Schedule 1 below references to the appointed day are to the day appointed for the purposes of those provisions by an order of the Secretary of State made by statutory instrument (*q*).

ILLUSTRATIONS

Section 24.—(1) A owns furs stored in a warehouse, where he owes for the storage charges. He sells the furs to the plaintiffs, promising to use the proceeds to pay the charges and then deliver the furs. Instead, he pledges the furs to the defendants, and with the proceeds of that transaction pays the storage charges and has the furs delivered to the defendants. The plaintiffs cannot recover the furs from the defendants without paying off their advance (*r*).

Section 25.—(2) A sells certain copper to B, forwarding bill of lading indorsed in blank and bill of exchange for acceptance. B, who is insolvent, does not accept the bill of exchange, but transfers the bill of lading to X in fulfilment of a contract to supply him with copper. X in good faith pays the price. A cannot stop the copper in transit (*s*).

(3) A delivers a motor cab to B under a hire-purchase agreement. The hire amounts to £374 payable by 24 monthly instalments, and B may purchase the cab at any time within the two years by paying a further sum of £100. B pledges the cab with C, being at that time £58 in arrears with his instalments. A can sue C for the conversion of the cab, for B is not a person who has "agreed to buy" the cab; he has merely an option to purchase (*t*).

(4) B agrees to buy a plot of land from A, and also a motor-car if his solicitor approves the title to the land. B gets the motor-car, does not pay for it, but sells it to a *bona fide* purchaser. Subsequently B's solicitor disapproves the conditions of sale of the land. The purchaser of the motor-car gets a good title thereto, for B "agreed to buy" it (*u*).

Derivation.—Section 24 is taken from s. 25 (1) of the 1893 Act. Section 25 is taken from s. 25 (2) of the 1893 Act as amended by Sch. 4 to the Consumer Credit Act 1974 from a date which was to have been appointed under s. 192 (4) of that Act.

Definitions.—For "delivery," "documents of title," "Factors

(*q*) Section 25 (2) comes into force only on the appointed day. As yet no date has been appointed, but a similar deeming provision in s. 54 of the Hire-Purchase Act 1965, as amended by Sch. 2, para. 6 to the Sale of Goods Act, *post* (which is to be repealed from a date to be appointed under s. 192 (4) of the Consumer Credit Act 1974) excludes conditional sale agreements from the operation of this section.

(*r*) *City Fur Manufacturing Co.* v. *Fureenbond*, [1937] 1 All E. R. 799. *Cf. Eastern Distributors* v. *Goldring*, [1957] 2 All E. R. 525; [1957] 2 Q. B. 600, C. A.

(*s*) *Cahn* v. *Pockett's Bristol Channel Co.*, [1899] 1 Q. B. 643, C. A.

(*t*) *Belsize Motor Supply Co.* v. *Cox*, [1914] 1 K. B. 244. As C has an interest in the cab, the measure of damages is not the full value, but only the amount which A has lost: *Wickham Holdings, Ltd.* v. *Brooke House Motors, Ltd.*, [1967] 1 All E. R. 117; [1967] 1 W. L. R. 295, C. A., so that payments made by the hirer after the action is brought will be taken into account in assessing damages: *Western Credit Pty., Ltd.* v. *Dragan Motors Pty., Ltd.*, [1973] W. A. R. 184. *Cf. Whiteley* v. *Hilt*, [1918] 2 K. B. 808, C. A., where a hire-purchase agreement, before default, was held to be assignable, so that the assignee succeeded to the rights of the assignor.

(*u*) *Marten* v. *Whale*, [1917] 2 K. B. 480, C. A.

Acts," "goods," "lien," "sale" and "seller," see s. 61 (1), *post*. For "good faith," see s. 61 (3), *post*. For "possession," see s. 1 (2) of the Factors Act 1889, *post*.

Cross-reference.—*Cf*. s. 48 (2), *post* (re-sale by unpaid seller).

COMMENT

These sections reproduce ss. 8 and 9 of the Factors Act 1889, *post*, but omitting in each section after "sale, pledge, or other disposition thereof" the further words, "or under any agreement for sale, pledge, or other disposition thereof." For further notes on these sections, see ss. 8 and 9 of the Factors Act, *post*. These sections may override s. 19, *ante*.

26. Supplementary to sections 24 and 25.—In sections 24 and 25 above "mercantile agent" means a mercantile agent having in the customary course of his business as such agent authority either—

(a) to sell goods, or
(b) to consign goods for the purpose of sale, or
(c) to buy goods, or
(d) to raise money on the security of goods.

Derivation.—This section adopts the same definition of "mercantile agent" as s. 1 (1) of the Factors Act 1889, *post*. This definition was incorporated by reference in s. 25 (3) of the 1893 Act.

Definitions.—For "goods" and "sale" see s. 61 (1), *post*.

COMMENT

See the comment to s. 1 (1) of the Factors Act 1889, *post*.

PART IV

PERFORMANCE OF THE CONTRACT

27. Duties of seller and buyer.—It is the duty of the seller to deliver the goods, and of the buyer to accept and pay for them, in accordance with the terms of the contract of sale (*a*).

Derivation.—Section 27 of the 1893 Act.

Definitions.—For "contract of sale," see s. 2 (1), *ante*, and s. 61 (1), *post*. For "buyer," "delivery," "goods," and "seller," see s. 61 (1), *post*.

(*a*) *Buddle* v. *Green* (1857), 27 L. J. Ex. 33; *Woolfe* v. *Horne* (1877), 2 Q. B. D. 355. See also 222 L. T. 129.

Cross-references.—Cf. ss. 29 to 32, *post* (rules as to delivery), and s. 35, *post* (acceptance).

COMMENT

"In every contract of sale," says WATSON, B.,

"there is involved a contract on the one side to accept, and on the other to deliver."

"If," says MARTIN, B., in the same case,

"one buys goods of another in the possession of a third party, the vendor undertakes that they shall be delivered in a reasonable time. . . . If I buy a horse of you in another man's field, it is part of the contract that if I go for the horse I shall have it" (*b*).

The general obligation to deliver may, however, be modified by the terms of the contract. As BLACKBURN, J. says, there is no rule of law to prevent the parties from making whatever bargain they please (*c*). Thus, when the seller gives the buyer a delivery order for the goods, it may be a condition that the order should be given up to the warehouseman before the buyer can get the goods (*d*). Again, a man with his eyes open may buy the chance of obtaining goods and not the goods themselves; see ss. 5 (2) and 12, *ante*.

As sale is a consensual contract, the parties may by agreement make the price payable how, when, and where they please (*e*); and when the time of payment arrives, the parties may agree that the debt shall be discharged by any means which amount to an accord and satisfaction. In one case the contract provided for payment of the price by instalments, the buyer to have possession, but the property not to pass until payment of the last instalment. The buyer made default in payment and the seller retook possession and sued for the instalments which ought to have been paid. It was held that the remedy was not for the price but for damages (*f*). See further, note to s. 49, *post* (action for price).

28. Payment and delivery are concurrent conditions.—Unless otherwise agreed (*g*), delivery of the

(*b*) *Buddle* v. *Green* (*supra*), at p. 34; *cf. Wood* v. *Baxter* (1883), 49 L. T. 45.

(*c*) *Calcutta Co.* v. *De Mattos* (1863), 32 L. J. Q. B. 322, at p. 328. See the passage cited at length, *post*, Note C, Appendix II; and see *per* BRETT, L. J., in *Honck* v. *Muller* (1881), 7 Q. B. D. 92, at p. 103, C. A.

(*d*) *Barlett* v. *Holmes* (1853), 13 C. B. 630; see, too, *Salter* v. *Woollams* (1841), 2 M. & Gr. 650, as explained in *Benjamin on Sale* (8th ed.), pp. 698, 699.

(*e*) But see the provisions as to credit-sale and conditional sale agreements in the Hire-Purchase Act 1965; 30 Halsbury's Statutes (3rd Edn.) 61, and in the Consumer Credit Act 1974, which repeals and replaces the Hire-Purchase Act 1965 from a date to be appointed under s. 192 (4) of and Schs. 3 and 5 to the 1974 Act.

(*f*) *Att.-Gen.* v. *Pritchard* (1928), 97 L. J. K. B. 561.

(*g*) As, for instance, in a c.i.f. contract: see *E. Clemens Horst Co.* v. *Biddell Brothers*, [1912] A. C. 18, 22; *Orient Co.* v. *Brekke*, [1913] 1 K. B. 531. See further as to c.i.f. contracts, p. 33, *ante*.

goods and payment of the price are concurrent conditions, that is to say, the seller must be ready and willing to give possession of the goods to the buyer in exchange for the price and the buyer must be ready and willing to pay the price in exchange for possession of the goods (*h*).

ILLUSTRATION

Sale of hops under c.i.f. contract to be shipped to Hull, "terms net cash." The seller tenders the shipping documents to the buyer while the goods are at sea. This operates as tender of the goods, and the buyer must pay the price without waiting for the actual arrival and examination of the goods (*i*).

Derivation.—Section 28 of the 1893 Act.

Definitions.—For "buyer," "delivery," "goods" and "seller," see s. 61 (1), *post*.

Cross-references.—*Cf*. ss. 2 (1) and 8, *ante* (price); s. 55, *post* ("unless otherwise agreed"). For a general note on conditions and warranties, see, *ante* p. 8. For their history, see Note A, *post*, Appendix II. For their effect, see s. 11, *ante*. *Cf*. also ss. 29–32, *post* (rules as to delivery), ss. 49 and 50, *post* (remedies of seller), and ss. 51 to 53, *post* (remedies of buyer).

COMMENT

"Where goods are sold," says BAYLEY, J.,

> "and nothing is said as to the time of delivery or the time of payment . . . the seller is liable to deliver them whenever they are demanded upon payment of the price; but the buyer has no right to have possession of the goods till he pays the price. . . . If goods are sold upon credit, and nothing is agreed upon as to the time of delivering the goods, the vendee is immediately entitled to the possession, and the right of possession and the right of property vest at once in him; but his right of possession is not absolute, it is liable to be defeated if he becomes insolvent before he obtains possession" (*k*).

The language of BAYLEY, J., might be taken to imply that in cash sales payment was a condition precedent to delivery, but a reference to the cases cited in the second footnote to the section shows that payment and delivery have always been considered concurrent conditions. It is not now necessary, as it was when the above cases were decided, for the plaintiff to allege that he had performed, or was ready and willing to perform, his part of the contract (*l*).

(*h*) *Morton* v. *Lamb* (1797), 7 Term Rep. 125; *Rawson* v. *Johnson* (1801), 1 East, 203; *Wilks* v. *Atkinson* (1815), 1 Marshall, 412; *Pickford* v. *Grand Junction Railway* (1841), 8 M. & W. 372, at p. 378; *cf. Bussey* v. *Barnett* (1842), 9 M. & W. 312; *Bankart* v. *Bowers* (1866), L. R. 1 C. P. 484; *Paynter* v. *James* (1867), L. R. 2 C. P. 348.

(*i*) *E. Clemens Horst Co.* v. *Biddell Brothers*, [1912] A. C. 18; approving the judgment of KENNEDY, L. J., [1911] 1 K. B. 934, C. A.

(*k*) *Bloxam* v. *Sanders* (1825), 4 B. & C. 941, at p. 948; *cf. Chinery* v. *Viall* (1860), 5 H. & N. 288, at p. 293, as to credit sales.

(*l*) It has been held in Canada that since nothing is "otherwise agreed" payment and

Where a man went into a restaurant and ordered dinner, and, after dining, said he could not pay for it, having only a halfpenny upon him, it was held that he could be convicted of obtaining credit by fraud but not of obtaining goods by false pretences (*m*). It seems therefore that under such circumstances there is an implied agreement for credit until the dinner is finished.

Evidence.—In an action for non-delivery, it seems that the buyer need not give evidence that he was ready and willing to pay, till the seller shows he was ready to deliver (*n*). By the same token, in an action for non-acceptance, the seller need not prove any tender of delivery. It is enough to show that he was ready and willing to deliver (*o*).

Where shares were sold, under a written contract, to be paid for at a future day, it was held that evidence might be received of a trade usage not to deliver till payment (*p*). On the other hand, where there was a contract in writing for the sale of hops at so much per cwt., evidence of a course of dealing between the parties to allow six months' credit was rejected (*q*). It is easier to draw imaginary distinctions between these cases than to harmonise the principles on which they rest.

29. Rules about delivery.—(1) Whether it is for the buyer to take possession of the goods or for the seller to send them to the buyer is a question depending in each case on

---

delivery are convenient conditions under the Ontario equivalent to this section not only where the parties are silent as to the time of payment but also where they fail to agree, so that there is a binding contract if all other terms are agreed: *Kay Corporation* v. *Dekeyser* (1977), 15 O. R. (2d) 697 (Ont. C. A.). This decision seems plainly wrong, however, at least where the goods have not been tendered and accepted (in the Canadian case they had been shipped but not delivered) since this section and its Canadian equivalent contemplate that there is an agreement between the parties and do not seek to impose one when there has never been an offer by one party which the other has accepted and where the terms imposed have been expressly rejected by the prospective buyer.

(*m*) *R.* v. *Jones*, [1898] 1 Q. B. 119.

(*n*) *Wilks* v. *Atkinson* (1815), 1 Marsh., 412. "The averment of the plaintiff's readiness and willingness to perform his part of the contract will be proved by showing that he called on the defendant to accomplish his part": notes to *Cutter* v. *Powell* (1795), 2 Smith's L. C. (13th ed.), p. 1, at p. 15. See also notes to *Pordage* v. *Cole* (1669), 1 Williams' *Notes to Saunders' Reports*, 319. But *cf. Longbottom & Co.* v. *Bass Walker & Co.*, [1922] W. N. 245, C. A. where the sellers were entitled to withhold delivery until they were paid for goods already delivered, and it was held to be immaterial that they were not ready to deliver at the contract date unless this showed that they would have been unable to perform the contract when the obligation to deliver arose.

(*o*) *Jackson* v. *Allaway* (1844), 6 M. & Gr. 942; *Baker* v. *Firminger* (1859), 28 L. J. Ex. 130; *Levey* v. *Goldberg*, [1922] 1 K. B. 688, at p. 692, *per* McCardie, J. "Whichever party," says Lord Halsbury, "was the actor, and is complaining of a breach of contract, is bound to show as a matter of law that he has performed all that was incident to his part of the concurrent obligations," *Forrestt* v. *Aramayo* (1900), 9 Asp. M. L. C. 134, C. A.

(*p*) *Field* v. *Lelean* (1861), 6 H. & N. 617, Ex. Ch.; overruling as to usage, *Spartali* v. *Benecke* (1850), 10 C. B. 212.

(*q*) *Ford* v. *Yates* (1841), 2 M. & Gr. 549; as explained, *Lockett* v. *Nicklin* (1848), 2 Exch. 93.

the contract, express or implied, between the parties (*r*).

(2) Apart from any such contract, express or implied, the place of delivery is the seller's place of business if he has one, and if not, his residence; except that, if the contract is for the sale of specific goods, which to the knowledge of the parties when the contract is made are in some other place, then that place is the place of delivery.

(3) Where under the contract of sale the seller is bound to send the goods to the buyer, but no time for sending them is fixed, the seller is bound to send them within a reasonable time (*s*).

(4) Where the goods at the time of sale are in the possession of a third person, there is no delivery by seller to buyer unless and until the third person acknowledges to the buyer that he holds the goods on his behalf (*t*); but nothing in this section affects the operation of the issue or transfer of any document of title to goods (*u*).

(5) Demand or tender of delivery may be treated as ineffectual unless made at a reasonable hour; and what is a reasonable hour is a question of fact.

(6) Unless otherwise agreed, the expenses of and incidental to putting the goods into a deliverable state must be borne by the seller.

ILLUSTRATIONS

(1) Sale of cotton seed to be shipped from Bombay in August or September. The goods are shipped in August, but the ship is stranded and cannot be got off for three months, and then has to be repaired. Unless the commercial object of the contract has been wholly defeated, the buyer cannot reject the goods on the ground that they have not been delivered within a reasonable time, but he may have claim in damages for the delay (*a*).

(2) Sale of a cask of wine to be delivered at buyer's house. The carrier delivers the wine there to an apparently respectable person, who signs for it, and then makes off with it. This is a good delivery to the buyer (*b*).

(*r*) As to f.o.b. contracts, see p. 31, *ante*.

(*s*) *Ellis* v. *Thompson* (1838), 3 M. & W. 445; see at p. 456 *per* ALDERSON, B.

(*t*) *Farina* v. *Home* (1846), 16 M. & W. 119, at p. 123; *Godts* v. *Rose* (1855), 17 C. B. 229; *Buddle* v. *Green* (1857), 27 L. J. Ex. 33; Pollock and Wright, *Possession in the Common Law*, p. 73.

(*u*) See the Bills of Lading Act 1885, *post*, Appendix I, and the Factors Act 1889, *post*; *cf. Hayman* v. *M'Lintock*, 1907 S. C. 936.

(*a*) *Re Carver & Co.* (1911), 17 Com. Cas. 59, at pp. 67, 70.

(*b*) *Galbraith and Grant* v. *Block*, [1922] 2 K. B. 155. *Cf. Thomas* v. *Alper*, [1953] C. L. Y. 3277.

Derivation.—Section 29 (1) and (2) are derived from s. 29 (1) of the 1893 Act. Subsections (3)–(6) are derived from s. 29 (2)–(5) of the 1893 Act.

Definitions.—For "contract of sale," see s. 2 (1), *ante*, and s. 61 (1), *post*. For "business," "buyer," "delivery," "document of title," "goods," "seller" and "specific goods," see s. 61 (1), *post*. For "deliverable state," see s. 61 (5), *post*.

Cross-references.—*Cf.* s. 10, *ante* (stipulations as to time); ss. 24 and 25, *ante*, and 47, *post* (effect of documents of title); s. 32, *post*, (delivery to carrier); s. 55, *post* ("express or implied"); and s. 59, *post* (reasonable time a question of fact).

COMMENT

The delivery of the key of the place where the goods are may, by agreement, operate as a delivery of the goods (*c*). But where the goods are kept in a room or container on the seller's premises, then in the absence of any express agreement the seller is not to be taken to have delivered the goods by handing over the key to the room or container (*d*) unless the buyer is also licensed to enter on the seller's premises to take possession of them (*e*).

Subsections (1) and (2).—*Place of delivery.*—Subsection (1) of the 1893 Bill was much considered and several times altered in Committee. The first part (now s. 29 (1) of the 1979 Act) deals incidentally with the mode of delivery, and the second part (now s. 29 (2) of the 1979 Act) with the place of delivery. As regards mode of delivery there was very little authority, but the assumed rule was that it was for the buyer to take delivery and that, in the absence of any different agreement, the duty of the seller to deliver was satisfied by his affording to the buyer reasonable facilities for taking possession of the goods at the agreed place of delivery (*f*). It seems a pity that a more definite *prima facie* rule was not laid down by the 1893 Act.

As regards place of delivery, there was no authority in point, and text-book writers seem to have thought that the place of delivery was where the goods were to be found. The 1893 Act adopted a rule which is more in accordance with ordinary practice.

Subsection (3).—*Delivery "as required"*.—In a contract for goods to be delivered "as required," the buyer must require delivery within a

(*c*) *Ellis* v. *Hunt* (1789), 3 Term Rep. 464; *Chaplin* v. *Rogers* (1800), 1 East, 192, at p. 195; *Elmore* v. *Stone* (1809), 1 Taunt, 458; *Ancona* v. *Rogers* (1876), 1 Ex. D. 285, at p. 290, C. A.; and see the question of so-called symbolic delivery discussed in Pollock and Wright, *Possession in the Common Law*, pp. 61–70; *cf.* note, p. 263, *post*.

(*d*) *Milgate* v. *Kebble* (1841), 3 M. & Gr. 100; *Wrightson* v. *McArthur and Hutchinson*, [1921] 1 K. B. 807, at p. 816.

(*e*) *Wrightson* v. *McArthur and Hutchinson, supra.*

(*f*) *Cf. Wood* v. *Tassell* (1844), 6 Q. B. 234; *Smith* v. *Chance* (1819), 2 B. & Ald. 753, at p. 755; *Salter* v. *Woollams* (1841), 2 M. & Gr. 650, as explained in *Benjamin on Sale* (8th ed.), pp. 698, 699.

reasonable time, but the seller cannot rescind the contract on the ground of delay without giving the buyer notice. "No doubt," says POLLOCK, C. B.,

> "where a contract is silent as to time, the law implies that it is to be performed within a reasonable time; but there is another maxim of law, viz., that *every reasonable condition is also implied*, and it seems to me reasonable that the party who seeks to put an end to a contract, because the other party has not, within a reasonable time, required him to deliver the goods, should in the first instance inquire of the latter whether he means to have them" (*g*).

A seller who is told to deliver goods at the purchaser's premises discharges his obligations if he delivers them without negligence to a person apparently having authority to receive them (*h*).

Subsection (4).—*Goods in possession of third party.*—As regards documents of title, the common law drew a hard-and-fast distinction between bills of lading and other documents. The lawful transfer of a bill of lading was always held to operate as a delivery of the goods themselves because, while goods were at sea, they could not be otherwise dealt with (*i*). But the transfer of a delivery order or dock warrant operated only as a token of authority to take possession, and not as a transfer of possession (*k*); and, as between immediate parties, there is nothing to modify the common law rule. If, however, a buyer or mercantile agent, who is lawfully in possession of any document of title to goods, transfers it for value to a third person, the original seller's rights of lien and stoppage in transit are thereby defeated.

Subsection (5).—*Hours for delivery.*—Subsection (4) in the 1893 Act, which this subsection re-enacts, altered the law in so far as it makes the question of what is a reasonable hour a question of fact. It was formerly a question of law, and some highly technical rules for determining it were laid down by PARKE, B. (*l*).

Subsection (6).—*Expenses of delivery.*—This is declaratory. "There is no implied contract," says Story,

> "that the vendee shall pay the vendor for any services in relation to the property rendered previous to the completion of the sale by delivery" (*m*).

30. Delivery of wrong quantity.—(1) Where the seller delivers to the buyer a quantity of goods less than he contracted to sell, the buyer may reject them, but if the

---

(*g*) *Jones* v. *Gibbons* (1853), 8 Exch. 920, at p. 922. But this rule is not absolute—the facts may show a mutual intention to abandon the contract: *Pearl Mill Co.* v. *Ivy Tannery Co.*, [1919] 1 K. B. 78.

(*h*) *Galbraith* v. *Grant and Block*, [1922] 2 K. B. 155, *ante*, illustration (2).

(*i*) *Sanders* v. *Maclean* (1883), 11 Q. B. D. 327, at p. 341, *per* BOWEN, L. J. and *Biddell Brothers* v. *E. Clemens Horst Co.*, [1911] 1 K. B. 934, at p. 956, *per* KENNEDY, L. J.

(*k*) *Blackburn on Sale* (1st ed.), p. 302; *M'Ewan* v. *Smith* (1849), 2 H. L. Cas. 309.

(*l*) *Startup* v. *Macdonald* (1843), 6 M. & Gr. 593, Ex. Ch.

(*m*) *Story on Sale*, §297*a*.

buyer accepts the goods so delivered he must pay for them at the contract rate (*n*).

(2) Where the seller delivers to the buyer a quantity of goods larger than he contracted to sell, the buyer may accept the goods included in the contract and reject the rest, or he may reject the whole.

(3) Where the seller delivers to the buyer a quantity of goods larger than he contracted to sell and the buyer accepts the whole of the goods so delivered he must pay for them at the contract rate (*o*).

(4) Where the seller delivers to the buyer the goods he contracted to sell mixed with (*p*) goods of a different description not included in the contract, the buyer may accept the goods which are in accordance with the contract and reject the rest, or he may reject the whole (*q*).

(5) This section is subject to any usage of trade, special agreement, or course of dealing between the parties (*r*).

ILLUSTRATIONS

Subsection (1).—(1) Contract for sale of two lots of cotton seed (200 and 500 tons) at different prices. Part of each lot is delivered, the whole of the contract price is paid, and the ship then goes on to another port. She returns two weeks later and tenders the rest. The buyer may keep what he has got, reject the rest, and recover back the price pre-paid for the rejected portion (*s*).

Subsection (2).—(2) Sale of a cargo of wheat, which, with a limit of variation allowed by the contract, may amount to 4950 tons. The actual amount tendered is 4950 tons and 55 lbs., but the seller does not insist on payment for the extra 55 lbs. This is a good tender, and the buyer cannot reject it (*t*).

(*n*) *Shipton* v. *Casson* (1826), 5 B. & C. 378, at p. 382; *Oxendale* v. *Wetherell* (1829), 4 Man. & Ry. 429; approved, *Colonial Ins. Co.* v. *Adelaide Ins. C.* (1886), 12 App. Cas. 128, at pp. 138, 140; *Morgan* v. *Gath* (1865), 3 H. & C. 487; *Harland & Wolf* v. *Burstall* (1901), 84 L. T. 324 (470 loads of timber out of 500); *Behrend & Co.* v. *Produce Brothers Co.*, [1920] 3 K. B. 530.

(*o*) *Hart* v. *Mills* (1846), 15 M. & W. 85; *Cunliffe* v. *Harrison* (1851), 6 Exch. 903; *Tamvaco* v. *Lucas* (1859), 1 E. & E. 581; *cf. Dixon* v. *Fletcher* (1837), 3 M. & W. 146.

(*p*) Mixed with="accompanied by" and does not connote physical confusion: *Moore & Co.* v. *Landauer & Co.*, [1921] 1 K. B. 73, at p. 76; affirmed, [1921] 2 K. B. 519, C. A.; *Ebrahim Dawood, Ltd.* v. *Heath*, [1961] 2 Lloyd's Rep. 512; but see the different view expressed *obiter* by SALTER, J., in *Barker & Co., Ltd.* v. *Agius, Ltd.* (1927), 33 Com. Cas. 120 at pp. 131–132.

(*q*) *Levy* v. *Green* (1859), 8 E. & B. 575, Ex. Ch.; *Nicholson* v. *Bradfield Union* (1866), L. R. 1 Q. B. 620, at pp. 624, 625, *per* Lord BLACKBURN.

(*r*) See pp. 13–15, *ante*.

(*s*) *Behrend & Co.* v. *Produce Brokers Co.*, [1920] 3 K. B. 530.

(*t*) *Shipton Anderson & Co.* v. *Weil Brothers*, [1912] 1 K. B. 574, 577: *de minimis non curat*

Subsection (3).—(3) Sale of 1500 tons "briquettes, size 2 inches." Only 25 tons correspond to this description, the remainder being larger. The buyer may accept the 25 tons and reject the remainder (*u*).

Derivation.—Section 30 of the 1893 Act. Subsection (2) in the 1893 Act is divided into sub-ss. (2) and (3) in the 1979 Act and sub-ss. (3) and (4) in the 1893 Act are now sub-ss. (4) and (5).

Definitions.—For "buyer," "delivery," "goods" and "seller," see s. 61 (1), *post.*

Cross-references.—*Cf.* s. 13, *ante* (description); ss. 29, *ante*, and 31 and 32, *post* (rules as to delivery); s. 35, *post* (acceptance and rejection); and s. 55, *post* (usage, etc.).

Comment

As the seller does not fulful his contract by delivering a less quantity than he contracted to sell, so, conversely,

> "if a man contracts to buy 150 quarters of wheat, he is not at liberty to call for the delivery of a small portion without being prepared to receive the entire quantity" (*a*)

unless, of course, he has stipulated for the right to do so.

When the seller delivers a larger quantity of goods than was ordered, such delivery operates as a proposal for a new contract (*b*). This, presumably, is the effect of any tender of goods which are not in conformity with the contract.

When the seller is uncertain as to the exact amount he can deliver, he may protect himself by using such terms as so many tons "more or less," or "about" so many tons, and he is then allowed a reasonable margin (*c*).

Frequently, in commercial contracts, a clause will be found providing that the "buyer shall not reject the goods herein specified, but shall accept or pay for the goods in terms of the contract against shipping documents," or like terms. The precise effect of such a clause may be hard to define, but it is clear that it can only operate where delivery of "the goods herein specified" is in fact made, and that if, for example, delivery of larger or smaller quantities is tendered, the buyer can reject

---

lex. Cf. Payne v. *Lillico & Sons* (1920), 36 T. L. R. 569 (2 per cent. more or less); *Rapalli* v. *K. L. Take, Ltd.*, [1958] 2 Lloyd's Rep. 469, C. A.; *Margaronis Navigation Agency, Ltd.* v. *Henry W. Peabody & Co. of London, Ltd.*, [1964] 3 All E. R. 333; [1965] 2 Q. B. 430, C. A.

(*u*) *Barker* v. *Agius* (1927), 33 Com. Cas. 120.

(*a*) *Kingdom* v. *Cox* (1848), 5 C. B. 522, at p. 526, *per* Wilde, C. J.

(*b*) *Cunliffe* v. *Harrison* (1851), 6 Exch. 903, at p. 906, *per* Parke, B.; *Gabriel Wade & English* v. *Arcos, Ltd.* (1929), 34 Ll. L. Rep. 306 (if buyer accepts the larger quantity he cannot then sue for delivery of wrong quantity).

(*c*) *McConnel* v. *Murphy* (1873), L. R. 5 P. C. 203; *Re Thornett & Fehr & Yuills*, [1921] 1 K. B. 219 (five per cent. more or less). As to importing such a term by usage, see *Moore* v. *Campbell* (1854), 10 Exch. 323.

since the "goods herein specified" have not, in the specified quantities, been tendered (*d*).

Subsection (3) in the 1893 Bill (now sub-s. (4)) was amended in Committee. It has been held in Scotland not to apply to a case where goods are of the kind or description ordered, but a portion of them are of inferior quality (*e*), unless the contract is severable (*f*). Where in a f.o.b. contract, at the end of a clause dealing with over- and under-shipment, it was provided that "each item of this contract to be considered a separate interest," it was held that the buyer might reject the whole if part of the goods delivered did not comply with the contract specification as to quality (*g*).

The buyer's right to recover that part of the purchase price which relates to goods properly rejected is a right to recover money for a consideration which has wholly failed, at least for a rejection under s. 30 (1) and (4) (*h*), and *semble* under s. 30 (2) also.

31. Instalment deliveries.—(1) Unless otherwise agreed, the buyer of goods is not bound to accept delivery of them by instalments (*i*).

(2) Where there is a contract for the sale of goods to be delivered by stated instalments, which are to be separately paid for, and the seller makes defective deliveries in respect of one or more instalments, or the buyer neglects or refuses to take delivery of or pay for one or more instalments, it is a question in each case depending on the terms of the contract and the circumstances of the case whether the breach of contract is a repudiation of the whole contract or whether it is a severable breach giving rise to a claim for compensation but not to a right to treat the whole contract as repudiated (*k*).

ILLUSTRATIONS

Subsection (1).—(1) Contract for sale of thirteen engraved plates "to be sent to me as published, the price of each plate £10 10s. 0d." This is an

(*d*) *Green* v. *Arcos, Ltd.* (1931), 47 T. L. R. 336, C. A.; *Wilensko* v. *Fenwick*, [1938] 3 All E. R. 429.

(*e*) *Aitken & Co.* v. *Boullen*, 1908 S. C. 490 (rejection of part).

(*f*) *Cf. Jackson* v. *Rotax*, [1910] 2 K. B. 937, C. A.; and see s. 11 (4), *ante*.

(*g*) *Raahe O. Y. Osakeytio* v. *Goddard* (1935), 154 L. T. 124. See also *London Plywood & Timber Co.* v. *Nasic*, [1939] 2 K. B. 343.

(*h*) *Ebrahim Dawood, Ltd.* v. *Heath*, [1961] 2 Lloyd's Rep. 512.

(*i*) *Reuter* v. *Sala* (1879), 4 C. P. D. 239, C. A. Nor can he demand it: see note to last section.

(*k*) *Mersey Steel & Iron Co.* v. *Naylor & Co.* (1884), 9 App. Cas. 434 (non-payment of one instalment in error): *Dominion Coal Co.* v. *Dominion Iron and Steel Co.*, [1909] A. C. 293, P. C.; *Steinberger* v. *Atkinson & Co.* (1914), 31 T. L. R. 110; *Payzu, Ltd.* v. *Saunders*, [1919] 2 K. B. 581, C. A. (failure to pay punctually). See *Workman Clark* v. *Lloyd Brazileno*, [1908] 1 K. B. 968, 979, C. A., as to meaning of "compensation" in this section.

instalment contract and the buyer is bound to accept and pay for each plate separately (*l*).

Subsection (2).—(2) Contract for sale of steel bars to be delivered over a period of three months, in about equal monthly quantities; payment cash in fourteen days after delivery, "all payments to be made on due date as a condition precedent to future deliveries." If the buyer does not pay according to contract, the seller may refuse unconditionally to make any further delivery (*m*).

(3) Contract for rosewood to be delivered by instalments during the year. The buyer, on what afterwards turns out to be erroneous grounds, refuses an offer to deliver the first instalment and repudiates the contract. The first instalment and the second instalment, which is according to contract, are subsequently tendered and refused. The buyer cannot afterwards set up, in mitigation of damages, that part of the first instalment was of slightly inferior character; *sed quaere?* (*n*).

(4) Sale of 1100 pieces of blue gumwood to be delivered in two instalments. The first instalment of 750 pieces is of very inferior quality, and the buyer refuses to accept it. If an arbitrator finds that the quality of the instalment is of such a character as to amount to a repudiation of the contract, the court will not disturb his finding (*o*).

(5) Contract for the sale of two ships. One ship is requisitioned by Government, and cannot be delivered. The buyer may refuse to accept the other ship (*p*).

Derivation.—Section 31 of the 1893 Act.

Definitions.—For "contract of sale," see s. 2 (1), *ante*, and s. 61 (1), *post*. For "buyer," "delivery," "goods" and "seller," see s. 61 (1), *post*.

Cross-references.—*Cf.* s. 10, *ante* (stipulation as to time of payment not usually of the essence); s. 11, *ante* (repudiation, severable breach); s. 28, *ante* (payment and delivery usually concurrent conditions); ss. 29, *ante*, and 32, *post* (rules as to delivery); s. 35, *post* (acceptance); s. 41, *post* (seller's lien); and s. 55, *post* ("unless otherwise agreed"). *Cf.* also ss. 49 and 50, *post* (remedies of seller), and ss. 51 to 53, *post* (remedies of buyer).

COMMENT

Subsection (1).—"Suppose," says BRAMWELL, L. J.,

"a man orders a suit of clothes, the price being £7—£4 for the coat, £2 for the

(*l*) *Howell* v. *Evans* (1926), 42 T. L. R. 310.

(*m*) *Ebbw Vale Steel Co.* v. *Blaina Iron Co.* (1901), 6 Com. Cas. 33, C. A.

(*n*) *Braithwaite* v. *Foreign Hardwood Co.*, [1905] 2 K. B. 543, C. A.; explained and followed, *Taylor* v. *Oakes, Roncoroni & Co.* (1922), 38 T. L. R. 349, 351; affd. 38 T. L. R. 517, C. A.; *Continental Contractors* v. *Medway* (1925), 23 Ll. L. Rep. 55, 124, C. A.; criticised, *British and Beningtons, Ltd.* v. *N. W. Cachar Tea Co.*, [1923] A. C. 48, at p. 70. The *Braithwaite* case is not to be taken as impugning the general rule that a buyer, who gives a wrong reason for refusing to perform his contract and afterwards discovers a sound reason, may then rely on the sound reason. See also *Universal Cargo Carriers Corporation* v. *Citati*, [1957] 2 All E. R. 70; [1957] 2 Q. B. 401.

(*o*) *Millars Karri & Co.* v. *Weddell & Co.* (1908), 100 L. T. 128. *Cf. Ballantine & Co.* v. *Cramp & Bosman* (1923), 129 L. T. 502 (sale of meat to be shipped by instalments).

(*p*) *Claddagh S. S. Co.* v. *Stevens & Co.*, 1919 S. C. (H. L.) 132.

> trousers, and £1 for the waistcoat; can he be made to take the coat only, whether they were all to be delivered together, or the trousers and waistcoat first?"

and he then proceeds to show that this cannot be (*q*). On the other hand, the circumstances of a contract may be such that an agreement for delivery by instalments will be implied.

> "In many cases of contract to supply a quantity of goods to be delivered within a fixed period the whole quantity cannot, from the very nature of the case, be delivered at one time,"

as, for instance, in the case of contracts for the supply of provisions for the army and navy (*r*).

Subsection (2).—A failure to perform the contract in accordance with its terms or an anticipatory breach of contract may entitle the other party to treat it as at an end either because the contract correctly construed so provides (*s*) or because the effect of the breach is such as to go to the root of the contract (*t*).

It is very difficult to reconcile some of the older decisions in which it has been held that the refusal to deliver, accept, or pay for a particular instalment is a breach going to the root of the contract, with those in which the contrary has been held (*u*).

Each case must be judged on its own merits, and the main tests to apply are, first, the quantitative ratio which the breach bears to the contract as a whole, and, secondly, the degreee of probability that such a breach will be repeated (*a*). The section in terms deals only with "stated instalments," but a similar principle applies where the instalments are not specified (*b*).

A refusal to accept goods which are tendered in respect of the first instalment on the erroneous ground that they are not of the quality

---

(*q*) *Honck* v. *Muller* (1881), 7 Q. B. D. 92, at p. 99, C. A.

(*r*) *Colonial Ins. Co. of New Zealand* v. *Adelaide Ins. Co.* (1886), 12 App. Cas. 128, at pp. 138, 139, P. C.

(*s*) See *Withers* v. *Reynolds* (1831), 2 B. & Ad. 882, as explained in *Decro-Wall International S. A.* v. *Practitioners in Marketing, Ltd.*, [1971] 2 All E. R. 216; [1971] 1 W. L. R. 361, C. A. See also the comment to s. 11 (3), *ante*.

(*t*) *Mersey Steel Co.* v. *Naylor & Co.* (1884), 9 App. Cas. 434, at p. 443, *per* Lord BLACKBURN; and see *per* JESSEL, M. R. in court below, 9 Q. B. D. 648, at p. 657; *Warinco A. G.* v. *Samor, supra*. See also *Fixby Engineering Co., Ltd.*, v. *Auchlochan Sand and Gravel Co., Ltd.*, 1974 S. L. T. (Sh. Ct.) 58.

(*u*) Compare *Honck* v. *Muller* (1881), 7 Q. B. D. 92, C. A. (repudiation) with *Jonassohn* v. *Young* (1863), 4 B. & S. 296; *Simpson* v. *Crippin* (1872), L. R. 8 Q. B. 14; *Freeth* v. *Burr* (1874), L. R. 9 C. P. 208 (no repudiation). In *Hoare* v. *Rennie* (1859), 5 H. & N. 19, the issue was whether a buyer had to accept and pay for a first instalment of goods much smaller than the instalment contracted for, and it was held that he did not. Notwithstanding observations in the later cases cited in this note, it was not decided in that case whether the seller's breach was a repudiation of the contract.

(*a*) *Maple Flock Co., Ltd.* v. *Universal Furniture Products (Wembley), Ltd.*, [1934] 1 K. B. 148, C. A.

(*b*) *Coddington* v. *Paleologo* (1867), L. R. 2 Exch. 193, 197; *Reuter* v. *Sala* (1879), 4 C. P. D. 239, C. A.; *Jackson* v. *Rotax Motor and Cycle Co.*, [1910] 2 K. B. 937, C. A.

contracted for, coupled with a refusal in advance to take future goods of the same quality, goes to the root of the contract (*c*). This is so even if there is an express provision in the contract that each delivery should be treated as a separate contract and failure to give or take delivery should not cancel the contract as to future deliveries (*d*), for whatever the effect of a simple failure to take delivery, an outright refusal to take future goods is a fundamental anticipatory breach of contract.

But repeated minor breaches causing only slight damage to the other party will not go to the root of the contract even where they are likely to be continued (*e*). Nor will a refusal to pay which is based upon incorrect advice and which does not cast doubt upon the ability of the buyer to pay if payment can properly be made amount to a repudiatory breach (*f*).

If a breach is reasonably capable of an explantation which would not go to the root of the contract, it may not be treated as repudiatory by itself, but the party in breach should be given an opportunity to account for it (*g*).

An incorrect claim to be entitled to treat the contract as rescinded does not of itself amount to a repudiatory breach of contract even if an action is brought claiming rescission (*h*), but a refusal to perform the contract at the time fixed for performance by reason of that incorrect claim could go to the root of the contract.

Where the passing of the property in specific goods is made dependent upon full payment of a price payable by instalments, the buyer may at any time pay the outstanding balance, even if it is not yet due, and the seller must then appropriate the payment to the goods (*i*).

Subject to s. 11 (4), *ante*, under an instalment contract, the buyer may reject defective instalments while retaining the rest of the goods (*k*).

32. Delivery to carrier.—(1) Where, in pursuance of a contract of sale, the seller is authorised or required to

---

(*c*) *Warinco A. G.* v. *Samor*, [1979] 1 Lloyd's Rep. 450, C. A.

(*d*) *Munro & Co.* v. *Meyer*, [1930] 2 K. B. 312, at p. 332.

(*e*) *Decro Wall International S. A.* v. *Practitioners in Marketing, Ltd.*, [1971] 2 All E. R. 216; [1971] 1 W. L. R. 361, C. A., where, however, SALMON, L. J., said at pp. 222 and 369 that it would have been different if the breaches had been such as reasonably to shatter the sellers' confidence in the buyers' ability to pay, and BUCKLEY, L. J. put the test as being whether the consequences of the breach would be such that it would be unfair to hold the injured party to the contract and leave him to his remedy in damages as and when a breach or breaches may occur: see at pp. 232 and 380.

(*f*) *Mersey Steel and Iron Co.* v. *Naylor & Co.* (1884), 9 App. Cas. 434, H. L.

(*g*) *Dumenil* v. *Ruddin*, [1953] 2 All E. R. 294; [1953] 1 W. L. R. 815, C. A.

(*h*) *Spettabile Consorzio Veneziano* v. *Northumberland Shipping Co., Ltd.* (1919), 121 L. T. 628, C. A.; and see *Woodar Investment Development, Ltd.* v. *Wimpey Construction U. K., Ltd.*, [1980] 1 All E. R. 571; [1980] 1 W. L. R. 277, H. L.

(*i*) *Lancs. Waggon Co.* v. *Nuttall* (1879), 42 L. T. 465, C. A.; *Croft* v. *Lumley* (1858), 6 H. L. Cas. 672.

(*k*) *The Hansa Nord*, [1974] 2 Lloyd's Rep. 216, at p. 226; reversed on other grounds, *sub nom. Cehave N. V.* v. *Bremer Handelsgesellschaft*, [1976] 3 All E. R. 739; [1976] Q. B. 44, C. A.

send the goods to the buyer, delivery of the goods to a carrier (whether named by the buyer or not) for the purpose of transmission to the buyer is prima facie deemed to be a delivery of the goods to the buyer (*l*).

(2) Unless otherwise authorised by the buyer, the seller must make such contract with the carrier on behalf of the buyer as may be reasonable having regard to the nature of the goods and other circumstances of the case; and if the seller omits to do so, and the goods are lost or damaged in course of transit, the buyer may decline to treat the delivery to the carrier as a delivery to himself (*m*) or may hold the seller responsible in damages.

(3) Unless otherwise agreed, where goods are sent by the seller to the buyer by a route involving sea transit, under circumstances in which it is usual to insure, the seller must give such notice to the buyer as may enable him to insure them during their sea transit; and if the seller fails to do so, the goods are at his risk during such sea transit.

ILLUSTRATIONS

Subsection (2).—(1) Contract for sale of electric engines, to be sent by rail. Sellers send them at owner's risk rate and they arrive damaged. Buyers can reject, as contract of carriage made by sellers not reasonable in the circumstances (*n*).

(2) C.i.f. contract for the sale of groundnuts Sudan/Hamburg with no term, express or implied, governing the route. The Suez Canal, which would be the normal route, then becomes closed to traffic. The sellers must ship *via* the Cape, which is a reasonable and practicable route in the circumstances (*o*).

Subsection (3).—(3) Goods sold Antwerp, to be shipped as required, payment cash against bill of lading. Buyer directs seller to ship the goods to Odessa, leaving him to select the ship. Ship sails on 25th August, and is lost on

---

(*l*) For statement of principle, see *Wait* v. *Baker* (1848), 2 Exch. 1, at p. 7, *per* PARKE, B.; *Dunlop* v. *Lambert* (1839), 6 Cl. & F. 600, at p. 620, *per* Lord COTTENHAM; *Calcutta Co.* v. *De Mattos* (1863), 32 L. J. Q. B. 322, at p. 328, *per* BLACKBURN, J., cited in full, *post*, Appendix II, Note B; *Badische Anilin Fabrik* v. *Basle Chemical Works*, [1898] A. C. 200, at pp. 203, 204. For illustrations, see *Dutton* v. *Solomonson* (1803), 3 B. & P. 582 (carrier by land); *Bryans* v. *Nix* (1839), 4 M. & W. 775 (canal-boat); *Alexander* v. *Gardner* (1835), 1 Bing. N. C. 671 (ship); *Ex p. Pearson* (1868), 3 Ch. App. 443 (railway); see also *Galbraith* v. *Grant & Block*, [1922] 2 K. B. 155; Bells' *Inquiries into the Contract of Sale of Goods and Merchandise*, p. 86. The same rules apply where goods are delivered to a carrier to convey to a pledgee; *Kum* v. *Wah Tat Bank*, [1971] 1 Lloyd's Rep. 439, P. C.

(*m*) *Clarke* v. *Hutchins* (1811), 14 East, 475; *Buckman* v. *Levi* (1813), 3 Camp. 414; *Young* v. *Hobson* (1949), 65 T. L. R. 365, C. A. *Story on Sale*, § 305.

(*n*) *Young* v. *Hobson* (1949), 65 T. L. R. 365, C. A.

(*o*) *Tsakiroglou & Co., Ltd.* v. *Noblee & Thorl*, [1961] 2 All E. R. 179; [1962] A. C. 93, H. L.

the 26th. Buyer receives no notice of shipment till 29th August. He must pay for the goods, even though he has not insured, for he had sufficient information to enable him to do so before the goods were shipped (*p*).

Derivation.—Section 32 of the 1893 Act.

Definitions.—For "contract of sale," see s. 2 (1), *ante*, and s. 61 (1), *post*. For "buyer," "delivery," "goods" and "seller," see s. 61 (1), *post*.

Cross-references.—*Cf.* s. 20, *ante* (risk); ss. 29 and 31, *ante* (rules as to delivery); ss. 51 to 53, *post* (remedies of the buyer); and s. 55, *post* ("unless otherwise agreed"). See also ss. 44 to 46, *post* (stoppage in transit), and Note B, *post*, Appendix II (delivery to carrier). For the law relating to customary international contracts, see p. 30, *ante*.

COMMENT

Subsection (1).—*Effect of delivery to carrier.*—The rule that delivery of goods to a carrier is *prima facie* delivery to the buyer, passing to him the property and the risk, if they have not passed before, is the natural complement of the rule that *prima facie* the proper place for delivery is the seller's abode, or the place where the goods are at the time of sale (s. 29, *ante*).

It is to be noted that, though the carrier is ordinarily the agent of the buyer to receive the goods, it has been held that he is not his agent to accept them. The cases on this point before the Act proceed on the ground that the carrier is not the buyer's agent to examine the goods, and that acceptance "means such an acceptance as precludes the purchaser from objecting to the quality of the goods" (*q*).

While the goods are in the hands of a carrier as such, they are liable to be stopped in transit; and of course they may be delivered to the carrier on such terms as to make him the seller's agent. When goods are sent "carriage forward" it is strong evidence that the delivery to the carrier was intended as a delivery to the buyer (*r*).

Subsection (2).—*Seller's duty.*—"Delivery of goods to a carrier or wharfinger," says Lord ELLENBOROUGH,

> "with due care and diligence is sufficient to charge the purchaser, but he has a right to require that in making this delivery due care and diligence shall be exercised by the seller" (*s*).

Subsection (3).—*Sea transit.*—As regards goods sent by sea, Bell, summing up the Scottish cases, says:

> "In delivering goods on ship-board, the seller is bound not only to charge

---

(*p*) *Wimble* v. *Rosenberg & Sons*, [1913] 3 K. B. 743, C. A., affirming BAILHACHE, J., on varying grounds—but see note (*a*), p. 189, *infra*.

(*q*) *Norman* v. *Phillips* (1845), 14 M. & W. 277, at p. 283; *Meredith* v. *Meigh* (1853), 2 E. & B. 364; *Hanson* v. *Armitage* (1822), 5 B. & Ald. 557; and see *Hammer and Barrow* v. *Coca-Cola*, [1962] N. Z. L. R. 723; 26 M. L. R. 194.

(*r*) See *post*, Appendix II, Note B.

(*s*) *Buckman* v. *Levi* (1813), 3 Camp. 414 at p. 415; *cf. Young* v. *Hobson* (1949), 65 T. L. R. 365, C. A.

the ship-master or shipping company with them effectually, but though not bound to insure, he must give such notice as to enable the buyer to insure" (*t*).

There appears to have been no English decision in point, but the Scottish rule has been adopted by the Act.

Subsection (3) has no application to c.i.f. (*u*) and ex-ship contracts, but it applies to f.o.b. contracts unless the buyer waives notice or has from the contract itself or from other sources sufficient information to enable him to insure (*a*). It will also apply to c. and f. contracts and to ex-work contracts where the seller sends goods to the buyer by a route involving sea transit.

For a consideration of these various types of contract see pp. 30–38, *ante*.

33. Risk where goods are delivered at distant place.—Where the seller of goods agrees to deliver them at his own risk at a place other than that where they are when sold, the buyer must nevertheless (unless otherwise agreed) (*b*) take any risk of deterioration in the goods necessarily incident to the course of transit (*c*).

Derivation.—Section 33 of the 1893 Act.

Definitions.—For "buyer," "delivery," "goods" and "seller," see s. 61 (1), *post.*

Cross-references.—*Cf.* ss. 6 and 7, *ante* (goods perishing before sale); s. 20, *ante* (risk generally); ss. 29 and 31, *ante* (rules as to delivery); s. 32 (2) and (3), *ante* (delivery to carrier); and s. 55 (1), *post* ("unless otherwise agreed").

COMMENT

"A manufacturer," says ALDERSON, B.,

(*t*) *Inquiries into the Contract of Sale of Goods and Merchandise*, p. 89. See a review of the Scottish cases by HAMILTON, L. J., in *Wimble* v. *Rosenberg*, [1913] 3 K. B. 743, at p. 762, C. A.

(*u*) *Law and Bonar, Ltd.* v. *British American Tobacco, Ltd.*, [1916] 2 K. B. 605 (leaving open the question whether the subsection could apply to a c.i.f. contract made at a time when insurance other than that to be provided by the seller was usual).

(*a*) *Northern Steel and Hardware Co.* v. *Batt & Co.* (1917), 33 T. L. R. 516, C. A.; following the majority of the court in *Wimble* v. *Rosenberg*, [1913] 3 K. B. 743, C. A.; but note the judgment of HAMILTON, L. J., commenting on the Scottish law, and holding (contrary to the majority) that the subsection can have no application to an f.o.b. contract, and the dissenting judgment of VAUGHAN WILLIAMS, L. J., at p. 751, holding that the seller's obligation to give notice is not dispensed with because the buyer has sufficient information from other sources to enable him to insure.

(*b*) See, *e.g.*, *Beaver Specialty, Ltd.* v. *Donald H. Bain, Ltd.* (1974), 39 D. L. R. (3d) 574 (Sup. Ct. of Can.) (sale f.o.b. the buyer's place of business).

(*c*) Compare the non-liability of the insurer in insurance law for *vice propre*, or inherent vice: Chalmers' *Marine Insurance Act* 1906 (6th ed.), s. 55, and notes.

"who contracts to deliver a manufactured article at a distant place, must indeed stand the risk of any extraordinary or unusual deterioration; but the vendee is bound to accept the article if only deteriorated to the extent that it is necessarily subject to in its course of transit from one place to the other" (*d*).

There appeared to be no reason for confining the rule to the case of a manufacturer, nor is the section inconsistent with the case of *Beer* v. *Walker* (*e*), where the buyer was held entitled to reject rabbits which arrived in Brighton in an unsaleable condition, though they were saleable when sent off from London. In the case of perishable goods, they are not really merchantable when sent off by the seller unless they are in such a condition as to continue to be saleable for a reasonable time (*f*).

34. Buyer's right of examining the goods.—(1) Where goods are delivered to the buyer, and he has not previously examined them, he is not deemed to have accepted them until he has had a reasonable opportunity of examining them for the purpose of ascertaining whether they are in conformity with the contract (*g*).

(2) Unless otherwise agreed (*h*), when the seller tenders delivery of goods to the buyer, he is bound on request to afford the buyer a reasonable opportunity of examining the goods for the purpose of ascertaining whether they are in conformity with the contract (*i*).

Derivation.—Section 34 of the 1893 Act.

Definitions.—For "contract of sale," see s. 2 (1), *ante*, and s. 61 (1), *post*. For "buyer," "delivery," "goods" and "seller," see s. 61 (1), *post*.

(*d*) *Bull* v. *Robison* (1854), 10 Exch. 342, at p. 346 (hoop-iron sent by canal).

(*e*) (1877), 46 L. J. Q. B. 677. See also *Ollett* v. *Jordan*, [1918] 2 K. B. 41, 47; *Healy* v. *Howlett & Son*, [1917] 1 K. B. 337; *Broome* v. *Pardess Co-operative Society*, [1940] 1 All E. R. 603; *Mash & Murrell* v. *Joseph I. Emanuel, Ltd.*, [1961] 1 All E. R. 485; [1961] 1 W. L. R. 862; reversed on an issue of fact, [1962] 1 All E. R. 77; [1962] 1 W. L. R. 16, C. A.; *Cordova Land Co., Ltd.* v. *Victor Brothers Incorporated*, [1966] 1 W. L. R. 793; *Oleificio Zucchi S.p.A.* v. *Northern Sales, Ltd.*, [1965] 2 Lloyd's Rep. 496, at pp. 517, 518.

(*f*) See comment to s. 14 (2), *ante*.

(*g*) *Lorymer* v. *Smith* (1822), 1 B. & C. 1; *Toulmin* v. *Hedley* (1845), 2 C. & K. 157, at p. 160; *Heilbutt* v. *Hickson* (1872), L. R. 7 C. P. 438, at p. 456, *per* BRETT, J.; *Bragg* v. *Villanova* (1923), 40 T. L. R. 154 (f.o.b. contract); *B. and P. Wholesale Distributors* v. *Marko*, [1953] C. L. Y. 3266 (opportunity for cursory examination not enough). As to waiver of inspection, see *Castle* v. *Sworder* (1861), 6 H. & N. 828, at p. 837; *Khan* v. *Duché* (1905), 10 Com. Cas. 87; *cf. Van den Hurk* v. *Martens & Co.*, [1920] 1 K. B. 850 (ultimate destination); *Thornett* v. *Beers & Son*, [1919] 1 K. B. 486 (a case on the original proviso to s. 14 (2) of the 1893 Act, now the provisio to s. 14 (3) as reproduced in para. 6 of Sch. 1, *post*).

(*h*) *Pettitt* v. *Mitchell* (1842), 4 M. & Gr. 819; *Polenghi Brothers* v. *Dried Milk Co.* (1904), 92 L. T. 64; *E. Clemens Horst Co.* v. *Biddell Brothers*, [1912] A. C. 18.

(*i*) *Isherwood* v. *Whitmore* (1843), 11 M. & W. 347, at p. 350 (goods in closed casks).

Cross-references.—*Cf.* s. 35, *post* (acceptance); s. 14 (2), *ante* (proviso as to examination); s. 15 (2) (b), *ante* (sale by sample); and s. 55 (1), *post* ("unless otherwise agreed").

COMMENT

Until 1967 s. 34 of the 1893 Act was governed by, and had to be read in the light of, s. 35 of that Act so that a buyer who did any act amounting to an acceptance within the meaning of s. 35 could not reject the goods even though he had no reasonable opportunity of examining them (*k*).

Section 35 of the 1893 Act was amended by s. 4 (2) of the Misrepresentation Act 1967 which inserted the words "(except where section 34 of this Act otherwise provides)" before the words "when the goods have been delivered to him, and he does any act in relation to them which is inconsistent with the ownership of the seller." Since that amendment a buyer is no longer deemed to have accepted the goods by doing an act inconsistent with the ownership of the seller unless and until he has had a reasonable opportunity of examining them in accordance with s. 34. What is a reasonable opportunity for examining the goods is a question of fact.

"Suppose," says BRAMWELL, B.,

> "I order a certain quantity of lime to be taken to a farm, and I am not there to object, and nobody else is there . . . to object to it, I shall not be at liberty afterwards to say: 'Those goods have not been accepted and received by me'; they have been, as much as it was possible, unless I had chosen to be there to make objection. So, on the other hand, if I go to a shop for an article I have previously ordered, and it is delivered to me, wrapped up, though I cannot see what it is, there cannot be the slightest question that I have received and accepted the goods, if they turn out to be in conformity with the order; yet nobody can say that I shall not have a right to object to them afterwards, if they are not in conformity with the contract" (*l*).

Place for examination.—As a general rule, the place of delivery is *prima facie* the place of examination; but the general rule is always liable to be displaced by the circumstances of the particular contract (*m*), and the parties may make terms of their own both as to place and

---

(*k*) *Hardy* v. *Hillerns & Fowler*, [1923] 2 K. B. 490, C. A.; followed in *E. & S. Ruben* v. *Faire Bros. & Co.*, [1949] 1 All E. R. 215; [1949] 1 K. B. 254; followed but doubted by ROXBURGH, J. in *Pelhams* v. *Mercantile Commodities Syndicate*, [1953] 2 Lloyd's Rep. 281. It may be noted that it is only when the buyer was held to have accepted the goods in the second of the three ways contemplated by s. 35 that there was any question of a conflict between that section and s. 34 (1).

(*l*) *Castle* v. *Sworder* (1860), 29 L. J. Ex. 235, at p. 238; reversed, (1861) 30 L. J. Ex. 310, Ex. Ch.; see at p. 312.

(*m*) *Saunt* v. *Belcher & Gibbons* (1920), 90 L. J. K. B. 541; distinguishing *Van den Hurk* v. *Martens*, [1920] 1 K. B. 850; *Boks* v. *Rayner & Co.* (1921), 37 T. L. R. 519, affirmed by C. A., *ibid.* 800 (f.o.b. contract); *cf. Scalaris* v. *Ofverberg & Co.* (1921), 37 T. L. R. 307, C. A. (f.o.b. contract); *B. & P. Wholesale Distributors* v. *Marko*, [1953] C. L. Y. 3266; and compare the position where delivery is made to a carrier; p. 188, *ante*.

kind of examination which may materially affect other terms in the contract (*n*).

35. Acceptance.—(1) The buyer is deemed to have accepted the goods when he intimates to the seller that he has accepted them, or (except when section 34 above otherwise provides) when the goods have been delivered to him (*o*) and he does any act in relation to them which is inconsistent with the ownership of the seller (*p*), or when after the lapse of a reasonable time he retains the goods without intimating to the seller that he has rejected them (*q*).

(2) Paragraph 10 of Schedule 1 below applies in relation to a contract made before 22 April 1967 or (in the application of this Act to Northern Ireland) 28 July 1967.

ILLUSTRATIONS

(1) C.i.f. contract for the sale of wheat. Buyers take delivery, and resell and deliver part to sub-purchasers. It is then discovered that the whole of the wheat is not in conformity with the contract. Prior to the coming into force of the Misrepresentation Act 1967, the buyers would always have lost their right to reject (*r*). Now the buyers will not lose their right to reject if they have not examined the wheat prior to delivery unless and until they have had a reasonable opportunity of examining it to ascertain whether it is in conformity with the contract.

(2) Sale of 25 sacks of flour. Buyer, after discovering that the flour does not

---

(*n*) *Potts & Co., Ltd.*, v. *Brown, Macfarlane & Co., Ltd.* (1925), 30 Com. Cas. 64 (where such a clause resulted in an extension of time for delivery); *Ruben* v. *Faire*, [1949] 1 All E. R. 215; [1949] 1 K. B. 254.

(*o*) If the goods are delivered to a sub-purchaser at the request of the buyer, there is a constructive delivery to the buyer within the meaning of the section: *E. & S. Ruben* v. *Faire Bros. & Co.*, [1949] 1 All E. R. 215; [1949] 1 K. B. 254; and see *Hammer and Barrow* v. *Coca-Cola*, [1962] N. Z. L. R. 723; 26 M. L. R. 194. In a c.i.f. contract the goods are "delivered" within the meaning of this section when they are put on board a ship at the port of shipment: *Chao* v. *British Traders*, [1954] 1 All E. R. 779; [1954] 2 Q. B. 459.

(*p*) *Parker* v. *Palmer* (1821), 4 B. & Ald. 387; *Chapman* v. *Morton* (1843), 11 M. & W. 534; *Harnor* v. *Groves* (1855), 15 C. B. 667; *Heilbutt* v. *Hickson* (1872), L. R. 7 C. P. 438, at p. 451 *per* BOVILL, C. J.; *Mechan* v. *Bow McLachlan & Co.*, 1910 S. C. 758; *Wallis, Son and Wells* v. *Pratt*, [1911] A. C. 394, H. L., and see also *per* FLETCHER MOULTON, L. J. in the Court of Appeal, [1910] 2 K. B. at pp. 1013, 1015; *Hardy* v. *Hillerns & Fowler*, [1923] 2 K. B. 490, C. A.; *Libau Wood Co.* v. *H. Smith & Sons, Ltd.* (1930), 37 Lloyd's Rep. 296; *E. & S. Ruben* v. *Faire Bros. & Co.*, [1949] 1 All E. R. 215; [1949] 1 K. B. 254; *Chao* v. *British Traders*, [1954] 1 All E. R. 779; [1954] 2 Q. B. 459; see also 108 L. J. 68.

(*q*) *Sanders* v. *Jameson* (1848), 2 Car. & Kir. 557; *Heilbutt* v. *Hickson* (1872), L. R. 7 C. P. 438, at p. 452 *per* BOVILL, C. J.; *Reeves* v. *Armour*, [1920] 3 K. B. 614; *Leaf* v. *International Galleries*, [1950] 1 All E. R. 693, C. A., *per* DENNING, L. J. at p. 695; [1950] 2 K. B. 86. See too the cases on "sale or return" noted to s. 18, rule (4), *ante*.

(*r*) *Hardy & Co.* v. *Hillerns & Fowler*, [1923] 2 K. B. 490, C. A.

answer the contract description, uses two of the sacks and sells another. He has lost his right to reject (*s*).

(3) Contract for the supply of 2 feed-tanks to a firm of shipbuilders for a tug which they are building for the Admiralty. By the contract, the tanks are to be made "to British Admiralty latest tests and requirements". The tanks are delivered without having been tested by the Admiralty inspector and the shipbuilders fit them into the tug in ignorance of this fact, although they could have ascertained it by examination of the tanks. Thereafter the Admiralty inspect and condemn the tanks. The shipbuilders have lost their right to reject (*t*).

(4) Contract for sale of 200,000 yo-yos by plaintiffs to C, 85,000 of which are to be delivered to N. Before deliveries begin, C re-sells the 85,000 yo-yos to N. The plaintiffs deliver them to N and they are found to be defective. Neither the delivery to N, which was in accordance with the terms of the contract, nor the re-sale, which was *before* delivery, disentitle C to reject the yo-yos (*u*).

Derivation.—Section 35 of the 1893 Act as amended by s. 4 (2) of the Misrepresentation Act 1967.

Definitions.—For "buyer," "delivery," "goods" and "seller," see s. 61 (1), *post*.

Cross-references.—*Cf.* s. 11 (4), *ante* (effect of acceptance); ss. 27 and 28, *ante* (buyer's duty to accept); s. 34, *ante* (buyer's right to examine); s. 36, *post* (rejected goods); s. 37, *post* (buyer's liability for non-acceptance); s. 50, *post* (seller's remedy for non-acceptance); and s. 59, *post* (reasonable time a question of fact).

COMMENT

Most of the numerous decisions relating to acceptance have arisen on the construction of the provisions of the Statute of Frauds relating to the sale of goods, or of s. 4 of the 1893 Act, all of which have now been repealed. For that reason they must be looked at critically. Before the repeal (*a*) there could be an acceptance within the meaning of s. 4, which yet was not an acceptance in performance of the contract. For the purpose of determing whether there is an acceptance in this latter sense those cases may still be of use. At one time acceptance within the meaning of the Statute of Frauds was interpreted in the same sense as acceptance in performance of the contract, but in the course of time two different interpretations of the word were developed and there was much learning on the distinction between the two. All this is now happily obsolete.

Rules for presuming acceptance.—The question whether the buyer has accepted the goods is a question of fact.

Section 35 (1) lays down three situations in which a buyer will be deemed to have accepted the goods. Only the second causes any difficulty. If goods are delivered to a buyer which he has not previously

(*s*) *Harnor* v. *Groves* (1855), 15 C. B. 667.

(*t*) *Mechan* v. *Bow McLachlan & Co.*, 1910 S. C. 758.

(*u*) *Hammer and Barrow* v. *Coca-Cola*, [1962] N. Z. L. R. 723; 26 M. L. R. 194.

(*a*) By s. 1 of the Law Reform (Enforcement of Contracts) Act 1954.

examined, he will not be deemed to have accepted them by doing an act inconsistent with the ownership of the seller unless and until he has had a reasonable opportunity of examining them for the purpose of ascertaining whether they conform with the contract (*b*). Subject to this, it is clear that if, after they are delivered to him, the buyer re-sells the whole of the goods he will be deemed to have accepted them (*c*), whether or not the defect or misdescription was discoverable on a reasonable examination (*d*). But a re-sale before delivery, even where the buyer has already examined the goods, but without finally accepting them, need not be an acceptance under s. 35, which covers acts inconsistent with the seller's ownership only if done after delivery (*e*). If, however, pursuant to such re-sale the buyer asks the seller to deliver the goods to the premises of the sub-purchaser, and the seller does so, then he may be held to have done so as agent for the buyer. In that case, the delivery will be an act, inconsistent with the seller's ownership, done by the buyer's agent, and, subject to s. 34 (1), will amount to an acceptance under s. 35 (*f*).

It might be thought that the rule as to re-sale after delivery would be the same when the buyer re-sells part only of the goods, but it seems that this is not always so. If none of the goods delivered are of the contract description, re-sale of part will subject to s. 34 (1), amount to an acceptance of the whole (*g*); but it has been held, applying what is now s. 30 (4), that if the seller delivers goods part of which answer the contract description and part of which do not, a re-sale by the buyer of the part which conforms with the contract will not preclude him from rejecting the part which does not (*h*).

In a c.i.f. contract, where the transfer of the shipping documents passes the property in the goods to the buyer, it is not at first sight easy to see how the buyer can after that point do an act inconsistent with the ownership of the seller when, *ex hypothesi*, the seller has no ownership. The problem was dealt with by DEVLIN, J. in *Chao* v. *British Traders* (*i*) where

---

(*b*) See s. 34 (1), *ante*.

(*c*) *Wallis* v. *Pratt and Haynes*, [1911] A. C. 394. See also *Commercial Fibres* v. *Zabaida*, [1975] 1 Lloyd's Rep. 27 (defective packing apparent to agents who forwarded goods to sub-buyer); *Hitchcock* v. *Cameron*, [1977] 1 N. Z. L. R. 85 (where the sale was made by the buyer pending an appeal from a decision holding him liable for the price).

(*d*) *Wallis* v. *Pratt and Haynes*, [1911] A. C. 394 (goods not complying with contract description); *Mechans, Ltd.* v. *Highland Marine Charters, Ltd.*, 1964 S. C. 48 (latent defect not discoverable when goods accepted).

(*e*) *Ruben* v. *Faire*, [1949] 1 All E. R. 215; [1949] 1 K. B. 254; *Hammer and Barrow* v. *Coca-Cola, supra*, illustration (4); 12 M. L. R. 368.

(*f*) *Ruben* v. *Faire, supra; cf. Hammer and Barrow* v. *Coca-Cola, supra*, illustration (4), where delivery to the sub-purchaser was a term of the main contract.

(*g*) *Hardy* v. *Hillerns and Fowler*, [1923] 2 K. B. 490, C. A.

(*h*) *Barker* v. *Agius* (1927), 33 Com. Cas. 120.

(*i*) [1954] 1 All E. R. 779; [1954] 2 Q. B. 459; *J. Rosenthal & Sons, Ltd.* v. *Esmail*, [1965] 2 All E. R. 860, at p. 869; [1965] 1 W. L. R. 1117, at p. 1131, H. L.; see also 12 M. L. R. 368; *Hammer and Barrow* v. *Coca-Cola*, [1962] N. Z. L. R. 723; 26 M. L. R. 194; *Pullman Trailmobile* v. *Hamilton Transport*, [1979] 23 O. R. 553.

he said that the transfer of the shipping documents was effective only to pass a *conditional* property to the buyer. Thus if the buyer subsequently deals with the shipping documents, he is dealing only with his own conditional property in the goods and will not be taken thereby to have accepted them; but if he deals physically with the goods themselves after they have been landed, e.g. if he delivers them to a sub-buyer, he will be doing an act inconsistent with the seller's reversionary interest in the goods, and may thus be taken to have accepted them. Neither a pledge of the goods nor a sale of the documents, however, is inconsistent with the seller's reversionary interest (*k*).

Quite apart from the right to reject for breach of condition, which is controlled by section 11(4) of the Act, a buyer may also have a right to rescind the contract for material misrepresentation. In that case also the right will be lost if the buyer accepts the goods (*l*), not by reason of the operation of section 11 (4), but as a result of the general limitations imposed by equity upon the right of rescission.

Rejection.—Rejection by the buyer must take place within a reasonable time. As SCRUTTON, L. J. has said,

> "When one party to a contract becomes aware of a breach of a condition precedent by the other, he is entitled to a reasonable time to consider what he will do, and failure to reject at once does not prejudice his right to reject if he exercises it within a reasonable time" (*m*).

By s. 59, *post*, what is a reasonable time is a question of fact. In determining what is a reasonable time, the conduct of the seller may be taken into consideration, so that the time for rejection will be extended if the seller has induced the buyer to prolong the trial of the goods by a misrepresentation (*n*), or by a promise which he cannot fulfil (*o*), or by acquiescing by silence to an extended trial (*p*), or by encouraging the buyer to give the goods a fair trial (*q*) or by threatening the buyer that

(*k*) *A fortiori* where the buyer rejects the shipping documents but unloads and stacks the cargo as agent for the shipowner he is not deemed to have accepted the goods: *Libau Wood Co.* v. *H. Smith & Sons, Ltd.* (1930), 37 Ll. L. Rep. 296.

(*l*) See *Leaf* v. *International Galleries*, [1950] 1 All E. R. 693; [1950] 2 K. B. 86, C. A.; *Long* v. *Lloyd*, [1958] 2 All E. R. 402; [1958] 1 W. L. R. 753, C. A.; *Diamond* v. *B. C. Thoroughbred Breeders Society and Boyd* (1966), 52 D. L. R. (2d.) 146.

(*m*) *Fisher Reeves & Co.* v. *Armour & Co.*, [1920] 3 K. B. 614, at p. 624, C. A. *Cf. Chao* v. *British Traders*, [1954] 1 All E. R. 779; [1954] 2 Q. B. 459.

(*n*) *Heilbutt* v. *Hickson* (1872), L. R. 7 C. P. 438; *Munro & Co.* v. *Bennet & Son*, 1911 S. C. 337; and see *Freeman* v. *Consolidated Motors, Ltd.* (1968), 69 D. L. R. (2d) 581 (right to reject not lost by accepting "forced alternative" imposed by seller); *Rafuse Motors* v. *Mardo Constructions* (1963), 41 D. L. R. (2d) 340 (settlement of claim to reject induced by misrepresentation of seller does not bind buyer); *Beldessi v. Island Equipment, Ltd.* (1974), 41 D. L. R. (3d) 147 (buyer showed "unusual patience" partly because of seller's representation that the fault was that of the operator of the machine sold).

(*o*) *Scholfield* v. *Emerson Brantingham Implements* (1918), 43 D. L. R. 509 (Sup. Ct. of Canada) (representation that the vehicle would be all right in time, or if not, then the seller would make it all right).

(*p*) *Lucy* v. *Mouflet* (1860), 5 H. & N. 229.

(*q*) *Rafuse Motors* v. *Mardo Constructions, supra.* See also *Barker* v. *Inland Truck Sales* (1970), 11 D. L. R. (3d) 469; *Finlay* v. *Metro Toyota* (1977), 82 D. L. R. (3d) 440 (buyer

any rejection will be treated as a breach of contract (*r*). Nor does a buyer necessarily lose the right to reject because he tries to put goods sold into working order (*s*), or because he seeks to have samples analysed and to ascertain the attitude of sub-buyers (*t*).

Where there are negotiations between the buyer and the seller with a view to settling the buyer's claim, these negotiations will also be taken into account (*u*).

A rejection must be clear and unequivocal or the buyer may be held to have accepted the goods on the strength of his subsequent conduct (*a*). Moreover, if the buyer continues to use the goods in a manner not consistent with a *bona fide* intention to reject them, he may not be entitled to rely on his rejection and may be treated as having accepted them (*b*). But once he has clearly rejected them and rescinded the contract, a subsequent inadvertent act on his part inconsistent with the seller's ownership of them cannot amount to an acceptance and give new life to a contract which he has elected not to perform (*c*). It has also been held in Canada that a buyer who continued to use a machine after rejecting it while obtaining a replacement, because the buyer's business could not function properly without it, did not lose the right to reject (*d*). Where an effective examination of the goods is possible only by consuming or destroying a sample of them a buyer is not debarred from rejecting the remainder merely because he has consumed or destroyed

---

retained possession of a vehicle for six months, giving seller every opportunity to correct defects in it and attempting to use it for the purpose for which he bought it: right to reject for breach of a fundamental term not lost). But these cases are difficult to reconcile with *Long* v. *Lloyd*, [1958] 2 All E. R. 402; [1958] 1 W. L. R. 753, C. A., discussed in *Benjamin's Sale of Goods*, para. 903. See also *Burrough's Business Machines, Ltd.* v. *Feed Rite Mills* (*1962*), *Ltd.* (1974), 42 D. L. R. (3d) 303; affirmed (1976), 64 D. L. R. (3d) 767 (Sup. Ct. of Can.); *Public Utilities Commission* v. *Burrough's Business Machines, Ltd.* (1975), 52 D. L. R. (3d) 481 (agreement for sale and installation of computer system: buyer entitled to reject after seller had tried unsuccessfully for several months to make it function satisfactorily).

(*r*) *Manifatture Tessile Laniera Wooltex* v. *J. B. Ashley, Ltd.*, [1979] 2 Lloyd's Rep. 28, C. A.

(*s*) *Beldessi* v. *Island Equipment, Ltd.* (1974), 41 D. L. R. (3d) 147; see also *Wathes* (*Western*), *Ltd.* v. *Austin* (*Menswear*), *Ltd.*, [1976] 1 Lloyd's Rep. 14, C. A. (overruled on other grounds in *Photo Production, Ltd.* v. *Securicor Transport, Ltd.*, [1980] 1 All E. R. 556, H. L.) where a buyer was held still to be entitled to reject a machine which it had retained for several months while trying to placate neighbours to whom it was a nuisance.

(*t*) *Manifatture Tessile Laniera Wooltex* v. *J. B. Ashley, Ltd.*, *supra.*

(*u*) *Polar Refrigeration Service, Ltd.* v. *Moldenhauer* (1967), 61 D. L. R. (2d) 462.

(*a*) *Chapman* v. *Morton* (1843), 11 M. & W. 534.

(*b*) *Cornwal* v. *Wilson* (1750), 1 Ves. Sen. 509 (re-sale in manner only consistent with there having been no rejection); *Electric Construction Co.* v. *Hurry and Young* (1897), 24 R. 312 (Ct. of Sess.) (continued user for 3 months after rejection); *Croom & Arthur* v. *Stewart & Co.* (1905), 7 F. (Ct. of Sess.) 563. See also *Central Farmers, Ltd.* v. *Smith*, 1974 S. L. T. (Sh. Ct.) 87.

(*c*) *Breckwoldt* v. *Hanna* (1963), 5 W. I. R. 356, applying *Hardy & Co.* v. *Hillerns and Fowler*, [1923] 2 K. B. 490, C. A.

(*d*) *Public Utilities Commission of City of Waterloo* v. *Burrough's Machines, Ltd.* (1975), 52 D. L. R. (3d) 481.

such a sample, or because he has sold such a sample for consumption (*e*).

If the seller refuses to take the goods back when tendered, the buyer may still not deal with the goods as his own, for the property in them has revested in the seller. In exceptional cases where the goods are liable to deteriorate, he may be able to sell them as agent of necessity for the seller (*f*). Generally, however, he would probably be better advised to commence proceedings against the seller and apply to the court for an order for sale (*g*).

If the buyer deals with the goods without an order for sale and in circumstances in which he cannot claim to be an agent of necessity, then unless perhaps the seller's refusal is in such terms as to entitle the buyer to do as he wishes with the goods, the buyer may be liable to the seller for conversion. Probably, however, in such a case the seller could not claim that the buyer's conduct in selling the goods was inconsistent with a *bona fide* intention to reject them.

Conditional acceptance.—Goods may, of course, by arrangement, be accepted conditionally and the acceptance may in such case be withdrawn on failure of the condition (*h*).

Scotland.—The right of rejecting goods as not being in conformity with the contract is larger in Scotland than in England. In Scotland a buyer may reject goods which he has accepted if he do so "timeously,"

(*e*) *Lucy* v. *Mouflet* (1860), 5 H. & N. 229 (beer); *Winnipeg Fish Co.* v. *Whitman Fish Co.* (1909), 41 S. C. R. 453 (Sup. Ct. of Canada) (frozen fish); *Georgetown Seafoods, Ltd.* v. *Usen Fisheries* (1977), 78 D. L. R. (3d) 542.

(*f*) *Kemp* v. *Pryor* (1802), 7 Ves. Jun. 237, at p. 247. *Cornwal* v. *Wilson* (1750), 1 Ves. Sen. 509 turned upon a mercantile custom that where a factor acquired goods for a principal in excess of authority, the principal could reject them, so that they became the property of the factor, and in certain circumstances the principal could deal with them as agent for the factor. It does not establish any general proposition as to agents of necessity. In *Benjamin's Sale of Goods*, para. 875, it is suggested that *Caswell* v. *Coare* (1809), 1 Taunt. 566 and *Chesterman* v. *Lamb* (1834), 2 Ad. & El. 129 are possibly also examples of agency of necessity. But those cases are clearly concerned with damages recoverable for breach of warranty where the buyer has no right to treat the contract as terminated, and establish that although the property remains in the buyer, if he wishes to recover the expenses of keeping the goods until he can resell them, he should first give the seller the opportunity to rescind the contract by agreement: see Selwyn's *Law of Nisi Prius* (13th ed.), Vol. I, pp. 577–578: *M'Kenzie* v. *Hancock* (1826), Ry. & M. 436; *Watson* v. *Denton* (1835), 7 C. & P. 85, 90. *Cf.* p. 218, *post*.

(*g*) The application will be under R. S. C., Order 29, r. 4 in the High Court, or under C. C. R., Order 13, r. 12 in the County Court. In *The Hansa Nord*, [1974] 2 Lloyd's Rep. 216 (reversed, on other grounds, *sub nom. Cehave N. V.* v. *Bremer Handelgesellschaft*, [1975] 3 All E. R. 739; [1976] Q. B. 44, C. A.) the buyer, fearing that the goods might become a total loss, obtained an order from a Dutch Court for their sale, the net proceeds to be deposited to the account of the legal owners. The goods were then sold by the court's agent to the buyers, who used them for their own purpose. MOCATTA, J., held that this was not an act inconsistent with the seller's ownership for the purposes of this section.

(*h*) *Lucy* v. *Mouflet* (1860), 5 H. & N. 229; *Heilbutt* v. *Hickson* (1872), L. R. 7 C. P. 438; *cf. Behrend & Co.* v. *Produce Brokers Co.*, [1920] 3 K. B. 530; *Adams* v. *Sprung*, *The Guardian*, 8th November 1961, C. A.

whereas in England he could only do so if the contract contained what the continental lawyers call a "resolutive condition" (*i*).

36. Buyer not bound to return rejected goods.—Unless otherwise agreed, where goods are delivered to the buyer, and he refuses to accept them, having the right to do so, he is not bound to return them to the seller, but it is sufficient if he intimates to the seller that he refuses to accept them (*k*).

Derivation.—Section 36 of the 1893 Act.

Definitions.—For "buyer," "delivery," "goods" and "seller," see s. 61 (1), *post.*

Cross-references.—*Cf.* s. 35, *ante* (acceptance), and s. 55 (1), *post* ("unless otherwise agreed").

COMMENT

"The buyer," says BRETT, J.,

> "may, in fact, return [the goods] or offer to return them, but it is sufficient I think, and the more usual course is to signify his rejection of them by stating that the goods are not according to contract, and that they are at the vendor's risk. No particular form is essential. It is sufficient if he does any unequivocal act showing that he rejects them" (*l*).

The buyer has no lien over the goods to secure repayment of the purchase price (*m*).

This section presupposes the relation of seller and buyer. It does not appear to touch the case of goods delivered to a man on the chance that he may buy them.

The buyer is entitled to take into account in claiming damages any expenses incurred by him in looking after the goods until the seller recovers them in accordance with the ordinary rules of assessing damages for breach of contract (*n*).

37. Buyer's liability for not taking delivery of goods.—(1) When the seller is ready and willing to deliver

(*i*) See s. 11 (5), *ante*, and *Couston* v. *Chapman* (1872), L. R. 2 Sc. & Div. 250, at p. 254. For resolutive conditions in England, see *Lamond* v. *Davall* (1847), 9 Q. B. 1030; *Head* v. *Tattersall* (1871), L. R. 7 Exch. 7.

(*k*) *Grimoldby* v. *Wells* (1875), L. R. 10 C. P. 391; as to the place of rejection, see *Heilbutt* v. *Hickson* (1872), L. R. 7 C. P. 438, at p. 456, *per* BRETT, J. As to where the buyer properly rejects goods and the seller refuses to take them back, see *ante*, p. 197.

(*l*) *Grimoldby* v. *Wells* (1875), L. R. 10 C. P. 391, at p. 395.

(*m*) *Lyons & Co.* v. *May & Baker*, [1923] 1 K. B. 685.

(*n*) *Kolfor Plant, Ltd.* v. *Tilbury Plant, Ltd.* (1977), *Times*, 18th May; *Tower Equipment Rental* v. *Joint Venture Equipment Sales* (1975), 9 O. R. (2d) 453. See also *post*, comment to ss. 53, 54. The authorities relied on in *MacGregor on Damages* (14th ed.), para. 629, and *Benjamin's Sale of Goods*, para. 875, are not in fact concerned with this situation, for the reasons given *ante*, n. (*f*) at p. 197.

the goods, and requests the buyer to take delivery, and the buyer does not within a reasonable time after such request take delivery of the goods, he is liable to the seller for any loss occasioned by his neglect or refusal to take delivery, and also for a reasonable charge for the care and custody of the goods (*o*).

(2) Nothing in this section affects the rights of the seller where the neglect or refusal of the buyer to take delivery amounts to a repudiation of the contract (*p*).

ILLUSTRATION

A contracts to build a steam launch for B by a fixed date, delivery to be made on a vessel found by B. A does not complete the launch by the contract time, but B does not notify A of a ship to receive the launch till A is ready to deliver. Neither party has any remedy against the other (*q*).

Derivation.—Section 37 of the 1893 Act.

Definitions.—For "buyer," "delivery," "goods" and "seller," see s. 61 (1), *post.*

Cross-references.—*Cf.* s. 20, *ante* (risk); ss. 27 and 28, *ante* (buyer's duty to accept); ss. 29, 31 and 32, *ante* (rules as to delivery); s. 50, *post* (seller's remedy for non-acceptance); and s. 59, *post* (reasonable time a question of fact).

COMMENT

Conversely, if the seller is in default in making delivery, and the buyer, notwithstanding the delay, accepts the goods, he may recover damages for any loss occasioned by the delay; see note to s. 51, *post.*

When the seller holds the goods in the exercise of his right of lien, he cannot charge for expenses of keeping them. See note to s. 41, *post.*

PART V

RIGHTS OF UNPAID SELLER AGAINST THE GOODS

Preliminary

38. Unpaid seller defined.—(1) The seller of goods is an unpaid seller within the meaning of this Act—

(*o*) *Greaves* v. *Ashlin* (1813), 3 Camp. 426; *cf. Bloxam* v. *Sanders* (1825), 4 B. & C. 941, at p. 950, and see also *Penarth Dock Engineering Co.* v. *Pounds*, [1963] 1 Lloyd's Rep. 359.

(*p*) *Cf. Mersey Steel Co.* v. *Naylor & Co.* (1884), 9 App. Cas. 434, at p. 443; *Braithwaite* v. *Foreign Hardwood Co.*, [1905] 2 K. B. 543, C. A., criticised, *British & Beningtons, Ltd.* v. *North Western Cachar Tea Co., Ltd.*, [1923] A. C. 48, at p. 70, *per* Lord SUMNER. See also s. 31, *ante.*

(*q*) *Forrestt* v. *Aramayo* (1900), 9 Asp. M. L. C. 134, C. A.

(a) when the whole of the price has not been paid or tendered (*r*);

(b) when a bill of exchange or other negotiable instrument has been received as conditional payment, and the condition on which it was received has not been fulfilled by reason of the dishonour of the instrument or otherwise (*s*).

(2) In this Part of this Act "seller" includes any person who is in the position of a seller, as, for instance, an agent of the seller to whom the bill of lading has been indorsed (*t*), or a consignor or agent who has himself paid (or is directly responsible for) the price (*u*).

Derivation.—Section 38 of the 1893 Act.

Definitions.—For "goods," see s. 61 (1), *post*. The definition of "seller" in sub-s. (2) of this section extends, for this and the succeeding ten sections, the definition given in s. 61 (1), *post*.

Cross-references.—*Cf.* ss. 2 (1), 8 and 9, *ante* (price), and ss. 27 and 28, *ante* (buyer's duty to pay the price).

COMMENT

Subsection (1).—In a case where the seller had discounted the buyer's acceptances, but the latter failed before the bills matured, it was held that the seller was unpaid, and MELLISH, L. J., says,

> "If the bill is dishonoured before delivery has been made, then the vendor's lien revives; or if the purchaser becomes openly insolvent before the delivery actually takes place, then the law does not compel the vendor to deliver to an insolvent purchaser" (*a*).

Subsection (2).—The courts show a strong inclination to give the rights of an unpaid seller against the goods to any one whose position

---

(*r*) *Hodgson* v. *Loy* (1797), 7 Term Rep. 440; *Feise* v. *Wray* (1802), 3 East, 93, at p. 102; *Van Casteel* v. *Booker* (1848), 2 Exch. 691, at pp. 702, 709; *Ex p. Chalmers* (1873), 8 Ch. App. 289 (severable contract). As to tender after the appointed day, see *Martindale* v. *Smith* (1841), 1 Q. B. 389.

(*s*) *Feise* v. *Wray* (1802), 3 East, 93; *Griffiths* v. *Perry* (1859), 1 E. & E. 680; *Ex p. Lambton* (1875), 10 Ch. App. 405, at p. 415; *cf. Ex p. Stapleton* (1879), 10 Ch. D. 586, C. A. As to conditional payment, see p. 225, *post*.

(*t*) *Morison* v. *Gray* (1824), 2 Bing. 260. See, too, the Bills of Lading Act 1855, *post*, Appendix I.

(*u*) *Feise* v. *Wray* (1802), 3 East, 93; *Tucker* v. *Humphrey* (1828), 4 Bing. 516; *cf. Ireland* v. *Livingston* (1872), L. R. 5 H. L. 395, at pp. 408, 409, *per* BLACKBURN, J. As to factors, see notes to *Kruger* v. *Wilcox* (1755), Tudor's *Merc. Cases* (3rd ed.), p. 370.

(*a*) *Gunn* v. *Bolckow, Vaughan & Co.* (1875), 10 Ch. App. 491, at p. 501, overruling on this point, it seems, *Bunney* v. *Poyntz* (1833), 4 B. & Ad. 568; but see *Benjamin on Sale* (8th ed.), p. 844.

can be shown to be substantially analogous to that of an ordinary seller (*b*).

But a buyer of goods who pays for them, and then on examination rejects them, has not the status of an unpaid seller, and has no lien on the goods for the price repayable to him (*c*).

39. Unpaid seller's rights.—(1) Subject to this and any other Act (*d*), notwithstanding that the property in the goods may have passed to the buyer, the unpaid seller of goods, as such, has by implication of law—

(a) a lien on the goods or right to retain them for the price while he is in possession of them;

(b) in case of the insolvency of the buyer, a right of stopping the goods in transit after he has parted with the possession of them;

(c) a right of re-sale as limited by this Act (*e*).

(2) Where the property in goods has not passed to the buyer, the unpaid seller has (in addition to his other remedies) a right of withholding delivery similar to and co-extensive with his rights of lien or retention and stoppage in transit where the property has passed to the buyer.

Derivation.—Section 39 of the 1893 Act.

Definitions.—For "buyer," "goods," "lien" and "property," see s. 61 (1), *post*. For "unpaid seller," see s. 38, *ante*.

Cross-references.—*Cf.* ss. 2 (1) and 8, *ante* (price); ss. 17 and 18, *ante* (passing of property); and ss. 27 and 28, *ante* (buyer's duty to pay price).

COMMENT

Subsection (1).—The origin of the seller's lien in English law is doubtful. It is probably founded in the custom of merchants (*f*). The term "lien" is unfortunate, because the seller's rights, arising out of his original ownership, in all cases exceed a mere lien. They

(*b*) *Cassaboglou* v. *Gibb* (1883), 11 Q. B. D. 797, at p. 804, *per* BRETT, M. R.; and, for examples, see *Jenkyns* v. *Usborne* (1844), 7 M. & Gr. 678, at p. 698 (re-sale by party who had contracted to buy goods); *Imperial Bank* v. *London & St. Katherine Docks Co.* (1877), 5 Ch. D. 195 (surety who has paid the price); *cf. Siffken* v. *Wray* (1805), 6 East, 371 (surety for price not entitled to stop goods in transit); *Longbottom & Co.* v. *Bass, Walker & Co.*, [1922] W. N. 245, C. A.

(*c*) *Lyons & Co.* v. *May & Baker*, [1923] 1 K. B. 685.

(*d*) See, as to lien, ss. 41 to 43 and ss. 47 and 48, *post*; as to stoppage in transit, ss. 44 to 48, *post*. See also the Factors Act 1889, *post*.

(*e*) See s. 48, *post*.

(*f*) *Blackburn on Sale* (1st ed.), p. 318.

"perhaps come nearer to the rights of a pawnee with a power of sale than to any other common law rights" (*g*).

Many of the cases fail to distinguish the seller's right of lien from his right of stoppage in transit. But it is important to keep them distinct, because, though the rights are analogous, they are in certain respects governed by different considerations (*h*). The seller's lien attaches when the buyer is in default, whether he be solvent or insolvent. The right of stoppage in transit only arises when the buyer is insolvent. Moreover, it does not arise until the seller's lien is gone, for it presupposes that the seller has parted with the possession as well as with the property in the goods. It is peculiar to contracts of sale, and can only be exercised by a seller or person in the position of a seller (*i*).

The courts look with great favour on the right of stoppage in transit on account of its intrinsic justice (*k*). The decisions on the subject are very numerous, but as JESSEL, M. R., observes,

"As to several of them there is great difficulty in reconciling them with principle; as to others there is great difficulty in reconciling them with one another; and as to the whole, the law on this subject is in a very unsatisfactory state" (*l*).

These decisions must now of course be read subject to the Act.

Subsection (2).—This subsection was necessary because it would be a contradiction in terms to speak of a man having a lien upon his own goods. The enactment is declaratory (*m*).

Scotland.— The words "or right to retain them" were inserted when the 1893 Bill was extended to Scotland.

The seller's "right of retention" in Scotland was more extensive than the seller's lien in England. Apart from statute the seller had the right to retain the goods not only for the price, but also for any other debt due from the buyer even if there had been a sub-sale (*n*). But the Mercantile Law Amendment (Scotland) Act 1856, s. 2 (now repealed), altered the law in the case of sub-sales, and the Sale of Goods Act appears to apply a uniform rule to both countries.

(*g*) *Blackburn on Sale* (1st ed.), p. 325; *cf. Bloxam* v. *Sanders* (1825), 4 B. & C. 941, at p. 948; *Schotsmans* v. *Lancashire and Yorkshire Rail. Co.* (1867), 2 Ch. App. 332, at p. 340.

(*h*) *Blackburn on Sale* (1st ed.), p. 308; *cf. Bolton* v. *Lancashire and Yorkshire Rail. Co.* (1866), L. R. 1 C. P. 431, at p. 439, *per* WILLES, J.

(*i*) *Sweet* v. *Pym* (1800), 1 East. 4; *Siffken* v. *Wray* (1805), 6 East, 371. See the definition of "seller" for this purpose in s. 38 (2), *ante*.

(*k*) See *Cassaboglou* v. *Gibbs* (1883), 11 Q. B. D. 797, at p. 804; *Kemp* v. *Falk* (1882), 7 App. Cas. 573, at p. 590.

(*l*) *Merchant Banking Co.* v. *Phœnix Co.* (1877), 5 Ch. D. 205, at p. 220 (case of seller's lien).

(*m*) *Griffiths* v. *Perry* (1859), 1 E. & E. 680, at p. 688; *Ex p. Chalmers* (1873), 8 Ch. App. 289, at p. 292. But see 19 L. Q. R. 113 *per* A. COHEN, K. C.

(*n*) Mercantile Law Commission, 1855, 2nd Report, pp. 8, 9, 44; *Melrose* v. *Hastie*, 1851, 13 Dunl. (Ct. of Sess.) 880.

The Scottish law as to stoppage in transit appears to be similar to English law (*o*).

40. Attachment by seller in Scotland.—In Scotland a seller of goods may attach the same while in his own hands or possession by arrestment or poinding; and such arrestment or poinding shall have the same operation and effect in a competition or otherwise as an arrestment or poinding by a third party.

Derivation.—Section 40 of the 1893 Act.

Definition.—For "seller," see s. 38 (2), *ante*.

COMMENT

The equivalent section in the 1893 Act was taken from s. 3 of the repealed Mercantile Law Amendment (Scotland) Act 1856. It is probably restrained by the provisions of s. 47, *post*. *Cf*. Green's *Encyclopaedia of Scots Law*, tit. "Poinding," as to the procedure generally.

Unpaid Seller's Lien

41. Seller's lien.—(1) Subject to this Act (*p*), the unpaid seller of goods who is in possession of them is entitled to retain possession of them until payment or tender of the price in the following cases:—

(a) where the goods have been sold without any stipulation as to credit(*q*);

(b) where the goods have been sold on credit, but the term of credit has expired (*r*);

(c) where the buyer becomes insolvent (*s*).

(2) The seller may exercise his right of lien notwithstanding that he is in possession of the goods as agent or bailee or custodier for the buyer (*t*).

Derivation.—Section 41 of the 1893 Act.

Definitions.—For "bailee," "buyer," "goods" and "lien," see s. 61

(*o*) *Allen* v. *Stein* (1790), M. 4949.

(*p*) See ss. 25 and 39, *ante*, and ss. 42, 43, 47 and 48, *post*.

(*q*) *Bloxam* v. *Sanders* (1825), 4 B. & C. 941, at p. 948; *Miles* v. *Gorton* (1834), 2 Cr. & M. 504, at p. 511.

(*r*) *New* v. *Swain* (1828), 1 Dan. & Lloyd, 193, *per* BAYLEY, J.; *Bunney* v. *Poyntz* (1833), 4 B. & Ad. 568, at p. 569, *per* LITTLEDALE, J.

(*s*) *Bloxam* v. *Sanders* (1825), 4 B. & C. 941; *Bloxam* v. *Morley* (1825), 4 B. & C. 951; *Griffiths* v. *Perry* (1859), 1 E. & E. 680; *Ex. p. Lambton* (1875), 10 Ch. App., at p. 415; *Gunn* v. *Bolckow, Vaughan & Co.* (1875), 10 Ch. App. 491, at p. 501.

(*t*) *Townley* v. *Crump* (1835), 4 Ad. & El. 58; *Grice* v. *Richardson* (1877), 3 App. Cas. 319, P. C.; *Poulton* v. *Anglo-American Oil Co.* (1911), 27 T. L. R. 216, C. A.

(1), *post*. For "unpaid seller," see s. 38, *ante*. For "insolvent," see s. 61 (3), *post*.

Cross-references.—*Cf.* ss. 2 (1) and 8, *ante* (price), and ss. 27 and 28, *ante* (buyer's duty to pay price).

COMMENT

Subsection (1).—The lien is a lien for the price only, and not for charges for keeping the goods, for they are kept against the buyer's will (*u*).

A sale on credit excludes the lien during the currency of the credit (*a*), unless there be a trade usage to the contrary (*b*).

As regards instalment contracts, MELLISH, L. J. says that, once the buyer has become insolvent,

> "The seller, notwithstanding he may have agreed to allow credit for the goods, is not bound to deliver any more goods under the contract until the price of the goods not yet delivered is tendered to him; and that if a debt is due to him for goods already delivered, he is entitled to refuse to deliver any more till he is paid the debt due for those already delivered, as well as the price of those still to be delivered . . . It would be strange if the right of a vendor who had agreed to deliver goods by instalments were less than that of a vendor who had sold specific goods" (*c*).

Even if the seller has broken his contract to deliver while the buyer is solvent, his lien revives on the buyer becoming insolvent, and the buyer's trustee is only entitled at most to nominal damages for the breach, unless the value of the goods at the time of breach was above the contract price (*d*).

When the seller exercises his right of lien, the buyer's trustee may affirm the contract and obtain the goods by tendering the price within a reasonable time (*e*), for it is clear law that the mere insolvency or bankruptcy of a party to a contract does not rescind it (*f*). But it seems that in the case of insolvency an agreement to rescind will be presumed on slight grounds (*g*).

A sub-purchaser also is probably entitled to obtain the goods by tendering the price to the original seller within a reasonable time (*h*).

Subsection (2).—This subsection was originally confined in the

(*u*) *Somes* v. *British Empire Shipping Co.* (1860), 8 H. L. Cas. 338, at p. 345 (shipwright's lien, but the rule was stated to apply to the seller's lien).

(*a*) *Spartali* v. *Benecke* (1850), 10 C. B. 212, at p. 223.

(*b*) *Field* v. *Lelean* (1861), 6 H. & N. 617, Ex. Ch.

(*c*) *Ex p. Chalmers* (1873), 8 Ch. App. 289, at p. 291; *cf. Ex p. Stapleton* (1879), 10 Ch. D. 586, C. A.

(*d*) *Valpy* v. *Oakeley* (1851), 16 Q. B. 941; *Griffiths* v. *Perry* (1859), 1 E. & E. 680.

(*e*) *Ex p. Stapleton* (1879), 10 Ch. D. 586, C. A.

(*f*) *Mess* v. *Duffus* (1901), 6 Com. Cas. 165 (action for damages for non-acceptance).

(*g*) *Morgan* v. *Bain* (1874), L. R. 10 C. P. 15. As to trustee's right to disclaim onerous contracts, see s. 54 of the Bankruptcy Act 1914.

(*h*) *Ex p. Stapleton*, (*supra*); and *cf. Kemp* v. *Falk* (1882), 7 App. Cas. 573, at p. 578, *per* Lord SELBORNE.

1893 Bill to the case where the buyer was insolvent (*i*). It was altered to its present form in Committee.

The seller may only rely upon this subsection so long as the lien or right of retention exists. If it is lost, as by the seller delivering the goods, it does not revive because the goods are returned to the seller as bailee for the buyer (*k*).

42. Part delivery.—Where an unpaid seller has made part delivery of the goods, he may exercise his right of lien or retention on the remainder, unless such part delivery has been made under such circumstances as to show an agreement to waive the lien (*l*) or right of retention.

Derivation.—Section 42 of the 1893 Act.

Definitions.—For "goods," "delivery" and "lien," see s. 61 (1), *post*. For "unpaid seller," see s. 38, *ante*.

Cross-references.—*Cf.* s. 29, *ante* (rules as to delivery); s. 31, *ante* (instalment deliveries); and ss. 39 and 41, *ante*, and s. 43, *post* (lien).

COMMENT

In a case where it was unsuccessfully contended that the delivery of part of a cargo to a sub-purchaser was a constructive delivery of the whole, Lord BLACKBURN says:

> "It is said that the delivery of a part is a delivery of the whole. It may be a delivery of the whole. In agreeing for the delivery of goods with a person, you are not bound to take an actual corporeal delivery of the whole in order to constitute such a delivery, and it may very well be that the delivery of a part of the goods is sufficient to afford strong evidence that it is intended as a delivery of the whole. If both parties intend it as a delivery of the whole, then it is a delivery of the whole; but if either of the parties does not intend it as a delivery of the whole, if either of them dissents, then it is not a delivery of the whole" (*m*).

The onus is on the party who relied upon the part delivery as a delivery of the whole to show that the part delivery took place under such circumstances as to make it a delivery of the whole (*n*).

Severable contract.—As regards severable contracts, if, for instance, delivery is to be made by three instalments, and the first instalment has been delivered and paid for, and the second has been delivered but not paid for, the seller cannot withhold delivery of the

(*i*) Thus following BLACKBURN, J. in *Cusack* v. *Robinson* (1861), 1 B. & S. 299, at p. 308.

(*k*) *Valpy* v. *Gibson* (1847), 4 C. B. 837; *United Plastics, Ltd.* v. *Reliance Electric*, [1977] 2 N. Z. L. R. 125.

(*l*) *Dixon* v. *Yates* (1833), 5 B. & Ad. 313, at p. 341 (lien); *Miles* v. *Gorton* (1834), 2 Cr. & M. 504; *cf. Ex p. Cooper* (1879), 11 Ch. D. 68, C. A. (stoppage in transit).

(*m*) *Kemp* v. *Falk* (1882), 7 App. Cas. 573, at p. 586; citing for the proposition *Dixon* v. *Yates* (*supra*).

(*n*) *Ex p. Cooper* (1879), 11 Ch. D. 68, C.A., at p. 73, *per* BRETT, L.J.

third instalment till he has been paid for both the second and third instalments, unless (1) the non-payment involves a repudiation of the contract under s. 31, *ante* (*o*), or (2) the buyer is insolvent (*p*). But any instalment which has been paid for must be delivered, even though the buyer be insolvent (*q*).

43. Termination of lien.—(1) The unpaid seller of goods loses his lien or right of retention in respect of them—

(a) when he delivers the goods to a carrier or other bailee or custodier for the purpose of transmission to the buyer (*r*) without reserving the right of disposal of the goods;

(b) when the buyer or his agent lawfully obtains possession of the goods (*s*);

(c) by waiver of the lien or right of retention.

(2) An unpaid seller of goods, who has a lien or right of retention in respect of them, does not lose his lien or right of retention by reason only that he has obtained judgment or decree for the price of the goods (*t*).

Derivation.—Section 43 of the 1893 Act.

Definitions.—For "bailee," "buyer," "delivery," "goods" and "lien," see s. 61 (1), *post*. For "unpaid seller," see s. 38, *ante*.

Cross-references.—*Cf.* ss. 2 (1) and 8, *ante* (price); s. 19, *ante* (reservation of right of disposal); s. 32, *ante* (delivery to carrier); and s. 49, *post* (action for price).

COMMENT

When goods are delivered to a carrier for transmission to the buyer the right of lien is lost, but a right of stoppage in transit arises should the

---

(*o*) *Steinberger* v. *Atkinson & Co.* (1914), 31 T. L. R. 110 (no repudiation).

(*p*) *Ex p. Chalmers* (1873), 8 Ch. App. 289.

(*q*) *Merchant Banking Co.* v. *Phœnix Bessemer Steel Co.* (1877), 5 Ch. D. 205; *Longbottom* v. *Bass Walker & Co.*, [1922] W. N. 245, C. A.

(*r*) *Bolton* v. *Lancashire and Yorkshire Rail. Co.* (1866), L. R. 1 C. P. 431, at p. 439, *per* WILLES, J.; Pollock and Wright, *Possession in the Common Law*, pp. 71, 72; and see the cases cited under s. 32, *ante*.

(*s*) *Hawes* v. *Watson* (1824), 2 B. & C. 540; *Cooper* v. *Bill* (1865), 3 H. & C. 722; *Dodsley* v. *Varley* (1840), 12 A. and E. 632; *Valpy* v. *Gibson* (1847), 4 C. B. 837 (goods returned to seller for purpose of repacking); *cf. Schotsmans* v. *Lancashire and Yorkshire Railway* (1867), 2 Ch. App. 332, at p. 335, as to stoppage in transit. The subsection in the 1893 Bill was amended in Committee. See also a Scottish case, *Paton's Trustees* v. *Finlayson*, 1923 S. C. 872 (potatoes lifted by buyer, but left on seller's land: right of retention upheld).

(*t*) *Houlditch* v. *Desanges* (1818), 2 Stark 337; *Scrivener* v. *Great Northern Rail. Co.* (1871), 19 W. R. 388. (*Quaere* whether the lien extends only to the price or also to costs on the judgment?)

buyer become insolvent, and if this is exercised the right of lien revives. Since, in the case of the buyer's insolvency, the two rights are similar in their effects, they are sometimes confused in the cases.

For the most part, the cases on what constituted an actual receipt within the meaning of the repealed section of the Statute of Frauds and the repealed s. 4 of the 1893 Act (*u*) appear to furnish the test for determining whether the seller's lien is gone or not. "The principle," says BLACKBURN, J.,

> "is that there cannot be an actual receipt by the vendee so long as the goods continue in the possession of the seller so as to preserve his lien" (*a*).

But the requirements of the two sections are not identical, for receipt of part of the goods by the buyer, coupled with acceptance, was enough to satisfy the old s. 4, though it would not wholly destroy the lien: s. 42, *ante*. And by s. 41 (2), *ante*, the seller may now exercise his right of lien notwithstanding that he is in possession of the goods as agent or bailee for the buyer, so that the cases before the 1893 Act are no longer of authority on this latter point (*b*).

Subject to s. 47, *post*, when goods, at the time of sale, are in the possession of a third person, there is no delivery to the buyer, and the seller's lien therefore is not divested till such third person attorns to the buyer (*c*).

Again, the seller may deliver the goods to the buyer on terms such that the buyer holds them as bailee for the seller; but in that case the seller has a special property in the goods arising out of the special agreement rather than a lien properly so called (*d*).

Waiver of lien.—The right of lien is given to the seller by implication of law: see s. 39, *ante*. It follows that it may be waived expressly. But it may also be waived by implication. The seller may reserve an express lien which excludes the implied one (*e*), or he may take a bill for the price which ordinarily would exclude his lien during its currency, though the lien would revive on its dishonour (*f*), or he may assent to a sub-sale (*g*), or he may part with the documents of title so as to exclude his lien under the provisions of the Factors Act, *post*, if the documents get into the hands of a holder for value. See, too, s. 55, *post*, as to negativing implied terms. The seller may also waive his lien by some wrongful act, such as dealing with the goods in a manner

(*u*) Repealed by s. 1 of the Law Reform (Enforcement of Contracts) Act 1954.

(*a*) *Cusack* v. *Robinson* (1861), 1 B. & S. 299, at p. 308; *cf. Baldey* v. *Parker* (1823), 2 B. & C. 37, at p. 44, *per* HOLROYD, J.

(*b*) *Baldey* v. *Parker* (*supra*), at p. 44; *Bill* v. *Bament* (1841), 9 M. & W. 36, at p. 41; *Cusack* v. *Robinson* (*supra*).

(*c*) *McEwan* v. *Smith* (1849), 2 H. L. Cas. 309, and *ante*, note to s. 29 (4).

(*d*) *Dodsley* v. *Varley* (1840), 12 A. & E. 632, at p. 634, *per* Lord DENMAN.

(*e*) *Re Leith's Estate* (1866), L. R. 1 P. C. 296, at p. 305. As to effect of taking subsequent security, see *Angus* v. *McLachlan* (1883), 23 Ch. D. 330.

(*f*) *Valpy* v. *Oakeley* (1851), 16 Q. B. 941, at p. 951; *Griffiths* v. *Perry* (1859), 1 E. & E. 680, at p. 688.

(*g*) *Knights* v. *Wiffen* (1870), L. R. 5 Q. B. 660; and see, too, s. 47, *post*.

inconsistent with the mere right to have possession of them, as by wrongfully re-selling or consuming them (*h*), or by claiming to keep them on some ground other than his right of lien. The practical result of this is that if sued for wrongful interference with goods by the buyer he cannot defeat the action by setting up his lien or pleading that the price was not tendered before action brought (*i*): but the damages will only be the value of the buyer's actual interest in the goods, that is, their value less the price, or that part of it which is unpaid (*k*).

Stoppage in transit

44. Right of stoppage in transit.—Subject to this Act (*l*), when the buyer of goods becomes insolvent the unpaid seller who has parted with the possession of the goods has the right of stopping them in transit, that is to say, he may resume possession of the goods as long as they are in course of transit, and may retain them until payment or tender of the price (*m*).

Derivation.—Section 44 of the 1893 Act.

Definitions.—For "buyer" and "goods," see s. 61 (1), *post*. For "unpaid seller," see s. 38, *ante*. For "course of transit," see s. 45, *post*.

Cross-references.—*Cf.* ss. 2 (1) and 8, *ante* (price), and ss. 27 and 28, *ante* (buyer's duty to pay price).

COMMENT

"The vendors being unpaid," says Lord ESHER,

> "and the purchasers having become insolvent, according to the law merchant the vendors had a right to stop the goods while *in transitu*, although the property in such goods might have passed to the purchasers. The doctrine of stoppage *in transitu* has always been construed favourably to the unpaid vendor" (*n*).

The right of stoppage in transit is a right against the goods themselves, and does not extend to policy moneys paid to the buyer by insurers for loss of or damage to the goods while in transit (*o*).

(*h*) *Gurr* v. *Cuthbert* (1843), 12 L. J. Ex. 309.

(*i*) See *Jones* v. *Tarleton* (1842), 9 M. & W. 675 (carrier); *Mulliner* v. *Florence* (1878), 3 Q. B. D. 484, C. A. (innkeeper); *Youngmann* v. *Briesemann* (1893), 67 L. T. 642, 644, C. A.

(*k*) *Chinery* v. *Viall* (1860), 5 H. & N. 288.

(*l*) See. s. 39, *ante*, and ss. 45 to 47, *post*.

(*m*) *Lickbarrow* v. *Mason* (1793), 6 East 22, *n*., H. L.; 1 Smith L. C. (13th ed.), p. 703; *Gibson* v. *Carruthers* (1841), 8 M. & W. 321; *Bolton* v. *Lancashire and Yorkshire Rail. Co.* (1866), L. R. 1 C. P. 431, at p. 439; *Bethell* v. *Clark* (1887), 19 Q. B. D. 553, at p. 561, affirmed, (1888), 20 Q. B. D. 615, C. A.; Pollock and Wright, *Possession in the Common Law*, pp. 72, 74, 214.

(*n*) *Bethell* v. *Clark* (1888), 20 Q. B. D. 615, at p. 617, C. A.

(*o*) *Berndtson* v. *Strang* (1868), 3 Ch. App. 588, at p. 591, *per* Lord CAIRNS; *cf. Phelps* v. *Comber* (1855), 29 Ch. D. 813, C. A.

The term "stoppage in transit" only applies in strictness to cases where the property in the goods has passed to the buyer (*p*). If the property has not passed, as when the seller has reserved the right of disposal, his rights depend upon s. 39 (2), *ante*, which is declaratory, as it was clear before the 1893 Act that the seller's right of withholding or countermanding delivery extended to executory, as well as executed, contracts when the buyer was insolvent (*q*).

As to the carrier's lien and rights when goods are stopped in transit, see s. 46 (4) *post*.

Since the right of stoppage in transit arises by implication of law (s. 39, *ante*), it follows that it may be waived by the seller under the provisions of s. 55, *post*.

45. Duration of transit.—(1) Goods are deemed to be in course of transit from the time when they are delivered to a carrier or other bailee or custodier for the purpose of transmission to the buyer, until the buyer or his agent in that behalf, takes delivery of them from the carrier or other bailee or custodier (*r*).

(2) If the buyer or his agent in that behalf obtains delivery of the goods before their arrival at the appointed destination, the transit is at an end (*s*).

(*p*) *Gibson* v. *Carruthers* (1841), 8 M. & W. 321.

(*q*) See *Griffths* v. *Perry* (1859), 1 E. & E. 680, at p. 688; *Ex p. Chalmers* (1873), 8 Ch. App. 289, at p. 292.

(*r*) For principle, see *Bolton* v. *Lancashire and Yorkshire Rail. Co.* (1866), L. R. 1 C. P. 431, at p. 439, *per* WILLES, J. For illustrations, see *Whitehead* v. *Anderson* (1842), 9 M. & W. 518 (promise by captain to deliver when satisfied as to freight, transit not ended); *Dodson* v. *Wentworth* (1842), 4 M. & Gr. 1080 (goods delivered by carrier to warehouse to await orders, transit ended); *Valpy* v. *Gibson* (1847), 4 C. B. 837 (goods delivered to shipping agent of buyer, transit ended); *Schotsmans* v. *Lancashire and Yorkshire Rail. Co.* (1867), 2 Ch. App. 332 (goods delivered to general ship owned by buyer, transit ended); *Coventry* v. *Gladstone* (1868), L. R. 6 Eq. 44 (overside orders given by mate to holder of bill of lading, transit not ended); *Ex p. Gibbes* (1875), 1 Ch. D. 101 (goods shipped to Liverpool and then put on railway for buyer, transit ended); *Ex p. Watson* (1877), 5 Ch. D. 35 (ineffectual interruption of transit); *Ex. p. Barrow* (1877), 6 Ch. D. 783 (goods warehoused by carrier as forwarding agent, transit not ended); *Ex p. Rosevear China Clay Co.* (1879), 11 Ch. D. 560 (goods shipped on ship hired by buyer, destination not stated, transit not ended); *Kemp* v. *Falk* (1882), 7 App. Cas. 573, at p. 584 (goods on ship, cash receipts instead of delivery orders given to buyer, transit not ended); *Ex p. Francis* (1887), 4 Morr. 146 (goods shipped in vessel of buyer's agent, transit ended); *Bethell* v. *Clark* (1888), 20 Q. B. D. 615, C. A. (goods ordered to be delivered to the *Darling Downs* to Melbourne, transit not ended by shipment); followed *Lyons* v. *Hoffnung* (1890), 15 App. Cas. 391, P. C.; *Ex p. Hughes* (1892), 9 Morr. 294 (break in transit); *Kemp* v. *Ismay* (1909), 100 L. T. 996 (goods bought by agent in his own name for transmission abroad).

(*s*) *Whitehead* v. *Anderson* (1842), 9 M. & W. 518, at p. 534; *Blackburn on Sale* (1st ed.), p. 249; *London and North Western Rail Co.* v. *Bartlett* (1861), 7 H. & N. 400 (alteration of

(3) If, after the arrival of the goods at the appointed destination, the carrier or other bailee or custodier acknowledges to the buyer or his agent that he holds the goods on his behalf and continues in possession of them as bailee or custodier for the buyer or his agent, the transit is at an end, and it is immaterial that a further destination for the goods may have been indicated by the buyer (*t*).

(4) If the goods are rejected by the buyer, and the carrier or other bailee or custodier continues in possession of them, the transit is not deemed to be at an end, even if the seller has refused to receive them back (*u*).

(5) When goods are delivered to a ship chartered by the buyer it is a question depending on the circumstances of the particular case whether they are in the possession of the master as a carrier or as agent to the buyer (*a*).

(6) Where the carrier or other bailee or custodier wrongfully refuses to deliver the goods to the buyer, or his agent in that behalf, the transit is deemed to be at an end (*b*).

(7) Where part delivery of the goods has been made to the buyer or his agent in that behalf, the remainder of the goods may be stopped in transit, unless such part delivery has been made under such circumstances as to show an agreement to give up possession of the whole of the goods (*c*).

Derivation.—Section 45 of the 1893 Act.

---

journey by agreement between carrier and consignee); see, too, dictum of BOWEN, L.J., in *Kendall* v. *Marshall, Stevens & Co.* (1883), 11 Q. B. D. 356, at p. 369.

(*t*) For principle, see *Kendall* v. *Marshall, Stevens & Co.* (1883), 11 Q. B. D. 356, C. A., where the carrier attorned to buyer's agent. In illustration, see *Dixon* v. *Baldwen* (1804), 5 East, 175; *Valpy* v. *Gibson* (1847), 4 C. B. 837, where a re-delivery to seller for special purpose did not revive right of stoppage; *Ex p. Miles* (1885), 15 Q. B. D. 39, C. A.

(*u*) *Bolton* v. *Lancashire and Yorkshire Rail. Co.* (1866), L. R. 1 C. P. 431; *James* v. *Griffin* (1837), 2 M. & W. 623.

(*a*) *Berndtson* v. *Strang* (1867), L. R. 4 Eq. 481, at p. 489; on appeal (1868), 3 Ch. App. 588, at p. 590, *per* Lord CAIRNS (the test is whether the master is the servant of the owner or the charterer); *Ex p. Rosevear China Clay Co.* (1879), 11 Ch. D. 560, C. A. (ship hired verbally); *cf. Schotsman* v. *Lancashire and Yorkshire Rail. Co.* (1867), 2 Ch. App. 332 (general ship owned by buyer, transit ended).

(*b*) *Bird* v. *Brown* (1850), 4 Exch. 786, at p. 790 (where carrier refused to deliver in consequence of an invalid notice to stop).

(*c*) *Bolton* v. *Lancashire and Yorkshire Railway* (1866), L. R. 1 C. P. 431, at p. 440, *per* WILLES, J.; *Ex p. Cooper* (1879), 11 Ch. D. 68, C. A.; *Kemp* v. *Falk* (1882), 7 App. Cas. 573, at p. 586, *per* Lord BLACKBURN; *cf.* s. 42, *ante*, as to seller's lien.

Definitions.—For "bailee," "buyer" and "goods," see s. 61 (1), *post*. For "seller," see s. 38 (2), *ante*, and s. 61 (1), *post*.

Cross-references.—*Cf.* ss. 39 and 44, *ante* (right of stoppage); s. 31, *ante* (part delivery); s. 32, *ante* (delivery to carrier); and s. 35, *ante* (rejection).

COMMENT

Duration of transit.—In order to form a clear notion of the meaning of the term "transit," two points should be noted: (1) The goods may be in transit although they have left the hands of the person to whom the seller intrusted them for transmission. It is immaterial how many agents' hands they have passed through if they have not reached their destination (*d*). (2) The term does not necessarily imply that the goods are in motion, for,

> "If the goods are deposited with one who holds them merely as an agent to forward and has the custody as such, they are as much *in transitu* as if they were actually moving" (*e*).

"The essential feature of a stoppage *in transitu*," says CAIRNS, L. J., "is that the goods should be . . . in the possession of a middleman . . ." (*f*).

When goods which have been sold are in the actual possession of a carrier or other bailee, three states of fact may exist with regard to them: First, the carrier or other bailee may hold them as agent for the seller; in that case the seller preserves his lien, and the right of stoppage in transit does not arise. Secondly, the goods may be *in medio*. The carrier or other bailee may hold them in his character as such, and not exclusively as the agent of either the seller or buyer. In that case the right of stoppage in transit exists. Thirdly, the carrier or other bailee may hold the goods, either originally or by subsequent attornment, solely as agent for the buyer. In that case there either has been no right of stoppage or it is determined. The difficulties that arise are rather difficulties of fact than of law.

Destination.—As regards the term "destination," BRETT, M. R. says that it means

> "sending [the goods] to a particular place to a particular person who is to receive them there, and not sending them to a particular place without saying to whom" (*g*);

(*d*) *Bethell* v. *Clark* (1888), 20 Q. B. D. 615, at p. 619, *per* FRY, L. J.; approved, *Lyons* v. *Hoffnung* (1890), 15 App. Cas. 391, P. C.

(*e*) *Blackburn on Sale* (1st ed.), p. 244.

(*f*) *Schotsmans* v. *Lancashire and Yorkshire Rail. Co.* (1867), 2 Ch. App. 332, at p. 338. *Cf.* the duration of transit for the purpose of insurance policies covering goods in transit: *Sadler Brothers Co.* v. *Meredith*, [1963] 2 Lloyd's Rep. 293; *Crows Transport, Ltd.* v. *Phoenix Assurance Co., Ltd.*, [1965] 1 All E. R. 596; [1965] 1 W. L. R. 383, C. A.

(*g*) *Ex p. Miles* (1885), 15 Q. B. D. 39, at p. 43, C. A.

and Lord FITZGERALD says,

> "Transit embraces not only the carriage of the goods to the place where delivery is to be made, but also delivery of the goods there according to the terms of the contract of conveyance" (*h*).

Termination of transit.—Where the attornment of the carrier is relied on, that attornment must be founded on mutual assent. If the carrier does not assent to hold the goods for the buyer, or if the buyer does not assent to his so holding them, there is no attornment (*i*).

The fact that the freight is unpaid is strong, though not conclusive, evidence that the carrier is in possession of the goods as carrier, and not as the buyer's agent (*k*).

In a case where goods were consigned to South Africa but were stopped by the buyer at Southampton, BAILHACHE, J., held that the transit was at an end, saying,

> "Where the original *transitus* is interrupted by the buyers, I think the test is whether the goods will be set in motion again without further orders from the buyers; if not, the transit is ended, and the right to stop lost" (*l*).

So, too, where goods which, under the contract, were to be delivered "free house, London," arrived in London port, and the buyer directed the carrier to warehouse them and await further instructions, it was held that the transit was at an end when the goods were collected from the steamer and warehoused in accordance with this instruction, and that in any case sub-s. (2) of the section would operate to terminate the transit (*m*).

Postal packets.—It has been held in New Zealand that packets containing goods sent by post by a seller to a buyer are not, while in the course of transit by post, delivered to or in the possession of "a carrier or other bailee" as no contract of bailment can arise. They cannot therefore be stopped in transit (*n*). The reasoning is difficult to follow, however, as a person may be a carrier without there being any contract of bailment (*o*). But the seller would seem to be prevented from exercising a right of stoppage in transit by s. 64 of the Post Office Act 1969, which protects postal packets from seizure under distress or in execution and from retention by virtue of a lien to the same extent as if they were the property of the Crown. Although there is no authority on

---

(*h*) *Kemp* v. *Falk* (1882), 7 App. Cas. 573, at p. 588.

(*i*) See *James* v. *Griffin* (1837), 2 M. & W. 623 (offer to attorn not accepted by buyer); *Kemp* v. *Falk* (1882), 7 App. Cas. 573, at pp. 584, 586 (carrier not agreeing to change his character). See also *Blackburn on Sale* (1st ed.), p. 248.

(*k*) *Kemp* v. *Falk* (1882), 7 App. Cas. 573, at p. 584.

(*l*) *Reddall* v. *Union Castle Steamship Co.* (1914), 84 L. J. K. B. 360, 362.

(*m*) *Plischke* v. *Allison Bros. Ltd.*, [1936] 2 All E. R. 1009.

(*n*) *Postmaster General* v. *W. H. Jones & Co.*, [1957] N. Z. L. R. 829, applying *Triefus & Co.* v. *Post Office*, [1957] 2 All E. R. 387; [1957] 2 Q. B. 352, C. A.

(*o*) *Cf. Badische Anilin and Soda Fabrik* v. *Basle Chemical Works*, [1898] A. C. 200, at p. 204; *Schotsman* v. *Lancashire and Yorkshire Rail. Co.* (1867), L. R. 2 Ch. 332, at p. 338.

the point, the right of stoppage in transit would probably be held to be in the nature of a lien for the purpose of this section.

46. How stoppage in transit is effected.—(1) The unpaid seller may exercise his right of stoppage in transit either by taking actual possession of the goods (*p*) or by giving notice of his claim to the carrier or other bailee or custodier in whose possession the goods are (*q*).

(2) The notice may be given either to the person in actual possession of the goods or to his principal.

(3) If given to the principal, the notice is ineffective unless given at such time and under such circumstances that the principal, by the exercise of reasonable diligence, may communicate it to his servant or agent in time to prevent a delivery to the buyer (*r*).

(4) When notice of stoppage in transit is given by the seller to the carrier, or other bailee or custodier in possession of the goods, he must re-deliver the goods to, or according to the directions of, the seller (*s*); and the expenses of the re-delivery must be borne by the seller.

ILLUSTRATIONS

(1) Goods are stopped in transit while in the hands of a railway company. The company has a lien for the charge of carrying these particular goods, but no general lien for other moneys due from the consignee, even though the consignment note purports to create such a lien (*t*).

(2) Goods sent by sea are stopped in transit at a port short of the destination. The unpaid seller declines to take any action with regard to the goods. He is liable for freight to destination and any landing charges that may have been incurred (*u*).

Derivation.—Subsections (1)–(3) are taken from s. 46 (1) in the 1893 Act. Subsection (4) is taken from s. 46 (2) in the 1893 Act.

Definitions.—For "bailee," "buyer," "delivery" and "goods," see

(*p*) *Snee* v. *Prescot* (1743), 1 Atk. 245, at p. 250, *per* Lord HARDWICKE; *Whitehead* v. *Anderson* (1842), 9 M. & W. 518, at p. 534, *per* PARKE, B.

(*q*) *Litt* v. *Cowley* (1816), 7 Taunt. 169, at p. 170, *per* GIBBS, C. J.

(*r*) *Whitehead* v. *Anderson* (1842), 9 M. & W. 518; *Ex p. Watson* (1877), 5 Ch. D. 35, C. A.; *Kemp* v. *Falk* (1882), 7 App. Cas. 573, at p. 585; *cf. Phelps* v. *Comber* (1885), 29 Ch. D. 813, C. A. (notice to consignee to hold proceeds ineffectual).

(*s*) *The Tigress* (1863), 32 L. J. P. M. & A. 97, at p. 102.

(*t*) *United States Steel Products Co.* v. *Great Western Rail. Co.*, [1916] 1 A. C. 189, 195, 916. It is not clear whether a forwarding agent in possession of goods has any lien over them. The point was raised in *Langley, Beldon and Gaunt, Ltd.* v. *Morley*, [1965] 1 Lloyd's Rep. 297, but was not decided as the forwarding agent was not in fact in possession of the goods.

(*u*) *Booth Steamship Co.* v. *Cargo Fleet Iron Co.*, [1916] 2 K. B. 570, C. A.

s. 61 (1), *post*. For "unpaid seller," see s. 38, *ante*, For "seller," see s. 38 (2), *ante*, and s. 61 (1), *post*.

Cross-references.—*Cf*. ss. 39 and 44, *ante* (right of stoppage), and s. 45, *ante* (duration of transit).

COMMENT

"The seller," says Dr. LUSHINGTON,

> "exercises his right of stoppage *in transitu* at his own peril, and it is incumbent upon the master to give effect to a claim, as soon as he is satisfied it is made by the vendor, unless he is aware of a legal defeasance of the claim" (*a*).

If, after notice, lawfully given, the carrier delivers to the consignee or refuses to deliver to the seller, he is guilty of a wrongful interference with the goods (*b*). In case of real doubt he should resort to an interpleader (*c*), for if the transit has ended and he wrongfully restores the goods to the seller, he is liable to the buyer in an action for wrongful interference (*d*). The seller also has a remedy by injunction (*e*), or, if the goods be in the hands of the master of a ship, by arrest of the ship (*f*).

In a case in the Court of Appeal, BRAMWELL, L. J., doubted whether there was any obligation on the part of the principal to send on a notice of stoppage to his agent (*g*); but, when the case went to the House of Lords, Lord BLACKBURN expressly repudiated this doubt (*h*). Though, as between seller and carrier, the expenses of stoppage and re-delivery fall on the seller, it may be that the seller would be able to prove for them against the buyer's estate.

Re-sale etc. by buyer

47. Effect of sub-sale etc. by buyer.—(1) Subject to this Act (*i*), the unpaid seller's right of lien or retention or stoppage in transit is not affected by any sale or other

(*a*) *The Tigress* (1863), 32 L. J. P. M. & A. 97, at p. 101.

(*b*) Under the Torts (Interference with Goods) Act 1977. See *ante*, p. 27.

(*c*) *The Tigress* (*supra*), at p. 102; *cf. Litt* v. *Cowley* (1816), 7 Taunt. 169 at p. 170; *Pontifex* v. *Midland Rail. Co.* (1877), 3 Q. B. D. 23; discussed, *Booth Steamship Co.* v. *Cargo Fleet Iron Co.*, [1916] 2 K. B. 570, C. A.

(*d*) *Taylor* v. *Great Eastern Rail. Co.*, [1901] 1 K. B. 774.

(*e*) *Schotsmans* v. *Lancashire and Yorkshire Rail. Co.* (1867), 2 Ch. App. 332, at p. 340.

(*f*) *The Tigress* (1863), 32 L. J. P. M. & A. 97.

(*g*) *Ex p. Falk* (1880), 14 Ch. D. 446, C. A.

(*h*) *Kemp* v. *Falk* (1882), 7 App. Cas. 573, at p. 585.

(*i*) See s. 25, *ante*, and *Cahn* v. *Pockett's Bristol Channel Co.*, [1899] 1 Q. B. 643, at p. 664, C. A.

disposition of the goods which the buyer may have made (*k*), unless the seller has assented to it (*l*).

(2) Where a document of title to goods has been lawfully transferred to any person as buyer or owner of the goods, and that person transfers the document (*m*) to a person who takes it in good faith and for valuable consideration, then—

(a) if the last-mentioned transfer was by way of sale the unpaid seller's right of lien or retention or stoppage in transit is defeated; and

(b) if the last-mentioned transfer was by way of pledge or other disposition for value, the unpaid seller's right of lien or retention or stoppage in transit can only be exercised subject to the rights of the transferee.

ILLUSTRATIONS

(1) A, an oil merchant, sells oil to B without appropriating any particular oil to the contract. B sells 2 tons of the oil to C, and gives him a delivery order. C lodges the delivery order with A, indorsing it "please wait our orders." B falls into arrears with his payments, and A refuses to deliver the 2 tons to C. He has not lost his seller's lien, and is entitled to refuse, since nothing he has done was an assent to the re-sale (*n*).

(2) A having 6,000 bags of mowra seed sells 2,600 to B, which B pays for by cheque. A gives B delivery orders for the 2,600 bags, and B sells the seed to C, and indorses the delivery orders to him. If B's cheque is dishonoured, A has lost his right of lien and must deliver the seed to C (*o*).

Derivation.—Section 47 of the 1893 Act. The division into subsections is new.

Definitions.—For "buyer," "document of title," "goods," "lien"

(*k*) As to seller's lien, see *Dixon* v. *Yates* (1833), 5 B. & Ad. 313, at p. 339; *Farmeloe* v. *Bain* (1876), 1 C. P. D. 445. As to stoppage in transit, see *Craven* v. *Ryder* (1816), 6 Taunt. 433; *Ex p. Golding Davis & Co.* (1880), 13 Ch. D. 628; *Kemp* v. *Falk* (1882), 7 App. Cas. 573. As to delivery orders before the Factors Act 1877, see *McEwan* v. *Smith* (1849), 2 H. L. Cas. 309; and *Blackburn on Sale* (1st ed.), p. 302, which shows the common law effects of these documents.

(*l*) *Blackburn on Sale* (1st ed.), p. 271; *Stoveld* v. *Hughes* (1811), 14 East, 308; *Pearson* v. *Dawson* (1858), E. B. & E. 448; *Woodley* v. *Coventry* (1863), 2 H. & C. 164; *Knights* v. *Wiffen* (1870), L. R. 5 Q. B. 660; *Merchant Banking Co.* v. *Phoenix Bessemer Co.* (1877), 5 Ch. D. 205; *Mount* v. *Jay & Jay*, [1959] 3 All E. R. 307; [1960] 1 Q. B. 159.

(*m*) It seems that this means the identical document as that transferred to the buyer, even though such a construction may lead to very artificial results: see *per* SALMON, J. in *Mount* v. *Jay & Jay* (*supra*).

(*n*) *Mordaunt Brothers* v. *British Oil and Cake Mills*, [1910] 2 K. B. 502; *cf. Mount* v. *Jay & Jay*, [1959] 3 All E. R. 307; [1960] 1 Q. B. 159.

(*o*) *Ant. Jurgens Margarinefabrieken* v. *Louis Dreyfus & Co.*, [1914] 3 K. B. 40 (*issue* of delivery order by A = *transfer* of document of title).

and "sale," see s. 61 (1), *post*. For "good faith," see s. 61 (3), *post*. For "unpaid seller," see s. 38, *ante*. For "seller," see s. 38 (2), *ante*, and s. 61 (1), *post*.

Cross-references.—*Cf.* ss. 39 and 41, *ante* (right of lien), and ss. 39 and 44, *ante* (right of stoppage).

COMMENT

Subsection (2) reproduces and develops s. 10 of the Factors Act 1889, *post*, the effect of which appears to be (i) to affirm the common law effect of the transfer of a bill of lading, and (ii) to put all the documents of title mentioned in s. 1 of that Act on the same footing as bills of lading for the purposes of that Act.

Transfer of bill of lading.—As regards bills of lading the law appears to be as follows:—

(1) As between buyer and seller, that is to say the immediate parties to the contract of sale, the indorsement of the bill of lading does not affect the right of stoppage, nor does a further indorsement by the buyer affect the right unless the indorsement be for value (*p*), but an antecedent debt may constitute such value (*q*).

(2) If the holder of the bill of lading re-sells the goods or otherwise disposes of them for value to a third person who pays the money, such third person acquires his interest in the goods subject to the original seller's right of stoppage in transit, unless he gets a transfer of the bill of lading (*r*).

(3) Since the Bills of Lading Act 1855, *post*, Appendix I, as well as before, a bill of lading may be indorsed by way of mortgage, pledge, or other security, and not only by way of absolute sale (*s*). Where a bill of lading is so transferred, the original seller retains his right of stoppage subject to the rights of the incumbrancer, and, further, he may compel the incumbrancer to resort to other goods pledged with him by his debtor, if such there be, before resorting to the goods covered by the bill of lading (*t*).

(4) The right of stoppage in transit is wholly defeated when the bill of lading is assigned absolutely for a consideration which is wholly paid (*u*).

(5) When the bill of lading is transferred to a sub-purchaser absolutely and for value, but that value is unpaid wholly or in part,

---

(*p*) *Lickbarrow* v. *Mason* (1793), 6 East, 22, *n*., H. L.; 1 Smith L. C. (13th ed.), p. 703.

(*q*) *Leask* v. *Scott* (1877), 2 Q. B. D. 376, C. A.; dissenting from *Rodger* v. *Comptoir d'Escompte* (1869), L. R. 2 P. C. 393.

(*r*) *Kemp* v. *Falk* (1882), 7 App. Cas. 573, at p. 582, *per* Lord BLACKBURN.

(*s*) *Sewell* v. *Burdick* (1884), 10 App. Cas. 74. But as to Scotland, see *Hayman* v. *McLintock*, 1907 S. C. 936.

(*t*) *Re Westzinthus* (1833), 5 B. & Ad. 817; *Spalding* v. *Ruding* (1843), 6 Beav. 376; approved *Kemp* v. *Falk* (1882), 7 App. Cas. 573 at p. 585; *cf. Coventry* v. *Gladstone* (1868), L. R. 6 Eq. 44.

(*u*) *Lickbarrow* v. *Mason* (1793), 1 Smith L. C. (13th ed.), p. 703; *Leask* v. *Scott* (1877), 2 Q. B. D. 376, C. A.

there is probably no right to stop against the sub-purchaser for the original purchase price, even to the extent of what remains to be paid by the sub-purchaser (*a*).

See further the Bills of Lading Act 1855, *post*, Appendix I.

Note that this section may override the operation of s. 19, *ante*, while according with the provisions of s. 25, *ante*.

Rescission: and re-sale by seller

48.—Rescission: and re-sale by seller.—(1) Subject to this section, a contract of sale is not rescinded by the mere exercise by an unpaid seller of his right of lien or retention or stoppage in transit (*b*).

(2) Where an unpaid seller who has exercised his right of lien or retention or stoppage in transit re-sells the goods, the buyer acquires a good title to them as against the original buyer (*c*).

(3) Where the goods are of a perishable nature (*d*), or where the unpaid seller gives notice to the buyer of his intention to re-sell, and the buyer does not within a reasonable time pay or tender the price, the unpaid seller may re-sell the goods and recover from the original buyer damages for any loss occasioned by his breach of contract (*e*).

(4) Where the seller expressly reserves the right of re-sale in case the buyer should make default, and on the buyer making default re-sells the goods, the original contract of sale is thereby rescinded but without prejudice to any claim the seller may have for damages (*f*).

Derivation.—Section 48 of the 1893 Act.

Definitions.—For "contract of sale," see s. 2 (1), *ante*, and s. 62 (1),

---

(*a*) See *Ex p. Golding Davis & Co.* (1880), 13 Ch. D. 628, C. A.; *ex p. Falk* (1880), 14 Ch. D. 446, C. A.; on appeal, *sub nom. Kemp* v. *Falk* (1882), 7 App. Cas. 573; *cf. Phelps* v. *Comber* (1885), 29 Ch. D. 813, at p. 821; and see *Scrutton on Charterparties, etc.* (18th ed.), p. 185, art. 98.

(*b*) For an examination of the decisions before the 1893 Act, and the effect of this section on those decisions, see *Benjamin on Sale* (8th ed.), pp. 935–952.

(*c*) *Milgate* v. *Kebble* (1841), 3 M. & Gr. 100; *cf. Lord* v. *Price* (1874), L. R. 9 Exch. 54; *cf.* also s. 24, *ante*.

(*d*) *Cf. Maclean* v. *Dunn* (1828), 4 Bing. 722, at p. 728, where there had been a refusal to accept.

(*e*) *Page* v. *Cowasjee* (1866), L. R. 1 P. C. 127, at p. 145; *Lord* v. *Price* (1874), L. R. 9 Exch. 54, at p. 55; *ex p. Stapleton* (1879), 10 Ch. D. 586, C. A.

(*f*) *Lamond* v. *Davall* (1847), 9 Q. B. 1030.

post. For "buyer" and "goods," see s. 61 (1), *post*. For "unpaid seller," see s. 38, *ante*.

Cross-references.—*Cf.* ss. 39 and 41, *ante* (right of lien); ss. 39 and 44, *ante* (right of stoppage); ss. 12 and 21 to 26, *ante* (transfer of title); ss. 2 (1) and 8, *ante* (price); ss. 27 and 28, *ante* (buyer's duty to pay price); ss. 49 and 50, *post* (remedies of seller); s. 10 (stipulations as to time); and s. 59, *post* (reasonable time a question of fact).

COMMENT

As long as the buyer is in default he is not entitled to the immediate possession of the goods, and therefore cannot maintain an action for wrongful interference even against a wrongdoer in possession (*g*).

Re-sale by seller.—In *ex p. Stapleton* (*h*) it was said that when the buyer was insolvent, the seller might re-sell unless the trustee or a sub-purchaser tendered the price within a reasonable time, and nothing was said about notice. But as a fact the seller in that case gave fair notice of his intention to re-sell.

Subsection (3) enables the seller to make the time of payment of the essence of the contract, so that when he later re-sells the seller is treating the buyer's failure to pay as a repudiation of the contract, and is re-selling as full owner (*i*). It would seem to follow that the seller is entitled to keep any extra profit, and that the law relating to deposits is that which generally governs deposits when a sale goes off through the fault of the buyer (*k*).

As to sale of perishable goods by order of the court, see R. S. C. O. 29, r. 4.

Quære whether in case of urgency, the seller in possession of the goods is justified in selling them on behalf of the buyer, acting as an "agent of necessity" (*l*).

Express reservation of title.—Contracts for the sale of goods commonly provide that although the buyer is entitled to immediate possession of the goods, property in the goods shall remain in the seller until the price is paid or some other condition performed.

Where there is such a provision, if the buyer repudiates the contract, for example by making it clear that he will not pay for the goods, the seller may terminate the contract and recover the goods (*m*). Until such

---

(*g*) *Lord* v. *Price* (1874), L. R. 9 Exch. 54 (auction sale, goods neither removed nor paid for).

(*h*) (1879), 10 Ch. D. 586, C. A.

(*i*) *R. V. Ward, Ltd.* v. *Bignall*, [1967] 2 All E. R. 449; [1967] 1 Q. B. 534, C. A., overruling *Gallagher* v. *Shilcock*, [1949] 1 All E. R. 921; [1949] 2 K. B. 765. Generally stipulations as to time of payment are not deemed to be of the essence of a contract of sale—see s. 10, *ante*.

(*k*) P. 24, *ante*.

(*l*) *Prager* v. *Blatspiel*, [1924] 1 K. B. 566, *per* MCCARDIE, J. But on the facts the sale was held not to be *bona fide*, and the dicta of MCCARDIE, J., were disapproved by SCRUTTON, L. J., in *Jebara* v. *Ottoman Bank*, [1927] 2 K. B. 254, at pp. 271, 272. See note on agency of necessity, *ante*, notes to s. 21 (2).

(*m*) Subject to special provisions where the Hire-Purchase Act 1965 or the Consumer Credit Act 1974 applies.

a termination the buyer has the right to possession and use of the goods. It will be a question of construction of each contract whether the buyer is also entitled to deal with the goods in any other way, as by disposing of them (*n*). Even if the contract forbids it, however, if a buyer does dispose of the goods, he may give a good title to a *bona fide* third party under s. 25, *ante*.

A reservation of title clause gives the seller (so long at least as the buyer continues to hold the goods sold in the form in which they are sold) a proprietary right which will prevent the goods forming part of the general assets of the buyer for distribution amongst his creditors in the event of his insolvency (*o*).

Reservation of equitable interest.—If only an equitable interest in the goods is reserved to the seller, the transaction is treated as a transfer of the goods to the buyer followed by a grant back of the equitable title by way of charge (*p*). In many cases where the buyer is a company such a charge will be either a floating charge or charge which would require registration as a bill of sale if executed by an individual and particulars of it must be submitted to the Companies Registrar for registration within 21 days of the notional re-transfer failing which it will be void against the liquidator and creditors of the company (*q*). Where the buyer is an individual the charge may have to be registered as a bill of sale and comply with the other requirements of the Bills of Sale Acts (*r*).

Goods incorporated with other goods or with land.—Where goods are incorporated with other goods in such a way that they have not lost their identity and are removable without injury to the remaining goods, such incorporation does not prevent the seller from relying upon a retention of title clause by which the legal title to the good is retained (*s*). The seller's rights over the goods are lost, however,

---

(*n*) *Re Anchor Line* (*Henderson Brothers*), *Ltd.*, [1936] 2 All E. R. 941; [1937] Ch. 1, C. A.

(*o*) *McEntire* v. *Crossley Brothers, Ltd.*, [1895] A. C. 457, H. L. If the buyer is an individual and goes bankrupt, the reputed ownership provisions of s. 38 of the Bankruptcy Act 1914 may, however, sometimes defeat the seller's claim: see *Re Keen*, [1902] 1 K. B. 555, D. C.; *Re Weibking*, [1902] 1 K. B. 713; *Re Fox*, [1948] 1 All E. R. 849; [1948] Ch. 407, D. C. There is no equivalent statutory provision in the case of company liquidations.

(*p*) *Re Bond Worth, Ltd.*, [1979] 3 All E. R. 919; [1980] Ch. 228.

(*q*) *Re Bond Worth, supra*. Where the legal title is retained by the seller the charge is not created by the buyer and therefore does not require registration: see *Aluminium Industrie Vaassen B. V.* v. *Romalpa Aluminium, Ltd.*, [1976] 2 All E. R. 552, at p. 557; [1976] 1 W. L. R. 676, at pp. 682, 683; *Re Bond Worth, supra*, at pp. 957 and 271; *Borden* (*U.K.*), *Ltd.* v. *Scottish Timber Products, Ltd.*, [1979] 3 All E.R. 961 at p. 973; [1981] Ch. 25, at p. 45. Note that it is sufficient to protect the charge to deliver the prescribed particulars, even if the registrar fails or refuses to register the charge: *N. V. Slavenburg's Bank* v. *Intercontinental Natural Resources, Ltd.*, [1980] 1 All E. R. 955; [1980] 1 W.L.R. 1076.

(*r*) See generally 4 Halsbury's Laws (4th Edn.) paras. 676 *et seq*. The formalities are such that a standard form retention of title clause which constitutes a bill of sale will never be valid in practice.

(*s*) *Firestone Tire & Rubber Co. of Canada, Ltd.* v. *Industrial Acceptance Corpn.* (1971), 17 D. L. R. (3d) 229 (Sup. Ct. of Can.)

if they are not capable of removal without material injury (*t*) or if only equitable and not legal ownership is retained (*u*).

If a seller of goods to a manufacturer, who knows his goods are to be used in the manufacturing process before they are paid for wishes to reserve to himself an effective security for the payment of the price, then, except as set out above, he cannot rely upon a simple reservation of title clause. If he wishes to acquire rights over the finished products, he can only do so by express contractual stipulation (*a*). But for such a provision to be valid in the case of a sale to an individual it would probably have to comply with the requirements of the Bills of Sale Acts as to form and registration (*b*). In the case of a sale to a company, the requirements of the Companies Act 1948 as to registration would again have to be met if it is not to be void against the liquidator and creditors of the company (*c*).

A retention of title clause will be ineffective, however, once goods are attached to land so that they become part of the land and lose their separate identity as goods (*d*).

Goods sold for resale.—Where goods are sold for resale and rights are reserved to the original seller over the proceeds of the re-sale as security for payment of the original price, the rights over the proceeds of sale normally take effect as a charge over book debts, so that in the case of a company the requirements of the Companies Act as to registration must again be complied with (*e*). But the Court of Appeal has held (*f*) that in a case in which the effect of the initial contract was that until payment the goods sold were to be held by the buyer as bailee and agent for the seller and that any resale effected by the buyer, although in the name of the buyer, was also to be made by it as agent for the original seller, the original seller was entitled to the proceeds of such resale as against a receiver of the assets of the buyer who had been appointed by a debenture holder, by the application of equitable principles of tracing (*g*).

(*t*) What is capable of removal without material injury will change in the light of technological advances: see Goode on *Hire Purchase Law and Practice* (2nd ed.), p. 750, cited with approval in *Ilford-Riverton Airways, Ltd.* v. *Aero Trades (Western), Ltd.*, [1977] 5 W. W. R. 193 (Manit. C. A.) (rented aircraft engine did not become part of aircraft by accession).

(*u*) *Regina Chevrolet Sales, Ltd.* v. *Riddell*, [1942] 3 D. L. R. 159 (Sask. C. A.).

(*a*) *Borden (U.K.), Ltd.* v. *Scottish Timber Products, Ltd.*, [1979] 3 All E. R. 961, at p. 971; [1981] Ch. 25, at p. 42.

(*b*) See *Borden (U.K.), Ltd.* v. *Scottish Timber Products, Ltd.*, (*supra*) at pp. 974 and 46–47, *per* BUCKLEY, L. J.

(*c*) *Borden (U. K.), Ltd.* v. *Scottish Timber Products, Ltd.*, *supra*, *per* BUCKLEY and TEMPLEMAN, L. JJ.; *Re Bond Worth, supra.*

(*d*) *Re Yorkshire Joinery Co., Ltd.* (1967), 111 Sol. Jo. 701.

(*e*) *Re Interview, Ltd.*, [1975] I. R. 382.

(*f*) *Aluminium Industrie Vaassen B. V.* v. *Romalpa Industries, Ltd.*, [1976] 2 All E. R. 552; [1976] 1 W. L. R. 676, C. A.

(*g*) The effect of such an arrangement in other respects seems unclear. For example, would the sub-buyer be able to sue the principal if the goods were defective or does the

Property and possession transferred to buyer.—It has commonly been assumed that if the buyer has acquired both title and possession under a contract, then in the absence of an express provision in the contract, or elsewhere, giving the seller rights over the goods, he will not be entitled to any such rights, even if he is entitled to treat the contract as at an end because it has been repudiated by the buyer (*h*).

But there is no clear authority in support of this proposition. Moreover, it has been decided that if property has passed but possession remains in the seller and the seller treats the contract as terminated by reason of the buyer's breach, the property in the goods automatically revests in the seller (*i*). There would seem to be no logical ground for holding that the question whether the property revests in the seller should turn on whether the seller or buyer is in possession at the material time (*k*).

If property does revest in the seller when he treats the contract as being at an end, he will have the same right to recover the property as if it had never passed to the buyer. This would seem to be so even if the buyer becomes bankrupt or, being a company goes into liquidation, or the trustee in bankruptcy takes the property subject to the rights of the seller (*l*).

Even if property does not remain or revest in the seller, in special circumstances, if an unpaid seller is entitled under the contract to give and does give special directions to the buyer as to the manner in which the goods are to be dealt with by the buyer, the seller may retain a beneficial interest in the goods until the price is paid (*m*).

---

agency extend only to the delivery of the goods and receipt of the price and not to the contract with the sub-buyer?

(*h*) See, *e.g.*, *Re Shackleton, Ex parte Whittaker* (1875), 10 Ch. App. 446, C.A.; *Re Wait*, [1927] 1 Ch. 606, at p. 640, *per* ATKIN L. J.

(*i*) *R. V. Ward, Ltd.* v. *Bignall*, [1967] 2 All E. R. 449; [1967] 1 Q. B. 534, C. A. *Cf. Page* v. *Cowasjee* (1866), L. R. 1 P. C. 127, at p. 145.

(*k*) There is nothing in *Ward* v. *Bignall*, *supra*, to suggest any basis for such a distinction, and indeed DIPLOCK, L. J., said, at pp. 457 and 550, "It is, of course, well established that where a contract for the sale of goods is rescinded after the property in the goods has passed to the buyer the rescission divests the buyer of his property in the goods". In using the terms "rescind" and "rescission" in this context, DIPLOCK, L. J., made it clear that he was referring to the seller's "right to treat the contract as repudiated by the buyer". While there does not appear to be any clear prior authority in support of this proposition, it would seem to be widely accepted where the contract is terminated before the buyer obtains possession.

(*l*) *Re Eastgate, Ex parte Ward*, [1905] 1 K. B. 465; *Tilley* v. *Bowman, Ltd.*, [1910] 1 K. B. 745, where goods were obtained by misrepresentation and the seller was allowed to rescind the contract and recover the goods from the trustees in bankruptcy.

(*m*) *Cf. Ex parte Banner* (1876), 2 Ch. D. 278, C. A.; *Tooke v. Hollingworth* (1793), 5 Term. Rep. 215; and compare the position where the seller is trustee of the purchase price, *post*, p. 252.

PART VI

ACTIONS FOR BREACH OF THE CONTRACT

Seller's remedies

49. Action for price.—(1) Where, under a contract of sale, the property in the goods has passed to the buyer, and he wrongfully neglects or refuses to pay for the goods according to the terms of the contract, the seller may maintain an action against him for the price of the goods (*n*).

(2) Where, under a contract of sale, the price is payable on a day certain irrespective of delivery and the buyer wrongfully neglects or refuses to pay such price, the seller may maintain an action for the price, although the property in the goods has not passed, and the goods have not been appropriated to the contract (*o*).

(3) Nothing in this section prejudices the right of the seller in Scotland to recover interest on the price from the date of tender of the goods, or from the date on which the price was payable, as the case may be.

ILLUSTRATIONS

(1) Contract for sale of goods to be paid for "net cash against documents on arrival of the steamer." If the buyer refuses the tender of the documents, the claim is for damages, and not for the price, for the price is not "payable on a day certain irrespective of delivery" (*p*).

(2) Goods sold and delivered, terms 6 months' credit, and then payment to be made by bills at 2 or 3 months at buyer's option. The cause of action does not arise till 9 months after date of the contract, and the Statute of Limitations begins to run from that time, and not from the time of delivery of the goods (*q*).

Derivation.—Section 49 of the 1893 Act.

Definitions.—For "contract of sale," see s. 2 (1), *ante*, and s. 61 (1),

---

(*n*) *Scott* v. *England* (1844), 2 D. & L. 520 (re-sale of goods bought at auction, but not yet paid for); *cf. Kymer* v. *Suwercropp* (1807), 1 Camp. 109 (goods stopped in transit); *Alexander* v. *Gardner* (1835), 1 Bing. N. C. 671 (goods lost at sea).

(*o*) *Dunlop* v. *Grote* (1845), 2 Car. & Kir 153.

(*p*) *Stein Forbes & Co.* v. *County Tailoring Co.* (1916), 86 L. J. K. B. 448, citing the notes to *Pordage* v. *Cole*, Saunders' Reports (ed. E. V. Williams) (6th ed.), Vol. I, p. 319 1. *Cf. Colley* v. *Overseas Exporters*, [1921] 3 K. B. 302 (f.o.b. contract); *Napier* v. *Dexters, Ltd.* (1926), 26 Ll. L. Rep. 62 (considering previous cases).

(*q*) *Helps* v. *Winterbottom* (1831), 2 B. & Ad. 431; *cf. Schneider* v. *Foster* (1857), 2 H. & N. 4 (where the buyer has an option to take credit or pay cash and opts to pay cash, the cause of action accrues at once).

post. For "action," "buyer," "delivery," "goods," "property" and "seller," see s. 61 (1), *post.*

Cross-references.—*Cf.* ss. 2 (1), 8 and 9, *ante* (price); s. 10 (1), *ante* (time for payment); ss. 17 and 18, *ante* (passing of property); ss. 27 and 28, *ante* (buyer's duty to pay price); and s. 54, *post* (interest and special damage).

History.—Before the Judicature Acts the price of goods sold could be recovered under the common *indebitatus* counts. The count for goods sold and delivered was applicable where the property had passed and the goods had been delivered to the buyer, and the price was payable at the time of action brought. The count for goods bargained and sold was applicable when the property had passed to the buyer and the contract had been completed in all respects except delivery, and the delivery was not a condition precedent to the payment of the price (*r*). Now it is sufficient to show facts disclosing either cause of action, but in practice the old counts are still largely used.

COMMENT

The general rule of English law is that, in the absence of any different agreement, when a debt becomes due, it is the duty of the debtor to go and tender the amount to his creditor, if in England, without waiting for any demand (*s*). Where goods are sold and delivered by a merchant in England to a buyer abroad, the price is payable in England, unless a different intention can be inferred from the contract (*t*).

Unless otherwise agreed (*u*), the price must be tendered in lawful money (*a*). Gold is legal tender up to any amount (*b*), silver or cupronickel coins of denominations of more than ten new pence are legal tender up to ten pounds; silver or cupronickel coins of up to ten new pence are legal tender up to five pounds; and bronze coins are legal tender up to twenty new pence (*c*). Bank of England notes payable to bearer on demand are legal tender for any amount notwithstanding

---

(*r*) Bullen & Leake's *Prec. of Pleading* (3rd ed.), pp. 38, 39; *Forbes* v. *Smith* (1863), 11 W. R. 574; *Colley* v. *Overseas Exporters*, [1921] 3 K. B. 302.

(*s*) *Cf. Walton* v. *Mascall* (1844), 13 M. & W. 452, at p. 458; *Fessard* v. *Mugnier* (1865), 18 C. B. N. S. 286; *Startup* v. *Macdonald* (1843), 6 M. & Gr. 593, at pp. 623, 624; cases cited in *Charles Duval* v. *Gans*, [1904] 2 K. B. 685, C. A. (service out of jurisdiction); *Joachimson* v. *Swiss Bank*, [1921] 3 K. B. 110, at p. 116, C. A.

(*t*) *Rein* v. *Stein*, [1892] 1 Q. B. 753, C. A., approved *Johnson* v. *Taylor Bros.*, [1920] A. C. 144, at p. 155.

(*u*) There may be an express or implied agreement to take payment by bill or cheque. As to payment by bill, note, or cheque, see Chalmers' *Bills of Exchange* (13th ed.), pp. 338–344; as to price expressed in foreign currency, see *post*, notes to s. 54.

(*a*) A debtor has no right to demand change: *Betterbee* v. *Davis* (1811), 3 Camp. 70; Roscoe, *Evidence in Civil Actions* (20th ed.), pp. 682, 683. As to mode of tender, see *International Sponge Co.* v. *Andrew Watt & Sons*, [1911] A. C. 279 (payment to agent); *Mitchell-Henry* v. *Norwich Union*, [1918] 2 K. B. 67 (payment through post).

(*b*) Coinage Act 1971, s. 2.

(*c*) *Ibid.*

that these are not now paid on demand in coin (*d*). When tender is pleaded as a defence, the sum tendered must be brought into court (*e*).

Where the property in the goods has passed.—The seller frequently insists that property in the goods is to pass only when he is paid. It has been suggested that this is a provision which the seller may in some circumstances be entitled to waive, it being for his benefit alone, thereby causing the property to pass to the buyer, so as to entitle him to sue for the price (*f*). This may assist him where the price is otherwise payable on delivery and the buyer refuses to take delivery. But in other circumstances, if the price is due, the seller may be entitled to claim it in any event at common law, apart from the provisions of sub-s. (2) of this section (*g*), and if the price is paid the property will then pass under the terms of the contract.

According to the terms of the contract.—The seller cannot sue unless the neglect or refusal to pay is wrongful. It does not necessarily follow that because the property has passed the price is payable forthwith. The buyer is only bound to pay according to the terms of the contract. The sale may have been on credit, or payment may have been made to depend on some specific condition or contingency (*h*). If the contract is silent as to the time of payment an action for the price can be maintained, provided that (1) the property has passed to the buyer, and (2) the goods have either been delivered or the seller is ready and willing to deliver them in exchange for the price, for by s. 28, *ante*, payment of the price and delivery of the goods are concurrent conditions.

On a day certain irrespective of delivery.—In order to succeed in a claim under sub-s. (2) it is necessary to prove that the price payable on a day certain irrespective of delivery. "Day certain" has been held to mean a time specified in the contract not depending on a future or contingent event (*i*), and it has frequently been held that where payment is against shipping documents it is not on a day certain irrespective of delivery, so that no action for the price may be maintained (*k*).

(*d*) Currency and Bank Notes Act 1954, s. 1; 2 Halsbury's Statutes (3rd Edn.) 771.

(*e*) R. S. C., O. 18, r. 16; C. C. R., O. 9, r. 4 (9).

(*f*) *Napier* v. *Dexters, Ltd.* (1926), 26 Ll. L. Rep. at pp. 63–64, *per* ROCHE, J., and on appeal at pp. 187–188, *per* BANKES, L.J.; *Martin* v. *Hogan* (1917), 24 C. L. R. 231 (H. C. of Aus.).

(*g*) See *post*, "On a day certain irrespective of delivery".

(*h*) See, for example, *Calcutta Co.* v. *De Mattos* (1863), 32 L. J. Q. B. 322, at p. 328.

(*i*) *Merchant Shipping Co.* v. *Armitage* (1873), L. R. 9 Q. B. 99; *Shell Mex, Ltd.* v. *Elton Cop. Dyeing Co.* (1928), 34 Com. Cas. 39; *Muller Maclean & Co.* v. *Lesley and Anderson*, [1921] W. N. 235. But in *Workman Clark & Co.* v. *Lloyd Brazileno*, [1908] 1 K. B. 968, the Court of Appeal all considered that s. 49 (2) applied in a case where an instalment of the price was payable when the keel of a ship was laid. The judgments as reported refer only to s. 49, but it is clear from the terms of the contract, under which the property had not passed, and from the arguments of counsel that only s. 49 (2) could apply. See also *Colley* v. *Overseas Exporters*, [1921] 3 K. B. 302, 306.

(*k*) *Muller Maclean & Co.* v. *Lesley and Anderson, supra; Stein Forbes & Co.* v. *County Tailoring Co.* (1916), 115 L. T. 215. But *cf. Polenghi* v. *Dried Milk Co., Ltd.* (1904), 10 Com. Cas. 42.

But if this construction is correct, it would seem that this section does not cover all the situations in which an action for the price might have been maintained at common law where the property in the goods have not passed. In *Workman Clark & Co.* v. *Lloyd Brazileno* (*l*), the Court of Appeal held that a seller was entitled at common law to summary judgment for an instalment of the price of a ship which under the terms of the contract was payable "when the keel . . . is laid". In principle there seems no reason why the rules of common law should be excluded by this section, and there is some authority that where a contract clearly provides for the unconditional (*m*) payment of the price in given circumstances which arise, then the seller may claim the price (*n*). Thus, if the buyer has accepted delivery and not rejected the goods, payment being 90 days after delivery, and there being a provision that property should not pass until payment, the seller cannot claim damages for non-acceptance for the buyer has accepted the goods, and there seems no good reason why he should not claim the price.

Payment by bill.—Where there is an agreement for payment of the price by a bill payable at a future day and the bill is not given, the seller cannot sue for the price till the bill would have matured. His remedy before that time is by action for damages for breach of the agreement (*o*). Where a bill or cheque is given for the price, the general rule is that it operates as conditional payment (*p*). If the bill be dishonoured, the debt revives, and the buyer may be sued either on the bill or on the consideration (*q*). When the seller agrees to take the

---

(*l*) [1908] 1 K. B. 968, C. A. In *Colley* v. *Overseas Exporters*, [1921] 3 K. B. 302, at pp. 309–310, McCardie, J., says that no action will lie for the price of goods until the property has passed except under the rule now embodied in s. 49 (2). But at p. 306, he clearly interprets the *Workman Clark* case, as coming within sub-s. (2).

(*m*) Payment "on delivery" or "against documents" is not unconditional in this sense.

(*n*) *Minister of Supply and Development* v. *Servicemen's Co-operative Joinery Manufacturers, Ltd.* (1951), 82 C. L. R. 621 (H. C. of Aus.) ("net cash before delivery"). See also *McEntire* v. *Crossley Brothers*, [1895] A. C. 497, *per* Lord Halsbury; *Sandford* v. *Dairy Supplies, Ltd.*, [1941] N. Z. L. R. 141. *Polenghi* v. *Dried Milk Co., Ltd.* (1904), 10 Com. Cas. 42 (payment on arrival of ship against documents) also supports this proposition, but the case is inconsistent with *Stein Forbes & Co.* v. *County Tailoring Co.* (1916), 115 L. T. 215, where Atkin, J., construed a similar provision as meaning payment upon delivery.

(*o*) *Paul* v. *Dod* (1846), 2 C. B. 800; distinguished, *Waynes Merthyr Steam Coal Co.* v. *Morewood* (1877), 46 L. J. Q. B. 746; but see *Bartholomew* v. *Markwick* (1864), 15 C. B. N. S. 711, where there was a repudiation of the contract. As to measure of damages, see *Gordon* v. *Whitehouse* (1846), 18 C. B. 747.

(*p*) *Goldshede* v. *Cottrell* (1836), 2 M. & W. 20; *Gunn* v. *Bolckow Vaughan & Co.* (1875), 10 Ch. App. 491, at p. 501; *Bolt and Nut Co.* (*Tipton*), *Ltd.* v. *Rowlands Nicholls & Co., Ltd.*, [1964] 1 All E. R. 137; [1964] 2 Q. B. 10, C. A.

(*q*) Chalmers on *Bills of Exchange* (13th ed.), p. 338; but a bill *may* be taken in absolute payment: see *ibid.*, p. 342; *Bolt and Nut Co.* (*Tipton*), *Ltd.* v. *Rowlands Nicholls & Co., Ltd.*, [1964] 1 All E. R. 137; [1964] 2 Q. B. 10, C. A. If the plaintiff sues on the consideration he must be the holder of the bill at the time of action brought: *Davis* v. *Reilly*, [1898] 1 Q. B. 1; *cf. Re a Debtor*, [1908] 1 K. B. 344, C. A. As to payment by cheque to agent authorised only to receive cash, see *Bradford & Sons* v. *Price* (1923), 92 L. J. K. B. 871; for the converse case, see *International Sponge Co.* v. *Watts*, [1911] A. C. 279. *Cf.* s. 38 (1) (b), *ante*.

buyer's acceptance for the price, it is his duty to tender a bill to the buyer to get his acceptance (*r*).

A bill of exchange is generally treated as cash not only as between remote parties, but also as between immediate parties. Where, therefore, the seller sues upon a bill given to him as payment for goods sold, he is entitled to judgment for the whole amount of the bill, without any stay of execution, even if the buyer has a cross-claim in damages against him in respect of the goods. The buyer must pay upon the bill and bring his cross-claim afterwards. But when a bill of exchange is given on the sale of goods, then, if the consideration wholly fails, as between the immediate parties the buyer who has accepted it is not liable upon it (*s*).

Payment by banker's irrevocable letter of credit.—This is considered at length p. 42, *ante*.

Interest.—For the English law, see the note to s. 3 of the Law Reform (Miscellaneous Provisions) Act 1934, reproduced in Appendix I, *post*.

In Scotland it was said that

> "the seller may sue the purchaser for the price *and interest*, whether the goods sold are specific or not, provided goods according to the contract have been tendered to the purchaser" (*t*).

The Act preserves this rule.

50. Damages for non-acceptance.—(1) Where the buyer wrongfully neglects or refuses to accept and pay for the goods, the seller may maintain an action against him for damages for non-acceptance.

(2) The measure of damages is the estimated loss directly and naturally resulting, in the ordinary course of events, from the buyer's breach of contract (*u*).

(3) Where there is an available market for the goods in question the measure of damages is primâ facie (*a*) to be ascertained by the difference between the contract price and the market or current price at the time or times (*b*)

(*r*) *Reed* v. *Mestaer* (1802), 2 *Comyn on Contract*, 229; Bullen & Leake's *Precedents of Pleading* (12th ed.), p. 1281.

(*s*) *All Trades Distributors, Ltd.* v. *Agencies Kaufman, Ltd.* (1969), 113 Sol. Jo. 995, C. A. And see *Thoni G.m.b.H. & Co.* v. *P.T.P. Equipment, Ltd.*, [1979] 2 Lloyd's Rep. 282 (amount of bill alleged to be excessive because of erroneous calculation of amount due: leave to defend in respect of alleged excess on bringing the money into court).

(*t*) Mercantile Law Commission, (1855) 2nd Report, p. 47. *Cf.* Green's *Encyclopædia of Scot's Law*, tit. "Interest."

(*u*) *Cort* v. *Ambergate Rail. Co.* (1851), 17 Q. B. 127; *Wayne's Merthyr Coal Co.* v. *Morewood* (1877), 46 L. J. Q. B. 746; *Re Vic. Mill Ltd.*, [1913] 1 Ch. 465, C. A.

(*a*) *Charter* v. *Sullivan*, [1957] 1 All E. R. 809; [1957] 2 Q. B. 117, C. A.

(*b*) See *Brown* v. *Muller* (1872), L. R. 7 Exch. 319; *Roper* v. *Johnson* (1873), L. R. 8 C. P. 167, as to non-delivery in instalment contracts.

when the goods ought to have been accepted (*c*) or (if no time was fixed for acceptance) at the time of the refusal to accept (*d*).

ILLUSTRATIONS

(1) V. Ltd. is in voluntary liquidation and in breach of an agreement, made before the winding-up, to buy and accept machines to be specially made by the sellers. The sellers can prove in the liquidation for the whole of the profit which they will lose on the machines which they have not yet begun to make (*e*).

(2) Buyers wrongfully refuse to accept a new motor car which they have agreed to buy from a dealer. The dealer returns the car to his suppliers, and can recover from the buyers the profit he would have made on the deal (*f*).

(3) Buyer wrongfully refuses to accept a new motor car which he has agreed to buy from a dealer. Cars of this kind are in short supply and the dealer can sell all he can get; he in fact re-sells this car within 10 days at the list price. He cannot recover any loss of profit from the defaulting buyer (*g*).

Derivation.—Section 50 of the 1893 Act.

Definitions.—For "action," "buyer," "goods" and "seller," see s. 61 (1), *post*.

Cross-references.—*Cf*. ss. 2 (1), 8 and 9, *ante* (price); s. 10, *ante* (stipulations as to time); ss. 27 and 28, *ante* (buyer's duty to pay price); s. 35, *ante* (acceptance); s. 37, *ante* (delay in taking delivery); s. 48 (3), *ante* (right of re-sale); s. 51, *post* (non-delivery); and s. 54, *post* (interest and special damage).

COMMENT

This section deals only with general damages.

In general, where the property in the goods has not passed to the buyer, the seller's only remedy is an action for non-acceptance (*h*).

(*c*) Thus if the market price is lower than the contract price at the time when the goods ought to have been accepted, the seller is entitled to the difference even though the market price has subsequently risen and he has re-sold for more than the contract price; *Campbell Mostyn* v. *Barnett*, [1954] 1 Lloyd's Rep. 65, C. A.

(*d*) *Phillpotts* v. *Evans* (1839), 5 M. & W. 475; *Barrow* v. *Arnaud* (1846), 8 Q. B. 595, at p. 609, Ex. Ch.; *cf. ex parte Stapleton* (1879), 10 Ch. D. 586, at p. 590, C. A. As to extension of time at buyer's request, see *Hickman* v. *Haynes* (1875), L. R. 10 C. P. 598.

(*e*) *Re Vic Mill*, [1913] 1 Ch. 465, C. A.

(*f*) *Thompson* v. *Robinson* (*Gunmakers*), [1955] 1 All E. R. 154; [1955] Ch. 177. See also *Victory Motors, Ltd*. v. *Bayda* (1973), 3 W. W. R. 747 (seller would have made loss selling trade-in car: loss taken into account in estimating seller's damages). But *cf. Jeremy's Garages, Ltd*. v. *MacAndrews Car Hire, Ltd*., unreported, 31st October 1974, C. A. (losses actually made on re-selling trade-in cars disregarded in assessing seller's damages). As to second-hand cars, see *Lazenby Garages* v. *Wright*, [1976] 2 All E. R. 770; [1976] 1 W. L. R. 459, C. A.; *J. Sargent* (*Garages*), *Ltd*. v. *Motor Auctions*, [1977] R. T. R. 121, C. A.

(*g*) *Charter* v. *Sullivan*, [1957] 1 All E. R. 809; (1957) 2 Q. B. 117, C. A. Nor will the seller be able to recover loss of profit if he delays selling the car until a time when supply exceeds demand: *Blythswood Motors, Ltd*. v. *Raeside*, 1966 S. L. T. 13 (Sheriff's Court).

(*h*) For cases in which he may sue for the price, see the comment to s. 49 (2), *ante*.

Where the property has passed he may sue either for the price (*i*) or for damages for non-acceptance. If the parties so choose, they can fix the damages by the contract itself (*k*).

The market price rule in sub-s. (3) is an obvious deduction from sub-s. (2), applicable in general to the ordinary goods of commerce for which there is more or less ready sale. The rule is so convenient that the courts apply it whenever and so far as practicable. But it is only a *prima facie* rule depending on its conformity with the general principle. For example, if a contract be repudiated before the time fixed for delivery, and the seller accept the repudiation, he may not be justified in holding back the goods on a falling market and thus enhancing the damages. He must act reasonably (*l*). But "he is not bound to nurse the interests of the contract breaker, and so long as he acts reasonably at the time it ill lies in the mouth of the contract breaker to turn round afterwards, and complain, in order to reduce his own liability to a plaintiff, that the plaintiff has failed to do that which perhaps with hindsight he might have been wiser to do" (*m*).

Where the seller has a discretion how much to deliver, as in a contract for x tonnes of wheat, 10 per cent more or less, in assessing damages where the buyer refuses to accept the goods before they are tendered, damages will be be assessed by reference to the quantity of goods which, on the balance of probabilities, the seller would have tendered (*n*).

Available market.—Various suggestions have been put forward as to what constitutes, or is required for there to be, an available market.

It was formerly suggested (*o*) that there had to be a particular place, such as an exchange where the goods could be sold, but this has been criticised (*p*) and expressly dissented from (*q*). An alternative view that "an available market merely means that the situation in the particular area was such that the particular goods could freely be sold, and that there was a demand sufficient to absorb readily all the goods that were thrust on it, so that if a purchaser defaulted, the goods in question could readily be disposed of" (*r*) was criticised in the Court of Appeal (*s*)

(*i*) Unless he has resold, in which case he must sue for damages: *Lamond* v. *Davall* (1847), 9 Q. B. 1030.

(*k*) *Diestal* v. *Stevenson & Co.*, [1906] 2 K. B. 345—subject of course to the general rules about penalties and, perhaps, to the provisions of the Unfair Contract Terms Act 1977, *post*, Appendix I. See p. 357, *post*.

(*l*) *Roth* v. *Taysen* (1895), 73 L. T. 628, and see note to s. 54, *post*; for general principle, see *British Westinghouse Co.* v. *Underground Electric Railway*, [1912] A. C. 673, at p. 689.

(*m*) *Harlow and Jones* v. *Panex (International), Ltd.*, [1967] 2 Lloyd's Rep. 509, at p. 530, *per* ROSKILL, J.

(*n*) *Toprak* v. *Finagrain*, [1979] 2 Lloyd's Rep. 98, C. A.

(*o*) *Dunkirk Colliery* v. *Lever* (1878), 9 Ch. D. 20, at p. 25, C. A.

(*p*) *Thompson* v. *Robinson (Gunmakers)*, [1955] 1 All E. R. 154; [1955] Ch. 177; *Charter* v. *Sullivan*, [1957] 1 All E. R. 809; [1957] 2 Q. B. 117, C. A.

(*q*) *A. B. D. (Metals and Waste), Ltd.* v. *Anglo-Chemical and Ore Co., Ltd.*, [1955] 2 Lloyd's Rep. 456, at p. 466.

(*r*) *Thompson* v. *Robinson (Gunmakers)*, *supra;* followed in *A. B. D. (Metals and Waste), Ltd.* v. *Anglo-Chemical and Ore Co., Ltd.*, *supra*.

(*s*) *Charter* v. *Sullivan*, *supra*.

where JENKINS, L. J., suggested that, since the subsection contemplates a difference between contract price and market price, there might only be an "available market" in the sense of the subsection where the market price was regulated by supply and demand and thus subject to fluctuation, and not where the only "market" was an existing demand for goods which, for other reasons, could be sold only at a standard retail price.

Where there is only one alternative buyer available, who is willing to purchase part only of the contract goods, that buyer is not an "available market" (*t*).

In some cases where the seller has re-sold, the re-sale price has been assumed to furnish the correct measure of damages (*u*).

Where there is no available market, the measure of the seller's loss will normally be the difference between the sale price and the value of the goods to the seller at the time of the breach (*a*).

Where new goods are sold at a fixed retail price, the "available market" test is inapplicable and the question is whether the seller has lost the opportunity of making an extra sale, so that he has lost the profit on that sale, or whether he has not in fact lost any profit, because he has been able quickly to re-sell the subject matter of the contract together with all other goods of that kind that he could obtain (*b*).

If goods are to be made specially for a buyer and the buyer repudiates before the seller begins to make the goods, the seller will be entitled to recover his loss of profit unless the buyer can prove that the seller acting reasonably and in the ordinary course of his business, has been able, as a result of the situation in which the buyer placed him, to take a course of action (such as taking on new orders) which diminished his loss. But if the buyer can prove that he has so diminished his loss then his damages would be reduced accordingly (*c*). The seller will not have to give credit for a profit arising from speculative work not in the ordinary course of his business (*d*).

Buyer's remedies

51. Damages for non-delivery.—(1) Where the seller wrongfully neglects or refuses to deliver the goods to

(*t*) *Harlow and Jones* v. *Panex* (*International*), *Ltd.*, [1967] 2 Lloyd's Rep. 509.

(*u*) *Maclean* v. *Dunn* (1828), 4 Bing. 722; *Ex p. Stapleton* (1879), 10 Ch. D. 586, C. A.; *Ryan* v. *Ridley* (1902), 8 Com. Cas. 105. But the seller must prove his actual loss; it is not enough merely to prove the re-sale price if, for instance, the re-sale was on conditions different from those of the original sale: *Macklin* v. *Newbury Sanitary Laundry* (1919), 63 Sol. Jo. 337. Note also *Campbell Mostyn* v. *Barnett*, [1954] 1 Lloyd's Rep. 65, C. A. (wrongfully rejected goods re-sold by seller at more than contract price; measure of damages nevertheless difference between contract price and market price at date of rejection).

(*a*) *Harlow & Jones* v. *Panex* (*International*), *Ltd.*, *supra*.

(*b*) *Thompson* v. *Robinson* (*Gunmakers*), *ante*, illustration (2); *Charter* v. *Sullivan*, *ante*, illustration (3).

(*c*) *Hill & Sons* v. *Showell & Sons, Ltd.* (1918), 87 L. J. Q. B. 1106, H. L.

(*d*) *Ibid.*

the buyer, the buyer may maintain an action against the seller for damages for non-delivery (*e*).

(2) The measure of damages is the estimated loss directly and naturally resulting, in the ordinary course of events, from the seller's breach of contract (*f*).

(3) Where there is an available market for the goods in question (*g*) the measure of damages is prima facie (*h*) to be ascertained by the difference between the contract price and the market or current price of the goods at the time (*i*) or times (*k*) when they ought to have been delivered, or (if no time was fixed) then at the time of the refusal to deliver (*l*).

ILLUSTRATIONS

(1) Sale of 10,000 tons of coal to be delivered at Lubeck, "penalty for non-execution of this contract, one shilling per ton." This is not a penalty, but liquidated damages; and, if default is made in delivery, this measure must be applied to the instalments undelivered (*m*).

(2) A in June sells a cargo of coal to B, to be shipped in November. In October B sells the cargo to C, assigning his rights against A. The cargo is not delivered. In an action by B the measure of damages is the difference between the contract price and the market price at the time of breach, i.e. in November. The sub-contract with C is to be disregarded, since it only affords evidence of the market value in October (*n*).

(3) Six contracts of sale of cotton waste on the terms that delivery is to be made within a reasonable time of the removal of a government embargo. The contracts are repudiated before the time has elapsed. Damages must be

---

(*e*) *Ramsden* v. *Gray* (1849), 7 C. B. 961; *Jones* v. *Gibbons* (1853), 8 Exch. 920 (non-delivery of goods agreed to be delivered "as required"); *Lewis* v. *Clifton* (1854), 14 C. B. 245 (refusal to permit growing timber, which had been sold by auction, to be carried away).

(*f*) *Smeed* v. *Foord* (1859), 1 E. & E. 602; *Grébert-Borgnis* v. *Nugent* (1885), 15 Q. B. D. 85, C. A. (specially manufactured goods); *cf. Hammond* v. *Bussey* (1887), 20 Q. B. D. 79, at p. 93, C. A.; and see note to s. 54, *post*.

(*g*) See *Marshall* v. *Nicoll*, 1919 S. C. (H. L.) 129, and *per* UPJOHN, J. in *Thompson* v. *Robinson (Gunmakers)*, [1955] 1 All E. R. 154, at p. 159; [1955] Ch. 177, at p. 186; *Mouat* v. *Betts Motors, Ltd.*, [1958] 3 All E. R. 402; [1959] A. C. 71, P. C., *post*, illustration (4). See also the comment to the previous section.

(*h*) *Charter* v. *Sullivan*, [1957] 1 All E. R. 809; [1957] 2 Q. B. 117, C. A.

(*i*) *Leigh* v. *Paterson* (1818), 8 Taunt. 540; *Hinde* v. *Liddell* (1875), L. R. 10 Q. B. 265. As to c.i.f. contract, see *Sharpe & Co.* v. *Nosawa*, [1917] 2 K. B. 814 (time when the shipping documents, not the goods, should have been tendered).

(*k*) As to instalment deliveries, see *Brown* v. *Muller* (1872), L. R. 7 Exch. 319; *Roper* v. *Johnson* (1873), L. R. 8 C. P. 167; *cf. Bergheim* v. *Blaenavon Co.* (1875), L. R. 10 Q. B. 319.

(*l*) *Shaw* v. *Holland* (1846), 15 M. & W. 136, 146; *Josling* v. *Irvine* (1861), 6 H. & N. 512; *Ashmore* v. *Cox*, [1899] 1 Q. B. 436, 443 (date of repudiation of contract).

(*m*) *Diestal* v. *Stevenson & Co.*, [1906] 2 K. B. 345.

(*n*) *Williams* v. *Agius*, [1914] A. C. 510, 523; see also *Williams* v. *Reynolds* (1865), 6 B. & S. 495; *Thol* v. *Henderson* (1881), 8 Q. B. D. 457.

assessed in accordance with sub-s. (2). The market price at the time of repudiation is inapplicable (*o*).

(4) A sells a car to B for £1,207. B promises to offer it to A at, in the event, £1,157, if he wishes to re-sell it within two years. Within the two years he re-sells it to C for £1,700 without first offering it to A. Because of similar covenants given by him to his seller, A could only have re-sold the car for £1,207; had he re-purchased it. The measure of A's damages is £543, being the difference between the contract price and the market price, the only available market being the black market upon which B had re-sold the car (*p*).

Derivation.—Section 51 of the 1893 Act.

Definitions.—For "action," "buyer," "delivery," "goods" and "seller," see s. 61 (1), *post.*

Cross-references.—*Cf.* ss. 2 (1), 8 and 9, *ante* (price); s. 10, *ante* (stipulations as to time); ss. 27 and 28, *ante* (seller's duty to deliver); ss. 29 to 31, *ante* (rules as to delivery); and s. 54, *post* (interest and special damage).

COMMENT

This section also, in terms, deals only with general damages. It is declaratory and is founded on *Hadley* v. *Baxendale* (*q*).

When the seller breaks his contract to deliver, one or more of four remedies may be open to the buyer, namely: (1) in all cases he may sue for damages for non-delivery; (2) if the price has been prepaid by him, he may recover it back as money had and received for a consideration which has wholly failed (*r*); (3) if the goods be specified or ascertained he may sue for specific performance; and (4) if the property in the goods has passed, and he is entitled to immediate possession, he has the ordinary remedies of an owner deprived of his goods, *viz.*, conversion or detinue as the case may be. The action for non-delivery lies when the goods are not delivered, or when goods which are not in conformity with the contract are tendered and rejected.

Section 51 does not in terms apply to actions for delay in delivery when the goods are ultimately accepted; and necessarily damages there are assessed on different lines from damages for non-delivery in order to give effect to the guiding principle stated in sub-s. (2), which applies throughout the law of contract.

Non-delivery.—The rule as to market price is clearly a deduction from the more general rule in sub-s. (2). "Where a contract to deliver goods at a certain price is broken," says TINDAL, C.J.,

---

(*o*) *Millett* v. *Van Heek & Co.*, [1921] 2 K. B. 369, C. A.; approved in *Tai Hing Cotton Mill* v. *Kamsing Knitting Factory*, [1978] 1 All E. R. 515; [1979] A. C. 91, P. C.

(*p*) *Mouat* v. *Betts Motors, Ltd.*, [1958] 3 All E. R. 402; [1959] A. C. 71, P. C.

(*q*) (1854), 9 Exch. 341, at p. 354; 2 Smith L. C. (13th ed.), p. 529; and see now *Victoria Laundry* v. *Newman Industries*, [1949] 1 All E. R. 997; [1949] 2 K. B. 528, C. A.

(*r*) But not if the contract itself was illegal; see, *e.g. Berg* v. *Sadler & Moore*, [1937] 1 All E. R. 637; [1937] 2 K. B. 158, C. A.

"the proper measure of damages in general is the difference between the contract price and the market price of such goods at the time when the contract is broken, because the purchaser having the money in his hands may go into the market and buy. So, if a contract to accept and pay for goods is broken, the same rule may be properly applied, for the seller may take his goods into the market and obtain the current price for them" (*s*).

Hence, if in an action for non-delivery no difference between the contract price and the market price is shown, the plaintiff in general is only entitled to nominal damages (*t*).

The English courts have applied this rule whenever possible, even where it produced hardship in individual cases (*u*). But it is not an absolute rule, and if to follow it would give rise to injustice, the court has power to fix such other date as may be appropriate in the circumstances (*a*). In Scotland the rule has not been so strictly applied (*b*).

But there are many cases in which the rule of market price is inapplicable. If it is partially applicable it will be applied with the necessary modifications, thus—

(1) The buyer may have prepaid the price. In that case he is entitled to recover back the money he has paid with interest (*c*), together with the difference between the price he paid and the full market price of the goods on the day when they ought to have been delivered (*d*).

(2) The exact sort of goods the buyer has contracted for may not be obtainable, but if it is reasonable for him to buy in similar goods he may charge the seller with the difference in price (*e*).

(3) The seller may have repudiated his contract before the time for delivery arrives. In such a case the buyer may either accept the

---

(*s*) *Barrow* v. *Arnaud* (1846), 8 Q. B. 604, at p. 609, Ex. Ch.

(*t*) *Valpy* v. *Oakeley* (1851), 16 Q. B. 941; *Erie Natural Gas Co.* v. *Carroll*, [1911] A. C. 105, P. C. (substituted performance); *Aryeh* v. *Lawrence Kostoris & Son, Ltd.*, [1967] 1 Lloyd's Rep. 63.

(*u*) *Brady* v. *Oastler* (1864), 3 H. & C. 112 (special price for early delivery ignored); *Williams* v. *Reynolds* (1865), 6 B. & S. 495 (profit on re-sale excluded); *Thol* v. *Henderson* (1881), 8 Q. B. D. 457 (sub-contract by buyer disregarded); *Williams* v. *Agius*, [1914] A. C. 510 (sub-contract disregarded); *cf. Victoria Laundry* (*Windsor*) v. *Newman Industries, Ltd.*, [1949] 1 All E. R. 997; [1949] 2 K. B. 528, C. A.; *Mouat* v. *Betts Motors, Ltd.*, [1958] 3 All E. R. 402; [1959] A. C. 71, P. C. (*ante*, illustration (4)); and see *Charter* v. *Sullivan*, [1957] 1 All E. R. 809; [1957] 2 Q. B. 117, C. A.

(*a*) *Johnson* v. *Agnew*, [1979] 1 All E. R. 883, at p. 896; [1980] A. C. 367, at p. 401, H. L.

(*b*) *Dunlop* v. *Higgins* (1848), 1 H. L. Cas. 381, at p. 403.

(*c*) As to interest, see s. 3 of The Law Reform (Miscellaneous Provisions) Act 1934; reproduced in Appendix I, *post*.

(*d*) *Startup* v. *Cortazzi* (1835), 2 C. M. & R. 165; *cf. Barrow* v. *Arnaud* (1846), 8 Q. B. 604, at p. 610.

(*e*) *Hinde* v. *Liddell* (1875), L. R. 10 Q. B. 265; *cf. Erie Natural Gas Co.* v. *Carroll*, [1911] A. C. 105, at p. 117, "the measure of damage is the cost of procuring the substituted article." This assumes that the article is a satisfactory and not an inferior substitute. *Cf.* also *Harbutt's Plasticine, Ltd.* v. *Wayne Tank and Pump Co., Ltd.*, [1970] 1 All E. R. 225; [1970] 1 Q. B. 447, C. A. (Old factory burnt down; measure of damages full cost of re-instating factory because not possible to acquire second-hand factory. *Aliter* in case of second-hand cars.)

repudiation and sue at once, or he may refuse to accept it and wait for the time for performance before suing. If he refuses to accept the repudiation the measure of damages is calculated by reference to the value of the goods at the time when they ought to have been delivered and it seems that in such a case the buyer is under no obligation to mitigate his loss and may sit tight on a rising market (*f*). But since the contract is still open, the seller has the opportunity of changing his mind and eventually performing, and he may also take advantage of any subsequent events which operate to release him from his obligation to perform (*g*).

Where, however, the buyer accepts the seller's repudiation and sues forthwith, although the damages are still calculated by reference to the value of the goods at the time fixed for delivery (*h*), the buyer is under a duty to mitigate his loss if he can by buying in against the contract (*i*).

The final words of sub-s. (3) "or (if no time was fixed) at the time of the refusal to deliver" do not apply in any case of anticipatory breach of contract, even where no time is fixed for delivery (*k*).

(4) The time for delivery may have been extended at the seller's request. In that case the extended time will be taken as the contract time (*l*).

(5) There may be no available market at the place of delivery, but regard may be had to the market price contemplated by the parties at the ultimate destination of the goods (*m*).

(6) The parties in their contract may have provided that in case of breach certain agreed damages should be paid by the party in default

---

(*f*) *Leigh* v. *Paterson* (1818), 8 Taunt. 540; *Roth* v. *Taysen* (1895), 73 L. T. 628, C. A.; *Michael* v. *Hart & Co.*, [1902] 1 K. B. 482, C. A.; *Tredegar Iron Co.* v. *Hawthorn* (1902), 18 T. L. R. 716, C. A. Dicta in *Nickoll* v. *Ashton* by MATHEW, J., at first instance, and VAUGHAN WILLIAMS, L. J., in the Court of Appeal, ([1900] 2 Q. B. 298 at p. 305 and [1901] 2 K. B. 126 at p. 138, respectively) might be taken to suggest the contrary, but it is not clear whether these remarks were based on accepted or non-accepted repudiation.

(*g*) *Avery* v. *Bowden* (1855), 5 E. & B. 714; (1856), 6 E. & B. 953, Ex. Ch.

(*h*) *Cf. Maredelanto Compania Naviera S.A.* v. *Bergbau-Handel G.m.b.H.*, [1970] 3 All E. R. 125; [1971] 1 Q. B. 164, C. A. (party in breach, had he waited, could lawfully have cancelled contract).

(*i*) *Roper* v. *Johnson* (1873), L. R. 8 C. P. 167; approved in *Garnac Grain Co., Inc.* v. *H. M. F. Faure and Fairclough, Ltd.*, [1967] 2 All E. R. 353, 360; [1968] A. C. 1130, 1140, H. L.

(*k*) *Tai Hing Cotton Mill* v. *Kamsing Knitting Factory*, [1978] 1 All E. R. 515; [1979] A. C. 91, P. C.; *Millet* v. *Van Heek & Co.*, [1921] 2 K. B. 369, C. A.

(*l*) *Ogle* v. *Earl Vane* (1868), L. R. 3 Q. B. 272 (non-delivery), Ex. Ch.; *Hickman* v. *Haynes* (1875), L. R. 10 C. P. 598 (non-acceptance); *Tyers* v. *Rosedale Co.* (1875), L. R. 10 Exch. 195, Ex. Ch. See also *Rickards* v. *Oppenheim*, [1950] 1 All E. R. 420, C. A.; [1950] 1 K. B. 616, and see p. 20, *ante*:

(*m*) *Wertheim* v. *Chicoutimi Pulp Co.*, [1911] A. C. 301, P. C.; applied in *Macauley & Culle* v. *Horgan*, [1925] 2 I. R. 1. *Cf. Sharpe & Co.* v. *Nosawa & Co.*, [1917] 2 K. B. 814, as to c.i.f. contract.

(*n*), and the question may then arise whether this is a penalty under the general law of contract (*o*).

(7) There may be a breach of a contract to deliver goods at a fixed date in a foreign country. In that case the court may give damages in the currency which best expresses the plaintiff's loss (*p*).

Again the market price test may be wholly inapplicable, and then recourse must be had to the wider general principle of sub-s. (2). This is the case where there is no available market for the goods in question, as, for example, where the buyer has ordered some special article or articles to be expressly manufactured for him (*q*). In the case of non-delivery, where there is no market and the sale is for the purpose of re-sale, the measure of damages is the difference between the contract price and the re-sale price (*r*). Each case turns on its particular circumstances, and is usually complicated by questions of special damage (*s*). As to mitigation of damages, see *post*, notes to s. 54.

Goods lawfully rejected.—The buyer's duty to accept the goods arises only where tender of delivery is made in accordance with the terms of the contract of sale (see s. 27, *ante*), and if goods other than goods of the contract description are delivered, or if the delivery is otherwise not in accordance with the conditions of the contract, the buyer may rightfully reject the goods (provided he has not done any act amounting to acceptance within s. 35 of the Act) by notifying the seller within a reasonable time that he refuses to accept them: see ss. 35 and 36, *ante*.

When the buyer is entitled to reject the goods, and does so, he can

---

(*n*) *Dunlop* v. *New Garage*, [1915] A. C. 79; *Cellulose Acetate Silk Co., Ltd.* v. *Widnes Foundry (1925), Ltd.*, [1933] A. C. 20; *Imperial Tobacco Co., Ltd.* v. *Parslay*, [1936] 2 All E. R. 515; *Stewart* v. *Carapanayoti*, [1962] 1 All E. R. 418; [1962] 1 W. L. R. 34.

(*o*) See, *e.g.*, *Dunlop* v. *New Garage* (*supra*); *Cooden Engineering* v. *Stanford*, [1952] 2 All E. R. 915; [1953] 1 Q. B. 86, C. A.; *Bridge* v. *Campbell Discount*, [1962] 1 All E. R. 385; [1962] A. C. 600; *Lombank, Ltd.* v. *Excell*, [1963] 3 All E. R. 486; [1964] 1 Q. B. 415, C. A.; *Robophone Facilities, Ltd.* v. *Blank*, [1966] 3 All E. R. 128; [1966] 1 W. L. R. 1428, C. A.

(*p*) *The Despina R*, [1979] 1 All E. R. 421; [1979] A. C. 685, H. L. overruling *Di Ferdinando* v. *Simon Smits & Co.*, [1920] 3 K. B. 409, C. A., and distinguishing, *S. S. Celia*, [1921] 2 A. C. 544. For the circumstances in which a loss caused by devaluation of a currency may be recovered, see *Aruna Mills, Ltd.* v. *Dhanrajmal Gobindram*, [1968] 1 All E. R. 113; [1968] 1 Q. B. 655; and see *post*, notes to s. 54. As to loss caused or aggravated by the injured party's impecuniosity, see p. 248, *post*. See further p. 252, *post*.

(*q*) *Grébert-Borgnis* v. *Nugent* (1885), 15 Q. B. D. 85, C. A.; *Elbinger A. G.* v. *Armstrong* (1874), L. R. 9 Q. B. 473, at p. 476; *Leavey (J.) & Co., Ltd.* v. *Hirst (George) & Co., Ltd.*, [1943] 2 All E. R. 581; [1944] K. B. 24, C. A.

(*r*) *Patrick* v. *Russo-British Grain Export Co.*, [1927] 2 K. B. 535; *Leavey* v. *Hirst*, [1943] 2 All E. R. 581; [1944] 1 K. B. 24; *Household Machines* v. *Cosmos Exporters*, [1946] 2 All E. R. 622; [1947] K. B. 217; *Kwei Tek Chao* v. *British Traders and Shippers*, [1954] 3 All E. R. 165; [1954] 2 Q. B. 459.

(*s*) *Hydraulic Co.* v. *McHaffie* (1878), 4 Q. B. D. 670, C. A. (special damage); *Grébert-Borgnis* v. *Nugent* (1885), 15 Q. B. D. 85, to C. A. (goods made to order); but see an attempt to apply the current price rule to specially manufactured goods: *Marshall* v. *Nicoll*, 1919 S. C. (H. L.) 129. See also another Scottish case, *British Motor Body Co.* v. *Shaw*, 1914 S. C. 922, 928 (motor-car made to order, undue delay).

recover back the price if he has paid it, for the consideration for its payment has wholly failed (*t*). Then arises the question: what further compensation, if any, is he entitled to? When he lawfully rejects the goods the position seems to be this: he has contracted for the supply of certain goods, and those goods have never been supplied to him. The seller, therefore, has failed in his obligation to deliver, and whatever damages would be recoverable in an action for non-delivery should on principle be recoverable in this case (*u*).

Where a contract for the supply of machinery contained a guarantee to replace defective parts, and concluded: "we do not give any other guarantee and we do not accept responsibility for consequential damages," it was held that the buyers were entitled to reject the goods delivered as not in accordance with the contract, and that the clause did not negative the seller's liability for extra expenses, etc., incurred in procuring other machinery, as this was damage arising naturally and directly from the failure to deliver according to contract (*a*).

Delay in delivery.—A similar rule applies to damages for delay, when goods of a particular description are ordered and are ultimately accepted after the delay (*b*), there being a *prima facie* rule that the damage is the difference between "the value of the article contracted for at the time when it ought to have been and at the time when it actually was delivered" (*c*). Accordingly, in the case of ordinary goods of commerce, the *prima facie* measure of damages is the difference between the market price at the time when the goods ought to have been delivered and the time when they actually were delivered. But if that price has fallen, and yet the buyer has on delivery resold at a price above the market price, it has been held that the re-sale must be taken into account in fixing the damages (*d*). In this respect the action for delay would seem to differ from the action for non-delivery in which (special damages apart) circumstances "personal" or "accidental" to the buyer cannot be taken into account (*e*).

On the other hand the market price may have no bearing on the damages. Thus where the sellers had refused to make delivery, in the

---

(*t*) See p. 252, *post*.

(*u*) See *Bridge* v. *Wain* (1816), 1 Stark. 504, as commented on in *Elbinger A. G.* v. *Armstrong* (1874), L. R. 9 Q. B. 473, at p. 476, where this position seems to be assumed.

(*a*) *Millar's Machinery Co., Ltd.* v. *Way & Son* (1935), 40 Com. Cas. 204, C. A.; *Croudace Construction, Ltd.* v. *Cawoods Concrete Products*, [1978] 2 Lloyd's Rep. 55, C. A.

(*b*) *Fletcher* v. *Tayleur* (1855), 17 C. B. 21; *Smeed* v. *Foord* (1859), 1 E. & E. 602; *Cory* v. *Thames Ironworks Co.* (1868), L. R. 3 Q. B. 181; *Re Carver* (1911), 17 Com. Cas. 59. As to damages against a carrier for delay in delivering ordinary goods of commerce, see *Koufos* v. *Czarnikow, Ltd., Heron II*, [1967] 3 All E. R. 686; [1969] 1 A. C. 350, H. L.

(*c*) *Elbinger A. G.* v. *Armstrong* (1874), L. R. 9 Q. B. 473, at p. 477, *per* BLACKBURN, J.

(*d*) *Wertheim* v. *Chicoutimi Pulp. Co.*, [1911] A. C. 301, P. C.; distinguished and criticised, *Slater* v. *Hoyle & Smith*, [1920] 2 K. B. 11, C. A. (action for breach of warranty); see s. 53 (2), *post*. See further, *Benjamin's Sale of Goods*, para. 1297.

(*e*) *Williams* v. *Agius*, [1914] A. C. 510, approving *Rodocanachi* v. *Milburn* (1886), 18 Q. B. D. 67, 77, C. A. See also *Victoria Laundry* v. *Newman Industries*, [1949] 1 All E. R. 997, C. A.; [1949] 2 K. B. 528; *Brading* v. *McNeill & Co.*, [1946] 1 Ch. 145.

mistaken belief that the Control of Timber (No. 1) Order 1939, made delivery illegal, the buyer, in addition to obtaining a declaration that he was entitled to delivery, claimed damages on the ground that if delivery had been made on the contract date he could have used the timber as he pleased, whereas now he would be subject to restrictions rendering the timber less valuable, and an inquiry as to damages was directed (*f*).

Wrongful interference with goods.—Subject to the provisions of ss. 8 to 10 of the Factors Act 1889 and of ss. 24, 25 and 47 of this Act, *ante*, where, under a contract of sale, the buyer is entitled to immediate possession of the goods, and the seller wrongfully neglects or refuses to deliver them, the buyer may maintain an action for wrongful interference with the goods against the seller or any other person in possession of the goods who has dealt with the goods under such circumstances as to amount to a conversion thereof (*g*).

The measure of damages for wrongful interference is the actual damage sustained by the buyer (*h*), provided, of course, that the damage is not too remote. The *prima facie* measure of damages is the value of the goods at the time of the wrongful act (*i*), but this will not be so if the damage suffered by the plaintiff is less than the value of the goods.

As between seller and buyer, the buyer cannot recover larger damages by suing in tort rather than in contract. Thus if he has not paid the price and, instead of delivering the goods, the seller wrongfully sells them to a third party, the buyer can only recover the difference between the contract price and the value of the goods, even if he frames his action in tort (*k*).

(*f*) *Rappaport* v. *London Plywood and Timber Co., Ltd.*, [1940] 1 All E. R. 576.

(*g*) See the Torts (Interference with Goods) Act 1977. The claim would formerly have been in detinue or conversion. As to detinue, see *Langton* v. *Higgins* (1859), 4 H. & N. 402; *Whiteley* v. *Hilt*, [1918] 2 K. B. 808, 819. As to conversion or trover, see *Hollins* v. *Fowler* (1875), L. R. 7 H. L. 757; *Delaney* v. *Wallis* (1884), 13 L. R. Ir. 31, C. A. (sale by auctioneer in market overt).

(*h*) Torts (Interference with Goods) Act 1977, s. 3; *Chinery* v. *Viall* (1860), 5 H. & N. 288; *Wickham Holdings* v. *Brooke House Motors, Ltd.*, [1967] 1 All E. R. 117; [1967] 1 W. L. R. 295, C. A.; and see *Whitely* v. *Hilt*, [1918] 2 K. B. 808, C. A.; *cf. Astley Industrial Trust* v. *Miller*, [1968] 2 All E. R. 36 (hire-purchase: detinue by third party; value of goods less than amount due to hirer at date of demand by him); *Aronson* v. *Mologa Holzindustrie A/G Leningrad* (1927), 32 Com. Cas. 276, C. A. (price paid by buyer; conversion by seller; fall in market price after conversion).

(*i*) *Chinery* v. *Viall, supra; France* v. *Gaudet* (1871), L. R. 6 Q. B. 199.

(*k*) This is because the seller, having failed to deliver, cannot sue for the price: *Chinery* v. *Viall, supra; cf. Johnson* v. *Stear* (1863), 15 C. B. N. S. 330; *Johnson* v. *Lancashire Rail. Co.* (1878), 3 C. P. D. 499, at p. 507; *Hiort* v. *London and North Western Rail. Co.* (1879), 4 Ex. D. 188, C. A. The position would seem to be different if the seller tortiously retakes the goods after delivery, since at that stage he has performed his part of the contract and may sue for the price notwithstanding his tort: *Stephens* v. *Wilkinson* (1831), 2 B. & Ad. 320; *Gillard* v. *Brittan* (1841), 8 M. & W. 575; *Page* v. *Cowasjee Edulgee* (1866), L. R. 1 P. C. 127, at pp. 146–147. This would seem to be so even though the tortious seizure is also a breach of the warranty of quiet possession implied by s. 12 (2) and, *semble*, could be set up under s. 53 (1) in diminution or extinction of the price: *Healing (Sales) Pty., Ltd.* v. *Inglis Electrix Pty., Ltd.* (1968), 121 C. L. R. 584 (High Ct. of Aus.).

As regards third parties, the *prima facie* measure of damages is not normally applied where the plaintiff immediately prior to the wrongful interference had only a limited interest in the goods (*l*).

When a man has sold goods to one person, a mere contract to sell them to another after the property has passed is not a conversion, but a delivery of them in pursuance of that contract is a conversion (*m*), unless at the time of re-sale the original buyer was in default in paying the price (*n*). Ordinarily a person who buys and receives goods (otherwise than in market overt) which the seller had no right to sell is guilty of a conversion, however innocently he may have acted (*o*), but his liability has been much restricted by ss. 8 and 9 of the Factors Act 1889, *post*, reproduced in ss. 24 and 25 of this Act; and note also s. 23, *ante*.

52. Specific performance.—(1) In any action for breach of contract to deliver specific or ascertained goods (*p*) the court may, if it thinks fit, on the plaintiff's application, by its judgment or decree direct that the contract shall be performed specifically, without giving the defendant the option of retaining the goods on payment of damages.

(2) The plaintiff's application may be made at any time before judgment or decree.

(3) The judgment or decree may be unconditional, or on such terms and conditions as to damages, payment of the price and otherwise, as seems just to the court.

(4) The provisions of this section shall be deemed to be supplementary to, and not in derogation of, the right of specific implement in Scotland.

Derivation.—Section 52 of the 1893 Act, which was not, however, divided into subsections.

Definitions.—For "action," "defendant," "delivery," "goods," "plaintiff" and "specific goods," see s. 61 (1), *post*.

Cross-references.—*Cf.* ss. 2 (1), 8 and 9, *ante* (price), and s. 51, *ante* (action for non-delivery).

(*l*) *Wickham Holdings* v. *Brooke House Motors, Ltd.*, [1967] 1 All E. R. 117; [1967] 1 W. L. R. 295, C. A.; and see *Whiteley* v. *Hilt*, [1918] 2 K. B. 808, C. A.; *cf. Astley Industrial Trust* v. *Miller*, [1968] 2 All E. R. 36.

(*m*) *Lancashire Waggon Co.* v. *Fitzhugh* (1861), 6 H. & N. 502.

(*n*) *Milgate* v. *Kebble* (1841), 3 M. & Gr. 100, decided before the Act; "default" in this sense would now have to be construed in the light of s. 48 (3), *ante*.

(*o*) *Wilkinson* v. *King* (1809), 2 Camp. 335; *Cooper* v. *Willomatt* (1845), 1 C. B. 672.

(*p*) "Specific goods bear the meaning assigned to them in the definition clause, 'goods identified and agreed upon at the time a contract of sale is made.' 'Ascertained' probably means identified in accordance with the agreement after the time a contract of sale is made." *Per* ATKIN, L. J., *Re Wait*, [1927] 1 Ch. 606, at p. 630.

COMMENT

This section applies to all cases where the goods are specific or ascertained, whether the property therein has passed to the buyer or not. An arbitrator can award specific performance to the same extent as the High Court unless a contrary intention is expressed in the arbitration agreement, and provided the contract does not relate to land or any interest in land (*q*).

If payment and delivery are concurrent, as they will be by virtue of s. 28, *ante*, unless otherwise agreed, it will be made a condition of an order for specific performance that the price is paid on delivery (*r*). So too, where all or part of the price is not payable immediately on delivery and the seller is entitled to a lien such as an unpaid seller's lien over the goods to secure payment of the price, the court will not order specific performance in a manner which will deprive the seller of his lien, but will seek to protect his rights while enforcing the contract against him (*s*).

In appropriate cases, a contract of sale may be rectified by the court, and then in the same action specifically enforced as so amended (*t*).

The court has power to order a distress to be levied on all the defendant's goods until he delivers the specific chattel (*a*).

The power of the court to order specific performance is a discretionary one. It is akin to the power of a court of equity to order specific performance of a contract and will be exercised on similar principles (*b*). In an action for detinue it was stated that:

> "The power vested in the Court to order the delivery up of a particular chattel is discretionary and ought not to be exercised when the chattel is an ordinary article of commerce, and of no special value or interest, and not alleged to be of any special value to the plaintiff, and where damages would fully compensate" (*c*).

The section deals only with claims for specific performance by a buyer against a seller. But a seller may also in a special case obtain

---

(*q*) Arbitration Act 1950, s. 15; 2 Halsbury's Statutes (3rd Edn.) 446.

(*r*) *Cf. Hart* v. *Herwig* (1873), 8 Ch. App. 860, at p. 864.

(*s*) *Cf. Langen and Wind, Ltd.* v. *Bell*, [1972] 1 All E. R. 296; [1972] Ch. 685 (sale of shares).

(*t*) *U.S. of America* v. *Motor Trucks, Ltd.*, [1924] A. C. 196, P. C.; but see *Rose* v. *Pim*, [1953] 2 All E. R. 739, C. A.; [1953] 2 Q. B. 450.

(*a*) See R. S. C., O. 45, rr. 4, 13 (2); Appendix A, Forms 64 and 65.

(*b*) *Société des Industries Metallurgiques S. A.* v. *Bronx Engineering Co.*, [1975] 1 Lloyd's Rep. 465, *per* BUCKLEY and ORMROD, L.JJ.

(*c*) *Whiteley* v. *Hilt*, [1918] 2 K. B. 808, at p. 819, C. A.; *Cohen* v. *Roche*, [1927] 1 K. B. 169 (order for specific delivery of Hepplewhite chairs refused); *Behnke* v. *Bede Shipping Co.*, [1927] 1 K. B. 649 (specific performance of contract of sale of ship "of peculiar and perhaps unique value to the plaintiff granted)"; *Société des Industries Metallurgiques S. A.* v. *Bronx Engineering Co.*, *supra* (machinery specially made to order; obtainable elsewhere but would take 9–12 months; damages would be substantial and difficult to quantify. Held: these factors did not of themselves justify an order for specific performance).

specific performance against a buyer at least where the goods are specific or ascertained (*d*).

Non-specific or unascertained goods.—This section does not apply to non-specific or unascertained goods. In general, the courts will not order a seller to specifically perform such a contract, as the buyer can be adequately compensated for breach in damages (*e*).

It has recently been held, however, on an application for interlocutory relief, that where damages are not an adequate remedy, as where the goods are not or may not be obtainable elsewhere, then on general equitable principles, and subject to the normal limitations on such relief, the court may order specific performance of such a contract or grant an injunction restraining a seller from acting in breach of it (*f*).

Scotland.—In Scotland specific performance, or, as it is called, specific implement, is an ordinary and not an extraordinary remedy, and it can be demanded as of right wherever it is practicable (*g*).

53. Remedy for breach of warranty.—(1) Where there is a breach of warranty by the seller (*h*), or where the buyer elects (or is compelled) to treat any breach of a condition on the part of the seller as a breach of warranty (*i*), the buyer is not by reason only (*k*) of such breach of warranty entitled to reject the goods; but he may—

(*d*) *Shell-Mex* v. *Elton Cop Dyeing Co.* (1928), 34 Com. Cas. 39, at p. 46. And see *Thomas Borthwick* v. *South Otago Freezing Co.*, [1977] 1 N. Z. L. R. 366; on appeal [1978] 1 N. Z. L. R. 538, where an injunction was granted restraining a buyer under an exclusive buying and selling agreement from obtaining goods elsewhere although this was in effect a round about way of ordering specific performance.

(*e*) *Re Clarke* (1887), 36 Ch. D. 348, at p. 352, *per* COTTON, L. J.; *Fothergill* v. *Rowland* (1873), 43 L. J. Ch. 252, especially at p. 255, *per* JESSEL, M.R. See also *Dominion Coal Co., Ltd.* v. *Dominion Iron and Steel Co., Ltd. and National Trust Co., Ltd.*, [1909] A. C. 293, P. C.

(*f*) *Sky Petroleum, Ltd.* v. *VIP Petroleum, Ltd.*, [1974] 1 All E. R. 954; [1974] 1 W. L. R. 576; *Decro-Wall International S. A.* v. *Practitioners in Marketing, Ltd.*, [1971] 2 All E. R. 216; [1971] 1 W. L. R. 361, C. A. (injunction restraining seller under sole concessionaire agreement from selling goods to anyone but the sole concessionaire); see also n. (*d*), *supra*. *Cf.* the conflicting opinions on this point of the members of the Court of Appeal in *Re Wait*, [1927] 1 Ch. 606., discussed p. 142, *ante*, *Fry on Specific Performance* (6th ed.) 82–86; *Humboldt Flour Mills Co.* v. *Boscher* (1975), 50 D. L. R. (3d) 477 (specific performance held not to be available apart from this section).

(*g*) *Stewart* v. *Kennedy* (1890), 15 App. Cas. 75, at pp. 102, 105. *Cf. The S.S. Elorio*, 1916 S. C. 882 (discretion).

(*h*) *Syers* v. *Jonas* (1848), 2 Exch. 111, at p. 117; *Dawson* v. *Collis* (1851), 10 C. B. 523, at p. 523; *Behn* v. *Burness* (1863), 3 B. & S. 751, at pp. 755, 756, Ex. Ch.; *Heilbutt* v. *Hickson* (1872), L. R. 7 C. P. 438, at p. 451.

(*i*) See s. 11 (4), *ante*, and *Street* v. *Blay* (1831), 2 B. & Ad. 456, at p. 463; *Gompertz* v. *Denton* (1832), 1 Cr. & M. 207; *Parsons* v. *Sexton* (1847), 4 C. B. 899; *Couston* v. *Chapman* (1872), L. R. 2 Sc. & Div. 250, at p. 254.

(*k*) *Bannerman* v. *White* (1861), 10 C. B. N. S. 844; *Behn* v. *Burness*, *supra*; *Heilbutt* v. *Hickson*, *supra*.

(a) set up against the seller the breach of warranty in diminution or extinction of the price (*l*); or

(b) maintain an action against the seller for damages for the breach of warranty (*m*).

(2) The measure of damages for breach of warranty is the estimated loss directly and naturally resulting, in the ordinary course of events (*n*), from the breach of warranty (*o*).

(3) In the case of breach of warranty of quality such loss is prima facie the difference between the value of the goods at the time of delivery to the buyer and the value they would have had if they had fulfilled the warranty (*p*).

(4) The fact that the buyer has set up the breach of warranty in diminution or extinction of the price does not prevent him from maintaining an action for the same breach of warranty if he has suffered further damage (*q*).

(5) Nothing in this section prejudices or affects the buyer's right of rejection in Scotland as declared by this Act (*r*).

ILLUSTRATIONS

(1) A sells sulphuric acid to B as commercially free from arsenic; B uses it for making glucose, which he sells to brewers, and the persons who drink the

---

(*l*) *Mondel* v. *Steel* (1841), 8 M. & W. 858, 870, 871 (diminution); *Poulton* v. *Lattimore* (1829), 9 B. & C. 259 (extinction); *cf. Kinnear* v. *Brodie*, 1901 3 F. (Ct. of Sess.) 540,(horse, warranted quiet, drowned as a result of its vice; buyer not liable for the price. But the warranty seems to have been treated as a condition).

(*m*) *Davis* v. *Hedges* (1871), L. R. 6 Q. B. 687. The effect of the corresponding sub-section in the New South Wales Sale of Goods Act is discussed at length in *Healing* (*Sales*) *Pty., Ltd.* v. *Inglis Electrix Pty., Ltd.* (1968), 121 C. L. R. 584, 280, where differing conclusions are reached by the various members of the High Court of Australia.

(*n*) See *Waitapu* v. *R. H. Tregowath, Ltd.*, [1975] 2 N. Z. L. R. 218 (sale of unsafe saw which caused injury when used in a manner not contemplated at the date of the sale).

(*o*) *Randall* v. *Raper* (1858), E. B. & E. 84 (seed barley of inferior quality sold with warranty. Re-sold with same warranty. Claim by sub-buyer. Seller liable to buyer for amount of sub-buyer's claim although buyer had not yet paid sub-buyer); *Smith* v. *Green* (1875), 1 C. P. D. 92 (cow with foot-and-mouth disease; sold to farmer and infected other cows); *Randall* v. *Newson* (1877), 2 Q. B. D. 102, C. A., at p. 111 (defective carriage-pole specially made for carriage); *Wilson* v. *Dunville* (1879), 4 L. R. Ir. 249 (brewers' grains which poisoned cattle); *Hammond* v. *Bussey* (1887). 20 Q. B. D. 79, C. A. (ship coal of particular quality; costs of reasonably defending actions by sub-buyer, re-sale to whom was contemplated by parties at time of sale); *Parsons* (*Livestock*), *Ltd.* v. *Uttley Ingham & Co., Ltd.*, [1978] 1 All E. R. 525; [1978] Q. B. 791, C. A., illustration (7), *post*.

(*p*) *Loder* v. *Kekulé* (1857), 3 C. B. N. S. 128; *Jones* v. *Just* (1868), L. R. 3 Q. B. 197; *cf. Heilbutt* v. *Hickson* (1872), L. R. 7 C. P. 438, at p. 453.

(*q*) *Mondel* v. *Steel* (1841), 8 M. & W. 858; *cf. Rigge* v. *Burbidge* (1846), 15 M. & W. 598.

(*r*) See s. 11 (5), *ante*, and s. 58, *post*.

beer made by the brewers are poisoned. A does not know the purpose for which the acid is required. In an action for breach of warranty, B can recover the price of the acid and the value of other goods which have been spoiled by it, but not the damages he has had to pay to the brewers or damages for injury to the goodwill of his business (*s*).

(2) An orchid, warranted a *Cattelaya Alba*, is bought at a sale for £20. Two years afterwards it produces purple flowers. The purple variety is worth a few shillings, the white is worth £50. The buyer is entitled to £50 damages for breach of warranty (*t*).

(3) A, a grocer, sells tinned salmon to B which is unfit for food. B's wife is poisoned and dies. B may recover the reasonable expenses of medical attendance and the funeral, and also a reasonable sum for loss of his wife's services (*u*).

(4) Contract for the sale of cotton cloth of certain quality. The cloth delivered is of inferior quality. The buyer can recover as damages the difference between the value of the cloth at the time of delivery, and the value it would have had if it had answered to the warranty. A sub-contract of which the seller had no notice must be disregarded (*a*).

(5) Contract for goods to be shipped in August. They are accepted and paid for. The buyer subsequently finds out that they were shipped in September. If this does not affect the market price of the goods at the time of delivery, the buyer can recover only nominal damages (*b*).

(6) A buys a fur coat from B for re-sale and sells it to X. By reason of a dye used on the collar, X contracts dermatitis and recovers damages from A. A is entitled to recover from B the damages and costs awarded against him in the action by X which he has reasonably defended, together with his own costs in that action as between solicitor and client (*c*).

(7) A sells a hopper for pig food to B, a farmer. The ventilation is faulty and the pig nuts stored in the hopper become mouldy, but the farmer, not realising that serious illness might result, feeds the nuts to his pigs, which become ill and die. The farmer's conduct is reasonable in the light of then existing knowledge. He is entitled to damages for the loss of his pigs. A ought to have foreseen that if mouldy nuts were fed to the pigs they might become ill and was liable even though the illness was much worse than could have been foreseen (*d*).

Derivation.—Section 53 of the 1893 Act.

Definitions.—For "action," "buyer," "delivery," "goods," "quality," "seller" and "warranty," see s. 61 (1), *post*.

Cross-references.—*Cf.* ss. 2 (1), 8 and 9, *ante* (price); ss. 10 to 15,

---

(*s*) *Bostock* v. *Nicholson*, [1904] 1 K. B. 725, C. A.; *cf. Holden* v. *Bostock* (1902), 50 W. R. 323, C. A., and see illustrations to s. 14, *ante*; and *Pinnock Brothers* v. *Lewis & Peat*, [1923] 1 K. B. 690, at p. 697.

(*t*) *Ashworth* v. *Wells* (1898), 78 L. T. 136, C. A.

(*u*) *Jackson* v. *Watson & Sons*, [1909] 2 K. B. 193, C. A.

(*a*) *Slater* v. *Hoyle & Smith*, [1920] 2 K. B. 11, C. A.

(*b*) *Taylor & Sons, Ltd.* v. *Bank of Athens* (1922), 27 Com. Cas. 142. *Cf. Kwei Tek Chao* v. *British Traders and Shippers*, [1954] 1 All E. R. 779; [1954] 2 Q. B. 459.

(*c*) *Bennett, Ltd.* v. *Kreeger* (1925), 41 T. L. R. 609; and see *Bowmaker (Commercial), Ltd.* v. *Day*, [1965] 2 All E. R. 856, n.; [1965] 1 W. L. R. 1396.

(*d*) *Parsons (Livestock), Ltd.* v. *Uttley Ingham & Co.*, [1978] 1 All E. R. 525; [1978] Q. B. 791, C. A.

ante (conditions and warranties); s. 61 (1) *post*, definition of "warranty"; Note A, *post*, Appendix II; s. 35, *ante* (acceptance and rejection); and s. 54 *post* (interest and special damage).

COMMENT

This section is the complement to s. 11, *ante*. Section 11 shows when goods may be rejected or when the buyer must resort to his remedy for breach of warranty under this section. Although the buyer may not be able to reject the goods for simple breach of warranty, he may be entitled to reject them for fraud or some other invalidating cause. This conclusion is pointed to by the words "by reason *only* of such breach of warranty" in sub-s. (1), and by the provisions of s. 62 (2), *post*, as to savings of common law.

The seller's breach of warranty not only provides the buyer with a right of action if he has suffered damage, but also with a defence against an action for price. Thus if the contract contains an arbitration clause limited to quality disputes, the seller's action for the price may still be stayed if the buyer insists on such an arbitration, notwithstanding that the buyer does not counterclaim for damages.

Subsection (2).—The measure of damages for breach of warranty provided by this subsection is the normal measure of damages for breach of contract. The general principles governing the award of damages for breach of contract are discussed in the comment to s. 54, *post*. Particular examples are considered later in the comment to this section.

Subsection (3).—This subsection lays down a *prima facie* measure of damages in the case of a breach of warranty of quality. It does not apply to any other breach of warranty (*e*), but appears to be based on the same principle as where the seller fails to deliver the goods at all (*f*), namely that if the contract is broken, the buyer may sell the defective goods and purchase goods of the required quality (*g*). This principle may well be relevant in assessing damages for other breaches of warranty by the seller.

The difference in value of the goods.—The value of the goods will be the market value where there is an available market (*h*), for in such a case the buyer can go into the market, buy new goods, and sell those delivered at the relevant market price (*i*).

The buyer must prove his damage by adducing evidence as to the reduction in value of the goods (*k*). The contract price cannot be

(*e*) For damages for the breach of the condition and warranties implied by s. 12, see the comments to that section, *ante*.

(*f*) See. s. 51 (3), *ante*.

(*g*) *Slater* v. *Hoyle and Smith*, [1920] 2 K. B. 11, C. A.

(*h*) *Ibid.*, at p. 22.

(*i*) See *Barrow* v. *Arnaud* (1846), 8 Q. B. 604, at p. 609, Ex. Ch., cited at length in the comment to s. 51, *ante*.

(*k*) *Aryeh* v. *Lawrence Kostoris & Son, Ltd.*, [1967] 1 Lloyd's Rep. 63. On the other hand, the Supreme Court of Canada has held that where goods are not fit for the purpose for

assumed to represent the value which the goods would have had if they had answered to the warranty, both because the buyer may have been getting a bargain, or overpaying, and also, where delivery does not immediately follow the making of the contract, because the value may have changed in the interval. It may, however, be a factor to be taken into account where there is little other evidence (*l*).

So, too, the price at which the purchaser has agreed to re-sell will not be taken into account where other goods can be bought to enable the buyer to fulfil his sub-sale, but may be an element in estimating the value where alternative goods cannot be acquired (*m*). Indeed, where no substitute can be obtained for the goods, the price which the buyer is entitled to receive on the sub-sale will be very strong evidence of the value of the goods to the buyer, although account would have to be taken of the terms of the contract under which the goods are re-sold.

In some cases it will be necessary to assess what would have been a fair market price at the time of the purchase if the defects had been known to the parties (*n*).

In other cases, the difference in value may be assessed as the amount necessary to make the goods in question answer the warranty (*o*), or as an amount equal to a fair allowance against the price in respect of the damage (*p*).

The respective values should *prima facie* be assessed at the date of delivery. But this rule is based on the proposition that the buyer can acquire alternative goods on that date to fulfil his requirements, and can sell the inferior goods on the same day. If the circumstances are such that the seller cannot reasonably expect the buyer to discover the defect until later, then the difference in value must be calculated at the time when the buyer can reasonably be expected to discover the defect (*q*). So, too, at least if the price falls, the relevant date may be postponed if the buyer is induced by the seller not to re-sell immediately (*r*).

Where damages are assessed by reference to the cost of repairs, the

---

which they are bought so as to be valueless for that purpose, the *prima facie* measure of damages is the price of the goods, and it is for the seller to show that they are still of some merchantable value: *Ford Motor Co. of Canada, Ltd.* v. *Haley*, [1967] S. C. R. 437, as explained in *Zack* v. *Kenworth* (1968), 65 W. W. R. 570; *Bouchard* v. *South Park Mercury Sales* (1978), 85 D. L. R. (3d) 404.

(*l*) *Minster Trust, Ltd.* v. *Traps Tractors, Ltd.*, [1954] 3 All E. R. 136; [1954] 1 W. L. R. 963.

(*m*) *Slater* v. *Hoyle and Smith*, [1920] 2 K. B. 11, at pp. 17, 18.

(*n*) *Jackson* v. *Chrysler Acceptances*, [1978] R. T. R. 474.

(*o*) *Minster Trust, Ltd.* v. *Traps Tractors, Ltd.*, *supra*.

(*p*) *Biggin & Co., Ltd.* v. *Permanite, Ltd.*, [1950] 2 All E. R. 859, at p. 871; [1951] 1 K. B. 422, at p. 439, *per* DEVLIN, J.; reversed on other grounds, [1951] 2 All E. R. 191; [1951] 2 K. B. 314, C. A.

(*q*) *Van den Hurk* v. *Martens*, [1920] 1 K. B. 850 (packaged goods which seller knew buyer intended to re-sell and which it was not practical to examine before they were required for use); *Ashworth* v. *Wells*, illustration (2), *ante*.

(*r*) *Loder* v. *Kekule* (1857), 3 C. B. N. S. 128. *Cf.* the cases on a reasonable time for rejection, discussed in the comment to s. 35, *ante*.

cost of the repairs is to be taken at the time when, having regard to all the relevant circumstances, the repairs can first reasonably be undertaken (*s*).

In general, however, fluctuations in the market price of the inferior goods after the date of delivery, or where appropriate the date on which the defect is discovered, will be ignored (*t*).

Other recoverable heads of damage.—The measure of damages set out in subsection (3) of this section is a *prima facie* measure only. It is always open to a buyer to prove that he has suffered other loss which directly and naturally resulted in the ordinary course of events from the breach of warranty, and in such a case he will be entitled to damages to compensate him for such loss. It is sufficient if damage of the type which occurred was a serious possibility even if the exact nature of the damage could not be foreseen (*u*).

The buyer may claim such damages even where he has set up the breach of warranty in diminution or extinction of the price under sub-s. (4) for his loss may greatly exceed the price.

In considering what loss is within sub-s. (2) of this section, it is necessary first to consider whether and if so when, the buyer ought to have discovered that there had been a breach of warranty.

Where the defect is patent or discoverable.—In general, a buyer cannot use an article at the risk of his seller if before he uses it he knows that it is defective (*a*). So, too, if he buys it for re-sale, but before he re-sells it he becomes aware that it is defective, he will not normally be able to recover from his seller extra damages which he has had to pay the sub-buyer as a result of delivering the defective goods over and above those he would have had to pay had he not delivered them (*b*).

If the buyer learns of the defects after the sub-sale, he ought to warn the sub-buyer if by so doing he can diminish his liability to him, and if he fails to do so, he will not be able to pass on the extra damages to his seller (*c*).

A party to a contract should act reasonably even when the other

---

(*s*) *Dodd Properties* (*Kent*), *Ltd.* v. *Canterbury City Council*, [1980] 1 All E. R. 928; [1980] 1 W. L. R. 433, C. A. (on facts, held reasonable to postpone extensive repairs to building until after judgment).

(*t*) *Jones* v. *Just* (1868), L. R. 3 Q. B. 197; *Campbell Mostyn* (*Provisions*), *Ltd.* v. *Barnett Trading Co.*, [1954] 1 Lloyd's Rep. 65, C. A.; and see *Jamal* v. *Moolla Dawood*, [1916] 1 A. C. 175, at p. 179, P. C.

(*u*) *Parsons* v. *Uttley Ingham & Co.*, *ante*, illustration (7). See further the distinction between general and special damages, considered in the comment to s. 54, *post*. For cases where the seller fails to deliver the goods and the buyer is able to recover more than the *prima facie* measure of damages, see *ante*, comment to s. 51.

(*a*) *British Oil and Cake* v. *Burstall* (1923), 39 T. L. R. 406, at p. 407.

(*b*) *Biggin & Co., Ltd.* v. *Permanite, Ltd.*, [1951] 1 K. B. 422, at p. 435; reversed on another ground [1951] 2 K. B. 314, C. A.; see also *Dobell & Co., Ltd.* v. *Barber Garratt*, [1931] 1 K. B. 219, at p. 238 (a buyer cannot increase the damages recoverable from his seller by making further deliveries of cattle cake to a sub-buyer after he learns that the cattle cake is unfit for use as cattle food).

(*c*) *Biggin & Co., Ltd.* v. *Permanite, Ltd.* *supra*.

party is in breach, and may not increase the liability of the other party by acting unreasonably. In some circumstances a buyer may reasonably use defective goods even with knowledge of the defect. Thus, if no alternative goods are available and there is a reasonable prospect that the defective goods will fulfil the purpose for which they were bought, it may sometimes be reasonable to use them for that purpose, and if in such a case the buyer in fact suffers additional loss, such loss might be recoverable from the seller (*d*).

Nor will a buyer normally be debarred from recovering damages just because the loss could have been avoided had he examined the goods, for he will normally be entitled to rely on the seller's warranty (*e*). It may be different if without any special examination the buyer is put on notice that something is wrong with the goods. The buyer must act reasonably.

He will not normally be held to have acted unreasonably just because, in the absence of any indication that there was anything wrong with the goods, he chooses to rely on the seller's warranty and does not subject the goods to a thorough examination (*e*), even if he is careless in failing to examine the goods (*f*). But once it is apparent to the buyer that the goods are defective and are no longer in the same state in which they were delivered, then, at least where the safety of others is involved, the buyer must take the precaution either to get them mended or at least to find out whether it is safe to continue to use them. If he does not do so he will not be able to recover from the seller in respect of any damages payable to third parties by reason of his negligent failure to take such precautions (*g*).

Loss of profits.—If the seller should realise at the date of the contract that goods which are sold are likely to be used by the buyer with a view

---

(*d*) In deciding what is reasonable, it would be necessary to take all factors into account, including the likely damage resulting from not using the goods, the prospect of successfully using them, and the extra loss which the buyer would suffer if he used them unsuccessfully. *Cf.* the rule that a party who acts reasonably in seeking to mitigate damages may recover additional loss which he thereby incurs: *Lloyds and Scottish Finance, Ltd.* v. *Modern Cars and Caravans* (*Kingston*), *Ltd.*, [1964] 2 All E. R. 732; [1966] 1 Q. B. 764; *The World Beauty*, [1970] P. 144, at p. 156, C. A.; *MacGregor on Damages* (14th. ed.), paras. 242–243.

(*e*) *Pinnock Brothers* v. *Lewis and Peat*, [1923] 1 K. B. 690, 698 (where only a small parcel of goods was involved, and an expert examination would have been required to discover the defect); *Dobell & Co., Ltd.* v. *Barber and Garratt*, [1931] 1 K. B. 219, C. A. (where an analysis of cattle cake would have been required). *Cf. Mowbray* v. *Merryweather*, [1895] 2 Q. B. 640, C. A. (where the defect in a chain could have been discovered but the owner's warranty was relied on instead by the hirers).

(*f*) *Mowbray* v. *Merryweather*, *supra*.

(*g*) *Lexmead* (*Basingstoke*) *Ltd.* v. *Lewis* (1981) Times, 9th April, as yet unreported except in the Times, where the House of Lords applied a dictum of WINN, L. J. in *Hadley* v. *Droitwich Construction Co. Ltd.*, [1968] 1 W. L. R. 37, that "in a case where A has been held liable to X, a stranger, for negligent failure to take a certain precaution, he may recover over from someone with whom he has a contract only if, by that contract, the other contracting party has warranted that he *need not* – there is no necessity – take the very precaution for the failure to take which he has been held liable in law to [X]".

to profit, then damages for breach of warranty may include a sum in respect of any profits which the buyer has lost (*h*).

If the goods have more than one use, it would not seem to be necessary that the seller should know the precise use to which they are to be put by the buyer (*i*).

Expenses.—Subject to the same proviso as to foreseeability, a buyer may also recover damages in respect of wasted expenditure (*k*). Where there is no claim for loss of profit, this claim may even extend to cover expenditure incurred before the contract in anticipation of it (*l*). But this will not be so if the party in breach proves that the loss would have occurred apart from the breach, for in such a case the expenditure is not wasted because of the breach (*m*).

Where costs are incurred in a reasonable attempt to mitigate damage, such costs are recoverable as part of the damages, even if the attempt to mitigate is unsuccessful (*n*).

It has sometimes been suggested that it is not possible to claim both for loss of profit and for expenses incurred. Such a general proposition cannot be supported either by authority (*o*) or in principle. The object of damages, however assessed, is to put the injured party as far as possible in the same position as if the contract had been performed (*p*). Damages cannot be recovered twice over. Net profits are calculated by deducting from gross profits the expenses necessary to earn them. If as a result of the breach, the buyer makes a smaller net profit or succeeds only in breaking even, then he is put in the same position as if the contract had been performed if he receives by way of damages a sum equivalent to the net profits which he ought to have made but did not

---

(*h*) See, *e.g.*, *Ashworth* v. *Wells*, *ante*, illustration (2); *Holden* v. *Bostock* (1902), 18 T. L. R. 317 (sugar contaminated with arsenic sold to brewers; damages included market value of beer made with the sugar which the brewers had to destroy).

(*i*) *Bostock & Co., Ltd.* v. *Nicholson & Sons, Ltd.*, [1904] 1 K. B. 725; *Kendall* v. *Lillico*, [1968] 2 All E. R. 444; [1969] 2 A. C. 31, H. L.; *Bunting* v. *Tory* (1948), 64 T. L. R. 353, a decision of HILBERY, J., which is sometimes cited for the proposition that the seller should know the precise use, would seem to be inconsistent with these authorities. In any event, in that case, the only possible use for the bull which was bought was for breeding, and it is difficult to see why it should affect the measure of the damages that the buyer might have, but did not, sell the bull to somebody else instead of breeding from it himself.

(*k*) See, *e.g.*, *Molling & Co.* v. *Dean & Son, Ltd.* (1901), 18 T. L. R. 217 (cost of bringing goods back from sub-buyer who rejected them); *Smith* v. *Johnson* (1899), 15 T. L. R. 179 (cost of pulling down and rebuilding wall).

(*l*) *Anglia Television* v. *Reed*, [1971] 3 All E. R. 690; [1972] 1 Q. B. 60, C. A.

(*m*) *Bowlay Logging, Ltd.* v. *Domtar, Ltd.*, [1978] 4 W. W. R. 105.

(*n*) *Hoffberger* v. *Ascot International Bloodstock Bureau* (1976), *Times*, 29 January, C. A.

(*o*) Such a claim was allowed in *Molling* v. *Dean*, *supra*, *Foaminol Laboratories* v. *British Artid Plastics*, [1941] 2 All E. R. 393; *Hydraulic Engineering Co., Ltd.* v. *McHaffie Goslett and Co.* (1878), 4 Q. B. D. 670 (delay in delivery); *Steam Herring Fleet, Ltd.* v. *Richards & Co., Ltd.* (1901), 17 T. L. R. 731 (delay in delivery).

(*p*) *Cullinane* v. *British Rema*, [1953] 2 All E. R. 1257; [1954] 1 Q. B. 292, *per* JENKINS, L. J., at pp. 1264 and 308; *Monarch SS Co., Ltd.* v. *A. B. Karl-shamns Oljefabriker*, [1949] 1 All E. R. 1, at p. 12; [1949] A. C. 196, at pp. 220–221. See also comment to s. 54, *post*.

make (*q*). But if he incurs an overall loss, then he can only be recompensed if he receives in addition to the net profits a sum equivalent to that loss.

Thus if a man buys a machine for £5,000 which is warranted to produce him £10,000 profit during its lifetime of one year after allowing for the cost of the machine and all other expenses, but after he has spent £1,000 by way of necessary preliminary expenditure, and £500 reasonably trying to make the machine work, it finally proves to be valueless, the amount necessary to put him in the same position as if the contract had been performed must include £1,500 to cover him for his loss, in addition to damages in respect of the profit he should have made (*r*).

Losses incurred by the buyer as a result of reselling the goods.—The question of re-sale has been considered in the House of Lords, where Lord PHILLIMORE said,

> "It is all a question of contract. . . Notice will not do of itself, nor will knowledge. But if the tribunal which tries the case comes to the conclusion that he contracted to sell . . . on terms that he should be responsible for damage which might accrue from his failure to provide for any one of certain objects, then he must be held liable" (*s*).

In order to recover damages in respect of such losses, a buyer must show that the seller ought to have contemplated the possibility of a sub-contract under which a claim might be made against the buyer (*t*). It is

(*q*) In *Cullinane* v. *British Rema, supra*, the buyer of a clay pulverising plant claimed loss of net profits for three years (deducting running expenses and an allowance for depreciation of the plant) plus the difference between the cost of the plant and its estimated residual value. The venture was a speculative one and the life expectancy of the plant was ten years. The plant failed to perform as warranted. The majority of the Court of Appeal held that in the absence of any claim for any loss of profit beyond three years and of any evidence or finding by the Official Referee as to what that profit would have been, the buyer was bound by his pleadings and they had to proceed on the assumption that no more profit would have been made after the three years—see *per* Lord EVERSHED at pp. 1263 and 305–306 and *per* JENKINS, L. J., at pp. 1266–1267 and 312. In those circumstances the buyer was put in the same position as if the contract had been performed, so far as was possible on the pleadings and the evidence. MORRIS, L. J., dissenting, considered that the evidence and the findings of the Official Referee indicated that further profit would have been made after the three years. The case is discussed at length by the High Court of Australia in *T. C. Industrial Plant Pty., Ltd.* v. *Roberts (Queensland), Pty., Ltd.* (1963), 37 A. L. J. R. 289. See also 1973 Can. Bar Rev. 490. See however *Anglia Television* v. *Reed*, [1971] 3 All E. R. 690, at p. 692; [1972] 1 Q. B. 60, at p. 64, where Lord DENNING, M. R. accepts *Cullinane* v. *British Rema* as authority for the proposition that in some cases at least a plaintiff cannot claim both wasted expenditure and loss of profit.

(*r*) *Cf. Jones Autos* v. *Volvo Distributors* (1975), 14 S. A. S. R. 297.

(*s*) *Hall, Ltd.* v. *Pim Junior & Co., Ltd.* (1928), 33 Com. Cas. 324, at p. 373 (construing contract of London Corn Association). This decision is commented upon by SCRUTTON, L. J., in *Finlay & Co.* v. *Kwik Hoo Tong Handel Maatschappij*, [1929] 1 K. B. 400, at pp. 409–412, and by SANKEY, L. J., at pp. 417 and 418.

(*t*) *James Finlay* v. *N. V. Kwik Hoo Tong*, [1929] 1 K. B. 400, at p. 411, *per* SCRUTTON, L. J.; *Biggin & Co.* v. *Permanite*, [1951] 1 K. B. 422, reversed on another ground [1951] 2 All E. R. 191; [1951] 2 K. B. 314, C. A.

also essential that any difference between the first contract and the sub-contract should not be such as to make it impossible to say whether the injury which ultimately resulted to the sub-buyer and for which the buyer was liable was a natural and foreseeable result of the breach of the first contract (*u*).

Inconvenience and frustration.—In a proper case, when this is a foreseeable consequence of the breach, damages may be awarded under this head (*a*).

Losses caused or aggravated by the buyer's impecuniosity.—Such losses will generally be irrecoverable (*b*), unless they can be shown to have been within the contemplation of the parties when the contract was made (*c*). But a seller will be unable to complain that a buyer has failed to take reasonable steps to mitigate his loss if he is unable to afford to take such steps (*d*).

Loss of goodwill.—Where goods are bought for re-sale or to enable the buyer to fulfil some other obligation, the buyer may suffer a loss of goodwill if as a result of a breach of contract by the seller, he is unable to fulfil his own obligations. He may recover damages in respect of any such loss, including the loss of repeat orders from the buyer's customers, if he pleads and proves with sufficient certaintly that he has suffered

---

(*u*) *Biggin* v. *Permanite, supra.* See also *Kasler and Cohen* v. *Slavonski*, [1928] 1 K. B. 78, at p. 85; *Dexters, Ltd.* v. *Hill Crest Oil Co.* (*Bradford*), *Ltd.*, [1926] 1 K. B. 348, at p. 359, C. A. For illustrations see *Hydraulic Engineering Co.* v. *McHaffie* (1878), 4 Q. B. D. 670, at p. 677, C. A. (part specially ordered to fulfil sub-contract); see also *Grébert-Bornis* v. *Nugent* (1885), 15 Q. B. D. 85, C. A. (goods ordered for French sub-contract); *Biggin & Co.* v. *Permanite*, [1951] 2 All E. R. 191; [1951] 2 K. B. 314, C. A. (buyers allowed to recover from sellers amount reasonably paid to sub-buyers in settlement of dispute). *Hammond* v. *Bussey* (1887), 20 Q. B. D. 79, C. A. (breach of warranty and sub-sale with similar warranty, costs of action reasonably defended), followed, *Agius* v. *Great Western Colliery Co.* (1899), 1 Q. B. 413, C. A.; *Bennett, Ltd.* v. *Kreeger* (1925), 41 T. L. R. 609; *Alison & Co.* v. *Wallsend Slipway & Engineering Co.* (1927), 43 T. L. R. 323, C. A. (damages including costs of compromising claim); *Kasler & Cohen* v. *Slavonski*, [1928] 1 K. B. 78 (costs of actions between successive sellers); *Slavonski* v. *La Pelleterie de Roubain S. A.* (1927), 137 L. T. 645; *Dobell & Co.* v. *Barber & Garratt*, [1931] 1 K. B. 219 (damages paid under sub-contract recoverable); *Slade* v. *Sinclair & Wilcox* (1930), 74 Sol. Jo. 122; *Lloyds and Scottish Finance, Ltd.* v. *Modern Cars and Caravans* (*Kingston*), *Ltd.*, [1964] 2 All E. R. 732; [1966] 1 Q. B. 764 (cost of interpleader proceedings reasonably incurred in an attempt to mitigate damages).

(*a*) *G. K. N. Centrax Gears, Ltd.* v. *Matbro, Ltd.*, [1976] 2 Lloyd's Rep. 555, C. A. (general disruption, inconvenience and expense resulting to commercial enterprise); *Gascoigne* v. *British Credit Trust*, [1978] C. L. Y. 711 (Cty. Ct.); *Jackson* v. *Chrysler Acceptances, Ltd.*, [1978] R. T. R. 474, C. A.

(*b*) *Trans Trust S. P. R. L.* v. *Danubian Trading Co., Ltd.*, [1952] 1 All E. R. 970; [1952] 2 Q. B. 297, C. A.; and see *Muhammad Tasa el Sheikh Ahmad* v. *Ali*, [1947] A. C. 414, P. C. Compare *Mrs. Eaton's Car Sales* v. *Thomesen*, [1973] N. Z. L. R. 686.

(*c*) *Cf. Freedhoff* v. *Pomalift* (1971), 19 D. L. R. (3d.) 153, in which it was held by the Ontario Court of Appeal that where there is a contract for the sale of a revenue generating asset, the forseeable damage is the loss of revenue, not the loss occasioned by the buyer's inability to make payments using that revenue.

(*d*) *Dodd Properties* (*Kent*), *Ltd.* v. *Canterbury City Council*, [1980] 1 All E. R. 928; [1980] 1 W. L. R. 433, C. A. *Cf. Robbins of Putney* v. *Meek*, [1971] R. T. R. 345; and see generally the passage on mitigation of damages, p. 249, *post*.

pecuniary loss, and that such pecuniary loss was within the contemplation of the seller when the contract was made (*e*).

Scotland.—In Scotland before the Act no distinction was drawn between warranties and conditions. Every material term was a condition, and the rule was that where the buyer could reject the goods, but had not done so, he could not sue for damages. The *actio quanti minoris* only applied to cases where the goods could not be returned; but now the buyer has a double remedy, guarded, however, by the court's power to order the consignation of the whole or part of the purchase price—see the comment to s. 59, *post*.

Interest, etc.

54. Interest etc.—Nothing in this Act affects the right of the buyer or the seller to recover interest or special damages in any case where by law interest or special damages may be recoverable, or to recover money paid where the consideration for the payment of it has failed.

Derivation.—Section 54 of the 1893 Act.

Definitions.—For "buyer" and "seller," see s. 61 (1), *post*.

Cross-references.—*Cf.* ss. 37 and 49 to 53, *ante* (rights of action).

Comment

Interest.—See note to s. 3 of the Law Reform (Miscellaneous Provisions) Act 1934, reproduced in Appendix I, *post*.

Object of damages.—In assessing damages for breach of contract the object aimed at is to put the injured party, so far as money can do it, into the same position as if the contract had not been broken, for this is the measure of the loss directly and naturally resulting from the breach (*f*).

Mitigation of damages.—But the injured party must act reasonably; and if it be open to him to take steps to mitigate the loss, he

---

(*e*) *G. K. N. Centrax Gears, Ltd.* v. *Matbro, Ltd.*, [1976] 2 Lloyd's Rep. 555, C. A.; *Foaminol Laboratories, Ltd.* v. *British Artid Plastics, Ltd.*, [1941] 2 All E. R. 393, at p. 400; *cf. Simon* v. *Pawson and Leafs, Ltd.* (1932), 38 Com. Cas. 151, C. A. The buyer may show either that the seller should have contemplated that the breach of contract would naturally lead to a loss of the buyer's business or that the seller knew that the breach would probably lead to a loss of business: *Doe* v. *W. H. Bowater, Ltd.*, [1916] W. N. 185. A claim for loss of goodwill was disallowed in *Bostock* v. *Nicholson*, [1904] 1 K. B. 725. For a Canadian case where a claim for loss of custom was allowed, see *Lakelse Dairy Produce, Ltd.* v. *General Dairy Machinery, Ltd.* (1970), 10 D. L. R. (3d.) 277.

(*f*) *Wertheim* v. *Chicoutimi Pulp Co.*, [1911] A. C. 301, P. C.; *British Westinghouse Electric Co.* v. *Underground Railway*, [1912] A. C. 673, at p. 689. *Cf. Taylor & Sons, Ltd.* v. *Bank of Athens* (1922), 27 Com. Cas. 142, at p. 147 (nominal damages only given on facts). *Quære* how far this principle applies to breach of warranty in respect of dangerous articles, where the cause of action may be framed in tort?

must do so. If he fails to take such steps, the defendant may set up the failure in mitigation of damages (*g*). This, in effect, is an application of the general rule of *causa proxima* to damages. If a man does not take reasonable steps to mitigate the loss arising from the other party's breach of contract, the resulting loss is proximately caused by his own conduct and not by the breach of contract. But a contracting party is not bound to take steps in mitigation of damages which would prove injurious to him in other ways (*h*). Provided he acts reasonably at the time, the other contracting party will not be permitted to complain that he failed to do that which, perhaps, with hindsight he might have been wiser to do (*i*). And if a contracting party takes a reasonable and prudent course to mitigate his loss, which naturally arises out of the circumstances in which he was placed by the breach, and which is not an independent or disconnected transaction, then any resulting diminution in the loss he has suffered will be taken into account although there was no duty on him so to act (*k*). Where a contracting party repudiates a wholly executory contract, the other contracting party is not bound to accept such repudiation, but can carry out his part of the contract and claim the full contract price, at least where he has a legitimate interest, financial or otherwise in so doing (*l*).

Special damages.—In pleading a care, a distinction is drawn, between general and special damages.

> "Special damage in such a context means the particular damage (beyond the general damage) which results from the particular circumstances of the case, and of the plaintiff's claim to be compensated, for which he ought to give

---

(*g*) *Roth* v. *Taysen* (1895), 73 L. T. 628, C. A.; *Nickoll* v. *Ashton*, [1900] 2 Q. B. 298; *Hill* v. *Showell* (1918), 87 L. J. K. B. 1106, H. L.; *Payzu, Ltd.* v. *Saunders*, [1919] 2 K. B. 581, C. A.; *Melachrino* v. *Nickoll and Knight*, [1920] 1 K. B. 693; *Houndsditch Warehouse Co., Ltd.* v. *Waltex, Ltd.*, [1944] K. B. 579.

(*h*) *Finlay & Co., Ltd.* v. *Kwik Hoo Tong Handel Maatschappij*, [1929] 1 K. B. 400 (buyer not bound to enforce sub-contracts when to do so would injure his commercial reputation); *Jewelowski* v. *Propp*, [1944] 1 All E. R. 483; [1944] 1 K. B. 510 (claimant not bound to expend money on a speculative venture in order to mitigate damages); *Lesters Leather and Skin Co.* v. *Home and Overseas Brokers* (1948), 64 T. L. R. 569, C. A. (no obligation to purchase from unfamiliar suppliers abroad goods which would only arrive long after contractual delivery date); *Heaven and Kesterten, Ltd.* v. *Etablissements Francois Albiac et cie*, [1956] 2 Lloyd's Rep. 316 (buyer who has rejected goods on grounds of defective quality is not bound to accept such goods if offered in mitigation of damages; *aliter*, perhaps where the rejection was for reasons unconnected with the quality of the goods); *Robbins of Putney* v. *Meek*, [1971] R. T. R. 345 (impecunious seller forced to re-sell prematurely). *Cf.*, pp. 233, 248, *ante*.

(*i*) *Harlow & Jones* v. *Panex (International), Ltd.*, [1967] 2 Lloyd's Rep. 509.

(*k*) *British Westinghouse Electric and Manufacturing Co., Ltd.* v. *Underground Electric Rail. Co., Ltd.*, [1912] A. C. 673, at pp. 689–692, H. L.; *R. Pagnan and Frateli* v. *Corbisa Industrial Agropacuaria Limitdator*, [1971] 1 All E. R. 165; [1970] 1 W. L. R. 1306, C. A.; contrast *Aruna Mills, Ltd.* v. *Dhanrajmal Gobindram*, [1968] 1 All E. R. 113; [1968] 1 Q. B. 655 (independent transaction).

(*l*) *White and Carter (Councils), Ltd.* v. *Macgregor*, [1961] 3 All E. R. 1178; [1962] A. C. 413.

warning in his pleadings in order that there may be no surprise at the trial" (*m*).

The Act deals only with general damages, and merely saves the law relating to special damages. Many of the cases fail to distinguish special from general damages, the reason being that both are governed by the same guiding rule. Given a particular contract, the measure of damages is the loss which naturally results from breach of a contract of the kind in question. Given a contract made under special circumstances to the knowledge of both parties, *e.g.*, a contract to fulfil a sub-contract, the measure of special damage is the loss which naturally results from the breach of a contract made under those particular circumstances. The underlying principles governing the award of damages for breach of contract were considered by the Court of Appeal in *Victoria Laundry* v. *Newman Industries* (*n*), where the following propositions were approved:

(1) The governing purpose of damages is to put the injured party in the same position, so far as money can do it, as if his rights had been observed, but this rule does not permit recovery of all loss resulting from a breach of contract, however improbable or unpredictable.

(2) Damages are recoverable only in respect of that part of the loss actually resulting as was the time of the contract reasonably foreseeable and liable to result from the breach.

(3) What was then reasonably foreseeable depends upon the knowledge then possessed by the parties, or, at all events, by the party who later commits the breach.

(4) For this purpose knowledge may be actual or imputed. A contract breaker is assumed to know what loss is liable to result in the ordinary course of things from his breach. He may also be shown to know of special circumstances outside the ordinary course of things of such a kind that a breach in those special circumstances would be liable to cause more loss. If so, the additional loss is also recoverable.

(5) For a contract breaker to be liable, it is not necessary that he should have asked himself what loss might result. As has often been pointed out, parties at the time of contracting contemplate performing the contract not breaking it. It is sufficient that, if he had considered the question, he would as a reasonable man have concluded that the loss in question was liable to result (*o*).

(6) It is not necessary to show that the loss was certain to result. It is enough if it is a "serious possibility" or "real danger" (*p*).

(*m*) *Ratcliffe* v. *Evans*, [1892] 2 Q. B. 524, at p. 528, *per* BOWEN, L. J.; see also *Anglo-Cyprian Trade Agencies* v. *Paphos Wine Industries*, [1951] 1 All E. R. 873.

(*n*) [1949] 1 All E. R. 997; [1949] 2 K. B. 528, C. A.

(*o*) Thus where the goods are misused and an injury is caused because they are defective which would not have occurred otherwise, damages in respect of that injury have been held to be unrecoverable by the buyer if that user was not in the contemplation of the parties when the contract was made: *Waitapu* v. *R. H. Tregoweth, Ltd.*, [1975] 2 N. Z. L. R. 218. And see *Lexmead (Basingstoke) Ltd.* v. *Lewis* (1981) Times, 9th April, considered *ante*, p. 245.

(*p*) *Koufos* v. *Czarnikow, Ltd.*, [1967] 3 All E. R. 686; [1969] 1 A. C. 350, H. L., where the use of the words "on the cards" in the *Victoria Laundry* case was disapproved.

It has further been held in *Parsons* v. *Uttley Ingham Co., Ltd.* (*q*) that the test of remoteness of damage is the same in contract and that a loss will be recoverable by action if a loss of that type was a serious possibility even though the actual loss would not have been contemplated.

Failure of consideration.—As to failure of consideration also, there is nothing peculiar to the contract of sale. Money paid on a consideration which has wholly failed can usually be recovered as money had and received (*r*). And where the plaintiff bought and paid for 175 tons of terra japonica, and only 156¾ tons were delivered, he was held entitled to recover a proportionate amount of the price under the common money counts (*s*).

Where the plaintiff bought a motor-car, used it for some months, and then found out that it had been stolen and had to be restored to its original owner, it was held that he was entitled to recover the full price he had paid. There was a total failure of consideration consequent on the breach of condition as to title (*t*).

If there is a total failure of consideration because the buyer has paid for the goods and the seller has then become bankrupt, or in the case of a company has gone into liquidation, before he supplies the goods, the buyer must normally prove in the bankruptcy or liquidation for the price. But in special circumstances, the seller may be held to be a trustee of the purchase price for the buyer, in which case the buyer will recover it in priority to the other creditors (*u*).

Rate of exchange.—Changes in the relative values of currencies are irrelevant if they occur after the date as at which damages fall to be assessed and are usually to be disregarded if they occur on or before that date, either because the loss flowing from the revaluation has no causal connection with the breach of contract, or because such a loss is not within the assumed contemplation of the parties (*a*). Until recently, it has also repeatedly been held that an English court cannot give judgment in foreign currency. But the House of Lords has now held that there is power to give judgment for payment of money in a foreign currency, and that one case in which that power ought to be exercised is where the action is brought to enforce a foreign monetary obligation

(*q*) [1978] 1 All E. R. 525; [1978] Q. B. 791, C. A.

(*r*) See Bullen, Leake and Jacob's *Precedents of Pleadings* (12th ed.), p. 665, and cases there collected. As to set-off of failure of consideration, see *Biggerstaff* v. *Rowatt's Wharf*, [1896] 2 Ch. 93, C. A.

(*s*) *Devaux* v. *Conolly* (1849), 8 C. B. 640; and see *Ebrahim Dawood, Ltd.* v. *Heath*, [1961] 2 Lloyd's Rep. 512; but *cf. Covas* v. *Bingham* (1853), 2 E. & B. 836, where by the contract the bill of lading was made conclusive as to quantity.

(*t*) *Rowland* v. *Divall*, [1923] 2 K. B. 500, at p. 505, C. A. See further the comment to s. 12, *ante*.

(*u*) *Re Kayford, Ltd.*, [1975] 1 All E. R. 604; [1975] 1 W. L. R. 279; and see *Barclays Bank, Ltd.* v. *Quistclose Investments, Ltd.*, [1968] 3 All E. R. 651; [1970] A. C. 567, H. L.

(*a*) *Aruna Mills, Ltd.* v. *Dhanrajmal Gobindram*, [1968] 1 All E. R. 113; [1968] 1 Q. B. 655 (where, on special facts, damages were awarded in respect of a loss flowing from a devaluation of the Indian rupee).

(*b*). Damages may also be awarded, where appropriate, in a foreign currency (*c*).

Even before this change in practice, where a foreign contract, *viz.* a hotel bill incurred in France, was sought to be enforced in England, and the defendant before the hearing paid the nominal amount of the debt in francs to the plaintiffs, it was held that this was a good satisfaction notwithstanding that the rate of exchange had moved heavily against the plaintiffs after the debt was incurred (*d*).

PART VII

SUPPLEMENTARY

55. Exclusion of implied terms.—(1) Where a right, duty, or liability would arise under a contract of sale of goods by implication of law, it may (subject to the Unfair Contract Terms Act 1977) be negatived or varied by express agreement, or by the course of dealing between the parties (*e*), or by such usage as binds both parties to the contract (*f*).

(2) An express condition or warranty does not negative a condition or warranty implied by this Act unless inconsistent with it.

(3) Paragraph 11 of Schedule 1 below applies in relation to a contract made on or after 18 May 1973 and before 1 February 1978, and paragraph 12 in relation to one made before 18 May 1973.

ILLUSTRATIONS

Note that the illustrations below do not apply to international supply contracts as defined by s. 26 of the Unfair Contract Terms Act 1977, post, *Appendix I.*

(1) "Seller gives no warranty express or implied as to description or any other matters": in Scotland this clause would seem to be void whether or not the contract is a consumer contract as "any other matters" must include the warranties implied by s. 12 of the Act—see s. 20 (1) of the Unfair Contract Terms Act 1977 (*g*). In the remainder of the United Kingdom its effect is limited. By virtue of s. 6 (1) of the Unfair Contract Terms Act 1977 (*g*) it will

(*b*) *Miliangos* v. *George Frank (Textiles), Ltd.*, [1975] 3 All E. R. 801; [1976] A. C. 443, H. L.

(*c*) *Kraut* v. *Albany Fabrics, Ltd.*, [1977] 2 All E. R. 116; [1977] Q. B. 182; *The Despina R*, [1979] 1 All E. R. 421; [1979] A. C. 685, H. L. Probably a plaintiff should make his claim in the currency which best expresses his loss: see *Ozalid Group* v. *African Continental Bank*, [1979] 2 Lloyd's Rep. 231.

(*d*) *Société des Hotels Le Touquet* v. *Cummings*, [1922] 1 K. B. 451, C. A.; see also *Cummings* v. *London Bullion Co.*, [1952] 1 All E. R. 383; [1952] 1 K. B. 327, C. A.

(*e*) See p. 13, *ante*.

(*f*) See p. 15, *ante*.

(*g*) *Post*, Appendix I. Contrast s. 173 (1) of the Consumer Credit Act 1974, under

not affect the warranties implied by s. 12 of the Sale of Goods Act, and as it purports to exclude only warranties, it will not affect the conditions implied by ss. 13–15 of the Sale of Goods Act (*h*).

(2) "No allowance will be made for errors in description quantity weight or measurement": this term purports to restrict the liability of the seller for breach of s. 13 of the Act. In Scotland, it is therefore void against a consumer in the case of a consumer contract (*i*) and in any other case in Scotland is of no effect if it was not fair and reasonable (*k*) to incorporate the term in the contract. In the remainder of the United Kingdom the term will be valid but its effect is limited by ss. 6 (2) and (3) of the Unfair Contract Terms Act (*l*). Against a person dealing as consumer (*m*) it cannot exclude or restrict liability for breach of ss. 13–15 of the Sale of Goods Act. In other cases it can exclude such liability but only insofar as the term satisfies the requirement of reasonableness (*n*).

(3) "The purchaser is deemed to have examined the vehicle prior to this agreement and satisfied himself as to its condition": this would have the effect of excluding or limiting the operation of s. 14 (2), in that it seeks to exclude or restrict rules of evidence relating to the term (*o*). Its effect is therefore limited as in illustration (2), above.

(4) "The purchaser acknowledges that he has not made known any particular purpose for which he requires the goods, and has fully examined them before entering into this agreement": An acknowledgement in this form is generally treated as not being part of the contract (*p*). If it genuinely represents the true position, it does not seek to limit or exclude any liability to which the seller would be subject (or restrict any right of the buyer) for the position is no different, except as to evidence, than would have been the case if nothing had been written. If it is not true, there seems no reason why it should bind the purchaser quite apart from this section (*q*) but insofar as it might, it would be caught by the provisions of the Unfair Contract Terms Act 1977 in the same way as in illustration (2), above.

(5) "Any claim must be made within 14 days from the final discharge of the goods": in Scotland this is invalid even in the case of a non-consumer sale, for it restricts the exercise of rights conferred by ss. 12–15 of the Act by limiting the time within which any such right must be exercised.

In the remainder of the United Kingdom it will be valid, but its effect will

---

which terms in regulated agreements are invalid if, *and to the extent that*, they are inconsistent with certain provisions in that Act or in regulations made under it.

(*h*) *Wallis, Son and Wells* v. *Pratt and Haynes*, [1911] A. C. 394, H. L.

(*i*) Unfair Contract Terms Act, ss. 20 (2), 25 (1), *post*, Appendix I.

(*k*) *Ibid.*, ss. 20 (2), 24.

(*l*) *Post*, Appendix I.

(*m*) See Unfair Contract Terms Act, s. 12, *post*, Appendix I, for the meaning of "dealing as consumer". In consumer transactions, terms of the kind illustrated here will also generally be unlawful by virtue of the Consumer Transactions (Restrictions on Statements) Order 1976 unless they are qualified in the manner provided in that Order: see *ante*, p. 63.

(*n*) As defined in the Unfair Contract Terms Act, s. 11, *post*, Appendix I.

(*o*) Unfair Contract Terms Act 1977, ss. 13 (1) (c), 25 (3) (c), *post*, Appendix I.

(*p*) *Lowe* v. *Lombank, Ltd.*, [1960] 1 All E. R. 611; [1960] 1 W. L. R. 196, C. A.

(*q*) There will generally be no estoppel, as in most cases where the representation is untrue, the seller must know that this is the case: *cf. Lowe* v. *Lombank, Ltd., supra*; and see *Blair* v. *Buckworth* (1908), 24 T. L. R. 474 (acknowledgment by borrower in moneylending transaction).

be limited as in illustration (2) above. In addition to general considerations of reasonableness para. (d) of Sch. 2 to the Unfair Contract Terms Act (*r*) requires it to be considered whether it was reasonable at the time of the contract to expect that compliance with the condition would be practicable.

The effect of the clause may also be limited by ss. 2 and 3 of the Unfair Contract Terms Act (*s*) subject, except where death or personal injury results from negligence, to the clause being shown to be reasonable (*t*), and by s. 3 of the Misrepresentation Act 1967 (*u*).

(6) "The buyer undertakes carefully to examine the goods immediately upon receipt and to notify the seller forthwith of any defect which such examination ought to reveal": if the buyer does not examine the goods, his loss as the result of a discoverable defect may be increased. In this case, he will be able to recover the full amount of his loss but the seller will be able, if the clause is valid, to recoup the amount by which the loss has been increased as a result of the failure to examine promptly or properly. This appears to have the effect of restricting the liability of the seller by subjecting the buyer to a prejudice if he pursues his claim against the seller and the term is therefore void as against a consumer in Scotland, and ineffective as against a consumer in the rest of the United Kingdom, so far as it relates to liability for breach of the obligations arising from ss. 13–15 of the Sale of Goods Act (*a*). But if it is clearly brought to the attention of the buyer in a sale which is not a consumer sale, it would seem to be fair and reasonable, and in most cases the courts would probably allow reliance on it, at least so long as such examination was practicable (*b*).

(7) "Compensation and damages payable under any claim or claims arising out of this contract shall not under any circumstances amount in aggregate to more than the contract price of the goods forming the subject of the claim or claims": once again, in Scotland this clause would seem to be void as it purports to restrict liability for breach of the obligations arising from s. 12 of the Sale of Goods Act (*c*). In the rest of the United Kingdom it is valid but is ineffective in relation to liability under s. 12 of the Sale of Goods Act and also against purchasers who are dealing as consumers (*d*) in relation to liability under ss. 13–15 of the Sale of Goods Act. In relation to persons who are not dealing as consumers it is ineffective in relation to liability under ss. 13–15 except insofar as it satisfies the requirement of reasonableness. It is capable of satisfying that requirement at least where the parties are of equal bargaining power and the seller has no reason to suppose when he enters into the contract that he will not be able to perform it properly (*e*).

(*r*) *Post*, Appendix I.

(*s*) In Scotland the relevant sections are ss. 16 and 17.

(*t*) For the reasonableness test, see ss. 11 and 24 of the Unfair Contract Terms Act, *post*, Appendix I.

(*u*) *Post*, Appendix I.

(*a*) See ss. 13 (1) (b) and 25 (3) (b) of the Unfair Contract Terms Act, *post*, Appendix I.

(*b*) Even in the case of a consumer sale, if it is clearly brought to the attention of the buyer, it may be arguable that even though the provision is void, extra loss suffered as a result of not examining the goods is too remote as it was in the contemplation of the parties that the buyer would examine the goods.

(*c*) Unfair Contract Terms Act 1977, s. 20 (1) (a), *post*, Appendix I.

(*d*) "Dealing as consumer" is defined in s. 12 of the Unfair Contract Terms Act, *post*, Appendix I.

(*e*) *Cf. R. W. Green* v. *Cade Bros.*, [1978] 1 Lloyd's Rep. 602; *Bahous* v. *Alcon International, Ltd.* (1976), unreported, Court of Appeal transcript 343A; and see *post*, p. 355.

Derivation.—See the comment below.

Definition.—For "Contract of sale," see s. 2 (1), *ante*, and s. 61 (1), *post*. For "warranty" and "business" see s. 61 (1), *post*.

Cross-references.—The words "unless otherwise agreed," or words to a similar effect, appear in ss. 10, 11 (1) (c), 18, 20, 28, 29, 30, 31 (1), 32 (2) and (3), 33, 34 (2) and 36, *ante*. For exemption clauses, see *ante*, p. 10. For statutory restrictions on exemption clauses see *ante*, p. 63, and the Misrepresentation Act 1967, s. 3, and the Unfair Contract Terms Act 1977, *post*, Appendix I. For questions as to conflict of laws see s. 27 of the Unfair Contract Terms Act, *post*, Appendix I. For international supply contracts see s. 26 of the Unfair Contract Terms Act 1977, *post*, Appendix I.

COMMENT

Subsection (1) is declaratory. The various ways in which rights duties and liabilities which would otherwise be implied by law may be negatived or varied are considered, *ante*, pp. 9–15.

New sub-ss. (2)–(11) were introduced into the 1893 Act by the Supply of Goods (Implied Terms) Act 1973 implementing recommendations of the Law Commission in its Report on Amendments to the Sale of Goods Act 1893 (Law Com. No. 24). Previously, the section was simply a declaratory section in terms similar to what is now s. 55 (1). The new sub-s. (2) was taken from the former s. 14 (4) of the Act.

The new sub-ss. (3)–(11), which are now reproduced in para. 11 of Sch. 1 to the 1979 Act, *post*, restricted the effect of exemption clauses affecting the provisions of ss. 12–15 of the 1893 Act except in the case of contracts for the international sale of goods. They were repealed and replaced with effect from 1st February 1978 by the Unfair Contract Terms Act 1977, *post*, Appendix I.

The combined effect of this section and the Unfair Contract Terms Act 1977, *post*, Appendix I, means that it is now necessary to distinguish between four different types of contract for the sale of goods. These are international supply contracts, as defined in s. 26 of the 1977 Act, *post*; contracts for the sale of goods which are not international supply contracts but which are sales to a person dealing as consumer within s. 12 of the 1977 Act, or in the case of Scotland sales which are to a consumer under a consumer contract within s. 25 (1) of the 1977 Act; sales on written standard terms of business within s. 3 (or in the case of Scotland, s. 17) of the 1977 Act; and contracts for the sale of goods which come within none of the foregoing categories.

56. Conflict of laws.—Paragraph 13 of Schedule 1 below applies in relation to a contract made on or after 18 May 1973 and before 1 February 1978, so as to make provision about conflict of laws in relation to such a contract.

Derivation.—Paragraph 13 of Sch. 1 is derived from s. 55A of the

1893 Act, which was introduced by s. 5 (1) of the Supply of Goods (Implied Terms) Act 1973.

Cross-reference.—For provision about conflict of laws in relation to contracts made on or after 1st February 1978, see s. 27 of the Unfair Contract Terms Act 1977, *post*, Appendix I.

57. Auction sales.—(1) Where goods are put up for sale by auction in lots, each lot is prima facie deemed to be the subject of a separate contract of sale (*f*).

(2) A sale by auction is complete when the auctioneer announces its completion by the fall of the hammer (*g*), or in other customary manner; and until the announcement is made any bidder may retract his bid (*h*).

(3) A sale by auction may be notified to be subject, to a reserve or upset price, and a right to bid may also be reserved expressly by or on behalf of the seller (*i*).

(4) Where a sale by auction is not notified to be subject to a right to bid on behalf of the seller, it is not lawful for the seller to bid himself or to employ any person to bid at the sale, or for the auctioneer knowingly (*k*) to take any bid from the seller or any such person.

(5) A sale contravening subsection (4) above may be treated as fraudulent by the buyer (*l*).

(6) Where, in respect of a sale by auction, a right to bid is expressly reserved (but not otherwise) the seller or any one person on his behalf, may bid at the auction (*m*).

ILLUSTRATION

Sale by auction subject to a reserve price. The auctioneer by mistake knocks down a lot for less than the reserve. On finding this out he refuses to

---

(*f*) *Emmerson* v. *Heelis* (1809), 2 Taunt. 38; *Roots* v. *Lord Dormer* (1832), 4 B. & Ad. 77; *cf. Couston* v. *Chapman* (1872), L. R. 2 Sc. & Div. 250, H. L. (a Scottish case).

(*g*) *Shankland* v. *Robinson & Co.*, 1920 S. C. (H. L.) 103.

(*h*) *Payne* v. *Cave* (1789), 3 Term Rep. 148; *Warlow* v. *Harrison* (1859), 1 E. & E. 309. And so may the seller retract his offer: *Fenwick* v. *Macdonald*, 1904 6 F. (Ct. of Sess.) 850.

(*i*) See cases cited in note (*l*), and *Howard* v. *Castle* (1796), 6 Term Rep. 642, at p. 645, *per* GROSE, J.

(*k*) *Mainprice* v. *Westley* (1865), 6 B. & S. 420; *cf.* Sale of Land by Auction Act 1867, s. 5; 2 Halsbury's Statutes (3rd Edn.) 500.

(*l*) *Bexwell* v. *Christie* (1776), Cowp. 395, *per* Lord MANSFIELD; *Thornett* v. *Haines* (1846), 15 M. & W. 367; *Green* v. *Baverstock* (1863), 14 C. B. N. S., 204; *cf. Mortimer* v. *Bell* (1865), 1 Ch. App. 10, at p. 13. As to fictitious bids by person interested in the sale, but not the seller, see *Union Bank* v. *Munster* (1887), 37 Ch. D. 51; and the maxim of Roman Law, *alterius circumventio alii non præbet actionem.*

(*m*) *Thornett* v. *Haines* (1846), 15 M. & W. 367, at p. 372; *Mortimer* v. *Bell* (1865), 1 Ch. App. 10 (where auctioneer and puffer both bid and sale was held void).

complete the sale or sign the necessary memorandum. The buyer has no remedy against the auctioneer, and it is immaterial that he did not know what the actual reserve was (*n*).

Derivation.—Section 58 of the 1893 Act. Subsections (1) and (2) are unchanged. Subsection (4) in the 1893 Act is now sub-s. (3); sub-s. (3) is now sub-ss. (4) and (5). What is now sub-s. (6) was included in s. 58 of the 1893 Act, but was not numbered.

Definitions.—For "contract of sale," see s. 2 (1), *ante*, and s. 61 (1) *post*. For "buyer," "seller," "goods" and "sale," see s. 61 (1), *post*.

Cross-references.—*Cf.* ss. 2 (1), 8 and 9, *ante* (price).

COMMENT

Subsection (2).—If the contract is resolved into offer and acceptance, the bid constitutes the offer. As the offer may be retracted before acceptance, so, conversely, it has been held that if a sale be advertised, but the lots are afterwards withdrawn, an intending bidder has no right of action (*o*). An auctioneer who sells goods which he has no right to sell may or may not be guilty of conversion, according to the circumstances (*p*). He has no implied authority to give a warranty on behalf of the seller (*q*).

At common law there is an implied contract between an auctioneer and a purchaser that the purchaser should pay the price to the auctioneer. The auctioneer has a lien on the goods until he is paid, and is entitled to sue in his own name for the price (*r*).

Subsection (3).—There is no express decision on what amounts to notification under this subsection. But in *Hills and Grant, Ltd.* v. *Hodson* (*s*), a case on s. 5 of the Sale of Land by Auction Act 1867, which is *in pari materia*, it was held that that section does not require that the words "with reserve" or "without reserve" and no others shall be used, and that so long as it is made plain, by whatever words may be chosen, that the sale is subject to a reserve, that is sufficient. Presumably this applies also to the present subsection.

After much doubt it was settled that an agreement for a "knock-out" (*i.e.* a combination between intending bidders to refrain from bidding against each other) was not illegal. The seller could protect himself by fixing a reserve price (*t*). Conversely, an agreement between bidders to

(*n*) *McManus* v. *Fortescue*, [1907] 2 K. B. 1, C. A., criticising *Rainbow* v. *Howkins*, [1904] 2 K. B. 322. But it seems that an auctioneer warrants that he has his principal's authority to sell: *Anderson* v. *Croall*, 1904 6 F. (Ct. of Sess.) 153.

(*o*) *Harris* v. *Nickerson* (1873), L. R. 8 Q. B. 286.

(*p*) See *National Mercantile Bank* v. *Rymill* (1881), 44 L. T. 767; *Consolidated Co.* v. *Curtis & Son*, [1892] 1 Q. B. 495, 498; *Barker* v. *Furlong*, [1891] 2 Ch. 172; see, too, 36 Sol. Jo. 480. It seems he is liable unless he acts as "a mere conduit pipe".

(*q*) *Payne* v. *Leconfield* (1882), 51 L. J. Q. B. 642.

(*r*) *Chelmsford Auctions, Ltd.* v. *Poole*, [1973] 1 All E. R. 810; [1973] Q. B. 542, C. A.

(*s*) [1934] Ch. 53.

(*t*) *Rawlings* v. *General Trading Co.*, [1921] 1 K. B. 635, C. A.; followed in *Cohen* v. *Roche*, [1927] 1 K. B. 169. *Cf. Fuller* v. *Abrahams* (1821), 6 Moore C. P. 316.

run up prices at an auction for a collateral purpose may not be illegal (*u*). But the common law has since been modified, and it is now provided by s. 3 of the Auctions (Bidding Agreements) Act 1969 (*a*) that where a person who buys goods at an auction has been a party to an agreement between potential bidders not to bid for the goods (other than an agreement to buy the goods *bona fide* on joint account) and one of the parties to that agreement was a dealer as defined in s. 1 (2) of the Auctions (Bidding Agreements) Act 1927 (*b*), then the seller may avoid the contract under which the goods were sold (*c*).

If the seller does avoid the contract and the goods are not restored to him, then s. 3 (2) of the 1969 Act provides that the parties to the agreement to abstain from bidding are jointly and severally liable to make good to the seller any loss he may have sustained because of the agreement.

As to an auctioneer's duty to put up his name, etc., during sale, see the Auctioneers Act 1845, s. 7, the Auctions (Bidding Agreements) Act 1927, s. 3, and the Auctions (Bidding Agreements) Act 1969, s. 4 (*d*).

A by-law prohibiting sales by auction in an open market is *ultra vires* (*e*).

Subsection (4).—Formerly it seems to have been the rule in equity that, when a sale by auction was not expressly stated to be without reserve, the seller might employ one person to bid, so as to prevent the property going at an undervalue. The Sale of Land by Auction Act 1867 (*f*), commonly called the Puffer's Act, was passed to abolish this rule. It first declares that any sale which would be invalid at common law, by reason of the employment of a puffer, shall be invalid in equity, and then proceeds to regulate sales at which a price is reserved or a right to bid is reserved, and in this it appears to go slightly further than the common law rule (*g*). That Act does not apply to the sale of goods by auction, but the present section is in substantial accordance with it (*h*).

Scotland.—As regards Scotland, this section seems to be declaratory (*i*).

(*u*) *Doolubdass* v. *Ramloll* (1850), 5 Moo. Ind. App. 109, at p. 133, P. C.; but *cf. Scott* v. *Brown & Co.*, [1892] 2 Q. B. 724, C. A. (making market in shares).

(*a*) *Post*, Appendix I.

(*b*) "A person who in the normal course of his business attends sales by auction for the purpose of purchasing goods with a view to reselling them."

(*c*) Even where there is an agreement to buy *bona fide* on joint account, the agreement must be in writing and a copy must be deposited with the auctioneer before the goods are purchased. If this is not done, an offence is committed under s. 1 of the Auctions (Bidding Agreements) Act 1927.

(*d*) 2 Halsbury's Statutes (3rd Edn.) 498.

(*e*) *Nicholls* v. *Tavistock Urban Council*, [1923] 2 Ch. 18.

(*f*) 2 Halsbury's Statutes (3rd Edn.) 499.

(*g*) *Parfitt* v. *Jepson* (1877), 46 L. J. Q. B. 529, at p. 533.

(*h*) See its provisions carefully discussed in Dart's *Vendors and Purchasers* (8th ed.), p. 188, and Fry's *Specific Performance* (6th ed.), pp. 341 *et seq.*

(*i*) See Bell's *Principles of the Law of Scotland*, §§ 130–132; but *cf.* Green's *Encyclopaedia of Scots Law*, tit. "Auction," as to withdrawing bids.

58. Payment into court in Scotland.—In Scotland where a buyer has elected to accept goods which he might have rejected, and to treat a breach of contract as only giving rise to a claim for damages, he may, in an action by the seller for the price, be required, in the discretion of the court before which the action depends, to consign or pay into court the price of the goods, or part of the price, or to give other reasonable security for its due payment.

Derivation.—Section 59 of the 1893 Act.

Definitions.—For "action," "buyer," "goods" and "seller," see s. 61 (1), *post*.

Cross-references.—*Cf.* ss. 2 (1), 8 and 9, *ante* (price); s. 35, *ante* (acceptance and rejection); ss. 11 (5) and 53 (5) *ante*, (right of rejection).

COMMENT

The section is intended to guard against the abuse of the alternative remedy given to the buyer by s. 11 (5) but it has been said to have no application to either of the buyer's remedies under s. 53 (1) (*k*). Under the common law of Scotland, however, where an action is brought for the price of goods the court has a discretionary power to order the consignation of the whole or part of the sum claimed where it appears from the pleadings that some sum at least will be due to the seller at the end of the day (*l*). In exercising its discretion both at common law (*l*) and under s. 58 (*m*) the court will take into account the buyer's financial stability. At common law, and *semble* under s. 58, the court will, *inter alia*, also take into account the fact that the buyer is continuing to use the goods and that he admits that they are of some use to him (*l*).

In England, unfortunately, the power of the court is far less, and it is a commonly practised fraud to keep the goods and then set up against the price an alleged breach of warranty. In some such cases, of course, leave to defend under R. S. C., O. 14, r. 6 may in practice only be granted upon the condition that the defendant pay the amount claimed into court, but there are substantial limitations on the Court's discretion in this respect (*n*). The right of rejection is larger in Scotland than in England.

59. Reasonable time a question of fact.—Where a reference is made in this Act to a reasonable time the

(*k*) *George Cohen Sons & Co., Ltd.* v. *Jamieson and Paterson*, 1963 S. C. 289, 291; where s. 53 (1) (b) was said to contemplate only a situation where the price had been paid: *sed quaere*; Brown, *Sale of Goods* (2nd ed.), p. 405. As to the *actio quanti minoris* and also the *actio redhibitoria* in Roman Law, see De Zulueta, *The Roman Law of Sale*, p. 50; and Arangio-Ruiz, *La compravendita in diritto romano*, pp. 361–399.

(*l*) *George Cohen Sons & Co., Ltd.* v. *Jamieson and Paterson, supra; Findlay Bannatyne & Co.* v. *Donaldson* (1842), 5 Bell, S. C. App. 105, H. L.

(*m*) *Porter Spiers* v. *Cameron*, [1950] C. L. Y. (Sc.), § 5324.

(*n*) See *Jacobs* v. *Booth's Distillery* (1901), 85 L. T. 262, H. L.

question what is a reasonable time is a question of fact.

Derivation.—Section 56 of the 1893 Act.

Cross-references.—This definition is required by ss. 18 (4), 29 (3), 35, 37 and 48 (3), *ante*. *Cf.* s. 29 (5) (reasonable hours).

COMMENT

It is often difficult to say whether reasonable time is a question of law or a question of fact, or a mixed question of law and fact. The Act resolves the doubt as regards sale, by making it in all cases a question of fact.

60. Rights etc. enforceable by action.—Where a right, duty or liability is declared by this Act, it may (unless otherwise provided by this Act) be enforced by action.

Derivation.—Section 57 of the 1893 Act.

Definition.—For "action," see s. 62 (1), *post*.

COMMENT

This section is possibly required in order to negative the rule of the common law that, when a statute is mandatory and provides no express penalty for disobedience to its provisions, any contravention of its provisions is punishable as a misdemeanour. The words "unless otherwise provided" refer to seller's lien and stoppage in transit; see ss. 38–48, *ante*.

61. Interpretation.—(1) In this Act, unless the context or subject matter otherwise requires.—

"action" includes counterclaim and set-off, and in Scotland condescendence and claim and compensation;

Cross-references.—This definition is required by ss. 9, 49 to 53, 58 and 60, *ante*.

COMMENT

The definition is inclusive, not exhaustive. For the purposes of the Judicature Acts, "action" is defined as meaning a civil proceeding commenced by writ or in such other manner as may be prescribed by Rules of Court, and does not include a criminal proceeding by the Crown (*o*).

Scotland and foreign systems.—As to compensation in Scotland, which is equivalent to set-off in England, see Green's *Encyclopædia of Scots Law*, tit. "Compensation."

(*o*) Supreme Court of Judicature (Consolidation) Act 1925, s. 225; 7. Halsbury's Statutes (3rd Edn.) 623; *cf. Cox* v. *Hoare* (1906), 95 L. T. 121.

"business" includes a profession and the activities of any government department (including a Northern Ireland department), or local or public authority;

Cross-references.—This definition was introduced into the 1893 Act by s. 7 (1) of the Supply of Goods (Implied Terms) Act 1973 and was amended by Sch. 3 of the Unfair Contract Terms Act 1977. It is required by ss. 14 and 29, *ante*. For the definitions of "business" applicable before 1st February 1978, see s. 61 (6) and Sch. 1, paras. 14 and 15, *post*.

COMMENT

The meaning of the word "business" must be construed in the context in which it appears (*p*), and although it has been said that "business" means almost anything which is an occupation as distinct from a pleasure (*q*), it is unlikely that what a man does with his spare time will be held to be a business unless it has some direct commercial involvement in it (*r*). An activity may be a business, however, even if there is no intention on the part of the person conducting it to make a profit (*s*), and this is recognised by the statutory definition above.

One or two isolated transactions will not by themselves be a business (*t*). But if they are proved to have been undertaken with the intent that they should be the first of several transactions, that is with the intent of carrying on a business, then they will be the first transactions in an existing business (*u*).

A sale of a capital asset of a business may in some circumstances at least be a sale in the course of a business (*a*).

"buyer" means a person who buys or agrees to buy goods;

Cross-references.—This definition is required by ss. 1, 7 to 9, 11, 12, 14 to 23, 27 to 37, 39, 41, 43 to 51, 53, 54, 57 and 58, *ante*, See definition of "goods" in this section, *post*.

(*p*) *Abernethie* v. *Kleiman, Ltd.*, [1969] 2 All E. R. 790, at p. 792; [1970] 1 Q. B. 10, at p. 18, *per* HARMAN, L. J.

(*q*) *Rolls* v. *Miller* (1884), 27 Ch. D. 71, at p. 88, *per* LINDLEY, L. J.

(*r*) *Abernethie* v. *Kleiman, Ltd., supra, per* WIDGERY, L. J. at pp. 794 and 20. See also *Southwell* v. *Lewis* (1880), 45 J. P. 206 (farming for pleasure; occasional sale, not part of regular practice: not business).

(*s*) *South-West Suburban Water Co.* v. *St. Marylebone Guardians*, [1904] 2 K. B. 174; *Paddington Burial Board* v. *Inland Revenue Commissioners* (1884), 13 Q. B. D. 9.

(*t*) *Cf.* s. 189 (2) of the Consumer Credit Act 1974.

(*u*) The business exists from the time of the commencement of the first transaction with the effect that it should be the first of its series: *Re Griffiths; ex parte Board of Trade* (1890), 60 L. J. Q. B. 235, at p. 237, *per* Lord ESHER, M. R.

(*a*) *London Borough of Havering* v. *Stevenson*, [1970] 3 All E. R. 609; [1970] 1 W. L. R. 1375, D. C.

"contract of sale" includes an agreement to sell as well as a sale;

Cross-references.—*Cf.* the definition of "sale" in this section, *post*, and note the substantive definition of "contract of sale" in s. 1 (1), *ante*. The definition is required by ss. 4, 5 to 19, 21, 27, 29, 31, 32, 48, 49, 55 and 57, *ante*, and s. 62, *post*.

COMMENT

The term "contract of sale" is used to include both executory and executed contracts of sale.

"credit-broker" means a person acting in the course of a business of credit brokerage carried on by him, that is a business of effecting introductions of individuals desiring to obtain credit—

(a) to persons carrying on any business so far as it relates to the provision of credit, or

(b) to other persons engaged in credit brokerage;

Cross-reference.—This definition is required by s. 14 (3), *ante*. For credit brokerage, see Consumer Credit Act 1974, s. 145 (2). See also the comment at p. 136, *ante*.

"defendant" includes in Scotland defender, respondent, and claimant in a multiplepoinding;

Cross-reference.—This definition is required by s. 52, *ante*.

COMMENT

Multiplepoinding in Scotland corresponds with interpleader in England.

"delivery" means voluntary transfer of possession from one person to another (*b*);

Cross-references.—This definition is required by ss. 2, 9, 11, 18 to 20, 24, 25, 27 to 37, 42, 43, 49, and 51 to 53, *ante*.

COMMENT

Delivery does not carry the same consequences in all circumstances. A delivery which is effectual for one purpose may be ineffectual for

(*b*) For a case where the "context of subject matter" was held to require a different meaning, see *W. E. Marshall & Co.* v. *Lewis and Peat (Rubber), Ltd.*, [1963] 1 Lloyd's Rep. 562.

other purposes. For instance, delivery to a carrier generally passes the property to the buyer, but does not defeat the right of stoppage in transit, while delivery by the carrier to the consignee does defeat that right.

Pollock defines delivery as "voluntary dispossession in favour of another," and proceeds to say that

> "in all cases the essence of delivery is that the deliveror by some apt and manifest act puts the deliveree in the same position of control over the thing, either directly or through a custodian, which he himself held immediately before that act" (*c*).

Delivery may be actual or constructive. Delivery is constructive when it is effected without any change in the actual possession of the thing delivered, as in the case of delivery by attornment or symbolic delivery. Delivery by attornment may take place in three classes of cases (*d*): first, the seller may be in possession of the goods, but after sale he may attorn to the buyer, and continue to hold the goods as his bailee (*e*); secondly, the goods may be in the possession of the buyer before sale, but after sale he may hold them on his own account (*f*); thirdly, the goods may be in the possession of a third person as bailee for the seller, and after sale such third person may attorn to the buyer and continue to hold them as his bailee (*g*).

Pollock and Wright have carefully discussed the so-called "symbolic delivery" by giving the buyer the key of the place where the goods are stored. They show that the key is not the symbol of the goods, but that the transaction

> "consists of such a transfer of control in fact as the nature of the case admits, and as will practically suffice for causing the new possessor to be recognised as such" (*h*).

But the transfer of a bill of lading appears to afford a genuine instance of symbolic delivery (*i*). While goods are at sea, they can be dealt with on land only through the instrumentality of the bill of lading which represents them. The transfer of the bill of lading has the like effect as a delivery of the goods themselves. But a clause in a c.i.f. contract that "no claims shall be valid unless made within two weeks after the goods are

---

(*c*) Pollock and Wright, *Possession in the Common Law*, pp. 43, 46.

(*d*) *Dublin City Distillery Co.* v. *Doherty*, [1914] A. C. 823, at p. 853, *per* Lord PARKER; and see cases reviewed by Lord ATKINSON, at p. 843.

(*e*) *Ibid.*; *Elmore* v. *Stone* (1809), 1 Taunt. 458; *Marvin* v. *Wallis* (1856), 6 E. & B. 726.

(*f*) *Story on Sale*, § 312*a*. *Cf. Cain* v. *Moon*, [1896] 2 Q. B. 283, 289; *Blundell-Leigh* v. *Attenborough*, [1921] 3 K. B. 235, C. A. (pledge).

(*g*) Pollock and Wright, *Possession in the Common Law*, p. 72; *Farina* v. *Home* (1846), 16 M. & W. 119, 123; and see s. 29 (4), *ante*.

(*h*) Pollock and Wright, *Possession in the Common Law*, p. 61.

(*i*) *Sanders* v. *Maclean* (1883), 11 Q. B. D. 327, at p. 341; *Biddell Bros.* v. *E. Clemens Horst Co.*, [1911] 1 K. B. 934, C. A., at p. 957, *per* KENNEDY, L.J. *The Prinz Adalbert*, [1917] A. C. 586, at p. 589, *per* Lord SUMNER.

delivered" was held to mean delivery from the ship to the buyers, and not delivery of the documents by which the property passed (*k*).

Where goods are taken possession of by the buyer under a licence to seize, the transaction is equivalent to a delivery by the seller (*l*) and should perhaps be regarded as a case of actual delivery. Where possession is ambiguous, it must be attributed to the person having the title to the goods (*m*).

A delivery by mistake may be inoperative (*n*). For certain purposes, *e.g.*, the termination of the seller's lien, part delivery may operate as a delivery of the whole: see s. 42, *ante*.

It is to be noted that the Act makes no attempt to define "possession." The term is too elusive. Its meaning is always relative (*o*). For instance, when goods are under the control of an agent or servant, they are for some purposes in the possession of the principal or master, while for other purposes they are in the possession of the agent or servant. But a definition of possession for the purposes of the Factors Acts is given by s. 1 (2) of the Factors Act 1889, *post*. The subject is exhaustively treated in Pollock and Wright, *Possession in the Common Law* (*p*), and O. W. Holmes' *The Common Law*, lectures 5 and 6. See also Harris: *Oxford Essays in Jurisprudence*, p. 61.

"document of title to goods" has the same meaning as it has in the Factors Acts;

Cross-references.—This definition is required by ss. 24, 25, 29 (3) and 47, *ante*.

COMMENT

See next definition. These Acts are reproduced with notes, *post*.

"Factors Acts" means the Factors Act 1889, the Factors (Scotland) Act 1890, and any enactment amending or substituted for the same;

Cross-references.—This definition is required by s. 21 (2), *ante*.

(*k*) *Scriven Bros.* v. *Schmoll Fils & Co., Inc.* (1924), 40 T. L. R. 677.

(*l*) *Congreve* v. *Evetts* (1854), 10 Exch. 298, at p. 308, *per* PARKE, B.

(*m*) *French* v. *Gething*, [1921] 3 K. B. 280, at p. 290 (gift of furniture to wife).

(*n*) *Godts* v. *Rose* (1855), 17 C. B. 229; Pollock and Wright, *Possession in the Common Law*, pp. 100–114. *Cf. Bishop* v. *Shillito* (1819), 2 B. & Ald. 329 *n.*, *per* BAYLEY, J. As to delivery by mistake as between two buyers, one lot of goods being lost, see *Denny* v. *Skelton* (1916), 115 L. T. 305.

(*o*) As to possession by wife when living with husband, see *French* v. *Gething*, [1922] 1 K. B. 236, C. A.

(*p*) Maitland, in an interesting article on the *Seisin of Chattels*, at 1 L. Q. R. 324, establishes that in early times the term "seisin" was applied to chattels as freely as the term "possession," and as its equivalent.

COMMENT

These Acts are reproduced with notes, *post*.

"fault" means wrongful act or default (*q*);

Cross-references.—This definition is required by ss. 7, 9 (2) and 20, *ante*.

COMMENT

This definition was inserted in the 1893 Bill at the instance of Lord WATSON.

"The rule of law applicable to contracts is that neither of the parties can by his own act or default defeat the obligations he has undertaken to fulfil" (*r*).

"future goods" means goods to be manufactured or acquired by the seller after the making of the contract of sale;

Cross-references.—This definition repeats that in s. 5 (1), *ante*. It is required by s. 18, rule (5), *ante*. *Cf.* definition of "goods" in this section, *post*.

COMMENT

The expression "future goods" has been criticised as awkward, but STIRLING, J., refers to it as "convenient" (*s*).

"goods" include all personal chattels other than things in action and money, and in Scotland all corporeal moveables except money; and in particular "goods" includes emblements, industrial growing crops, and things attached to or forming part of the land which are agreed to be severed before sale or under the contract of sale;

Cross-references.—This definition is required by ss. 2, 5 to 7, 9, 11, 12, 14 to 16, 18 to 51, 53, 57 and 58, *ante*. *Cf.* "contract of sale" defined in s. 2 (1) and in this section, *ante*, and "sale" defined in this section, *post*.

COMMENT

A definition was needed because the expression "goods" is a term of uncertain extent, and is used in different Acts in different senses (*t*).

(*q*) *Cf. Asiatic Petroleum Co.* v. *Lennards Carrying Co.*, [1914] 1 K. B. 419.
(*r*) *Sailing Ship Blairmore Co.* v. *Macredie*, [1898] A. C. 593, at p. 607.
(*s*) *Ajello* v. *Worsley*, [1898] 1 Ch. 274, at p. 280.
(*t*) *Cf. The Noordam*, [1920] A. C. 904, at p. 908, *per* Lord SUMNER.

Compare the definitions of "goods" given by s. 167 of the Bankruptcy Act 1914 (*u*), by s. 10 of the Trading Stamps Act 1964 and by s. 137 (2) of the Fair Trading Act 1973, and contrast the definition of "personal chattels" given by s. 4 of the Bills of Sale Act 1878, *post*, Appendix I. See also the definition of "property" in s. 4 and of "goods" in s. 34 (2) of the Theft Act 1968, *post*, Appendix I.

It is to be noted (1) that this definition is *inclusive*, not exhaustive, and (2) that it is guarded by the opening words of the section, "unless the subject matter or context otherwise requires."

Chattels personal.—These include all tangible moveable property, except money. They are "properly and strictly speaking things moveable which may be annexed to or attendant on the person of the owner, and carried about with him from one part of the world to another"; and they are commonly classified as chattels animate, chattels vegetable, and chattels inanimate (*a*). The property in, or right to, chattels personal is either *in possession* or *in action*. Property is in possession "where a man has the enjoyment, either actual or constructive, of the thing or chattel" (*b*).

Gas and water may be the subjects of theft (*c*), and there seems to be no reason why they should not be capable of being sold as goods (*d*). Electricity, however, is probably not goods for the purposes of this Act (*e*).

Things in action.—Property is in action where a man has not the enjoyment of the thing in question, but merely a right to recover it by legal process, whence the thing so recoverable is called a thing (or chose) *in action*. "Choses in action," says CHANNELL, J.—

> "is a known legal expression used to describe all personal rights of property which can only be claimed or enforced by action, and not by taking physical possession" (*f*).

Scrip and shares are things in action, and so of course are bills, notes, and cheques (*g*).

(*u*) 3 Halsbury's Statutes (3rd Edn.) 159.

(*a*) Williams & Mortimer, *Executors Administrators and Probate*, pp. 472 *et seq.*

(*b*) *Dicey on Parties to an Action*, p. 66.

(*c*) *Cf. Russell on Crimes* (12th ed.) pp. 887 *et seq.*; *Ferens* v. *O'Brien* (1883), 11 Q. B. D. 21. Electricity is the subject of a separate offence: see the Theft Act 1968, s. 13.

(*d*) In Canada, steam and gas have been held to be tangible personal property capable of being sold: *Re Social Services Tax Act, Re Central Heat Distribution, Ltd.* (1970), 74 W. W. R. 246 (steam); *Marleau* v. *People's Gas Supply Co., Ltd.*, [1940] 4 D. L. R. 433 (Sup. Ct. of Can.) (acetylene gas); *Bradshaw* v. *Booth's Marine, Ltd.*, [1973] 2 O. R. 646 (propane gas). But supplies of gas and water by statutory boards under a duty to supply are probably not sales: *cf. Pfizer* v. *Ministry of Health*, [1965] 1 All E. R. 450; [1965] A. C. 512, H. L.

(*e*) *Low* v. *Blease*, [1975] Crim. L. R. 513, D. C. See also *County of Durham Electrical Power Co.* v. *Inland Revenue*, [1909] 2 K. B. 604, at p. 608, C. A. (stamp question); *Bentley Brothers* v. *Metcalfe*, [1906] 2 K. B. 548, at pp. 552–553.

(*f*) *Torkington* v. *Magee*, [1902] 2 K. B. 427, at p. 430.

(*g*) *Humble* v. *Mitchell* (1839), 11 A. & E. 205; *Colonial Bank* v. *Whinney* (1886), 11 App. Cas. 426 (shares), approving the definition given by FRY, L. J., in the Court of Appeal,

Money.—Money (*i.e.*, current money) is necessarily excluded, because in sale the goods and the price are contrasted, and wholly different considerations apply to them. But a Jubilee five-pound gold piece, bought as a curiosity, may be treated as goods and not as money (*h*).

Emblements.—These are "such vegetable products as are the annual result of agricultural labour" (*i*).

The term "Industrial growing crops" was added when the 1893 Bill was extended to Scotland. It is probably a wider term than emblements or the Scottish equivalent, "way-going crops." Its possible effect may be to include in "goods" such crops as grass or clover, which did not come within the term of "emblements" (*k*).

Things attached to or forming part of land.—These words appear intended to give a rule for determining whether trees, fixtures and other things attached to or forming part of the soil are to be treated as goods or not.

Where an owner of land agrees to sell something attached to or forming part of his land, such as slate or slag, then unless the agreement obliges the buyer to sever the slate, slag, or other thing to be sold, the agreement will not normally be a contract for the sale of goods (*l*).

Ships.—These are clearly chattels personal, but they are governed by so many special rules that it is doubtful how far they come under the denomination of "goods" for the purposes of the Act. "A ship," says TURNER, L. J.,

> "is not like an ordinary chattel. It does not pass by delivery, nor does the possession of it prove the title to it. There is no market overt for ships. In the case of American ships the laws of the United States provide the means of evidencing the title to them" (*m*);

as the Merchant Shipping Act 1894 does for British ships (*n*). But unless

---

(1885), 30 Ch. D. 261; *Lang* v. *Smyth* (1831), 7 Bing. 284 (foreign bonds); *Freeman* v. *Appleyard* (1862), 32 L. J. Ex. 175 (certificate of railway stock).

(*h*) *Moss* v. *Hancock*, [1899] 2 Q. B. 111. As to price, see *ante*, s. 8; *cf. Banque Belge* v. *Hambrouck*, [1921] 1 K. B. 321, at p. 326, C. A., discussing the various meanings of "currency" and contrasting money and goods.

(*i*) *Williams on Personal Property* (18th ed.), p. 162; *cf.* Williams & Mortimer, *Executors Administrators and Probate*, pp. 476 *et seq.*

(*k*) See *Kingsbury* v. *Collins* (1827), 4 Bing. 202 (teazles); *Graves* v. *Weld* (1833), 5 B. & Ad. 105 (clover); *Paton's Trustees* v. *Finlayson*, 1923 S. C. 872 (potatoes sold growing).

(*l*) *Morgan* v. *Russell & Sons*, [1909] 1 K. B. 354 (agreement to sell such cinders and slag as the buyer may desire to remove from the land); *Mills* v. *Stokman* (1967), 116 C. L. R. 61 (H. C. of Aus.) (licence to enter on land and remove slate); *Atlantic Concrete Co., Ltd.* v. *Le Vatte Construction Co., Ltd.* (1975), 62 D. L. R. (3d) 663; contrast *Amco* v. *Wade*, [1968] Qd. R. 445 (buyer agreed to enter land and remove sand and gravel within fixed time; sale of goods). See further, *Benjamin's Sale of Goods*, paras. 81 *et seq.*

(*m*) *Hooper* v. *Gumm* (1867), 2 Ch. App., 282, at p. 290; *cf. Lindley on Partnership* (14th ed.), p. 351.

(*n*) *Cf. Stapleton* v. *Haymen* (1864), 2 H & C. 918 (sale of ship to infant); *Manchester Ship Canal* v. *Horlock*, [1914] 2 Ch. 199, C. A. (sale of abandoned ship sunk in fairway).

and except in so far as there is some provision to the contrary, the Sale of Goods Act appears to apply (*o*).

"plaintiff" includes pursuer, complainer, claimant in a multiplepoinding and defendant or defender counter-claiming;

Cross-reference.—This definition is required by s. 52, *ante*.

"property" means the general property in goods, and not merely a special property;

Cross-references.—This definition is required by ss. 2, 3, 11, 12, 16 to 20, 26, 39 and 49, *ante*. *Cf.* the definition of "goods" in this section, *ante*.

COMMENT

The essence of sale is the transfer of the ownership or general property in goods from seller to buyer for a price. See "the" property (that is, the general property), distinguished from "a" property (that is, merely a special property) by Lord BOWEN (*p*). The use of the term "special property" is inveterate in English law. But it would have conduced to clearness if the term "special interest" had been used instead, while "property" was confined to its primary meaning as ownership or *dominium* (*q*).

The general property in certain goods may be in one person, while a special property in them is in another person: as in the case of a pledge where the pledgee has only a special property or interest, the general property remaining in the pledgor (*r*). The general property in goods may be transferred to one person subject to a special property or interest in another (*s*).

Again, the right of property in goods must be distinguished from the right to their present possession. The right of property may be in one person, while the right to possession may be in another, as in the case of a lien (*t*). So, too, property may be divided between owners, but the

---

(*o*) *Lloyd del Pacifico* v. *Board of Trade* (1930), 35 Ll. L. Rep. 217 (ship assumed to be goods for purpose of s. 14).

(*p*) *Burdick* v. *Sewell* (1884), 13 Q. B. D. 159, at p. 175, and (1884), 10 App. Cas. 74, at p. 93. This distinction is not recognised in Scotland: *Hayman* v. *M'Lintock*, 1907 S. C. 936, at p. 949; and see the term "special property" discussed, *Attenborough* v. *Solomon*, [1913] A. C. 76, at pp. 83, 84 (pledge).

(*q*) *The Odessa*, [1916] A. C. 145, at p. 159, P. C.

(*r*) *Halliday* v. *Holgate* (1868), L. R. 3 Exch. 299, Ex. Ch.

(*s*) *Franklin* v. *Neate* (1844), 13 M. & W. 481; *Jenkyns* v. *Brown* (1849), 14 Q. B. 496. See a lien distinguished from a pledge: *Donald* v. *Suckling* (1866), L. R. 1 Q. B. 585, at p. 612; *cf. Howes* v. *Ball* (1827), 7 B. & C. 481 (hypothecation); as to pledge, see p. 86, *ante*.

(*t*) *Mulliner* v. *Florence* (1878), 3 Q. B. D. 484, C. A.; *Blackburn on Sale* (1st ed.), pp. 198,

right to possession may be in one alone (*u*); and where there is a sale of specific goods for cash, the property passes by the contract, but the seller may (unless otherwise agreed) retain the goods till the price is paid. Again, goods may be sold which are in the possession of a third person, such as a carrier or warehouseman, who has no property in the goods but has a right to retain them till his charges are paid.

The Prize Court, when dealing with enemy goods, takes cognisance only of the general property in the goods, and disregards any special property or interest (*a*).

"quality", in relation to goods, includes their state (*b*) or condition (*c*);

Cross-references.—This definition is required by ss. 14, 15 and 53 (3), *ante*. *Cf.* the definition of "goods" in this section, *ante*.

COMMENT

Flour or tobacco may be of excellent kind, but if it is sea-damaged it may not be of merchantable quality.

Lord DUNEDIN points out the distinction between the "description" of goods in the contract and their quality:

> "The tender of anything that does not tally with the specified description is not compliance with the contract. But when the article tendered does comply with the specified description, and the objection on the buyer's part is an objection to quality alone, then I think s. 14 (1) [now s. 14 (3)] settles the standard, and the only standard by which the matter is to be judged" (*d*).

But, of course, in many cases, it will be the standard set by s. 14 (2) and (6) that has to be considered.

"sale" includes a bargain and sale as well as a sale and delivery;

Cross-references.—The word occurs in ss. 3, 23 to 25, 47 and 57, *ante*.

316; *Milgate* v. *Kebble* (1841), 3 M. & Gr. 100; Pollock and Wright, *Possession in the Common Law*, p. 120.

(*u*) *Nyberg* v. *Handelaar*, [1892] 2 Q. B. 202, C. A.

(*a*) *The Odessa*, [1916] A. C. 145; *The Ningchow*, [1916] P. 221 (enemy goods pledged with neutral).

(*b*) See *Tesco Stores, Ltd.* v. *Roberts*, [1974] 3 All E. R. 74; [1974] 1 W. L. R. 1253, D. C., where the meaning of "in the same state as when he purchased it" in s. 115 (1) of the Food and Drugs Act 1955 is considered.

(*c*) See *Beer* v. *Walker* (1877), 46 L. J. Q. B. 677; *Niblett* v. *Confectioners' Materials Co.*, [1921] 3 K. B. 387, at pp. 396, 402; *Mash & Murrell* v. *Emanuel*, [1961] 1 All E. R. 485; [1961] 1 W. L. R. 862, reversed on an issue of fact, [1962] 1 All E. R. 77; [1962] 1 W. L. R. 16, C. A.

(*d*) *Manchester Liners, Ltd.* v. *Rea*, [1922] 2 A. C. 74, at p. 80.

COMMENT

This definition follows from the definition of "contract of sale" given by s. 2 (1) and this section, *ante*. See notes to ss. 2 and 49, *ante*. See also headings "sale" and "seller" in Stroud's *Judicial Dictionary* (4th ed.).

"seller" means a person who sells or agrees to sell goods;

Cross-references.—This definition is required by ss. 2, 5 to 7, 9, 11, 12, 14, 18 to 25, 27 to 38, 40, 45 to 47, 49 to 51, 53, 54, 57 and 58, *ante*. *Cf.* the definition of "goods" in this section, *ante*.

COMMENT

As to seller selling to himself, see p. 78, *ante*. In other Acts the expression "seller" must, of course, be construed according to its context, and the subject-matter dealt with (*e*).

"specific goods" means goods identified and agreed on at the time a contract of sale is made;

Cross-references.—This definition is required by ss. 6, 7, 11 (4), 17, 18, rules (1) to (3), 19 (1), 29 (2) and 52 (1), *ante*. *Cf.* definition of "contract of sale" in s. 2 (1) and this section, *ante*, and the definition of "goods" in this section, *ante*.

COMMENT

Specific goods must be distinguished from unascertained goods. Where there is a contract for the sale of specific goods, the seller would not fulfil his contract by delivering any other goods than those agreed upon. Where there is a contract for unascertained goods the seller fulfils his contract by delivering at the appointed time any goods which answer to the description in the contract. It is clear that "future goods," even though particularly described, do not come within the definition of specific goods, but for most purposes would be subject to the same considerations as unascertained goods; see notes to ss. 17 and 18, *ante*.

"warranty" (as regards England and Wales and Northern Ireland) means an agreement with reference to goods which are the subject of a contract of sale, but collateral to the main purpose of such contract, the breach of which gives rise to a claim for damages, but not to a right to reject the goods and treat the contract as repudiated (*f*).

(*e*) See, *e.g.*, *Pharmaceutical Society* v. *White*, [1901] 1 K. B. 601, C. A. As to who is a "hawker," see *O'Dea* v. *Crowhurst* (1899), 68 L. J. Q. B. 655. As to "seller" or "sale" in the Licensing Acts, see *Titmus* v. *Littlewood*, [1916] 1 K. B. 732, and the cases about clubs, p. 83, *ante*.

(*f*) For the distinction between a condition and a warranty, see p. 8, *ante*.

Cross-references.—This definition is required by ss. 11, 12, 14 and 53, *ante*. *Cf.* the definition of "contract of sale" in s. 2 (1) and this section, *ante*, "goods" defined in this section, *ante*, and s. 35, *ante* (acceptance and rejection).

History.—Anson, in the 13th edition of his work on contracts, had collected six different senses in which the word warranty was used in the cases (*g*), but it is submitted that the definition selected by the Act is the most convenient. See Note A, *post*, Appendix II, where the history of the word is discussed at length.

COMMENT

Conditions and warranties contrasted.—The Act draws throughout a distinction between the terms "condition" and "warranty," and defines the circumstances under which a condition may be treated as a warranty.

See further p. 8, *ante*.

---

(2) As regards Scotland a breach of warranty shall be deemed to be a failure to perform a material part of the contract (*h*).

COMMENT

This subsection was included as part of the definition of "warranty" in the 1893 Act.

---

(3) A thing is deemed to be done in good faith within the meaning of this Act when it is in fact done honestly, whether it is done negligently or not (*i*).

Cross-references.—This definition is required by ss. 22 (1), 23 to 25 and 47, *ante*.

COMMENT

What constitutes fraud.—The House of Lords in *Derry* v. *Peek* (*k*) has exploded the notion of "legal fraud," and has established the principle that there is no *tertium quid* between good faith on the one hand and bad faith or fraud on the other. "First," says Lord HERSCHELL,

"in order to sustain an action of deceit, there must be proof of fraud, and

(*g*) *Anson on Contracts* (13th ed.), p. 368.

(*h*) *Cf.* ss. 11 (5) and 53 (5), *ante*, saving Scottish rules.

(*i*) Taken from the Bills of Exchange Act 1882, s. 90; 2 Halsbury's Statutes (3rd Edn.) 235; *cf. Jones* v. *Gordon* (1877), 2 App. Cas. 616, 629.

(*k*) (1889), 14 App. Cas. 337, at p. 374; and see *Weir* v. *Bell* (1878), 3 Ex. D. 238, at p. 243, *per* BRAMWELL, L. J. See fraud and illegality contrasted: *Ex p. Watson* (1888), 21 Q. B. D. 301, at p. 309.

nothing short of that will suffice. Secondly, fraud is proved when it is shewn that a false representation has been made (1) knowingly, or (2) without belief in its truth, or (3) recklessly, careless whether it be true or false. Although I have treated the second and third as distinct cases, I think the third is but an instance of the second; for one who makes a statement under such circumstances can have no real belief in the truth of what he states. To prevent a false statement being fraudulent, there must, I think, always be an honest belief in its truth. And this probably covers the whole ground; for one who knowingly alleges that which is false, has obviously no such honest belief. Thirdly, if fraud be proved, the motive of the person guilty of it is immaterial. It matters not that there was no intention to cheat or injure the person to whom the statement was made."

Gross negligence may be evidence of bad faith, but it is not the same thing, and does not entail the same consequences (*l*).

Though fraud avoids sale like any other contract it must be remembered, as Lord DUNEDIN says, that sale

"is a contract made at arm's length, not a contract *uberrimæ fidei* such as insurance" (*m*).

---

(4) A person is deemed to be insolvent within the meaning of this Act if he has either ceased to pay his debts in the ordinary course of business or he cannot pay his debts as they become due, whether he has committed an act of bankruptcy or not, and whether he has become a notour bankrupt or not (*n*).

Cross-references.—This definition is required by ss. 39, 41 and 44, *ante*.

COMMENT

For the relevance of the reference to a notour bankrupt, see the Bankruptcy (Scotland) Act 1913, ss. 5 and 6.

---

(5) Goods are in a deliverable state within the meaning

(*l*) *Jones* v. *Gordon* (1877), 2 App. Cas. 616, at p. 629, *per* Lord BLACKBURN. As to *dolus dans locum contractui*, see *Price & Pearce* v. *Bank of Scotland*, 1912 S. C. (H. L.) 19. In *Houghland* v. *Low, Ltd.*, [1962] 2 All E. R. 159; [1962] 1 Q. B. 694, C. A., ORMEROD, L. J., said: "I am not sure what is meant by the term 'gross negligence' which has been in use for a long time in cases of this kind. . . . I have always found some difficulty in understanding just what was 'gross negligence.'"

(*m*) *Shankland & Co.* v. *Robinson & Co.*, 1920 S. C. (H. L.) 103, at p. 111; *cf. Ward* v. *Hobbs* (1877), 3 Q. B. D. 150, at p. 157, *per* BRAMWELL, L. J.

(*n*) *Biddlecombe* v. *Bond* (1835), 4 A. & E. 332 (general inability to pay debts); *Ex p. Carnforth Co.* (1876), 4 Ch. D. 108, C. A., at p. 122 (inability to pay avowed either in act or word, and consequent intention not to pay debts); see *The Feliciana* (1915), 59 Sol. Jo. 546, as to an alien enemy dishonouring his acceptance in wartime.

of this Act when they are in such a state that the buyer would under the contract be bound to take delivery of them (*o*).

Cross-references.—This definition is required by s. 18, rules (1), (2), (3) and (5), and s. 29 (6) *ante*. *Cf.* the definitions of "buyer," "delivery," "goods" and "quality" in this section, *ante*.

(6) As regards the definition of "business" in subsection (1) above, paragraph 14 of Schedule 1 below applies in relation to a contract made on or after 18 May 1973 and before 1 February 1978, and paragraph 15 in relation to one made before 18 May 1973.

62. Savings: rules of law etc.—(1) The rules in bankruptcy relating to contracts of sale apply to those contracts notwithstanding anything in this Act.

(2) The rules of the common law, including the law merchant (*p*), except in so far as they are inconsistent with the provisions of this Act, and in particular the rules relating to the law of principal and agent (*q*) and the effect of fraud, misrepresentation, duress or coercion, mistake, or other invalidating cause, apply to contracts for the sale of goods (*r*).

(3) Nothing in this Act or the Sale of Goods Act 1893 affects the enactments relating to bills of sale, or any enactment relating to the sale of goods which is not expressly repealed or amended by this Act or that.

(*o*) See *Blackburn on Sale* (1st ed.), p. 152; *Pritchett & Co.* v. *Currie*, [1916] 2 Ch. 515, C. A.; *Underwood* v. *Burgh Castle Brick and Cement Synd. Co.*, [1922] 1 K. B. 343, C. A.; *Morison* v. *Lockhart*, 1912 S. C. 1017; *Kursell* v. *Timber Operators, Ltd.*, [1927] 1 K. B. 298 (timber to be cut by purchaser not in a deliverable state until so cut).

(*p*) As to the law merchant, and its power of expansion, see *Blackburn on Sale* (2nd ed.), p. 317; *Edelstein* v. *Schuler*, [1902] 2 K. B. 144, *per* BIGHAM, J.

(*q*) See, *e.g.*, *Keighley* v. *Durant*, [1901] A. C. 240 (contract made by one person in his own name, on behalf of another as undisclosed principal, but without the authority of the latter, cannot be ratified); *Universal Steam Navigation Co.* v. *McKelvie*, [1923] A. C. 492 (effect of signature "as agent"); *Prager* v. *Blatspiel*, [1924] 1 K. B. 566 (sale by "agent of necessity"); but see *Jebara* v. *Ottoman Bank*, [1927] 2 K. B. 254, at pp. 270, 271.

(*r*) *Clarke* v. *Army and Navy*, [1903] 1 K. B. 155, C. A.; *Wren* v. *Holt*, [1903] 1 K. B. 610, at p. 616 (liability for dangerous goods); *Leaf* v. *International Galleries*, [1950] 1 All E. R. 693, C. A.; [1950] 2 K. B. 86 (innocent misrepresentation); *Petrofina* (*Gt. Britain*), *Ltd.* v. *Martin*, [1966] 1 All E. R. 126; [1966] Ch. 146, C. A.; *Esso Petroleum Co., Ltd.* v. *Harper's Garage* (*Stourport*), *Ltd.*, [1967] 1 All E. R. 699; [1968] A. C. 269, H. L. (unreasonable restraint of trade).

(4) The provisions of this Act about contracts of sale do not apply to any transaction in the form of a contract of sale which is intended to operate by way of mortgage, pledge, charge, or other security (*s*).

(5) Nothing in this Act prejudices or affects the landlord's right of hypothec or sequestration for rent in Scotland (*t*).

Derivation.—Section 61 of the 1893 Act.

Definition.—For "contract of sale," see ss. 2 (1), *ante*, and 61 (1), *ante*.

COMMENT

Subsection (1).—The Act now in force in England is the Bankruptcy Act 1914 (*u*). See in particular s. 34 (2), reputed ownership; s. 44, fraudulent preferences; s. 45, protected *bona fide* transactions; ss. 55, 56, power of trustee to sell; and s. 54, power of trustee to disclaim onerous contracts. As to Scotland, see the Bankruptcy (Scotland) Act 1913.

Subsection (2).—The word "coercion" was added when the Bill was extended to Scotland, as "duress" is not an indigenous term in Scottish law.

For the nature of fraud, see p. 272, *ante*,

For the effect of misrepresentation, whether fraudulent, negligent or innocent, see p. 5, *ante*,

As to mistake, see p. 3, *ante*,

As to illegality, see p. 16, *ante*,

The object of this saving is (1) to fill up any *lacunæ* in the Act itself (*a*), and (2) to emphasise the fact that the law of sale is merely a chapter in the general law of contract. Rules of law common to the whole field of contract apply to contracts of sale unless they contravene some express provision of the Act embodying some special rule peculiar to sale.

Subsection (3).—The Bills of Sale Acts at present in force in England are the Acts of 1878, 1882, 1890 and 1891 (*b*). The Act of 1878 alone effects sales as defined and dealt with by this Act. As to these Acts, see Appendix I, *post*. The bill of sale by which a British ship is transferred has nothing to do with bills of sale under the Bills of Sale Acts.

For examples of other Acts relating to sales, see p. 51, *ante*.

(*s*) See *Maas* v. *Pepper*, [1905] A. C. 102; *The Orteric*, [1920] A. C. 724, 733, P. C.; and cases cited, *ante*, p. 79, note (*e*). As to mortgages and pledges, see *ante*, p. 85. In view of this express provision, some of the decisions before the Act must be looked at critically, *e.g.*, *McBain* v. *Wallace* (1881), 6 App. Cas. 588 (motive immaterial). See this subsection discussed in *Gavin's Trustee* v. *Fraser*, 1920 S. C. 674.

(*t*) As to hypothec, see Green's *Encyclopædia of Scots Law*, tit. "Hypothec."

(*u*) 3 Halsbury's Statutes (3rd Edn.) 33.

(*a*) See, *e.g.*, *Booth Steamship Co.* v. *Cargo Fleet Iron Co.* [1969] 2 K. B. 570, C. A.

(*b*) 3 Halsbury's Statutes (3rd Edn.) 245 *et seq.*

63. Consequential amendments, repeals and savings.—(1) Without prejudice to section 17 of the Interpretation Act 1978 (repeal and re-enactment), the enactments mentioned in Schedule 2 below have effect subject to the amendments there specified (being amendments consequential on this Act).

(2) The enactments mentioned in Schedule 3 below are repealed to the extent specified in column 3, but subject to the savings in Schedule 4 below.

(3) The savings in Schedule 4 below have effect.

64. Short title and commencement.—(1) This Act may be cited as the Sale of Goods Act 1979.

(2) This Act comes into force on 1 January 1980.

SCHEDULES

SCHEDULE 1

Modification of Act for Certain Contracts

Preliminary

1.—(1) This Schedule modifies this Act as it applies to contracts of sale of goods made on certain dates.

(2) In this Schedule references to sections are to those of this Act and references to contracts are to contracts of sale of goods.

(3) Nothing in this Schedule affects a contract made before 1 January 1894.

Section 11: *condition treated as warranty*

2. In relation to a contract made before 22 April 1967 or (in the application of this Act to Northern Ireland) 28 July 1967, in section 11 (4) after "or part of them," insert "or where the contract is for specific goods, the property in which has passed to the buyer,".

Section 12: *implied terms about title etc.*

3. In relation to a contract made before 18 May 1973 substitute the following for section 12:—

12. Implied terms about title, etc. In a contract of sale, unless the circumstances of the contract are such as to show a different intention, there is—

(a) an implied condition on the part of the seller that in the case of a sale he has a right to sell the goods, and in the case of an agreement to sell he will have such a right at the time when the property is to pass;

(b) an implied warranty that the buyer will have and enjoy quiet possession of the goods;

(c) an implied warranty that the goods will be free from any charge or encumbrance in favour of any third party, not declared or known to the buyer before or at the time when the contract is made.

Section 13: *sale by description*

4. In relation to a contract made before 18 May 1973, omit section 13 (3).

Section 14: *quality or fitness* (*i*)

5. In relation to a contract made on or after 18 May 1973 and before the appointed day, substitute the following for section 14:—

14. Implied terms about quality or fitness.—(1) Except as provided by this section and section 15 below and subject to any other enactment, there is no implied condition or warranty about the quality or fitness for any particular purpose of goods supplied under a contract of sale.

(2) Where the seller sells goods in the course of a business, there is an implied condition that the goods supplied under the contract are of merchantable quality, except that there is no such condition—

(a) as regards defects specifically drawn to the buyer's attention before the contract is made; or

(b) if the buyer examines the goods before the contract is made, as regards defects which that examination ought to reveal.

(3) Where the seller sells goods in the course of a business and the buyer, expressly or by implication, makes known to the seller any particular purpose for which the goods are being bought, there is an implied condition that the goods supplied under the contract are reasonably fit for that purpose, whether or not that is a purpose for which such goods are commonly supplied, except where the circumstances show that the buyer does not rely, or that it is unreasonable for him to rely, on the seller's skill or judgment.

(4) An implied condition or warranty about quality or fitness for a particular purpose may be annexed to a contract of sale by usage.

(5) The preceding provisions of this section apply to a sale by a person who in the course of a business is acting as agent for another as they apply to a sale by a principal in the course of a business, except where that other is not selling in the course of a business and either the buyer knows that fact or reasonable steps are taken to bring it to the notice of the buyer before the contract is made.

(6) Goods of any kind are of merchantable quality within the meaning of subsection (2) above if they are as fit for the purpose or purposes for which goods of that kind are commonly bought as it is reasonable to expect having regard to any description applied to them, the price (if relevant) and all the other relevant circumstances.

(7) In the application of subsection (3) above to an agreement for the sale of goods under which the purchase price or part of it is payable by instalments any reference to the seller includes a reference to the person by whom any antecedent negotiations are conducted: and section 58 (3) and (5) of the Hire-Purchase Act 1965, section 54 (3) and (5) of the Hire-Purchase (Scotland) Act 1965 and section 65 (3) and (5) of the Hire-Purchase Act (Northern Ireland) 1966 (meaning of antecedent negotiations and related expressions) apply in relation to this subsection as in relation to each of those Acts, but as if a reference to any such agreement were included in the references in subsection (3) of each of those sections to the agreements there mentioned.

Section 14: *quality or fitness* (*ii*)

6. In relation to a contract made before 18 May 1973 substitute the following for section 14:—

14. Implied terms about quality or fitness.—(1) Subject to this and any other Act, there is no implied condition or warranty about the quality or fitness for any particular purpose of goods supplied under a contract of sale.

(2) Where the buyer, expressly or by implication, makes known to the seller the particular purpose for which the goods are required, so as to show that the buyer relies on the seller's skill or judgment, and the goods are of a description which it is in the course of the seller's business to supply (whether he is the manufacturer or not), there is an implied condition that the goods will be reasonably fit for such purpose, except that in the case of a contract for the sale of a specified article under its patent or other trade name there is no implied condition as to its fitness for any particular purpose.

(3) Where goods are bought by description from a seller who deals in goods of that description (whether he is the manufacturer or not), there is an implied condition that the goods will be of merchantable quality; but if the buyer has examined the goods, there is no implied condition as regards defects which such examination ought to have revealed.

(4) An implied condition or warranty about quality or fitness for a particular purpose may be annexed by the usage of trade.

(5) An express condition or warranty does not negative a condition or warranty implied by this Act unless inconsistent with it.

Section 15: *sale by sample*

7. In relation to a contract made before 18 May 1973, omit section 15 (3).

Section 22: *market overt*

8. In relation to a contract under which goods were sold before 1 January 1968 or (in the application of this Act to Northern Ireland) 29 August 1967, add the following paragraph at the end of section 22 (1):—

"Nothing in this subsection affects the law relating to the sale of horses."

Section 25: *buyer in possession*

9. In relation to a contract under which a person buys or agrees to buy goods and which is made before the appointed day, omit section 25 (2).

Section 35: *acceptance*

10. In relation to a contract made before 22 April 1967 or (in the application of this Act to Northern Ireland) 28 July 1967, in section 35 (1) omit "(except where section 34 above otherwise provides)".

Section 55: *exclusion of implied terms* (*i*)

11. In relation to a contract made on or after 18 May 1973 and before 1 February 1978 substitute the following for section 55:—

55. Exclusion of implied terms.—(1) Where a right, duty or liability would arise under a contract of sale of goods by implication of law, it may be negatived or varied by express agreement, or by the course of dealing between the parties, or by such usage as binds both parties to the contract, but the preceding provision has effect subject to the following provisions of this section.

(2) An express condition or warranty does not negative a condition or warranty implied by this Act unless inconsistent with it.

(3) In the case of a contract of sale of goods, any term of that or any other contract exempting from all or any of the provisions of section 12 above is void.

(4) In the case of a contract of sale of goods, any term of that or any other contract exempting from all or any of the provisions of section 13, 14 or 15 above is void in the case of a consumer sale and is, in any other case, not enforceable to the extent that it is shown that it would not be fair or reasonable to allow reliance on the term.

(5) In determining for the purposes of subsection (4) above whether or not reliance on any such term would be fair or reasonable regard shall be had to all the circumstances of the case and in particular to the following matters—

(a) the strength of the bargaining positions of the seller and buyer relative to each other, taking into account, among other things, the availability of suitable alternative products and sources of supply;

(b) whether the buyer received an inducement to agree to the term or in accepting it had an opportunity of buying the goods or suitable alternatives without it from any source of supply;

(c) whether the buyer knew or ought reasonably to have known of the existence and extent of the term (having regard, among other things, to any custom of the trade and any previous course of dealing between the parties);

(d) where the term exempts from all or any of the provisions of section 13, 14 or 15 above if some condition is not complied with, whether it was reasonable at the time of the contract to expect that compliance with that condition would be practicable;

(e) whether the goods were manufactured, processed, or adapted to the special order of the buyer.

(6) Subsection (5) above does not prevent the court from holding, in accordance with any rule of law, that a term which purports to exclude or restrict any of the provisions of section 13, 14 or 15 above is not a term of the contract.

(7) In this section "consumer sale" means a sale of goods (other than a sale by auction or by competitive tender) by a seller in the course of a business where the goods—

(a) are of a type ordinarily bought for private use or consumption; and

(b) are sold to a person who does not buy or hold himself out as buying them in the course of a business.

(8) The onus of proving that a sale falls to be treated for the purposes of this section as not being a consumer sale lies on the party so contending.

(9) Any reference in this section to a term exempting from all or any of the provisions of any section of this Act is a reference to a term which purports to exclude or restrict, or has the effect of excluding or restricting, the operation of all or any of the provisions of that section, or the exercise of a right conferred by any provision of that section, or any liability of the seller for breach of a condition or warranty implied by any provision of that section.

(10) It is hereby declared that any reference in this section to a term of a contract includes a reference to a term which although not contained in a contract is incorporated in the contract by another term of the contract.

(11) Nothing in this section prevents the parties to a contract for the international sale of goods from negativing or varying any right, duty or liability which would otherwise arise by implication of law under sections 12 to 15 above.

(12) In subsection (11) above "contract for the international sale of goods" means a contract of sale of goods made by parties whose places of business (or, if they have none, habitual residences) are in the territories of different States (the Channel Islands and the Isle of Man being treated for this purpose as different States from the United Kingdom) and in the case of which one of the following conditions is satisfied:—

(a) the contract involves the sale of goods which are at the time of the conclusion of the contract in the course of carriage or will be carried from the territory of one State to the territory of another; or

(b) the acts constituting the offer and acceptance have been effected in the territories of different States; or

(c) delivery of the goods is to be made in the territory of a State other than that within whose territory the acts constituting the offer and the acceptance have been effected.

Section 55: *exclusion of implied terms* (*ii*)

12. In relation to a contract made before 18 May 1973 substitute the following for section 55:—

55. Exclusion of implied terms.—Where a right, duty or liability would arise under a contract of sale by implication of law, it may be negatived or varied by express agreement, or by the course of dealing between the parties, or by such usage as binds both parties to the contract.

Section 56: *conflict of laws*

13.—(1) In relation to a contract made on or after 18 May 1973 and before 1 February 1978 substitute for section 56 the section set out in sub-paragraph (3) below.

(2) In relation to a contract made otherwise than as mentioned in sub-paragraph (1) above, ignore section 56 and this paragraph.

(3) The section mentioned in sub-paragraph (1) above is as follows:—

56. Conflict of laws.—(1) Where the proper law of a contract for the sale of goods would, apart from a term that it should be the law of some other country or a term to the like effect, be the law of any part of the United Kingdom, or where any such contract contains a term which purports to substitute, or has the effect of substituting, provisions of the law of some other country for all or any of the provisions of sections 12 to 15 and 55 above, those sections shall, notwithstanding that term but subject to subsection (2) below, apply to the contract.

(2) Nothing in subsection (1) above prevents the parties to a contract for the international sale of goods from negativing or varying any right, duty or liability which would otherwise arise by implication of law under sections 12 to 15 above.

(3) In subsection (2) above "contract for the international sale of goods" means a contract of sale of goods made by parties whose places of business (or, if they have none, habitual residences) are in the territories of different States (the Channel Islands and the Isle of Man being treated for this purpose as different States from the United Kingdom) and in the case of which one of the following conditions is satisfied:—

(a) the contract involves the sale of goods which are at the time of the conclusion of the contract in the course of carriage or will be carried from the territory of one State to the territory of another; or

(b) the acts constituting the offer and acceptance have been effected in the territories of different States; or

(c) delivery of the goods is to be made in the territory of a State other than that within whose territory the acts constituting the offer and the acceptance have been effected.

Section 61 (1): *definition of "business"* (*i*)

14. In relation to a contract made on or after 18 May 1973 and before 1 February 1978, in the definition of "business" in section 61 (1) for "or local or public authority" substitute, "local authority or statutory undertaker".

Section 61 (1): *definition of "business"* (*ii*)

15. In relation to a contract made before 18 May 1973 omit the definition of "business" in section 61 (1).

SCHEDULE 2

Consequential Amendments

War Risks Insurance Act 1939 (2 & 3 Geo. 6 c. 57)

1. In section 15 (1)(e) of the War Risks Insurance Act 1939 for "section sixty-two of the Sale of Goods Act 1893" substitute "section 61 of the Sale of Goods Act 1979".

Law Reform (Frustrated Contracts) Act 1943 (6 & 7 Geo. 6 c. 40)

2. In section 2 (5)(c) of the Law Reform (Frustrated Contracts) Act 1943 for "section seven of the Sale of Goods Act 1893" substitute "section 7 of the Sale of Goods Act 1979".

Frustrated Contracts Act (Northern Ireland) 1947 (c. 2)

3. In section 2 (5)(c) of the Frustrated Contracts Act (Northern Ireland) 1947 for "section seven of the Sale of Goods Act 1893" substitute "section 7 of the Sale of Goods Act 1979".

Hire-Purchase Act 1964 (c. 53)

4. In section 27 (5) of the Hire-Purchase Act 1964 (as originally enacted and as substituted by Schedule 4 to the Consumer Credit Act 1974)—

(a) in paragraph (a) for "section 21 of the Sale of Goods Act 1893" substitute "section 21 of the Sale of Goods Act 1979";

(b) in paragraph (b) for "section 62 (1) of the said Act of 1893" substitute "section 61 (1) of the said Act of 1979".

Hire-Purchase Act 1965 (c. 66)

5. In section 20 of the Hire-Purchase Act 1965—

(a) in subsection (1) for "Section 11 (1)(c) of the Sale of Goods Act 1893" substitute "Section 11 (4) of the Sale of Goods Act 1979";

(b) in subsection (3) for "sections 12 to 15 of the Sale of Goods Act 1893" substitute "sections 12 to 15 of the Sale of Goods Act 1979".

6. In section 54 of the Hire-Purchase Act 1965 for "section 25 (2) of the Sale of Goods Act 1893" substitute "section 25 (1) of the Sale of Goods Act 1979".

7. In section 58 (1) of the Hire-Purchase Act 1965 for "the Sale of Goods Act 1893" substitute "the Sale of Goods Act 1979".

Hire-Purchase (Scotland) Act 1965 (c. 67)

8. In section 20 of the Hire-Purchase (Scotland) Act 1965 for "1893" substitute "1979".

9. In section 50 of the Hire-Purchase (Scotland) Act 1965 for "section 25 (2) of the Sale of Goods Act 1893" substitute "section 25 (1) of the Sale of Goods Act 1979".

10. In section 54 (1) of the Hire-Purchase (Scotland) Act 1965 for "the Sale of Goods Act 1893" substitute "the Sale of Goods Act 1979".

Hire-Purchase Act (Northern Ireland) 1966 (c. 42)

11. In section 20 of the Hire-Purchase Act (Northern Ireland) 1966—

(a) in subsection (1) for "Section 11 (1)(c) of the Sale of Goods Act 1893" substitute "Section 11 (4) of the Sale of Goods Act 1979";

(b) in subsection (3) for "1893" substitute "1979".

12. In section 54 of the Hire-Purchase Act (Northern Ireland) 1966

for "section 25 (2) of the Sale of Goods Act 1893" substitute "section 25 (1) of the Sale of Goods Act 1979".

13. In section 62 (5) of the Hire-Purchase Act (Northern Ireland) 1966 (as originally enacted and as substituted by Schedule 4 to the Consumer Credit Act 1974)—

(a) in paragraph (a) for "1893" substitute "1979";

(b) in paragraph (b) for "section 62 (1) of the said Act of 1893" substitute "section 61 (1) of the said Act of 1979".

14. In section 65 (1) of the Hire-Purchase Act (Northern Ireland) 1966 for "the Sale of Goods Act 1893" substitute "the Sale of Goods Act 1979".

Uniform Laws on International Sales Act 1967 (c. 45)

15. For section 1 (4) of the Uniform Laws on International Sales Act 1967 substitute the following:—

"(4) In determining the extent of the application of the Uniform Law on Sales by virtue of Article 4 thereof (choice of parties)—

(a) in relation to a contract made before 18 May 1973, no provision of the law of any part of the United Kingdom shall be regarded as a mandatory provision within the meaning of that Article;

(b) in relation to a contract made on or after 18 May 1973 and before 1 February 1978, no provision of that law shall be so regarded except sections 12 to 15, 55 and 56 of the Sale of Goods Act 1979;

(c) in relation to a contract made on or after 1 February 1978, no provision of that law shall be so regarded except sections 12 to 15 of the Sale of Goods Act 1979".

Supply of Goods (Implied Terms) Act 1973 (c. 13)

16. In section 14 (1) of the Supply of Goods (Implied Terms) Act 1973 (as originally enacted and as substituted by Schedule 4 to the Consumer Credit Act 1974) for "Section 11 (1)(c) of the principal Act" substitute "Section 11 (4) of the Sale of Goods Act 1979".

17. For the definition of "consumer sale" in section 15 (1) of the Supply of Goods (Implied Terms) Act 1973 substitute—

"consumer sale" has the same meaning as in section 55 of the Sale of Goods Act 1979 (as set out in paragraph 11 of Schedule 1 to that Act).

Consumer Credit Act 1974 (c. 39)

18. In section 189 (1) of the Consumer Credit Act 1974, in the definition of "goods", for "section 62 (1) of the Sale of Goods Act 1893" substitute "section 61 (1) of the Sale of Goods Act 1979".

Unfair Contract Terms Act 1977 (c. 50)

19. In section 6 of the Unfair Contract Terms Act 1977—

(a) in subsection (1)(a) for "section 12 of the Sale of Goods Act 1893" substitute "section 12 of the Sale of Goods Act 1979";

(b) in subsection (2)(a) for "section 13, 14 or 15 of the 1893 Act" substitute "section 13, 14 or 15 of the 1979 Act".

20. In section 14 of the Unfair Contract Terms Act 1977, in the definition of "goods", for "the Sale of Goods Act 1893" substitute "the Sale of Goods Act 1979".

21. In section 20 (1)(a) and (2)(a) of the Unfair Contract Terms Act 1977 for "1893" substitute (in each case) "1979".

22. In section 25 (1) of the Unfair Contract Terms Act 1977, in the definition of "goods", for "the Sale of Goods Act 1893" substitute "the Sale of Goods Act 1979".

SCHEDULE 3

Repeals

Chapter	Short title	Extent of repeal
56 & 57 Vict. c. 71.	Sale of Goods Act 1893.	The whole Act except section 26.
1967 c. 7.	Misrepresentation Act 1967.	Section 4. In section 6 (3) the words, "except section 4 (2),".
1967 c. 14. (N. I.)	Misrepresentation Act (Northern Ireland) 1967.	Section 4.
1973 c. 13.	Supply of Goods (Implied Terms) Act 1973.	Sections 1 to 7. Section 18 (2).
1974 c. 39.	Consumer Credit Act 1974.	In Schedule 4, paragraphs 3 and 4.
1977 c. 50.	Unfair Contract Terms Act 1977.	In Schedule 3, the entries relating to the Sale of Goods Act 1893.

SCHEDULE 4

Savings

Preliminary

1. In this Schedule references to the 1893 Act are to the Sale of Goods Act 1893.

Orders

2. An order under section 14 (8) or 25 (4) above may make provision that it is to have effect only as provided by the order (being provision corresponding to that which could, apart from this Act, have been made by an order under section 192 (4) of the Consumer Credit Act 1974 bringing into operation an amendment or repeal making a change

corresponding to that made by the order under section 14 (8) or 25 (4) above).

Offences

3. Where an offence was committed in relation to goods before 1 January 1969 or (in the application of this Act to Northern Ireland) 1 August 1969, the effect of a conviction in respect of the offence is not affected by the repeal by this Act of section 24 of the 1893 Act.

1893 Act, section 26

4. The repeal by this Act of provisions of the 1893 Act does not extend to the following provisions of that Act in so far as they are needed to give effect to or interpret section 26 of that Act, namely, the definitions of "goods" and "property" in section 62 (1), section 62 (2) and section 63 (which was repealed subject to savings by the Statute Law Revision Act 1908).

Things done before 1 January 1894

5. The repeal by this Act of section 60 of and the Schedule to the 1893 Act (which effected repeals and which were themselves repealed subject to savings by the Statute Law Revision Act 1908) does not affect those savings, and accordingly does not affect things done or acquired before 1 January 1894.

6. In so far as the 1893 Act applied (immediately before the operation of the repeals made by this Act) to contracts made before 1 January 1894 (when the 1893 Act came into operation), the 1893 Act shall continue so to apply notwithstanding this Act.

THE SALE OF GOODS ACT 1893

(56 & 57 VICT. c. 71)

An Act for codifying the Law relating to the Sale of Goods [20th February 1894.]

26. Effect of writs of execution.—(1) A writ of fieri facias or other writ of execution against goods shall bind the property in the goods of the execution debtor as from the time when the writ is delivered to the sheriff to be executed; and, for the better manifestation of such time, it shall be the duty of the sheriff, without fee, upon the receipt of any such writ to endorse upon the back thereof the hour, day, month, and year when he received the same (*a*).

Provided that no such writ shall prejudice the title to such goods acquired by any person in good faith and for valuable consideration (*b*), unless such person had at the time when he acquired his title notice that such writ or any other writ by virtue of which the goods of the execution debtor might be seized or attached had been delivered to and remained unexecuted in the hands of the sheriff (*c*).

(2) In this section the term "sheriff" includes any officer charged with the enforcement of a writ of execution (*d*).

(3) The provisions of this section do not apply to Scotland.

Definitions.—For "goods" and "property," see s. 61 (1) of the 1979 Act, *ante*, and for "good faith," see s. 61 (3) of the 1979 Act, *ante*, in each case substantially reproducing the definitions in s. 62 of the 1893 Act. The definitions in s. 62 of the 1893 Act are preserved so far as they are needed to give effect to or interpret this section by the Sale of Goods Act 1979, Sch. 4, para. 4, *ante*.

(*a*) See further, s. 10 of the Sheriffs Act 1887; 30 Halsbury's Statutes (3rd Edn.) 582, as to giving a receipt.

(*b*) Thus a trustee in bankruptcy, who gives no value but derives his title by operation of law, will not be protected by this proviso: *Re Cooper*, [1958] 2 All E. R. 97, at p. 100; [1958] Ch. 922, at p. 928.

(*c*) As to the origin of the provision, see 2nd Report of the Mercantile Law Commission 1855, p. 8.

(*d*) *Cf.* the definition of "sheriff" in s. 167 of the Bankruptcy Act 1914; 3 Halsbury's Statutes (3rd Edn.) 159; and s. 29 of the Sheriff's Act 1887; 30 Halsbury's Statutes (3rd Edn.) 592.

History.—The first part of subsection (1) reproduces s. 15 (*e*) of the Statute of Frauds, with the addition that the sheriff is required to indorse the *hour* on the writ, but this accords with the practice. The proviso reproduces s. 1 of the Mercantile Law Amendment (Scotland) Act 1856. Both these enactments were repealed by this Act.

COMMENT

It has been held that where goods are sold, otherwise than in market overt, after delivery of the writ, the words "shall bind the property in the goods" do not prevent the property from passing by the sale, but constitute the execution a charge upon the goods (*f*).

The effect of "shall bind the property" is that on delivery of the writ the sheriff acquires a legal right to seize enough of the debtor's goods to satisfy the amount specified in the writ (*g*). The proviso protects a purchaser against that right of seizure if the stated conditions are fulfilled, but it has no scope for operation where an actual seizure has already been effected (*g*).

The registration of a *lis pendens* does not affect goods (*h*).

As to practice, see R. S. C., O. 46 and 47, and notes in the Supreme Court Practice.

A creditor trustee under a deed of assignment is a purchaser for valuable consideration (*i*).

County Courts.—In the application of this section to county courts, the Registrar now corresponds with the sheriff, and "the time when the writ is delivered to the sheriff" must be construed as meaning the time when application is made to the Registrar for the writ (*k*).

(*e*) Section 15 of the Revised Edition is commonly cited as s. 16.

(*f*) *Woodland* v. *Fuller* (1840), 11 Ad. & El. 859, at p. 867. See also *Re Ferrier, Ex p. the Trustee* v. *Donald*, [1944] Ch. 295, at p. 297, where the effect of the seizure in execution of goods which were held on sale or return was discussed.

(*g*) *Lloyds and Scottish Finance, Ltd.* v. *Modern Cars and Caravans (Kingston), Ltd.*, [1964] 2 All E. R. 732; [1966] 1 Q. B. 764.

(*h*) *Wigram* v. *Buckley*, [1894] 3 Ch. 483, at p. 492, C. A.

(*i*) *Beebee & Co.* v. *Turner's Successors* (1931), 48 T. L. R. 61.

(*k*) *Murgatroyd* v. *Wright*, [1907] 2 K. B. 333; as to execution issued from one county court to another or from a local court as defined by s. 140 (3) of the County Courts Act 1959, to a county court, see the Administration of Justice Act 1965, s. 22; 7 Halsbury's Statutes (3rd Edn.) 760.

THE FACTORS ACT 1889

(52 & 53 VICT. c. 45)

An Act to amend and consolidate the Factors Acts.

[26th August 1889.]

The Factors Act 1889, which repeals the previous enactments dealing with similar subject-matter, is a partial application to English law of the French maxim, "en fait de meubles possession vaut titre." The present Act is the result of a long struggle between the mercantile community on the one hand and the principles of the common law on the other. The general rule of the common law was *nemo dat quod non habet* (*a*), and it was held that the mere fact that a person was in possession of goods or documents of title to goods did not enable him to dispose of those goods in contravention of his instructions about them. The merchants and bankers contended that, in the interests of commerce, if a person was put or left in the possession of goods or documents of title, he ought, as regards innocent third parties, to be treated as the owner of the goods. As BOWEN, L. J., has pointed out, the object of the courts is to prevent fraud,

> "the object of mercantile usages is to prevent the risk of insolvency, not of fraud, and any one who attempts to follow and understand the law merchant will soon find himself lost if he begins by assuming that merchants conduct their business on the basis of attempting to insure themselves against fraudulent dealing. The contrary is the case. Credit, not distrust, is the basis of commercial dealings; mercantile genius consists principally in knowing whom to trust" (*b*).

To express the principle in other words, lawyers see only the pathology of commerce, and not its healthy physiological action, and their views are therefore apt to be warped and one-sided.

The first Factors Act was passed in 1823, the second in 1825 and the third in 1842. These enactments were a model of the art of saying few things in many words. They dealt with the powers of factors and other mercantile agents intrusted with the possession of goods or documents of title to goods, and their conjoint effect is carefully summed up by BLACKBURN, J., in *Cole* v. *North Western Bank* (*c*). After reviewing the history and policy of the Acts, he proceeds to say:

(*a*) See s. 21 of the Sale of Goods Act, *ante*, and *Fuentes* v. *Montis* (1868), L. R. 3 C. P. 268, at p. 277, *per* WILLES, J.

(*b*) *Sanders* v. *Maclean* (1883), 11 Q. B. D. 327, at p. 343, C. A.; *cf. Speight* v. *Gaunt* (1883), 9 App. Cas. 1, at p. 20, *per* Lord BLACKBURN.

(*c*) *Cole* v. *North Western Bank* (1875), L. R. 10 C. P. 354, at p. 372, Ex. Ch.; *cf. Weiner* v. *Harris* (1910), 15 Com. Cas. 39, at p. 48, *per* FARWELL, L. J.

"We do not think that the legislature wished to give to all sales and pledges in the ordinary course of business the effect which the Common Law gives to sales in market overt . . . The general rule of law is, that where a person is deceived by another into believing he may safely deal with property he bears the loss, unless he can show that he was misled by the act of the true owner. The legislature seems to us to have wished to make it the law that, where a third person has intrusted goods or the documents of title to goods to an agent who, in the course of such agency, sells or pledges the goods, he should be deemed by that act to have misled any one who *bonâ fide* deals with the agent, and makes a purchase from or an advance to him without notice that he was not authorised to sell or to procure the advance."

The Factors Act 1877 dealt with a new subject-matter. After providing that a secret revocation of agency should be inoperative, it proceeded to deal with the case, not of agents, but of buyers or sellers left in possession of the documents of title to goods. The present Act reproduces and somewhat extends the effect of the four above-mentioned Acts.

"The Act," says Lord HERSCHELL,

"is divided into parts. The first headed 'Preliminary' consists of a definition clause. The last part headed 'Supplemental' contains provisions as to the mode of transfer 'for the purposes of the Act' and certain savings. The other two parts are headed respectively 'Dispositions by Mercantile Agents,' and 'Dispositions by Buyers and Sellers of Goods.' These headings are not, in my opinion, mere marginal notes, but the sections in the group to which they belong must be read in connection with them, and interpreted by the light of them. It appears to me that the Legislature has clearly indicated the intention that the provisions of s. 3 should not be treated as an enactment relating to all pledges of documents of title, but only to those effected by mercantile agents" (*d*).

By s. 21 (2) of the Sale of Goods Act, *ante*, nothing in that Act is to affect the provisions of the Factors Acts, or any enactment enabling the apparent owner of goods to dispose of them as if he were the true owner thereof.

Preliminary

1. Definitions.—(1) For the purposes of this Act—

The expression "mercantile agent" shall mean a mercantile agent having in the customary course of his business as such agent authority either to sell goods, or to consign goods for the purpose of sale, or to buy goods, or to raise money on the security of goods:

Definition.—For "goods," see sub-s. (3), *post*.

Cross-references.—This definition is required by ss. 2 (1), (2) and (3), 4 to 6, 7 (2), 8, 9, 12 and 13, *post*. *Cf.* s. 6, *post* (agreements through

(*d*) *Inglis* v. *Robertson*, [1898] A. C. 616, at p. 630.

clerks, etc.) and the definition of mercantile agent in s. 26 of the Sale of Goods Act 1979, *ante*.

COMMENT

This definition is new, but is mainly declaratory. It extends the construction put on the repealed Acts in so far as it applies to agents "to buy goods," and perhaps also in so far as it applies to forwarding agents (*e*).

Under the repealed Acts, the terms used were simply "person" or "agent" intrusted with the possession of goods, but it was held that the Acts only applied to mercantile transactions, and that the term person or agent did not include a mere servant or caretaker, or one who had possession of goods for carriage, safe custody, or otherwise as an independent contracting party; but only persons whose employment corresponded to that of some known kind of commercial agent like that class (factors) from which the Acts took their name (*f*). Thus, a person intrusted with furniture to keep in her own house for the plaintiff was held not to be an "agent" within the meaning of the Acts (*g*); and a wine merchant's clerk who, as such, was possessed of delivery orders, was held not to be an agent, within the meaning of the Acts, as to to be able to make a valid pledge in fraud of his master (*h*). It was further held that if a mercantile agent received goods in some other capacity the Act did not apply; for instance, where goods were warehoused with a warehouseman who was also a broker, he could not pledge them in his capacity of broker (*i*). Under the present Act it was once held that a person employed to sell jewellery for a firm of jewellers at a small commission was not a mercantile agent (*k*), but that case has been expressly overruled (*l*).

On the other hand, it was held that the repealed Acts applied to an isolated instance of employment, if the employment was such that persons who ordinarily carried on that kind of business would come within the Acts, and this is still the law (*m*).

(*e*) *Quære* how far *Hellings* v. *Russell* (1875), 33 L. T. 380, and *City Bank* v. *Barrow* (1880), 5 App. Cas. 664, are affected?

(*f*) *Cole* v. *North Western Bank* (1875), L. R. 10 C. P. 354, at pp. 372, 373, *per* BLACKBURN, J.; *City Bank* v. *Barrow* (1880), 5 App. Cas. 664, at p. 678.

(*g*) *Wood* v. *Rowcliffe* (1846), 6 Hare, 183.

(*h*) *Lamb* v. *Attenborough* (1862), 31 L. J. Q. B. 41; *cf. Oppenheimer* v. *Attenborough*, [1908] 1 K. B. 221, at p. 226, C. A.

(*i*) *Cole* v. *North Western Bank* (1875), L. R. 10 C. P. 354, Ex. Ch.

(*k*) *Hastings* v. *Pearson*, [1893] 1 Q. B. 62; see also *Tremoille* v. *Christie* (1893), 37 Sol. Jo. 650.

(*l*) *Weiner* v. *Harris*, [1910] 1 K. B. 285.

(*m*) *Hayman* v. *Flewker* (1863), 32 L. J. C. P. 132 (pictures entrusted to insurance agent to sell on commission); *Lowther* v. *Harris*, [1927] 1 K. B. 393; *Budberg* v. *Jerwood and Ward* (1934), 51 T. L. R. 99; *Thoresen* v. *Capital Credit Corporation* (1962), 37 D. L. R. (2d.) 317; *R.* v. *Eaton* (1966), 50 Cr. App. Rep. 189. *Cf. Biggs* v. *Evans*, [1894] 1 Q. B. 88, decided on the repealed Acts, where it was held that an opal matrix table-top entrusted (but not for the purpose of sale) to a dealer in jewels and gems, and sold by him outside the ordinary course of his business, was not within the Act.

The court will look behind any document purporting to regulate the relationship of the parties to it, if in fact it is a cloak designed to hide the true nature of that relationship so as to deprive a third party of rights he would otherwise possess (*n*).

---

(2) A person shall be deemed to be in possession of goods or of the documents of title to goods, where the goods or documents are in his actual custody or are held by any other person subject to his control or for him or on his behalf:

Definitions.—For "goods," "documents of title" and "person," see sub-ss. (3), (4) and (6), *post*, respectively.

Cross-references.—This definition is required by ss. 1 (4), 2 (1), (2) and (3), 7 (1), 8 and 9, *post*.

COMMENT

This definition is taken from words used in s. 4 of the Factors Act 1842, but it is generalised by the substitution of the word "person" for the word "agent." See note to definition of "delivery" in s. 61 (1) of the Sale of Goods Act, *ante*.

---

(3) The expression "goods" shall include wares and merchandise:

Cross-references.—This definition is required by ss. 1 (1) and (2), *ante*, 1 (4) and (5), 2 (1), (2) and (3), 3 to 5, 7 (1), 8 to 11, 12 (2) and (3), *post*.

COMMENT

The term used in the repealed s. 17 of the Statute of Frauds is "goods, wares, and merchandise." This definition, therefore, probably incorporates the numerous (and now otherwise obsolete) decisions on the meaning of those words in that Act. A different definition of "goods" is given by s. 61 (1) of the Sale of Goods Act for the purposes of that Act, *ante*.

---

(4) The expression "document of title" shall include any bill of lading, dock warrant, warehouse-keeper's certificate, and warrant or order for the delivery of goods (*o*), and any

---

(*n*) *St. Margaret's Trust* v. *Castle*, [1964] C. L. Y. 1685, C. A.; and see generally pp. 79–80, *ante*.

(*o*) As to delivery orders, see *Morgan* v. *Gath* (1865), 3 H. & C. 748, at p. 760 (definition); *Re Hall* (1884), 14 Q. B. D. 386; *Re Cunningham & Co.* (1885), 54 L. J. Ch. 448 (distinguished from bill of sale); *Union Credit Bank* v. *Mersey Docks*, [1899] 2 Q. B. 205.

other document used in the ordinary course of business as proof of the possession or control of goods, or authorising or purporting to authorise, either by endorsement or by delivery, the possessor of the document to transfer or receive goods thereby represented:

Definitions.—For "goods" and "possession," see sub-ss. (3) and (2), *ante*, respectively.

Cross-references.—This definition is required by ss. 1 (2), *ante*, and 2 (1), (2) and (3), 3, 5, 8 to 11 and 12 (2), *post*. *Cf.* s. 11, *post* (transfer of documents of title).

COMMENT

This definition is taken from s. 4 of the Act of 1842, with the addition of the "warehouse-keeper's certificate." It is incorporated by s. 61 (1) of the Sale of Goods Act, *ante*. The Act of 1825 included warehouse-keepers' certificates, but the Act of 1842 omitted them, and in a case in 1875 the Lords Justices held that these documents were not documents of title (*p*).

Cash receipts given in place of delivery orders are not documents of title (*q*), nor are the registration books of motor vehicles (*r*).

Ordinarily, when the title to goods depends upon a written instrument, the document requires to be registered as a bill of sale for the purposes of the Bills of Sale Acts; but most of the usual commercial documents of title are excluded by s. 4 of the Bills of Sale Act 1878, reproduced *post*, Appendix I. And by the Bills of Sale Act 1890 (*c*), as amended by the Bills of Sale Act 1891 (*s*), certain mercantile letters of hypothecation are exempted from the provisions of the Bills of Sale Acts.

---

(5) The expression "pledge" shall include any contract pledging, or giving a lien or security on, goods, whether in consideration of an original advance or of any further or continuing advance or of any pecuniary liability:

(*p*) *Gunn* v. *Bolckow, Vaughan & Co.* (1875), 10 Ch. App. 491.

(*q*) *Kemp* v. *Falk* (1882), 7 App. Cas. 573, at p. 585, *per* Lord BLACKBURN. As to mate's receipts, see *Cowas-Jee* v. *Thompson* (1845), 5 Moo. P. C. C. 165; *Hathesing* v. *Laing* (1873), L. R. 17 Eq. 92; and compare *Kum* v. *Wah Tat Bank*, [1971] 1 Lloyd's Rep. 439, P. C.

(*r*) *Joblin* v. *Watkins and Roseveare*, [1949] 1 All E. R. 47; *Central Newbury Car Auctions* v. *Unity Finance*, [1956] 3 All E. R. 905, C. A.; [1957] 1 Q. B. 371, but the sale of a motor vehicle without its registration book is not normally a sale in the ordinary course of a mercantile agent's business: see p. 297, *post*. In a contract of hire-purchase, and presumably also in a contract of sale, the provision of a car log book is a suspensive condition on which the existence of the contract depends, though the condition may be waived by taking delivery of the car and using it: *Bentworth Finance, Ltd.* v. *Lubert*, [1967] 2 All E. R. 810; [1968] 1 Q. B. 680, C. A. See also 99 L. J. 243 and 101 L. J. 481.

(*s*) 3 Halsbury's Statutes (3rd Edn.) 262.

Definition.—For "goods," see sub-s. (3), *ante*.

Cross-references.—This definition is required by ss. 2 (1), 3 to 6, 7 (2), 8, 9 and 12 (2), *post*.

COMMENT

This definition is new. Its terms seem wide enough to include a mortgage, that is, a contract transferring conditionally the general property in goods in consideration of a loan, and also perhaps a letter of hypothecation without possession. As to the common law definition of "pledge", see *ante*.

The words "any pecuniary liability" are very wide, and are probably intended to meet cases such as the granting of a letter of credit to be operated by bills of exchange in consideration of the pledge of goods or documents.

---

(6) The expression "person" shall include any body of persons corporate or incorporate.

Cross-references.—This definition is required by ss. 1 (2), *ante*, and 2 (1), (2) and (3), 7 (1), 8 to 10 and 12 (2), *post*.

COMMENT

Cf. Sch. 1 to the Interpretation Act 1978, by which "person" includes a body of persons corporate or unincorporate. But by Sch. 2, para. 4 (1) of the 1978 Act that definition applies only to Acts passed after 1889.

Dispositions by Mercantile Agents

2. Powers of mercantile agent with respect to disposition of goods.—(1) Where a mercantile agent is with the consent (*t*) of the owner, in possession of goods (*u*) or of the documents of title to goods, any sale, pledge, or other disposition of the goods, made by him when acting in the ordinary course of business of a mercantile agent, shall, subject to the provisions of this Act, be as valid as if he were expressly authorised by the owner of the goods to make the same; provided that the person taking under the disposition acts in good faith, and has not at the time of the disposition notice that the person making the disposition has not authority to make the same.

(*t*) As to "consent," see note to s. 23 of the Sale of Goods Act, *ante*.

(*u*) The word "goods" here bears its ordinary meaning; thus a car is still "goods" though it lack both ignition key and registration book and so cannot be used: *Stadium Finance* v. *Robbins*, [1962] 2 All E. R. 633; [1962] 2 Q. B. 664, C. A. But see *Pearson* v. *Rose & Young*, [1950] 2 All E. R. 1027; [1951] 1 K. B. 275.

ILLUSTRATIONS

(1) A diamond broker obtains a parcel of diamonds from a diamond merchant on the pretence that he has a prospective customer in K. Instead of taking them to K, he pledges them with a pawnbroker. It is against the custom of the diamond trade for brokers to have authority to pledge, but the pawnbroker, who has had previous dealings with the broker, believes him to be a principal. The pledge stands good (*a*).

(2) A diamond broker obtains a parcel of diamonds from a diamond merchant on the pretence that he has a prospective customer in K. Instead of taking them to K, he hands them to B, requesting him to sell them. B arranges with another firm of diamond merchants to purchase the diamonds on joint account with him, and the price is paid to the broker. B, who shares an office with the broker, does not act in good faith, but the purchasing firm does. The purchasing firm is not protected, and they and B are jointly liable in an action for conversion (*b*).

(3) The owner of a car entrusts it to a motor-car agent to sell it on commission subject to a reserve price. The agent sells it to a *bona fide* purchaser below the reserve price, and misappropriates the money. The agent is a "mercantile agent," and the purchaser gets a good title to the car (*c*).

(4) A hires a car to B on hire-purchase terms for use in B's self-drive hire business. B also sells cars as a mercantile agent. B sells this car to C. B is not in possession of the car in his capacity of a mercantile agent. C, therefore, does not get a good title to the car by virtue of this subsection (*d*).

Definitions.—For "mercantile agent," "possession," "goods," "document of title," "pledge" and "person," see s. 1 (1), (2), (3), (4), (5) and (6), *ante*, respectively.

Cross-references.—*Cf.* s. 4, *post* (pledges for antecedent debt); s. 5, *post* (necessary consideration); s. 7, *post* (provisions as to consignors and consignees); Sale of Goods Act 1979, s. 23, *ante* (sale under voidable title).

History.—This subsection supersedes and reproduces, in altered language, ss. 2 and 4 of the Act of 1825 and s. 4 of the Act of 1842.

COMMENT

The consent of the owner: (1) the owner.—For the purposes of this subsection, the owner must be a person in a position to give the mercantile agent express authority to dispose of the goods. Where rights of ownership are divided among two or more persons in such a way that the acts which the subsection is contemplating could never be authorized save by both or all of them, those persons together constitute

(*a*) *Oppenheimer* v. *Attenborough*, [1908] 1 K. B. 221, C. A.

(*b*) *Oppenheimer* v. *Frazer & Wyatt*, [1907] 2 K. B. 50, C. A.; not followed in *Du Jardin* v. *Beadman*, [1952] 2 All E. R. 160; [1952] 2 Q. B. 712.

(*c*) *Folkes* v. *King*, [1923] 1 K. B. 282, C. A.; distinguished, *Heap* v. *Motorists Advisory Agency, Ltd.*, [1923] 1 K. B. 577 (larceny by trick, but the thief was not a mercantile agent).

(*d*) *Astley Industrial Trust, Ltd.* v. *Miller*, [1968] 2 All E. R. 36. Note, however, that if C is a private purchaser as defined by s. 29 (2) of the Hire-Purchase Act 1964, he may now get a good title to the car by virtue of s. 27 of that Act, as substituted by Sch. 4 to the Consumer Credit Act 1974 and as amended by Sch. 2, para. 4 to the Sale of Goods Act 1979, *ante*.

the owner (*e*). The mercantile agent himself may be part owner of the goods (*e*).

(2) The consent.—This subsection no longer requires the goods or documents to be "intrusted" to the agent, but it suffices that they are in his possession with the owner's consent. How far this alteration of language extends the operation of the Act is not very clear; but it is now established that where a mercantile agent is intrusted with goods in some other capacity than that of mercantile agent, he cannot sell or pledge those goods contrary to instructions (*f*). Goods are in the possession of a mercantile agent in that capacity if his possession is in some way connected with his business of mercantile agent even if he has no authority to dispose of the goods (*g*).

The consent is not vitiated by fraud on the part of the mercantile agent (*h*) even, it seems, where the fraud would before the Theft Act 1968 have amounted to larceny by a trick (*i*). It is irrelevant that the consent has determined if the buyer has no notice that this is so: see s. 2 (2), *post*.

Sale pledge or other disposition.—Pledge is defined by s. 1 (5), *ante*, to include any contract pledging or giving a lien or security on goods. Such a contract would give only an equitable interest in the goods to the pledgee. A disposition must involve a transfer of property (*k*), but in the context it would seem that it would be sufficient to transfer an equitable interest in the goods. There are two cases in which the expression "sale pledge or other disposition" has been restrictively construed (*l*), but it is doubtful whether they would now be followed on this point (*m*).

Ordinary course of business of a mercantile agent.—It is a question of fact in each case whether a mercantile agent is acting in the

(*e*) *Lloyds Bank, Ltd.* v. *Bank of America, National Trust and Savings Association*, [1938] 2 All E. R. 63; [1938] 2 K. B. 147, C. A.

(*f*) *Astley Industrial Trust, Ltd.* v. *Miller*, [1968] 2 All E. R. 36 (reviewing earlier cases) (*ante*, illustration (4)); *Belvoir Finance Co., Ltd.* v. *Harold G. Cole & Co., Ltd.*, [1969] 2 All E. R. 904. As to former rule, see *Monk* v. *Whittenbury* (1831), 2 B. & Ad. 484 (flour factor and wharfinger); *Cole* v. *North Western Bank* (1875), L. R. 10 C. P. 354 (warehouse-keeper and broker); *Biggs* v. *Evans*, [1894] 1 Q. B. 88 (dealer in jewels and gems intrusted with table-top to be sold on certain conditions only). As to meaning of "intrusted," see *Lake* v. *Simmons*, [1927] A. C. 487.

(*g*) *Pearson* v. *Rose & Young*, [1950] 2 All E. R. 1027, at p. 1032; [1951] 1 K. B. 275, at p. 288, *per* DENNING, L. J.; *Turner* v. *Sampson* (1911), 27 T. L. R. 200 (agent to obtain offers for picture and report back).

(*h*) *Lowther* v. *Harris*, [1927] 1 K. B. 393.

(*i*) See the comment to s. 23 of the Sale of Goods Act, *ante*.

(*k*) *Worcester Works Finance, Ltd.* v. *Cooden Engineering Co., Ltd.*, [1971] 3 All E. R. 708; [1972] 1 Q. B. 210, C. A.

(*l*) *Waddington & Sons* v. *Neale & Sons* (1907), 96 L. T. 786; *Jobling* v. *Watkins and Roseveare (Motors), Ltd.*, [1949] 1 All E. R. 47.

(*m*) They would seem to be inconsistent with *Worcester Works Finance, Ltd.* v. *Cooden Engineering Co., Ltd. supra*, and can be justified, if at all, only on the basis that the dispositions in question were not in the ordinary course of the agent's business. *Cf.* also *Stoneleigh Finance, Ltd.* v. *Phillips*, [1965] 1 All E. R. 513, C. A.; [1965] 2 Q. B. 537, C. A.

ordinary course of his business. The situation may vary from place to place and from trade to trade. Even where it is in the ordinary course of a mercantile agent's business to sell or pledge goods, it may be necessary to consider whether the manner in which the sale or pledge is effected is within the ordinary course of such business (*n*), "that is to say, within business hours, at a proper place of business, and in other respects in the ordinary way in which a mercantile agent would act" (*o*).

There may be a general rule that agents should only sell for cash, cheque or bill (*p*), but there seems no inherent reason why an agent may not dispose of goods by way of exchange of for other valuable consideration, or even by way of set-off (*q*), as long as it is, on the facts, within the ordinary course of business of such a mercantile agent.

A sale will not normally be in the ordinary course of business of a mercantile agent, where the mercantile agent sells the goods as agent and not as principal, and the buyer knows that the profits on the sale are to go to the agent and not the principal (*r*).

The sale of a second-hand car without a log book has been held not to be in the ordinary course of business of a mercantile agent (*s*), but the opposite conclusion was reached in another case where a new car was sold and a satisfactory explanation was given as to the absence of the log book (*t*).

The circumstances in which the vendor acquires possession of the goods has been held to affect the question of whether the mercantile agent is acting in the ordinary course of business (*u*). The better view, however, would seem to be that such circumstances are irrelevent in this context, although they may be important in deciding whether the goods have been given to the mercantile agent in his capacity as a mercantile agent (*a*).

Agent purporting to act as principal.—The third party cannot be in a worse position if the agent purports to be the owner of the goods than would have been the case if the agent had acted as agent (*b*). Accordingly, if he would have acquired a good title if the agent had acted as agent, he will still acquire a good title if the agent acts as owner

---

(*n*) *Janesich* v. *Attenborough* (1910), 102 L. T. 605 (not commercial rate of interest); *De Gorter* v. *Attenborough* (1904), 21 T. L. R. 19 (friend asked to pledge article for mercantile agent); *Mortimer-Rae* v. *Barthel* (1980), 11 Alta L. R. (2d) 66 (sale of entire stock-in-trade amounting to sale of business not in ordinary course of business).

(*o*) *Oppenheimer* v. *Attenborough & Son*, [1907] 2 K. B. 221, at pp. 230–231, *per* BUCKLEY, L. J.

(*p*) *Biggs* v. *Evans*, [1894] 1 Q. B. 88, at p. 91.

(*q*) *Tingey & Co., Ltd.* v. *Chambers, Ltd.*, [1967] N. Z. L. R. 785.

(*r*) *Raffoul* v. *Essanda, Ltd.* (1970), 72 S. R. (N. S. W.) 633.

(*s*) *Pearson* v. *Rose and Young, Ltd.*, [1950] 2 All E. R. 1027; [1951] 1 K. B. 275, C. A.; *Lambert* v. *G. and C. Finance Corporation, Ltd.* (1963), 107 Sol. Jo. 666.

(*t*) *Astley Industrial Trust* v. *Miller*, [1968] 2 All E. R. 36. See further the comment to s. 1 (4), *ante*.

(*u*) *Stadium Finance* v. *Robbins*, [1962] 2 All E. R. 633, at p. 639; [1962] 2 Q. B. 664, at p. 675, *per* WILLMER, L. J.

(*a*) *Astley Industrial Trust* v. *Miller, supra.*

(*b*) *Oppenheimer* v. *Attenborough*, [1908] 1 K. B. 221, C. A. (illustration (1), *ante*).

(*c*). But it would seem that to come within this section, the transaction must still be one that would have been within the ordinary course of business of the agent had he acted as such (*d*).

A transaction would still be within the ordinary course of a mercantile agent's business, where the agent holds himself out as principal, although payment is made to the agent in a manner that would be outside his apparent or actual authority as agent (*e*).

The powers of the mercantile agent.—It was held under the repealed Acts that the mercantile agent's powers were not exhausted by a single transaction. Thus, where the consignee of cotton pledged the bill of lading with a broker, authorising him to sell the cotton, and then with the broker's consent pledged the net proceeds to D, it was held that the latter transaction was valid as well as the former one (*f*). This case would seem still to be good law.

Under s. 1 of the Factors Act 1842, no protection was given to a pledgee under a general pledge or lien, where goods which had been entrusted to a mercantile agent by their owner were pledged by him, together with other goods, as security for a loan (*g*). Section 2 (1) of the present Act is worded in more general terms. So far only the Supreme Court of British Columbia has considered the change of wording, holding that it has not altered the law (*h*).

Notice.—The term "notice" in this section probably means actual, though not formal, notice (*i*); that is to say, either knowledge of the facts, or grounds for a suspicion of something wrong combined with a wilful disregard of the means of knowledge. The same construction would probably be put on it as upon the term "notice" in s. 29 of the Bills of Exchange Act 1882, or in ss. 30 and 45 of the Bankruptcy Act 1914 (*k*). Under this section, which creates an exception to the rule that

(*c*) *Oppenheimer* v. *Attenborough, supra; Janesich* v. *Attenborough* (1910), 102 L. T. 605.

(*d*) Thus in *Janesich* v. *Attenborough, supra*, a pledge was made by an agent acting as principal at 15 per cent interest, and the court considered whether this was a commercial rate for interest such as an agent might agree to in the ordinary course of his business.

(*e*) *Oppenheimer* v. *Attenborough, supra; Janesich* v. *Attenborough, supra; Raffoul* v. *Essanda, Ltd.* (1970), 72 S. R. (N. S. W.) 633.

(*f*) *Portalis* v. *Tetley* (1867), L. R. 5 Eq. 140.

(*g*) *Kaltenbach* v. *Lewis* (1883), 24 Ch. D. 54, C. A.; see especially at pp. 79–80. The point was not raised in the appeal to the House of Lords, (1885), 10 App. Cas. 617, but the decision of the Court of Appeal on this point received the approval of Lord BRAMWELL, at p. 635.

(*h*) *Thoresen* v. *Capital Credit Corporation, Ltd. and Active Bailiff* (1962) 37 D. L. R. (2d.) 317; and see *Re the Farmers' and Settlers' Co-operative Society, Ltd., City Bank of Sydney* v. *Barden* (1908), 9 S. R. (N. S. W.) 41.

(*i*) There is no room for the doctrine of constructive notice in the world of commerce: *Manchester Trust* v. *Furness*, [1895] 2 Q. B. 539, C. A.; *Greer* v. *Downs Supply Co.*, [1927] 2 K. B. 28, C. A.; *By Appointment (Sales), Ltd.* v. *Harrods* (1977), unreported, Court of Appeal Transcript No. 465.

(*k*) 3 Halsbury's Statutes (3rd Edn.) 204, 78, 96. See the term discussed, *Navulshaw* v. *Brownrigg* (1852), 21 L. J. Ch. 908, at p. 911 (Factors Act); *Raphael* v. *Bank of England* (1855), 17 C. B. 161, at p. 174, *per* WILLES, J. (bill of exchange); *Ex p. Snowball* (1872), 7 Ch. App. 534, at p. 549 (act of bankruptcy). See further, the comment to s. 8 of the Factors, Act, *post*.

no one can give a better title than he himself has, the person claiming the benefit of the proviso must prove his good faith and absence of notice; while under s. 23 of the Sale of Goods Act, *ante*, which embodies an exception recognised by the common law to that rule, the onus is on the person who seeks to impeach the title of a buyer from a seller with a voidable title to prove in bad faith or notice (*l*).

(2) Where a mercantile agent has, with the consent of the owner, been in possession of goods or of the documents of title to goods, any sale, pledge, or other disposition, which would have been valid if the consent had continued, shall be valid notwithstanding the determination of the consent: provided that the person taking under the disposition has not at the time thereof notice that the consent has been determined.

ILLUSTRATIONS

(1) A picture dealer in Paris sends pictures to an agent in London, some for sale, others for exhibition only. After revocation of his authority the agent pledges both lots of pictures with B, who takes them without notice of the revocation. B gets a good title (*m*).

(2) A, by fraud, induces plaintiff to sell him a car. On learning of the fraud, plaintiff rescinds the contract. Subsequently A sells the car in the Warren Street car market to B who acts in good faith and without notice of A's lack of title. By virtue of s. 9 of the Factors Act, A is in the same position as a mercantile agent. He obtained possession of the car initially with the consent of the owner, albeit the consent was obtained by fraud. The consent has since determined, but A may nevertheless give a good title to the car in a manner which would be within the ordinary course of a mercantile agent's business (*n*).

Definitions.—See note to sub-s. (1) of this section.

History.—See last note. This subsection reproduces in altered language the provisions of s. 2 of the Factors Act 1877, which was passed to override the decision in *Fuentes* v. *Montis* (*o*) where it was held that a mercantile agent was not intrusted with goods or documents within the meaning of the earlier Acts if his authority had been revoked.

---

(3) Where a mercantile agent has obtained possession of

(*l*) *Cf. Heap* v. *Motorists Advisory Agency, Ltd.*, [1923] 1 K. B. 577 (Factors Act); *Halfway Garage* (*Nottingham*) v. *Lepley* (1964), *Guardian*, 8th February, C. A. (s. 25, Sale of Goods Act); and *Whitehorn Brothers* v. *Davison*, [1911] 1 K. B. 463 (s. 23, Sale of Goods Act). The Law Reform Committee in its Report on the Transfer of Title to Chattels (Cmd., 2958) has recommended that in a s. 23 situation it should be for the buyer to prove that he bought in good faith.

(*m*) *Moody* v. *Pall Mall Deposit Co.* (1917), 33 T. L. R. 306.

(*n*) *Newtons of Wembley, Ltd.* v. *Williams*, [1964] 3 All E. R. 532; [1965] 1 Q. B. 560, C. A.

(*o*) (1868), L. R. 3 C. P. 268; affirmed L. R. 4 C. P. 93, Ex. Ch.

any documents of title to goods by reason of his being or having been, with the consent of the owner, in possession of the goods represented thereby, or of any other documents of title to the goods, his possession of the first-mentioned documents shall, for the purposes of this Act, be deemed to be with the consent of the owner.

Definitions.—See note to sub-s. (1) of this section.

History.—This subsection reproduces in somewhat different language a provision in s. 4 of the Factors Act 1842, which was intended to alter the law as laid down in *Phillips* v. *Huth* (*p*) and *Hatfield* v. *Phillips* (*q*). In the latter case it was held that a person intrusted with a bill of lading for the purpose of selling the goods mentioned in it was not, in consequence of being so intrusted, to be considered as intrusted with the dock warrant, notwithstanding that his possession of the bill of lading enabled him to obtain the dock warrant.

---

(4) For the purposes of this Act the consent of the owner shall be presumed in the absence of evidence to the contrary.

History.—This subsection reproduces in somewhat different language the concluding paragraph of s. 4 of the Factors Act 1842.

3. Effect of pledges of documents of title.—A pledge of the documents of title to goods shall be deemed to be a pledge of the goods.

Definitions.—For "goods," "documents of title" and "pledge," see s. 1 (3), (4) and (5), *ante*, respectively.

History.—This section is taken from a paragraph in s. 4 of the Factors Act 1842.

COMMENT

The section, though general in its terms, is controlled by the heading "Dispositions by Mercantile Agents" of the part in which it occurs. It therefore applies only to pledges by "mercantile agents" as defined by s. 1 (1) (*r*).

4. Pledge for antecedent debt.—Where a mercantile agent pledges goods as security for a debt or liability due from the pledgor to the pledgee before the time of the

---

(*p*) (1860), 6 M. & W. 572; see the comments on this case in *Cole* v. *North Western Bank* (1875), L. R. 10 C. P. 354, at p. 370.

(*q*) (1842), 9 M. & W. 647; affirmed (1845), 14 M. & W. 665.

(*r*) *Inglis* v. *Robertson*, [1898] A. C. 616.

pledge, the pledgee shall acquire no further right to the goods than could have been enforced by the pledgor at the time of the pledge.

Definitions.—For "mercantile agent," "goods" and "pledge," see s. 1 (1), (3) and (4), *ante*, respectively.

History.—This section reproduces in altered language the clumsily worded s. 3 of the Factors Act 1825, as read with the proviso contained in s. 3 of the Factors Act 1842. The substitution of the words "debt *or liability*" for "antecedent debt" is material (*s*).

COMMENT

The use of the word "due," though appropriate to the term "debt," seems inappropriate to the term "liability." The section should perhaps be read as if it ran "debt due from or liability incurred by."

The object of this section seems to be to draw a marked distinction between past consideration and present or future consideration (*t*). In terms it applies only to pledges of goods, but having regard to the language of s. 3, *ante*, it may be intended to apply also to pledges of documents.

5. Rights acquired by exchange of goods or documents.—The consideration necessary for the validity of a sale, pledge, or other disposition, of goods, in pursuance of this Act, may be either a payment in cash, or the delivery or transfer of other goods, or of a document of title to goods, or of a negotiable security, or any other valuable consideration; but where goods are pledged by a mercantile agent in consideration of the delivery or transfer of other goods, or of a document of title to goods, or of a negotiable security, the pledgee shall acquire no right or interest in the goods so pledged in excess of the value of the goods, documents, or security when so delivered or transferred in exchange.

Definitions.—For "mercantile agent," "goods," "document of title" and "pledge," see s. 1 (1), (3), (4) and (5), *ante*, respectively.

History.—By s. 4 of the Factors Act 1842, it was provided, *inter alia*, that "any payment made, whether by money or bills of exchange, or other negotiable security, shall be deemed and taken to be *an advance* within the meaning of this Act." The first sentence of the present section

---

(*s*) For cases on the repealed sections, see *Jewan* v. *Whitworth* (1866), L. R. 2 Eq. 692; *Macnee* v. *Gorst* (1867), L. R. 4 Eq. 315; *Kaltenbach* v. *Lewis* (1885), 10 App. Cas. 617.

(*t*) But see *Industrial Acceptance Corpn.* v. *Whiteshall Finance Corporation* (1966), 57 D. L. R. (2d) 670, where the equivalent provision in the Manitoban Factors Act is considered in relation to a revolving credit given by a finance company to a car dealer.

considerably extends the scope of the old enactment, by substituting "valuable consideration" for "an advance" as above defined.

The second sentence of the section reproduces in somewhat different language the provisions of s. 2 of the Factors Act 1842, which was intended to protect exchanges of goods and securities made in good faith, and to alter the law as laid down in *Taylor* v. *Kymer* and *Bonzi* v. *Stewart* (*u*).

Scotland.—As regards the application of this section to Scotland, see s. 1 (2) of the Factors (Scotland) Act 1890, *post*.

6. Agreements through clerks, &c.—For the purposes of this Act an agreement made with a mercantile agent through a clerk or other person authorised in the ordinary course of business to make contracts of sale or pledge on his behalf shall be deemed to be an agreement with the agent.

Definitions.—For "mercantile agent" and "pledge," see s. 1 (1) and (5), *ante*, respectively.

History.—This section is taken from, and generalises, a paragraph in s. 4 of the Factors Act 1842.

7. Provisions as to consignors and consignees.—(1) Where the owner of goods has given possession of the goods to another person for the purpose of consignment or sale, or has shipped the goods in the name of another person, and the consignee of the goods has not had notice that such person is not the owner of the goods, the consignee shall, in respect of advances made to or for the use of such person, have the same lien on the goods as if such person were the owner of the goods, and may transfer any such lien to another person.

(2) Nothing in this section shall limit or affect the validity of any sale, pledge, or disposition, by a mercantile agent.

Definitions.—For "mercantile agent," "possession," "goods," "pledge" and "person," see s. 1 (1), (2), (3), (5) and (6), *ante*, respectively.

History.—The first subsection reproduces in different language the provisions of s. 1 of the Factors Act 1825 (*a*).

(*u*) (1832), 3 B. & Ad. 320; and (1842), 4 M. & Gr. 295; and see the comments on these cases in *Cole* v. *North Western Bank* (1875), L. R. 10 C. P. 354, at p. 370.

(*a*) See that enactment discussed in *Cole* v. *North Western Bank* (1875), L. R. 10 C. P. 354, at pp. 361–367; and *Johnson* v. *Crédit Lyonnais* (1877), 3 C. P. D. 32, at pp. 44, 45.

COMMENT

It is to be noted that the section applies only to goods and not to documents of title, and to cases where the consignee has not had notice that the consignor is not the owner. Lord BLACKBURN raised a doubt on the repealed enactment whether "notice" was co-extensive with knowledge (*b*). The term "advance" must probably be interpreted in the light of s. 5, *ante*.

The second subsection shows that the present section is to be construed as amplifying, and not as derogating from, the powers of mercantile agents under s. 2, *ante*. Section 13, *post*, further saves the common law powers of factors and agents of that class.

Dispositions by Sellers and Buyers of Goods

8. Disposition by seller remaining in possession.—Where a person, having sold goods, continues, or is, in possession of the goods or of the documents of title to the goods, the delivery or transfer by that person, or by a mercantile agent acting for him, of the goods or documents of title under any sale, pledge, or other disposition thereof, or under any agreement for sale, pledge, or other disposition thereof, to any person receiving the same in good faith and without notice of the previous sale, shall have the same effect as if the person making the delivery or transfer were expressly authorised by the owner of the goods to make the same.

Definitions.—For "mercantile agent," "possession," "goods," "document of title," "pledge" and "person," see s. 1 (1), (2), (3), (4), (5) and (6), *ante*, respectively.

Cross-references.—*Cf.* Sale of Goods Act 1979, s. 24, *ante* (sale, etc. by seller in possession), and s. 48 (3), *ante* (re-sale by unpaid seller).

History.—This section and the next are reproduced by ss. 24 and 25 of the Sale of Goods Act, slightly modified by omitting the words "or under any agreement for sale, pledge, or other disposition thereof."

The Sale of Goods Bill 1893 originally proposed to repeal these two sections, but the repeal was afterwards omitted, as the provisions of the Sale of Goods Act are slightly narrower (*c*).

COMMENT

This section alters the law as laid down about sellers in possession in *Johnson* v. *Crédit Lyonnais* (*d*). It was there held that if the buyer, for his

(*b*) *Mildred* v. *Maspons* (1833), 8 App. Cas. 874, at p. 885.

(*c*) The repeal of these two sections was again proposed by the Law Reform Committee in its Report on the Transfer of Title to Chattels (Cmd. 2958).

(*d*) (1877), 3 C. P. D. 32, 40.

own convenience, left the goods and documents of title in the hands of the seller, who fraudulently re-sold or pledged them, he could nevertheless recover the goods from the innocent purchaser or pledgee.

Continues, or is, in possession.—The words "continues . . . in possession" refer to the continuity of physical possession regardless of any private transaction between seller and buyer which might alter the legal title under which the seller is in possession (*e*). The words "or is" refer only to a case where the person who sold the goods had not got the goods when he sold them but they came into his possession afterwards (*f*).

So, if the seller continues in possession in another capacity such as bailee or hirer by virtue of a term in the contract of sale itself (*g*) or of some other arrangement (*h*) he "continues in possession" within the meaning of the section even if he is in breach of such arrangement and his right to possession of the goods has determined so that he holds them as trespasser (*h*).

But there must be continuity of possession. If the seller delivers the goods to a purchaser who then leases them back to the seller, then at least as a general rule the section has no application (*i*).

By s. 1 (2) of the Factors Act 1889, *ante*, a person is deemed to be in possession of the goods or of the documents of title to goods where the goods are held by any other person subject to his control or on his behalf.

Where the seller sold goods which were at the time of the sale deposited with a warehouseman, who had a lien thereon for his charges and promised to discharge the lien and to send the delivery orders to the buyer, but instead of so doing sold the goods to a second buyer who obtained delivery, it was held that the second sale was a sale by a seller in possession of the goods and the section accordingly operated in favour of the second buyer (*k*).

Delivery or transfer.—So that the section may apply there must be either delivery of the goods or a transfer of a document of title so that

---

(*e*) *Worcester Works Finance, Ltd.* v. *Cooden Engineering Co., Ltd.*, [1971] 3 All E. R. 708; [1972] 1 Q. B. 182, C. A. *Pacific Motor Auctions Pty., Ltd.* v. *Motor Credit* (*Hire Finance*), *Ltd.*, [1965] 2 All E. R. 105, at p. 114; [1965] A. C. 867, at p. 888, P. C.; *Mercantile Credit, Ltd.* v. *Upton & Son Pty., Ltd.* (1974), 48 A. L. J. R. 301 (H. C. of Aus.).

(*f*) *Worcester Works Finance, Ltd.* v. *Cooden Engineering Co., Ltd.*, *supra*.

(*g*) *Worcester Works Finance, Ltd.* v. *Cooden Engineering Co., Ltd.*, *supra*, following *Pacific Motor Auctions Pty., Ltd.* v. *Motor Credit* (*Hire Finance*), *Ltd.*, *supra*, and not following *Eastern Distributors* v. *Goldring*, [1957] 2 All E. R. 523; [1957] 2 Q. B. 600, C. A.

(*h*) *Worcester Works Finance, Ltd.* v. *Cooden Engineering Co., Ltd.*, *supra*. See further 1972 J. B. L. 149; 88 L. Q. R. 239.

(*i*) *Mitchell* v. *Jones* (1905), 24 N. Z. L. R. 932; approved in *Pacific Motor Auctions Proprietary, Ltd.* v. *Motor Credits* (*Hire Finance*), *Ltd.*, [1965] 2 All E. R. 105; [1965] A. C. 867, P. C.; *cf. Worcester Works Finance, Ltd.* v. *Cooden Engineering Co., Ltd.*, [1971] 3 All E. R. 708, at p. 712; [1972] 1 Q. B. 182, at pp. 217–218, where Lord DENNING, M. R., referred to a "substantial break in the continuity".

(*k*) *City Fur Manufacturing Co., Ltd.* v. *Fureenbond* (*Brokers*), *London, Ltd.*, [1937] 1 All E. R. 799.

there is a change in the physical possession of the goods or of the documents of title (*l*).

In a case where wine stored in a warehouse was sold, and the seller afterwards, by executing a memorandum of charge, pledged the wine to the warehouseman who had no notice of the sale, it was held that the warehouseman acquired no title, as there was no delivery of the goods and no transfer of a document of title to him (*m*).

In another case A bought a car from B but paid for it by a cheque which bounced. While in possession of the car A re-sold the car to C but did not deliver it to him. The car was re-possessed by B with the consent of A, and it was held by the Court of Appeal that this was a delivery or transfer of the car by A to B under a disposition of the car, so that B and not C was entitled to it (*n*).

Sale pledge or other disposition.—To constitute a disposition there must be more than a mere transfer of goods; there must be a disposal involving the transfer of an interest in property (*n*). As there is nothing in this section which requires the recipient to give value for the goods, a gift would seem to be sufficient for this purpose (*o*).

Notice.—Notice in this context would seem to mean actual notice so that a person receiving the goods need only show that he did not know of the sale and did not deliberately turn a blind eye (*p*).

The same effect . . . as if expressly authorised by the owner.—This is a wider provision than in s. 9, *post*, by virtue of which a disposition by a buyer in possession only has the same effect as if he was a mercantile agent in possession of the goods with the consent of the owner.

It is for the second purchaser to show that his case comes in all respects within this section or s. 24 of the Sale of Goods Act (*q*).

9. Disposition by buyer obtaining possession.—Where a person, having bought or agreed to buy goods, obtains with the consent of the seller possession of the goods or the documents of title to the goods, the delivery or transfer, by that person or by a mercantile agent acting for him, of the goods or documents of title (*r*), under any sale,

---

(*l*) *Nicholson* v. *Harper*, [1895] 2 Ch. 415, 418; *Bank of N. S. W.* v. *Palmer*, [1970] 2 N. S. W. R. 532; *N. Z. Securities and Finance, Ltd.* v. *Wrightcars, Ltd.*, [1976] 1 N. Z. L. R. 77.

(*m*) *Nicholson* v. *Harper*, [1895] 2 Ch. 415.

(*n*) *Worcester Works Finance, Ltd.* v. *Cooden Engineering Co., Ltd.*, *supra*.

(*o*) *Cf. Kitto* v. *Bilbie, Hobson & Co.* (1895), 72 L. T. 266; *Worcester Works Finance, Ltd.* v. *Cooden Engineering Co., Ltd.*, *supra*.

(*p*) *Worcester Works Finance, Ltd.* v. *Cooden Engineering Co., Ltd.*, *supra*, at pp. 712 and 219, *per* Lord DENNING, M. R. See also *Re Funduck and Horncastle* (1974), 39 D. L. R. (3d) 94. *Cf.* the comment to s. 2, *ante*.

(*q*) *Heap* v. *Motorists Advisory Agency, Ltd.*, [1923] 1 K. B. 577; *Halfway Garage (Nottingham)* v. *Lepley* (1964), *Guardian*, 8th February, C. A.

(*r*) It seems that these need not be the same documents as those of which the buyer has

pledge, or other disposition thereof, or under any agreement for sale, pledge, or other disposition thereof, to any person receiving the same in good faith and without notice of any lien or other right of the original seller in respect of the goods, shall have the same effect as if the person making the delivery or transfer were a mercantile agent in possession of the goods or documents of title with the consent of the owner (*s*).

For the purposes of this section—

(i) the buyer under a conditional sale agreement shall be deemed not to be a person who has bought or agreed to buy goods, and

(ii) "conditional sale agreement" means an agreement for the sale of goods which is a consumer credit agreement within the meaning of the Consumer Credit Act 1974 under which the purchase price or part of it is payable by instalments, and the property in the goods is to remain in the seller (notwithstanding that the buyer is to be in possession of the goods) until such conditions as to the payment of instalments or otherwise as may be specified in the agreement are fulfilled (*t*).

Definitions.—For "mercantile agent," "possession," "goods," "document of title," "pledge" and "person," see s. 1 (1), (2), (3), (4), (5) and (6), *ante*, respectively.

Cross-references.—*Cf.* Sale of Goods Act 1979, s. 25, *ante* (sale by buyer in possession), and ss. 2 to 5, *ante* (dispositions by mercantile agents).

History.—As to the reason for not repealing this section by the Sale of Goods Act 1893, see note to s. 8, *ante*.

---

obtained possession. See *per* SALMON, J., in *Mount* v. *Jay & Jay*, [1959] 3 All E. R. 307 at p. 311; [1960] 1 Q. B. 159 at pp. 168–169.

(*s*) See illustration (2) to s. 2 (2), *ante*.

(*t*) The provision relating to conditional sale agreements was introduced by Sch. 4 to the Consumer Credit Act 1974 with effect from a date to be appointed under s. 192 (4) of that Act. At present no date has been appointed, but the provisions of this section and of s. 25 of the Sale of Goods Act do not apply to conditional sale agreements by virtue of s. 54 of the Hire-Purchase Act 1965, as amended by Sch. 2, para. 6 to the Sale of Goods Act 1979, *ante*. There are special provisions which apply to the sale of motor vehicles by a purchaser under a conditional sale agreement; see ss. 27–29 of the Hire-Purchase Act 1964, which sections have been amended by Sch. 2, para. 4 to the Sale of Goods Act 1979, *ante*, and, from a date to be appointed, by the Consumer Credit Act 1974, Sch. 4, para. 22.

COMMENT

This section alters the former law as regards buyers in possession, which was thus stated by BLACKBURN, J. (*u*):

> "It has been repeatedly decided that a sale or pledge of a delivery order or other document of title (not being a bill of lading) by the vendee does not defeat the unpaid vendor's rights, because the vendee is not intrusted as an agent" (*a*).

Bought or agreed to buy.—Possession under an agreement for sale or return is not within the Act (*b*): nor is possession under a hire-purchase agreement which confers a mere option to buy the goods at the end of the period of hiring on payment of a further, and usually nominal, sum, whether or not the hirer is obliged to continue the hiring for any specified period (*c*). This is so even though a promissory note is given as collateral security for , and not as payment of, the instalments to become due under the agreement (*d*). But possession under a conditional contract of sale (*e*), or under a so-called hire-purchase agreement in which there is no right to return the goods, but a mere provision that the goods shall not belong to the hirer until the last instalment has been paid, is within the Act (*f*). Such an agreement is a binding contract of sale, with a provision that the payment of the purchase price shall be deferred and that the property shall not pass until the full price is paid. It is a question of construction whether the contract is a contract of hire-purchase or a contract of sale (*g*).

It has also been held that if a buyer or mercantile agent is in possession of goods under an illegal contract, a third party acquiring the goods from that buyer or mercantile agent cannot prove that the possession is with the consent of the seller or owner because the consent is only under and subject to those agreements (*h*).

The consent of the seller.—Though the buyer must obtain possession with the consent of the seller, however fraudulent the buyer may have been in obtaining the possession (even, it seems, if he was

(*u*) *Cole* v. *North Western Bank* (1875), L. R. 10 C. P. 354, at p. 373. *Cf. Jenkyns* v. *Usborne* (1844), 7 M. & Gr. 678; *McEwan* v. *Smith* (1849), 2 H. L. Cas. 309.

(*a*) This refers to the distinction formerly existing between a buyer in possession and a mercantile agent to whom goods had been intrusted; see s. 2, *ante* (replacing in altered language ss. 2 and 4 of the Factors Act 1842).

(*b*) *Edwards* v. *Vaughan* (1910), 26 T. L. R. 545, C. A.

(*c*) *Helby* v. *Matthews*, [1895] A. C. 471, and see *Belsize Motor Supply Co.* v. *Cox*, [1914] 1 K. B. 244. But see the exception to this rule for motor vehicles in note (*t*), above.

(*d*) *Modern Light Cars, Ltd.* v. *Seals*, [1934] 1 K. B. 32.

(*e*) *Marten* v. *Whale*, [1917] 2 K. B. 480, C. A.

(*f*) *Lee* v. *Butler*, [1893] 2 Q. B. 318, C. A.; *Hull Rope Works Co.* v. *Adams* (1896), 65 L. J. Q. B. 114; *Thompson* v. *Veale* (1896), 74 L. T. 130, C. A.; *Wylde* v. *Legge* (1901), 84 L. T. 121.

(*g*) *McEntire* v. *Crossley Brothers*, [1895] A. C. 457, 467.

(*h*) *Belvoir Finance Co., Ltd.* v. *Harold G. Cole & Co., Ltd.*, [1969] 2 All E. R. 904; [1969] 1 W. L. R. 1877. *Sed quaere*, for the effect of such a principle is that a party to a contract derives an advantage over an innocent third party which he would not have obtained but for his own illegality.

guilty of larceny by a trick (*i*)) and however grossly he may abuse the confidence reposed in him or violate the mandate under which he got possession, he can by his disposition give a good title to the purchaser from him (*k*). Nor does it matter for this purpose that the seller's consent has since been withdrawn (*l*).

The first seller must probably be a person who is able to give a good title to the first buyer. A thief cannot be "the seller" within the meaning of this section nor can a person who has bought in good faith from a thief (*m*). The word "seller" would seem to be used here in contrast with the word "owner" later in the section because other persons than the owner are often able to confer a good title (*n*).

Delivery or transfer.—The delivery must be under a sale, pledge or other disposition or, in the case of s. 9 of the Factors Act, but not under s. 25 of the Sale of Goods Act, under any agreement for such sale, pledge or other disposition (*o*).

As if the person . . . were a mercantile agent in possession.—It would seem from this limitation that the buyer in possession will only give a good title if he disposes of the goods in a way which would be in the ordinary course of a mercantile agent's business (*p*), so as to satisfy the requirements of s. 2, *ante*. If so, the buyer could not give a good title by making a gift of the goods.

It is not clear how literally this requirement is to be interpreted in the case of a private buyer—for example if a sale from a private house is excluded (*q*).

But courts in Australia, New Zealand and Canada all held that the equivalent sections in those countries validate a sale as if the buyer in possession were a mercantile agent but without requiring him to act as such, so that if the other conditions of the section are satisfied the delivery or transfer of the goods has the same effect as if a sale of goods had been effected by a mercantile agent acting in the ordinary course of his business (*r*).

(*i*) See the comment to s. 23 of the Sale of Goods Act, *ante*.

(*k*) *Cahn* v. *Pockett's Bristol Channel Co.*, [1899] 1 Q. B. 643, at p. 659. As to larceny by a trick, see *ante*, notes to s. 23 of the Sale of Goods Act.

(*l*) *Newtons of Wembley, Ltd.* v. *Williams*, [1964] 3 All E. R. 532; [1965] 1 Q. B. 560, C. A.; *ante*, illustration (2) to s. 2 (2).

(*m*) *Brandon* v. *Leckie* (1972), 29 D. L. R. (3d) 633. There are several English cases in which a thief or a hirer sold goods and the buyer has subsequently re-sold them, but in no case has the ultimate purchaser sought to rely on this section. See also *Elwin* v. *O'Regan and Maxwell*, [1971] N. Z. L. R. 1124.

(*n*) See examples at p. 160, note (*u*), *ante*.

(*o*) See the comment to s. 8 of this Act, *ante*.

(*p*) See *Newtons of Wembley, Ltd.* v. *Williams*, [1964] 3 All E. R. 532; [1965] 1 Q. B. 560, C. A., where, however, the Court of Appeal held as a fact that the sale was in the ordinary course of business and PEARSON, L.J. said, at pp. 539 and 579, "It is an obscure provision and I do not wish to define too precisely what the effect is." DIPLOCK, L.J. appears to have agreed: see at pp. 540 and 580.

(*q*) See further *Benjamin's Sale of Goods*, para. 538.

(*r*) *Langmead* v. *Thyer Rubber Co., Ltd.*, [1947] S. A. S. R. 29; *Jeffcote* v. *Andrews Motors*,

10. Effect of transfer of documents on vendor's lien or right of stoppage in transitu.—Where a document of title to goods has been lawfully transferred to a person as a buyer or owner of the goods, and that person transfers the document to a person who takes the document in good faith and for valuable consideration, the last-mentioned transfer shall have the same effect for defeating any vendor's lien or right of stoppage in transitu as the transfer of a bill of lading has for defeating the right of stoppage in transitu.

Definitions.—For "goods," "document of title" and "person," see s. 1 (3), (4) and (5), *ante*, respectively.

Cross-references.—*Cf.* Sale of Goods Act 1979, s. 47, *ante* (effect of sub-sale or pledge by buyer).

History.—This section, which is now reproduced and developed by s. 47 of the Sale of Goods Act, was substituted for s. 5 of the Factors Act 1877. It applies to all the documents of title mentioned in s. 1, *ante*, the common law rules relating to the effect of the transfer of a bill of lading on the seller's right of lien or stoppage in transit, as to which see *ante*, notes to s. 47 of the Sale of Goods Act.

COMMENT

To some extent this section covers the same ground as the preceding section. But s. 9 requires that the transferee shall have no notice of the seller's lien or other rights, because it applies to cases where the buyer has obtained the goods or documents under a contract voidable on the ground of fraud. The present section omits the requirement as to absence of notice. The mere fact that the price is unpaid does not make it a fraud to transfer the goods or documents so as to defeat the seller's lien or right of stoppage in transit (*s*).

Supplemental

11. Mode of transferring documents.—For the purposes of this Act, the transfer of a document may be by endorsement, or, where the document is by custom or by its express terms transferable by delivery, or makes the goods deliverable to the bearer, then by delivery.

Definitions.—For "goods" and "document of title," see s. 1 (3) and (4), *ante*, respectively.

History.—This section is taken from words used in s. 5 of the Factors

---

Ltd., [1960] 79 N. Z. L. R. 721 (N. Z. C. A.); *General Motors Acceptance Corporation of Canada* v. *Hubbard* (1978), 87 D. L. R. (3d) 39.

(*s*) *Cuming* v. *Brown* (1808) 9 East. 506; *Murdoch* v. *Wood*, [1921] W. N. 299.

Act 1877, which are now generalised by being put into a separate section.

12. Saving for rights of true owner.—(1) Nothing in this Act shall authorise an agent to exceed or depart from his authority as between himself and his principal, or exempt him from any liability, civil or criminal, for so doing.

Definition.—For "mercantile agent," see s. 1 (1), *ante*.

(2) Nothing in this Act shall prevent the owner of goods from recovering the goods from an agent or his trustee in bankruptcy at any time before the sale or pledge thereof, or shall prevent the owner of goods pledged by an agent from having the right to redeem the goods at any time before the sale thereof, on satisfying the claim for which the goods were pledged, and paying to the agent, if by him required, any money in respect of which the agent would by law be entitled to retain the goods or the documents of title thereto, or any of them, by way of lien as against the owner, or from recovering from any person with whom the goods have been pledged any balance of money remaining in his hands as the produce of the sale of the goods after deducting the amount of his lien (*t*).

Definitions.—For "mercantile agent," "goods," "document of title," "pledge" and "person," see s. 1 (1), (3), (4), (5) and (6), *ante*.

COMMENT

As a general rule, goods or documents of title, held by an agent for his principal, are considered as trust property, and do not pass to the agent's trustee in bankruptcy, though in some cases the reputed ownership provisions might apply: see Bankruptcy Act 1914, s. 38 (*u*). Whether the proceeds of sale of goods entrusted to a factor and intermixed with his own moneys pass to his trustee in bankruptcy, or whether the principal can trace them as trust moneys will, it seems, depend on whether the relationship was a fiduciary one or merely one of debtor and creditor in account. Although it has been said that in the

---

(*t*) See the effect of a similar section in the British Columbian Sale of Goods Act discussed in *Thoresen* v. *Capital Credit Corporation, Ltd. and Active Bailiff* (1962), 37 D. L. R. (2d.) 317, and see the comment to s. 2 (1), *ante*.

(*u*) 3 Halsbury's Statutes (3rd Edn.) 87. But see the limitation placed upon the operation of this section by s. 53 of the Hire-Purchase Act 1965; 30 Halsbury's Statutes (3rd Edn.) 105, and by the new s. 38A of the Bankruptcy Act 1914, introduced with effect from a date to be appointed by s. 192 and Sch. 4 to the Consumer Credit Act 1974.

general course of business merchants voluntarily become the creditors, and not the *cestuis que trustent*, of their factors (*a*), each case must be decided on its own facts and a fiduciary relationship will be readily inferred (*b*). See *Williams and Muir Hunter on Bankruptcy* (19th ed.), pp. 275 *et seq.*

(3) Nothing in this Act shall prevent the owner of goods sold by an agent from recovering from the buyer the price agreed to be paid for the same, or any part of that price, subject to any right of set-off on the part of the buyer against the agent (*c*).

Definitions.—For "mercantile agent" and "goods," see s. 1 (1) and (3), *ante.*

13. Saving for common law powers of agent.—The provisions of this Act shall be construed in amplification and not in derogation of the powers exerciseable by an agent independently of this Act.

Definition.—For "mercantile agent," see s. 1 (1), *ante.*

COMMENT

This section is new. It recognises what the judges have frequently pointed out, namely that the Factors Acts are partly declaratory and partly enacting (*d*). In dealing with the exceptions to the general rule, *nemo dat quod non habet*, WILLES, J., observes:

> "A third case in which a man may convey a better title to goods than he himself had . . . is where an agent, who carries on a public business, deals with the goods in the ordinary course of it, though he has received secret instructions from his principal to deal with them contrary to the ordinary course of that trade. In that case he has . . . an ostensible authority to deal in such a way with the goods as agents ordinarily deal with them, and if he deals with them in the ordinary way of the trade he binds his principal" (*e*).

[14. Repeals.—*Repealed.*]

This section and the schedule, having done their work, are repealed by the Statute Law Revision Act 1908. The Acts repealed by s. 14 were

---

(*a*) *Pennell* v. *Deffell* (1853), 23 L. J. Ch. 115; see also *Henry* v. *Hammond*, [1913] 2 K. B. 515.

(*b*) *Re Hallet's Estate Knatchball* v. *Hallett* (1879), 13 Ch. D. 696, C. A.; *Ex p. Cooke, re Strachan* (1876), 4 Ch. D. 123; *Re Cotton* (1913), 108 L. T. 310.

(*c*) As to the buyer's rights of set-off against an agent with whom he dealt, under the belief that he was a principal, see *Kaltenbach* v. *Lewis* (1885), 10 App. Cas. 617; *Cooke* v. *Eshelby* (1887), 12 App. Cas. 271.

(*d*) See *Cole* v. *North Western Bank* (1875), L. R. 10 C. P. 354, at pp. 360 *et seq.*

(*e*) *Fuentes* v. *Montis* (1868), L. R. 3 C. P. 268, at p. 277; *cf. Johnson* v. *Crédit Lyonnais* (1877), 3 C. P. D. 32, at pp. 37–40; *Lloyds and Scottish Finance, Ltd.* v. *Williamson*, [1965] 1

the Factors Act 1823; the Factors Act 1825; the Factors Act 1842 and the Factors Act 1877.

[15. Commencement.—*Repealed.*]

[16. Extent.—*Repealed.*]

Sections 15 and 16 are repealed by the Statute Law Revision Act 1908. Section 16 excluded Scotland, but the Factors Act 1889 was applied to Scotland the next year by the Factors (Scotland) Act 1890, *post*. It may be noted that the provisions of the Factors Acts are more nearly declaratory of Scottish common law than they were of English common law (*f*). See the subject discussed in Bell's *Principles of the Laws of Scotland* (9th ed.), pp. 824 *et seq*.

17. Short title.—This Act may be cited as the Factors Act 1889.

Though the Act is called the Factors Act, the word "factor" does not occur in it. It applies to any mercantile agent within the meaning of s. 1. It might have been more appropriate to call it the "Mercantile Agents Act," as has been done in some colonies which have adopted it, but there was convenience in retaining the familiar name (*g*).

All E. R. 641; [1965] 1 W. L. R. 404, C. A.; and see the comment to s. 21 of the Sale of Goods Act, *ante*.

(*f*) *Vickers* v. *Hertz* (1871), L. R. 2 Sc. & Div. 113, at p. 119.

(*g*) For definitions of "factor," see *Story on Agency* (9th ed. revised), § 33, and *Ex p. Dixon* (1876), 4 Ch. D. 133, at p. 137.

THE FACTORS (SCOTLAND) ACT 1890

(53 & 54 VICT. c. 40)

An Act to extend the Provisions of the Factors Act 1889 to Scotland.
[14th August 1890.]

1. Application of 52 & 53 Vict. c. 45 to Scotland.—Subject to the following provisions, the Factors Act 1889 shall apply to Scotland:—

(1) The expression "lien" shall mean and include right of retention; the expression "vendor's lien" shall mean and include any right of retention competent to the original owner or vendor; and the expression "set-off" shall mean and include compensation.

(2) In the application of section five of the recited Act, a sale, pledge, or other disposition of goods shall not be valid unless made for valuable consideration.

COMMENT

See s. 5 of the Factors Act 1889, *ante*, and Green's *Encyclopaedia of Scots Law*, tit. "Factors Acts."

2. Short title.—This Act may be cited as the Factors (Scotland) Act 1890.

APPENDIX I—STATUTES

THE BILLS OF LADING ACT 1855

(18 & 19 VICT., c. 111)

An Act to amend the Law relating to Bills of Lading

[4th August 1855.]

Whereas, by the custom of merchants, a bill of lading of goods being transferable by endorsement, the property in the goods may thereby pass to the endorsee, but nevertheless all rights in respect of the contract contained in the bill of lading continue in the original shipper or owner; and it is expedient that such rights should pass with the property: And whereas it frequently happens that the goods in respect of which bills of lading purport to be signed have not been laden on board, and it is proper that such bills of lading in the hands of a bona fide holder for value should not be questioned by the master or other person signing the same on the ground of the goods not having been laden as aforesaid:

1. Consignees, and endorsees of bills of lading empowered to sue.—Every consignee of goods named in a bill of lading, and every endorsee of a bill of lading, to whom the property in the goods therein mentioned shall pass upon or by reason of such consignment or endorsement, shall have transferred to and vested in him all rights of suit, and be subject to the same liabilities in respect of such goods as if the contract contained in the bill of lading had been made with himself.

COMMENT

"A bill of lading," says Lord BLACKBURN,

> "is a writing signed on behalf of the owner of the ship in which goods are embarked, acknowledging the receipt of the goods, and undertaking to deliver them at the end of the voyage, subject to such conditions as may be mentioned in the bill of lading" (*a*).

A bill of lading running "Received for shipment" instead of "Shipped" is, it seems, within the Act (*b*).

A "through bill of lading" is a bill of lading "made for the carriage of goods from one place to another by several shipowners or railway companies" (*c*). It

---

(*a*) *Blackburn on Sale* (1st ed.), p. 275; see also *Sewell* v. *Burdick* (1884), 10 App. Cas. 74, at p. 105.

(*b*) *The Marlborough Hill*, [1921] 1 A. C. 444, P. C. But such a bill of lading would not comply with the requirements of a c.i.f. contract except in trades where it is shown to be usual: see p. 37, *ante*.

(*c*) *Scrutton on Charterparties, etc.* (18th ed.), art. 177. *Cf. Hansson* v. *Hamel and Horley*, [1922] 2 A. C. 36 (c.i.f. contract).

seems doubtful how far the Act applies to these documents, which are of modern origin (*d*).

At common law the property in the goods could be transferred by the endorsement of the bill of lading, but the contract created by the bill of lading could not, therefore the endorsee could not sue on the contract in his own name (*e*). The Act confers this right while confirming the common law rights.

The property must pass "upon or by reason of the consignment or endorsement" (*f*). Where, therefore, a number of bills of lading are issued in respect of unseparated bulk cargoes, and are endorsed to different c.i.f. purchasers, so that no property (legal or equitable) passes to the buyer at least until the goods are appropriated to such contract and ascertained (*g*), this section would seem not to apply (*h*). A contractual relationship may however arise between the bill of lading holder and the ship by implication from presentation of the bill on delivery by the ship (*i*).

2. Saving as to stoppage in transitu, and claims for freight, &c.—Nothing herein contained shall prejudice or affect any right of stoppage in transitu, or any right to claim freight against the original shipper or owner, or any liability of the consignee or endorsee by reason or in consequence of his being such consignee or endorsee, or of his receipt of the goods by reason or in consequence of such consignment or endorsement.

Comment

As to non-liability of pledgee of bill of lading for freight, see *Sewell* v. *Burdick* (*k*). As to pledge of bill of lading and conversion before plaintiff's title accrued, see *Bristol Bank* v. *Midland Railway* (*l*).

3. Bill of lading in hands of consignee, etc., conclusive evidence of shipment as against master, etc.—Every bill of lading in the hands of a consignee or endorsee for valuable consideration representing goods to have been shipped on board a vessel, shall be conclusive evidence of such shipment (*m*) as against the master or other

(*d*) See *Scrutton, supra,* and *British Shipping Laws*, Vol. 2, §§ 200–203, where their effect is fully discussed.

(*e*) *Thompson* v. *Dominy* (1845), 14 M. & W. 403.

(*f*) If property is reserved to the seller until delivery ex installation at the port of discharge, the section does not apply; *Gardano and Giamperi* v. *Greek Petroleum, George Mamidakis & Co.*, [1961] 3 All E. R. 919; [1962] 1 W. L. R. 40.

(*g*) See the comment to s. 16 of the Sale of Goods Act, *ante*. See also p. 34, *ante*, concerning c.i.f. contracts.

(*h*) It is clear that no property passes upon consignment or endorsement, and it would seem to be stretching the meaning of the words to say that it passes by reason of the consignment or endorsement.

(*i*) *Brandt* v. *Liverpool, Brazil and River Plate Steam Navigation Co.*, [1924] 1 K. B. 575; *cf. The "Dona Mari"*, [1973] 2 Lloyd's Rep. 366.

(*k*) (1884), 10 App. Cas. 74.

(*l*) [1891] 2 Q. B. 653, C. A., commented upon in *Margarine Union G.m.b.H.* v. *Cambay Prince S. S. Co.*, [1967] 3 All E. R. 775; [1969] 1 Q. B. 219.

(*m*) The estoppel relates only to the essentials of the goods as described in the bill (*i.e.*, those denoting or effecting the nature, quality or commercial value of the goods: *Parsons* v. *New Zealand Shipping Co.*, [1901] 1 Q. B. 548).

person signing the same, notwithstanding that such goods or some part thereof may not have been so shipped, unless such holder of the bill of lading shall have had actual notice at the time of receiving the same that the goods had not been in fact laden on board (*n*): Provided, that the master or other person so signing may exonerate himself in respect of such misrepresentation by showing that it was caused without any default on his part, and wholly by the fraud of the shipper, or of the holder, or some person under whom the holder claims.

The section is of limited effect only. Where a bill is signed by an agent the principal is not an "other person signing the same", and so is not affected by the provisions of the section (*o*). Moreover, the bill is conclusive evidence only of shipment and by itself imposes no liability upon the signatory for non-delivery (*o*).

General Note.—"A cargo at sea," says BOWEN, L. J.,

> "while in the hands of the carrier, is necessarily incapable of physical delivery. During this period of transit and voyage, the bill of lading by the law merchant is universally recognised as its symbol, and the indorsement and delivery of the bill of lading operates as a symbolical delivery of the cargo. Property in the goods passes by such indorsement and delivery of the bill of lading whenever it is the intention of the parties that the property should pass, just as under similar circumstances the property would pass by an actual delivery of the goods" (*p*).

Bills of lading are commonly made out in several parts, one part being usually retained by the ship, the others being handed to the shipper. This practice has often given rise to frauds. The subject of bills of lading is fully dealt with in *Scrutton on Charter Parties, etc.* (18th ed.) and *Carver on Carriage by Sea, British Shipping Laws*, Vol. 2 and 3; but the following salient points may be noted:

(1) So long as the contract of carriage is not discharged, the bill of lading remains a document of title, by endorsement and delivery of which the property in the goods can be transferred, even though the goods have been landed (*q*), or wrongfully delivered to a third party without production of the bill (*r*).

(2) When two or more parts of a bill of lading are transferred to two or more different *bona fide* transferees for value, the property in the goods passes to the transferee who is first in point of time (*q*).

(*n*) But at common law the shipowner was not liable if the master signed a bill of lading for goods not received on board: *Grant* v. *Norway* (1851), 10 C. B. 665: see *Scrutton on Charterparties, etc.* (18th ed.), pp. 112–113. Under the Carriage of Goods by Sea Act 1971, which was brought into effect on 23rd June 1977 (S. I. 1977 No. 981), the final sentence of Article III, Rule 4 of the Hague Rules as amended is aimed at reversing the common law rule as between the shipowner and a person acting in good faith to whom the bill of lading has been transferred. Such a person may now rely on the bill of lading where the Act applies as conclusive evidence of the shipment of the goods of which it acknowledges receipt.

(*o*) *V/O Rasnoimport* v. *Guthrie & Co., Ltd.*, [1966] 1 Lloyd's Rep. 1, where the signatory to the bill signed as agent only and could not be regarded as contracting to carry or accept charge of the goods.

(*p*) *Sanders* v. *Maclean* (1883), 11 Q. B. D. 327, at p. 341; *cf. The Prinz Adalbert*, [1917] A. C. 586, at p. 589, *per* Lord SUMNER.

(*q*) *Barclays Bank, Ltd.* v. *Customs and Excise Commissioners*, [1963] 1 Lloyd's Rep. 81; *Barber* v. *Meyerstein* (1870), L. R. 4 H. L. 317.

(*r*) See *Short* v. *Simpson* (1866), L. R. 1 C. P. 248, which appears to confirm this despite

(3) Nevertheless, the person who has the custody of the goods may safely deliver them to the person who first presents the bill of lading (or a part thereof) to him, provided he acts in good faith and without notice of any prior claim (*s*).

(4) A contract to deliver a bill of lading is complied with by delivering one part, though the others are not accounted for (*t*).

(5) Except for the purposes of the Factors Act and of defeating the right of stoppage in transit, the transferee of a bill of lading acquires no better title to the goods represented thereby than the transferor had. In this respect a bill of lading differs from a bill of exchange, or rather it resembles an overdue bill of exchange, which can only be negotiated subject to all equities attaching to it (*u*). As to the effect of the transfer of a bill of lading on the right of stoppage in transit, see *ante*, notes to s. 47 of the Sale of Goods Act. See also the Factors Act 1889, *ante*.

(6) Stipulations in a bill of lading must be construed according to the proper law of the contract; see note "conflict of laws," p. 47, *ante*.

(7) When a bill of exchange, with bill of lading attached, is presented for acceptance or payment, the person who in good faith presents it is not responsible for the authenticity of the bill of lading (*a*).

Foreign systems.—As to the United States and the Harter Act, see *Scrutton, loc. cit.*, App. III, and as to Australia, Canada, and New Zealand, *ibid.*, App. IV. The German Commercial Code, arts. 642–663, minutely regulates Bills of Lading.

THE BILLS OF SALE ACT 1878 (*b*)

(41 & 42 VICT., c. 31)

An Act to consolidate and amend the Law for preventing Frauds upon Creditors by secret Bills of Sale of Personal Chattels.

[22nd July 1878.]

* * * * *

4. Interpretation of terms.—In this Act the following words and expressions shall have the meanings in this section assigned to them respectively, unless there be something in the subject or context repugnant to such construction; (that is to say),

The expression "bill of sale" shall include bills of sale, assignments, transfers, declarations of trust without transfer, inventories of goods with receipt thereto attached, or receipts for purchase-moneys of goods, and other assurances of personal chattels, and also powers of attorney, authorities, or licences to take possession of personal chattels as security for any debt, and also any agreement, whether intended or not to be

---

the doubt expressed in the headnote. See also *Bristol and West of England Bank* v. *Midland Railway*, [1891] 2 Q. B. 653, C. A., as explained in *Margarine Union G.m.b.H.* v. *Gambay Prince S. S. Co.*, [1967] 3 All E. R. 775; [1969] 1 Q. B. 219, for a case where a fresh pledge passed the right to possession after a misdelivery.

(*s*) *Glyn, Mills & Co.* v. *East & West India Dock* (1882), 7 App. Cas. 591.

(*t*) *Sanders* v. *Maclean* (1883), 11 Q. B. D. 327, C. A.

(*u*) *Gurney* v. *Behrend* (1854), 3 E. & B. 622. As to fraud, however, see *The Argentina* (1867), L. R. 1 A. & E. 370

(*a*) *Guaranty Trust Co. of New York* v. *Hannay & Co.*, [1918] 2 K. B. 623, C. A.

(*b*) For the rest of this Act, see 3 Halsbury's Statutes (3rd Edn.) 245.

followed by the execution of any other instrument, by which a right in equity to any personal chattels, or to any charge or security thereon, shall be conferred, but shall not include the following documents; that is to say, assignments for the benefit of the creditors of the person making or giving the same, marriage settlements, transfers or assignments of any ship or vessel or any share thereof, transfers of goods in the ordinary course of business of any trade or calling (*c*), bills of sale of goods in foreign parts or at sea, bills of lading, India warrants, warehouse-keepers' certificates, warrants or orders for the delivery of goods, or any other documents used in the ordinary course of business as proof of the possession or control of goods, or authorising or purporting to authorise, either by indorsement or by delivery, the possession of such document to transfer or receive goods thereby represented:

The expression "personal chattels" shall mean goods, furniture, and other articles capable of complete transfer by delivery, and (when separately assigned or charged) fixtures and growing crops, but shall not include chattel interests in real estate, nor fixtures (except trade machinery as hereinafter defined), when assigned together with a freehold or leasehold interest in any land or building to which they are affixed, nor growing crops when assigned together with any interest in the land on which they grow, nor shares or interest in the stock, funds, or securities of any government, or in the capital or property of incorporated or joint stock companies, nor choses in action, nor any stock or produce upon any farm or lands which by virtue of any covenant or agreement or of the custom of the country ought not to be removed from any farm where the same are at the time of making or giving of such bill of sale:

Personal chattels shall be deemed to be in the "apparent possession" of the person making or giving a bill of sale, so long as they remain or are in or upon any house, mill, warehouse, building, works, yard, land, or other premises occupied by him, or are used and enjoyed by him in any place whatsoever, notwithstanding that formal possession thereof may have been taken by or given to any other person (*d*):

"Prescribed" means prescribed by rules made under the provisions of this Act.

COMMENT

This Act has been amended by the Bills of Sale Act (1878) Amendment Act 1882 (*e*), but the Act of 1882 only relates to bills of sale by way of security, and does not affect sales within the meaning of the Sale of Goods Act 1979; see s. 62 (4) of the Act, *ante*. The Bills of Sale Acts 1890 and 1891 (*f*), merely exempt

---

(*c*) *Stephenson* v. *Thompson*, [1924] 2 K. B. 240, C. A. (sale of growing crops).

(*d*) As to the meaning of apparent possession, see *Koppel* v. *Koppel*, [1966] 2 All E. R. 187; [1966] 1 W. L. R. 802, C. A., reviewing the earlier cases. As to distinction between apparent possession and "possession, order, and disposition" in the reputed ownership provision in bankruptcy, see *Ancona* v. *Rogers* (1876), 1 Ex. D. 285, at p. 291, C. A.

(*e*) 3 Halsbury's Statutes (3rd Edn.) 261.

(*f*) 3 Halsbury's Statutes (3rd Edn.)270, 271.

certain mercantile letters of hypothecation from the definition of "bill of sale." These Acts apply only to England (*g*). There are corresponding enactments for Ireland, but there are no corresponding enactments for Scotland (*h*).

The Bills of Sale Acts strike at documents, and not at the transactions themselves (*i*). When the seller of goods remains in possession of them, and the buyer has to base his title or right to possession on some document which comes within the definition of a bill of sale, the document must be registered in accordance with the Act of 1878. If it be not so registered, the contract, though valid as between the parties, is void as against the seller's execution creditors, trustee in bankruptcy, or assignee for the benefit of creditors. See *Reed on the Bills of Sale Acts* (14th ed.), pp. 141 *et seq.*, where all the authorities are exhaustively reviewed. It may be noted that where the seller remains in possession, an entry of the sale by the auctioneer, or a note of the contract drawn up by the sheriff who has sold privately, constitutes a bill of sale (*k*). A delivery order for furniture is not a bill of sale (*l*), nor is an unregistered transfer of a ship or vessel (*m*), nor a letter of lien to bankers (*n*).

THE FINANCE ACT 1901

(1 Edw. 7, c. 7)

An Act to grant certain duties of Customs and Inland Revenue, to alter other duties, and to amend the Law relating to Customs and Inland Revenue . . .

[26th July 1901.]

* * * * *

10. Addition or deduction of new or altered duties in the case of contract.—(1) Where any new customs import duty or new excise duty is imposed, or where any customs import duty or excise duty is increased, and any goods in respect of which the duty is payable are delivered after the day on which the new or increased duty takes effect in pursuance of a contract made before that day, the seller of the goods may, in the absence of agreement to the contrary, recover, as an addition to the contract price, a sum equal to any amount paid by him in respect of the goods on account of the new duty or the increase of duty, as the case may be.

(*g*) *Cf. Coote* v. *Jecks* (1872), L. R. 13 Eq. 597 (English bill of sale cannot affect property in Scotland).

(*h*) Green's *Encyclopædia of Scots Law.* tit. "Bill of Sale."

(*i*) *North Central Wagon Co.* v. *Manchester, Sheffield and Lincolnshire Rail Co.* (1887), 35 Ch. D. 191, at p. 207.

(*k*) *Re Roberts* (1887), 36 Ch. D. 196 (auctioneer); *Ex p. Blandford* (1893), 10 Morr. 231 (sheriff).

(*l*) *Grigg* v. *National Guardian Assurance Co.*, [1891] 3 Ch. 206.

(*m*) *Gapp* v. *Bond* (1887), 19 Q. B. D. 200 (dumb-barge which did not require registration under Merchant Shipping Act).

(*n*) *Ex p. Carter*, [1905] 2 K. B. 772.

(2) Where any customs import duty or excise duty is repealed or decreased, and any goods affected by the duty are delivered after the day on which the duty ceases or the decrease in the duty takes effect in pursuance of a contract made before that day, the purchaser of the goods, in the absence of agreement to the contrary, may, if the seller of the goods has had in respect of those goods the benefit of the repeal or decrease of the duty, deduct from the contract price a sum equal to the amount of the duty or decrease of duty, as the case may be.

(3) Where any addition to, or deduction from, the contract price may be made under this section on account of any new or repealed duty, such sum as may be agreed upon or in default of agreement determined by the Commissioners of Customs in the case of a customs duty, and by the Commissioners of Inland Revenue in the case of an excise duty, as representing in the case of a new duty any new expenses incurred, and in the case of a repealed duty any expenses saved, may be included in the addition to or deduction from the contract price, and may be recovered or deducted accordingly.

* * * * *

COMMENT

This section is amended by s. 7 of the Finance Act 1902, which is as follows:—

> "Section ten of the Finance Act 1901, applies although the goods have undergone a process of manufacture or preparation, or have become a part or ingredient of other goods."

Under s. 4 of the Finance Act 1908, now replaced by s. 1 (1) of the Customs and Excise Act 1952, excise was transferred from the Inland Revenue to the Customs, and the Commissioners are now known as the Commissioners of Customs and Excise.

As to the construction of s. 10 of the Act of 1901, see generally *Corn Products Co.* v. *Fry* (*o*). Even though an action for the price of the goods is pending when the new duties are imposed, the seller can add the new duty to the price (*p*). It has been held that the words "duty paid" do not constitute an agreement to the contrary within the above section so as to disentitle the seller to recover the amount of an increase (*q*), but more recently an agreement to sell "free house London" was held to be an agreement to the contrary, and the foreign seller was held liable to pay duty imposed by the Abnormal Importations (Customs Duties) Act 1931 (*r*). When a temporary customs duty was imposed under s. 3 of the Finance (No. 2) Act 1964 these problems were avoided by s. 3 (8) which provided that for the purposes of s. 10 of the Act of 1901:

> "any terms in a contract expressly or impliedly making a seller liable for all customs duties (or all customs duties with exceptions not affecting duty under this section) shall not be deemed to amount to an agreement to the contrary (that is to say to an agreement that the said section 10 shall not apply)."

(*o*) [1917] W. N. 224.

(*p*) *Conway Brothers and Savage* v. *Mulheirn & Co., Ltd.* (1901), 17 T. L. R. 730. *Cf. Newbridge Rhondda Brewery Co.* v. *Evans* (1902), 86 L. T. 453 (a case of a conditional agreement for sale).

(*q*) *American Commerce Co., Ltd.* v. *Boehm* (*Frederick*), *Ltd.* (1919), 35 T. L. R. 224.

(*r*) *Lanificio Di Manerbio S. A.* v. *Gold* (1932), 76 Sol. Jo. 289.

As to the adjustment of rights between seller and buyer on the commencement or variation of rates of charge of value added tax, see s. 42 of the Finance Act 1972, *post.*

THE LAW REFORM (MISCELLANEOUS PROVISIONS) ACT 1934

(24 & 25 Geo. 5, c. 41)

An Act to amend the law as to the effect of death in relation to causes of action and as to the awarding of interest in civil proceedings.

[25th July 1934.]

* * * * *

3. Power of courts of record to award interest on debts and damages.—(1) In any proceedings tried in any court of record (*s*) for the recovery of any debt (*t*) or damages, the court may, if it thinks fit, order that there shall be included in the sum for which judgment is given interest at such rate as it thinks fit on the whole or any part of the debt or damages for the whole or any part of the period between the date when the cause of action arose and the date of the judgment:

Provided that nothing in this section—

(a) shall authorise the giving of interest upon interest (*u*); or

(b) shall apply in relation to any debt upon which interest is payable as of right whether by virtue of any enactment or otherwise; or

(c) shall affect the damages recoverable for the dishonour of a bill of exchange.

History.—At common law interest was not payable, even on a debt or other liquidated claim, *e.g.*, for the price of goods sold and delivered, unless there was a contract, express or implied, to pay it, though interest was apparently always payable when a bill of exchange was dishonoured (see now s. 57 of the Bills of Exchange Act 1882 (*a*)).

Section 28 of the Civil Procedure Act 1833 (*b*), allowed the jury to award interest as damages, if they thought fit, where a debt or sum of money was due by virtue of some written instrument at a certain time, or, if payable otherwise,

---

(*s*) Including proceedings under R. S. C., O. 14: *Gardner Steel, Ltd.* v. *Sheffield Brothers (Profiles), Ltd.*, [1978] 3 All E. R. 399; [1978] 1 W. L. R. 916, C. A.

(*t*) Including proceedings for an award under s. 1 of the Law Reform (Frustrated Contracts) Act 1943: *B. P. Exploration Co. (Libya), Ltd.* v. *Hunt (No. 2)*, [1979] 1 W. L. R. 783.

(*u*) But see *Bushwall Properties, Ltd.* v. *Vortex Properties Ltd.*, [1975] 2 All E. R. 214 (where it was held that the court may give interest on damages awarded to cover interest lost by plaintiff through breach of contract). The award of damages in that case was subsequently set aside by the Court of Appeal: see [1976] 2 All E. R. 283; [1976] 1 W. L. R. 591.

(*a*) 3 Halsbury's Statutes (3rd Edn.) 220.

(*b*) Repealed by sub-s. (2) of this section.

then from the time when demand for payment had been made in writing, giving notice that interest would be claimed. Section 29 of the same Act (*c*) similarly allowed interest to be awarded as damages in actions of trover and trespass *de bonis asportatis* and in actions on policies of assurance.

Under neither of these two sections could there be any award of interest in an action for breach of a contract of sale where the claim was for damages for non-delivery, late delivery, non-acceptance, breach of warranty, or other unliquidated claim. And similarly, in actions for the price of goods, interest could only be claimed as of right if there was an agreement to pay it, though such an agreement might be inferred from the course of dealing between the parties or from trade usage (*d*). It could be awarded in the discretion of the court under s. 28 of the Civil Procedure Act 1833, *supra*, but only if the conditions specified by that section were satisfied, which in practice was not commonly the case.

COMMENT

The present section leaves untouched those cases where interest is payable as of right by virtue of contract or otherwise, and does not affect the measure of damages, which includes interest, on the dishonour of a bill of exchange. In all other actions for the recovery of debt or damages it gives the court a discretion whether interest should be awarded or not; it is for the court to specify the rate of interest and whether it is to be payable on the whole or part only of the sum in question, and the period during which, between the date the cause of action arose and judgment, the interest is to be allowed.

Interest is not awarded on the basis of anybody's fault but on the simple commercial basis that if the money had been paid at the appropriate commercial time, the other party would have had the use of it (*e*). It is a well-recognised rule of practice that *prima facie* the losing party should be ordered to pay interest at a reasonable rate running from the date when the amount due should reasonably have been paid (*f*).

The onus is on the losing party to show sufficient reason why the usual practice should not apply in any particular case (*g*). Mere delay is not normally a ground for modifying the general rule as to interest, and an unexplained delay, as opposed to a delay which is shown to be unjustified (*h*) cannot be a basis for refusing to award interest (*i*). But if the plaintiff has been indemnified

---

(*c*) Also repealed by sub-s. (2) of this section.

(*d*) *Re Anglesey* (*Marquis*), *Willmot* v. *Gardner*, [1901] 2 Ch. 548, C. A.

(*e*) *Cookson* v. *Knowles*, [1978] 2 All E. R. 604, at p. 616; [1979] A. C. 556, at p. 578, *per* Lord FRASER

(*f*) *Panchaud Frères S. A.* v. *R. Pagnan and Fratelli*, [1974] 1 Lloyd's Rep. 394, *per* KERR, J., at p. 409; *Harbutt's Plasticine, Ltd.* v. *Wayne Tank and Pump Co., Ltd.*, [1970] 1 All E. R. 225; [1970] 1 Q. B. 447, C. A.; *General Tire & Rubber Co.* v. *Firestone Tyre & Rubber Co., Ltd.*, [1975] 1 W. L. R. 819, at p. 836, H. L. See also *Kemp* v. *Tolland*, [1956] 2 Lloyd's Rep. 681.

(*g*) *Cremer* v. *General Carriers S. A.*, [1974] 1 All E. R. 1; [1974] 1 W. L. R. 341.

(*h*) *Tire and Rubber Co.* v. *Firestone Tyre and Rubber Co., Ltd.*, [1975] 2 All E. R. 173, at pp. 188, 192; [1975] 1 W. L. R. 819, at pp. 836, 841, *per* Lords WILBERFORCE and SALMON; *Cookson* v. *Knowles*, [1978] 2 All E. R. 604, at p. 616; [1979] A. C. 556, at p. 578, *per* Lord FRASER.

(*i*) *Panchaud Frères S. A.* v. *R. Pagnan and Fratelli*, [1974] 1 Lloyd's Rep. 394, *per* KERR, J., at p. 409; affirmed in the Court of Appeal, at pp. 411, 414. For a case where interest was reduced, see *United Fresh Meat Co.* v. *Charterhouse Cold Storage*, [1974] 2 Lloyd's Rep. 286.

by an insurance company, he will not normally be awarded interest on the money when he has not been kept out of it (*k*).

It has been said (*l*) that the approach of the Commercial Court has been to compensate successful parties by awarding interest at a rate which broadly represents the rate at which they would have had to borrow the amount recovered over the period for which interest is awarded. But in practice, while the courts have taken account of the market rate, a borrower would have been fortunate to have been able to borrow at the rates awarded.

A rate of 1 per cent over Bank Rate was commonly awarded (*m*). This principle was reviewed because of the replacement of Bank Rate by minimum lending rate, and what were then more realistic interest rates on judgment debts and on money in court placed on short-term investment (*n*). Interest is now commonly awarded by reference to minimum lending rate or the base rate of the major banks (*o*).

By virtue of the new subsection (1A) of the 1934 Act, introduced by s. 22 of the Administration of Justice Act 1969, where damages are awarded in respect of personal injuries, interest will be awarded on those damages unless the defendant can show that there are special reasons why such interest should not be awarded.

There is no obligation to claim interest under the Act on the indorsement of claim, the writ of summons, or in the pleadings (*p*). The claim for interest is not a cause of action and the defendant cannot and should not make a payment into court in respect of it. If a case proceeds to trial after a payment into court, any amount awarded at the trial on account of interest will be disregarded in determining the incidence of costs after the payment into court (*q*). Where money is paid into court, and the court makes an order for payment out under R. S. C., O. 22, r. 5, in satisfaction of the cause of action, that order is not a judgment within s. 3 (1) of the 1934 Act, so that the plaintiff will not be entitled to interest on the sum paid in (*r*). It is nevertheless submitted that it is the better

---

(*k*) *Harbutt's Plasticine, Ltd.* v. *Wayne Tank and Pump Co., Ltd.*, *supra.*

(*l*) *Cremer* v. *General Carriers S. A.*, *supra.*

(*m*) *F. M. C. (Meat), Ltd.* v. *Fairfield Cold Stores, Ltd.*, [1971] 2 Lloyds' Rep. 221.

(*n*) *Cremer* v. *General Carriers S. A.*, *supra.* Judgment was delivered on 5th July 1973, when interest on judgment debts was 7½ per cent. and interest on money in court of short-term investments was 8 per cent. The rate awarded by KERR, J., of 7½ per cent. was very close to the rate of 7·9 per cent. claimed by the plaintiff, whose calculations were based on average Bank Rate and Bank of England minimum lending rate. The subsequent rise in interest rates in general has not always been reflected in interest rates on judgment debts or on money in court on short-term investment and they do not therefore at present seem to be a reliable basis for calculating the rate of interest to be awarded.

(*o*) For awards of interest on foreign currency debts and damages, see *Helmsing Schiffahrts G.m.b.h.* v. *Malta Drydocks Corporation*, [1977] 2 Lloyd's Rep. 444; *B. P. Exploration Co. (Libya), Ltd.* v. *Hunt (No. 2)*, [1979] 1 W. L. R. 783, at p. 849; on appeal, (1981), 125 Sol. Jo. 165, C. A. *Cia Barca de Panama S. A.* v. *George Wimpey & Co., Ltd.* (1979), 129 N. L. J. 1264, C. A.

(*p*) *Riches* v. *Westminster Bank, Ltd.*, [1943] 2 All E. R. 725, C. A.; *Jefford* v. *Gee*, [1970] 1 All E. R. 1202; [1970] 2 Q. B. 130, C. A.

(*q*) *Jefford* v. *Gee*, *supra.*

(*r*) *Waite* v. *Redpath Dorman Long, Ltd.*, [1971] 1 All E. R. 513; [1971] 1 Q. B. 294. Interest can be awarded by the court when giving judgment under R. S. C., Order 14: *Gardner Steel* v. *Sheffield Brothers (Profiles), Ltd.*, [1978] 3 All E. R. 399; [1978] 1 W. L. R. 916, C. A. *Quaere* whether interest can be claimed under the Act if judgment is signed in default of appearance or pleadings, for there would not seem to be any "proceedings tried in any court of record".

practice to claim interest. It is clearly desirable that the defendant should know what exactly is claimed, and if the plaintiff causes embarrassment by not telling him, it is conceivable that it might in certain circumstances influence the exercise by the court of its discretion. It is therefore suggested that in all appropriate cases, such as, for example, claims by the buyer for the return of the price where no delivery has been made or claims by the seller for the price, etc., a claim for interest should be included in the prayer for relief on both writ and statement of claim. A county court is a court of record (s. 1 (2) of the County Courts Act 1959); and what is said above applies also to the filling in of the *praecipe* and the settling of particulars of claim in county court actions.

Scotland.—The present section does not apply to Scotland, but s. 49 (3) of the Sale of Goods Act 1979, *ante*, preserves the right which the seller has by Scottish law to receive interest from the date of tender of the goods pursuant to the contract, or the date of delivery, or the date the price otherwise becomes payable.

* * * * *

LAW REFORM (FRUSTRATED CONTRACTS) ACT 1943

(6 & 7 Geo. 6, c. 40)

1. Adjustment of rights and liabilities of parties to frustrated contracts.—(1) Where a contract governed by English law (*s*) has become impossible of performance or been otherwise frustrated, and the parties thereto have for that reason been discharged from the further performance of the contract, the following provisions of this section shall, subject to the provisions of section two of this Act, have effect in relation thereto.

(2) All sums paid or payable to any party in pursuance of the contract before the time when the parties were so discharged (in this Act referred to as "the time of discharge") shall, in the case of sums so paid, be recoverable from him as money received by him for the use of the party by whom the sums were paid, and, in the case of sums so payable, cease to be so payable:

Provided that, if the party to whom the sums were so paid or payable incurred expenses before the time of discharge in, or for the purpose of, the performance of the contract, the court may, if it considers it just to do so having regard to all the circumstances of the case, allow him to retain or, as the case may be, recover the whole or any part of the sums so paid or payable, not being an amount in excess of the expenses so incurred.

(3) Where any party to the contract has, by reason of anything done by any other party thereto in, or for the purpose of, the performance of the contract, obtained a valuable benefit (other than a payment of money to which the last foregoing subsection applies) before the time of

(*s*) As to Scottish law, which is unaffected by this Act, see *Cantiare Sau Rocco* v. *Clyde Shipbuilding and Engineering Co., Ltd.*, [1924] A. C. 226.

discharge, there shall be recoverable from him by the said other party such sum (if any), not exceeding the value of the said benefit to the party obtaining it, as the court considers just, having regard to all the circumstances of the case and, in particular,—

(a) the amount of any expenses incurred before the time of discharge by the benefited party in, or for the purpose of, the performance of the contract, including any sums paid or payable by him to any other party in pursuance of the contract and retained or recoverable by that party under the last foregoing sub-section, and

(b) the effect, in relation to the said benefit, of the circumstances giving rise to the frustration of the contract.

(4) In estimating, for the purposes of the foregoing provisions of this section, the amount of any expenses incurred by any party to the contract, the court may, without prejudice to the generality of the said provisions, include such sum as appears to be reasonable in respect of overhead expenses and in respect of any work or services performed personally by the said party.

(5) In considering whether any sum ought to be recovered or retained under the foregoing provisions of this section by any party to the contract, the court shall not take into account any sums which have, by reason of the circumstances giving rise to the frustration of the contract, become payable to that party under any contract of insurance unless there was an obligation to insure imposed by an express term of the frustrated contract or by or under any enactment.

(6) Where any person has assumed obligations under the contract in consideration of the conferring of a benefit by any other party to the contract upon any other person, whether a party to the contract or not, the court may, if in all the circumstances of the case it considers it just to do so, treat for the purposes of subsection (3) of this section any benefit so conferred as a benefit obtained by the person who has assumed the obligations as aforesaid.

COMMENT

See generally, the note on frustration, p. 17, *ante*. The fundamental principle underlying the Act is the prevention of the unjust enrichment of either party to a contract at the other's expense (*t*).

Subsection (2).—See Sale of Goods Act 1979, ss. 31 (2) and 49 (2), *ante*. It will be observed that it is not necessary that the consideration for the payment should have wholly failed, as was necessary at common law (*u*). This provision must be read in conjunction with sub-s. (3).

The proviso is an attempt to modify the hardship suffered by the seller at

---

(*t*) *B. P. Exploration Co.* (*Libya*), *Ltd.* v. *Hunt* (*No.* 2), [1979] 1 W. L. R. 783, where the history and effect of the Act are considered at length. An appeal has been dismissed: see (1981), 125 Sol. Jo. 165, C. A.

(*u*) See *Fibrosa S. A.* v. *Fairbairn Lawson Combe Barbour, Ltd.*, [1942] 2 All E. R. 122; [1943] A. C. 32.

common law, and pointed out by Lord SIMON, L. C. in the *Fibrosa Case* (*a*). It can only be invoked by the seller when the price or part of it was paid or payable under the contract of sale before the date of frustration. See further, sub-s. (4).

Subsection (3).—This provision is new, but so far as contracts of sale of goods are concerned, it may be unnecessary to have recourse to it: for, if the buyer receives and keeps goods, he must as a general rule pay for them: in some cases he must pay a reasonable price, in others he must pay for them at the contract rate. See, *e.g.*, Sale of Goods Act 1979, ss. 8 (2), 9 (1), 30 (1), (2), (3), *ante*. The same rule would no doubt apply if a case relating to a contract of sale arose under sub-s. (6).

2. Provision as to application of this Act.—

* * * * *

(2) This Act shall apply to contracts to which the Crown is a party in like manner as to contract between subjects.

(3) Where any contract to which this Act applies contains any provision which, upon the true construction of the contract, is intended to have effect in the event of circumstances arising which operate, or would but for the said provision operate, to frustrate the contract, or is intended to have effect whether such circumstances arise or not, the court shall give effect to the said provision and shall only give effect to the foregoing section of this Act to such extent, if any, as appears to the court to be consistent with the said provision.

(4) Where it appears to the court that a part of any contract to which this Act applies can properly be severed from the remainder of the contract, being a part wholly performed before the time of discharge, or so performed except for the payment in respect of that part of the contract of sums which are or can be ascertained under the contract, the court shall treat that part of the contract as if it were a separate contract and had not been frustrated and shall treat the foregoing section of this Act as only applicable to the remainder of that contract.

(5) This Act shall not apply—

(a) to any charterparty, except a time charterparty or a charterparty by way of demise, or to any contract (other than a charterparty) for the carriage of goods by sea; or

(b) to any contract of insurance, save as is provided by subsection (5) of the foregoing section; or

(c) to any contract to which section 7 of the Sale of Goods Act 1979 (*b*) (which avoids contracts for the sale of specific goods which perish before the risk has passed to the buyer) applies, or to any other contract for the sale, or for the sale and delivery, of specific goods (*c*), where the contract is frustrated by reason of the fact that the goods have perished.

(*a*) [1942] 2 All E. R. 122, at pp. 129, 130; [1943] A. C. 32, at p. 49.

(*b*) As amended by Sale of Goods Act 1979, Sch. 2, para. 2, *ante*.

(*c*) For the definition of specific goods, see s. 61 (1) of the Sale of Goods Act 1979, *ante*.

COMMENT

See generally, the note on frustration, p. 17, *ante*, and *B. P. Exploration Co. (Libya), Ltd.* v. *Hunt (No. 2)* (*d*).

Subsection (3).—Parties to contracts are free to make whatever bargain they wish, provided that it is lawful. A clause, however, dealing with frustration may itself be or become illegal (*e*). It will be for the court to decide whether, in a case where the contract is abrogated by the outbreak of war, an alien enemy will, on the conclusion of peace, be able to take advantage of the provisions of this Act.

Subsection (4).—A contract for the sale of goods providing for delivery by instalments and payment for each instalment may be of such a nature that each delivery is equivalent to delivery under a separate contract to be paid for separately, and in such cases the contract is clearly severable, and no difficulty will arise. But even though the contract provides for delivery by instalments, it may still be an entire contract (*i.e.*, the whole of what is to be done on one side is the consideration of the whole of what is to be done on the other (*f*), though divisible in performance) and

> "where there is an entire contract to deliver a large quantity of goods consisting of distinct parcels within a specified time, and the seller delivers part, he cannot, before the expiration of that time, bring an action to recover the price of that part delivered, because the purchaser may, if the vendor fail to complete his contract, return the part delivered. But if he retain the part delivered after the seller has failed in performing his contract, the latter may recover the value of the goods which he has so delivered" (*g*).

Even if the buyer under the contract must pay for each instalment as delivered, the contract may still be entire, so that the seller's failure to complete may entitle the buyer to return the instalments received and recover the sums that he has paid; for the consideration, being entire, fails entirely by failing partially (*h*). How far the buyer's rights in such cases are affected by this subsection and other provisions of this Act is a question which must await judicial interpretation.

Subsection (5) (c).—These words are inserted perhaps to make it clear that the Act does not apply to cases where the property in the goods has passed to the buyer, but have perished before delivery to him, or to cases falling within s. 6 of the Sale of Goods Act; though it may be doubtful whether in either of these cases the contract can properly be said to be frustrated. As to what contracts fall within ss. 6 and 7 of the Sale of Goods Act, see p. 19 and the notes to those sections, *ante*, and also the note to s. 61 (1) of that Act, *ante*.

3. Short title and interpretation.—(1) This Act may be cited as the Law Reform (Frustrated Contracts) Act 1943.

(2) In this Act the expression "court" means, in relation to any matter, the court or arbitrator by or before whom the matter falls to be determined.

(*d*) [1979] 1 W. L. R. 783; affirmed on appeal (1981), 125 Sol. Jo. 165, C. A.
(*e*) *Ertel Bieber & Co.* v. *Rio Tinto Co.*, [1918] A. C. 260.
(*f*) *Honck* v. *Muller* (1881), 7 Q. B. D. 92, 100.
(*g*) *Oxendale* v. *Wetherell* (1829), 9 B. & C. 386, at p. 387, *per* PARKE, B.
(*h*) *Chanter* v. *Leese* (1840), 5 M. & W. 698, 702.

THE EXCHANGE CONTROL ACT 1947 (*i*)

(10 & 11 Geo. 6, c. 14)

An Act to confer powers, and impose duties and restrictions, in relation to gold, currency, payments, securities, debts, and the import, export, transfer and settlement of property, and for purposes connected with the matters aforesaid.

[11th March 1947.]

* * * * *

33. Contracts, legal proceedings, etc.—(1) It shall be an implied condition in any contract that, where, by virtue of this Act, the permission or consent of the Treasury is at the time of the contract required for the performance of any term thereof, that term shall not be performed except in so far as the permission or consent is given or is not required:

Provided that this sub-section shall not apply in so far as it is shown to be inconsistent with the intention of the parties that it should apply, whether by reason of their having contemplated the performance of that term in despite of the provisions of this Act or for any other reason.

* * * * *

Schedule IV

* * * * *

4. (1) In any proceedings in a prescribed court and in any arbitration proceedings, a claim for the recovery of any debt shall not be defeated by reason only of the debt not being payable without the permission of the Treasury and of that permission not having been given or having been revoked.

* * * * *

Comment

This Act revised and perpetuated the Exchange Control system introduced, in the first instance as a war-time measure, by the Defence (Finance) Regulations 1939.

Broadly speaking, the permission or consent of the Treasury is required for any transaction effected by a United Kingdom resident as a result of which a financial benefit accrues to a person resident outside the "sterling area." In practice, since October 1979 consent has been altogether dispensed with for most transactions; moreover, the provisions of the "Bretton Woods" Agreement (*k*) and the Anglo-American Loan Agreement (*l*) bind the U.K. Government

---

(*i*) For the rest of this Act, see 22 Halsbury's Statutes (3rd Edn.) 900 *et seq.*

(*k*) Cmd. 6885; see Bretton Woods Agreements Act 1945; 22 Halsbury's Statutes (3rd Edn.) 886; and S. R. & O. 1946, No. 36.

(*l*) Cmd. 6968.

not to refuse permission for "current transactions" (*m*), which include "payments due in connection with foreign trade" (*n*).

The effect of s. 33 (1) is to imply the condition therein set out into any contract in which the parties have not themselves made a provision of their own governing the subject-matter of the condition.

If the case falls within the proviso, the effect on the rights and liabilities of the parties of failure to obtain Treasury consent will be determined, according to the ordinary law governing the performance and discharge of contracts, by whatever arrangement the parties have come to. So if, for example, the statutory condition is not implied because the parties have agreed to make a payment in contravention of the provisions of the Act without obtaining the requisite consent, the court would no doubt treat the contract as void for illegality, with the usual consequences to the parties.

If, however, the case does not fall within the proviso, it seems that the combined effect of the subsection and of paragraph 4 (1) of the Fourth Schedule is that the debtor need not (and indeed must not) pay so long as Treasury consent has not been given, but if the creditor sues him he cannot defend merely because there has been no Treasury consent (*o*). His proper course then is to pay into court under the appropriate Rules (*p*), and the creditor in his turn will require Treasury consent before he can take the money out of court (*q*).

MISREPRESENTATION ACT 1967

(1967, c. 7)

An Act to amend the law relating to innocent misrepresentation and to amend sections 11 *and* 35 *of the Sale of Goods Act* 1893.

[22nd March 1967.]

1. Removal of certain bars to rescission for innocent misrepresentation.—Where a person has entered into a contract after a misrepresentation has been made to him, and—

(a) the misrepresentation has become a term of the contract; or

(b) the contract has been performed;

or both, then, if otherwise he would be allowed to rescind the contract without alleging fraud, he shall be so entitled, subject to the provisions of this Act, notwithstanding the matters mentioned in paragraphs (a) and (b) of this section.

COMMENT

Before this Act, it was doubtful whether a party could ever rescind a contract

---

(*m*) International Monetary Fund Agreement, Art. VIII (2) (a); Anglo-American Loan Agreement, Art. 7.

(*n*) I.M.F. Agreement, Art. XIX.; A.A.L. Agreement, Art. 11.

(*o*) *Cummings* v. *London Bullion Co.*, [1951] W. N. 102; reversed, [1952] 1 All E. R. 383; [1952] 1 K. B. 327, C. A.; applied, *Contract & Trading Co.* v. *Barbey*, [1959] 3 All E. R. 846; [1960] A. C. 244, H. L.

(*p*) R. S. C., O. 6, r. 2; O. 22, r. 9; O. 45, r. 2; O. 46, r. 6 (4), 7; O. 49, r. 7; O. 51, r. 1 (2).

(*q*) Fourth Schedule, paragraph 2.

for non-fraudulent misrepresentation where the misrepresentation had become a term of the contract or where the contract had been performed. This section removes these possible bars to rescission but without affecting any other possible bar, as to which see *ante*, p. 6, note (*k*).

2. Damages for misrepresentation.—(1) Where a person has entered into a contract after a misrepresentation has been made to him by another party thereto and as a result thereof he has suffered loss, then, if the person making the misrepresentation would be liable to damages in respect thereof had the misrepresentation been made fraudulently, that person shall be so liable notwithstanding that the misrepresentation was not made fraudulently, unless he proves that he had reasonable ground to believe and did believe up to the time the contract was made that the facts represented were true.

(2) Where a person has entered into a contract after a misrepresentation has been made to him otherwise than fraudulently, and he would be entitled, by reason of the misrepresentation, to rescind the contract, then, if it is claimed, in any proceedings arising out of the contract, that the contract ought to be or has been rescinded, the court or arbitrator may declare the contract subsisting and award damages in lieu of rescission, if of opinion that it would be equitable to do so, having regard to the nature of the misrepresentation and the loss that would be caused by it if the contract were upheld, as well as to the loss that rescission would cause to the other party.

(3) Damages may be awarded against a person under subsection (2) of this section whether or not he is liable to damages under subsection (1) thereof, but where he is so liable any award under the said subsection (2) shall be taken into account in assessing his liability under the said subsection (1).

COMMENT

Subsection (1).—This subsection creates a statutory right to damages for non-fraudulent misrepresentation.

It is not clear whether the provision that a party is to be liable for misrepresentation under this section if he would have been liable had he been fraudulent equates such misrepresentation in all respects with fraudulent misrepresentation. Taken literally it seems to do so, but strange results would follow. Thus, the limitation period for fraud would have to be applied—as to which see s. 26 of the Limitation Act 1939—so that an action under this subsection may survive after any action on the contract has been barred. Moreover, no exclusion clause could exclude liability for damages under this subsection, for had the misrepresentation been fraudulent the party making it would have been liable as the exclusion clause could not have been construed as excluding liability for fraud (*r*). This point in no way conflicts with s. 3 of this Act, which is concerned with the effect to be given to an exclusion clause which, if valid, would be construed as excluding liability. To avoid these results, it is possible that the courts will construe the subsection restrictively, perhaps

(*r*) *Pearson & Son, Ltd.* v. *Dublin Corporation*, [1907] A. C. 351.

holding that "if the person making the misrepresentation would be liable to damages in respect thereof had the misrepresentation been made fraudulently" means that if damages would have been a possible remedy had the misrepresentation been fraudulent, then they shall be available under this subsection, but subject to the limitations appropriate in a case of negligence.

However, the right given by this subsection is a statutory right (*s*). It is not based upon the tort of negligence despite being commonly described as negligent misrepresentation. Thus, there is no requirement that the person making the representation should owe any duty of care to the representee, or that he should voluntarily or otherwise take upon himself any liability for the accuracy of what he says (*t*). It seems more likely, therefore, that the person making the representation cannot exclude his liability by notice as he can exclude his liability for negligent mis-statement (*u*).

In early cases under the 1967 Act the courts appear to have assumed that the appropriate measure of damages was the same as that for breach of contract (*a*). Subsequently, however, it has been held at first instance that the measure of damages is the same as in an action for damages for deceit (*b*).

A contractual measure of damages cannot, it is submitted, be reconciled with the wording of the section. Damages for breach of contract are estimated to put the injured party in the same position as if the contract had been performed, for this is the measure of the loss directly and naturally resulting from the breach (*c*). It is not necessary that the injured party should have suffered any loss as a result of entering into the contract. It is sufficient that he has not made the profit that he should have made. But it is a necessary pre-condition to liability under this subsection that the representee should have

---

(*s*) In *Andre & Cie S. A.* v. *Ets Michel Blanc and Fils*, [1979] 2 Lloyd's Rep. 427, the members of the Court of Appeal considered whether damages were recoverable under this section for a misrepresentation of law, and Lord DENNING, M. R. and LANE, L. J. expressed conflicting views.

(*t*) *Howard Marine and Dredging Co., Ltd.* v. *Ogden & Sons (Excavations), Ltd.*, [1978] 2 All E. R. 1134, at pp. 1145, 1149; [1978] Q. B. 574, at pp. 596, 601, C. A.

(*u*) *Cf. Hedley Byrne & Co.* v. *Heller & Partners*, [1963] 2 All E.R. 575; [1964] A. C. 465, H. L. But in *Howard Marine* v. *Ogden, supra*, the Court of Appeal assumed that liability for misrepresentation under this subsection could be excluded, subject to the provisions of s. 3, *post*, and by a majority held that it would not be reasonable to allow reliance on the exclusion clause in that case.

(*a*) In *Gosling* v. *Anderson* (1972), *Times*, 8th February, the Court of Appeal appears to have assumed that the measure of damages was the same as in contract, but in that case the point was not argued and the Court of Appeal did not have to decide it, but simply directed an inquiry as to damages. A similar assumption was made, *obiter*, by Lord DENNING, M. R., in *Jarvis* v. *Swan Tours, Ltd.*, [1973] 1 All E. R. 71; [1973] Q. B. 233, C. A. Lord DENNING'S dictum was applied by Judge FAY in *Davis & Co.* v. *Afa-Minerva, (E.M.I.), Ltd.*, [1974] 2 Lloyd's Rep. 27, but again the point does not seem to have been argued.

(*b*) *Watts* v. *Spence*, [1975] 2 All E. R. 528; [1976] Ch. 165, where, however, GRAHAM, J. held, following *Gosling* v. *Anderson, supra*, and apparently overlooking *Doyle* v. *Olby, supra*, where the contrary was held, that damages for loss of bargain could be recovered in an action for fraud; *F. & B. Entertainments, Ltd.* v. *Leisure Enterprises, Ltd.* (1976), 240 Estate Gazette 455; *Andre & Cie S. A.* v. *Ets. Michel Blanc*, [1977] 2 Lloyd's Rep. 166, at p. 181; on appeal [1979] 2 Lloyd's Rep. 427, C. A.; *McNally* v. *Welltrade International, Ltd.*, [1978] I. R. L. R. 497.

(*c*) See the comment to s. 54 of the Sale of Goods Act, *ante*.

suffered loss as a result of entering into the contract, and if he has suffered no such loss, he should get no damages although he has not got the bargain he expected.

Nor can the measure of damages be the same as for negligence. Damages for negligence and for deceit are calculated in the same manner—so as to compensate the injured party for the loss he has suffered. But in negligence, damages are limited to such loss as may reasonably have been foreseen at the time of the negligent act or representation. Damages for deceit are not so limited (*d*). It is possible for a party to suffer loss as a result of a misrepresentation which would be recoverable in an action for deceit, but not in an action for negligence. It is clear from the subsection that in such a case the person making the representation is liable to damages.

It would seem, therefore, that the appropriate measure of damages must be the same as that for the tort of deceit, the measure suggested by the equation of the statutory liability with liability for fraud (*e*).

If the representor is to avoid liability under this subsection, he must show that he had reasonable grounds to believe, and did believe, the representation to be true not only when he made it, but also at all times up to the time the contract was made. Should new facts come to his notice before that time, he must disclose them to the other party. The question is not whether the representor was negligent. The Act imposes an absolute obligation not to state facts which the representor cannot prove that he had reasonable grounds to believe (*f*).

Subsection (2).—It is open to a party who is entitled to rescind a contract for misrepresentation either to seek rescission from the court or to rescind without taking any proceedings. In either case, if the misrepresentation was fraudulent, even if it was negligent, and either party brings any proceedings in respect of the contract, then the court has a discretion to declare the contract subsisting and award damages instead. The court has no power to award damages under this subsection as well as rescission, and it would seem that it cannot award damages if the right to rescind has been lost (*g*).

3. Avoidance of provision excluding liability for misrepresentation.—If a contract contains a term which would exclude or restrict—

(a) any liability to which a party to a contract may be subject by reason of any misrepresentation made by him before the contract was made; or

(b) any remedy available to another party to the contract by reason of such a misrepresentation,

that term shall be of no effect except insofar as it satisfies the requirement of reasonableness as stated in section 11 (1) of the Unfair Contract Terms Act 1977; and it is for those claiming that the term satisfies that requirement to show that it does (*h*).

(*d*) *Doyle* v. *Olby* (*Ironmongers*), *Ltd.*, [1969] 2 All E. R. 119; [1969] 2 Q. B. 158, C. A.

(*e*) See *n.* (*b*) on p. 331, *ante*.

(*f*) *Howard Marine and Dredging Co., Ltd.* v. *Ogden & Sons* (*Excavation*), *Ltd.*, [1978] 2 All E. R. 1134; [1978] Q. B. 574, C. A.

(*g*) See generally 30 M. L. R. 369; [1967] C. L. J. 239; 31 Conv. 234.

(*h*) This section was substituted for the original s. 3 by s. 8 of the Unfair Contract Terms Act 1977.

COMMENT

The original section (*i*) provided that the term was to be of no effect except to the extent (if any) that, in any proceedings arising out of the contract, the court or arbitrator allowed reliance on it as being fair and reasonable in the circumstances. The question under the original section was thus whether and to what extent it was fair and reasonable to rely on the term. Under the present section the question is whether and to what extent the term is reasonable (*j*). Factors arising after the date of the contract could formerly be taken into account but are now to be disregarded.

The section only applies to a term contained in a contract. But such provisions are frequently contained in sales brochures, auction particulars and similar documents. It is not clear how far liability for misrepresentation may be limited or excluded by a provision in such a document. The position would seem, however, to be as follows:

(1) Whether such a provision becomes a term of any contract between the parties is a question of construction of the contract and of the provision (*k*).

(2) Liability for fraud cannot be excluded because no exemption clause will be construed as extending to cover a fraudulent misrepresentation (*l*).

(3) Liability for misrepresentation under section 2 (1) of this Act cannot be excluded by a provision other than a term of a contract and arguably cannot be excluded even by such a term (*m*). If a term of a contract should be held to be capable of excluding liability under s. 2 (1), by virtue of this section it will still only be valid to the extent that it satisfies the requirement of reasonableness (*n*). In general it seems unlikely that a term which purports to exempt a person from liability for a misrepresentation which he had no reasonable grounds to believe was true will be held to satisfy that requirement (*n*).

(4) Liability for misrepresentation other than for fraud and for damages under s. 2 (1) may be excluded by a suitably worded clause in an agreement, but by virtue of this section, such a clause will be valid only to the extent that it satisfies the requirement of reasonableness. Liability for damages for negligent mis-statement under the law stated in *Hedley Byrne* v. *Heller Brothers* (*o*) may also be excluded by a suitably worded disclaimer independently of any contract, but that is because liability depends upon the assumption by the person making the statement of a duty of care, and he is therefore free to make it clear to the person to whom he makes the statement that he will not assume such a duty.

(5) The right to rescind for non-fraudulent misrepresentation is an equitable right, and while a court of equity may give some weight to an

---

(*i*) See *n*. (*h*) on p. 332, *ante*.

(*j*) See Unfair Contract Terms Act 1977, s. 11, and comment to that section, *post*.

(*k*) See, *e.g.*, *Cremdean Properties* v. *Nash* (1977), 244 Estate Gazette 837 affirmed (1977), 244 Estate Gazette 547, C. A. where a notice forming a footnote to conditions of tender which sought to exclude liability for misrepresentation, and to provide that representations in the tender form should not form part of any contract, was held to be a provision of the agreement within the original s. 3, since the contract was entered into on the basis that the notice should be applicable to it.

(*l*) *Pearson & Son, Ltd.* v. *Dublin Corporation*, [1907] A. C. 351, H. L.

(*m*) See the comment to that section, *ante*.

(*n*) *Howard Marine* v. *Ogden & Sons*, [1978] 2 All E. R. 1134, at pp. 1147, 1149; [1978] Q. B. 574, at pp. 599, 601, C. A. *Cf.* the dissenting judgment of Lord DENNING, M. R., at pp. 1143 and 594.

(*o*) [1963] 2 All E. R. 575; [1964] A. C. 465, H. L.

exclusion clause which is not in a contract, there seems no reason why, in doing what is equitable, it should allow reliance on such a provision unless it is fair and reasonable in all the circumstances to do so.

(6) Representors frequently seek to forestall any claim for misrepresentation either by warning the person to whom the representation is made that he should not rely on it, or by requiring him to sign an acknowledgment that he has not relied on any representation in entering into the contract. Such provisions are probably outside the scope of this section. But it does not follow that they will necessarily be effective. A warning not to rely on a representation will not normally assist the representor if he is fraudulent, and will therefore probably not assist him if he is sued for damages under s. 2 (1) (*p*). In other cases, the question will be whether he intended the representations to be relied on, and while the warning not to rely on them may be evidence that he did not so intend, it will not be conclusive. So too, an acknowledgment by a party to a contract that he has not relied on any representation may be evidence of that fact, and may sometimes give rise to an estoppel if the other party can show that the acknowledgment was intended to be acted upon, that he believed it, and that he did act upon it. But, if a person is required to sign such an acknowledgment as condition of entering into a contract, such an acknowledgement is unlikely to be given very much weight, particularly if the other evidence shows that the representor must have been aware that the representee was only entering the contract as a result of what he had been told.

(7) A provision that "notwithstanding any statement of fact included in these particulars the vendor shall be conclusively deemed to have made no misrepresentation within the Misrepresentation Act 1967" was a provision of an agreement which would exclude or restrict liability for misrepresentation within the original s. 3 (*q*) and would equally appear to be a term of a contract within the present section.

(8) The section does not apply to clauses excluding or restricting liability or remedies for breach of contractual terms as such. However, if one provision excludes liability for both misrepresentation and breaches of contract, it would seem that the entire provision would be of no effect subject to the discretion of the court under this section, unless perhaps the part referring to misrepresentation can be severed from the rest (*r*). Moreover, if a misrepresentation is made in such circumstances that it becomes a term of the contract, it would seem that by reason of the misrepresentation the party making it is subjected to liability for breach of contract and the other party is entitled to certain remedies in respect of that breach. A provision excluding or restricting such liability or remedies would therefore seem to come within this section. If so, then a new distinction must be drawn between terms which are representations and terms which are not. The wording of the section is obscure, however, and it is unlikely that either of the interpretations suggested in this paragraph was considered or intended by the draftsman.

The section does not apply to clauses which prevent liability from arising, for example where a principal gives notice that an agent has no power to make representations on his behalf (*s*).

(*p*) See the comment to that section, *ante*.

(*q*) See *Cremdean Properties* v. *Nash* (1977), 242 Estate Gazette 547, *per* BRIDGE, L. J.

(*r*) *Cf*. the rules relating to severance of covenants in restraint of trade.

(*s*) *Overbrooke Estates, Ltd.* v. *Glencombe Properties, Ltd.*, [1974] 3 All E. R. 511; [1974] 1 W. L. R. 1335, approved and distinguished by the Court of Appeal in *Cremdean Properties* v. *Nash, supra*.

The section probably applies to agreed damage clauses, for such clauses, like other compromises, restrict the remedies available to the parties, but if the agreed damage clause is a fair one the court will generally allow reliance on it.

4. Amendments of Sale of Goods Act 1893.—[*Repealed by s.* 63 *and Sch.* 3 *of the Sale of Goods Act* 1979.]

5. Savings for past transactions.—Nothing in this Act shall apply in relation to any misrepresentation or contract of sale which is made before the commencement of this Act.

COMMENT

Exclusion clauses agreed before the Act came into force are expressly affected by s. 3, but only when they apply to misrepresentations made after that date.

6. Short title, commencement and extent.—(1) This Act may be cited as the Misrepresentation Act 1967.

(2) This Act shall come into operation at the expiration of the period of one month beginning with the date on which it is passed.

(3) This Act . . . does not extend to Scotland (*t*).

(4) This Act does not extend to Northern Ireland.

COMMENT

The Act came into operation on 22nd April 1967.

The English law of misrepresentation does not apply to Scotland.

The Parliament of Northern Ireland has passed a similar Misrepresentation Act.

(*t*) As amended by s. 63 and Sch. 3 of the Sale of Goods Act 1979.

THEFT ACT 1968

(1968, c. 60)

An Act to revise the law of England and Wales as to theft and similar or associated offences . . . and for other purposes connected therewith.

[26th July 1968.]

1. Basic definition of theft.—(1) A person is guilty of theft if he dishonestly appropriates property belonging to another with the intention of permanently depriving the other of it; and "thief" and "steal" shall be construed accordingly.

(2) It is immaterial whether the appropriation is made with a view to gain, or is made for the thief's own benefit.

* * * * *

COMMENT

The terms "dishonestly", "appropriates", "property", "belonging to another" and "permanently depriving" are defined in ss. 2–6 of the Act. "Gain" is defined in s. 34 (2).

* * * * *

24. Scope of offences relating to stolen goods.—(1) The provisions of this Act relating to goods which have been stolen shall apply whether the stealing occurred in England or Wales or elsewhere, and whether it occurred before or after the commencement of this Act, provided that the stealing (if not an offence under this Act) amounted to an offence where and at the time when the goods were stolen; and references to stolen goods shall be construed accordingly.

* * * * *

(4) For purposes of the provisions of this Act relating to goods which have been stolen (including subsections (1) to (3) above) goods obtained in England or Wales or elsewhere either by blackmail or in the circumstances described in section 15 (1) of this Act shall be regarded as stolen; and "steal", "theft" and "thief" shall be construed accordingly.

* * * * *

28. Orders for restitution.—(1) Where goods have been stolen, and a person is convicted of any offence with reference to the theft (whether or not the stealing is the gist of his offence), the court by or before which the offender is convicted may on the conviction exercise any of the following powers:—

(a) the court may order anyone having possession or control of the goods to restore them to any person entitled to recover them from him; or

(b) on the application of a person entitled to recover from the person convicted any other goods directly or indirectly representing the first-mentioned goods (as being the proceeds of any disposal or realisation of the whole or part of them or of goods so representing them), the court may order those other goods to be delivered or transferred to the applicant; or

(c) on the application (*a*) of a person who, if the first-mentioned goods were in the possession of the person convicted, would be entitled to recover them from him, the court may order that a sum not exceeding the value of those goods shall be paid to the applicant out of any money of the person convicted which was taken out of his possession on his apprehension.

(2) Where under subsection (1) above the court has power on a person's conviction to make an order against him both under paragraph (b) and under paragraph (c) with reference to the stealing of the same goods, the court may make orders under both paragraphs provided that the applicant for the orders does not thereby recover more than the value of those goods.

(3) Where under subsection (1) above the court on a person's conviction makes an order under paragraph (a) for the restoration of any goods, and it appears to the court that the person convicted has sold the goods to a person acting in good faith, or has borrowed money on the security of them from a person so acting, then on the application (*a*) of the purchaser or lender the court may order that there shall be paid to the applicant, out of any money of the person convicted which was taken out of his possession on his apprehension, a sum not exceeding the amount paid for the purchase by the applicant or, as the case may be, the amount owed to the applicant in respect of the loan.

(4) The court shall not exercise the powers conferred by this section unless in the opinion of the court the relevant facts sufficiently appear from evidence given at the trial or the available documents, together with admissions made by or on behalf of any person in connection with any proposed exercise of the powers; and for this purpose "the available documents" means any written statements or admissions which were made for use, and would have been admissible, as evidence at the trial, the depositions taken at any committal proceedings and any written statements or admissions used as evidence in those proceedings.

(5) Any order under this section shall be treated as an order for the restitution of property within the meaning of sections 30 and 42 of the Criminal Appeal Act 1968 (which relate to the effect on such orders of appeals).

(6) References in this section to stealing are to be construed in accordance with section 24 (1) and (4) of this Act.

(*a*) An application is no longer essential: see s. 6 (2), Criminal Justice Act 1972.

COMMENT

The court should apply the same principles in considering whether to exercise its discretion under this section as formerly were applied under s. 45 of the Larceny Act 1916 (*b*).

If any doubt exists whether money or goods belong to a third party the criminal courts are not the correct forum in which that issue should be decided. It is only in the plainest cases, when there can be no doubt, that the court should make a restitution order (*c*).

The trial concludes when sentence is given. Evidence cannot be admitted after that time to assist the court in determining whether to make an order under this section (*d*).

By virtue of s. 6 (3) of the Criminal Justice Act 1972 a court may now also make a restitution order under this section where on the conviction of a person of any other offence, it takes an offence with reference to the theft of the goods in question into consideration in determining sentence.

Moreover, s. 6 (2) of the 1972 Act enables the court to exercise its powers under subsections (1) (c) and (3) of this section without any application being made in that behalf.

An appeal lies from an order made under this section (*e*), and the Court of Appeal has power to vary or annul such order although the conviction is not quashed (*f*).

Section 30 of the Criminal Appeal Act 1968 and s. 6 (5) of the Criminal Justice Act 1972 provide for the suspension of an order for the restitution of property (unless the court otherwise orders in a case where, in its opinion, the title to the property is not in dispute) for an initial period of 28 days and thereafter, in the event of an appeal, until the determination of the appeal. Section 42 of the Criminal Appeal Act 1968, provides for a further suspension of the order in the event of an appeal to the House of Lords.

31. Effect on civil proceedings.—

* * * * *

(2) Notwithstanding any enactment to the contrary, where property has been stolen or obtained by fraud or other wrongful means, the title to that or any other property shall not be affected by reason only of the conviction of the offender.

COMMENT

Under s. 24 (1) of the Sale of Goods Act 1893, where goods were stolen and the offender was prosecuted to conviction, the property in the stolen goods revested in the person who was the owner at the time of the theft notwithstanding any intermediate dealing with them, whether by sale in market overt or otherwise. Section 24 (2), however, limited the law as to revesting of property on conviction to cases of larceny, whereas prior to the enactment of the Sale of Goods Act 1893 the rule had extended to cover cases where the goods had been

(*b*) *R.* v. *Ferguson*, [1970] 2 All E. R. 820; [1970] 1 W. L. R. 1246, C. A.

(*c*) *Ibid.*, and see *Stamp* v. *United Dominions Trust* (*Commercial*), *Ltd.*, [1967] 1 All E. R. 251; [1967] 1 Q. B. 418, D. C.; *R.* v. *Church* (1970), 55 Cr. App. Rep. 65, D. C.

(*d*) *R.* v. *Church*, *supra*.

(*e*) *R.* v. *Parker*, [1970] 2 All E. R. 458; [1970] 1 W. L. R. 1003, C. A.; Criminal Justice Act 1972, s. 6 (4).

(*f*) Criminal Appeal Act 1968, s. 30 (4).

obtained by false pretences, but under a *de facto* contract (*g*). Section 24 of the Sale of Goods Act 1893 was repealed by the Theft Act 1968 (*h*), and the present subsection is required in lieu of s. 24 (2).

(*g*) For the history of the rule, see p. 104 of the 15th edition of the present work.
(*h*) Sch. 3, Pt. III.

THE AUCTIONS (BIDDING AGREEMENTS) ACT 1969

(1969, c. 56)

An Act . . . to make fresh provision as to the rights of a seller of goods by auction where an agreement subsists that a person or persons shall abstain from bidding for the goods . . .

[22nd October 1969.]

* * * * *

3. Rights of seller of goods by auction where agreement subsists that some person shall abstain from bidding for the goods.—(1) Where goods are purchased at an auction by a person who has entered into an agreement with another or others that the other or the others (or some of them) shall abstain from bidding for the goods (not being an agreement to purchase the goods bona fide on a joint account (*i*)) and he or the other party, or one of the other parties, to the agreement is a dealer, the seller may avoid the contract under which the goods are purchased.

(2) Where a contract is avoided by virtue of the foregoing subsection, then, if the purchaser has obtained possession of the goods and restitution thereof is not made, the persons who were parties to the agreement that one or some of them should abstain from bidding for the goods the subject of the contract shall be jointly and severally liable to make good to the seller the loss (if any) he sustained by reason of the operation of the agreement.

(3) Subsection (1) above applies to a contract made after the commencement of this Act whether the agreement as to the abstention of a person or persons from bidding for the goods the subject of the contract was made before or after that commencement.

(4) Section 2 of the Auctions (Bidding Agreements) Act 1927 (right of vendors to treat certain sales as fraudulent) shall not apply to a sale the contract for which is made after the commencement of this Act.

(5) In this section, "dealer" has the meaning assigned to it by section 1 (2) of the Auctions (Bidding Agreements) Act 1927.

* * * * *

COMMENT

"Dealer" is defined by s. 1 (2) of the Auction (Bidding Agreements) Act 1927 as "a person who in the normal course of his business attends sales by auction for the purpose of purchasing goods with a view to reselling them."

* * * * *

(*i*) But such an agreement will involve the commission of an offence under s. 1 of the Auction (Bidding Agreements) Act unless it is in writing and a copy is deposited with the auctioneer before the goods are purchased.

4. Copy of the Act to be exhibited at sale.—Section 3 of the Auctions (Bidding Agreements) Act 1927 (copy of Act to be exhibited at sale) shall have effect as if the reference to that Act included a reference to this Act.

* * * * *

FINANCE ACT 1972

(1972, c. 41)

An Act to grant certain duties . . .

[27th July 1972.]

PART I

VALUE ADDED TAX

* * * * *

42. Adjustment of contracts on changes in tax.—(1) Where, after the making of a contract for the supply of goods or services and before the goods or services are supplied, there is a change in the tax charged on the supply, then, unless the contract otherwise provided, there shall be added to or deducted from the consideration for the supply an amount equal to the change.

(2) References in this section to a change in the tax charged on a supply include references to or from no tax being charged on the supply.

* * * * *

COMMENT

The Finance Act 1972 replaced purchase tax, with value added tax. It is not within the scope of this book to deal with value added tax (*k*). In general, however, it is charged in the case of a contract for the sale of goods only where the supply is a taxable supply (*l*) by a taxable person in the course of a business carried on by him, and is payable by the person supplying the goods (*m*). But this does not mean that a seller is entitled to add the amount attributable to value added tax to the contract price at which he has agreed to sell the goods, unless there is a provision in the contract entitling him to do so. The price has still to be ascertained in accordance with s. 8 of the Sale of Goods Act 1979, *ante*, though where a supplier will be liable for value added tax, he will naturally take this into account when making his quotation, or will quote a price of £x + value added tax.

The tax is chargeable in respect of any sale when the goods are treated as having been supplied in accordance with the rules set out in the Finance Act 1972. If this is later than the date of the contract, the rate at which the tax charged may have been changed in the meantime, and in such a case, unless the parties have otherwise agreed, the section reproduced above provides for the price charged to be adjusted to take account of the increase or decrease in tax.

A similar provision in respect of customs and excise duties is contained in s. 1 of the Finance Act 1901, *ante*, while a similar provision in respect of purchase tax was contained in s. 35 of the Purchase Tax Act 1963.

(*k*) See, *e.g.*, *De Voil on Value Added Tax*.

(*l*) "Taxable supply" is defined by s. 46 (1) of the Finance Act 1972 to include any supply of goods other than an exempt supply. At present no sales of goods are exempt supplies. Some sales of goods are zero-rated, however, so that the supplier will not be liable for tax on the supply of those goods.

(*m*) Finance Act 1972, s. 2 (2).

POWERS OF CRIMINAL COURTS ACT 1973

(1973, c. 62)

An Act to consolidate certain enactments relating to the powers of courts to deal with offenders . . .

[25th October 1973.]

* * * * *

35. Compensation orders against convicted persons.—(1) Subject to the provisions of this Part of this Act, a court by or before which a person is convicted of an offence, in addition to dealing with him in any other way, may, on application or otherwise, make an order (in this Act referred to as "compensation order") requiring him to pay compensation for any personal injury, loss or damage resulting from that offence or any other offence which is taken into consideration by the court in determining sentence.

(2) In the case of an offence under the Theft Act 1968, where the property in question is recovered, any damage to the property occurring while it was out of the owner's possession shall be treated for the purposes of subsection (1) above as having resulted from the offence, however and by whomsoever the damage was caused.

(3) No compensation order shall be made in respect of loss suffered by the dependants of a person in consequence of his death, and no such order shall be made in respect of injury, loss or damage due to an accident arising out of the presence of a motor vehicle on a road, except such damage as is treated by subsection (2) above as resulting from an offence under the Theft Act 1968.

(4) In determining whether to make a compensation order against any person, and in determining the amount to be paid by any person under such an order, the court shall have regard to his means so far as they appear or are known to the court.

(5) The compensation to be paid under a compensation order made by a magistrates' court in respect of any offence of which the court has convicted the offender shall not exceed £1,000 (*n*); and the compensation or total compensation to be paid under a compensation order or compensation orders made by a magistrates' court in respect of any offence or offences taken into consideration in determining sentence shall not exceed the difference (if any) between the amount or total amount which under the foregoing provisions of this subsection is the maximum for the offence or offences of which the offender has been convicted and the amount or total amounts (if any) which are in fact ordered to be paid in respect of that offence or those offences.

COMMENT

This section, which re-enacts s. 1 of the Criminal Justice Act 1972, gives a court before which a person is convicted of an offence (*o*) a new and wide

(*n*) Increased from £400 by Criminal Law Act 1977, s. 60.

(*o*) If magistrates commit an offender convicted by them to the Crown Court for

discretionary power to order the person convicted to pay compensation to persons suffering injury, loss or damage as a result either of that offence or of any other offence which is taken into consideration by the court in determining sentence.

The 1972 Act made available such compensation for the first time to persons suffering loss as a result of an offence under the Trade Descriptions Act 1968 and other statutes for the protection of consumers, thereby providing a simple way for consumers to obtain recompense in a clear case.

In most cases brought under the Trade Descriptions Act 1968 and other consumer protection legislation, a person convicted of an offence is likely to be able to afford to pay compensation. In general, therefore, a person who seeks compensation in such a case, and who can show that he has suffered loss as a result of an offence, ought, if the facts are clear, to obtain compensation. But it is not the sole object of the court in making a compensation order to provide a quick and easy civil remedy for the victim (*p*). While compensation orders are not restricted to cases where the defendant can easily pay (*q*), an order will not normally be made which involves a large sum (*r*), or which will take the offender a long time to discharge (*s*).

There is no authority whether a court can award compensation in circumstances in which there is no civil liability, but the wording of subsection (1) above seems wide enough to extend to such a case (*t*). The concepts of causation which apply to the assessment of damages under the law of contract and tort do not apply in assessing compensation (*u*), so that, for example, an innocent buyer of goods from a dishonest handler was held entitled to compensation from the handler after he had returned the goods to the true owner (*a*). Compensation for loss may include a sum in respect of interest (*b*).

Cases where the facts are in dispute should normally be brought in the civil courts (*c*). But it does not follow that a criminal court cannot make a compensation order except where all the facts are before it. Both justices and judges in Crown Courts must do what they can to make a just order on such information as they have, even though they may not be apprised of the detailed

---

sentence under s. 29 of the Magistrates Court Act 1952, it is the Crown Court and not the magistrates court which should consider whether to order compensation to be paid: *R.* v. *Brogan*, [1975] 1 All E. R. 879; [1975] 1 W. L. R. 393, C. A.

(*p*) *R.* v. *Oddy*, [1974] 2 All E. R. 666; [1974] 1 W. L. R. 1212, C. A.; *R.* v. *Inwood*, (1975) Cr. App. Rep. 70, C. A.

(*q*) *R.* v. *Bradburn* (1973), 57 Cr. App. Rep. 948, C. A.

(*r*) *R.* v. *Kneeshaw*, [1974] 1 All E. R. 896; [1975] Q. B. 57, C. A.

(*s*) *R.* v. *Bradburn, supra* (£400 at £2 per week reduced to £100 at £2 per week); *R.* v. *Daly*, [1974] 1 All E. R. 290; [1974] 1 W. L. R. 133, C. A. (£1,200 at £3.50 per week reduced to £600 at the same rate); *R.* v. *Wylie*, [1975] R. T. R. 94, C. A.

(*t*) In particular, sub-s. (2) specifically authorises the award of compensation which might not be recoverable as damages in a civil action. The absence of a civil remedy would presumably be a factor which would encourage the court to be more ready to award compensation, since one of the factors which influenced the Court of Appeal in *R.* v. *Bradburn* and *R.* v. *Daly, supra*, was the fact that the victims in those cases still had their civil remedies in damages even if an order was made: see s. 38 of the Powers of Criminal Courts Act 1973.

(*u*) *R.* v. *Thomson Holdings, Ltd.*, [1974] 1 All E. R. 823; [1974] Q. B. 592, C. A.

(*a*) *R.* v. *Howell* (1978), 66 Cr. App. Rep. 179, C. A.

(*b*) *R.* v. *Schofield* (1978), 67 Cr. App. Rep. 282, C. A.

(*c*) *R.* v. *Kneeshaw, supra.*

facts of an offence (*d*), and must ask themselves on the facts available whether loss or damage can fairly be said to have resulted to anyone from the offence for which the accused has been convicted or which has been taken into account (*e*).

Evidence is admissible to enable the court to decide whether to order compensation. Although, therefore, it is not necessary for an application to be made by the victim before the court can make a compensation order, there may be some advantage in doing so. In *R.* v. *Kneeshaw* (*f*), the Court of Appeal held that the court has a discretion as to the evidence which it will admit, even though it should hesitate to embark on a complicated investigation even at the suit of an applicant making a positive application (*g*).

An order should only be made where the legal position is quite clear (*h*), and where the sum claimed by way of compensation is either agreed or proved (*i*).

Where there is more than one victim, or more than one injury or loss in respect of which the victim seeks compensation, the court in awarding compensation should specify how it is to be apportioned and in respect of what claims (*k*). Several compensation orders may be needed (*l*).

There is power to make a joint and several order against more than one offender, but this could lead to complications and should not normally be done (*m*).

Section 36 of this Act provides for the suspension of a compensation order pending an appeal and applies ss. 30 and 42 of the Criminal Appeal Act 1968 to compensation orders as they apply to restitution orders under s. 28 of the Theft Act 1968, *ante*. Section 37 enables a compensation order to be reviewed in certain circumstances, and s. 38 provides that damages subsequently awarded in civil proceedings should be reduced by the amount paid under the compensation order, and should not be enforced without the leave of the court to the extent that any sum remains to be paid under a compensation order.

(*d*) As in the case of many offences which are taken into consideration in determining sentence.

(*e*) *R.* v. *Thomson Holidays, Ltd.*, [1974] 1 All E. R. 823; [1974] Q. B. 592, C. A.

(*f*) [1974] 1 All E. R. 896; [1975] Q. B. 57, C. A.

(*g*) Under the law before 1972, the victim could instruct prosecuting counsel to make the application for compensation on his behalf, and a simple form which was in use in some police forces and which the victim signed authorising the prosecuting counsel to act on his behalf was approved and commended by the Court of Appeal for this purpose; *R.* v. *Salem Mohammed Monsoor Ali* (1972), 56 Cr. App. Rep. 301, C. A. The same procedure would seem to be equally effective under the new law at least so long as it is not necessary for the applicant to adduce any evidence in support of his application.

(*h*) *R.* v *Inwood* (1975), 60 Cr. App. Rep. 70, C. A.; *R.* v. *Miller*, [1976] Crim. L. R. 694, C. A.

(*i*) *R.* v. *Vivian*, [1979] 1 All E. R. 48, C. A.

(*k*) *R.* v. *Oddy*, [1974] 2 All E. R. 666; [1974] 1 W. L. R. 1212, C. A.

(*l*) *R.* v. *Inwood* (1975), 60 Cr. App. Rep. 70, C. A.

(*m*) *R.* v. *Grundy*, [1974] 1 All E. R. 292; [1974] 1 W. L. R. 139, C. A. But the loss must result from an offence. No compensation order may be made, therefore, in respect of obligations arising or which might have arisen out of civil proceedings between the victim and the offender which determine before the offender is convicted: *Hammerton Cars* v. *Redbridge London Borough*, [1974] 2 All E. R. 216; [1974] 1 W. L. R. 484, D. C., where the court left open the question whether liability for costs in civil proceedings can be loss or damage resulting from the offence and whether, if it could be, it would be too remote. In principle, there seems no reason why such costs should not be capable of being a loss resulting from an offence at least in the case of an action between the victim and a third party over a state of affairs which resulted from the offence, provided that such litigation was reasonably undertaken by the victim. *Cf.* the rule on mitigation of damages discussed, p. 249, *ante*.

UNFAIR CONTRACT TERMS ACT 1977 (*n*)

(1977, c. 50)

An Act to impose further limits on the extent to which under the law of England and Wales and Northern Ireland civil liability for breach of contract, or for negligence or other breach of duty, can be avoided by means of contract terms and otherwise, and under the law of Scotland civil liability can be avoided by means of contract terms.

[26th October 1977]

PART I

AMENDMENT OF LAW FOR ENGLAND AND WALES AND NORTHERN IRELAND

Introductory

1. Scope of Part I.—(1) For the purposes of this Part of this Act, "negligence" means the breach—

(a) of any obligation, arising from the express or implied terms of a contract, to take reasonable care or exercise reasonable skill in the performance of the contract;

(b) of any common law duty to take reasonable care or exercise reasonable skill (but not any stricter duty);

(c) of the common duty of care imposed by the Occupiers' Liability Act 1957 or the Occupiers' Liability Act (Northern Ireland) 1957.

(2) This Part of this Act is subject to Part III; and in relation to contracts, the operation of sections 2 to 4 and 7 is subject to the exceptions made by Schedule 1.

(3) In the case of both contract and tort, sections 2 to 7 apply (except where the contrary is stated in section 6 (4)) only to business liability, that is liability for breach of obligations or duties arising—

(a) from things done or to be done by a person in the course of a business (whether his own business or another's); or

(b) from the occupation of premises used for business purposes of the occupier;

and references to liability are to be read accordingly.

(4) In relation to any breach of duty or obligation, it is immaterial for any purpose of this Part of this Act whether the breach was inadvertent or intentional, or whether liability for it arises directly or vicariously.

Definitions.—For "business", see s. 14, *post*, and compare s. 61 of the Sale of Goods Act, *ante*.

(*n*) This Act gives effect in a modified form to the proposals of the Law Commission and the Scottish Law Commission in their Second Report on Exemption Clauses (Law Com. No. 69; Scottish Law Com. No. 39).

Cross-references.—Sections 2, 4 and 5, *post*, limit the effect of provisions purporting to exclude liability for negligence. Contrast the definition of "breach of duty" in relation to Scotland in s. 25 (1), *post*. For comment on the scope of "business" see the comment on that expression in s. 61 of the Sale of Goods Act, *ante*.

COMMENT

Subsection (1).—This subsection defines negligence for the purposes of Part I of the Act. The equivalent definition in relation to Scotland is in s. 25 (1) of the Act.

The Sale of Goods Act 1979 does not imply any term into a contract for the sale of goods to take reasonable care or exercise reasonable skill in the performance of any contract, but such an obligation may arise by reason of the special provisions of individual contracts.

A common law duty may often arise to take reasonable care even between contracting parties, particularly where potentially dangerous goods are sold or where advice is offered concerning goods.

By virtue of sub-s. (4) of this section it is immaterial whether a breach is intentional or inadvertent.

Subsection (2).—The limitations imposed by this part of the Act upon the effect of exemption clauses do not apply to certain specified categories of contract, the most important of which is that of international supply contracts (*o*).

Subsection (3).—The definition of business in s. 14, *post*, is the same as in s. 61 of the Sale of Goods Act, *ante* and is commented on *ante*, p. 262.

Avoidance of liability for negligence, breach of contract, etc.

2. Negligence liability.—(1) A person cannot by reference to any contract term or to a notice given to persons generally or to particular persons exclude or restrict his liability for death or personal injury resulting from negligence.

(2) In the case of other loss or damage, a person cannot so exclude or restrict his liability for negligence except in so far as the term or notice satisfies the requirement of reasonableness.

(3) Where a contract term or notice purports to exclude or restrict liability for negligence a person's agreement to or awareness of it is not of itself to be taken as indicating his voluntary acceptance of any risk.

Definitions.—For "negligence" see s. 1 (1), *ante*. For "liability" *cf.* s. 1 (3), *ante*. For the requirement of reasonableness, see s. 11 (1), *post*, and Sch. 2. For an extension of the meaning of "exclude or restrict" see s. 13, *post*. For "notice" and "personal injury" see s. 14, *post*.

Cross-references.—*Cf.* s. 5 (exclusion clauses in guarantees of consumer goods), s. 9 (effect of exclusion clause after termination of contract), s. 10 (evasion by means of secondary contract), s. 16 (equivalent provision for Scotland), s. 26 and Sch. 1 (contracts to which this section does not apply or is of restricted application).

(*o*) See s. 26, *post*. Note also the limitations in Sch. 1, *post*, on the application of this part of the Act to contracts involving the carriage of goods by sea.

3. Liability arising in contract.—(1) This section applies as between contracting parties where one of them deals as consumer or on the other's written standard terms of business.

(2) As against that party, the other cannot by reference to any contract term—

(a) when himself in breach of contract, exclude or restrict any liability of his in respect of the breach; or

(b) claim to be entitled—

(i) to render a contractual performance substantially different from that which was reasonably expected of him, or

(ii) in respect of the whole or any part of his contractual obligation, to render no performance at all,

except in so far as (in any of the cases mentioned above in this subsection) the contract term satisfies the requirement of reasonableness.

Definitions.—For "the requirement of reasonableness" see s. 11. For "deals as a consumer" see s. 12. For exclusion or restriction of liability see s. 13.

Cross-references.—As to the scope of breach of contract see s. 1 (4). As to the equivalent provision in Scotland see s. 17. For the evidence of provisions excluding liability for misrepresentation, see Misrepresentation Act 1967, s. 3, *ante*.

COMMENT

Subsection (1).—The Act does not define "written standard terms of business", but the expression would seem to be wide enough to include those cases where all or most of the written standard terms of one party are incorporated in a contract even if they only cover some aspects of that contract and even if they have been modified by agreement between the parties. Their scope and the extent to which they are modified by agreement would, however, be material factors in considering whether they satisfy the requirement of reasonableness (*p*).

Subsection (2).—The subsection draws no distinction between a business transaction with a consumer and a business transaction with another person dealing in the course of a business but on the first party's written standard terms of business.

Any contract term.—Even where the transaction is between two parties dealing in the course of a business the party incorporating his written terms of business cannot rely on any terms for the purposes set out in this subsection whether or not that term is one of his standard terms unless he can satisfy the requirement of reasonableness.

In breach of contract.—Sub-s. (2)(a) only applies in respect of a breach of contract. It does not prevent a term being relied on which prevents what would normally be a breach of contract from being such a breach. But sub-s. (2) (b) applies even where there is no breach of contract and in effect creates a breach where under the terms of the contract alone there would be none.

Substantially different.—In considering whether a contractual performance is substantially different from that which is reasonably expected, it is

(*p*) See s. 11, *post*.

necessary to have regard to all the circumstances, including discussions and correspondence between the parties, any previous dealings between them, whether the contractual term sought to be relied on was brought to the attention of and explained to the other party and whether the other party was informed that there was a real possibility of its being relied on in circumstances in which the first party seeks to rely on it.

The whole or any part of his contractual obligation.—A party to whom this section applies cannot rely on a contract term to excuse him from a total failure to perform any part of his contractual obligation unless the term satisfies the requirement of reasonableness.

The requirement of reasonableness.—This is defined and considered in s. 11, *post*, and the comment to that section. A contract term to which the present section applies can only be relied on insofar as it satisfies that requirement, that is, in so far as it was a fair and reasonable term to be included. It is not struck down completely because it is not wholly reasonable (*q*). The position would seem to be different in Scotland, where the term is of no effect if it was not fair and reasonable to incorporate the term in the contract (*r*), so that the term stands or falls as a whole and cannot be given effect to the extent to which it is reasonable.

4. Unreasonable indemnity clauses.—(1) A person dealing as consumer cannot by reference to any contract term be made to indemnify another person (whether a party to the contract or not) in respect of liability that may be incurred by the other for negligence or breach of contract, except in so far as the contract term satisfies the requirement of reasonableness.

(2) This section applies whether the liability in question—

(a) is directly that of the person to be indemnified or is incurred by him vicariously;

(b) is to the person dealing as consumer or to someone else.

Definitions.—For negligence see s. 1 (1), *ante*. For "the requirement of reasonableness" see s. 11, *post*. For "dealing as a consumer" see s. 12, *post*. For "liability" see s. 1 (3), *ante*.

Cross-references.—For the equivalent provision in Scotland see s. 18, *post*. For the effect of the words "in so far as" see the comment to s. 3, *ante*.

COMMENT

This section does not affect an agreement by a person who is not a consumer to indemnify another person. Nor does it apply where the liability incurred by the other person is not a business liability within s. 1 (3), *ante*.

Such indemnities may, however, be affected, as may consumer indemnities within the section by the restrictions imposed by other sections of the Act, in cases in which they are to be treated as exemption clauses by virtue of s. 13 (1) (a) or (b), *post*, or where they fall within s. 10, *post* (*s*).

(*q*) See further the comment to s. 3 of the Misrepresentation Act 1967, *ante*, and s. 6 of this Act, *post*.

(*r*) See s. 17, *post*.

(*s*) *Cf.* illustration (6) to s. 55 of the Sale of Goods Act, *ante*.

Liability arising from sale or supply of goods

5. "Guarantee" of consumer goods.—(1) In the case of goods of a type ordinarily supplied for private use or consumption, where loss or damage—

(a) arises from the goods proving defective while in consumer use; and

(b) results from the negligence of a person concerned in the manufacture or distribution of the goods,

liability for the loss or damage cannot be excluded or restricted by reference to any contract term or notice contained in or operating by reference to a gurantee of the goods.

(2) For these purposes—

(a) goods are to be regarded as "in consumer use" when a person is using them, or has them in his possession for use, otherwise than exclusively for the purposes of a business; and

(b) anything in writing is a gurantee if it contains or purports to contain some promise or assurance (however worded or presented) that defects will be made good by complete or partial replacement, or by repair, monetary compensation or otherwise.

(3) This section does not apply as between the parties to a contract under or in pursuance of which possession or ownership of the goods passed.

Definitions.—For "negligence" see s. 1 (1), *ante*. For exclusion or restriction of liability see s. 13, *post*. For "goods" and "notice" see s. 14, *post*.

Cross-reference.—For the equivalent provision in Scotland, see s. 19, *post*. Note in particular the differing effects of sub-s. (3) of this section and s. 19 (1) (b), *post*.

COMMENT

By virtue of sub-s. (3) this section will not normally apply as between parties to a contract for the sale of goods as possession of the goods will almost inevitably have passed before the goods prove defective while in consumer use.

The section will apply, however, in relation to claims by the consumer against somebody other than the person who sold the goods to him, as, for example, the manufacturer.

6. Sale and hire-purchase.—(1) Liability for breach of the obligations arising from—

(a) section 12 of the Sale of Goods Act 1979 (*t*) (seller's implied undertakings as to title, etc.);

(b) section 8 of the Supply of Goods (Implied Terms) Act 1973 (the corresponding thing in relation to hire-purchase),

cannot be excluded or restricted by reference to any contract term.

(2) As against a person dealing as consumer, liability for breach of the obligations arising from—

(*t*) Amended by Sale of Goods Act 1979, Sch. 2, para. 19.

(a) section 13, 14 or 15 of the 1979 Act (*u*) (seller's implied undertakings as to confirmity of goods with description or sample, or as to their quality or fitness for a particular purpose);

(b) section 9, 10 or 11 of the 1973 Act (the corresponding things in relation to hire-purchase),

cannot be excluded or restricted by reference to any contract term.

(3) As against a person dealing otherwise than as consumer, the liability specified in subsection (2) above can be excluded or restricted by reference to a contract term, but only in so far as the term satisfies the requirement of reasonableness.

(4) The liabilities referred to in this section are not only the business liabilities defined by section 1 (3), but include those arising under any contract of sale of goods or hire-purchase agreement.

Definitions.—For the requirement of reasonableness see s. 11, *post.* For "dealing as consumer" see s. 12, *post.* For "exclusion or restriction of liability" see s. 13, *post.*

Cross-references.—For contracts to which this section does not apply see s. 1 (2), *ante,* and s. 26, *post,* and Sch. 1, *post.* For evasion by means of a secondary contract, see s. 10, *post.* For the equivalent provision in Scotland see s. 20, *post.* For the avoidance of provisions excluding liability for misrepresentation, see Misrepresentation Act 1967, s. 3, *ante.*

COMMENT

Subsection (1).—Under s. 55 (3) of the Sale of Goods Act 1893 (*v*) any term of any contract exempting (*a*) from all or any of section 12 of the 1893 Act was void.

This is still the position in Scotland (*b*), with the result that there a term may be wholly invalid because it relates in part to liability under s. 12 of the Sale of Goods Act (*c*). In the remainder of the United Kingdom, however, sub-s. (1) of this section does not invalidate the term but simply prevents it affecting liability under s. 12 (*c*).

Subsection (2).—Under s. 55 (4) of the Sale of Goods Act 1893 (*v*) any term of any contract exempting (*a*) from all or any of the provisions of ss. 13, 14 or 15 of that Act were void in the case of a consumer sale (*d*) and in any other case was not enforceable to the extent that it was shown that it would not be fair or reasonable to allow reliance on the term (*e*).

The position in Scotland in the case of a consumer contract (*f*) is the same as in the case of a consumer sale under s. 55 (4), while in any other case in Scotland the term has no effect if it was not fair and reasonable to incorporate the term in

(*u*) Amended by Sale of Goods Act 1979, Sch. 2, para. 19.

(*v*) Introduced by s. 4 of the Supply of Goods (Implied Terms) Act 1973 and repealed by Sch. 4 to this Act with effect from 1st February 1978, it is now reproduced in the Sale of Goods Act 1979, Sch. 1, para. 11, *ante.*

(*a*) As defined in sub-s. (9) of that section.

(*b*) See s. 20 (1), *post.*

(*c*) See illustrations (1), (5) and (7) to s. 55 of the Sale of Goods Act, *ante.*

(*d*) As defined in sub-s. (7) of that section.

(*e*) As determined in accordance with sub-s. (5) of that section.

(*f*) As defined in s. 25 (1), *post.*

the contract. The Scottish law differs from the law under s. 55 (4) of the 1893 Act in that,

(1) it is the reasonableness of the term and not of the reliance upon it that is now material,

(2) the onus is now on the seller to show that the term is fair and reasonable (*g*) not upon the buyer to prove the contrary.

In the remainder of the United Kingdom the term is not void or unenforceable or of no effect at all if it covers other matters (*h*), but is ineffective to exclude or restrict liability (*i*) for breach of the obligations implied by ss. 13, 14 and 15 of the Sale of Goods Act except that as against a person dealing otherwise than as consumer (*k*) liability may be excluded or restricted (*i*) insofar as the term satisfies the requirement of reasonableness (*l*). This differs from the law under the 1893 Act in that,

(1) the validity of the term is unaffected,

(2) as in Scotland, the onus is upon the seller to prove that it is reasonable (*m*) and it is the reasonableness of the term and not of the reliance upon it that is material (*n*).

7. Miscellaneous contracts under which goods pass.—[*This section is not relevant to the law relating to the sale of goods.*]

8. Misrepresentation.—[*This section substitutes a new s.* 3 *in the Misrepresentation Act* 1967 *which is dealt with* ante *in the context of that Act, and substitutes the same section for s.* 3 *of the Misrepresentation Act* (*Northern Ireland*) 1967.]

9. Effect of breach.—(1) Where for reliance upon it a contract term has to satisfy the requirement of reasonableness, it may be found to do so and be given effect accordingly notwithstanding that the contract has been terminated either by breach or by a party electing to treat it as repudiated.

(2) Where on a breach the contract is nevertheless affirmed by a party entitled to treat it as repudiated, this does not of itself exclude the requirement of reasonableness in relation to any contract term.

Definitions.—For the requirements of reasonableness see s. 11, *post.*

Cross references.—For the equivalent provision in Scotland see s. 22, *post.* For fundamental breach and exemption clauses see *ante*, p. 10.

(*g*) Whether it was fair and reasonable to incorporate the term is determined in the manner provided by s. 24, *post.*

(*h*) Unless rendered of no effect by the Misrepresentation Act 1967, s. 3, *ante.*

(*i*) See s. 13, *post*, for the extended meaning of "excluding or restricting liability".

(*k*) For "dealing as consumer" see s. 12, *post.*

(*l*) For the requirement of reasonableness see s. 11, *post.*

(*m*) See s. 11 (5), *post.*

(*n*) For illustrations of the effect of this section upon typical exemption clauses see the illustrations to s. 55 of the Sale of Goods Act, *ante*. Where regulations have been made in respect of goods under the Consumer Protection Act 1961 or the Consumer Safety Act 1978, a term in a contract for the sale of such goods which has the effect of excluding any obligation imposed by those regulations or liability for breach of such an obligation is void: see *ante*, p. 55.

COMMENT

This section was made necessary by the decision of the Court of Appeal in *Harbutt's Plasticine, Ltd.* v *Wayne Tank & Pump Co., Ltd.* (*o*) that where, as the result of a breach of contract, the innocent party has, and exercises, a right to bring the contract to an end or where the breach automatically brings the contract to an end, then the guilty party cannot rely on an exemption clause to escape from his liability for the breach.

This decision was subsequently overruled by the House of Lords (*p*) which reaffirmed the law as being that the question whether an exemption clause was applicable where there was a fundamental breach of contract was one of the true construction of the contract, and that if it does apply, it does not cease to be applicable because the contract comes to an end as a result of such a breach.

Subsection (1) of this section therefore accords with the common law as restated by the House of Lords.

10. Evasion by means of secondary contract.—A person is not bound by any contract term prejudicing or taking away rights of his which arise under, or in connection with the performance of, another contract, so far as those rights extend to the enforcement of another's liability which this Part of this Act prevents that other from excluding or restricting.

Definition.—For excluding or restricting liability see s. 13, *post*.

Cross references.—For the equivalent provision in Scotland see s. 23, *post*.

Explanatory provisions

11. The "reasonableness" test.—(1) In relation to a contract term, the requirement of reasonableness for the purposes of this Part of this Act, section 3 of the Misrepresentation Act 1967 and section 3 of the Misrepresentation Act (Northern Ireland) 1967 is that the term shall have been a fair and reasonable one to be included having regard to the circumstances which were, or ought reasonably to have been, known to or in the contemplation of the parties when the contract was made.

(2) In determining for the purposes of section 6 or 7 above whether a contract term satisfies the requirement of reasonableness, regard shall be had in particular to the matters specified in Schedule 2 to this Act; but this subsection does not prevent the court or arbitrator from holding, in accordance with any rule of law, that a term which purports to exclude or restrict any relevant liability is not a term of the contract.

(3) In relation to a notice (not being a notice having contractual effect), the requirement of reasonableness under this Act is that it should be fair and reasonable to allow reliance on it, having regard to all the circumstances obtaining when the liability arose or (but for the notice) would have arisen.

(4) Where by reference to a contract term or notice a person seeks to restrict liability to a specified sum of money, and the question arises (under this or any other Act) whether the term or notice satisfies the

(*o*) [1970] 1 All E. R. 225; [1970] 1 Q. B. 447.

(*p*) *Photo Productions, Ltd.* v. *Securicor Transport, Ltd.*, [1980] 1 All E. R. 556; [1980] A. C. 827, H. L.

requirement of reasonableness, regard shall be had in particular (but without prejudice to subsection (2) above in the case of contract terms) to—

(a) the resources which he could expect to be available to him for the purpose of meeting the liability should it arise; and

(b) how far it was open to him to cover himself by insurance.

(5) It is for those claiming that a contract term or notice satisfies the requirement of reasonableness to show that it does.

Definition.—For "notice", see s. 14, *post.*

Cross references.—For the equivalent provision in Scotland see s. 24, *post.* For terms incorporated or approved by or incorporated pursuant to a decision or ruling of certain authorities, which are deemed to be reasonable, see s. 29 (2), *post.* For the effect upon this requirement of a party electing either to terminate or not to terminate a contract see s. 9, *ante.* For other terms not restricted by this Act, see s. 29 (1), *post.* This definition is required for the purposes of ss. 2 (2), 3, 4, 6 (3) and 7 (3) of this Act and s. 3 of the Misrepresentation Act 1967 as amended by s. 8 of this Act.

COMMENT

Under s. 55 of the Sale of Goods Act 1893 as amended by the Supply of Goods (Implied Terms) Act 1973, and the original s. 3 of the Misrepresentation Act 1967 the test was whether it was reasonable to allow *reliance* on the term in all the circumstances. Regard could therefore be had to the nature and circumstances of the alleged breach and to other circumstances arising after the date of the contract, so that it was open to a court to hold that although a term was reasonable it would not be reasonable to allow reliance on it in particular circumstances or that a term which overall was unreasonable could reasonably be relied on in some circumstances.

The test now is whether the term was a fair and reasonable one to be included, and it is only circumstances which were or ought reasonably to have been known to or in the contemplation of the parties at that time which may be taken into account.

For the purposes of s. 6, *ante*, which relates to the liability of the seller in a sale other than to a person dealing as consumer for breach of the obligations imposed by ss. 13–15 of the Sale of Goods Act, particular regard is to be had to the matters specified in Sch. 2, *post.* The matters listed in that Schedule will also be relevant in applying the reasonableness test under ss. 2–5, of this Act and under s. 3 of the Misrepresentation Act 1967, *ante*, but their importance may vary in those cases.

Under s. 55 of the 1893 Act it was for the party claiming that the provision was void to show that it would not be fair to allow reliance on it. Subsection (5) of this section places the burden of showing that the term was fair and reasonable upon the party seeking to rely on it.

Since the present Act came into force (*q*), in commercial matters generally, where the parties are not of unequal bargaining power, and where risks are normally borne by insurance, the apportionment of risk by the parties to a contract as they see fit will generally be upheld as reasonable by the courts (*r*).

Even in the absence of insurance, it also seems likely that standard terms

(*q*) On 1st February 1978: s. 31(1), *post.*

(*r*) *Photo Production, Ltd.* v. *Securicor Transport, Ltd.*, [1980] 1 All E. R. 556, at pp. 561, 570; [1980] 2 W. L. R. 283, at pp. 289, 298, H. L.

negotiated by trade organisations acting for both the buyer and the seller will be upheld by the courts (*s*) unless there are special circumstances which ought to have been known to or to the contemplation of the seller which makes it unreasonable for him to rely on the term (*t*).

The position would seem to be akin to that relating to the reasonableness as between the parties of contracts in restraint of trade, and there the courts have repeatedly stressed the importance of giving full weight to commercial practices and to the generality of contracts made freely by parties bargaining on equal terms (*u*). But a standard form clause imposed by a stronger party upon a weaker one will not be presumed to be fair by virtue of its being in common use (*a*), and even between parties of equal bargaining power, if the clause is included in a set of conditions which have not been freely negotiated the court will be more ready to find it to be unreasonable than where the provision has been negotiated between the parties or their trade associations (*b*).

In restraint cases, the courts have also held that if a term is unreasonable in the sense that it may work unfairly in circumstances which may reasonably be anticipated, the courts will refuse to enforce it, but it will not be treated as unreasonable simply because it might work unfairly in certain exceptional

---

(*s*) *Cf. R. W. Green, Ltd.* v. *Cade Bros. Farms*, [1978] 1 Lloyd's Rep. 602 (decided under s. 55 of the Sale of Goods Act 1893 upon the basis of whether it was fair to allow reliance on such a term in all the circumstances where, unknown to the seller, seed potatoes were infected with a virus). In *Schroeder Music Publishing* v. *Macaulay*, [1974] 3 All E. R. 616; [1974] 1 W. L. R. 1308, H. L., Lord DIPLOCK observed at pp. 624 and 1316 that if fairness or reasonableness were relevant to the enforceability of standard terms in contracts such as commodity contracts "the fact that they are widely used by parties whose bargaining power is fairly matched would raise a strong presumption that their terms are fair and reasonable".

(*t*) In *Rasbora, Ltd.* v. *J. C. L. Marine*, [1977] 1 Lloyds' Rep. 645, a boat was sold which had been negligently built by the seller and which contained a serious engineering defect which caused its total loss soon after it was delivered. It was held to be unreasonable under s. 55 of the Sale of Goods Act 1893 for the seller to rely on an exemption clause which would have left the buyer without a remedy. If the boat had already been built when the contract of sale was made no doubt such a clause would not be a reasonable one to incorporate in the contract, but it is by no means clear that this would be so if, as was in fact the position in the *Rasbora* case, the contract was made before the boat was built unless the defect was in the design rather than the construction of the boat. See also *Bahous* v. *Alcor International, Ltd.* (1976), unreported, Court of Appeal Transcript 343A, where seriously defective cloth was supplied under a contract of sale containing a term restricting the seller's liability to the invoice value of the cloth and it was held at first instance that it would not be fair and reasonable to allow the seller to rely on the term. The Court of Appeal left the point open as it held that the clause did not cover the breach in question.

(*u*) See *e.g. Esso Petroleum Co., Ltd.* v. *Harper's Garage* (*Stourport*), *Ltd.*, [1967] 1 All E. R. 699; [1968] A. C. 269, H. L.

(*a*) *Schroeder Music Publishing* v. *Macaulay*, [1974] 3 All E. R. 616, at pp. 623, 624; [1974] 1 W. L. R. 1308, at p. 1316, *per* Lord DIPLOCK. See also *Foley Motors, Ltd.* v. *McGhee*, [1970] N. Z. L. R. 649, where in applying a statute protecting hirers under hire-purchase agreements RICHMOND, J. commented that it might be argued that it is unfair and unreasonable to exclude an express warranty without at least drawing the attention of the purchaser to the clause in the contract and explaining its effect. He drew an analogy with moneylending contracts, where the failure by a lender to explain a clause in a loan agreement making the whole of the principal and interest due on default has been held to make the transaction harsh and unconscionable. See further *Meston on Moneylenders*, 5th ed., pp. 196–197.

(*b*) *Esso Petroleum* v. *Harper's Garage*, *supra*, at pp. 708 and 300.

circumstances outside the reasonable expectation of the parties at the time of making the agreement (*c*).

12. "Dealing as consumer".—(1) A party to a contract "deals as consumer" in relation to another party if—

(a) he neither makes the contract in the course of a business nor holds himself out as doing so; and

(b) the other party does make the contract in the course of a business; and

(c) in the case of a contract governed by the law of sale of goods or hire-purchase, or by section 7 of this Act, the goods passing under or in pursuance of the contract are of a type ordinarily supplied for private use or consumption.

(2) But on a sale by auction or by competitive tender the buyer is not in any circumstances to be regarded as dealing as consumer.

(3) Subject to this, it is for those claiming that a party does not deal as consumer to show that he does not.

Definition.—For "business" and "goods" see s. 14, *post*.

Cross-references.—For the equivalent provision in Scotland see the definition of "consumer contract" in s. 25 (1), *post*. The definition in this section is required by ss. 3, 4, 6 (2) and 7 (2) of this Act.

COMMENT

Under s. 55 of the Sale of Goods Act 1893 as amended by the Supply of Goods (Implied Terms) Act 1973, the distinction was drawn between a consumer sale and other sales, so that clauses exempting from any of the provisions of ss. 13–15 of the 1893 Act were void in the case of a consumer sale. In that context it was held that where there was a consumer sale, to A, followed by a novation of the contract in which B Ltd. was substituted as buyer, on the facts B Ltd. was in the same contractual position as A had been, and the exemption clause therefore remained void (*d*).

The present Act is differently worded in this respect both in this Part and in Part II, relating to Scotland, so that the relevant exemption clauses cannot be relied on as against a person dealing as consumer in England and is of no effect or is void against the consumer in Scotland. It is not clear whether the offending provision is wholly ineffective or void in the case of consumer contracts as against the consumer or anybody standing in his shoes, or whether the restrictions contained in the Act operate solely in favour of the consumer so that the substituted buyer is not entitled to the same rights as the consumer. It may be that different results follow from the different provisions.

13. Varieties of exemption clause.—(1) To the extent that this Part of this Act prevents the exclusion or restriction of any liability it also prevents—

(a) making the liability or its enforcement subject to restrictive or onerous conditions;

(*c*) *Commercial Plastics, Ltd.* v. *Vincent*, [1964] 3 All E. R. 546, at p. 553; [1965] 1 Q. B. 623, at p. 644, C. A.; *Home Counties Dairies, Ltd.* v. *Skilton*, [1970] 1 All E. R. 1227 at pp. 1231, 1234, 1235; [1970] 1 W. L. R. 526 at pp. 533, 536, C. A.

(*d*) *Rasbora, Ltd.* v. *J. C. L. Marine, Ltd.*, [1977] 1 Lloyds' Rep. 645.

(b) excluding or restricting any right or remedy in respect of the liability, or subjecting a person to any prejudice in consequence of his pursuing any such right or remedy;

(c) excluding or restricting rules of evidence or procedure; and (to that extent) sections 2 and 5 to 7 also prevent excluding or restricting liability by reference to terms and notices which exclude or restrict the relevant obligation or duty.

(2) But an agreement in writing to submit present or future differences to arbitration is not to be treated under this Part of this Act as excluding or restricting any liability.

Definitions.—For "notice", see s. 14 *post.*

Cross references.—For liability see ss. 1 (3), 6 (4), *ante.* References to excluding or restricting inability appear in ss. 2, 3, 5, 6, 7, 10 and 11, *ante*, and in s. 3 of the Misrepresentation Act 1967, *ante.* For the equivalent provision in Scotland see s. 25 (3), *post.* For illustration showing the operation of this section see the illustrations to s. 55 of the Sale of Goods Act, *ante.*

COMMENT

Under s. 55 (9) of the Sale of Goods Act 1893, as amended by the Supply of Goods (Implied Terms) Act 1973, any term was an exempting term which purported to exclude or restrict, or had the effect of excluding or restricting the operation of all or any of ss. 12–15 of the 1893 Act or the exercise of a right conferred by any of those sections, or any liability of the seller for breach of any condition or warranty implied by any of those sections.

Among the provisions caught by the extended definitions in the present section and in s. 25 (3), relating to Scotland, are clauses limiting the time within which any claim must be made, clauses limiting damages, clauses excluding any of the conditions and warranties implied by ss. 12–15 of the Sale of Goods Act, and clauses deeming certain facts to be true, for example that goods have been examined before being bought (*e*).

Agreed damages clauses are caught by this section although they are not normally treated as exemption clauses (*f*) in so far as they restrict the exercise of a right conferred by ss. 12–15 of the Sale of Goods Act or of any other right the restriction of which is prohibited by this Act. It is irrelevant that it does so in the interests of both parties, except in so far as it is necessary to consider the reasonableness of the clause.

14. Interpretation of Part I.—In this Part of this Act—

"business" includes a profession and the activities of any government department or local or public authority;

"goods" has the same meaning as in the Sale of Goods Act 1979 (*g*);

"hire-purchase agreement" has the same meaning as in the Consumer Credit Act 1974;

"negligence" has the meaning given by section 1 (1);

"notice" includes an announcement, whether or not in writing,

---

(*e*) See the illustrations to s. 55 of the Sale of Goods Act, *ante.*

(*f*) *Suisse Atlantique Société D'Armement Maritime S. A.* v. *N. V. Rotterdamsche Kolen Centrale*, [1966] 2 All E. R. 61; [1967] 1 A. C. 361, H. L.

(*g*) As amended by the Sale of Goods Act 1979, Sch. 3, para. 20.

and any other communication or pretended communication; and

"personal injury" includes any disease and any impairment of physical or mental condition.

Cross-references.—For comment on the definitions of "business" and "goods" see the comment to the definitions of those words in s. 61 (1) of the Sale of Goods Act, *ante*.

PART II

AMENDMENT OF LAW FOR SCOTLAND

15. Scope of Part II.—(1) This Part of this Act applies only to contracts, is subject to Part III of this Act and does not affect the validity of any discharge or indemnity given by a person in consideration of the receipt by him of compensation in settlement of any claim which he has.

(2) Subject to subsection (3) below, sections 16 to 18 of this Act apply to any contract only to the extent that the contract—

(a) relates to the transfer of the ownership or possession of goods from one person to another (with or without work having been done on them);

(b) constitutes a contract of service or apprenticeship;

(c) relates to services of whatever kind, including (without prejudice to the foregoing generality) carriage, deposit and pledge, care and custody, mandate, agency, loan and services relating to the use of land;

(d) relates to the liability of an occupier of land to persons entering upon or using that land;

(e) relates to a grant of any right or permission to enter upon or use land not amounting to an estate or interest in the land.

(3) Notwithstanding anything in subsection (2) above, sections 16 to 18—

(a) do not apply to any contract to the extent that the contract—

(i) is a contract of insurance (including a contract to pay an annuity on human life);

(ii) relates to the formation, constitution or dissolution of any body corporate or unincorporated association or partnership;

(b) apply to—

a contract of marine salvage or towage;
a charter party of a ship or hovercraft;
a contract for the carriage of goods by ship or hovercraft; or,
a contract to which subsection (4) below relates,

only to the extent that—

(i) both parties deal or hold themselves out as dealing in the course of a business (and then only in so far as the contract purports to exclude or restrict liability for breach of duty in respect of death or personal injury); or

(ii) the contract is a consumer contract (and then only in favour of the consumer).

(4) This subsection relates to a contract in pursuance of which goods are carried by ship or hovercraft and which either—

(a) specifies ship or hovercraft as the means of carriage over part of the journey to be covered; or

(b) makes no provision as to the means of carriage and does not exclude ship or hovercraft as that means,

in so far as the contract operates for and in relation to the carriage of the goods by that means.

Definitions.—For "business", "consumer contract" and "goods" see s. 25 (1), *post.*

Cross-references.—For the equivalent provisions in the remainder of the United Kingdom, see s. 1 (2), *ante*, and Sch. 1, *post.* For the exclusion of international supply contracts from this part of the Act, see s. 26, *post.*

16. Liability for breach of duty.—(1) Where a term of a contract purports to exclude or restrict liability for breach of duty arising in the course of any business or from the occupation of any premises used for business purposes of the occupier, that term—

(a) shall be void in any case where such exclusion or restriction is in respect of death or personal injury;

(b) shall, in any other case, have no effect if it was not fair and reasonable to incorporate the term in the contract.

(2) Subsection (1) (a) above does not affect the validity of any discharge and indemnity given by a person, on or in connection with an award to him of compensation for pneumoconiosis attributable to employment in the coal industry, in respect of any further claim arising from his contracting that disease.

(3) Where under subsection (1) above a term of a contract is void or has no effect, the fact that a person agreed to, or was aware of, the term shall not of itself be sufficient evidence that he knowingly and voluntarily assumed any risk.

Definitions.—For "breach of duty", "business" and "personal injury" see s. 25 (1), *post.* For "fair and reasonable" see s. 24, *post.* For excluding or restricting liability, see s. 25 (3), *post.*

Cross-references.—For the equivalent provision in the remainder of the United Kingdom, see s. 2, *ante.*

COMMENT

Unlike s. 2, this section, and indeed the other sections in Part II of the Act, applies only to contractual terms which seek to exclude or restrict liability, and not to exclusion of liability by means of a non-contractual notice.

Also, unlike s. 2, a term to which this section applies is rendered wholly void or of no effect, so that an otherwise innocuous provision may be struck down in its entirety because it falls foul of sub-s. (1) of this section in some minor respect.

17. Control of unreasonable exemptions in consumer or standard form contracts.—(1) Any term of a contract which is a consumer contract or a standard form contract shall have no effect for the purpose of enabling a party to the contract—

(a) who is in breach of a contractual obligation, to exclude or restrict any liability of his to the consumer or customer in respect of the breach;

(b) in respect of a contractual obligation, to render no performance, or to render a performance substantially different from that which the consumer or customer reasonably expected from the contract;

if it was not fair and reasonable to incorporate the term in the contract.

(2) In this section "customer" means a party to a standard form contract who deals on the basis of written standard terms of business of the other party to the contract who himself deals in the course of a business.

Definitions.—For "fair and reasonable" see s. 24, *post*. For "business" and "consumer contract", see s. 25 (1), *post*. For "exclude or restrict liability", see s. 25 (3), *post*.

Cross-reference.—For the equivalent provision in the remainder of the United Kingdom, see s. 3, *ante*. For the scope of "breach of obligation", see s. 25 (2), *post*.

COMMENT

This section appears to differ from s. 3, *ante*, in that sub-s. (1) (b) renders a term ineffective for the purpose of enabling a party to a contract to render a performance *in respect of a contractual obligation* substantially different from that which the other party reasonably expected from the contract, whereas s. 3 (2) (b) (i), *ante*, relates only to the contractual performance as a whole and not the performance in respect of any single obligation. See further the comment to s. 3, *ante*.

18. Unreasonable indemnity clauses in consumer contracts.—(1) Any term of a contract which is a consumer contract shall have no effect for the purpose of making the consumer indemnify another person (whether a party to the contract or not) in respect of liability which that other person may incur as a result of breach of duty or breach of contract, if it was not fair and reasonable to incorporate the term in the contract.

(2) In this section "liability" means liability arising in the course of any business or from the occupation of any premises used for business purposes of the occupier.

Definitions.—For "breach of duty", "business" and "consumer contract", see s. 25 (1), *post*. For "fair and reasonable" see s. 24, *post*.

Cross-references.—For the equivalent provision in the remainder of the United Kingdom, see s. 4, *ante*. For evasion by means of a secondary contract see s. 23, *post*.

COMMENT

See the comment to s. 4, *ante*, and illustration (6) to s. 55 of the Sale of Goods Act, *ante*.

19. "Guarantee" of consumer goods.—(1) This section applies to a guarantee—

(a) in relation to goods which are of a type ordinarily supplied for private use or consumption; and

(b) which is not a guarantee given by one party to the other party to a contract under or in pursuance of which the ownership or possession of the goods to which the guarantee relates is transferred.

(2) A term of a guarantee to which this section applies shall be void in so far as it purports to exclude or restrict liability for loss or damage (including death or personal injury)—

(a) arising from the goods proving defective while—

(i) in use otherwise than exclusively for the purposes of a business; or

(ii) in the possession of a person for such use; and

(b) resulting from the breach of duty of a person concerned in the manufacture or distribution of the goods.

(3) For the purposes of this section, any document is a guarantee if it contains or purports to contain some promise or assurance (however worded or presented) that defects will be made good by complete or partial replacement, or by repair, monetary compensation or otherwise.

Definitions.—For "breach of duty", "business" and "goods" see s. 25 (1), *post*. For "exclude or restrict liability", see s. 25 (3), *post*.

Cross-reference.—For the equivalent provision in the remainder of the United Kingdom, see s. 5, *ante*.

COMMENT

By virtue of sub-s. (1) (b) this section will not normally apply as between parties to a contract for the sale of goods except in so far as a guarantee given by a third party purports to exclude or restrict the seller's liability, as possession of the goods will almost inevitably have passed before the goods prove defective while in use otherwise than exclusively for the purposes of a business.

The section will apply, however, in relation to claims by the consumer against somebody other than the person who sold the goods to him, as, for example, the manufacturer.

20. Obligations implied by law in sale and hire-purchase contracts.—(1) Any term of a contract which purports to exclude or restrict liability for breach of the obligations arising from—

(a) section 12 of the Sale of Goods Act 1979 (*h*) (seller's implied undertakings as to title etc.);

(b) section 8 of the Supply of Goods (Implied Terms) Act 1973 (implied terms as to title in hire-purchase agreements),

shall be void.

(*h*) As amended by the Sale of Goods Act 1979, Sch. 3, para. 21.

(2) Any term of a contract which purports to exclude or restrict liability for breach of the obligations arising from—

(a) section 13, 14 or 15 of the said Act of 1979 (*i*) (seller's implied undertakings as to conformity of goods with description or sample, or as to their quality or fitness for a particular purpose);

(b) section 9, 10 or 11 of the said Act of 1973 (the corresponding provisions in relation to hire-purchase),

shall—

(i) in the case of a consumer contract, be void against the consumer;

(ii) in any other case, have no effect if it was not fair and reasonable to incorporate the term in the contract.

Definitions.—For "fair and reasonable" see s. 24, *post.* For "consumer contract", see s. 25 (1), *post.* For "exclude or restrict liability", see s. 25 (3), *post.*

Cross-references.—For the equivalent provision in the remainder of the United Kingdom, see s. 6, *ante.* For contracts to which this section does not apply, see ss. 15, *ante* and 26, *post.* For evasion by means of a secondary contract, see s. 23, *post.*

COMMENT

This section is considered together with s. 6 in the comment to that section, *ante.*

21. Obligations implied by law in other contracts for the supply of goods.—[*This section is not relevant to the law relating to the sale of goods.*]

22. Consequence of breach.—For the avoidance of doubt, where any provision of this Part of this Act requires that the incorporation of a term in a contract must be fair and reasonable for that term to have effect—

(a) if that requirement is satisfied, the term may be given effect to notwithstanding that the contract has been terminated in consequence of breach of that contract;

(b) for the term to be given effect to, that requirement must be satisfied even where a party who is entitled to rescind the contract elects not to rescind it.

Definitions.—For "fair and reasonable" see s. 24, *post.*

COMMENT

The background to this section, and its effect, are the same as the background to and effect of s. 9, *ante,* the equivalent provision in relation to the remainder of the United Kingdom and are set out in the comment to that section, *ante.*

23. Evasion by means of secondary contract.—Any term of any contract shall be void which purports to exclude or restrict, or has the effect of excluding or restricting—

(*i*) As amended by the Sale of Goods Act 1979, Sch. 3, para. 21.

(a) the exercise, by a party to any other contract, of any right or remedy which arises in respect of that other contract in consequence of breach of duty, or of obligation, liability for which could not by virtue of the provisions of this Part of this Act be excluded or restricted by a term of that other contract;

(b) the application of the provisions of this Part of this Act in respect of that or any other contract.

Definitions.—For "breach of duty" see s. 25 (1), *post*. For "excluding or restricting any liability" see s. 25 (3), *post*.

COMMENT

This section differs from s. 10, *ante*, the equivalent provision in relation to the remainder of the United Kingdom in that:

(1) It invalidates terms caught by it whereas s. 10 provides only that a person is not bound by such terms so far as they extend to the enforcement of another's liability which Part I of the Act prevents that other from excluding or restricting.

(2) It invalidates terms of *any* contract which purports to exclude or restrict or have the effect of excluding or restricting the application of the provisions of Part II of the Act in respect of *that or any other contract*. There is no equivalent provision in s. 10. It would therefore seem to invalidate in Scotland a provision in a contract of a kind provided for in s. 26 (4), *post*, if the effect of such a provision would be to exclude or restrict the application of Part II of the Act. It would also seem to invalidate a choice of law clause which is not affected by s. 27 (2), *post*, if apart from that clause Part II of the Act would apply. Thus both a clause providing for English law to apply and a clause providing bona fide for a foreign law to apply would seem to be struck down if apart from that clause the relevant law would be the law of Scotland and the contract is not an international supply contract within s. 26, *post*.

24. The "reasonableness" test.—(1) In determining for the purposes of this Part of this Act whether it was fair and reasonable to incorporate a term in a contract, regard shall be had only to the circumstances which were, or ought reasonably to have been, known to or in the contemplation of the parties to the contract at the time the contract was made.

(2) In determining for the purposes of section 20 or 21 of this Act whether it was fair and reasonable to incorporate a term in a contract, regard shall be had in particular to the matters specified in Schedule 2 to this Act; but this subsection shall not prevent a court or arbiter from holding, in accordance with any rule of law, that a term which purports to exclude or restrict any relevant liability is not a term of the contract.

(3) Where a term in a contract purports to restrict liability to a specified sum of money, and the question arises for the purposes of this Part of this Act whether it was fair and reasonable to incorporate the term in the contract, then, without prejudice to subsection (2) above, regard shall be had in particular to—

(a) the resources which the party seeking to rely on that term could expect to be available to him for the purpose of meeting the liability should it arise;

(b) how far it was open to that party to cover himself by insurance.

(4) The onus of proving that it was fair and reasonable to incorporate a term in a contract shall lie on the party so contending.

Cross-references.—For the equivalent provision in the remainder of the United Kingdom see s. 11, *ante*. For terms incorporated or approved by or incorporated pursuant to a decision or ruling of certain authorities see s. 29 (2), *post*. For other terms not restricted by this Act, see s. 29 (1), *post*. This definition is required for the purposes of ss. 16 (1) (b), 17, 18, 20 (2) and 21, *ante*.

COMMENT

This section is substantially the same as s. 11, *ante*, and the comment to s. 11 applies equally to this section.

25. Interpretation of Part II.—(1) In this Part of this Act—

"breach of duty" means the breach—

(a) of any obligation, arising from the express or implied terms of a contract, to take reasonable care or exercise reasonable skill in the performance of the contract;

(b) of any common law duty to take reasonable care or exercise reasonable skill;

(c) of the duty of reasonable care imposed by section 2 (1) of the Occupiers' Liability (Scotland) Act 1960;

"business" includes a profession and the activities of any government department or local or public authority;

"consumer" has the meaning assigned to that expression in the definition in this section of "consumer contract";

"consumer contract" means a contract (not being a contract of sale by auction or competitive tender) in which—

(a) one party to the contract deals, and the other party to the contract ("the consumer") does not deal or hold himself out as dealing, in the course of a business, and

(b) in the case of a contract such as is mentioned in section 15 (2) (a) of this Act, the goods are of a type ordinarily supplied for private use or consumption;

and for the purposes of this Part of this Act the onus of proving that a contract is not to be regarded as a consumer contract shall lie on the party so contending;

"goods" has the same meaning as in the Sale of Goods Act 1979 (*j*);

"hire-purchase agreement" has the same meaning as in section 189 (1) of the Consumer Credit Act 1974;

"personal injury" includes any disease and any impairment of physical or mental condition.

(2) In relation to any breach of duty or obligation, it is immaterial for any purpose of this Part of this Act whether the act or omission giving rise to that breach was inadvertent or intentional, or whether liability for it arises directly or vicariously.

(*j*) As amended by the Sale of Goods Act 1979, Sch. 3, para. 22.

(3) In this Part of this Act, any reference to excluding or restricting any liability includes—

(a) making the liability or its enforcement subject to any restrictive or onerous conditions;

(b) excluding or restricting any right or remedy in respect of the liability, or subjecting a person to any prejudice in consequence of his pursuing any such right or remedy;

(c) excluding or restricting any rule of evidence or procedure;

(d) excluding or restricting any liability by reference to a notice having contractual effect,

but does not include an agreement to submit any question to arbitration.

(4) In subsection (3) (d) above "notice" includes an announcement, whether or not in writing, and any other communication or pretended communication.

(5) In sections 15 and 16 and 19 to 21 of this Act, any reference to excluding or restricting liability for breach of an obligation or duty shall include a reference to excluding or restricting the obligation or duty itself.

Cross-references.—For the equivalent definitions in Part I of the Act see as to "breach of duty" s. 1 (1); as to "consumer" and "consumer contract" *cf.* s. 12, and as to the other definitions, s. 14, *ante*. For excluding or restricting liability see s. 13, *ante*.

COMMENT

These definitions and the provisions as to excluding or restricting liability are substantially similar to the equivalent provisions in Part I of the Act and the comments to those equivalent provisions and to the definitions of "business" and "goods" in s. 61 (1) of the Sale of Goods Act, *ante*, apply equally to this section.

PART III

PROVISIONS APPLYING TO WHOLE OF UNITED KINGDOM

Miscellaneous

26. International supply contracts.—(1) The limits imposed by this Act on the extent to which a person may exclude or restrict liability by reference to a contract term do not apply to liability arising under such a contract as is described in subsection (3) below.

(2) The terms of such a contract are not subject to any requirement of reasonableness under section 3 or 4: and nothing in Part II of this Act shall require the incorporation of the terms of such a contract to be fair and reasonable for them to have effect.

(3) Subject to subsection (4), that description of contract is one whose characteristics are the following—

(a) either it is a contract of sale of goods or it is one under or in pursuance of which the possession or ownership of goods passes; and

(b) it is made by parties whose places of business (or, if they have none, habitual residences) are in the territories of different States (the Channel Islands and the Isle of Man being treated for this purpose as different States from the United Kingdom).

(4) A contract falls within subsection (3) above only if either—

(a) the goods in question are, at the time of the conclusion of the contract (*k*), in the course of carriage, or will be carried (*l*), from the territory of one State to the territory of another; or

(b) the acts constituting the offer and acceptance have been done in the territories of different States; or

(c) the contract provides for the goods to be delivered to the territory of a State other than that within whose territory those acts were done.

Derivation.—This section replaces, so far as the sale of goods is concerned, s. 61 (6) and the definition of "contract for the international sale of goods" in s. 62 (1) of the Sale of Goods Act 1893, which was introduced into that Act by s. 7 of the Supply of Goods (Implied Terms) Act 1973. So far as it relates to other contracts this section is new.

COMMENT

Contracts of the description defined in sub-ss. (3) and (4) ("international supply contracts" in the language of the side-note) are not subject to the limits otherwise imposed by the Act on a person's freedom to exclude or restrict liability by reference to contract terms and their terms are not subject to any requirement of reasonableness under s. 3 or s. 4, *supra*, or under the equivalent provisions applying to Scotland in Part II of the Act, *supra*. To fall within that description it must be shown, first, that the contract is one of sale of goods or one under or in pursuance of which the possession or ownership of goods passes, second, that the contract was between parties whose places of business (or if none habitual residences) were in different states and third that one of the conditions (a), (b) or (c) in sub-s. (4) applies.

In the ordinary meaning of the words a person may have more than one "place of business" (*m*). In sub-s. (3) (b), words may refer to the principal place of business but it is more likely that they will be interpreted as meaning the place of business through or from which the contract was made.

"Habitual residence" has been held (in the context of matrimonial legislation) to be residence of a particular quality rather than duration, and to involve an intention (albeit not of the same order as the "animus" required to establish domicile) to reside in a country on a basis which is neither temporary nor secondary (*n*).

(*k*) I.e. when formed by offer and acceptance: *Rasbora* v. *J. C. L. Marine, Ltd.*, [1977] 1 Lloyd's Rep. 645 (a decision upon the meaning of contract for the international sale of goods as defined in s. 62 of the Sale of Goods Act 1893 and amended by the Supply of Goods (Implied Terms) Act 1973).

(*l*) This probably does not cover the use of a boat or vehicle moving under its own power: *Rasbora* v. *J. C. L. Marine, Ltd.*, *supra*.

(*m*) *Davies* v. *British Geon, Ltd.*, [1956] 3 All E. R. 389; [1957] 1 Q. B. 1, C. A.

(*n*) *Cruse* v. *Chittum*, [1974] 2 All E. R. 940, also comparing the phrase with "ordinary

In relation to sub-s. (4) (a), it has been held that the contract must actually contemplate by its terms the goods being in the course of carriage or being carried from one to another state (*o*). An f.o.b. contract would normally involve this. A contract for sale by an international haulier of his stock of lorries (half of which are in the United Kingdom and half of which are returning home from abroad) would not contemplate the goods being in the course of carriage, since it is pure chance where the lorries are when the contract is concluded.

The place where "the acts constituting the offer and acceptance have been done" probably need not be the same as the place where the offer is made and the place where it is accepted (*p*).

27. Choice of law clauses.—(1) Where the proper law of a contract is the law of any part of the United Kingdom only by choice of the parties (and apart from that choice would be the law of some country outside the United Kingdom) sections 2 to 7 and 16 to 21 of this Act do not operate as part of the proper law.

(2) This Act has effect notwithstanding any contract term which applies or purports to apply the law of some country outside the United Kingdom, where (either or both)—

(a) the term appears to the court, or arbitrator or arbiter to have been imposed wholly or mainly for the purpose of enabling the party imposing it to evade the operation of this Act; or

(b) in the making of the contract one of the parties dealt as consumer, and he was then habitually resident in the United Kingdom, and the essential steps necessary for the making of the contract were taken there, whether by him or by others on his behalf.

(3) In the application of subsection (2) above to Scotland, for paragraph (b) there shall be substituted—

"(b) the contract is a consumer contract as defined in Part II of this Act, and the consumer at the date when the contract was made was habitually resident in the United Kingdom, and the essential steps necessary for the making of the contract were taken there, whether by him or by others on his behalf."

Cross-reference.—On the proper law of a contract see p. 47, *ante*. For dealing as a consumer see s. 12, *ante*. For "consumer contract", see s. 25 (1), *ante*. For "habitually resident" see the comment to s. 26, *ante*.

---

residence". See also *Oundjian* v. *Oundjian* (1979), 10 Fam. Law 90; Dicey and Morris, *Conflict of Laws* (10th ed.), pp. 141 *et seq*.

(*o*) *Rasbora* v. *J. C. L. Marine, Ltd.*, *supra*.

(*p*) Under the definition in s. 62 (1) of the Sale of Goods Act 1893, as amended, the question was where those acts had been effected. *Cf.* art. 1 (4) of the Uniform Law on the International Sale of Goods, which provides for this purpose that in the case of contracts by correspondence, offer and acceptance shall be considered to have been effected in the territory of the same State only if the letters and telegrams or other documentary communications which contain them have been sent and received in the territory of that State. The provisions of the Uniform Law may also be relevant in considering condition (c): see s. 1 (5) of the Uniform Law on International Sales Act 1967 and arts. 1 (5) and 19 of the Uniform Law on the International Sale of Goods. See also the definition of delivery in s. 61 (1) of the Sale of Goods Act 1979, *ante*.

COMMENT

"Choice of the parties" in sub-s. (1) probably refers only to express choice, and not to the inferred selection which may exist where, for example, parties have agreed that disputes be resolved by litigation or arbitration in some forum outside the United Kingdom (*q*). The distinction (*r*) between choice of law by inferred selection and choice of law by judicial determination of the system of law with which the transaction has the closest and most real connection is in any event fine and it is submitted that this is not the relevant distinction under sub-s. (1).

Under sub-s. (2)(a), whether or not the term was imposed for the purpose of enabling the party imposing it to evade the operation of the Act would seem ultimately to be a matter of subjective intention, which would have to be decided as a matter of fact and in the light of any evidence available. Where the term is one of a set of standard written terms of business (*s*), the party imposing it might well have no specific intention, but would presumably answer for the intention of the draughtsman which the court or arbitrator would in practice no doubt have to infer from the standard terms in the context of the contract as a whole.

The concept of "the essential steps necessary for the making of the contract" is an unfamiliar one; the phrase "whether by him or by others on his behalf" indicates that sub-s. (2)(b) is concerned with the process by which the contract was made on the consumer's side. Notwithstanding s. 27 (2) (b), the contract may of course be taken wholly outside the Act by s. 26, *ante*.

28. Temporary provision for sea carriage of passengers.—[*This section is not relevant to the law relating to sale of goods.*]

29. Saving for other relevant legislation.—(1) Nothing in this Act removes or restricts the effect of, or prevents reliance upon, any contractual provision which—

(a) is authorised or required by the express terms or necessary implication of an enactment; or

(b) being made with a view to compliance with an international agreement to which the United Kingdom is a party, does not operate more restrictively than is contemplated by the agreement.

(2) A contract term is to be taken—

(a) for the purposes of Part I of this Act, as satisfying the requirement of reasonableness; and

(b) for those of Part II, to have been fair and reasonable to incorporate,

if it is incorporated or approved by, or incorporated pursuant to a decision or ruling of, a competent authority acting in the exercise of any statutory jurisdiction or function and is not a term in a contract to which the competent authority is itself a party.

(3) In this section—

(*q*) See p. 48, *ante*.

(*r*) See p. 48, *ante*, Dicey and Morris: *Conflict of Laws* (10th ed.), Rule 145 and 8 Halsbury's Laws (4th Edn.), Title "Conflict of laws", para. 583.

(*s*) See s. 3 (1), *ante*.

"competent authority" means any court, arbitrator or arbiter, government department or public authority;

"enactment" means any legislation (including subordinate legislation) of the United Kingdom or Northern Ireland and any instrument having effect by virtue of such legislation; and

"statutory" means conferred by an enactment.

30. Obligations under Consumer Protection Acts.—(1) In section 3 of the Consumer Protection Act 1961 (provisions against marketing goods which do not comply with safety requirements), after subsection (1) there is inserted—

"(1A) Any term of an agreement which purports to exclude or restrict, or has the effect of excluding or restricting, any obligation imposed by or by virtue of that section, or any liability for breach of such an obligation, shall be void."

(2) The same amendment is made in section 3 of the Consumer Protection Act (Northern Ireland) 1965.

General

31. Commencement; amendments; repeals.—(1) This Act comes into force on 1st February 1978.

(2) Nothing in this Act applies to contracts made before the date on which it comes into force; but subject to this, it applies to liability for any loss or damage which is suffered on or after that date.

(3) The enactments specified in Schedule 3 to this Act are amended as there shown.

(4) The enactments specified in Schedule 4 to this Act are repealed to the extent specified in column 3 of that Schedule.

32. Citation and extent.—(1) This Act may be cited as the Unfair Contract Terms Act 1977.

(2) Part I of this Act extends to England and Wales and to Northern Ireland; but it does not extend to Scotland.

(3) Part II of this Act extends to Scotland only.

(4) This Part of this Act extends to the whole of the United Kingdom.

SCHEDULES

SCHEDULE 1

SCOPE OF SECTIONS 2 TO 4 AND 7

1. Sections 2 to 4 of this Act do not extend to—

(a) any contract of insurance (including a contract to pay an annuity on human life);

(b) any contract so far as it relates to the creation or transfer of an interest in land, or to the termination of such an interest, whether by extinction, merger, surrender, forfeiture or otherwise;

(c) any contract so far as it relates to the creation or transfer of a right or interest in any patent, trade mark, copyright, registered design, technical or commercial information or other intellectual property, or relates to the termination of any such right or interest;

(d) any contract so far as it relates—

(i) to the formation or dissolution of a company (which means any body corporate or unincorporated association and includes a partnership), or

(ii) to its constitution or the rights or obligations of its corporators or members;

(e) any contract so far as it relates to the creation or transfer of securities or of any right or interest in securities.

2. Section 2 (1) extends to—

(a) any contract of marine salvage or towage;

(b) any charterparty of a ship or hovercraft; and

(c) any contract for the carriage of goods by ship or hovercraft;

but subject to this sections 2 to 4 and 7 do not extend to any such contract except in favour of a person dealing as consumer.

3. Where goods are carried by ship or hovercraft in pursuance of a contract which either—

(a) specifies that as the means of carriage over part of the journey to be covered, or

(b) makes no provision as to the means of carriage and does not exclude that means,

then sections 2 (2), 3 and 4 do not, except in favour of a person dealing as consumer, extend to the contract as it operates for and in relation to the carriage of the goods by that means.

4. Section 2 (1) and (2) do not extend to a contract of employment, except in favour of the employee.

5. Section 2 (1) does not affect the validity of any discharge and indemnity given by a person, on or in connection with an award to him of compensation for pneumoconiosis attributable to employment in the coal industry, in respect of any further claim arising from his contracting that disease.

SCHEDULE 2

"GUIDELINES" FOR APPLICATION OF REASONABLENESS TEST

The matters to which regard is to be had in particular for the purposes of sections 6 (3), 7 (3) and (4), 20 and 21 are any of the following which appear to be relevant—

(a) the strength of the bargaining positions of the parties relative to each other, taking into account (among other things) alternative means by which the customer's requirements could have been met;

(b) whether the customer received an inducement to agree to the term, or in accepting it had an opportunity of entering into a similar contract with other persons, but without having to accept a similar term;

(c) whether the customer knew or ought reasonably to have known of the existence and extent of the term (having regard, among other things, to any custom of the trade and any previous course of dealing between the parties);

(d) where the term excludes or restricts any relevant liability if some condition is not complied with, whether it was reasonable at the time of the contract to expect that compliance with that condition would be practicable;

(e) whether the goods were manufactured, processed or adapted to the special order of the customer.

SCHEDULE 3

[AMENDMENT OF ENACTMENTS]

SCHEDULE 4

[REPEALS]

APPENDIX II—NOTES

NOTE A.—ON THE HISTORY OF THE TERMS CONDITION AND WARRANTY

I.—"CONDITION"

The term "condition" as applied to contracts of sale (*a*) appears to mean indifferently (1) an uncertain event on the happening of which the obligation of the contract is to depend, and (2) a term of the contract making its obligation depend on the happening of the event. Though the Act uses the term, it does not define it explicitly in the definition section (s. 62): but s. 11 (1) (*b*) implicitly defines it as "a stipulation . . . the breach of which may give rise to a right to treat the contract as repudiated" (*c*).

The term seems to have been imported into the law of contract from the law of conveyancing. In conveyancing a distinction was drawn between "conditions" and "covenants" (*b*) which, in contracts, has now become obliterated.

The classification of conditions in English law is imperfect and unsatisfactory.

The division of conditions into positive and negative (*e.g.*, "if my horse wins the Derby"—"if my horse does not win the Derby") is obvious and requires no comment.

JAMES, L. J., divides conditions into conditions precedent, subsequent and inherent, a classification which seems to involve a cross-division (*d*). Ordinarily they are divided into conditions precedent and conditions subsequent, that is to say, conditions which must be fulfilled before the obligation of the contract arises, and conditions on the happening of which an existent obligation is dissolved. This division corresponds generally, in sale at any rate, with the distinction drawn by Scottish law and the Continental codes between suspensive and resolutive conditions (*e*).

Conditions precedent have again (*f*) been divided into conditions precedent strictly so called and concurrent conditions. A condition is concurrent where the parties to a contract have reciprocally to perform certain acts at the same time. In the case of the failure of one party to perform his part of the contract, it is sufficient if the other party shows

(*a*) For the modern view about contracts other than contracts of sale, see the judgment of DIPLOCK, L. J., in *Hong Kong Fir Shipping Co., Ltd.* v. *Kawasaki Kisen Kaisha, Ltd.*, [1962] 1 All E. R. 474 at pp. 485–489; [1962] 2 Q. B. 26 at pp. 65–73, C. A.

(*b*) *Bacon's Abridgement* (7th ed.), vol. ii, p. 116.

(*c*) The references are to the 1893 Act. The relevant sections in the 1979 Act are ss. 61 and 11 (3).

(*d*) *Ex p. Collins, Re Lees* (1875), 10 Ch. App. 367, at p. 372 (bill of sale case).

(*e*) Pothier's *Obligations*, by Evans, p. 112; French Civil Code, arts. 1181–1184; Italian Civil Code, arts. 1353, 1354; Bell's *Principles of the Law of Scotland* (9th ed.), pp. 47–50.

(*f*) And, in the editor's submission, confusingly.

that he was ready and willing to perform his part, although he did not actually perform it.

Pothier's further division of condition precedent into potestative, casual, and mixed conditions, though followed in Scotland and by the Continental codes, is not recognised in England. But for accuracy some such subdivision is required.

The important distinction from the point of view of English law is between what may be called promissory conditions and contingent or casual conditions. Where there is a constitution of the latter kind, the obligations of both parties are suspended till the event takes place. Where there is a promissory condition, the non-performance of the condition by the promisor (unless excused by law), gives a right to the promisee to treat the contract as repudiated, that is to say he is discharged from his part of the contract, and, further, he has a claim for damages. In the one case the obligations of the contract never attach: in the other case they attach, but the contract is broken. If A says to B, "I will hire your horse and trap to-morrow if the day be fine," and B assents to this, the obligations of both parties depend on the agreed condition being fulfilled: but if A agrees with B to sell him a ton of hay and deliver it "on Monday for certain," there is a breach of contract by A if the hay be not so delivered.

In the older cases promissory conditions were referred to as "dependent covenants or promises" and were contrasted with independent covenants or promises, namely, stipulations the breach of which gives rise to a claim for damages, but not to a right to treat the contract as repudiated. Now the term "dependent promise" appears to be merged in the wider term "condition precedent."

The Indian Contract Act discards the term "condition," but seeks to preserve the distinction referred to above by dealing separately with "contingent contracts" and "reciprocal promises." The same result is arrived at by the distinction which is sometimes drawn between conditions *of* the contract and conditions *in* the contract.

II.—"WARRANTY"

The term "warranty" seems also to have been imported into the law of contract from the old law of conveyancing, where it signified an express or implied covenant by the grantor of real estate to indemnify the grantee if he should be evicted.

Its meaning was considerably widened in the law of contract, and before the Act was passed it was a term of very uncertain signification. It was sometimes used as strictly equivalent to "condition precedent," yet sometimes it was sought to contrast it with "condition precedent," or rather with a certain kind of condition precedent, namely, a promissory condition precedent. When used in the latter sense the distinction between "condition" and "warranty" corresponded with the distinction drawn by the older cases between what were known as "dependant" and "independent" covenants or promises.

In insurance law its use is curious. When it relates to any undertaking by the assured, it is used to denote a condition precedent of the strictest kind, the breach of which destroys the contract, as in the case of a sailing warranty. But the term is also used as a mere term of exclusion or limitation, as where goods are insured, warranted free from particular average under 3 per cent.

The chief controversy over the proper meaning of the term "warranty" arose in the law of sale, and the ambiguity of its use may have resulted from the want of a clear distinction in English law between sale—*i.e.*, the transfer of property in a thing—and the contract by which that transfer is effected. The term was used in two different senses, and judges and text-writers continually oscillated between them.

First, the term "warranty" was opposed to the term "condition precedent," and denoted a stipulation in a contract of sale, the breach of which gave rise to a claim for damages, but not to a right to reject the goods and treat the contract as repudiated. This is the meaning which, after much consideration, was adopted by the Act as regards England and Ireland (see ss. 11 and 62) (*g*). The objection to this use of the term appears to be that it does not cover the whole field of independent stipulations. For instance, where there is a contract for instalment deliveries, the obligation to pay for a particular instalment may be an independent promise, but it would not ordinarily be called a warranty.

Secondly, the term "warranty" was used to denote any auxiliary stipulation to a contract of sale, and in particular a stipulation relating to the title to, or the quality, condition, or fitness of, goods contracted to be sold. In this sense of the term a breach of warranty might give rise either to a mere claim for damages, or to a right to reject the goods and treat the contract as repudiated, according as the goods might have been accepted or not.

The weight of judicial authority before the Act was in favour of the first meaning, though etymologically and historically the second meaning appears more correct. [Warranty = Guarantee.] The objection to this use of the term is that it does not mark the distinction between a condition precedent and a collateral promise or undertaking. Using the term in the first sense, it is to be noted that many stipulations which in their inception are conditions (*e.g*, the implied undertakings as to merchantableness and fitness for a particular purpose) may become contracted into warranties by virtue of subsequent events, and this fact doubtless explains much of the confusion of language to which the term has given rise.

Citations

1.—"A *warranty* (concerning freeholds and inheritances) is a covenant real annexed to lands or tenements whereby a man and his heirs are bound to warrant the same, and either by voucher or by judgment in a writ of *warrantia chartæ* to yield other lands and tenements to the

---

(*g*) The reference is to the 1893 Act. The relevant sections in the 1979 Act are ss. 11 and 61. But note the saving for Scotland in those sections.

value of those that shall be evicted by a former title, else it may be used by way of rebutter" (*h*).

2.—"A *warranty* is an arrangement by which a seller assures to a buyer the existence of some fact affecting the transaction, whether past, present, or future" (*i*).

3.—"A *warranty*, properly so called, can only exist where the subject-matter of the sale is ascertained and existing, so as to be capable of being inspected at the time of the contract, and is a collateral engagement that the specific thing so sold possesses certain qualities, but the property passing by the contract of sale, a breach of the warranty cannot entitle the vendor to rescind the contract, and revest the property in the vendor without his consent. . . . But when the subject-matter of the sale is not in existence, or not ascertained at the time of the contract, an engagement that it shall, when existing or ascertained, possess certain qualities, is not a mere *warranty*, but a *condition*, the performance of which is precedent to any obligation on the vendee under the contract, because the existence of those qualities, being part of the description of the thing sold, becomes essential to its identity, and the vendee cannot be compelled to receive and pay for a thing different from that for what he contracted" (*k*).

4.—"An express *warranty* is a stipulation inserted in writing on the face of the policy, upon the literal truth or fulfilment of which the validity of the entire contract is dependent. These written stipulations either allege the existence of some fact or state of things at the time, or previous to the time, of making the policy, or they undertake for the happening of future events, or the performance of future acts. In the former case Mr. Marshall terms the stipulation an affirmative, and in the latter a promissory warranty" (*l*).

5.—"When it appears that the consideration has been executed in part, that which before was a warranty or condition precedent, loses the character of a condition, or, to speak more properly, ceases to be available as a condition and becomes a *warranty* in a narrower sense of the word, viz., a stipulation by way of agreement for the breach of which a compensation must be sought in damages" (*m*).

6.—"If upon a treaty about the buying of certain goods, the buyer should ask the seller if he would warrant them to be of such a value and his own goods, and the seller should warrant them, and then the buyer should demand the price and the seller should set the price, and then the

---

(*h*) *Bacon's Abridgement* (7th ed.), pp. 356, 359, 361; and see *Williams's Real Property* (24th ed.), p. 714.

(*i*) New York Draft Code, § 877.

(*k*) Notes to *Cutter* v. *Powell* (1795), 2 Smith L. C. (7th ed.), p. 30.

(*l*) *Arnould's Marine Insurance* (6th ed.), p. 599; *Cranston* v. *Marshall* (1850), 5 Exch. 395, at p. 402; and see *Barnard* v. *Faber*, [1893] 1 Q. B. 340, at p. 343, *per* BOWEN, L. J., as to fire insurance.

(*m*) Williams, *Notes to Saunders' Reports*, vol. i, p. 554, cited and approved *Heilbut* v. *Hickson* (1872), L. R. 7 C. P. 438, at p. 450; *cf. Stanton* v. *Richardson* (1872), L. R. 7 C. P. 421, at p. 436.

buyer should take time for two or three days to consider, and then should come and give the seller his price, though the warranty here was before the sale yet this will be well, because the *warranty* is the ground of the treaty, and this is *warrantizando venditit*" (*n*).

7.—"It was rightly held by HOLT, C. J., and has been uniformly adopted ever since, that an affirmation at the time of a sale is a *warranty*, provided it appear on evidence to have been so intended" (*o*).

8.—"Here, when F., a mutual acquaintance of the parties, introduced them to each other, he said, 'Mr. J. is in want of copper for sheathing a vessel,' and one of the defendants answered, 'We will supply him well.' As there was no subsequent communication, that constituted a contract and amounted to a *warranty*. But I wish to put the case on a broad principle. If a man sells an article he thereby *warrants* that it is merchantable—that is, fit for some purpose. If he sells it for a particular purpose he thereby *warrants* it fit for that purpose. . . . In every contract to furnish manufactured goods, however low the price, it is an implied *term* that the goods should be merchantable" (*p*).

9.—"Although the vendee of a specific chattel, delivered with a *warranty*, may not have a right to return it, the same reason does not apply to cases of executory contracts, where an article, for instance, is ordered from a manufacturer, who contracts that it shall be of a certain quality, or fit for a certain purpose, and the article sent is such as is never completely accepted by the party ordering it" (*q*).

10.—"A good deal of confusion has arisen in many of the cases on this subject from the unfortunate use made of the word '*warranty*.' Two things have been confounded together. A *warranty* is an express or implied statement of something which the party undertakes shall be part of a contract; and though part of the contract, yet collateral to the express object of it. But in many of the cases, some of which have been referred to, the circumstances of a party selling a particular thing by its proper description has been called a *warranty*, and the breach of such contract a breach of warranty; but it would be better to distinguish such cases as a non-compliance with a contract which a party has engaged to fulfil, as if a man offers to buy peas of another, and he sends him beans, he does not perform his contract; but that is not a warranty; there is no warranty that he should sell him peas; the contract is to sell peas, and if he sends him anything else in their stead, it is a non-performance of it" (*r*).

11.—"We avoid the term '*warranty*,' because it is used in two senses, and the term 'condition,' because the question is whether that term is applicable. Then the effect is that the defendants required and the

(*n*) *Lysney* v. *Selby* (1705), 2 Ld. Raym. 1118.

(*o*) *Per* BULLER, J., *Pasley* v. *Freeman* (1789), 3 Term. Rep. 51.

(*p*) *Per* BEST, C. J., *Jones* v. *Bright* (1829), 5 Bing. 533, at p. 543.

(*q*) *Per* Lord TENTERDEN, *Street* v. *Blay* (1831), 2 B. & Ad. 456, at p. 463 (horse case).

(*r*) *Per* Lord ABINGER, *Chanter* v. *Hopkins* (1838), 4 M. & W. 399, at p. 404. *Cf. Kennedy* v. *Panama Mail Co.* (1867), L. R. 2 Q. B. 580, at p. 587; *Wallis* v. *Pratt*, [1910] 2 K. B. 1003, 1012, *per* FLETCHER MOULTON, L. J.

plaintiff gave his undertaking that no sulphur had been used. This undertaking was a preliminary stipulation; and if it had not been given, the defendants would not have gone on with the treaty which resulted in the sale. In this sense it was the condition upon which the defendants contracted, and it would be contrary to the intention expressed by this stipulation that the contract should remain valid if sulphur had been used. The intention of the parties governs in the making and in the construction of all contracts. If the parties so intend, the sale may be absolute, with a warranty superadded, or the sale may be conditional to be null if the warranty is broken; and upon this statement of facts we think that the intention appears to have been that the contract should be null if sulphur had been used" (*s*).

12.—"I agree with what MAULE, J., and CROWDER, J., say in *Hopkins* v. *Tanqueray*. CROWDER, J., says, in the plainest terms, in that case, that the conversation 'was a mere representation, and was evidently not made with an intention to warrant the horse. A representation to constitute a *warranty* must be shown to have been intended to form part of the contract.' It seems to me that that is perfectly correct" (*t*).

13.—"But with respect to statements in a contract descriptive of the subject-matter of it, or of some material incident thereof, the true doctrine established by principle, as well as authority, appears to be, generally speaking, that if such descriptive statement was intended to be a substantive part of the contract, it is to be regarded as a *warranty*, that is to say, a condition on the failure or non-performance of which the other party may, if he is so minded, repudiate the contract *in toto* and so be relieved from performing his part of it, provided it has not been partially executed in his favour. If, indeed, he has received the whole, or any substantial part, of the consideration from the promise on his part, the *warranty* loses the character of a *condition*, or, to speak perhaps more properly, perhaps, ceases to be available as a condition, and becomes a *warranty* in the narrower sense of the word, viz., a stipulation by way of agreement for the breach of which a compensation must be sought in damages" (*u*).

14.—"The wools are 'guaranteed about similar to samples.' Now such a clause may be a simple guarantee or *warranty*, or it may be a condition. Generally speaking when the contract is as to any goods, such a clause is a condition going to the essence of the contract; but when the contract is as to specific goods the clause is only collateral to the contract, and is the subject of a cross action or matter in reduction of damages. Here there is, I think, merely a *warranty* as distinguished from a *condition*" (*a*).

15.—"If the subject-matter of the contract is a specific existing chattel, a representation as to some quality attached to it or possessed by

(*s*) *Per* ERLE, C. J., *Bannerman* v. *White* (1861), 10 C. B. N. S. 844, at p. 860.
(*t*) *Per* MARTIN, B., *Stucley* v. *Baily* (1862), 31 L. J. Ex. 483, at p. 489.
(*u*) *Per* WILLIAMS, J., *Behn* v. *Burness* (1863), 3 B. & S. 751, at p. 755.
(*a*) *Per* BLACKBURN, J., *Heyworth* v. *Hutchinson* (1867), L. R. 2 Q. B. 447, at p. 451.

it is only a warranty unless the absence of that quality or the possession of it in a less degree makes the thing essentially different from that described in the contract" (*b*).

16.—"As a matter of law I think every item in a description which constitutes a substantial ingredient in the identity of the thing sold is a *condition*" (*c*).

17.—"It has been said many times, and particularly in *Wallis, Son & Wallis* v. *Pratt & Haynes*, that whether any statement is to be regarded as a *condition* or a *warranty* must depend on the intention to be properly inferred from the particular statement made. A statement that an animal is sound in every respect would *primâ facie* be but a *warranty*, but in this case the learned judge found as a fact that the defendant went further and promised that he would take the animal back if she were no good . . . it seems to me plain that the language he used could not have been intended merely as a *warranty*, for a *warranty* would give no right of rejection to the purchaser" (*d*).

NOTE B.—DELIVERY TO CARRIER

Frequent reference has been made to the rule that delivery of goods to a carrier is *prima facie* a delivery to the buyer and a performance of the seller's contract which passes both the property and the risk to the buyer. It follows that, as a rule, if the goods are lost or destroyed, the buyer or consignee is the proper person to sue the carrier. The most authoritative statement of the principle is in the judgment of the House of Lords in *Dunlop* v. *Lambert* (*e*), where it was held that if there was a special contract the consignor might sue the carrier though the goods might be the property of the consignee. Lord COTTENHAM there says (*f*):

> "It is no doubt true as a general rule that the delivery by the consignor to the carrier is a delivery to the consignee, and that the risk is after such delivery the risk of the consignee. This is so if, without designating the particular carrier, the consignee directs that the goods shall be sent by the ordinary conveyance: the delivery to the ordinary carrier is then a delivery to the consignee, and the consignee incurs all the risks of the carriage. And it is still more strongly so if the goods are sent by a carrier specially pointed out by the consignee himself, for such carrier then becomes his special agent.
>
> But, though the authorities all establish the general inference I have stated, yet that general inference is capable of being varied by the circumstances of any special arrangement between the parties, or of any particular mode of

(*b*) *Per* BAILHACHE, J., *Harrison* v. *Knowles and Foster*, [1917] 2 K. B. 606, at p. 610.

(*c*) *Per* SCOTT, L. J. (TUCKER and BUCKNILL, L. JJ., concurring) in *Couchman* v. *Hill*, [1947] 1 All E. R. 103, at p. 105; [1947] K. B. 554, at p. 559.

(*d*) *Per* EVERSHED, M. R., in *Harling* v. *Eddy*, [1951] 2 All E. R. 212, at p. 215; [1951] 2 K. B. 739, at pp. 741–742.

(*e*) (1839), 6 Cl. & Fin. 600.

(*f*) *Ibid.*, at pp. 620, 621.

dealing between them. If a particular contract be proved between the consignor and the consignee, and the circumstance of the payment of the freight and insurance is not alone a conclusive evidence of ownership—as where the party undertaking to consign undertakes to deliver at a particular place—the property, till it reaches that place and is delivered according to the terms of the contract, is at the risk of the consignor. And again, though in general the following of the directions of the consignee, and delivering the goods to a particular carrier, will relieve the consignor from the risk, he may make such a special contract that, though delivering the goods to the carrier specially intimated to the consignee, the risk may remain with him; and the consignor may, by a contract with the carrier, make the carrier liable to himself. In an infinite variety of circumstances, the ordinary rule may turn out not to be that which regulates the liabilities of the parties" (*g*).

Delivery to carrier to pass property.—This passage is discussed by BLACKBURN, J., in an instructive judgment in *The Calcutta Co.* v. *De Mattos* (*h*), which has often been referred to in the text, but which was too long for insertion there. He says (*i*):

"What was the effect of the contract as regards the property in the goods and the right to the price, from the time of the handing over the shipping documents and paying half of the invoice value? There is no rule of law to prevent the parties, in cases like the present, from making whatever bargain they please. If they use words in the contract showing that they intend that the goods shall be shipped by the person who is to supply them, on the terms that when shipped they shall be the consignee's property, and at his risk, so that the vendor shall be paid for them whether delivered at the port of destination or not, this intention is effectual. Such is the common case where goods are ordered to be sent by a carrier to a port of destination. The vendor's duty is, in such cases, at an end when he has delivered the goods to the carrier, and, if the goods perish in the carrier's hands, the vendor is discharged and the purchaser is bound to pay him the price. If the parties intend that the vendor shall not merely deliver the goods to the carrier, but also undertake that they shall actually be delivered at their destination, and express such intention, this also is effectual; in such a case, if the goods perish in the hands of the carrier, the vendor is not only not entitled to the price, but he is liable for whatever damage may have been sustained by the purchaser in consequence of the breach of the vendor's contract to deliver at the place of destination. But the parties may intend an intermediate state of things; they may intend that the vendor shall deliver the goods to the carrier, and that, when he has done so, he shall have fulfilled his undertaking, so that he shall not be liable in damages for a breach of contract if the goods do not reach their destination; and yet they may intend that the whole or part of the price shall not be payable unless the goods do arrive. They may bargain that the property shall vest in the purchaser, as owner, as soon as the goods are shipped, that they shall then be both sold and delivered, and yet that the price (in whole or in part) shall be payable only on the contingency of the goods arriving, just as they might, if they pleased, contract that the price should not be payable unless a particular tree fall; but without any contract on the vendor's part in the one case to procure the goods to arrive, or in the

(*g*) *Cf. Young* v. *Hobson* (1949), 65 T. L. R. 365.
(*h*) (1863), 32 L. J. Q. B. 322.
(*i*) *Ibid.*, at p. 328.

other to cause the tree to fall. Where the contract is of this kind, the position of the vendor and purchaser, in case the goods do not arrive, is analogous to that of freighter and shipowner, in the ordinary contract of carriage on board a ship, in case the goods are prevented from arriving by one of the excepted perils. The shipowner is not bound to carry and deliver at all events; but, though he is excused if prevented by the excepted perils, yet no freight is earned or payable unless the goods are delivered. In the case of freight, also, the question often arises, whether a payment made at the port of shipment is an advance of part of the freight, returnable if the goods are not delivered and freight earned, or is an absolute payment, leaving only the balance contingent on the safe delivery of the goods—a question very analogous to the one that arises on the present contract" (*k*).

"Carriage forward."—The effect of the ordinary "carriage forward" contract is thus expressed by MELLOR, J.:

"There is evidence in the present case that these goods were, with the consent or by the authority of the purchaser, consigned by the vendors, as consignors, to be carried by the defendants as common carriers, to be delivered to the purchaser as consignee, and that the name of the consignee was made known to the defendants at the time of the delivery. Under such circumstances the ordinary inference is that the contract of carriage is between the carrier and the consignee, the consignor being the agent for the consignee to make it. It appears to us that there is evidence also that at the time of the delivery there was a specific mention that the freight was to be paid by the consignee. Under such circumstances the inference is almost irresistible that the contract for carriage in the present case was the ordinary contract for carriage at the cost and risk and under the control of the consignee" (*l*).

(*k*) See the cases as to prepayment of freight collected in *M'Lachlan on Shipping* (7th ed.) p. 434.

(*l*) *Cork Distilleries Co.* v. *Great Southern and Western Rail. Co.* (1874), L. R. H. L. 269, at p. 277.

INDEX